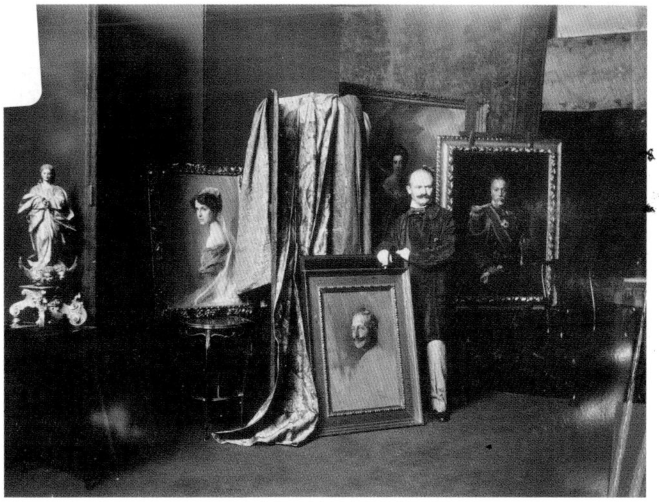

A BRUSH WITH GRANDEUR

Philip Alexius de László (1869–1937)

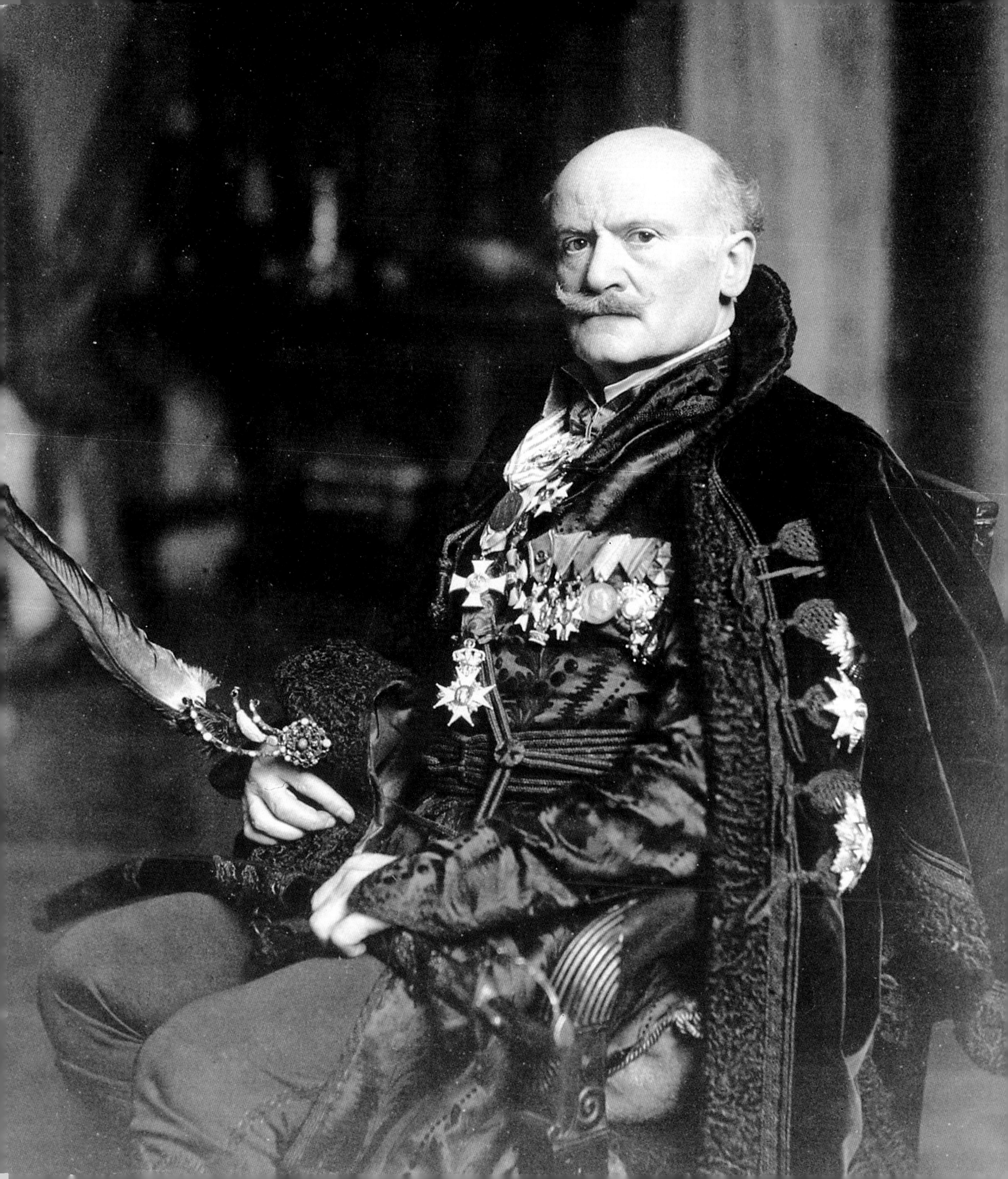

A BRUSH WITH GRANDEUR

Philip Alexius de László

(1869–1937)

Essays by Suzanne Bailey, Gábor Bellák,

Christopher Lloyd, Richard Ormond, Christopher Wood

Catalogue by Sandra de Laszlo

Paul Holberton publishing

London 2004

First published 2004

Accompanies an exhibition held at CHRISTIE'S London, 6–22 January 2004. The exhibition has been presented by the Hungarian Cultural Centre in collaboration with Christie's as part of Magyar Magic–Hungary in Focus 2004, a year-long celebration of Hungarian culture in the United Kingdom

www.magyarmagic.com

www.hungarytourism.hu
www.hungarywelcomesbritain.com

MINISTRY OF CULTURAL HERITAGE

ISBN (hardcover) 1 903470 18 8

ISBN (softcover) 1 903470 19 6

British Library Cataloguing in Publication Data

A catalogue record for this book is available from the British Library

Produced by Paul Holberton publishing
37 Snowsfields, London SE1 3SU
www.paul-holberton.net

Designed by Roger Davies
davies design@onetel.net.uk

Printed in Verona, Italy

Distributed in UK and Europe and the rest of the world through Greenhill Books
Distributed in USA and Canada through University of Washington Press
See further www.paul-holberton.net

Jacket/ cover image: Mrs Edmund Buchanan (detail), cat. 119
Back jacket/ cover: The Baronesses Dorothee and Marga Schröder, cat. 39
Half title: The artist in his studio at West House, Campden Hill, London, with portraits of the Countess of Rosse (1911) and Emperor William II (1910), photograph by Paul Laib, 1911
Frontispiece: The artist in Hungarian ceremonial dress in his studio at Fitzjohn's Avenue, London, photograph by Paul Laib, 1929

CONTENTS

A Message from Katalin Bogyay Director of the Hungarian Cultural Centre

It was ten years ago that we started our discussions with Edmund de Unger, the renowned art collector, about the ways in which we might assemble an exhibition showing the life and works of a painter who emerged from Hungary to conquer Europe at the beginning of the twentieth century. He lived at time when his talent was free to spread its wings beyond Hungary, enchanting the whole world. He lived and worked where he was needed. Events later in the twentieth century prevented Hungarian artists from moving around Europe: few of them received the acclaim they deserved in the patchwork that is European culture.

For me, Fülöp László's career serves as a model for the kind of free European life that we hope will once again become the reality for Hungarian artists after we join the European Union. Once again, they will enjoy the freedom to learn, to gain experience, to indulge their creativity, to spread their wings.

I should like to thank the de Unger family, Christopher Wood and Richard Ormond for helping us realise our desire to make Fülöp László's career known to the world. I should like to thank Nöel Annesley and Paul Hewitt at Christie's for their strong support, for placing their faith in us and for agreeing to house this exhibition as part of the Magyar Magic festival. I should also like to thank the owners of the paintings and the Hungarian National Gallery for making these pictures available to us. And my special thanks are due to Sandra de Laszlo and my colleague Beáta Somfalvi for their great hard work and commitment.

I am very glad that we have been able to realise this old dream. Let us discover who Fülöp László was, and how that lesser-known Hungarian painter became the famous and greatly admired genius Philip de László.

Acknowledgements

Without the generosity of the owners of Philip de László's pictures the exhibition this book accompanies could not have taken place. I thank them all, especially the artist's descendants, whose patience has been legendary, for their support.

Heartfelt thanks go to our leading sponsors, Richard de Unger and the Harmsworth and Schroder families, without whom this catalogue would not be in creation.

I am incredibly grateful to Christopher Wentworth-Stanley for his scholarly improvements to my text. As an extension of this co-operation Christopher has agreed to work with me in the determination to produce at least Volume I of the Catalogue Raisonné of the Works of P.A. de László for 2007. That year marks the hundredth anniversary of the artist's settling in England, and of his first London exhibition, at the Fine Art Society; also the seventieth anniversary of his death, in November 1937.

I am much indebted also to so many individuals, historians, art historians and curators, who have given freely of their time to assist me in my research – notably Dr. Paul d'Orbán in Canada, Charles Noble L.V.O., Keeper of the Devonshire Collections, Gabriel Badéa Päun in Paris, andChristophe Vachaudez in Belgium. In the early years, Revd Dr Ed Hanson gave me invaluable support from Boston not least by transcribing and editing de László's Sitters' Book (twice, as the first was consumed by technology), giving me an accessible index to the some 1,700 signatures. The teams at the Royal Collection and the Bridgeman Art Library offices have been particularly helpful in the preparations for this exhibition and its catalogue.

The descriptions herein will be used also in the forthcoming Catalogue Raisonné. My friend Fiona Potter started the work more than sixteen years ago, using the Paul Laib photographs of his work at the Witt Library in the Courtauld Institute. I have since been ably assisted by Nicky Wardell, Alice Whitehead, Henrietta Cartwright, Lucia Cannon and Victoria Lynne to date. Emilia Holt is still hard at work correcting our huge database. They have all brought their individual talents to the task.

Many of the portraits in the exhibition are sporting their original frames. To de László the frame was an integral part of the portrait. He had strong views about their appearance and mostly designed and ordered them himself, chiefly using E. Remy, 153 King's Road, Chelsea. He completed most of his paintings with the canvas in the frame on the easel. The original frames have not been individually identified in this catalogue, as that alone could be the subject of an entire exhibition. Suffice it to say that the frames the viewer most admires will in all probability be the original ones.

I am grateful indeed to the Hungarian Ministry of Cultural Heritage who are presenting this exhibition and to Katalin Bogyay and Edmund de Unger, whose idea it was in the first place. Their contribution to the photography expenditure is much appreciated. Dr. Gert Rudolf Flick has also been very generous. Beáta Somfalvi at the Hungarian Cultural Centre in London has been unreservedly supportive and I look forward to her co-operation in the future, too. Working with my co-curators, Richard Ormond and Christopher Wood, has been an enjoyable and enlightening experience, after so many years of toiling away on my own. Christie's have supported us even beyond the call of duty. Paul Hewitt's energy and tenacity has enabled us to achieve this exhibition in an almost impossibly short span of time. His staff, alas too many to name individually, have been efficient and thoroughly professional at every turn.

My deepest thanks go to my husband Damon, one of the artist's seventeen grandchildren, for his patience and generosity, and to the de Laszlo Foundation for the considerable contribution towards the photography, framing, cleaning and restoration of the drawings and paintings for the exhibition.

Sandra de Laszlo
Glebe House, Chelsea, November 2003

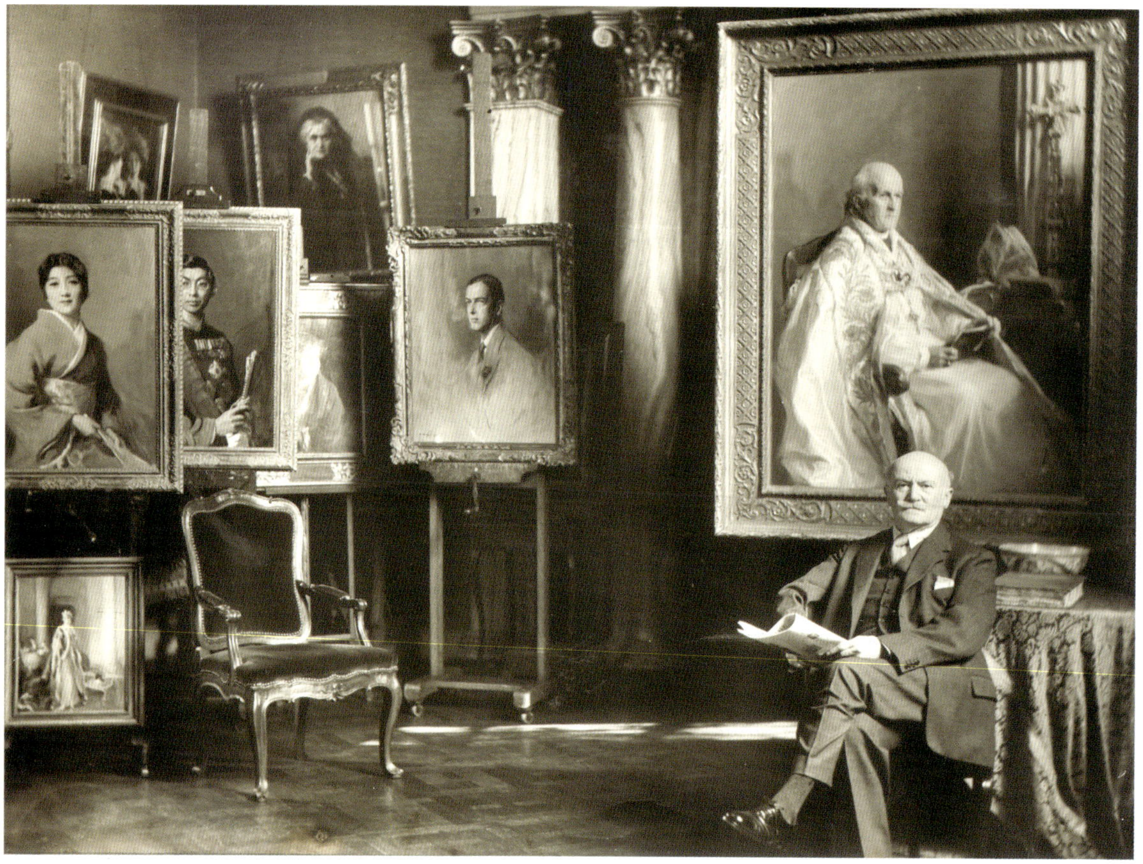

FIG. 1 Philip de László in his studio, in front of portraits of, among others, Prince and Princess Chichibu of Japan, the artist's mother (cat. 62), Archbishop Lang (see cat. 122) and his 'Zoffany' of the Duchess of Northumberland (cat. 138), in the year of his death, 1937

The de Laszlo Foundation

Special thanks are due to the Schroder and Harmsworth family foundations for supporting and sponsoring this catalogue, together with the de Laszlo Foundation.

On their behalf as well as my own I would like to thank the contributors – Suzanne Bailey, Gábor Bellák (Curator at the Hungarian National Gallery), Christopher Lloyd (Surveyor of the Queen's Pictures), Richard Ormond (The John Singer Sargent Catalogue Raisonné) and Christopher Wood – who have provided key articles.

Special thanks are due to the publisher, Paul Holberton, for dealing with the production of the catalogue under tremendous time pressure, and to Sandra de Laszlo, who has masterminded the selection of the representative exhibits and, as Archivist to the Foundation, has written the catalogue entries.

Damon de Laszlo

Chairman, The de Laszlo Foundation

Preface
Richard de Unger

For nearly three decades, until his death in 1937, Philip de László enjoyed an unassailable position as the leading portrait painter in England and indeed in Europe. Having made his name rapidly as a young man, he consolidated his reputation in the first decade of the twentieth century, and by the time of his death held twenty-two orders and seventeen medals of merit (see frontispiece). Contemporary appreciation of his extraordinary achievement is encapsulated in Lord Selborne's question, "Has any one painter ever before painted so many interesting and historical personages?" However, since the Second World War de László has undeniably fallen into comparative obscurity, however undeserved.

What should explain this dramatic change in status? Why should de László's contemporaries such as John Singer Sargent and John Lavery be better established in the public consciousness than a man who, as a portraitist, enjoyed an even more prominent and celebrated clientèle? Might it be that the works do not hold up to posthumous scrutiny? Even a cursory glance at these will categorically refute such a notion. Another factor may be that, indeed, little of his work is generally seen, since the great majority of it remains in private ownership, in the collections of the families of his sitters or of the artist's own descendants. Clearly, the reasons why de László has been deprived of his rightful place in the history of twentieth-century painting are not artistic; they are more complex, the consequence of changes of attitude that need briefly to be discussed before considering the paintings themselves.

The radical social changes brought about by the upheavals of the Second World War and the election of a Labour government in 1945 affected most that slice of the social strata who were predominantly de László's patrons. The hardship and austerity of the post-war years epitomized by the continuation of rationing hardened the puritanical perceptions of the opulence and what came to seem the frivolous gaiety of the immediately preceding period. Meanwhile those who had once 'indulged' now faced pressing difficulties simply in maintaining their homes and the walls on which such portraits hung against an unenviable combination of crippling tax increases, dwindling incomes and rising labour costs. The situation was so bleak that demolition frequently became the practical option (for instance, to name but one tragedy among many, that of the main house at Bowood in Wiltshire). A passage from a letter written in 1948 by one of de Lászlo's sitters, Vita Sackville West (cat. 44), to her husband, Harold Nicolson, illustrates a typical situation:

"And as the wages alone come to £45 a week, or £1,340 a year, you will readily see that there is not much balance left for such things as house-books, electric light and heat, rates, insurance, the motor car, coal and coke (I have just had a bill for £149 for these), telephone, and the thousand things involved in the upkeep of a house."

It was surely owing to the speed of this transformation of circumstances and the psychological need to move forward that de László's portraits were now abandoned together with the memories of a more secure and comfortable past. Inextricably linked with those 'Indian Summer' years of the earlier twentieth century, de László was unfairly viewed as a participant who recorded in paint rather than as the artist he so clearly was.

Portraiture, where it continued, mirrored these social and political changes. With the exception of institutional commissions canvases shrank to more modest proportions. No longer adorning the large wall space provided by the country house, where it would be influenced in choice of pose and gesture by the presence of preceding traditions, portraits submitted to a trend of studied informality. The relaxed manner in which King George VI sits with his legs crossed at the tea table in Gunn's *Conversation Piece at the Royal Lodge in Windsor* marks a remarkable transition from the uncompromisingly hierarchical representation by Lavery of his father and his family. In the former the intimacy of the family, fluidly engaging one another in a harmonious unity, is very remote from the air of dynastic certainty reflected in the stance of the monarch in the latter – his hands resting on his ceremonial sword while his wife and children attend dutifully. Derek Hill's portrait of Anthony Eden in an open-necked checked shirt would have been inconceivable as a depiction of a former Prime Minister in de László's heyday. Indeed the ethos conveyed in this commission would no doubt have seemed equally inconceivable to the sitter in his younger years, when a comparable portrait would instead have emphasized attributes associated with statesmanship and office. De László was remarkably capable of studying and conveying character but he also deliberately played up to and endorsed the historic formulae of formal portraiture. His works deserve to be assessed in sympathy with the criteria of the period and with the expectations of his sitters.

Communism had even less sympathy with the world of de László. After his death de László was ignored and forgotten in his native Hungary, and the collection of his pictures in the National Gallery in Budapest was relegated to its basement. Fittingly, as Hungary is about to join a European Union offering a very different perspective on the world, de László's reputation is about to be revived in his native land. He will take his rightful place as the last of the great court painters of Europe.

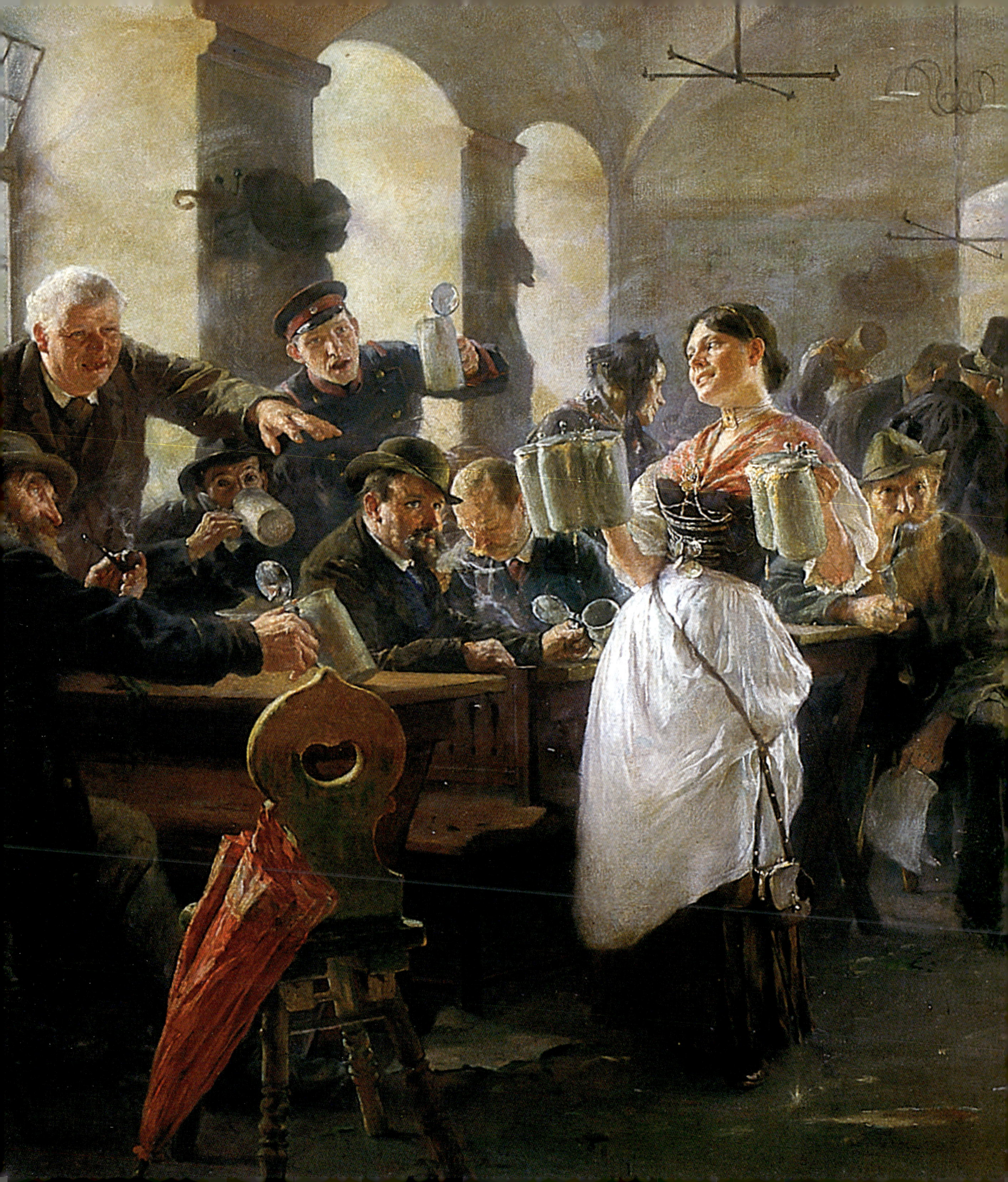

Philip de László in Hungary

Gábor Bellák

At the end of a letter written in September 1908 Philip de László (Fülöp László) underlined a passage stating "the artificiality of writing irritates me".[1] From this we might conclude that the painter (who was by then known and celebrated throughout Europe) did not like writing. He was a man of the brush, not of the pen. But the huge volume of letters held in the collection of the Hungarian National Gallery contradicts this, as does the fact that the passage quoted is on the eleventh page of the letter concerned. If we also consider that the artist dictated an autobiography which, edited after his death by Owen Rutter, ran to almost four hundred printed pages,[2] then we will be obliged to revise any such earlier conclusion. De László's career was not built on paintings alone: he took great care to polish his image as a painter through his letters and speeches.

We should not, however, therefore imagine that he promoted himself as a kind of brand, as if he were the product of an advertising agency. De László's image as an artist was not a composite, not a pose or a manipulated stereotype, but was founded on a precise and conscientious practice and on certain definite artistic and moral values. His value system was a very particular one, although not rare among artists of the ninteenth and twentieth centuries. Nature was at the heart of his credo. Of course, few artists or movements of the time failed to make reference to nature – their diversity is defined precisely by their differing interpretations of nature. But de László's art was also characterized by another idea, which he strongly emphasized, that of appropriate recognition. That de Lászlo was passionate about art is shown by many passages of his autobiography and by his letters, but he did not see himself simply as a footsoldier in the army of artists. In the pages of his autobiography the humiliations he had to endure during his childhood rankle strongly – not so much wounds inevitably inflicted by teachers and classmates, but indignities like that to which he was put by the likes of his first teacher, Moritz Lehmann, a stage designer, who used his knowledge-hungry pupil as a go-between to deliver his love letters.[3] De László soon developed a fierce self-esteem that refused to cede either to jealousy or to malice, or to laziness or shoddy work. He was not arrogant about his conscientious hard work or his skill, but modesty did not prevent him from feeling justified in attempting to garner greater respect. In a letter of June 1899 he asks an unidentified well-wisher to petition the King of Hungary to honour him. "I have been working at a German court all summer, and I would be very glad if I could receive an honour from my own King alongside these foreign distinctions. As far as I know, many people have been honoured who have done far less to deserve it than I. I was reluctant to mention it in Vienna. I am happy to make this request of you, because I know you to wish me well, that you understand my ambitions, and you know how dedicated I am to my art."[4] It is rare to find an artist expressing such an undisguised desire for recognition.

We should respect de László's honesty, and we should add that his desire for honour was entirely understandable. The artist grew up in an atmosphere overshadowed by the conflict between an irresponsible father and a mother who would make any sacrifice for her poor and populous family. The children, including the future famous painter, were forced to work from an early age in order to ward off abject poverty. Thus they learned to respect work but also to expect just payment in return. A similar expectation guided the boy not just through life, but through the art world of the end of the nineteenth century, where it was still the case that achievement was

opposite
The Hofbräuhaus (cat. 8, detail)

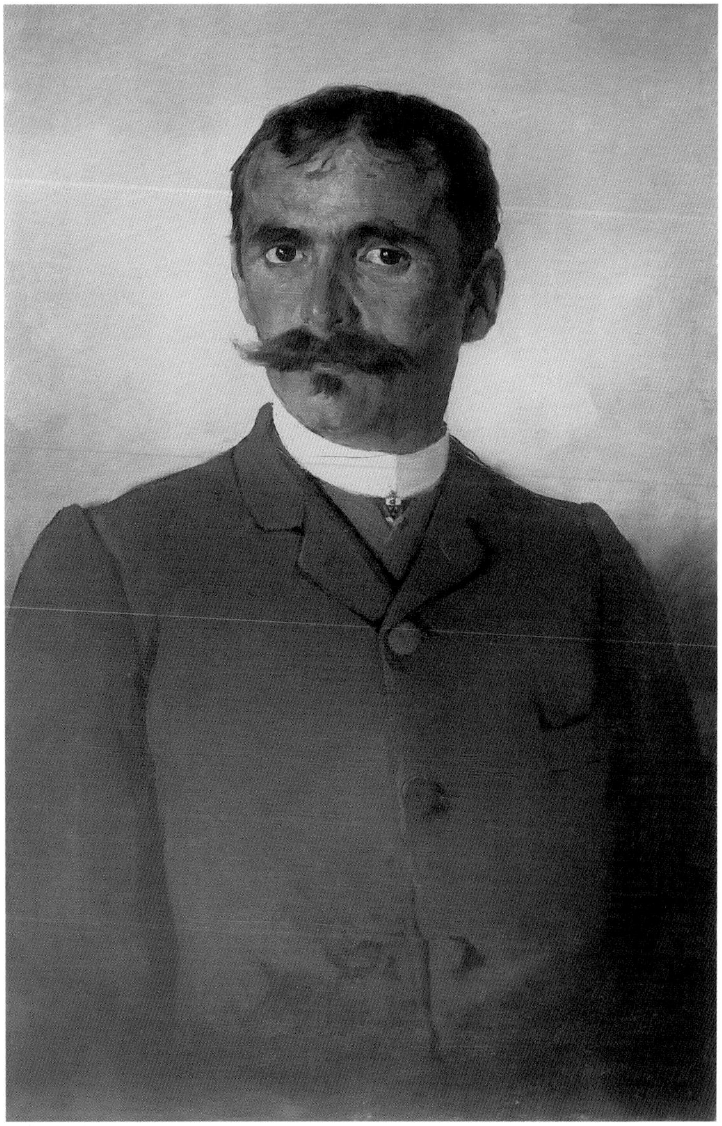

FIG. 2
Dr Paul Galambos, O-Becse, 1888
Oil on canvas, untraced

measured and the rewards to be obtained – medals, prizes, titles – determined the station of the artist, as if art were some kind of athletic competition.[5] The surest indicator of artistic success was the kind of social acceptance that raised the artist into the ranks of the élite. In this sense, de László (he obtained the 'de' in 1912, after painting the Austrian Emperor Francis Joseph, see below) was certainly ambitious. By the time he was thirty, the poor boy from Pest had become very wealthy: his studio-villa (fig. 8) was one of the most luxurious in Budapest.

Our knowledge of most aspects of Fülöp László's early career depend on his own accounts, which sometimes vary. For example, when, in London in March 1917, he began dictating his memoirs, initially in German, he began: "It was in the year 1869, on 30 April, that my dear mother bore me, in humble circumstances, in Budapest".[6] And yet on a questionnaire he completed around 1910[7] and in the letter of 1908 referred to above[8] he gives his date of birth as 28 April. While there is a fuller account in Rutter's biography, based on his dictations of 1917, in the letter of 1908 he describes his studies as follows: "In the midst of great difficulties I spent the years of my youth as an apprentice to [Moritz] Lehmann, the Pest set designer (the most famous of the time). I dealt with architectural sculpture above all, and then I moved on to painting maiolica and porcelain, and then I came to art photography. In 1884 I attended the School of Applied Arts, run at the time by the late János Vidéky, to whom I owe a great deal. He supported my passion for art. In 1886 I became Gusztáv Keleti's pupil at the Drawing School, although I could only go to two classes a day. At the end of that year I competed for and won my first state art scholarship. At the beginning of 1887 I became a full-time apprentice of Károly Lotz, now deceased."[9] Thus he received his first significant training as an artist in the two most important art teaching institutions of the Budapest of the time, the School of Applied Arts and the Drawing School, which would be later the Academy of Fine Art. Among his teachers, not only Károly Lotz but Bertalan Székely deserves particular mention. They were the two outstanding portrait painters of their era, but Székely's principal achievements were in historical paintings on canvas, whereas Lotz's were in genre painting and frescos. László's early interest in genre and historical painting was doubtless due to these two.

Although de László had painted his first portraits in 1888 – of the mathematics teacher Márton Hajnal and of the influential provincial lawyer Paul Galambos (fig. 2) and his wife respectively – he became known on the national stage through his genre paintings (see figs. 4, 5 and cat. 8–14). He began the first studies for the painting entitled *Goose Girl* whilst still in O-Becse as a guest of the Galambos family in summer 1888. De László gives a lively and detailed account of the *Goose Girl*'s career before the competition juries and at exhibition[10] and of his joy when it was chosen for the 1888 Christmas Exhibition. The truth is, however, that it was not de László's first exhibition piece. At the Hungarian Fine Arts Society, which regularly exhibited the latest 'crop' of Hungarian art – indeed its exhibitions were its most important forum – de László had in autumn 1888 already exhibited a portrait of a child. From this point on his pictures regularly featured in the winter exhibitions. In 1889 he exhibited a picture called *First Wash,* in 1890 *Sunday Morning* and *Family Joy,* all of which were genre paintings. Genre was the most popular theme of the late nineteenth century. Every significant Hungarian painter of

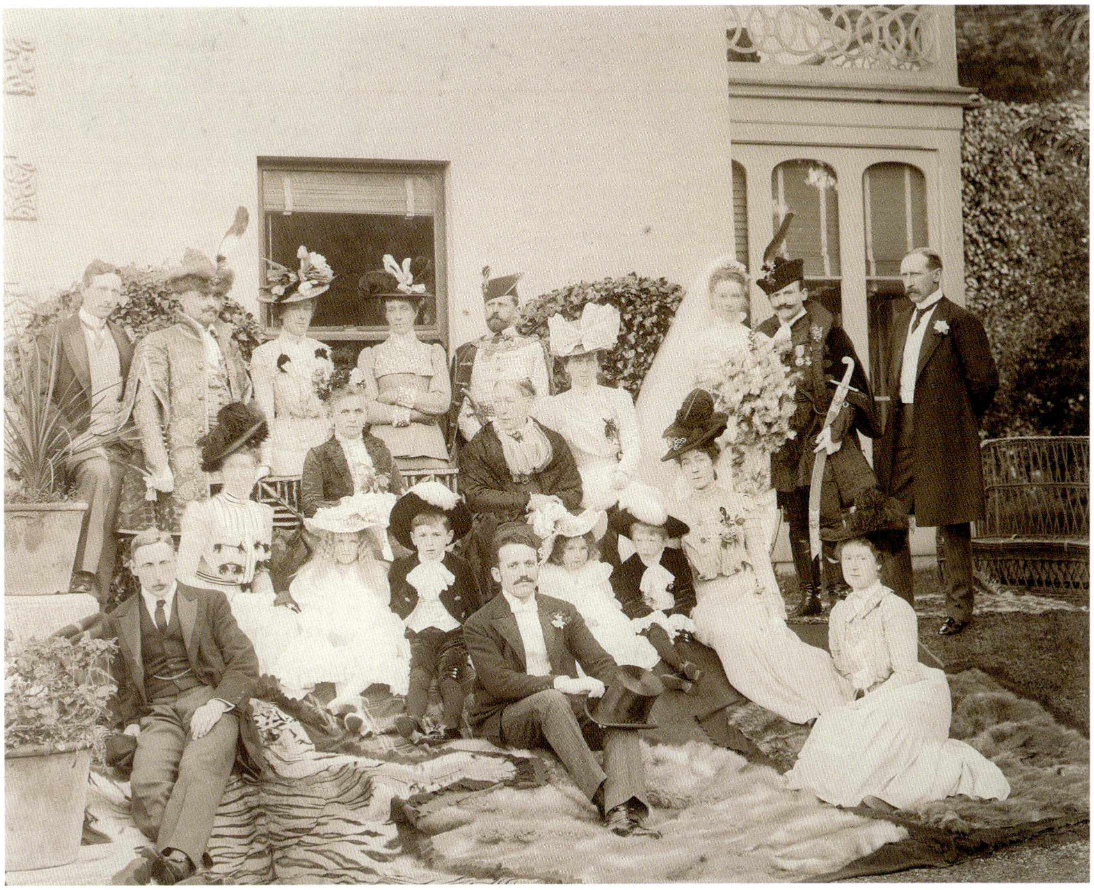

FIG. 3
Philip de László and Lucy Guinness on their wedding day, 7 June 1900, at Burton Hall, Stillorgan, Co. Dublin, after their marriage at St Bridget's, Stillorgan

Lucy Madeleine Guinness and Philip Alexius László (later de László) are standing at the back, far right

Second from left in the back row, Alexius de Lippich, de László's early mentor; on his right two of the bride's sisters; Dr Gabriel de Térey, another friend of the groom

In the middle row, seated, second and third from left, Johanna László, the mother of the groom; Mrs Henry Guinness, the mother of the bride and widow of Henry Guinness of Burton Hall

the period developed his characteristic genre subjects – the great masters, like Lotz, Székely or Benczúr, as much as the many lesser masters, who by specializing in well composed and easily understandable genre paintings became famous and frequently rich as well.

The popularity of genre painting can be explained not only by changes in taste but also by the fact that 'great', heroic, or historical themes had become less attractive, once the era of revolutions was over. Bertalan Székely, de László's cherished teacher, was forced to conclude in spite of himself and his own work that historical painting was the past, genre painting the future. As the generation of artists born around the 1860s came on to the scene, artists who no longer knew the revolutionary years 1848–67 through personal experience, they took as their theme not Man and his destiny but the ethnographically, psychologically or socially definable individual – the child, the agricultural labourer, the small-town official, the Bohemian, the old man or woman, the cripple; or else the Gypsy, the Slovak (*Tóth*), the Swabian etc. Such painting demanded the creation of a perfect illusion by the precise, painstaking documentation of authentic detail. Indeed the creation of a major genre painting demanded the participation of something approximating a small film-crew. The choice of location and the organization of appropriate models and clothes and attributes, the assembly of all these closely studied elements into a unified whole – this could take months, or even years, of work. It is characteristic, for instance, of the procedure employed in such paintings that the head and body of one of the figures were painted from two different models.[11] De László enthusiastically describes the stages in the birth of one of the major works of his early period, *The Hofbräuhaus* (cat. 8; see detail p.10). His enthusiasm was due in no small part to the fact that one of his models – the English lady standing on the far right – was the same Lucy Guinness whom the artist had met at a fancy-dress ball in February 1892, and with whom he had promptly fallen in love. Seven years later, in June 1900 – de Lászlo showed truly biblical patience in his unwavering devotion to Lucy and in gradually winning over her sceptical family – Miss Guinness became his wife (fig. 3). It is an affectingly romantic story, as related in his own words in Rutter's biography.

By 1892 de László was living in Munich. He had already spent a year at the Academy there as a pupil of Sándor Liezen-Mayer, himself

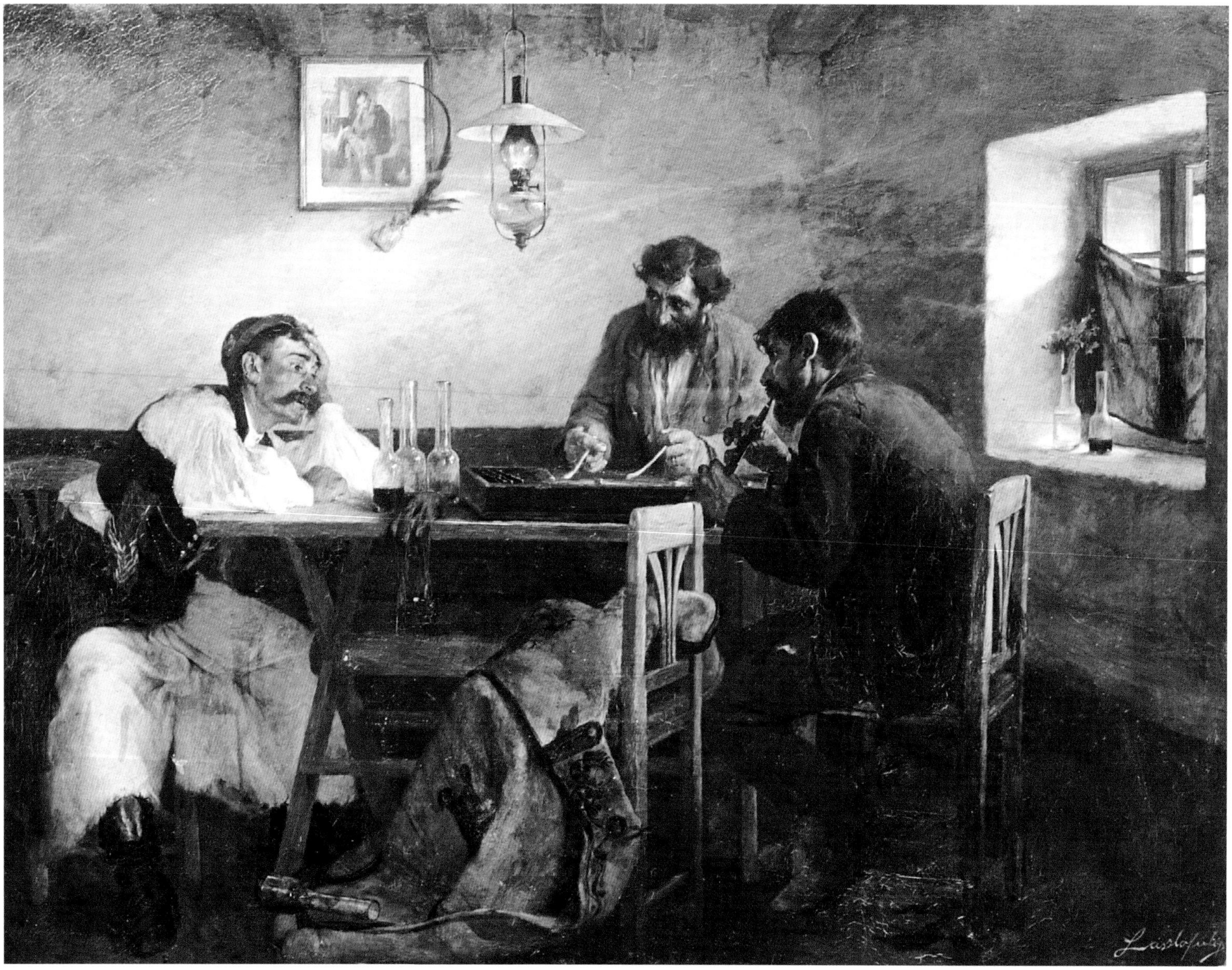

FIG. 4 *Regret* or *Love Spurned*, 1892
Oil on canvas, 83.8 × 118.1 cm
Hungarian National Gallery, Budapest

of Hungarian origin, in 1889–90. After another year studying in Paris at the Académie Julian, László returned to Liezen-Mayer's classes in 1891, remaining there until the summer of 1892. During these years he continued to take part in the Budapest exhibitions. In winter 1891 he exhibited four paintings in Budapest, including the genre painting *Storyteller*, which that year won the Art Lovers' Circle's prize of 1500 *forints*. This was László's first significant Hungarian distinction. Five new paintings by de László appeared in the 1892 Winter Exhibition in Budapest. In this outstanding collection we find the *Hofbräuhaus*, now at last finished, on sale for the unusually high price of 1800 *forints*, although the figure was justified by the respect the work commanded. De László also exhibited a historical character picture, *L'Incroyable* (cat. 7), a portrait in costume recreating a dandy of the French Revolution. The genre painting *Regret*, also known as *Love Spurned* (fig. 4), showing a young man drowning his sorrows in a village tavern, reprised Hungarian folklore. It was also a kind of

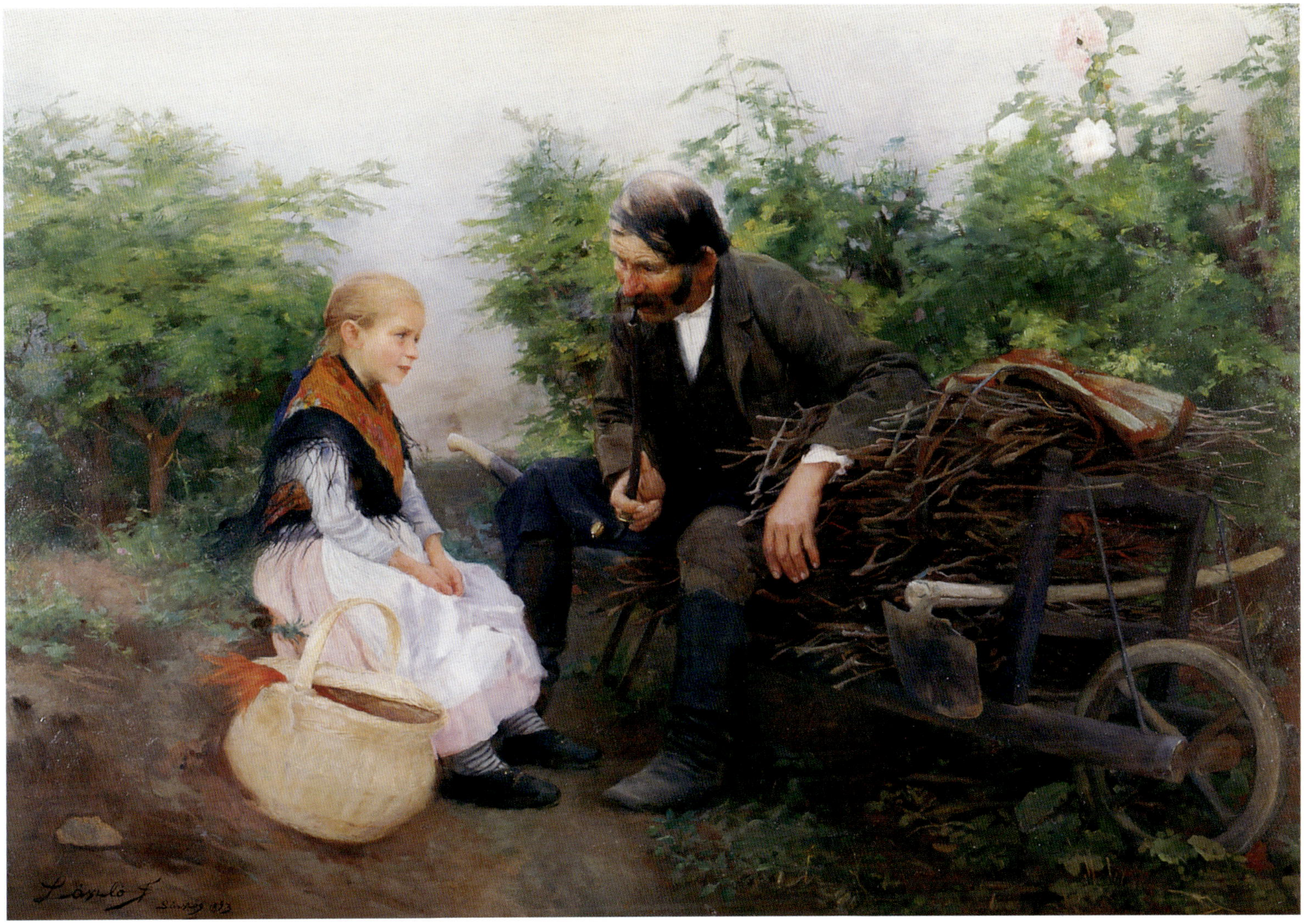

FIG. 5 *The Little Girl and the Gardener* or *Taking a Rest*, 1893
Oil on canvas, 68.5 × 96 cm
Private collection

hommage to Sándor Petőfi, the greatest poet of the Hungarian popular romanticism of the 1840s, whose portrait can be seen on the wall of the tavern, in a pose similar to that of the lovelorn young man. Characters and scenes of Hungarian peasant life constitute the main material of de László's genre painting, even though his greatest successes were not such Hungarian themes. Frequently these genre scenes embodied references to transience and the passing of time, for instance *Taking a Rest* (fig. 5). After the *Hofbräuhaus*, de László's second most famous genre painting was his 1895 *Falling Leaves* (cat. 14). In this widely reproduced work, depicting a veteran of the 1848 struggle for freedom, the aged fighter wearing his old Hussar uniform sits in an autumnal park surrounded by falling leaves, thinking of his youth and of battles for the homeland.

By the middle of the 1890s de László was becoming increasingly well known internationally as a portraitist, but his works were not to be found in the Hungarian national collections. It is for this reason that his 1895 *At Vesper Bell* (cat. 13) is important: it was purchased by the state in 1896 and entered the collections of the National Gallery. This picture, the first of László's works to find its way into a museum, was a reinterpretation of the Angelus theme that was so widespread in nineteenth-century national genre painting. An elderly peasant drops his work and prays at the sound of the tolling bell. The face of the little girl with him radiates deeply held faith, whereas the old man's broken expression betrays a kind of bitter resignation. The most enchanting feature of the painting is the landscape that shimmers in the background in the twilight, already showing the qualities of de László's late landscape paintings. His final genre painting was *Tired*, which was exhibited in 1897. Its title suggests that it was similar to the artist's other peasant genre paintings. He unveiled a portrait of Sándor Liezen-Mayer, his teacher, before Budapest audiences in 1893 and 1896.[12]

The biggest showcase for Hungarian fine art in the nineteenth century was the 1896 Millennium Exhibition, commemorating the thousandth anniversary of Hungarians' arrival in the Carpathian basin. Like all other ambitious painters, de László was keen to contribute a serious historical composition for this occasion. He wrote to a senior civil servant, Miklós Szmrecsányi, in the summer of 1895 in order to obtain a commission from him.[13] His painting of Prince Ferenc Rákóczi II was completed in 1896 and may well have been exhibited. Only one serious historical painting by de László, *Zách Felicián* (cat. 15), featured amongst the thirty historical paintings chosen. Zách was a favourite figure in Hungarian historical painting as in Hungarian ballads. He was, according to legend, a powerful landowner who in 1330 sought revenge against the king for seducing his daughter, attacking the queen. De László represented him in his own likeness, as he imagined it transformed by old age.

Besides such genre paintings, de László from time to time showed portraits. Many artists studied and practised portrait painting, but most considered it merely a means to supplement their income. Compared to the complex task of history or genre painting, painting a head was mere bagatelle. However, the portrait is to figure composition as chamber music is to a symphony. In it every stroke, every note has a specific purpose. In the depiction of a battle, who notices one badly drawn figure, or in the performance of a symphony one poor player among twenty to thirty violinists? But in a portrait one inexact, misplaced line can ruin an otherwise powerful effect.

Though he, too, had greater ambitions, after his Munich years de László was forced to paint bust portraits to earn a living and to support his mother, with whom he had a very close relationship. From the 1890s onwards, however, he acquired ever more distinguished patrons, of whom the Bulgarian Prince Ferdinand was possibly the most important. In 1894 the Sofia publishing house Cosmos asked Elek Koronghi Lippich, a department head in the Ministry of Culture, to recommend a young and none too expensive portrait painter who could paint a portrait of Ferdinand for reproduction.[14] Lippich, who had known the artist from his Munich days and who would continue to support him, recommended de László. De László's journey to Sofia and his encounter with Ferdinand opened the door to other rulers and persons of distinction.

The portrait of Ferdinand (fig. 6) suggests a comparison of de László's career with that of another great figure of the period, Gyula Benczúr. Benczúr was twenty-five years older than de László and had just completed his own portrait of Ferdinand, in 1891 (fig. 7). De László was poised to supplant Benczúr at the top of the Hungarian portrait painting tree, but, by contrast to Benczúr, who painted the bulk of his portraits at home, commissioned by Hungarians, de László became an international who painted more abroad than in Hungary. De László's activity took him all over Europe, his subjects coming from all strata of society. Benczúr and de László differed, too, not simply in style but also in philosophy or approach. If Benczúr clung to the objective, material world, de László saw endlessly changing people with unchanging souls. De László gives a lengthy and exciting description of his visit to Sofia,[15] and his recollections always show insight and sensitivity. All we have from Benczúr from Sofia is two letters to his family. He himself was taciturn, and what he says in the letters is truculent: "I don't yet know what I'll paint tomorrow. On Monday the Prince will be photographed in several poses and on Tuesday, God willing, I'll set off for home!"[16] Benczúr had no qualms about painting from a photograph; in fact he painted his own self-portrait from one. De László, on the other hand, always worked from the living model. He made his sitters converse with him, bringing them into an emotionally active state that guaranteed genuine facial features, expressions and gestures. For him the picture was born during the conversation and itself flowed and twisted in the making. Here he drew a line, there he covered one over only to go in a new direction. Sometimes he would repeat the stroke, or stop to seek an answer, until he got a malleable, sensitive, exact idea of the other person. For him a portrait was an interactive project. His method and results were consistent. It was the secret of his success. He was a kind of Professor Higgins, able to tell after a couple of words the origins and education of the person he was talking to, sometimes even his age, and whether you could make a lady out of a Doolittle by teaching her to talk. A de László portrait is like a good conversation – reserved, deliberate, and perhaps even unemotional, but also magnificent, humorous and exact. It reveals at least as much about the person as a touching, spiritual depiction. De László's subjects were distinguished people. Their elegance was revealed in their dress and postures alike. De László represented this elegance in graceful, virtuoso paintings. He stressed that dignity was not pompous, bombastic or histrionic, but rather the display of inherent grace – sharing a general trend at the end of the nineteenth century towards a more quotidian, direct depiction of the subject in portrait painting. The heroic, boasting swagger portrait was giving way to a more 'natural' representation, even in prestigious paintings.

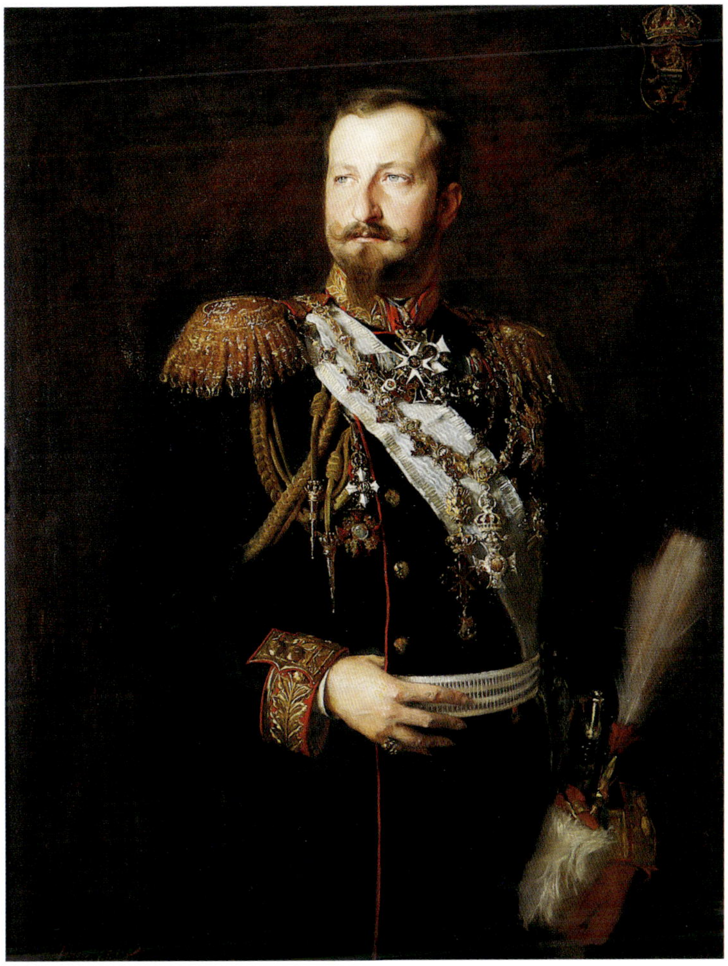

FIG. 6
H.R.H. Prince Ferdinand of Bulgaria (1861–1948), 1894
Oil on canvas, 119.4 × 91.4 cm
Private collection, Spain

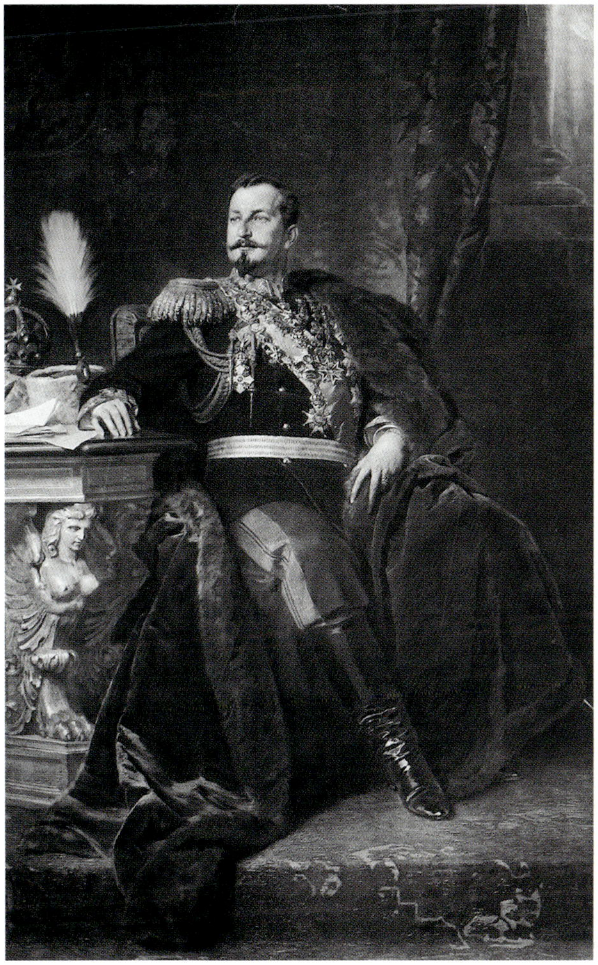

FIG. 7
Gyula Benczúr (1844–1920)
H.R.H. Prince Ferdinand of Bulgaria
Engraving

In comparison with László's interactive, conversational paintings, Benczúr's resemble a speech. He used props, costumes and draperies to enliven his works. He left nothing to chance; every tiny detail was carefully planned, defined and explicitly declared. His precision was a consequence, too, of his use of photographs, since in a photograph every part is equal, without distinction of emphasis. "Photography is based on that well-calculated moment when the model is waiting in anticipation, a huge detriment to authenticity," said László in a 1901 interview.[17] Even when Benczúr was not working from a photograph, he employed a similar approach. The Emperor Francis Joseph (King of Hungary) was used to Benczúr's painting method. When de László came to paint him (see fig. 18, p.32), revealingly, the Emperor reacted with great surprise when de László began working at the first sitting on an empty canvas. The Emperor had expected that the painter should already have outlined the portrait from a photograph and was to meet his sitter only to ensure the likeness and to put in final touches. Francis Joseph repeated the story of de László's empty canvas frequently, to many different people.[18]

In his early years László usually managed to lay down the finishing touches after four or five sittings. To many the paintings seemed finished after just one – indeed some were. De László himself claimed that he worked on the entire surface of the painting on each occasion. He laid down the main features, colour schemes and background contrasts without any preliminary sketches, and then later brought them up. His method is well illustrated in one of his most famous pictures, his portrait of Pope Leo XIII (cat. 18). The Hungarian Catholic Church had commissioned the painting in 1900 to celebrate the nine-hundredth anniversary of the Hungarian Christian state, and arranged the sitting in Rome. Seeing his portrait after three sittings, the Pope found his face to be too much like Voltaire's. With the Pope's permission de László began the entire work anew, and after another four sittings produced a painting that was awarded a gold medal by an international panel of judges that same year at the Paris world exhibition.

During the portrait sittings, de László worked out every detail not only of the sitter's face, but of the sitter's clothing as well. De László's technique is illustrated again in his portrait of Cardinal Rampolla (cat. 19). De László was so taken by the Cardinal's exquisite, fragile hands, in sharp contrast to his strapping physique, that he spent one and a half hours painting only his hands: "In the afternoon of the same day I was occupied with the picture of Cardinal Rampolla, and when I came to paint his hands, I found them more difficult to express than those of the Pope, which rested, simply and naturally, on the arms of the chair with the object of emphasizing his age. I placed the hands of the Cardinal so that they rested one on the other on the biretta. My object was to express through his hands the self-control manifested in his expression. Like the Pope, he was a splendid sitter. I explained to him that it would be very difficult to get the same position for the hands and that I wished to begin and finish both hands in the same sitting. 'How long will you need?' he asked. 'An hour and a half, Your Eminence', I replied. 'Bene', he said, and did not move his hands throughout the sitting. Painting with great concentration, I finished the work and I do not think I have ever painted a better pair of hands."[19]

De László's paintings continued a recent academic tradition – typified by the style of the Franz von Lenbach in Germany, who was greatly appreciated by de László – based on the flamboyant style of eighteenth-century English portraiture. His work involved a high level of technical skill; it was exact, but never over-detailed, it was not a psychological description but rather expressive of social status; he would use a number of Baroque devices in the composition; he laid in creamy, impasto brushstrokes apparently with great ease, with confident elegance and with calligraphic freedom. The free-floating, fanciful and seemingly instinctive contours, blurred strokes and ridges and furrows of paint looked as if they had emerged spontaneously, even if they were actually the product of a feverish, temperamental work tempo. As an Hungarian obituarist wrote of him, "His lines simply ran, in our age no one compares to his mastery of painted calligraphy."[20] Except in his earliest works he never sketched his sitters' faces before beginning. He simply took up his brush and started the picture, beginning by shaping the principal contours. He considered drawing more important than painting, and found it more valuable to grasp the characteristic features with a monochromatic pencil or chalk rather than with colour. He thought that using colours created a more general impression. Drawing required reduction, and in this sense called for more attention, understanding and skill.

De László produced more than three thousand portraits, an astonishing number in itself, even if they had not included many like that of the German Imperial Chancellor Hohenlohe-Schillingsfürst, which so greatly impressed Kaiser William II (cat. 40) that he at once wanted to meet the artist, whom he would later consider a lifelong friend. In general it can be said of de László that his consistently excellent portraits not only meant orders and satisfied clients, but good friends as well. At a London award dinner in 1932 he offered the following statement of his art: "To sum up, I feel that a great portrait should, in substance, be as follows: It must represent the painter in its composition and its colour scheme. It must represent a combination of the painter and the sitter in that the sitter is shown in an atmosphere and a pose which the painter has selected to characterise the mind and soul and walk of life of the sitter. And it must represent the sitter, in that he who sees the picture sees not only the human form of the sitter but sees the revelation of all his potentialities."[21]

When he moved with his new wife to Budapest in 1900 he already owned the city's most luxurious studio-villa (figs. 8, 9). His son Henry was born there, as was his daughter, Eva, who died young. It was largely for family reasons that he decided to settle in London in 1907, holding his first solo exhibition in England that same year, at the London Fine Art Society. But for some time before he had hardly been living in Budapest. He was more often to be seen working in elegant spa towns, in the palaces of his distinguished patrons, or in hotels in world cities. After 1903 Vienna had become a more frequent place of stay for him than Budapest. But, with a curious asymmetry, in the year 1907 he also had a solo exhibition in Budapest. The collection of almost a hundred exhibits embraced his entire life's work, from the very beginning to the lavish portraits on which he was working at the time. Thereafter he returned to Hungary on only three occasions (in 1910, 1927 and 1935), but he did not lose all contact with the land of his birth. He immortalized several Hungarian aristocrats in his later portraits, and even painted several portraits of the Regent Miklós Horthy (see cat. 109). In 1925, a small exhibition opened at the National Fine Arts Society, but thereafter the Hungarian press had nothing much to say about him, until his death. Yet, in 1907, Budapest could at last make the acquaintance of this painter: the city could see in its entirety the astonishing oeuvre that had brought acclaim and distinction to its creator. With this exhibition, de László may be said to have truly arrived in Budapest, but he had also left his home town behind.[22]

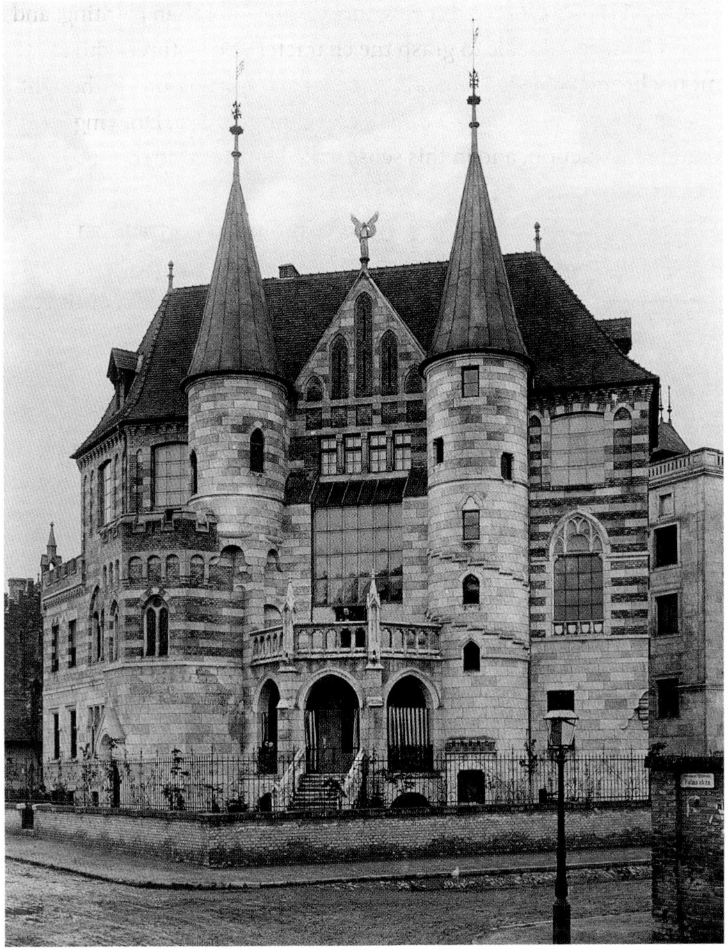

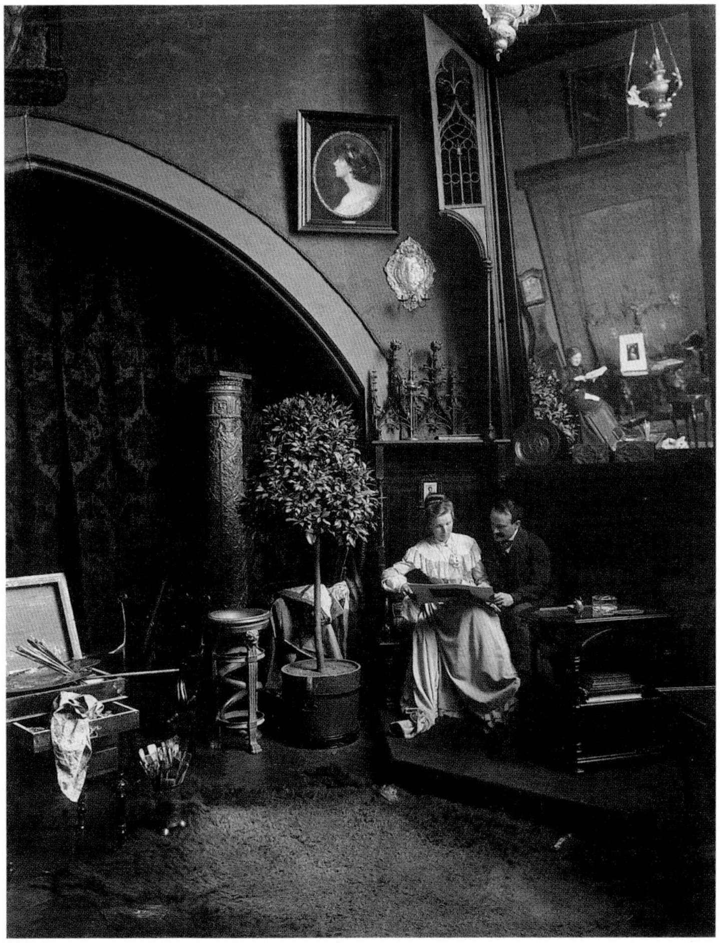

FIG. 8 (LEFT) *Philip de László's studio-villa, Pálma utea 10, Budapest*, photograph, 1900

FIG. 9 (RIGHT) *Philip de László and his wife, née Lucy Guinness, in the artist's studio at home in Budapest*, photograph, 1903

NOTES

1. Bad Kissingen, 10 September 1908, addressee unknown: MNG Adattár 1029/1920.
2. Owen Rutter, *Portrait of a Painter. The Authorized Life of Philip de László*, London (Hodder & Stoughton) 1939.
3. See Rutter 1939, p.23.
4. 26 June 1899, London, addressee unknown: (Archives of the Hungarian National Gallery) MNG Adattár 3495/1937.
5. This issue was addressed in the 1995 exhibition at the Hungarian National Gallery entitled 'Medals, Silver Wreaths. The Cult and Patronage of Art in 19th-century Hungary', curated by Katalin Sinkó.
6. Rutter 1939, p.17.
7. MNG Adattár 1030/1920.
8. See note 1.
9. See note 1.
10. Rutter 1939, pp.42–43.
11. Rutter 1939, p.85.
12. *Sándor Liezen-Mayer*, oil on canvas, 102.5 x 72 cm, Staatliche Galerie, Munich, inv. no. G. 11144.
13. Letter by de László to Miklós Szmrecsányi, 8 August 1895: MNG Adattár 4353/1-3.
14. Rutter 1939, pp.131–32.
15. Rutter 1939, pp.132–44.
16. Gyula Benczúr's letter to his family, no date (end of 1891): MNG Adattár, 6018/1954. The original text of the letter runs: *"Was ich morgen male, weiß ich noch nicht. Montag wird der Fürst in mehreren Stellungen photographiert und Dienstag reise ich, so Gott will heimwärts!"*
17. *Új Idok* [New Times], 1901, p.186.
18. *Müvcsarnok* [Art Gallery], 1899, pp.298–300.
19. Rutter 1939, p.200.
20. Fülöp László and János Thorma: 'Ervin Ybl: Képzömüvészeti halottai', *Budapesti Szemle*, CCXLVIII, 1938, pp.108–14.
21. The Art of the Painter. The response of Mr Philip de Laszlo to the toast of G.W. Jones', 1932.
22. It is indeed time that he should come home. The Ernst Museum, the founder of which, Lajos Ernst, was painted by de László in 1907, is preparing a de László exhibition for spring 2004.

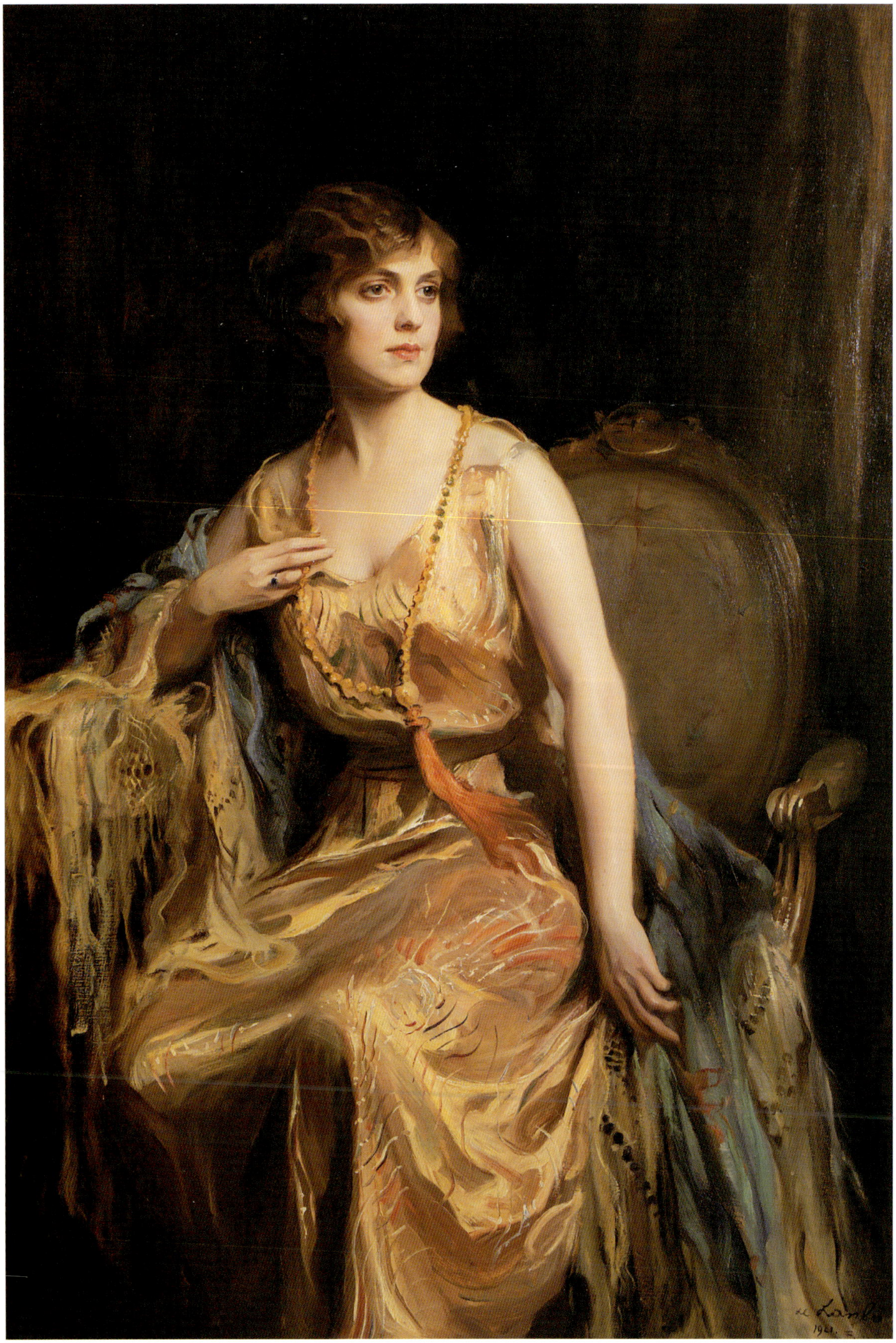

Philip de László in England

Christopher Wood

By 1907, Philip de László was thirty-eight years old, and had conquered Europe. Now he was to conquer England and America. His move to London in 1907 was for him a new artistic and social challenge; yet again, it was to prove a spectacular success, although not without its setbacks. Over the next thirty years, until his death in 1937, he was to become England's leading portrait painter. At the same time he maintained and consolidated his reputation in Europe, and built up a remarkable clientèle in America, painting four Presidents and many distinguished citizens.

In 1907 Sargent decided to give up portrait painting, and, as Richard Ormond demonstrates in his essay (pp.37–45), de László literally stepped into Sargent's shoes, painting many of the same sitters. But de László's motives for coming to London were largely personal. His English wife Lucy wanted to come home, and to bring up their children in England. By 1907 they had three sons, Henry, born in 1901, Stephen, born in 1904, and Paul, born in 1906. A girl, Eva, was born in 1903, but died in the same year. In England, they were to have two more sons, Patrick, born in 1909, and John, born in 1912.

De László began writing the story of his life in 1917, but by the time of his sudden death in 1937 he had not finished it. His account was then used by his friend and biographer, Owen Rutter, as the basis of his book on de László, published in 1939. Rutter quoted at length from de László's writings, which are the basis for most of our knowledge of his career. He also left a huge archive of letters and memorabilia, hitherto largely untouched, but now used by Suzanne Bailey as the basis of her article in this catalogue (see pp.47–60). We know from Rutter that de László was already a great admirer of England before he came here. He appreciated England's history, and its democratic traditions. He particularly appreciated its great tradition of portrait painting, and wanted to be part of it. He also knew of England's traditional hospitality towards foreign artists, from Holbein and Van Dyck, through to Lely and Kneller, and on to the nineteenth and twentieth centuries. In de László's lifetime, such artists as Tissot, Whistler, Sargent, Alma-Tadema and Herkomer had all settled successfully in England; so had the sculptor Joseph Edgar Boehm, a fellow Hungarian. "All this," wrote de László, "led me to feel that here indeed I could make my life, in this home of the art to which I was devoted, and that I might aspire to become a link, however humble, in the great chain of foreign artists who had been received and treated by England as her own sons."[1]

Before 1907, de László had already painted several English sitters, including Lord Stanley, Lord O'Neill and Sir George White. In 1904, two of his finest early portraits, of *Pope Leo XIII* (cat. 18) and of *Cardinal Rampolla* (cat. 19), had been shown at the International Society of Arts exhibition. To launch his career in England, de László decided to hold an exhibition in London, which was held at the Fine Art Society in May 1907. It contained fifty pictures, of both European and English sitters, including the Duke and Duchess of Teck, the Grand Duke and Duchess of Hesse (who he had just painted in Darmstadt), the King of Portugal and Princess Louise of Battenberg. *Pope Leo XIII* and *Cardinal Rampolla* were shown again, and a charming early picture of a girl, *Daniela Grunelius*, plus a few family pictures. It was an impressive collection, and a typical de László mixture.

Count Mensdorff, the Austro-Hungarian ambassador, was a friend of de László, and an extremely popular figure in London society. He agreed to open the exhibition, and also ensured that it would be attended by the rich, the royal and the fashionable. On 7 June the exhibition was visited by King Edward VII and Queen

FIG. 10
Miss Irene Hurst, later the Hon. Mrs Rose, 1921
Oil on canvas, 129.5 × 104.1 cm
Private collection

Alexandra. On the very same day, de László was commanded by the king and queen to come to Buckingham Palace and paint their daughter, Princess Victoria. He got there by 2.30 pm, and began the portrait at 3.00. Thus on that day de László's career in England was well and truly launched. This commission led to his painting both the King and Queen (figs. 26, 27, p. 36) and her parents, the King and Queen of Denmark. He painted King Edward VII in civilian dress, and found him an impatient sitter. His main concern was his necktie: "Please notice that it is not a ready-made tie," he said to the artist, "I arrange it myself, so see that you make that plain in the picture, for no gentleman wears a ready-made tie." The result was not one of de László's best works, as he was only allowed three short sittings. But he was to find many other better sitters in the English royal family over the next thirty years.

The reviews of the Fine Art Society exhibition were mixed, as one might expect, but all of them acknowledged his extraordinary technical skill in depicting grand and interesting sitters in a relaxed and informal way. *The Studio* commented in particular on his success "in catching the special fascination of women", always to be one of de László's strong points (fig. 10). Both *The Observer* and *The Sketch* referred to him as "the Hungarian Sargent", but *The Academy*, edited by the contentious and quarrelsome Lord Alfred Douglas, compared him unfavourably to Sargent. Douglas also pointed out that "as a portrait painter he had several equals and a few superiors in our country". Douglas does not name any names, but is clearly referring to such Edwardian painters as John Lavery, William Orpen, Frank Dicksee or Glyn Philpot.

De László was not a man to be deterred by criticism, and the Fine Art Society exhibition resulted not only in royal commissions, but in other important contacts. Arthur Lee M.P. (later Lord Lee of Fareham) became both a friend and patron (see cat. 88), introducing him to numerous clients, including James Lowther, Speaker of the House of Commons (cat. 38). It was Lee who commissioned de László to go to Washington and paint President Theodore Roosevelt (fig. 11). In March 1908, de László and his wife made the first of their five trips to the United States. He painted not only Roosevelt but several other important American sitters, including Andrew Mellon and George Eastman, who later gave him a ciné camera, of which he became an enthusiastic amateur. His American portraits were shown at Knoedler's in New York, and the critics praised his portrait of Roosevelt as the best of him ever painted – better even than Sargent's. So de Lászlo returned well pleased from his American trip, and £2,000 the richer.

Back in England, de László's life was to settle into the pattern he was to follow for the rest of his life – a busy and successful career in London, punctuated by regular trips to Europe and America. In 1908, the de László family moved to a new house in Kensington, 3 Palace Gate. It had no studio, but de László found one within walking distance, on Campden Hill. He was to remain in Kensington until 1921, when he made his final move to a large house and studio in Hampstead, at 3 Fitzjohn's Avenue. Like Alma-Tadema, who died in 1912, de László was quickly accepted into the London art world. The landscape painter Alfred East (cat. 34) became a close friend, and introduced him to many other artists. He became an Honorary member of the Royal Society of Portrait Painters , and a member of the Arts Club in Dover Street. Although he never became an R.A., de László was popular, and very much part of the London art scene. He did not belong to the inner establishment, but he did not need to.

The years leading up to the First World War were to be tremendously busy and fruitful for de László, in England, Europe and America. The First World War was to lead, however, to the biggest setback of his career. The golden years of the Edwardian age had given no inkling of this. He was painting the royal family, and this royal cachet meant that many of the great families of the aristocracy wanted his services, too. Among his most loyal and faithful clients were the families of the Dukes of Portland, Devonshire, Wellington and Northumberland. who all commissioned numerous pictures over many years. Other families for whom he painted many portraits included those of Aberconway, Selborne, Londonderry, Brocket, Bowlby, Harmsworth, Schröder (cat. 39, 73), Cazalet, Chamberlain (cat. 89, 90), Cromer, Croft, d'Erlanger (cat. 27), Devonport (cat. 61), Haldane, Lansdowne, Minto, Stanley, Trouton (cat. 47, 66) and Verulam. He was also particularly popular in Scotland, painting the Strathmore (cat. 120, 121), Mansfield, Balfour, Airlie (cat. 127), Buchanan (cat. 119), Elphinstone (cat. 101) and Graham (cat. 71, 103) families. In addition to the aristocracy, de László painted many of the famous personalities of the day, including politicians, soldiers, scientists, writers, and actresses. Before the First War, his sitters included Field Marshall Byng (cat. 118), Mrs Asquith, Arthur Balfour (fig. 23, p.33), Lord Roberts (also painted by Sargent; figs. 33, 34, p.45), Admiral Beatty (fig. 12), Lord Curzon (cat. 54), Vita Sackville-West (cat. 44) and Elinor Glyn (cat. 55) – this last commissioned by Lord Curzon, who thought the picture "a masterpiece of modern times".

In Europe, de László's career also went from strength to strength. In 1908 he went to Berlin to paint the Kaiser William II, the Empress, the Crown Prince and the Princess Victoria Louise. The Princess said of the portrait of the Kaiser, a half length, in a fur collar (fig. 62, p.105), "*Endlich der Papa und nicht der Kaiser*" (At last my father, not the Emperor). The Kaiser was so delighted that he commissioned de László to come back in 1909 to paint a full-length portrait of him with a white charger and borzoi dog (cat. 40). In 1910 de László went to Madrid to paint the King of Spain, the Queen and the Queen Mother. In 1910 the Uffizi asked him to present a self-portrait. (Holman Hunt had done the same three years earlier.) In Paris he had

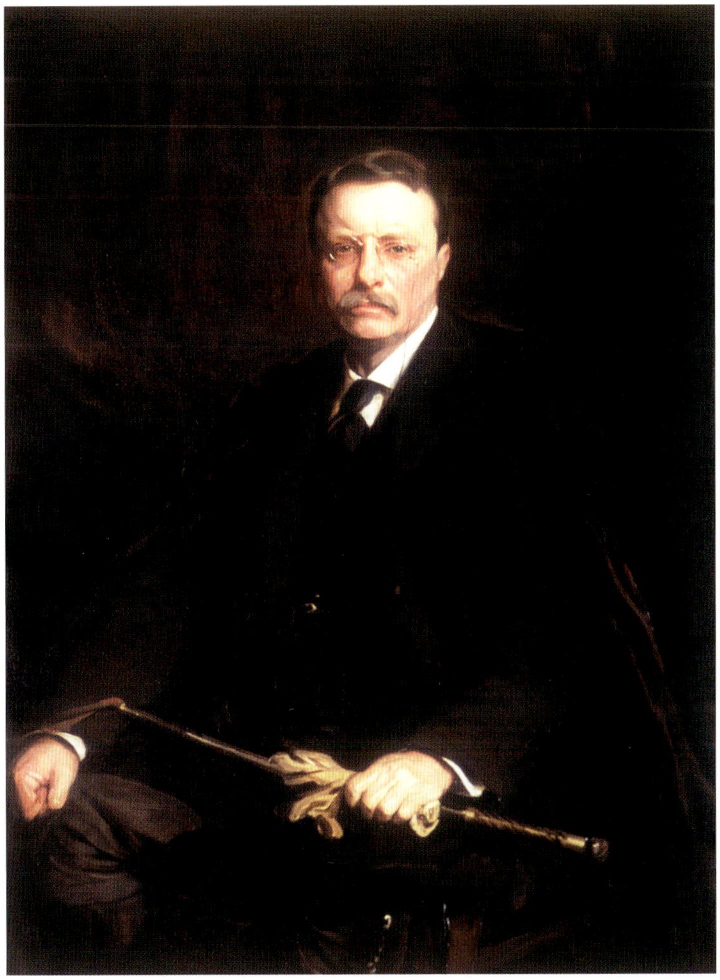

FIG. 11
President Theodore Roosevelt, 1908
Oil on canvas, 160 × 124.5 cm
The American Museum of Natural History, New York

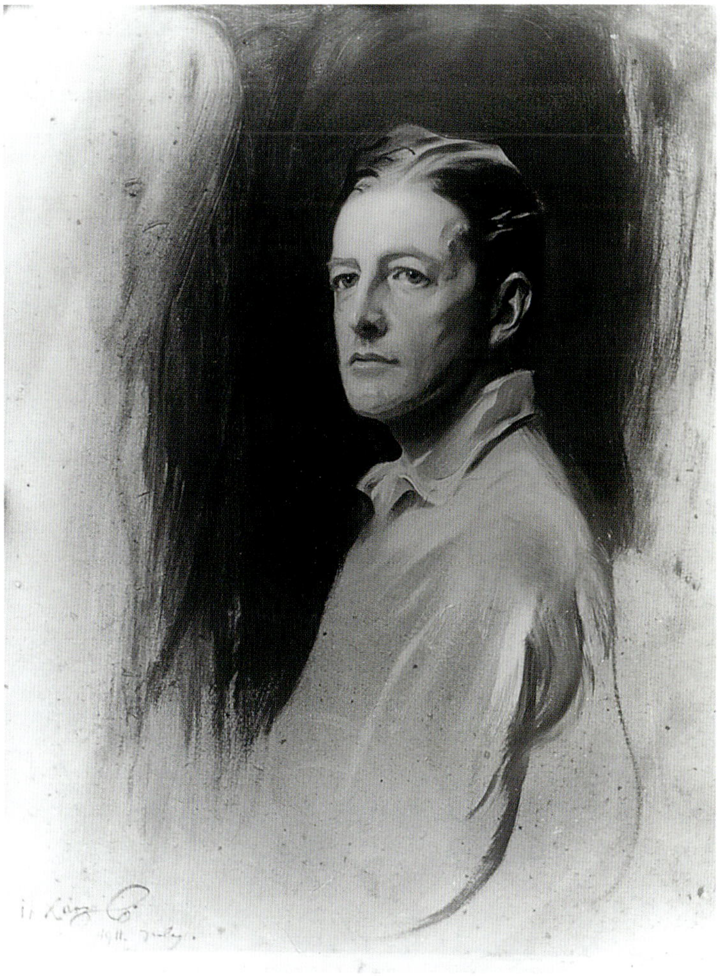

FIG. 12
Rear Admiral David Beatty, 1911
Oil on board, 79 × 63.4 cm (31 × 25 in.)
Private collection

many famous sitters, including the comtesse de Noailles, the comtesse Greffuhle (the original for Proust's Duchesse de Guermantes), Robert de Montesquiou, and numerous members of the de Gramont family (cat. 29). He also travelled to Athens to paint the Greek royal family (cat. 58–60). In 1912, the Emperor of Austria and King of Hungary, Francis Joseph, conferred on de László the hereditary title of de Lómbos. Henceforward, he was able to sign himself de László. It was the summit of his extraordinary career. But nemesis was in waiting, just around the corner.

It was the First World War which led to the first and only setback of de László's career. Just before the outbreak of war, de László was granted naturalization as an English citizen. His sponsors were Lord Devonport, Arthur Balfour, Arthur Lee and Howard Guinness, his brother-in-law. Though he had thought of seeking it sooner, the timing was unfortunate, as Hungary entered the war on the German side. As a result, de László was attacked in the Hungarian press, and his money in Austria seized. It also meant that he fell under suspicion in England, which was to intensify as the war progressed. Despite his giving generously to the Red Cross auctions and other war charities, his pictures began to be refused at exhibitions. Desperate to keep in touch with his family in Budapest, and to continue supporting them, he sent money to them via friends in Holland and Spain. Although innocent enough, these letters were intercepted, and in 1917 de László had to appear before Sir Charles

Matthews, the Director of Public Prosecutions, who gave him a warning. Not long after this, de László unwisely gave £1 to a Hungarian internee who came to his house, begging for help. He later reported this, but as a result he was arrested, and confined in Brixton Prison. Paranoia about foreigners had become intense by this stage of the war, and de László was denounced by the newspapers owned by Lord Northcliffe, whom he had painted in 1909. After a trial, at which many loyal friends and patrons spoke up for him, he was moved to Holloway Internment Camp, and finally released only in 1918. His experiences led to a nervous breakdown, and he ended the war, still confined, in a nursing home. He consoled himself at this time painting many charming studies of his wife and children (cat. 74–87). He was able to recuperate at the country house of his lawyer and friend Sir Charles Russell. However, it was not until 1919, after a further trial, that he was exonerated and his naturalization re-confirmed.

This ordeal left its mark on de László, but, being a man of resolve, he threw himself back into his work with frenetic energy. His capacity for work was prodigious: he could often see three sitters each day, and is estimated to have painted over 3,000 portraits by the time of his death. He simply wore himself out with overwork. Even after the war he was still attacked by *John Bull* magazine, edited by the odious Horatio Bottomley, but soon his clientèle began to build up again. By 1923, he was ready for his first exhibition since the war, at the French Gallery in Pall Mall. In 1925 he was received at court by King George V and Queen Mary, thus marking his official re-acceptance into royal circles, and English society. In 1930, he became President of the Royal Society of British Artists, in succession to Walter Sickert. The pattern of his life resumed, but with one important change: he began to take holidays – to Egypt, North Africa, Italy and the South of France. On these trips he was able for the first time to develop his considerable talents as a landscape painter. The oil sketches made on these trips, which mostly still belong to his family (cat. 105–9, 112–5), will come as a revelation to those who think of de László only as a portrait painter.

De László was painting right up to the end, with no visible decline in his powers. The 1920s and 1930s were hugely busy for him, with royalty, aristocrats and famous personalities still knocking on his door. Perhaps no portrait painter has painted such an extraordinary range of famous people. In 1923 he went to Rome to paint Mussolini, of whom he was a great admirer. In 1929 he was in Egypt painting King Fouad (fig. 83, p.176) and his son Prince Farouk. He then took a trip up the Nile, where he painted some of his best oil sketches of landscapes and buildings (cat. 112–5). The list of his famous sitters at this period is astonishing: Montagu Norman, Lloyd George, Lord Inchcape, Queen Marie of Rumania (cat. 128), the Duchess of York, later Queen Elizabeth the Queen Mother (cat. 98), Admiral Horthy (cat. 109), Sir Flinders Petrie, Princess Marina (cat. 126), Prince Chichibu of Japan, Anny Ahlers (cat. 123), Gwen Frangcon-Davies (cat. 125), Philip Sassoon (fig. 13), Gladys Cooper – the list goes on and on. Certainly Sargent never painted such a range of sitters as this. In this respect the only artist with whom de László can be compared is Franz Xavier Winterhalter, who also painted all the crowned heads of Europe.

But the comparison ends there: Winterhalter's range was much narrower, and he never settled permanently in England. At this point, it seems a good moment to look at de László's style and technique. Like Alma-Tadema, de László came to London in his late thirties, when his style and his reputation were already firmly established. His training had been entirely European – he studied in Budapest, Munich and Paris, and spent several years living in Vienna. De László's style emanates from mid-Europe, although living in England had a definite influence on his later work. De László certainly admired the Hungarian artist Gyula Benczúr, who was twenty-five years older than him, and enjoyed considerable success as portrait painter to the Austro-Hungarian empire. We also know of de László's admiration for the Austrian painter Franz von Lenbach, although he deplored his use of photographs. The influence of both these artists is detectible in de László's work, but he was also much influenced by the old masters, in particular Titian and Velázquez. His list of paintings he most admired is revealing – Michelangelo's Sistine Chapel, Rembrandt's *Night Watch*, Frans Hals's portrait of himself and his wife, Velázquez's *Pope Innocent X*, Dagnan-Bouvert's *Country Wedding*, Reynolds's *Nelly O'Brien*.[2] This is an eclectic list, to say the least, with Dagnan-Bouveret perhaps the most surprising name there. The artists whose influence can most obviously be seen in de László's work are Velázquez, Hals and Reynolds. Van Dyck, surprisingly, does not get a mention. De László certainly took many of his repertoire of poses from Old Masters.

De László's early portraits such as *Pope Leo XII* (cat. 18) and *Cardinal Rampolla* (cat. 19) are painted with tight brushwork and polished colours, and look decidedly European, and of their time. By the time de László came to England in 1907, a complete transformation had taken place. His style had become bolder, his technique looser, his brushstrokes broader. From being a mid-European painter to the Austro-Hungarian Empire he had suddenly developed into an Edwardian painter in the international style. So whence did this new stylistic panache come? In his memoirs de László makes reference to the Old Masters, Velázquez and Reynolds in particular. But in Paris, and in London, he must also have become aware of the work of John Singer Sargent, Giovanni Boldini and the Impressionists. It is much more likely that their influence, and their success, propelled him along the same path, to become one of the masters of the broad brush. It was a style that had its followers all over Europe, from

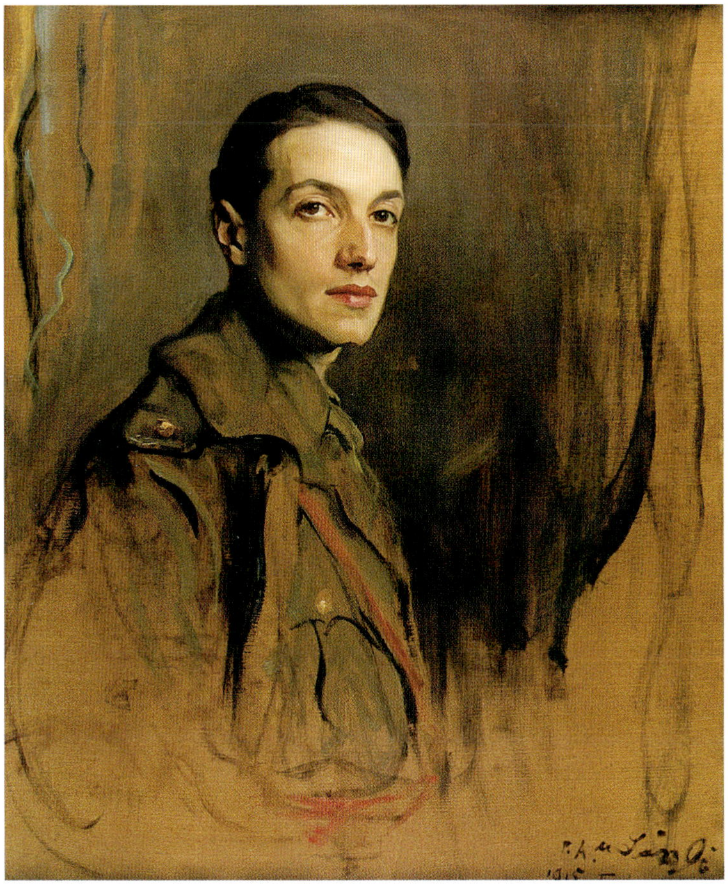

FIG. 13
Sir Philip Sassoon, 3rd Bt, 1915
Oil on canvas, 88.9 × 71.2 cm
Private collection

Sorolla in Spain to Serov in Russia. It remained the dominant high style for fashionable portrait painting from the 1880s up to the First World War, and beyond. De László was to carry it on nearly up to the Second World War. At its best, it was a style brilliantly suited to portrait painting, and produced what are arguably some of the most striking portraits of all time.

In his early period, de László made figurative drawings and studies for his pictures, in the approved academic style of the day. Examples of these studies, for *The Hofbraühaus* (cat. 8) and *Zách Felicián* (cat. 15), show what a highly accomplished draughtsman he was. But, as his portrait style developed, and his facility as a painter increased, he used preparatory drawings less and less, preferring to work directly on the canvas, usually in monochrome, then in colour, picking first on some salient feature, such as eyes, or nose, and then working outwards and downwards to details of dress and background. It was a technique which demanded incredible sureness of touch. Often de László would discard one or two sketches, and then start again. But when it worked, the resulting portrait would have an immediacy and spontaneity that more laboured portraits could never have. "I draw with my brush, and all my painting is drawing," he wrote.[3]

Before the First World War, de László taught briefly at an art school, The London and New Art School. He gave his services for free, as he liked encouraging younger painters. He would not allow preliminary drawing on the canvas, and insisted that his pupils work only with oil, first monochrome, then colour. "More luminous, more luminous", he would say.[4] In 1934, de László published a book, *How to Paint a Portrait*, using the Welsh actress Gwen Ffrangcon-Davies as a model (cat. 125). Here de László explained his methods. Working on a blank canvas, already in its frame, he would start with three lines of the brush to indicate the angles of the eyes, nose and mouth; this was the foundation of the whole design. Then he would paint the shape of the head, but only by means of light and shade. Often he used a mirror. It was a technique that required extraordinary dexterity, and great powers of concentration. Usually he would work for three hours at a time without a break.

Like Sargent, de László did occasionally make portrait drawings, using pencil and black or coloured chalks, such as *The Duchess of Portland* (cat. 49), *Miss Diana Chamberlain* (cat. 90) or *Major-General Sir John Hanbury Williams* (fig. 13). He also made many charming drawings of children, such as *Robin Vane-Tempest-Stewart* as a page (cat. 50), and even made a drawing of his golf professional (cat. 69).

De László's technique naturally lent itself to the portrait sketch, of which he was an absolute master. Whether painting a simple head or a head and shoulders, de László would rapidly complete the face and head, and then deliberately leave the rest of the canvas blank. Often a flurry of brush strokes would spill out in all directions, giving the impression that de László had literally just stopped and put down his brushes, in mid-session. This technique can be seen in many portraits, such as *James Lowther* (cat. 38), *Baron Sir Rudolph Slatin Pasha* (cat. 110), *Lord Louis Mountbatten* (cat. 43), or in the study of two Sikh officers (cat. 70). These have a freshness and spontaneity that many have admired more than his finished portraits. The backgrounds are often a distinctive buff colour and de László was fond of greeny-blue colours, which make them instantly recognizable. De László's range of colours is highly distinctive, and quite different from those of any of his other contemporaries; they are probably a legacy of his mid-European background.

Inevitably, the majority of de László's sitters were women, and it is as a painter of women he will be chiefly remembered. Nearly all his male sitters, be they kings, emperors, dukes or commoners, wanted him to paint their wives, their daughters and their little children. This is in no way to disparage the quality of de László's portraits of men, which were certainly just as good. But de László obviously responded to the attractions of beautiful, fascinating and stylish women, and he enjoyed painting them. As both Richard Ormond and Christopher Lloyd here point out, de László made queens and princesses look both regal and natural, interesting and modern, all at the same time. He re-invented royalty for the twentieth century. His picture of the beautiful and tragic Queen Marie of Roumania is a classic example of this (cat. 128). And he did just the same for his other sitters. However grand, distinguished or beautiful they were, de László could make them look interesting, make them come alive. That was what his sitters called "László's magic".[5]

De László liked his sitters to talk during sittings, so that their expressions and positions might look as lively and natural as possible. De László himself was an ebullient and entertaining character. To a particularly beautiful lady, he would say, "What an ugly girl you are".[6] Rutter wrote that de László rarely painted a sitter without making a friend, whereas Sargent rarely painted a sitter without making an enemy,[7] which is perhaps being unfair to Sargent. But it is certainly true of de László, and is confirmed by the many letters from sitters in the family archive.

De László was at his best painting a full-length portrait of a beautiful and elegant woman, such as *Mrs George Owen Sandys* of 1915 (cat. 64) or *Mrs. Archie Graham* of 1917 (cat. 71). These are both conventional Edwardian portraits, but with a distinctly stylish European chic. De László could be more daring on occasion, as in the extraordinary *Viscountess Castlereagh* of 1913 (cat. 57), represented full-length in a ballgown, in a moorland landscape, holding her pet lurcher, a dog at that time still largely associated with poaching. Later he was to paint her in uniform, with a restraint more suited to wartime (cat. 56). *Lady Alastair Graham* (cat. 103) he turns into an Italianate Madonna, in profile, holding lilies. *Vita Sackville-West* (cat. 44), in her large black hat, looks more like a Frans Hals. With *Mrs. Edmund Buchanan* (cat. 119) of 1929, a marvellously lively and animated portrait, we are instantly in the world of the 1920s, flappers and Bright Young Things. De László could move with the times, and his portraits of the 1920s and 1930s are as vivid a record of that unhappy era as one could wish. If a grand sitter wanted to look regal, then de László could oblige, as he did for *The Duchess of Northumberland* (cat. 138) in her robes for the Coronation of 1937. De László responded better to the charms of a beautiful actress or writer, as demonstrated by the mysterious, iconic portrait of the sensational novelist *Elinor Glyn* (cat. 55), commissioned by her admirer Lord Curzon. Another admirer or 'protector', as the phrase went, paid for the portrait of the beautiful German actress *Anny Ahlers* (cat. 123), who was to die tragically before her portrait was finished, making the liveliness and animation of the picture even more poignant.

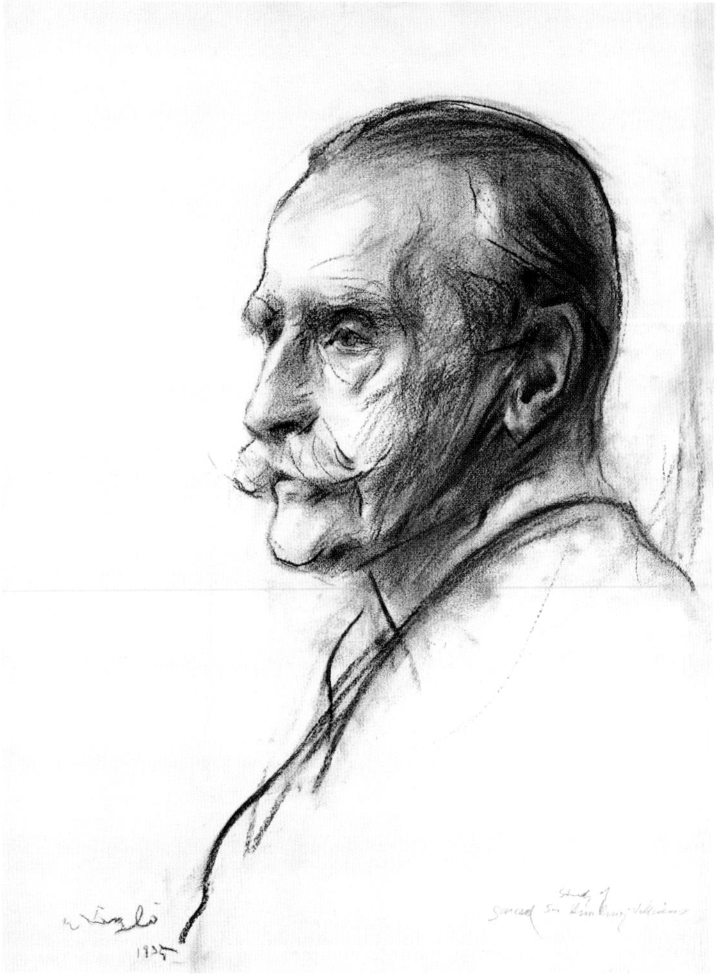

FIG. 14
Major General Sir John Hanbury-Williams, 1935
Charcoal on paper, 54 × 38.1 cm
Untraced

De László could also be extremely good at painting older women. His portrait of *Mabel, Countess of Airlie* (cat. 127) is marvellously aristocratic as well as sympathetic, and the redoubtable *Lady Wantage* (cat. 46) was greatly admired when shown at the Royal Academy in 1911. Many of de László's royal sitters were older women, and these could be some of his more sensitive and penetrating portraits, such as the wonderful *Queen Mother Maria Christina of Spain* of 1910, or *The Queen Mother Olga of Greece* (cat. 58). Equally serious, and sensitive, is the portrait of a female academic, *Elizabeth Guinness* (cat. 45), the Vice-Principal of Holloway College, and a relation of de László's wife.

One of the many popular misconceptions of de László is that he was only a painter of smart society women. It is one of the aims of the exhibition this book accompanies to demonstrate that he was also an extremely good painter of men. If called upon to depict a major public figure in official robes, de László could certainly rise to the occasion. He was particularly good at painting clerics. Before coming to England, he had already painted *Pope Leo XIII* (cat. 18), *Cardinal Rampolla* (cat. 19) and *The Archimandrite Gregorius*.[8] In England he was to paint two Archbishops of Canterbury, *Randall Davidson* in 1926 (fig. 34, p.44) and *Cosmo Gordon Lang* in 1932 (cat. 122). These are arguably two of the best clerical portraits ever painted in England, even though de László makes them look more like Catholic cardinals than leaders of the Anglican Church. Indeed Randall Davidson, a retiring and modest Scotsman, was astonished to find himself depicted with a grandeur worthy of Titian or Velázquez.[9]

As a painter to most of the kings and emperors of Europe, de László found no difficulty in painting grand sitters in their robes of office. For his close friend and supporter *Lord Devonport* (cat. 61) he pulled out all the stops: the very picture of senatorial splendour, he stands in robes of a Privy Councillor by a classical column. Devonport not only loyally supported de László during his troubles during the Great War, but also commissioned other portraits from him, of Lloyd George and of Field Marshal Lord Roberts. De László greatly admired Reynolds's famous portrait of *Lord Heathfield*, the hero of the siege of Gibraltar. This is evident in de László's grand portraits of famous men, many of which are now rarely seen, because they hang in colleges and institutions. Hopefully, they will come to light in the future, and demonstrate that de László was the last great European painter in the grand manner. One grateful client, Wilfrid Ashley, wrote to de László, "The portraits by Van Dyck, Romney, Opie, Raeburn, Reynolds, Lely, Hoppner and Lawrence in this house will welcome so distinguished an addition to their company".[10]

Inevitably, de László was called on to paint a great many generals, admirals and other servicemen who served and, in many cases, died in the First World War. At their best, his portraits of high-ranking officers are commandingly stern and powerful, but also full of character. A good example *is Field-Marshal Lord Byng of Vimy* (cat. 118); equally strong, if smaller, is *The Earl of Albemarle* (cat. 67). *Lieutenant Desmond Trouton* (cat. 66), who died at Passchendaele in 1917, is one of de László's many moving tributes to the doomed youth of that generation. As well as painting admirals and other naval officers, including Beatty (fig. 12, p. 23) and the Mountbattens (cat. 43, 94), de László was summoned back to Budapest twice to paint *Admiral Horthy* (cat. 109), the Regent of Hungary in 1927 and 1935.

In his half and three-quarter lengths, de László was more able to concentrate on the sitter's personality rather than on the trappings of office. The steely gaze of *Lord Curzon* (cat. 54) and *Sir Austen Chamberlain* (cat. 89) make it clear that these men wished to be remembered for their powerful intellects as well as the appointments they may have held. De László was also particularly good at academics: his portraits of *Sir Ernest Rutherford* (cat. 99), *Dr Alfred Haddon* (cat. 100) and *Sir Flinders Petrie* are among the best of his male portraits. Inevitably, he painted the art world, too; his portrait of *Sir Alfred East* (cat. 34), the landscape painter, is particularly sympathetic. Painting the bearded art critic and historian Alfred Lys Baldry, a great supporter and friend, he put him in robes and made him look like a figure from the Renaissance (cat. 81). His portrait of the art dealer *William Lockett Agnew* (cat. 53) is both penetrating and sympathetic, and very like a Sargent. It was said of Sargent that the Edwardians did not realise how rich they were until he painted them. De László, too, painted many successful bankers, financiers and newspaper proprietors. *Baron Bruno von Schröder* (cat. 73) looks every inch the prosperous financier. *Lord Joicey* (cat. 116), on the other hand, looks more like a distinguished professor than a great coal owner.

De László was often asked to paint the children of his earlier sitters. For the Schröders, he painted their daughters Marga and Dorothee (cat. 39) and for the Troutons a delightful study of their daughter Olive (cat. 47) *à la* Gainsborough. For the Rallis he painted their two children Godfrey and Diana (cat. 91) with a Pekinese. For the Elphinstones, he painted a particularly delightful picture of their son Andrew (cat. 101), wearing a kilt and holding a fishing rod. Many of de László's most charming pictures of children are of his own sons. As these have all remained in the de László family, they will feature as one of the delights of the exhibition. I would single out *Top of the Morning* (cat. 76), of his son Stephen, and one of his youngest son John with a goldfish bowl (cat. 79) as two of the best. De László also frequently painted his wife Lucy, both on her own and in family groups. These are some of his most delightful and appealing portraits, particularly one in which she looks in a mirror (cat. 77). Some of the portraits of Lucy and of her unmarried sister, Eva (fig. 15), particularly reflect the influence of Gainsborough on de László's style in the 1920s and 1930s.[11] De László would certainly have seen the exhibition of *English Conversation Pieces* mounted by that arbiter of taste, Philip Sassoon, in 1930 at his house in Park Lane, which helped to revive the reputation of Zoffany.

Another revelation of the exhibition will be de László's landscape sketches, all of which have remained in the artist's family, unseen until the present day. His landscapes painted in France, Italy and England, usually done for relaxation when he was on holiday, combine brilliance of colour and observation with a confident, flowing technique. Some of his best oil studies of places were painted

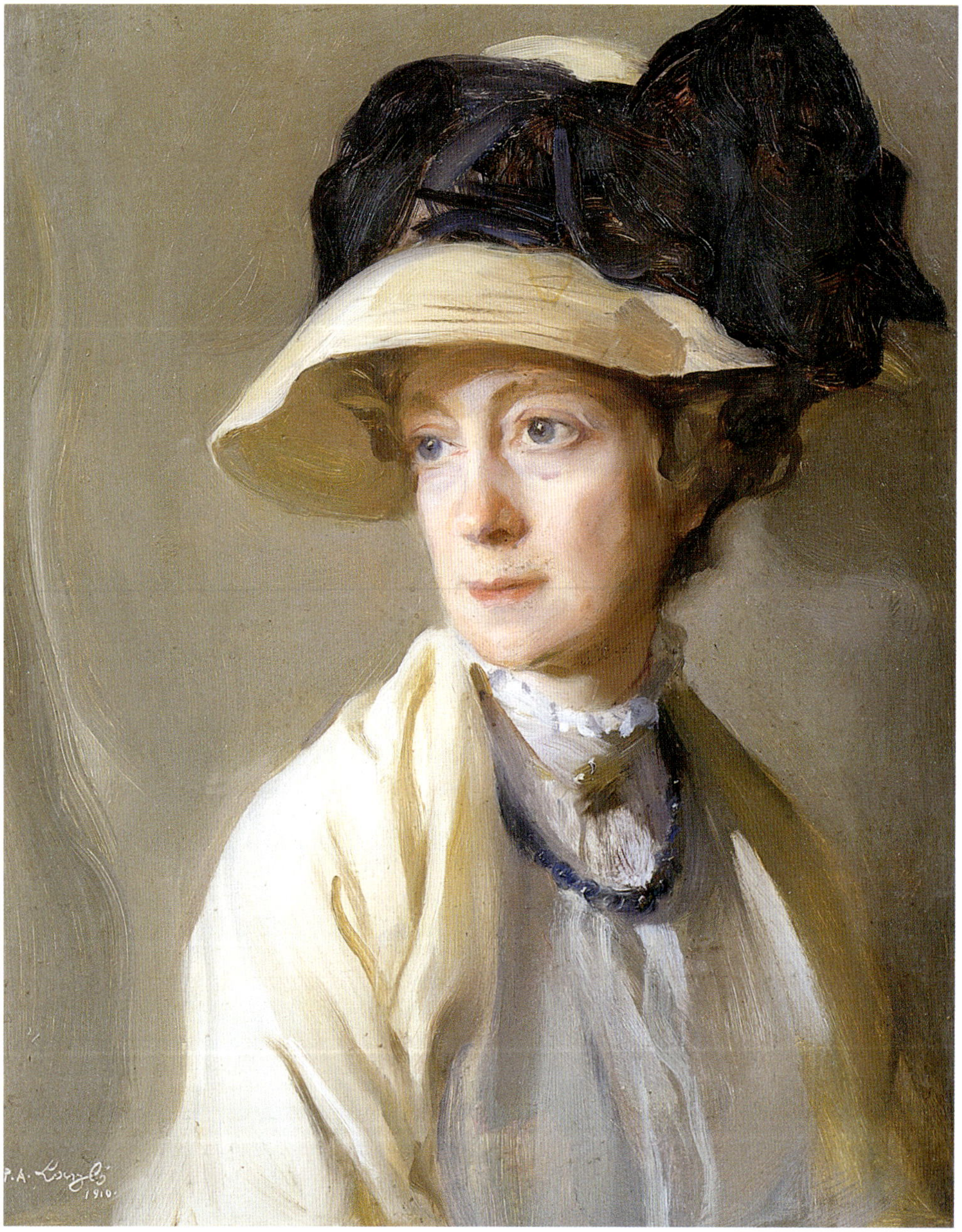

FIG. 15
Miss Eva F. Guinness, 1910
Oil on canvas, 39.5 × 32.4 cm
Private collection

on the Nile and in Venice (cat. 105–9, 112–5). Like so many artists, Lavery included, de László was hugely taken with North Africa, painting not only landscapes (fig. 17) but also heads of Arabs (fig. 16), street and market scenes, even nudes (cat. 129). His *Orange Seller* (cat. 97), painted in Rome, is as good as anything Sargent or Sorolla could do. At home, de László even found time to paint flowers, still life and their pet dog, Chinky (cat. 131–7). He simply could not stop painting.

De László was working right up to the end. He lost none of his zest for life, or his enthusiasm for painting, even though he knew he had a weak heart. "Life is so glorious!" he exclaimed to his wife after his first heart attack. Even in his last year, 1937, he painted numerous portraits (fig. 1, p. 8), including *The Duke of Portland in Garter Robes*, *Prince Chichibu of Japan*, *The Duchess of Northumberland* (cat. 138) in her court dress as Mistress of the Robes, and the Duke of Connaught. On 22 November, just before an exhibition at Wildenstein's in aid of the Artists' General Benevolent Institution, he had another heart attack, and died. His last words were. "I know I am going to die .... But it is a pity, because there is still so much to do."

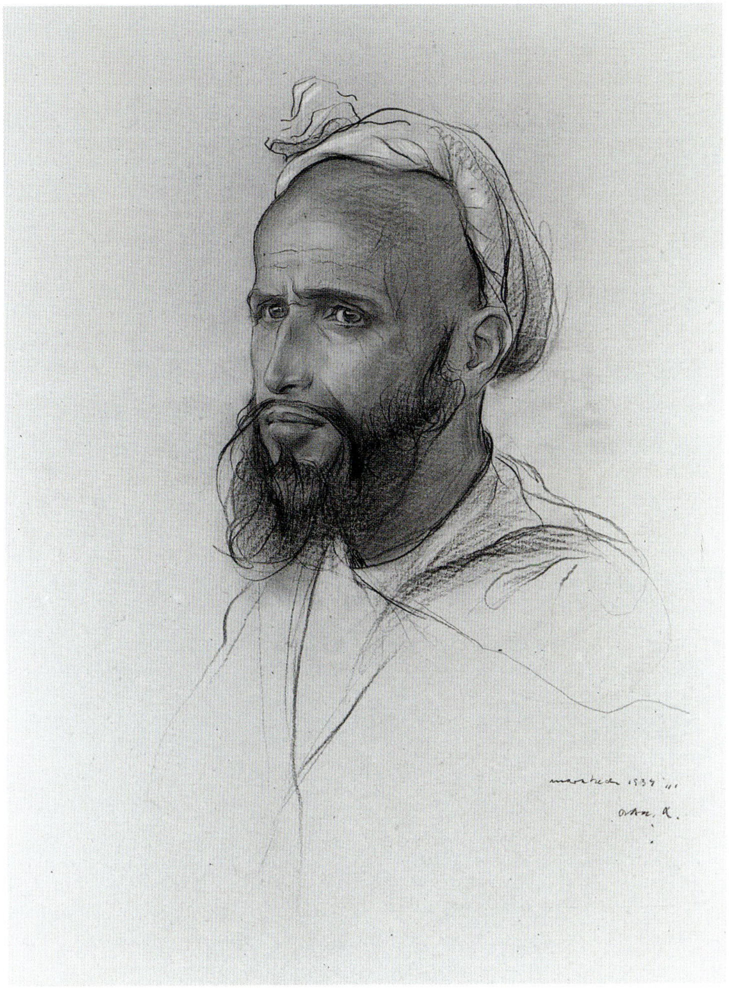

FIG. 16
An Arab, 1934
Chalk on paper, 52.4 × 40.2 cm
Ashmolean Museum, Oxford

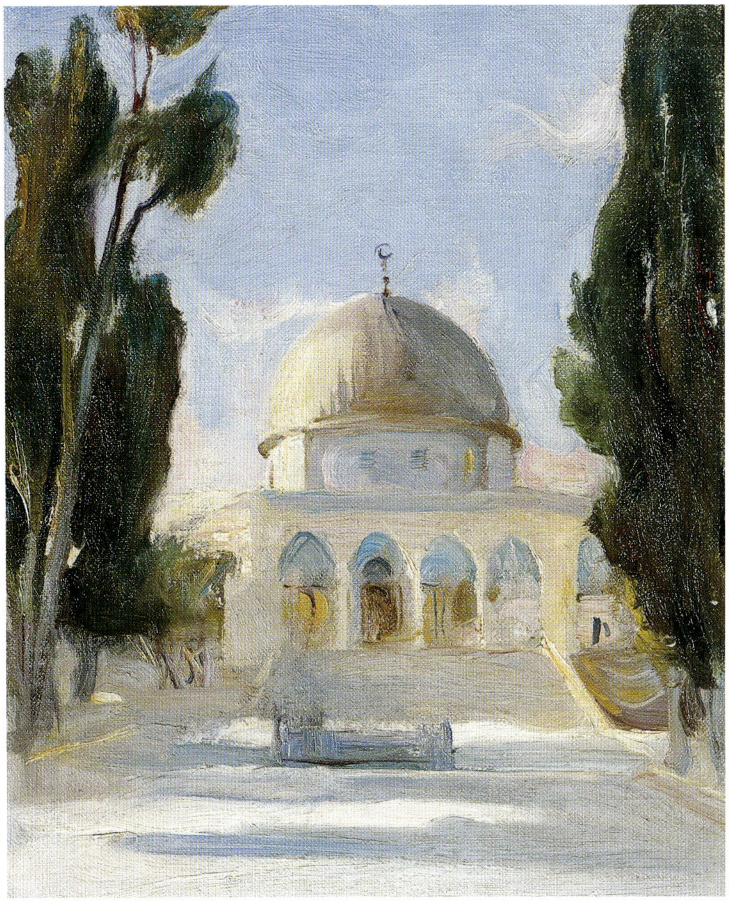

FIG. 17
The Dome of the Rock, Temple Mount, Jerusalem, 1936
Oil on canvasboard, 39.4 × 32.39 cm
Private collection

De László wrote a great deal about his work, and about portrait painting, much of it faithfully recorded by Owen Rutter. Like any portrait painter who painted rich and famous people, he had to face a great deal of sarcastic and unpleasant criticism. Fortunately, he was resilient enough to shake it off. And there were critics who praised him. One of the most perceptive articles appeared in *The Studio* magazine as early as 1901, before he settled in England. The writer, Anthony Tahi, credited de László with all the gifts needed by a portrait painter – "charming conception, harmonious colouring, sureness of drawing, intense expression, and sound technique". He also put his finger on de László's greatest strength, his ability to make his sitters look relaxed, animated and natural. "He insists that the eye should not seem to be *painted*, but should actually *see*; that the lips should not be painted and drawn but really exist on the canvas. Thus it comes about that there is a certain charm in all de László's portraits .... Everyone has some good point in his face, if it can only be discovered, be he prince or peasant."

NOTES
1. Owen Rutter, *Portrait of a Painter, The Authorised Life of Philip de László*, London 1939, p.233.
2. *Ibid.*, p.381. 3. *Ibid.*, p.383. 4. *Ibid.*, p.280. 5. *Ibid.*, p.390. 6. *Ibid.*, p.394.
7. *Ibid.*, p.366. 8. *Ibid.*, p.144. 9. *Ibid.*, p.362. 10. *Ibid.*, p.390. 11. *Ibid.*, p.320.

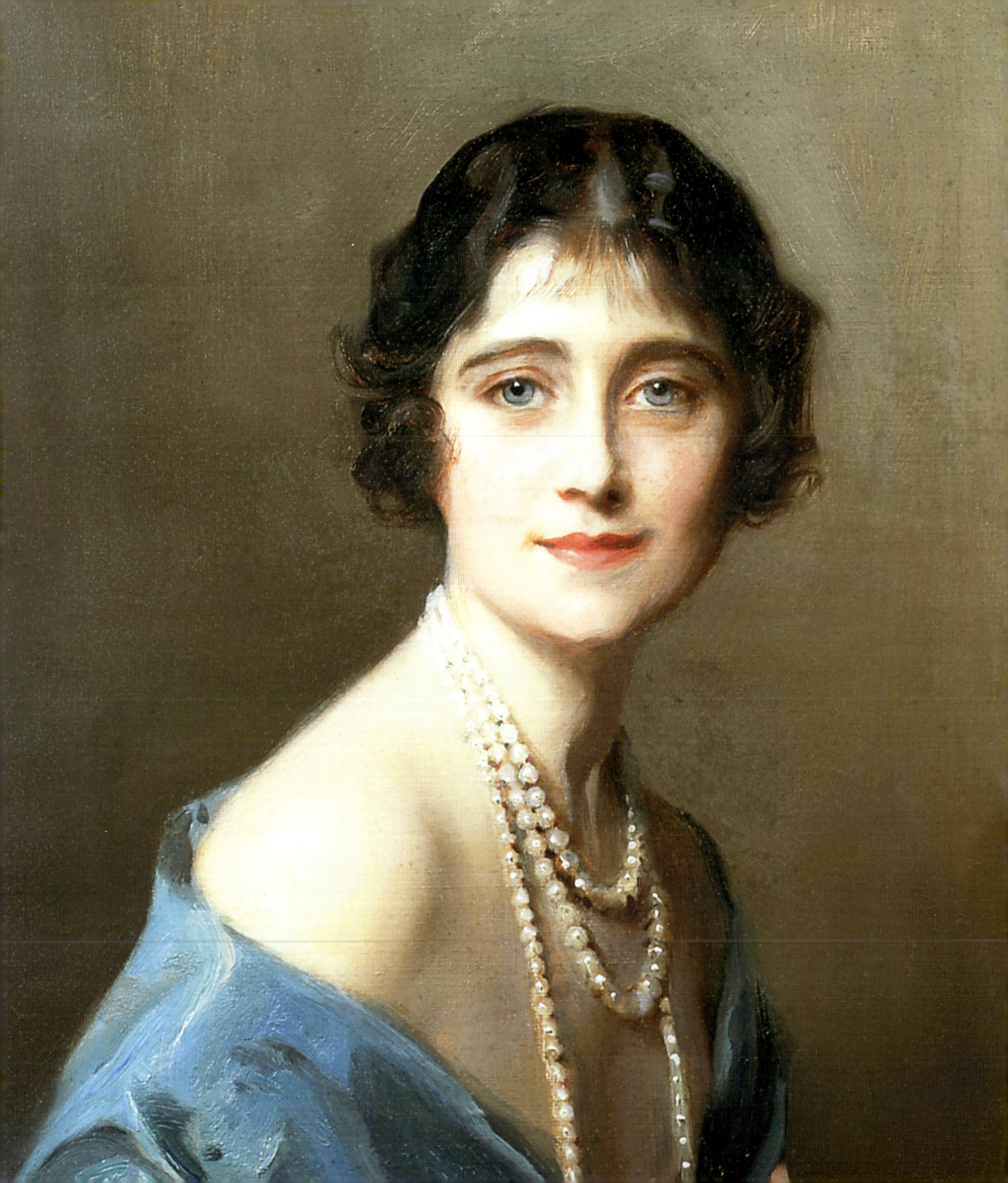

De László, Royalty and Tradition

Christopher Lloyd

Statistically, it is probably safe to assert that Philip de László depicted more royal sitters than any other painter in the history of art. Perhaps only Franz Xavier Winterhalter (1805–1873) offers a serious challenge in this respect, but then de László's oeuvre extends further, to include Popes, Archbishops and Presidents of the United States, in addition to the highest ranks of society. Certainly, de László benefited from historical circumstances in so far as the traditional fabric of European society remained intact while he was establishing his reputation and continued in being even in a diluted or fragmented state for the rest of his lifetime. Added to this is the fact that de László was a cosmopolitan figure who was able to move throughout Europe with ease, gaining the confidence of his far-flung and distinguished clientèle by his artistic skills and personal charm. To paint "an extraordinary succession of portraits of great personages and of notable people who have taken their fair share in the affairs of the world" became de László's mission, to the extent that his "portraits should last and continue to be available many generations hence for the information of students of humanity and for the enlightenment of the historian".[1] Such an ambition, which he surely abundantly fulfilled, immediately places de László's work in a sequence of artists extending from Holbein through Titian, Van Dyck and Velázquez to Goya, Lawrence and Ingres.

No intelligent portrait painter when confronted by a royal sitter can remain unaware of the tradition in which he is being asked to work, and de László was sensitive to such issues. When, for example, he was commissioned to paint Francis Joseph, Emperor of Austria and King of Hungary (fig. 19), it would have been unwise of him to discount the success that Titian had achieved with the Habsburgs, notably Charles V, or his son Philip II (fig. 18). As a result, de László's image of 1899 echoes the earlier master in the restrained formality of pose, colour, lighting and background. Similarly, the portrait of Queen Marie of Roumania, the daughter of Alfred, Duke of Edinburgh, the second son of Queen Victoria, and his wife the Grand Duchess Marie Alexandrovna (fig. 21), dressed in shimmering silk and wearing her Russian sapphire and diamond-encrusted tiara, brings to mind the elaborate Persian costume worn by Teresia, Lady Shirley by Van Dyck (fig. 20).

These are, of course, not quotations or direct borrowings, but rather associations. Such comparisons may be seen in the light of a shared heritage, like a pattern book or memory bank, that a portraitist might automatically call upon – even unconsciously – when confronted by a sitter. The swirling red academic gown encircling the body of the Prime Minister A.J. Balfour (fig. 23) might in this way owe its origins to Van Dyck's animated portrait of Lucas van Uffelen (fig. 22). Not surprisingly, after de László had settled in London in 1907, eighteenth-century British portraiture became a source of reference to him. The dramatic full-length state portrait of Kaiser William II in full-dress uniform standing with his charger in front of the Neues Palace at Potsdam (cat. 40) is reminiscent of *Captain Robert Orme* by Sir Joshua Reynolds (fig. 24). De László greatly admired the work of Reynolds, describing him as "the finest English portrait painter" and singling out the image of Lord Heathfield of Gibraltar (in the National Gallery) for special praise. Having been prompted to look also at Gainsborough's paintings, he must have found an affinity in the earlier artist's unorthodox technique and bravura brushwork, as well as in the element of risk-taking that Gainsborough relished. However, Gainsborough's attitude to his sitters, unless they were his friends ("they have but one part worth

Her Late Majesty Queen Elizabeth the Queen Mother, when Duchess of York
(cat. 98, detail)

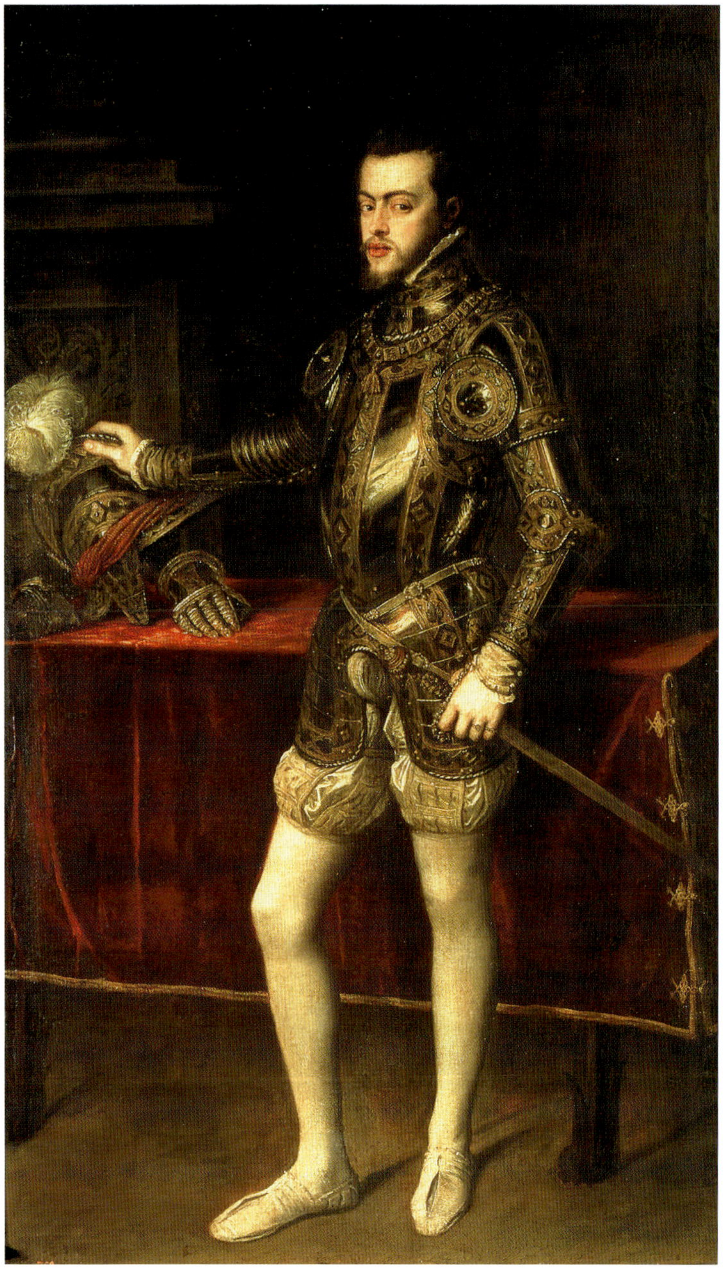

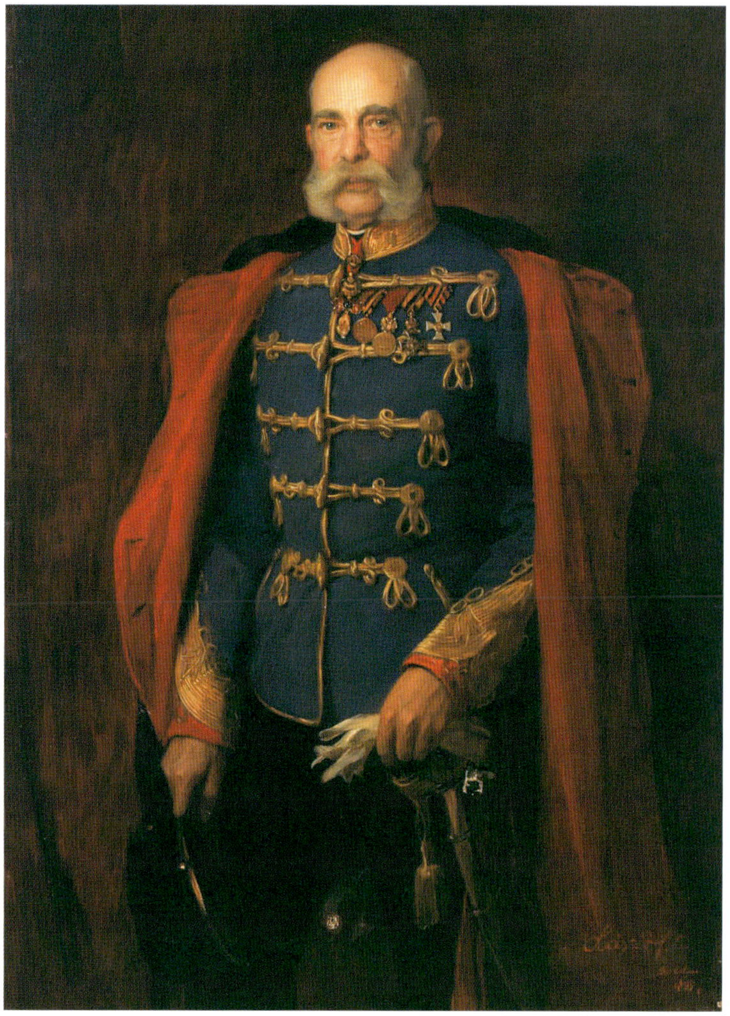

ABOVE FIG. 19 *Emperor Francis Joseph of Austria, King of Hungary*, 1899
Oil on canvas, 146 × 95.3 cm
The Historical Gallery, Hungarian National Museum, Budapest

OPPOSITE PAGE
ABOVE RIGHT FIG. 20 Sir Anthony van Dyck, *Teresia, Lady Shirley*, 1622
Oil on canvas, 200 × 133.4 cm, Petworth House

ABOVE FAR RIGHT FIG. 21 *Queen Marie of Roumania*, 1924
Oil on canvas, 92 × 70 cm, National Museum of Peles Castle, Sinaia, Roumania

BELOW RIGHT FIG. 22 Sir Anthony van Dyck, *Lucas van Uffelen*, 1622
Oil on canvas, 124 × 100.6 cm
The Metropolitan Museum of Art, Bequest of Benjamin Altman, 1913

BELOW FAR RIGHT FIG. 23 *Arthur James Balfour*, 1914
Oil on canvas, 152.4 × 111.8 cm (60 × 44 in.), Trinity College Library, Cambridge

FIG. 18
Titian
Philip II, 1550
Oil on canvas,
193 × 111 cm
Museo del Prado, Madrid

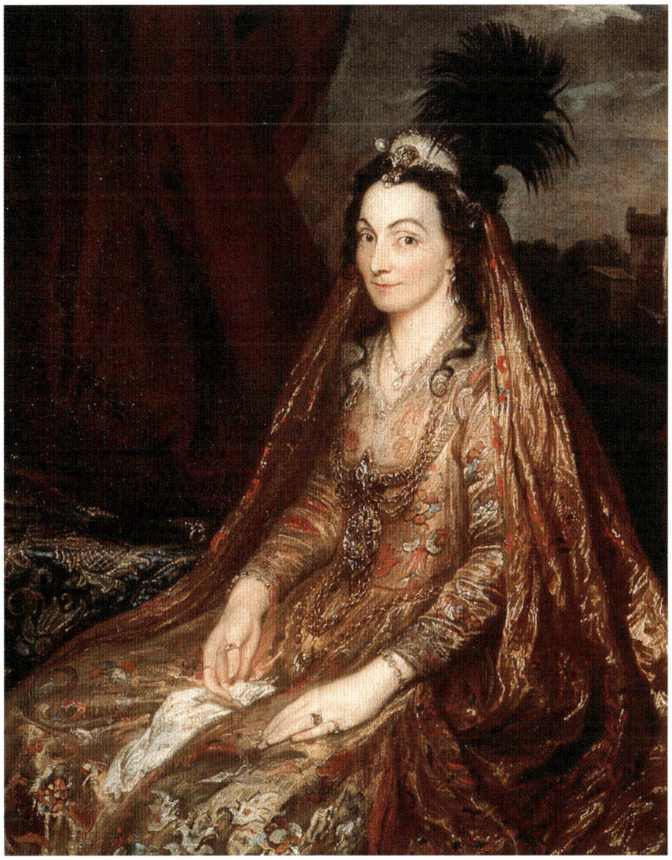
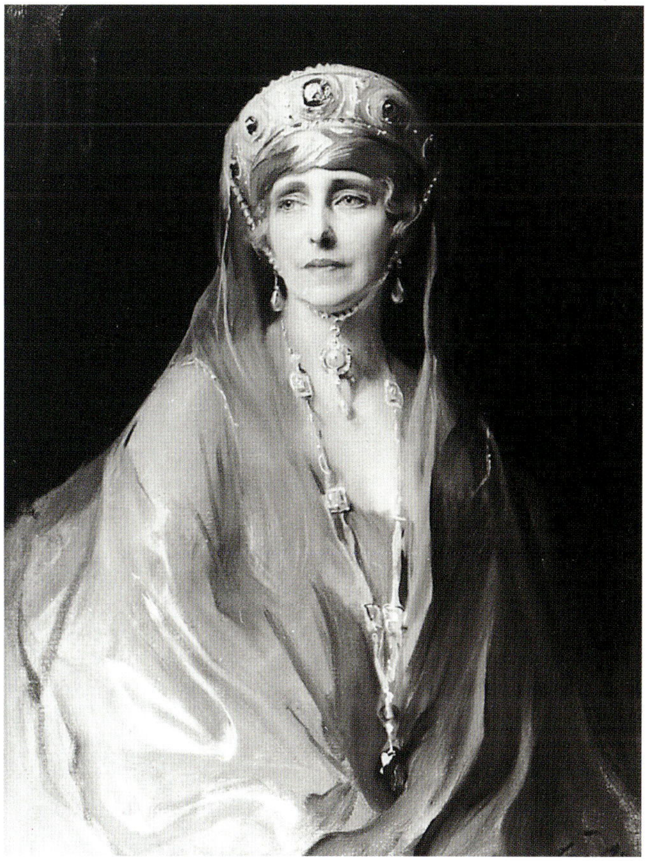
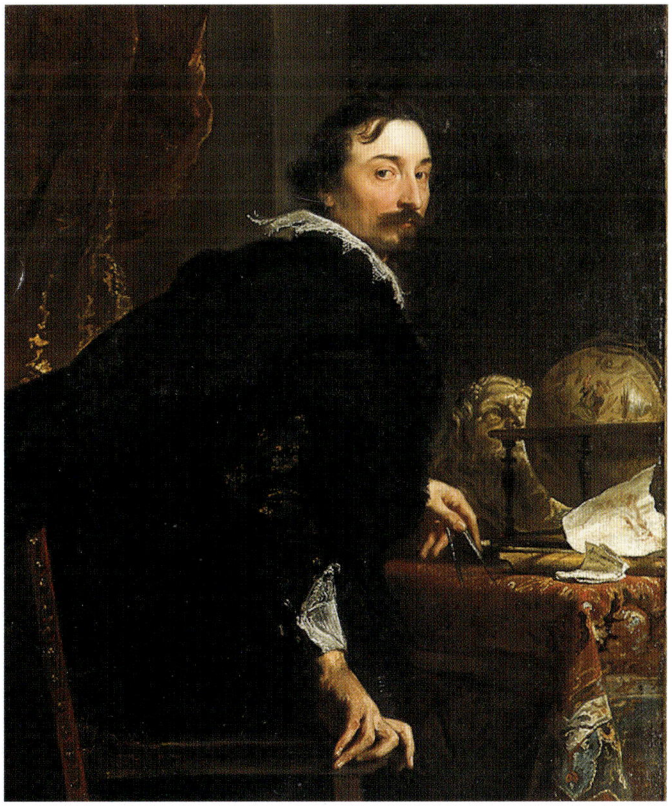
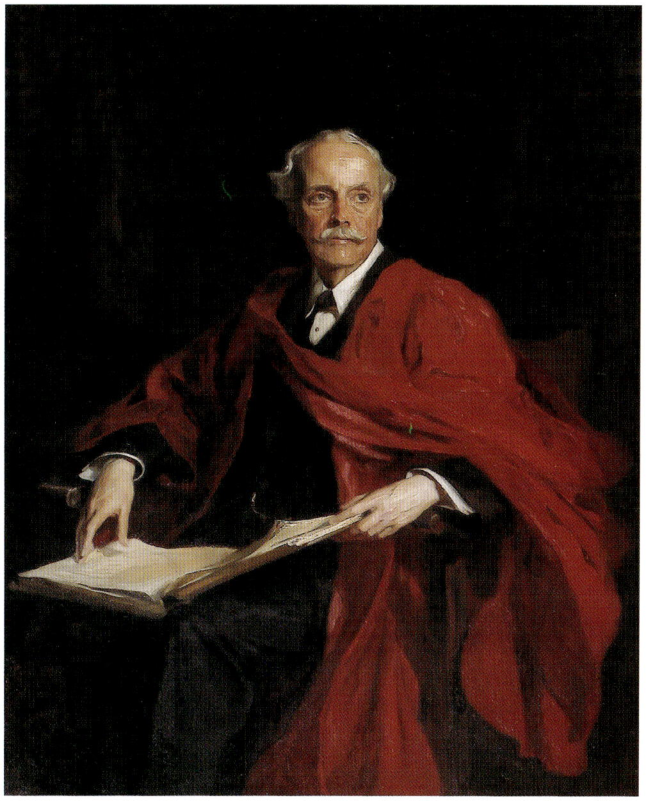

looking at, and that is their purse"), was diametrically opposed to de László's, and in this respect his situation more closely resembles that of Sir Thomas Lawrence, also a dazzling technician.

Lawrence's commission from George IV to paint the portraits of those statesmen, military commanders and diplomats involved in the overthrow of the Emperor Napoleon parallels de László's own relationship with his sitters. Lawrence's portraits were eventually installed in the Waterloo Chamber at Windsor Castle and reveal the artist at the height of his powers, in the variety of poses within the given formats dictated by status and in the dazzling application of paint. The portrait of *Pope Pius VII* (fig. 25) is a masterpiece in which Lawrence consciously strove to rival Raphael, Titian and Velázquez, and in so doing advanced the standing of British artists immeasurably. As it happens, de László was specially commissioned by the Hungarian government in the Pope's Silver Jubilee year of 1900 to paint a portrait of Pope Leo XIII to hang in the Museum of Fine Arts at Budapest. A comparison of the well documented experiences of both Lawrence and de László is instructive. Both were immediately made nervous by the inevitable comparisons that would be made with their predecessors; both drew inspiration from their surroundings in the Vatican; both prepared carefully by observing the respective popes at audiences and while performing their official duties; and both established a good rapport with their sitters that is reflected in the finished portraits. Pius VII was aged seventy-seven when painted by Lawrence and Leo XIII aged ninety when painted by de László: their portraits succeed in combining the outward authority with the inner spirituality of two of the greatest popes in history. Lawrence observed of Pius VII, "He has a fine countenance – stoops a little – with firm yet sweet-toned voice … and through all the storms of the past he retains the jet black of his hair".[2] De László described Leo XIII coming into the room for his first sitting: "The bent, ascetic figure entered, with his intelligent and alert expression, clad in a heavy ivory silk cassock, white shoes, a white cappelletto, and the crimson silk cloak which had come down from the Roman Emperors and is worn only by the Pope".[3] In such descriptions the reader senses the artist's visual appetite for his subject. As it happens, de László made a false start and Leo XIII was dismissive of his first attempt opining, '*Mais mon cher fils, ça ressemble à Voltaire, et je déteste cette creature*'.[4] The portrait was begun again (cat. 18), and the outcome of the second attempt acknowledge to be hugely successful. The artist was created a Chevalier of the Order of Pope Pius IX and the portrait won a gold medal in the Paris Salon of 1900.

A measure of de László's absorption of British portraiture is reflected in the way in which his own work was so readily perceived as being part of the national canon in spite of the political difficulties and prejudices he encountered during the First World War. For example, the vibrant portrait of the popular romantic novelist Mrs

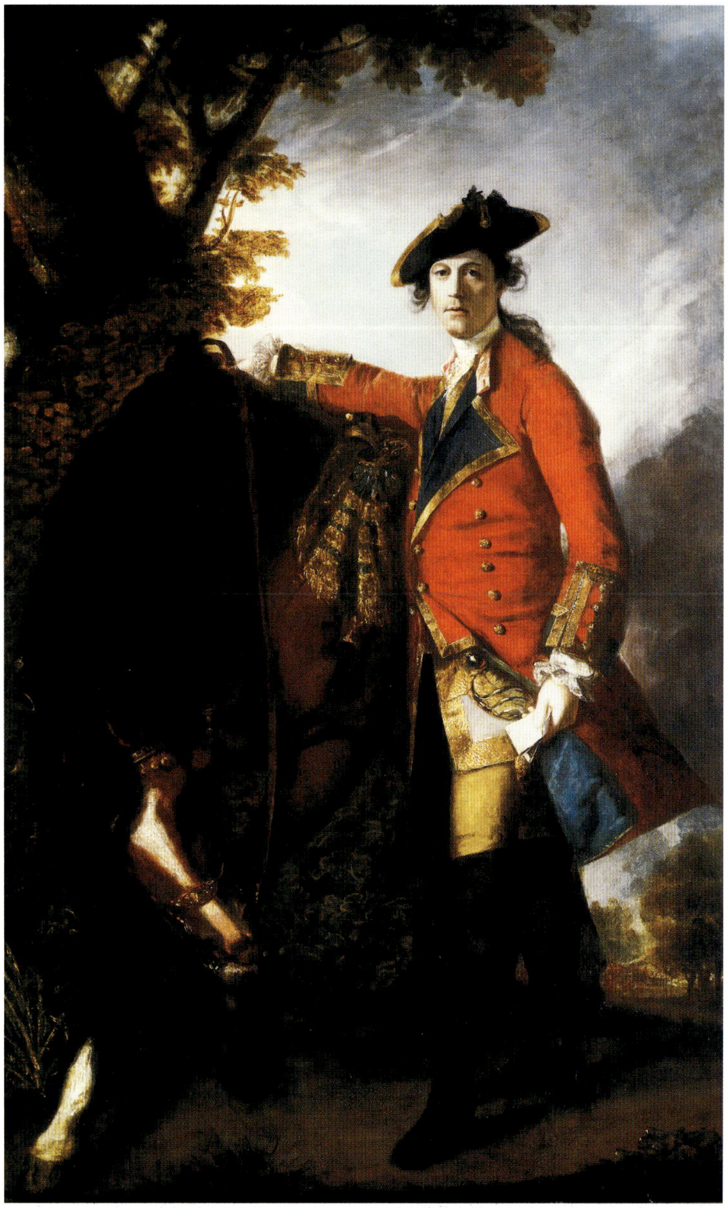

Elinor Glyn (cat. 55) was declared by her lover, Lord Curzon, who had proposed the commission, to "rank with the best of all ages".[5] This startling image, born of late Pre-Raphaelitism and verging on Symbolism, caused quite a furore when it was first exhibited in London. Similarly, when Mrs Wilfrid Ashley, the daughter of Sir Ernest Cassel, was painted, her husband wrote to the artist declaring that the portrait "shows clearly that there is at least one artist of the twentieth century whose works can challenge the best productions of former times. The portraits by Van Dyck, Romney, Opie, Raeburn, Reynolds, Lely, Hoppner and Laurence [*sic*] in this house will welcome so distinguished an addition to their company."[6] An equal

FIG. 24 (LEFT)
Sir Joshua Reynolds
Captain Robert Orme, 1756
Oil on canvas, 240 × 147.3 cm
National Gallery, London

FIG. 25 (RIGHT)
Sir Thomas Lawrence
Pope Pius VII, 1819
Oil on canvas, 269.4 × 178.3 cm
The Royal Collection © 2004
Her Majesty Queen Elizabeth II

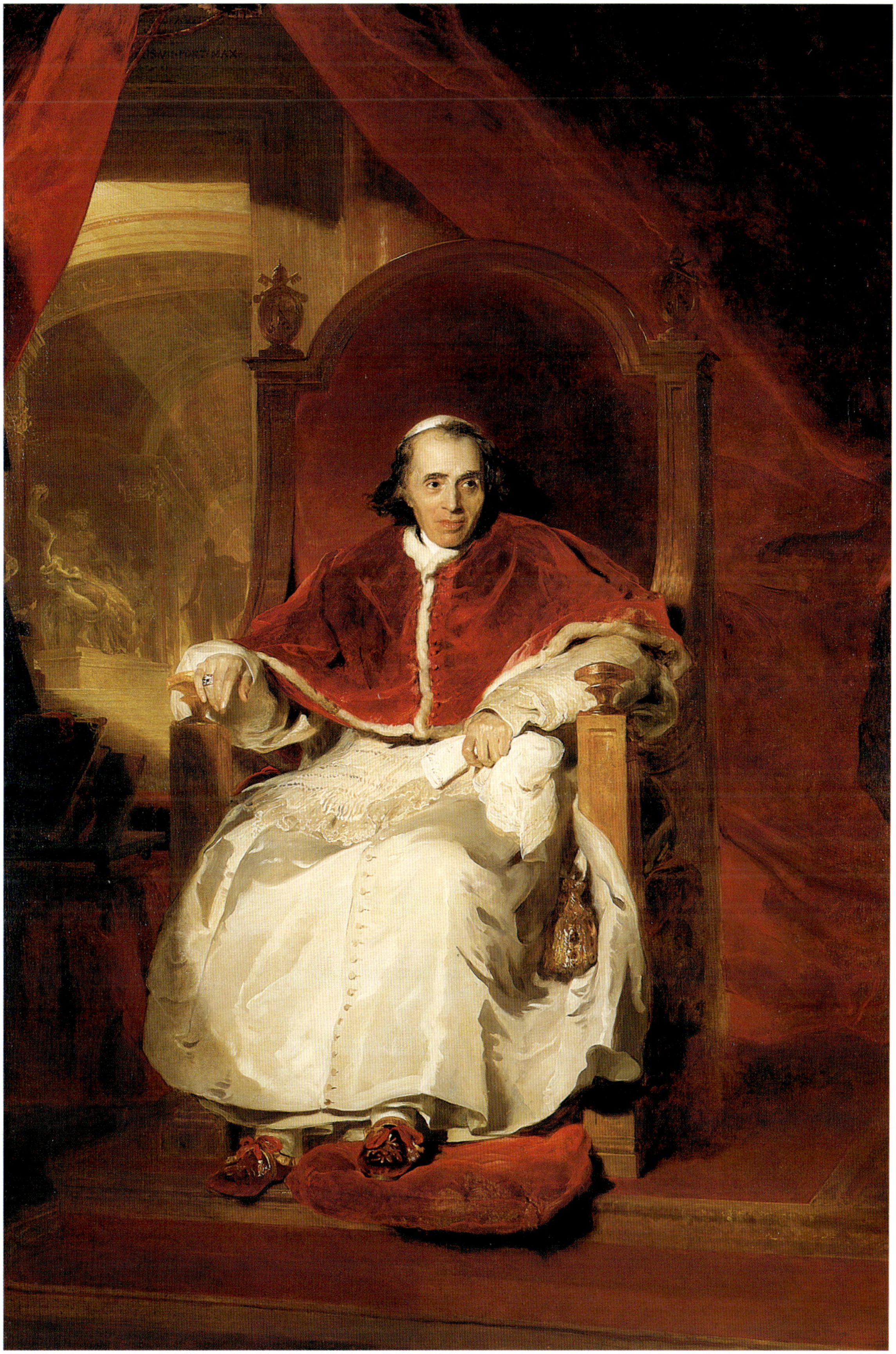

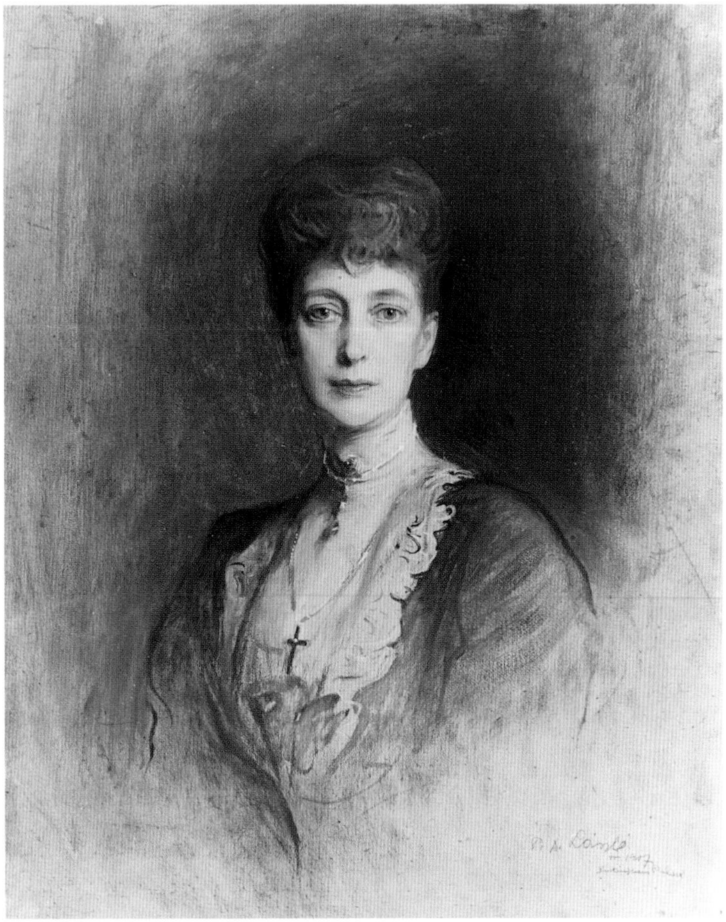

FIG. 26
Queen Alexandra, 1907
Oil on canvas
Untraced

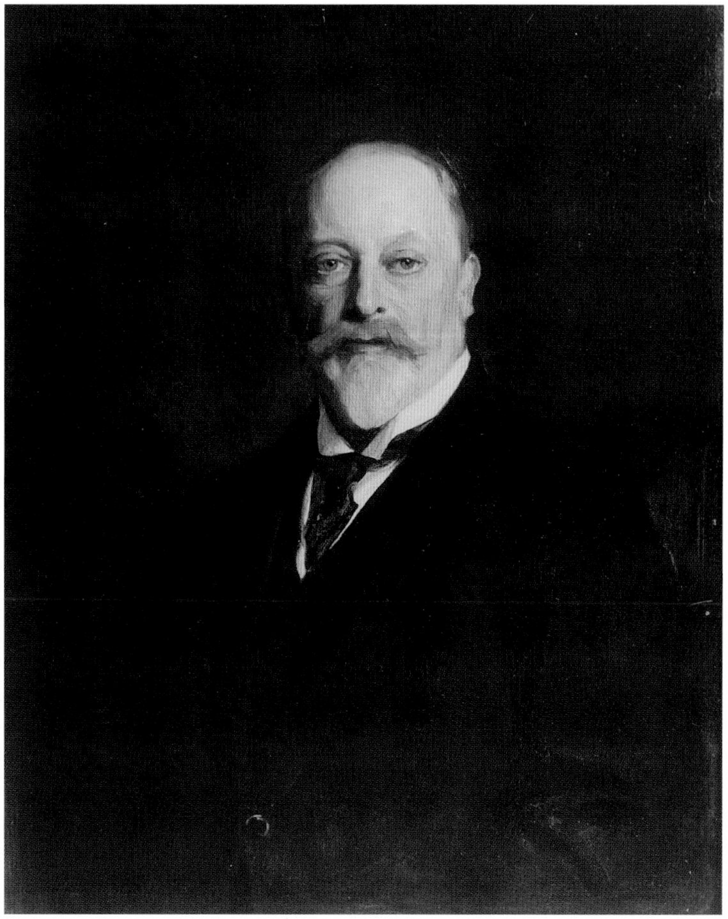

FIG. 27
King Edward VII, 1907
Oil on canvas
Untraced

admiration was felt for the artist by the Duke of Portland, who made a direct comparison with Van Dyck and set up a de László Room at Welbeck Abbey, where there was already a famed collection of pictures.

Royal sitters, perhaps more than most, will almost certainly have expectations, and de László's introduction to British monarchy was not auspicious. Having recommended the artist to her mother Queen Victoria, the Empress Frederick of Germany instructed her secretary to write to de László in 1898 as follows:

"I beg to inform you that Her Majesty the Queen of England has expressed the wish to see some of your paintings .... I must tell you in confidence that Her Majesty is not very enthusiastic about modern art, especially when applied to portraits. Her Majesty likes correct drawing and clean colours as used, for example, by the painter [Heinrich von] Angeli. Her Majesty has no feeling for the paintings of [Franz von] Lenbach."[7] De László was not asked to paint Queen Victoria, but was commissioned to undertake a portrait of Field Marshal Sir George White, who had conducted the defence of Ladysmith in 1899–1900. This did finally meet with royal approval, after an objection was raised about the format. However, de László had greater success with the next generation, beginning in 1907 with portraits of Edward VII and Queen Alexandra, both now lost (figs. 26, 27), and of their second daughter Princess Victoria (now in the National Portrait Gallery). A commission for a portrait of Princess Andrew of Greece (cat. 36), also of 1907, followed, but her husband, Prince Andrew (cat. 37), was not painted until 1913. The contrast between these two figures is marked and typifies other such pairings in the artist's oeuvre. While Prince Andrew is a dignified, reflective figure silhouetted against a sombre background evoking Dutch seventeenth-century portraiture, Princess Andrew exudes a charm and allure redolent of the French or British eighteenth-century schools.

A decade later, in 1925, de László painted the Duchess of York, later Queen Elizabeth, The Queen Mother (cat. 98), in three-quarters length swathed in a blue stole with pearls. The position of the figure on the canvas, the direct gaze of the sitter, the angle of the shoulders and the play of the hands makes a fine, adroit composition. Sir Peter Lely used this format to similarly good effect and it is possible that the artist recalled Lely's winning images of the 'Windsor Beauties' painted for Anne Hyde, Duchess of York, *ca.* 1662–5 (fig. 28). The success of this portrait led to the commission for a pair of portraits of the sitter's parents, the Earl and Countess of Strathmore (cat. 120, 121). These are both good examples of de László's habit of bringing a portrait to the requisite degree of finish without actually overpainting the whole canvas.

The degree to which de László exploited lack of finish as an artistic principle becomes apparent in his portrait of Queen Victoria's third son, Arthur, Duke of Connaught and Strathearn (fig. 29), who pursued a military career before becoming Governor-General of Canada. The Duke of Connaught and his wife Louise, Duchess of Connaught, were painted by John Singer Sargent in 1910 (fig. 30). Conceived as a pair at three-quarters length in subdued tones (perhaps inspired by Frans Hals), both sitters are imbued by Sargent with a suitable hauteur, but he clearly felt more at ease in rendering the silk/satin of the Duchess of Connaught's dress than with the Duke's uniform. The Duke of Connaught is presented as a reserved figure with whatever aspects of personality he might have had masked by the cramping crispness of his uniform which has been so acutely observed by Sargent. On the other hand, de László, in what turned out to be his last portrait, created a pyramidal composition firmly anchoring the Duke of Connaught in the picture space with the blue of the robe of the Order of the Garter. The robe is treated functionally and not descriptively, so that the viewer concentrates on the head, which is seen slightly from below. The duke's personality is no longer suppressed and he is revealed as alert, humorous and approachable, even playful – everyone's favourite uncle. De László has in fact treated the head as sculpture and his brush moves in and out of the concavities of the face like the incoming tide filling rock pools. The portrait is a perfect example of how an artist can reveal so much through a calculated process of understatement.

By contrast, the portrait of Queen Elizabeth II when Princess Elizabeth of York (cat. 124) is heavily worked. This was painted in 1933, when the sitter was seven. The artist found her "intelligent and full of character", but "very sleepy and restless" at the second sitting, after having been to Queen Mary's birthday luncheon party.[8] The results, however, are the quintessence of girlhood – a confection of soft powder-blues set in a fresh, verdant landscape. Positioned right in the front of the picture space, as though tilting slightly forward in the gold-backed chair, and holding a small basket of flowers to add variety of colour, this image, if expressed in allegorical terms, would be entitled *Innocence*. It is a portrait conceived in the tradition of Reynolds's *Lady Caroline Howard* (National Gallery of Art, Washington) or Lawrence's *Miss Julia Peel* (fig. 31), the elder daughter of the Prime Minister, Sir Robert Peel. However, silhouetted in the background of Princess Elizabeth's portrait is a reference (albeit summarily painted) to her royal status, for in the distance on the right, raised on its pedestal, is depicted the bronze equestrian figure of George III by Sir Richard Westmacott.

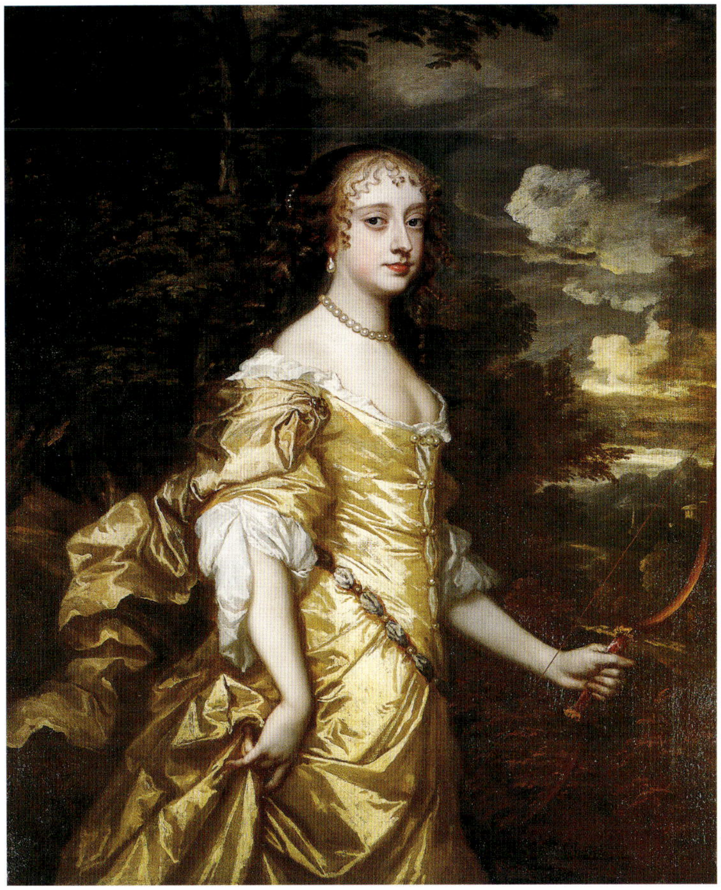

FIG. 28
Sir Peter Lely, *Frances Stuart, Duchess of Richmond, ca.* 1662–5
Oil on canvas, 125.8 × 102.7 cm
The Royal Collection © 2003
Her Majesty Queen Elizabeth II

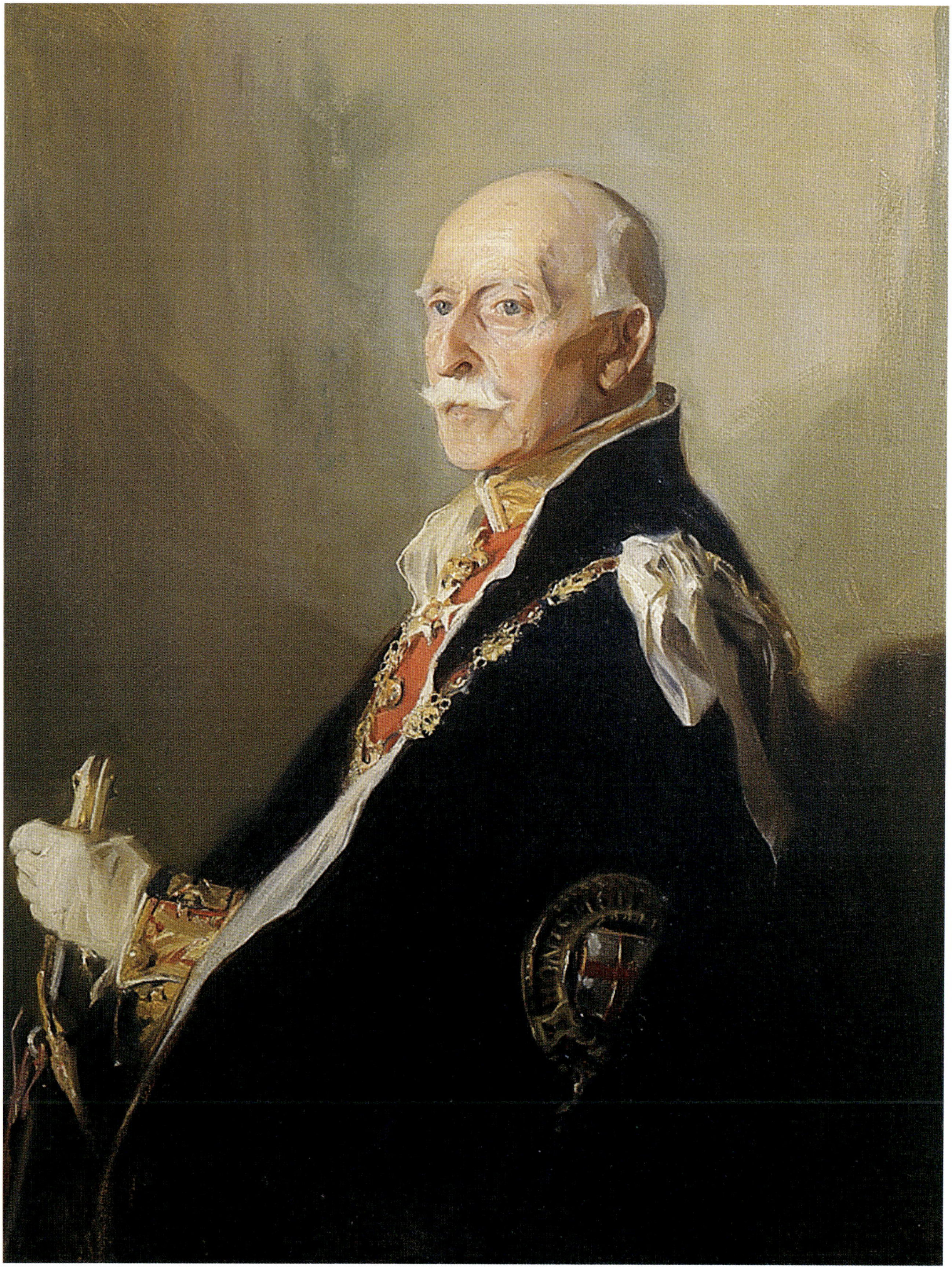

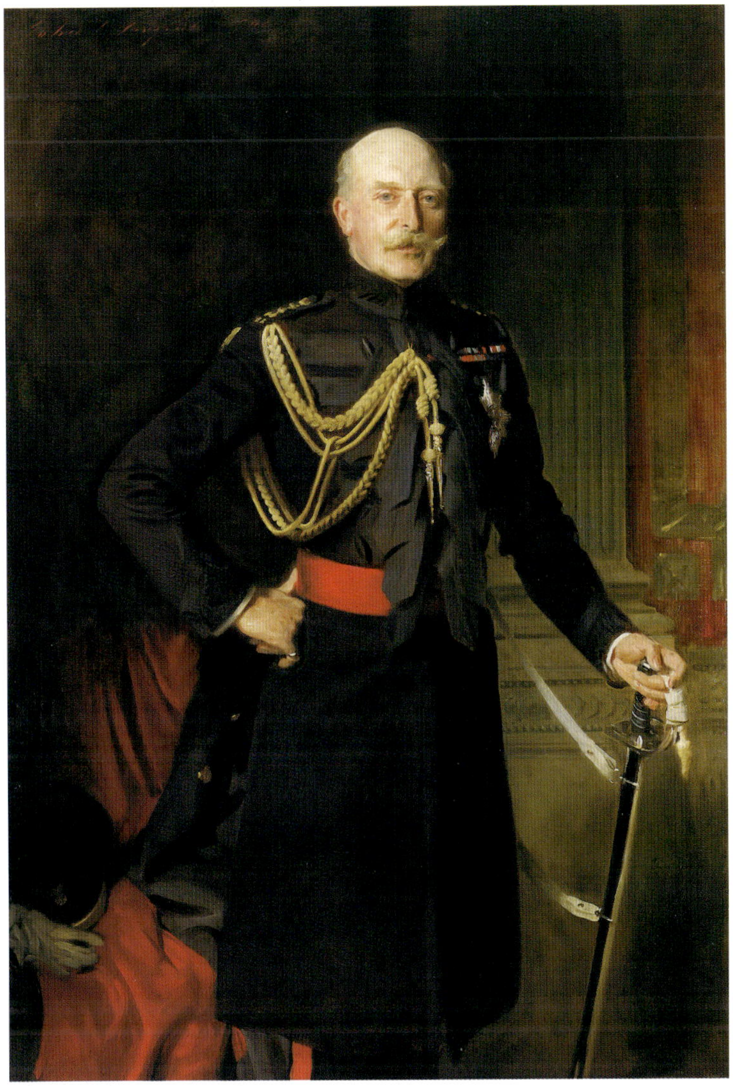

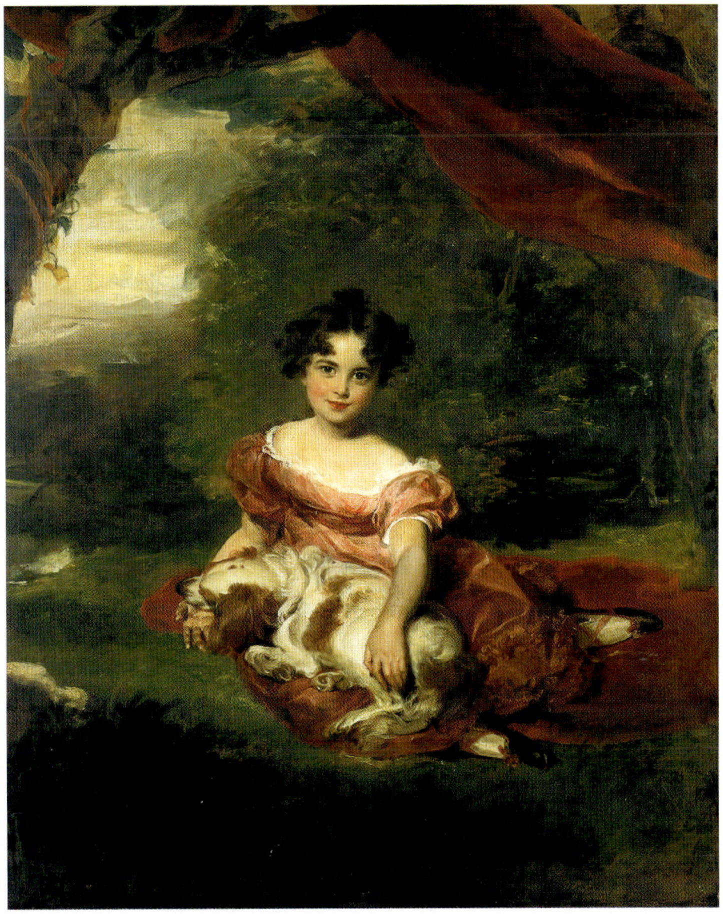

OPPOSITE LEFT FIG. 29 *Prince Arthur, Field Marshal the Duke of Connaught and Strathearn*, 1937
Oil on canvas, 99.7 × 74.9 cm, The Royal Society for the Encouragement of Arts, Manufactures and Commerce, London

ABOVE FIG. 30 John Singer Sargent, *Prince Arthur, Field Marshal the Duke of Connaught and Strathearn*, 1908
Oil on canvas, 163.8 × 110.2 cm
The Royal Collection © 2004 Her Majesty Queen Elizabeth II

RIGHT FIG. 31 Sir Thomas Lawrence, *Miss Julia Beatrice Peel*, 1828
Oil on canvas, 142.1 × 111.7 cm. private collection, Canada (courtesy Christie's)

De László's success as a painter of royalty lies in his skill in breaking down the barrier between formality and informality adhered to in earlier centuries. By using more relaxed and unusual poses matched by a spontaneity of brushwork and different degrees of finish de László was able to penetrate the veneer that so often occluded royal portraiture. In so far as the ruling families of Europe were in themselves becoming more closely integrated with society de László's strategies as an artist account for his considerable success as a painter.

1. A.L. Baldry, 'Recent Portraits by Mr. P. A. de László', *The Studio*, LXVIII, 1916, p.145.
2 D.E. Williams, *The Life and Correspondence of Sir Thomas Lawrence*, K^{t}, II, London 1831, p.153: Letter to Joseph Farington, 19 May 1819.
3. O. Rutter, *Portrait of a Painter. The Authorized Life of Philip de László*, London 1939, p.187.
4. *Ibid.*, pp 189–90. 5. *Ibid.*, p.299. 6. *Ibid.*, p.390. 7. *Ibid.*, pp.165–6. 8. *Ibid.*, p.374.

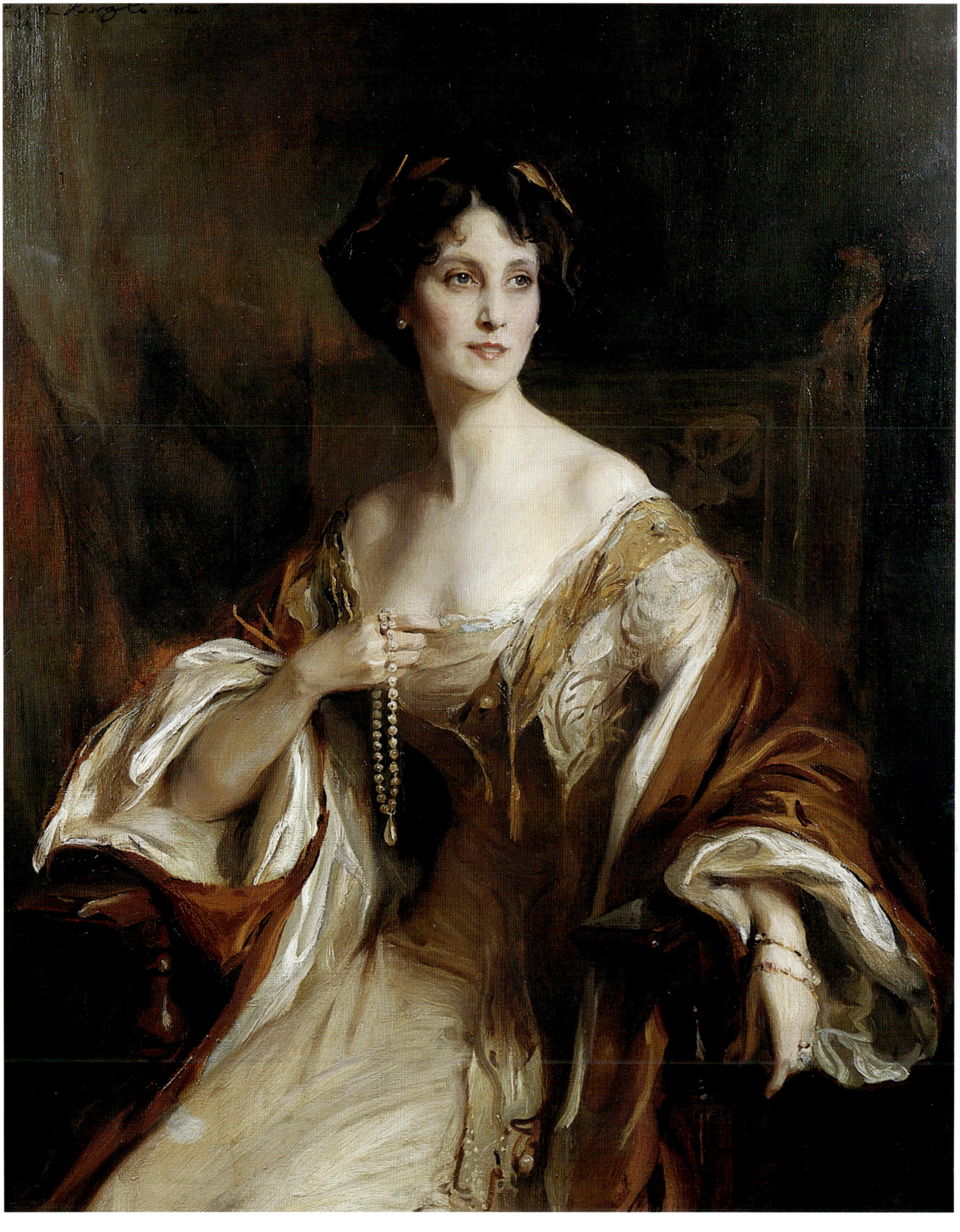

De László and Sargent

Richard Ormond

In the year 1907 Philip de László set up as a portrait painter in London and John Singer Sargent retired. Society's favourite portrait painter, an American, was succeeded by an Hungarian in a seamless transfer of patronage from one to the other. The people Sargent had painted in the early 1900s de László would portray a decade or more later, and occasionally the other way about. Their sitters came from the highest ranks of the British establishment. Both artists sought employment in America, and de László enjoyed a privileged position as court painter to most of Europe's royal families. Both were cosmopolitan, international in outlook, and masters of high style and painterly panache. They understood their role in giving fresh impetus to the grand tradition of formal portraiture by harnessing a modern sense of psychology and sensibility to the age-old claims of rank and status. Portraits by Sargent and de László are marked by flowing brushwork and scintillating effects of light and colour that bring their subjects vividly to life. At the same time their sitters are invested with the aura of wealth and glamour, power and prestige, through the devices of grand design and pictorial invention.

"Ask me to paint your gates, your fences, your barns, which I should gladly do, *but not the human face*", Sargent told Lady Radnor in 1907.[1] After twenty years of unparallelled success, he was giving up as a portraitist in order to concentrate on his mural projects and his landscapes and figure subjects. Lady Radnor was not the only person to remonstrate with him, and the artist came under intense pressure to lift his embargo. It seemed bizarre that the greatest portrait painter of his generation should renege on his contract to paint the great and the good and shut up shop. Except in rare instances, however, Sargent held firm to his resolve and refused to contemplate further portrait commissions.

Sargent's career had not always been marked by effortless success. The son of expatriate American parents, he had been born and brought up in Europe, and he had trained as a painter in the atelier of the fashionable French portrait painter Emile Carolus-Duran. Early successes at the Paris Salon with portraits and subject pictures came to an abrupt end when his celebrated portrait of *Mme Gautreau* (Metropolitan Museum of Art, New York) caused outrage at the Salon exhibition of 1884. In the wake of the scandal, Sargent transferred himself from Paris to London, but in one sense this was a case of out of the frying pan into the fire. The British public was far more conservative than its French counterpart, and in Sargent's own words his style was thought "beastly French".[2] Disheartened, he even talked at this time of giving up art altogether.

It was in America rather than England that he finally made his breakthrough, on two important visits in 1887 and 1890. To his surprise, he was awarded celebrity status, and showered with more commissions than he had time to paint. Success in London followed in 1893 when his portraits of *Lady Agnew* and *Mrs Hugh Hammersley* (National Gallery of Scotland, Edinburgh, and Metropolitan Museum of Art, New York, respectively) swept all before them at the Royal Academy and New Gallery exhibitions of that year. Election as an associate of the Royal Academy sealed recognition of his triumph.

Previously disparaged, Sargent's daring and sophisticated style now seemed to encapsulate the spirit of the age. A directness of characterization, revealing complicated modern people as they really were, distinguished his work from the beginning. Sargent's ability to

FIG. 32 *Winifred, Duchess of Portland*, 1912
Oil on canvas 127 × 101.5 cm, private collection

capture the illusion that his sitters are inhabiting real space came from his study of Velázquez and Frans Hals. Carolus-Duran had taught him how to paint exactly what he saw in terms of precisely rendered tonal values. And from the Impressionists he had learnt how to capture fleeting effects of light and how to model form through colour. Sargent's exacting training meant that his brilliant, bravura style of painting was grounded in a thorough understanding of the processes of art. He was acutely sensitive both to the individual and to the social type, and in those portraits where he really engaged with his sitter he could match the sense of who they were and what they represented in designs of great originality. The pale and pencil-thin *Graham Robertson* (1894; Tate, London), in his long black coat, holding a jade-topped cane, remains the epitome of the 1890s aesthete, as Mrs Phelps Stokes in the double portrait with her husband (1896; Metropolitan Museum of Art, New York), wearing white skirt and boater, is quintessentially a 'new woman'.

Many of Sargent's sitters in the 1890s had been members of the thrusting new class of financiers and entrepreneurs, both British and American, and the same is true of de László's early sitters. The glamorous, cosmopolitan style of both artists appealed to the extrovert instincts of this new class, their desire for prestige and recognition. By 1900, it was the turn of the aristocracy, who had finally woken up to Sargent's genius as an image-maker. In the full-length portraits and groups he painted for Blenheim and Chatsworth, Welbeck and Warwick Castle, Sargent proved himself heir to the great portrait tradition. His pictures looked quite at home with works by Van Dyck and Lely, Reynolds and Gainsborough, Romney and Lawrence, in the great houses of Britain. His portraits exemplify the grandeur and wealth, the dynastic tradition and the patent of nobility of these Edwardian grandees, who had ruled Britain for generations, at the very moment when power was slipping from their grasp.

Sargent adapted his vibrant bravura style to the demands of formal composition. His deep knowledge of the Old Masters, going back to his itinerant childhood, assisted by his mural work for the Boston Public Library, gave him the necessary resources to raise his game. His portraits of *Lord Dalhousie* (1900; private collection) and *Lord Ribblesdale* (1902; Tate, London), the *Duchess of Portland* (fig. 39) and the *Countess of Warwick and her Son* (1905; Worcester Art Museum, Massachusetts), and the groups of the *Wyndham Sisters* (1899; Metropolitan Museum of Art, New York), the *Misses Acheson* (1902; Chatsworth, Derbyshire) and the *Marlborough Group* (1905; Blenheim Palace, Oxfordshire), are magisterial creations that capture the Edwardian aristocracy in its heyday. Sargent's achievement was recognized in his own day: he was treated as a kind of living Old Master, and his friend Auguste Rodin aptly dubbed him "the Van Dyck of our times".[3]

And then in 1907 Sargent threw it all up. He had always been an artist first and a portraitist second. He was tired of the demands that portraiture made on his time and his creative energy, he was financially independent, and there were other things he wanted to do more. First and foremost were his murals for the Boston Public Library, first commissioned in 1890, which had been progressing all too slowly. Secondly, there was his desire to paint more landscape and figure subjects on the long summer and autumn tours he made to the Alps and Southern Europe. Occasionally he was forced out of retirement to paint a friend, like *Henry James* (1913; National Portrait Gallery, London), or in time of war to offer his services on behalf of the Red Cross, or to undertake a national commission like his *Generals of the First World War* (1920–2; National Portrait Gallery, London), but these were exceptions that proved the rule. His one concession to those who clamoured for his services as a portraitist was the charcoal drawing, an image of head and shoulders, executed in a sitting of an hour or two. Sargent did more than six hundred of these in the last part of his career, and they form a parallel portrait gallery to the oils, but in a minor key.

Those who deplored the void left by Sargent's departure did not have long to wait. Philip de László, arriving in London in the very year that Sargent retired, had all the right credentials to succeed him. He already enjoyed royal and aristocratic patronage in Europe; he was, like Sargent, a conjuror with the brush, and like him he successfully combined a modern style of painting and a modern sense of psychology with the traditional props of formal portraiture. His foreign polish and panache appealed to the British establishment, who recognized in him a mythologist who would help them to re-invent themselves. László's vivid sense of people, his forceful brushwork and flowing style of painting quickly won him admirers. His arrival in London was heralded by an exhibition of fifty recent portraits at the Fine Art Society, which included those of a number of prominent British sitters. Critics gave the artist vigorous reviews and a somewhat mixed reception, and inevitable comparisons were made to the work of Sargent, but the show helped to establish de László's credentials as his successor. Commissions flowed in, from the king downwards; Edward VII commanded the artist to begin a portrait of his daughter, Princess Victoria, on the day he visited the exhibition, and the artist's career in Britain quickly took off.[4]

What did the two artists think of each other? We know that de László admired Sargent's work and regarded him as the benchmark against which to measure his own success. When in Boston, in 1908, he made a point of going to see Sargent's great Spanish Dance picture, *El Jaleo* (1880–2; Isabella Stewart Gardner Museum, Boston), and he wrote: "No contemporary picture has impressed me so profoundly. It displays Sargent's mastery of his art and reproduces the very atmosphere of Spain, together with the lovely figure of the passionate and graceful dancer".[5] Painting Edward VII's portrait in 1907, de László was present when the names of Hubert von Herkomer and Sargent were proposed for knighthoods, "for I admired the work of both artists, particularly Sargent's". The king expressed his regret that he could not confer the honour on Sargent because he was not a British subject: "'I am very sorry to hear that', said the King. 'There is no one on whom I would more willingly have conferred that honour. Sargent is a great artist whose work will live'."[6]

That cordial relations existed between the two men we know from a small group of surviving letters from Sargent to de László. Two of these concern a proposed exhibition in Vienna to which Sargent had been invited to contribute. In the first letter, Sargent writes cordially to "My dear Laszlo" from Amsterdam, where he was recovering from a bout of influenza: "I hope to be well enough to go back to London in a few days, and I will try to borrow some good portraits, or if I do not succeed in that, I will send one of the few things that belong to me". Sargent approached the Duke and Duchess of Connaught about the possibility of borrowing their portraits, and he told de László that the Vienna authorities would have to solicit them officially: "So I have written to Prof von Angeli to explain this, and I hope they will send a formal request – If you are in Vienna would you tell him that seems to be a condition".[7] So far it has not been possible to confirm what the exhibition was or whether the portraits travelled there.

A third letter concerns another exhibition, this time in Berlin, where de László again seems to have had a co-ordinating role. Sargent was unclear whether inclusion in the show was "by *invitation*, or whether the exhibition defrays the expense of transport etc .... I am thinking of sending a very large and heavy thing in bronze, besides a picture or two, & I should like to know this point".[8] Apart from the letters there are two note cards from Sargent warmly inviting de László to visit him in his studio. In one of these, dating from 1909, he writes: "I shall be delighted to show you Lord Wemyss' portrait. Can you come some morning before you go to your own work? I am generally at my other studio now, but if you will name any morning I will be delighted to see you."[9] Both Sargent and de László were to paint this grand old Scottish aristocrat and sportsman in celebration of his ninetieth birthday, and both did justice to their subject's leonine head and majestic personality. That Sargent had an eye for de László's work is made clear in a letter from Margot Asquith to the Hungarian artist about her own portrait by him: "As you know I think it wonderfully clever & much more interesting than I am. The only people who have seen it, admire it hugely. Sargent found (in the studio) the only fault that I ever did: that it gives an impression of a bigger face than mine."[10] In 1919, during de László's internment, Sargent urged the President of the Royal Academy to write to the Home Secretary to allow the artist the use of a model.[11]

Though Sargent and de László were both expatriates and shared a common style of bravura painting, derived from training in Paris, they came from very different backgrounds, and they were poles apart in outlook and temperament. The reserved and stolid Sargent, reared on New England principles, was a complete contrast to the impulsive and romantic Hungarian. Though he never relinquished his American citizenship, Sargent was rooted in the British art establishment as de László, who did become a British citizen, never really was. Every year, Sargent sent his major portraits to the annual Royal Academy exhibition – over fifty of them between 1900 and 1908 – and they were the subject of extensive notice in the media. He exhibited widely elsewhere, especially in America, but his chosen forum was the Royal Academy and he was a pillar of the institution.

De László, by contrast, exhibited only a handful of works at the Academy, and he realized early on that he was unlikely to be accepted there.[12] He was too blatantly foreign, in a way that Sargent was not, and his style was not generally admired in academic circles. It would be wrong, however, to think of him as isolated in the art world. Surviving correspondence shows that he was friendly with many leading British painters, among them Sir Luke Fildes, an R.A. who was especially supportive, the Hon. John Collier, W.F. Calderon, Herbert Draper, Frank Brangwyn and Sir John Lavery. De László did exhibit occasionally at the Royal Society of Portrait Painters and he became president of the Royal Society of British Artists in 1930, but his favourite exhibition vehicle was the one-man show, carefully orchestrated and promoted, which put the spotlight on him as a cosmopolitan artist with an international clientèle. Recognition in Britain mattered to him as long as it was on his terms, and he was not dependent on it. His network of influential patrons ensured that he was in constant demand. Both he and Sargent enjoyed considerable patronage in America, but Sargent was native-born and his professional links with his home country went back to the very start of his career in the 1870s. On the other hand, de László had a flourishing European practice which Sargent lacked after 1885, and de László had made a speciality of royal portraiture.

Not since F.X. Winterhalter had any artist serviced the courts of Europe so expertly and comprehensively. Monarchs were charmed by de László personally and enchanted with his art, which made them appear far more regal and glamorous than they really were. Like Winterhalter before him, he re-invented the state portrait, and gave the royals he painted a fresh modern look. The contacts he established gave him opportunities to move from one court to another, from Stockholm to Madrid, London to Berlin, Vienna to Athens. A first commission would inevitably lead to others, so that whole dynasties ended up being painted by him. He could be relied on to produce images of power and authority that were also human and engaging. His style slid effortlessly across borders to establish an

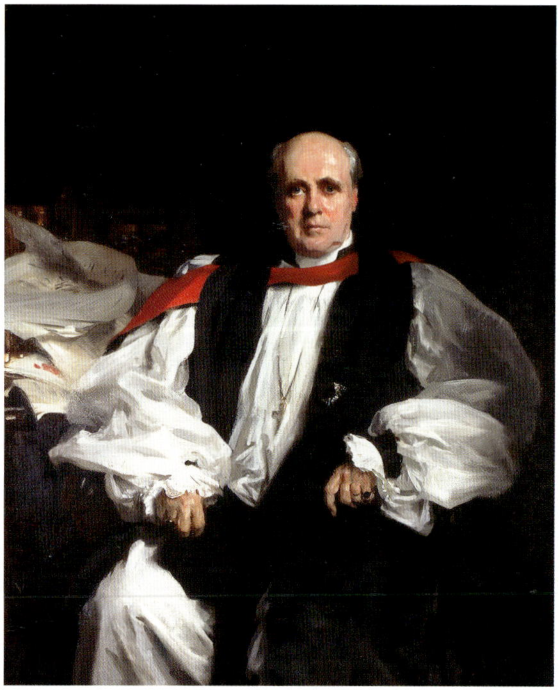

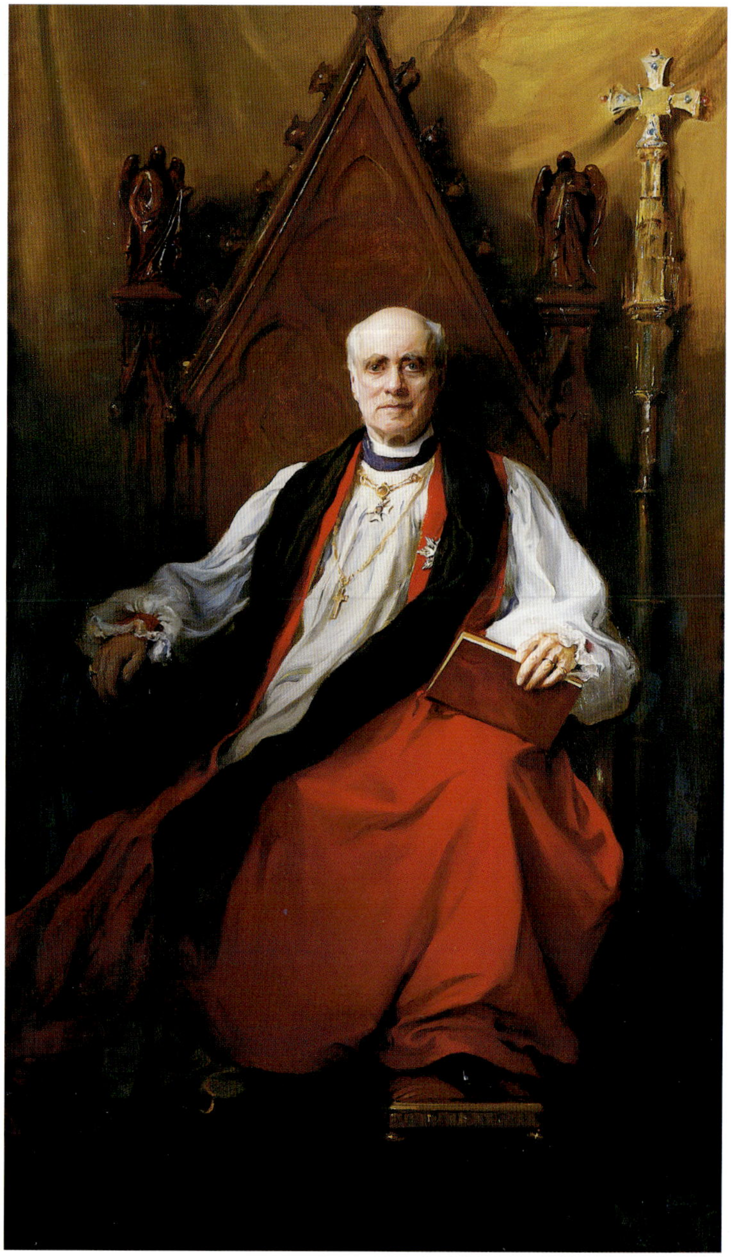

international iconography of royalty that underlined the close family relationships which bound the European courts so closely together.

Sargent, by contrast, shied away from royalty. He refused the commission to paint Edward VII's coronation and his only portrait of the king was a drawing after death (Royal Library, Windsor Castle). He did paint a pair of portraits of Queen Victoria's fourth son, Prince Arthur, Duke of Connaught, and his wife Princess Louise (1906; Royal Collection Trust), but this was no substitute for a state portrait of the king, which would have tested his powers to the full and might have produced a masterpiece. Maybe his democratic principles stood in the way of such a commission, for Edward VII, an admirer as we have seen, would surely have sat to him if asked. De László did paint the king but only in mufti, and his portrait, like that of Queen Alexandra (see figs. 26, 27, p.36), sadly remains untraced.

In painting the great and the good of the British establishment, Sargent and de László adopted strategies that point up the similarities and differences that distinguish their portraits. Sargent had made a exception to his portrait embargo in agreeing to paint Randall Davidson, Archbishop of Canterbury, in 1910 for Lambeth Palace (fig. 33), because they had met in the Alps and were friends. Sargent's portrait of Davidson in his surplice and robes draws on the traditional imagery reserved for princes of the church, but plays it in a minor key. We see this modest and conscientious churchman in the private setting of his study with a jumble of books and documents on the table beside him. De László's 1926 full-length of the Archbishop

ABOVE LEFT FIG. 33
John Singer Sargent
Randall Davidson, Archbishop of Canterbury, 1910
Oil on canvas, 130.8 × 105.4 cm
Lambeth Palace, London

ABOVE FIG.34
Randall Davidson, Archbishop of Canterbury, 1926
Oil on canvas, 251.5 × 139.7 cm
The Corporation of the Church House, London

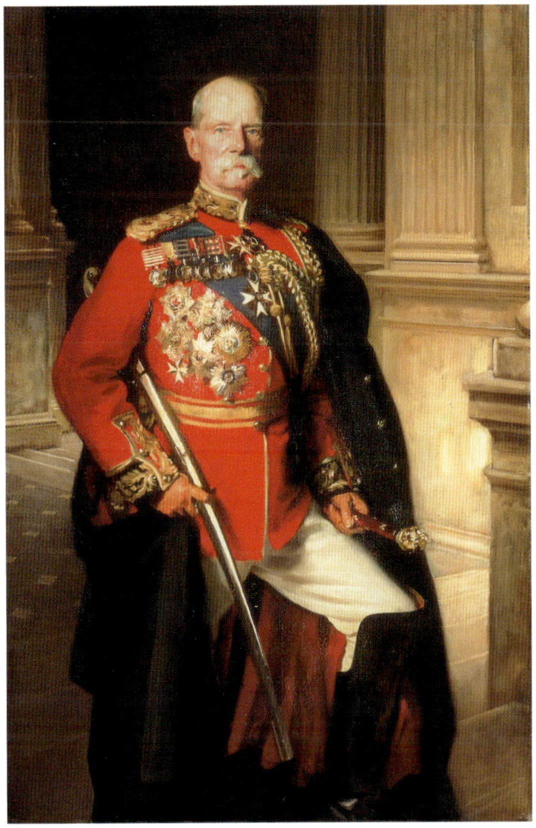

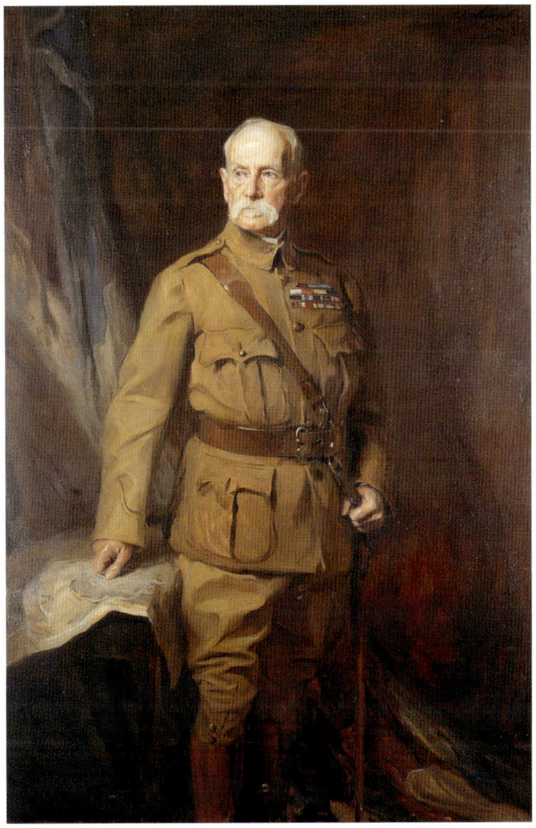

FAR LEFT FIG. 35
John Singer Sargent
Field Marshal Earl Roberts of Kandahar, 1908
Oil on canvas, 161.9 × 102.9 cm
National Portrait Gallery, London

LEFT FIG. 36
Field Marshal Earl Roberts of Kandahar, 1911
Oil on canvas, 172.8 × 113.7 cm
Eton College, Windsor

for Church House, London (fig. 33), draws on the same iconographical conventions as Sargent does, but goes for the full panoply of ecclesiastical splendour and symbol. The Gothic throne on which Davidson sits had been used by him at the coronations of Edward VII and George V, and it invests him with the aura of authority as leader of the Church. He holds a book on his knee and his crozier stands beside the throne. De László records the nervousness of the Archbishop when shown the preliminary sketches because he feared the picture would be thought too artificial and 'showy'. Interestingly, de László hides Davidson's Garter Star in the fold of the vestments, exactly as Sargent had done sixteen years earlier.

In the case of the veteran Field Marshal Earl Roberts, a much loved figure familiarly known as 'Bobs', it is Sargent who invests the sitter with pageant and symbol, while de László portrayts him as a straightforward military man (figs. 35 and 36). So encrusted with medals and order is Roberts in Sargent's portrait that one critic complained of the way the "truculent splendour of the uniform overshadows the individuality of the wearer".[13] The baroque swagger of the figure is set off by a receding vista of columns and pilasters in a grand staircase hall. De László's portrait, painted three years later for Eton College, shows an older and more careworn figure, his hand resting on a map as if still in active command. The background is bare of accessories except for a cascading piece of drapery, perhaps a flag.

Another pair of portraits painted within a short space of time are those of George Curzon, Earl Curzon (cat. 54; fig. 37), the brilliant but arrogant statesman who held high office but was never Prime Minister. This time it was de László's portrait that came first, in 1913, for All Souls College, Oxford. There is something forbidding and mask-like about the sitter, who gazes out with a fixed and penetrating expression on his features. One hand is held to his chin, in the traditional image of the thinker, while the claw-like fingers of the other hand are inserted between the pages of a book. He is dressed in his robes as Chancellor of Oxford University, and the artist paints the lace cravat and cuffs and the gold braid of the robe in that lovely, flowing, impressionistic style that is his hallmark. Sargent's characterization is less intense and more human, but there is surely irony in this image of self-conceit. Curzon is dressed here in Garter Robes as the embodiment of steely will-power and aristocratic hauteur. The portrait was painted a year after the de László, in July 1914, and one month before the outbreak of the Great War, in

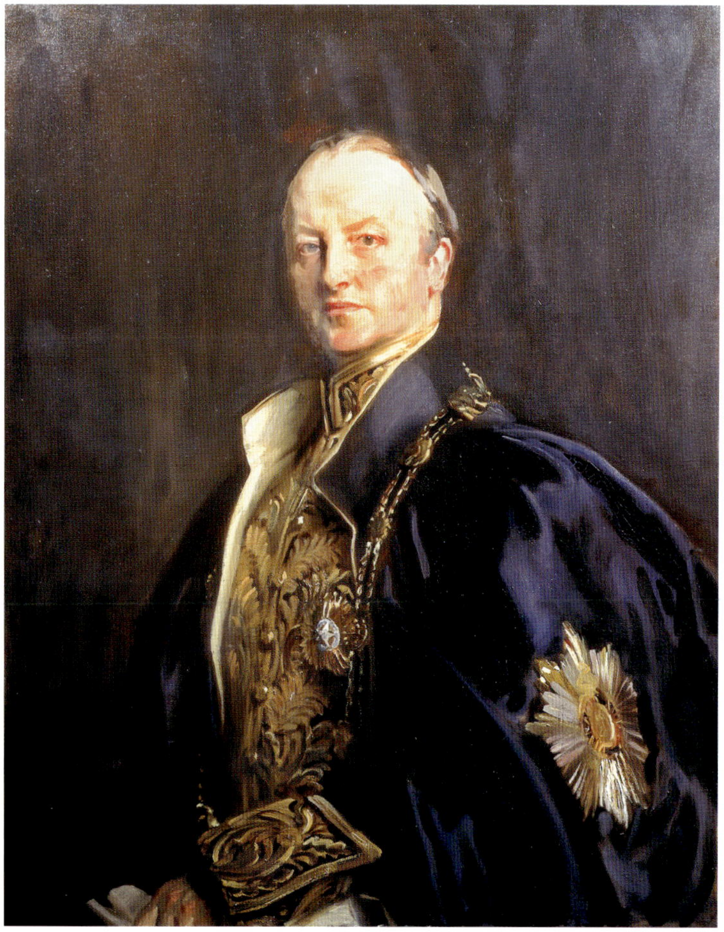

FIG. 37
John Singer Sargent
Earl Curzon of Kedleston, 1914
Oil on canvas, 100.3 × 77.5 cm
Royal Geographical Society, London

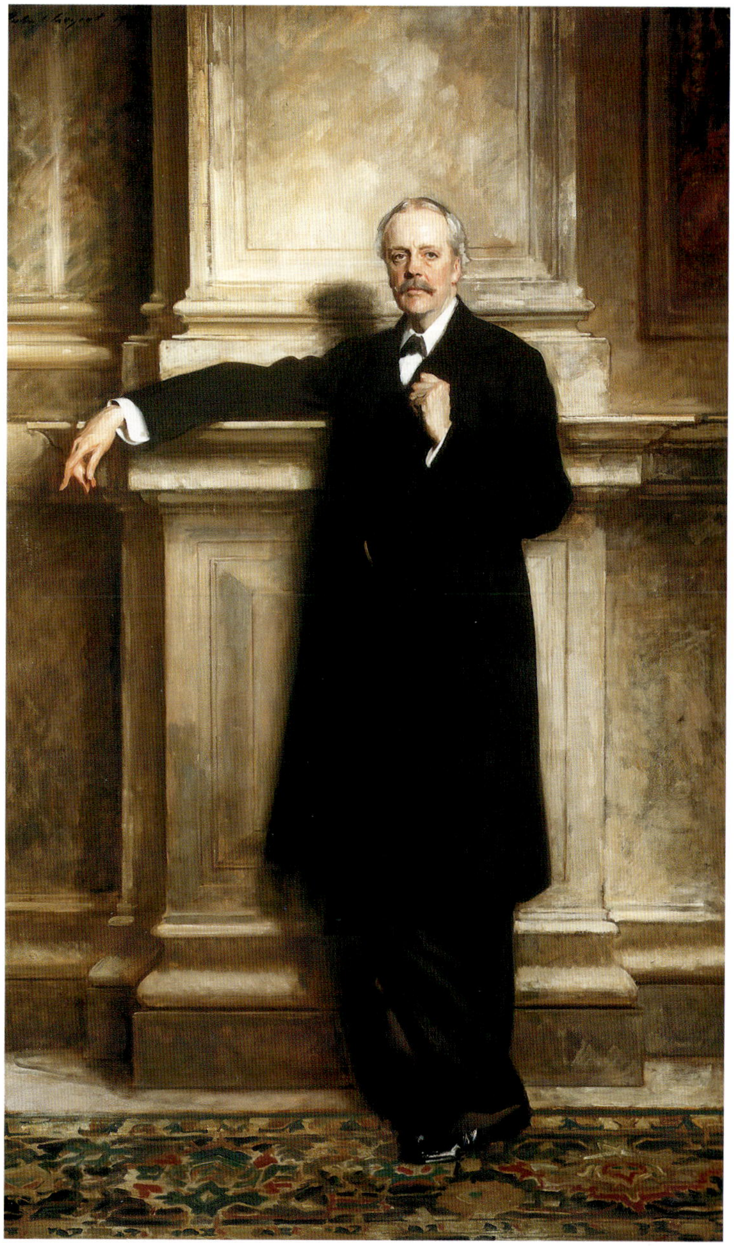

FIG. 38
John Singer Sargent
A.J. Balfour, 1908
Oil on canvas, 256.5 × 147.3 cm
National Portrait Gallery, London

recognition of Curzon's services to the Royal Geographical Society, of which he was president. Both artists would paint portraits of Lady Curzon, and de László also made a memorable portrait of Curzon's mistress, *Elinor Glyn* (cat. 55), together with two studies.

Another of the dominating political figures of the age painted by both artists was A.J. Balfour, conservative Prime Minister, philosopher and leading member of the 'Souls', a patrician group intellectuals and aesthetes (fig. 38). Both painted pictures of him in the same year, 1908 (László again in 1914), and the two were exhibited contemporaneously, Sargent's at the Royal Academy, de László's at a one-man exhibition at Dowdeswell's Galleries in New Bond Street. Critics were not slow to draw comparisons between the two works:

"As against Mr. Sargent's masterly full-length and its subtle seizure of the intellectual character of the subject, Mr. Laszlo has attempted a 'kit-kat' with a fresher complexion than Mr. Sargent's and has tried no subtleties at all."[14] De László's portrait is missing, although there is a related oil sketch in the National Portrait Gallery, but this time he was up against one of Sargent's most brilliant creations, a full-length figure, eloquent of intelligence and sensitivity; it was commissioned by the Carlton Club and has recently been acquired by the National Portrait Gallery.

The cross-over between Sargent and de László in terms of sitters is prodigious: they portrayed more than fifty of the same people. These range from royalty, the Duke and Duchess of York (later George VI and Queen Elizabeth) and the Duke of Connaught; statesmen, President Roosevelt and Lord Cromer; military commanders, Lord Byng of Vimy and the Earl of Cavan; aristocrats, the Duke and Duchess of Portland, the Duchess of Devonshire, the Duchess of Wellington and the Marchioness of Londonderry; leading society women, Gladys Vanderbilt (Countess Széchényi) and Mrs William Cazalet; musicians, Joseph Joachim and Sir George Henschel. The list is even longer if members of the same families are included.

Comparison of the female portraits is particularly instructive, because it is as painters of women that both artists are best known. A decade or more invariably separates their respective portraits of the same sitter, Sargent painting them as young or young middle-aged, de László as mature matrons. Winifred, Duchess of Portland, one of the great beauties of the age, was painted by Sargent in 1902, when she was thirty nine, though you would never guess that from Sargent's youthful-looking image (fig. 39). Dressed in a white evening gown with stand-up Van Dyck collar, cerise cape, and strings of pearls draped across her corsage, she stands perched momentarily on the edge of the marble fireplace in the Gobelins Tapestry room at Welbeck Abbey, the Portland family home. She is a mixture of nervous vitality, high breeding and aristocratic grandeur. De László's three-quarter length portrait (fig. 32), painted exactly ten years later, and only just recently traced, is a more stately and reflective image, showing the Duchess seated and gazing into space, lips parted, as if in thought. She is again dressed in evening gown and cape, and she fingers Queen Mary's pearl necklace in one hand like a rosary, with a classical filet of leaves in her hair. She is still stunningly beautiful at fifty, and de László grasps the essence of her radiant personality in one of his most accomplished works. Other portraits of the Duchess were to follow, including a half-length oil sketch of this same period, a drawing (cat. 49), and a head and shoulders study of 1925 in tiara and black chiffon veil (private collection).

A more conventional parallel is to be found in the portraits of Mrs Julius (later Lady) Wernher, the wife of a prominent diamond tycoon, whose house at Luton Hoo, Hertfordshire, was the setting for a

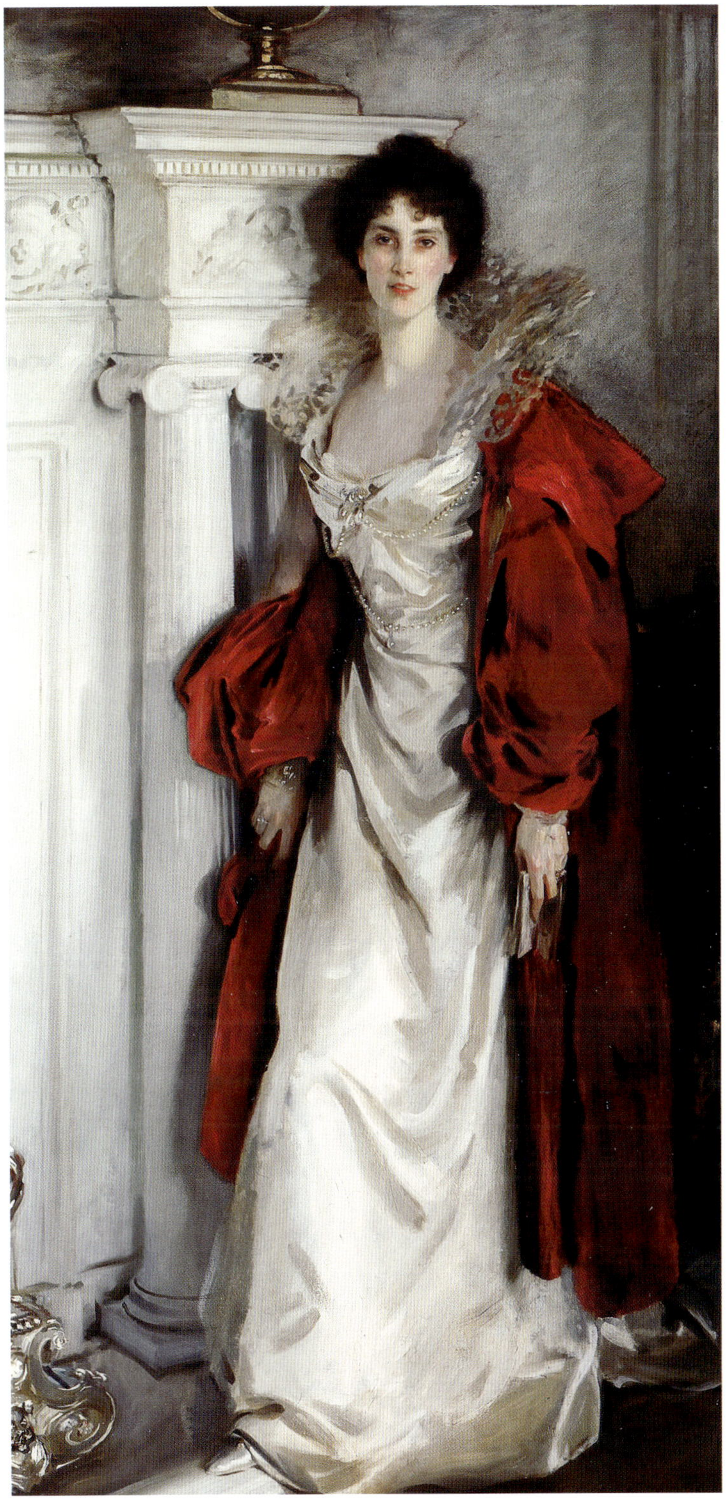

FIG. 39 John Singer Sargent, *Winifred, Duchess of Portland*, 1902
Oil on canvas, 228.6 × 111.8 cm
Private collection

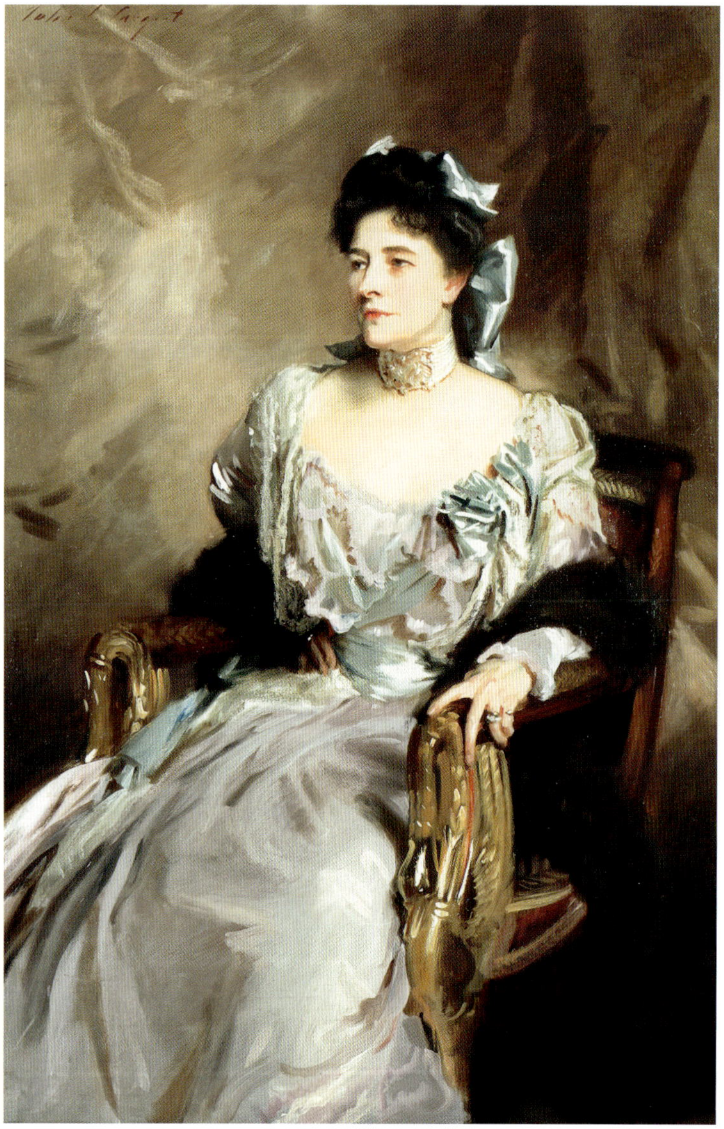

FIG. 40
John Singer Sargent, *Mrs Julius Wernher (later Lady Wernher)*, 1902
Oil on canvas, 147.3 × 95.3 cm
The Wernher Collection

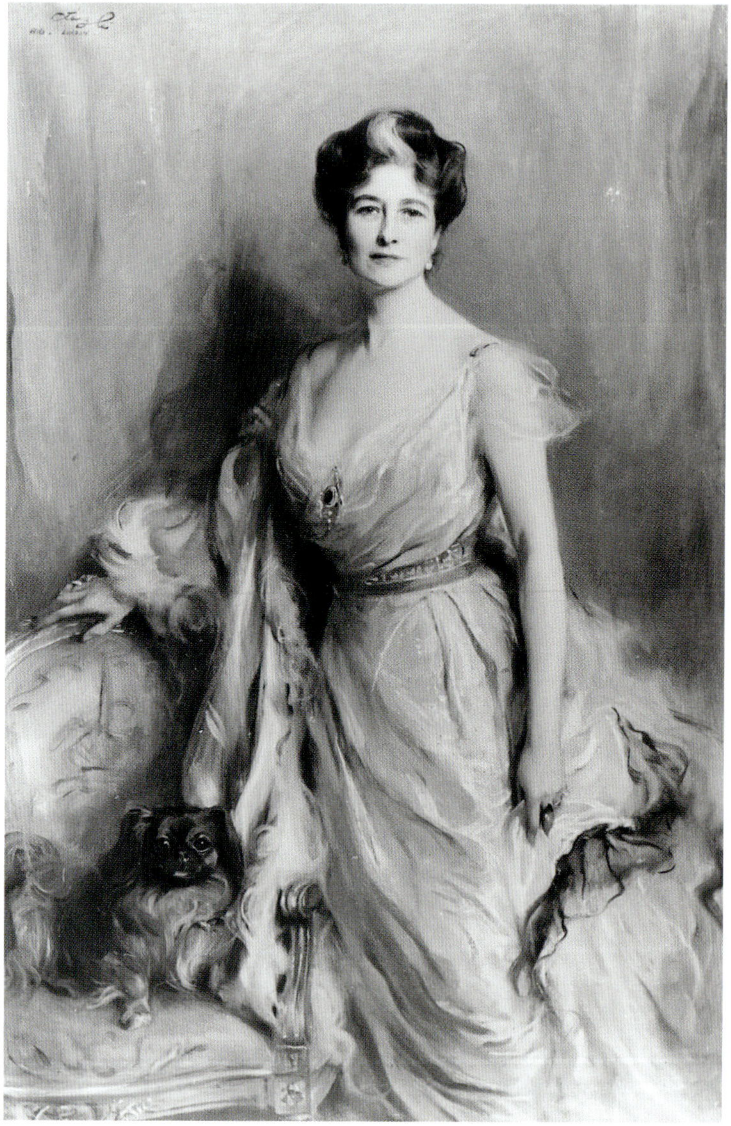

FIG. 41
Lady Wernher, 1916
Oil on canvas, 175.3 × 111.8 cm
Private collection

magnificent collection of old master paintings and works of art. Sargent's portrait of her (fig. 40) is one of those luxuriant studies of women in white that goes back to the famous portrait of *Lady Agnew*. *Mrs Julius Wernher*, as she then was, is dressed in an evening gown with lilac and light blue trimmings, sash and ribboned headdress, a dramatic choker and fur stole, and she is seated in an Empire-style *fauteuil* with swan's head scroll-ends. Behind is one of the *boiserie* panels in Sargent's Tite Street studio. Mrs Wernher has all the attributes of wealth and social distinction, but they do not seem to sit easily with her, and the sense of make-believe is too evident. No such doubts inform de László's portrait of the same sitter, by now *Lady Wernher*, painted a dozen years later (fig. 41). The style of dress is opulently eighteenth-century revival, like the Louis XVI chair occupied by a pekinese, and Lady Wernher stands in a resolutely commanding pose amidst the soft flutter of dress and drapes.

Such parallels could be multiplied. The innocent-looking debutantes in Sargent's three-quarter-length portraits of *Gladys Vanderbilt*, later Countess Széchényi, and *Maud Coats*, later Marchioness of Douro and Duchess of Wellington (both 1906; private collections), turn into the experienced women of the world in the greater realism of de László's post-war images (1921 and 1922; private collections). In the case of the autocratic Lady Londonderry, wife of the sixth Marquess, both artists arrived at the same conclusion. The marchioness swept aside Sargent's objections and offer of a charcoal, and insisted on being painted in oils (1909; private collection). The only defence he offered was to limit the number of sittings, telling her that he would spoil the sketch if he touched it again, "by losing all its lightness and freshness. I have done a tiny thing here and there, and you are as beautiful as the morning star, and nothing will induce me to mar it with a brush!"[15] Sargent portrayed the marchioness in a flamboyant plumed hat, with a voluminous cloak, feather boa and pearl necklace. Her head is tilted up, eyes heavy lidded, nostrils flared, the incarnation of aristocratic hauteur and disdain. De László's portrait study of 1912 (cat. 51) also shows her with her nose in the air in a style no less intimidating, in evening dress with black choker, swept-back hair, drop earrings and triple pearl necklace. Both artists play up to Lady Londonderry's persona as terrifying grand dame, who could reduce the greatest of statesmen to quivering wrecks, for she ran a political salon. Sargent also painted her husband in one of his grandest compositions, with the marquess posed before a view of Westminster Abbey, carrying the sword of state as he had at Edward VII's coronation, attended by his page (recently acquired by the Museum of Fine Arts, Boston).

It would be wrong to make too much of such comparisons. Sargent had effectively ceased painting portraits in 1907, while de László was to continue for another thirty years, and his style changed markedly in the post-war period in response to the changing mood and fashion of the time. He was infinitely more prolific than Sargent, producing his characteristic portrait studies, so instinct with life and panache, often in a single sitting. He amassed a vastly greater clientèle, that spanned Europe and America, and he remained a portrait painter through and through. There would be no grand mural scheme or landscape ambitions to lure him away from the thing he did best and push him into early retirement. The demands made on him never wore down his patience or dulled his spirit. He remained buoyant to the end, painting his late portraits with all the energy and flair he had displayed as a young man, with no loss of force or character. Like Sargent before him, he left behind a portrait gallery of many of the great figures of the age, and his contribution deserves greater recognition.

1. Quoted in Stanley Olson, *John Singer Sargent His Portrait*, London and New York 1986, p.228
2. Letter to Edward Russell, 10 September 1885, Tate Gallery Archives.
3. Rodin's comment recorded in an interview, 'Rodin in London', *Daily Chronicle*, London, 16 May 1902.
4. De László later painted portraits of Edward VII and Queen Alexandra and received the M.V.O., the personal gift of the Monarch, in 1910; see Owen Rutter, *Portrait of a Painter The Authorized Life of Philip de László*, London 1939, pp.235–42.
5. *Ibid.*, p.255.
6. *Ibid.*, p.241.
7. Both letters in the de László family archive. I am grateful to Suzanne Bailey for these references.
8. Ditto; the bronze must have been Sargent's crucifix, later placed in the crypt of St. Paul's as a memorial to the artist
9. Ditto.
10. Letter of 30 March 1910, from 10 Downing Street, de László family archive.
11. See the letter from de László's solicitor, Sir Charles Russell, to the artist's wife of 11 February 1919, de László family archive.
12. His portrait of Lord Stanley of Alderley was rejected by the Royal Academy in 1905. His first picture to be shown there was *Lady Wantage* (cat. 46). In 1915 *Lord Devonport* was rejected because the Academy had decided not to show any works by natives of countries with whom Britain was at war, even if (as de László was) they were naturalized.
13. *Academy*, London, 12 May 1906, p.455.
14. Quoted in Rutter 1939, p.264. There is a 1914 portrait of Balfour by de László in Cambridge.
15. Londonderry Papers, North Ireland Public Record Office, 2846/2/23/60.

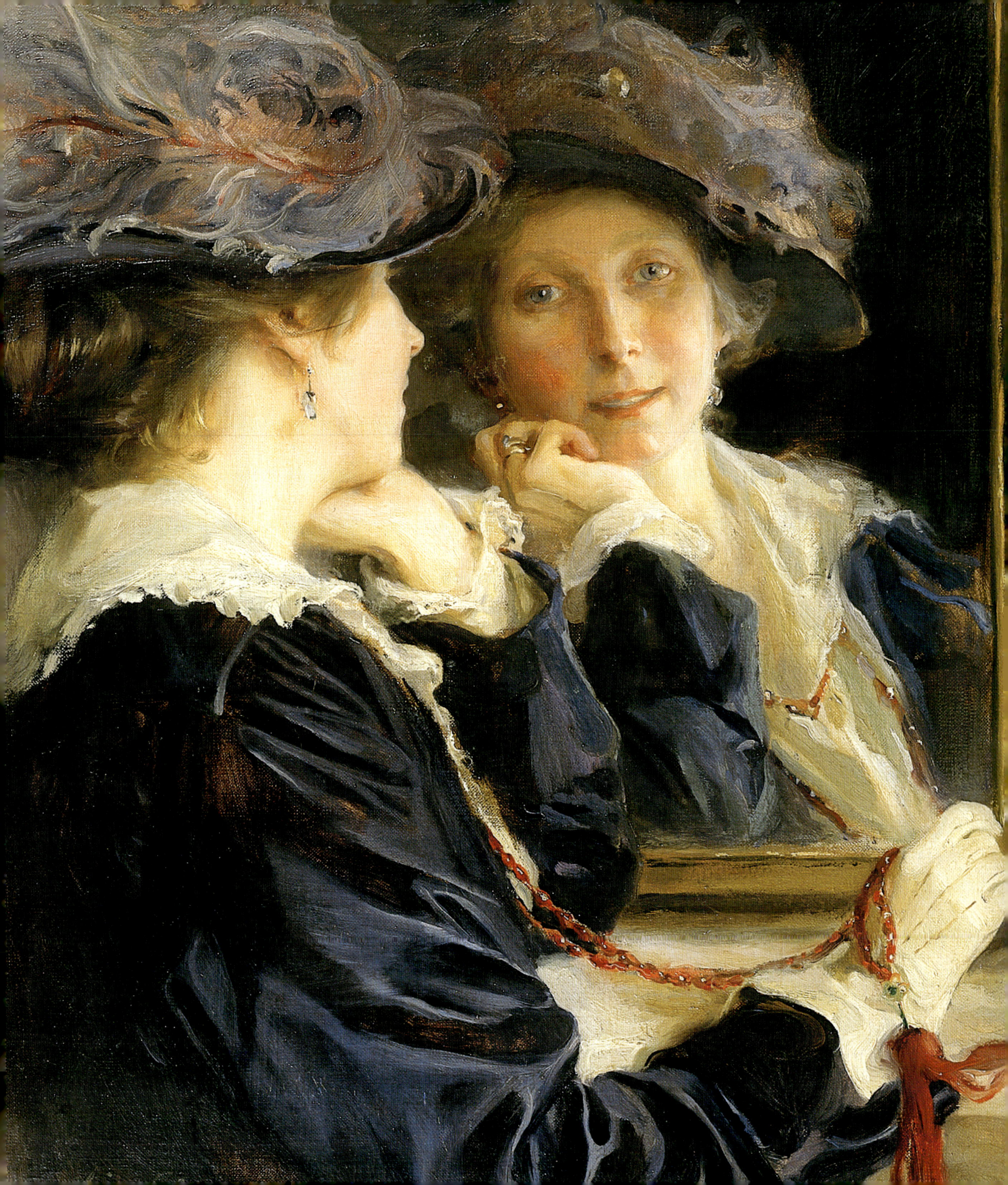

De László's Relationships with his Patrons and Sitters

Suzanne Bailey

In 1929 a question in a general knowledge quiz in the *Daily Express* asked: "Who is the most prolific portrait painter of the present time?" The answer: "Philip de László".[1] De László painted over 3,000 portraits in a career spanning fifty years. While some critics have dismissed de László as "the pet portrait-painter to Society with a big, big S",[2] and others have labelled him the "painter of kings", both ignore the enormous variety of sitters he painted. Unquestionably, his so-called society and royal sitters make an impressive list. A headline in *Time* magazine in 1932 declared that he had painted "Every Court But China".[3] But add to the list four Presidents of the United States, three British Prime Ministers, two Archbishops of Canterbury, two Popes, numerous statesmen, industrialists, financiers, members of the armed forces, academics, teachers, actors, musicians, writers, fellow artists, children, family members, favourite dogs, those who worked for him – his children's nanny, his secretary, his photographer, physician, gardener, even his golf professional – and we see a much more accurate account.

Notwithstanding the number or range of people he painted, it is his relationships with his sitters that are particularly significant. Owen Rutter, de László's biographer, commented: "It has been said of Sargent that he rarely painted a sitter without making an enemy. De László rarely painted a sitter without making a friend."[4] Evidence of the artist's enormous gift for friendship is to be found in the de László family archive. The archive, virtually untouched since the artist's death in 1937 when his wife, Lucy and their sons sorted through it, stands as an impressive testament to a man who loved and was loved by his patrons and sitters. Obsessively, he kept everything – every letter, calling card, telegram and invitation received; and drafts and carbon copies of many of his replies. Press cuttings, photographs and exhibition catalogues fill yet more boxes and trunks. His two sitters' books, now in the British Library, bear signatures and more eulogies. No doubt kept as copy for his proposed memoirs, unfinished at the time of his death, the archive is also a proud record of his rise from humble birth to a role of intimate and valued friend of many key figures of the period. In spite of his self-imposed and punishing workload as a painter, the volume and quality of his epistolary output was extraordinary: "I do not know how you find the time to transform even business letters in to a work of art and a most friendly missive. You are an example to us all," the Revd Chavasse wrote.[5]

opposite: Lucy de László, the Artist Wife (cat. 77, detail)

Whether de László was writing to kings and queens or commoners his warmth towards and interest in his correspondents did not differ. Nevertheless, corresponding with de László was a challenge when the recipient was faced with the artist's handwriting rather than his secretary's typing, as the author Mrs Alec Tweedie remarked: "Thank you for your very charming letters, all of which I have not yet been able to read, so it is absolutely imperative for you to come and see me some day, to decipher your own calligraphy".[6]

De László's correspondence, besides illustrating his propensity and aptitude for friendship with those he painted, also demonstrates that the relationship he formed with each sitter was part of the process of being painted by de László, and directly contributed to his impressive results. Acclaimed for his skill at capturing a likeness, de László saw portrait painting as more:

"It is my task to discover the character of the sitter and transfer it to the canvas. If it does not reflect the real inner spirit, the true person, it is not a good portrait. The physical is nothing. The personality within, which is human and spiritual, everything."[7]

One sitter described the psychological element to de László's portraits as an ability "even to paint the bones of the soul".[8] How he achieved this inevitably led to a friendship forming:

"I always try, when my sitters enter the studio for the first time, to make them feel at home and quite at their ease. I talk about matters which I hope will interest them and help them to forget themselves. Before starting a portrait it is essential that the sitter should be in sympathy with the artist."[9]

The talks continued during the sittings:

"... he prefers to represent his models as they would appear when engaged in pleasant converse, or listening to some fascinating discourse ... To effect this, László never ceases to engage his models in conversation while they are sitting, so that they may come out of themselves and appear perfectly natural."[10]

Many sitters remembered with fondness their talks with the artist and highlights from the archive show his versatility in relating to a variety of people on a variety of levels. Lt-Colonel McKergow, Master of Foxhounds, wrote of his sittings: "I think de Laszlo a most fascinating man & I love talking to him as he is a live wire".[11] "I love those hours of peace, combined with the charm of conversation & interest of watching the creative work which springs from your great art," wrote Ruby, Countess of Cromer.[12] "How I miss those hours!" wrote the suffragette and pacifist Dr Maude Royden.[13] In a later letter to Royden de László admitted he was not just making conversation: "I know I was a kind of Grand Inquisitor, but the result was good, and no one in generations to come will know about my cruelty, they will only see the result, which I must say, however conceited it sounds, is one of my best works".[14]

So insightful was the artist that some sitters, such as Lady Alastair Graham (cat. 103), worried what they had revealed:

"Thank you for painting such a wonderful picture in spite of the evil qualities you discovered in your sitter. It is also to ask if my husband may come and knock at your studio door on Thursday .... If he may – *please don't answer.* He so much wants to see the picture of his wicked wife."[15]

Sitters came to de László in a variety of ways. At the beginning of his career his friends and family sat to him, but once his reputation was established introductions came from former sitters; direct approaches were made to him and commissions were arranged through galleries such as the French Gallery or Grosvenor Galleries. He also painted a number of posthumous portraits, working from photographs.

Occasionally the artist himself solicited sitters. In 1924 he set off for Rome to persuade Pope Pius XI to sit for him. Others he pursued included a Spanish dancer spotted in a Noel Coward revue, Lady Alexandra Haig, whom he met at a cocktail party, and a Native American picked out by his son Patrick at the London Pavilion (cat. 95). He enlisted Bertram Park to find him "a few really good nudes".[16] He also set Albert Einstein in his sights, procuring the help of Professor Nuttall (a past sitter) and Nuttall's colleagues at Cambridge University:

"Einstein is apparently an erratic genius. Eddington said he could not help because one never knows what Einstein may do ... he (Eddington) had two invitations to meet Einstein at dinner, the one in London, the other in Manchester, on the same day and hour (Do not laugh too loudly when you read this, and keep it private my friend!). Such are the ways of GENIUS. If we catch him for you, Ramsey and I will have to hold on to his coat tails & back hair or hire a lion tamer."[17]

Einstein was indeed caught but regrettably de László had to sacrifice painting him to a previously planned trip to America.

Portraiture calls for varying degrees of collaboration between artist and sitter – depending on the attitude of the artist and the demands of his patrons. Letters in the archive record detailed preparations for each portrait – revealing de László's unfailingly polite but rather dictatorial views on how each sitter should be presented. It was explained: "Mr de László always paints in the frame, so that it harmonises with the portrait", and that he would be choosing the frame himself. Sitters were invited to the studio and de László often did sketches before decisions were made as to what type of portrait would be commissioned – head-and-shoulders, head-and-shoulders-with-hands, three-quarter-length or full-length.

"Exceptional" (reduced) prices were quoted for the favoured few, who were consequently asked to keep them secret. Those less fortunate were often given special prices, too, or given portraits as gifts. Some were assessed as to what they could afford:

"I saw Mr and Mrs Norie-Miller, both very nice people, but (this is of course confidential) I have since heard that he is a very wealthy man, and I regret that I promised to paint the portraits of him and his wife, of the size with hands, for such a very reduced sum as five hundred guineas each."[18]

Clothes received the artist's particular attention and he often painted his sitters in the costume belonging to their rank or office. The Marquis of Reading was sent instructions:

"May I ask you kindly to let me have your full uniform, with the Stars and Ribbon, (excepting the brilliant collar Badge of the Star of India), stockings, shoes and sword – all that is necessary for the picture, and I will send Webster, my butler ... to call for these."[19]

He and his sitters also appreciated the impact of some of the costumes. Monsignor Count Peter Vay saw his portrait as an opportunity to advertise his status: "I think the violet robe of a Prelate will be more artistic than the plain black – and now after the lectures I held in Paris my name will be better known too".[20] Female sitters were asked: "Please bring with you various costumes and a few evening cloaks to choose from". For some sitters de László sketched gowns to be made up by dressmakers. Lady Duff Gordon owned the fashion house Maison Lucile and in her column in the *Daily Sketch* she described her work for de László:

"He has asked me, to please him, to design dresses for evening wear long and trailing and draped, and I have done so, and I call them the Laszlo dresses. People who have seen them adore them, and so do I, but you others who jazz and Charleston I expect will hate the idea of covering up your legs so that they show only now and then as the drapery moves."[21]

De László dismissed the modern clothes of the 1920s: "I do not like these clothes. I do not wish to see those arms and legs, so persistently displayed. To see a dozen young women sitting in a row, twenty-four legs and twenty-four knees – could anything be more distressing?"[22] The press challenged de László for "fostering this unfashionable fashion for 'period' dress in modern portraits", but he remained dogged in his determination to present his sitters in his own way:

"'But,' he was asked, 'you admit that modern clothes express the modern spirit – and portraits surely should be historical. Don't you think that if modern portraits all present women in beautiful picture frocks, that are only worn for the sittings, they will fail to give an accurate historical impression of our period to posterity?' 'That is true,' he admitted gravely. Then, with a delicious flash of mischief, he added: 'So perhaps for the sake of historical accuracy … I will soon paint two or three ugly and inartistic pictures of women in these awful dresses – all ugly legs and poor arms! But it will be just a historical record'."[23]

Patrons and sitters did express their own ideas but these were more often cast aside. Dress that did not meet de László's exacting standards was likely to be attacked, with one sitter's blouse falling victim to the artist's scissors as he cut a more revealing neckline. Ultimately, little resistance was put up, and sitters were happy to collaborate with the artist and his image of them. Indeed some sitters, such as Lady Alastair Graham, worried they might not live up to de László's romantic ideals: "You have no idea what a sunburnt rustic you are proposing to dress up in ivory satin! I look more like a Hogarth than a Bronzino I assure you."[24]

Lengthy correspondence between de László and Lady Buchanan Jardine (fig. 42) illustrates the organization and collaboration necessary to arrange times, places, props and clothing for a successful sitting:

"Dear Lady Buchanan Jardine,

I am sending you the enclosed picture as promised, by Botticelli, and would prefer the blue which I think would suit you very well – very pale nattier blue chiffon – not exactly cut as it is here on the picture, but as you will see it on my drawing …. I think if you get the right green blue chiffon and a little silver for the girdle, it would look very attractive, and we could put some kind of silver decoration on your hair, something similar to what you see on the picture. May I ask you to let me have various patterns of pale bluish chiffon that I could choose from and you could have the dress made."[25]

Instructions for Simmonds, the dressmakers, followed. Dogs were sometimes included in portraits and auditions held. Lady Jardine's secretary wrote:

"Lady Jardine wishes me to tell you that she now has another dog which she is sure you will think is just the kind for the picture, he is an Irish wolf hound, but he is far too big to take to London, and could not be got into a car. Lady Jardine wondered whether it would not be possible for you to bring the picture here, and finish it, and the dog would be here …. Sir John and Lady Jardine would be delighted to see you if you could come north; and stay for a time …. I am sending you a snapshot of the Irish wolf hound [fig. 43]."[26]

Especially when they busy or lived far away, de László sometimes did stay with his sitters. These domestic arrangements are chronicled in the correspondence and give further insights into the close relationships which developed. The solemnity of the Archbishop of York's portrait is somewhat softened after reading his cosy letters to the artist: "I must ask you what sort of refreshment you like when you get home at about 10.0 after 'high tea' at about 5.0 – sandwiches? tea? cocoa? or something else? Personally I don't like eating much late, and generally have biscuits and barley-water."[27]

Despite his naturalization in 1914, which made de László an honorary Englishman, to many of his sitters his 'foreignness', along with his open and teasing nature, broke down some of the social formalities of the day. He relaxed sitters by gently teasing them, as was the case with Lady Davson (daughter of Elinor Glyn, cat. 55), whose permission he sought when planning an exhibition: "I need not say how pleased I shall be for it to be shown – as apart from its 'ugly subject with her huge mouth'! – I think is it artistically one of your most interesting pictures."[28]

De László's quick style of painting was well suited to child portraiture. Mrs Ralli wrote regarding her children (cat. 91): "I wonder how soon you would like to start the portrait of my two children? I should like it to be very soon as Godfrey may at any moment lose his top front teeth & then he will be a terrible sight for some time."[29]

Some children had their own ideas of how they should be presented. One ten-year-old sitter suggested in vain she be painted in a bathing suit. De László often included props in his child portraits – dolls, footballs, animals and so on. Others, like Robin, Lord Stewart (cat. 50), had grander responsibilities and needed coaxing: "Dear Mr.

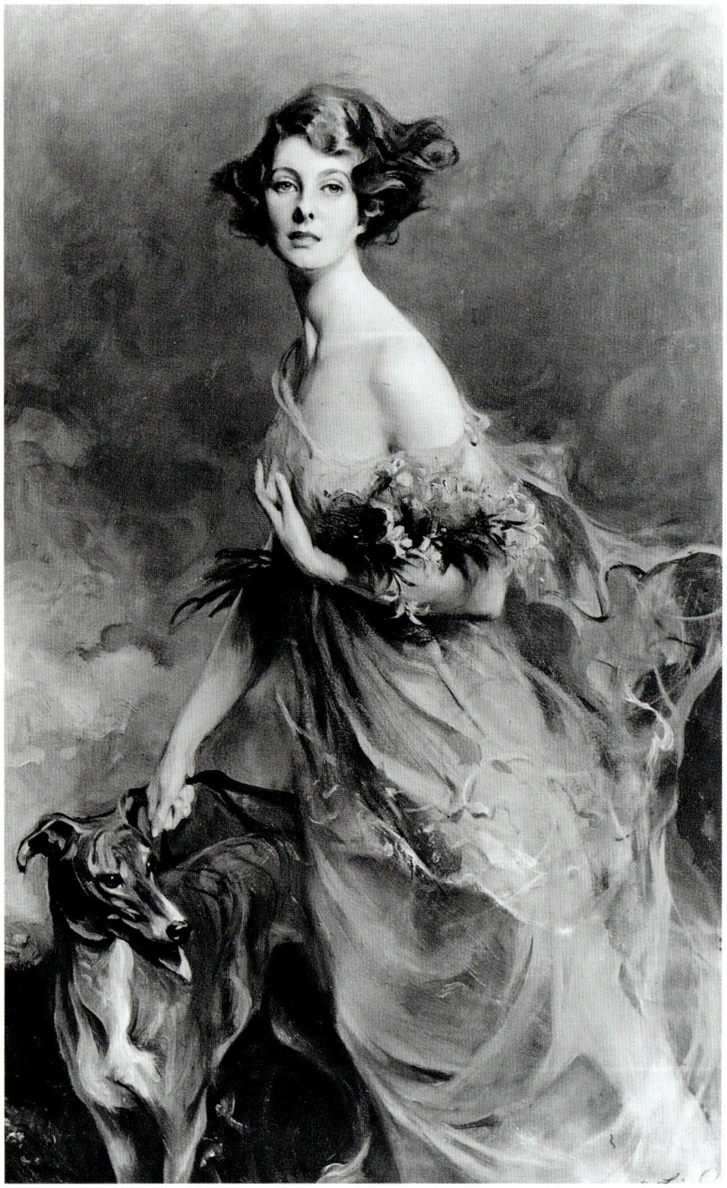

FIG. 42
Lady Buchanan Jardine, 1928
Oil on canvas; destroyed in the Blitz
Photograph courtesy of the National Portrait Gallery, London

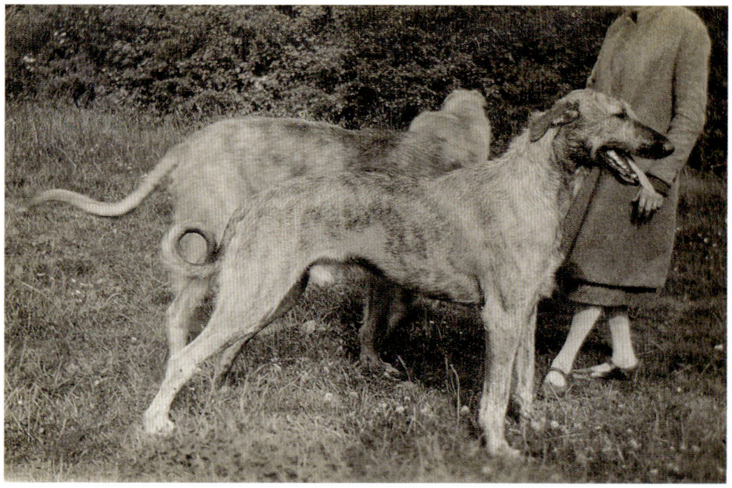

FIG. 43
Carlyn, Lady Buchanan Jardine's Irish wolf-hound

Laszlo," wrote his mother, "Here is Robin. He was rather tired to-day – but I think he will be good. Will you let him off for his biscuits at 11 o'c."[30] The artist was not popular with all his child sitters and one remembered him as "a very foreign gentleman, an egotist, small in stature and 'a clutcher'". Another sitter remembered, some sixty years on, that her mother read *Winnie the Pooh* to entertain her and the artist made her stop reading. One of the artist's own children recalled running up the back stairs of the house to avoid being called into the studio by his father.

Some children enchanted de László and some exasperated him. Jane Bendir was one of the former, and so keen was he to paint the six-year-old that he reduced his honorarium for a full-length portrait from £2000 to £1050: "I must reiterate that the hours I spent painting your beautiful little daughter, were an unusual pleasure to me, and she was a constant inspiration".[31]

Lady Pallas Blair Drummond was not so easy (figs. 44, 45). The adopted daughter of the Countess of Cottenham, she enchanted de László on first meeting: "Mr. de László is so impressed by the child's beauty and intelligence – she will, he feels sure make an exceptionally interesting picture".[32] De László made two unfinished studies of the subject – in one Pallas wears a hat and holds a doll and in the other she holds a white cockatoo – perhaps indicating the fractious nature of the sittings. The final portrait, however, was a success and her mother thought it a tribute to Pallas's character and the artist's:

"I simply love that portrait .... You know – you have left an echo

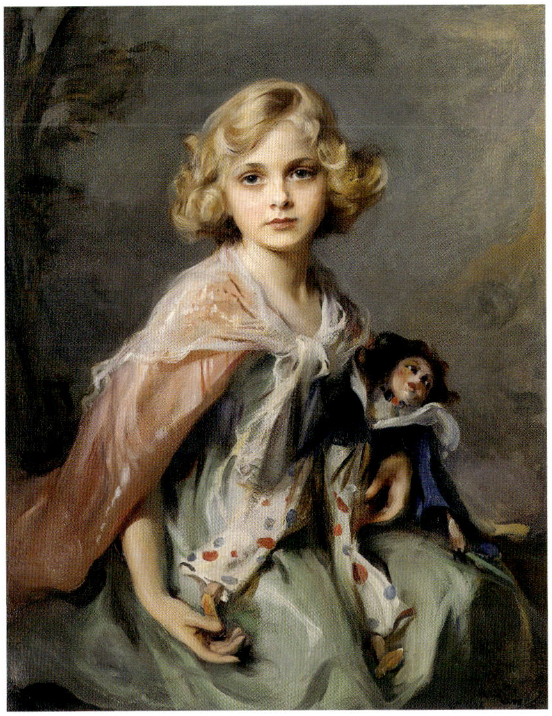

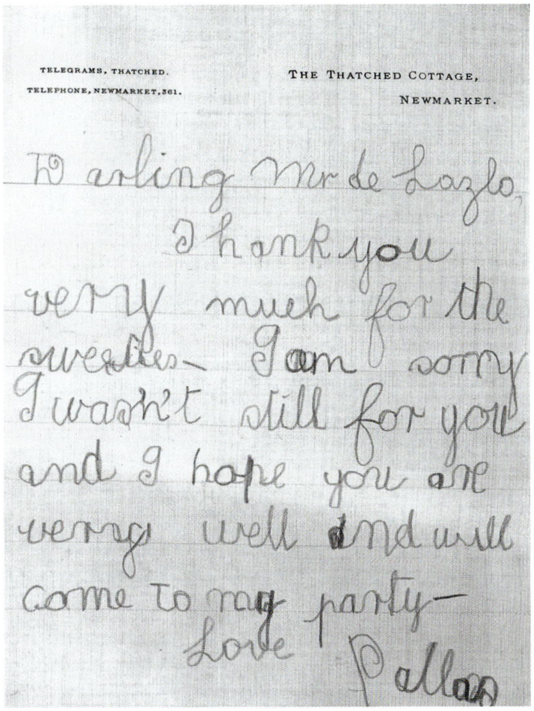

TELEGRAMS, THATCHED.
TELEPHONE, NEWMARKET, 361.

THE THATCHED COTTAGE,
NEWMARKET.

Darling Mr de Lazlo,
Thank you
very much for the
sweater. I am sorry
I wasn't still for you
and I hope you are
verry well and will
come to my party –
Love Pallas

FIG. 44
Lady Pallas Blair Drummond, 1936
Oil on canvas, 91.5 × 71 cm
Courtesy of Sotheby's, London

FIG. 45
Letter from Lady Pallas Blair Drummond to Philip de László

of your *own* self in this portrait. I assure you I can *hear* you say, 'Now *look* at me'. I can see you turn to *me* – in anguish throw out your hands and say 'Why *won't* she be good?' and then a lecture *at me* which makes me sink & disappear into my clothes like a mud turtle."[33]

One small complaint was made by Lady Cottenham: "... in case that very nice head of yours becomes too swollen – I must tell you that no one likes the doll!"[34] Intentionally or not, the artist seems to have transferred the rather difficult nature of the child on to the doll.

De László's female sitters could be just as demanding in different ways. Love letters between de László and his wife, Lucy, show nothing but devotion; however, his relationships with his women sitters obviously called for some flirting, as Lucy knew: "Hope you are a good boy – flirt a little – not too much. Love me in plenty. Your loving good companion. Lucie."[35] The artist was teased about the prettiness of so many of his sitters. Sibyl Colefax, the decorator, sketched in 1916, invited the artist to lunch with: "two popular beauties!!! Gladys Cooper & Winifred Baines as a contrast to all your beautiful friends in the 'other world'. Most will amuse you I am sure – I'll be very interested to see if you do think Gladys the beauty – a real one!"[36] It is thought that Gladys Cooper was painted in 1916 but the picture remains untraced.

Contact with and cultivation of his patrons and his sitters did not end at the completion of a portrait. The delivery of the portrait was carefully stage-managed. First Paul Laib, de László's official photographer, was called and a photograph sent to the sitter and patron. The recipients were delighted with the photograph and a little while later the delivery of the painting itself pleased them even more. De László was often a guest of honour at the unveilings of his portraits and he included some of his portraits in exhibitions. To those who lent pictures but were unable to attend the artist sent photographs of the gallery's rooms so the lenders could see the display. De László flattered his patrons by continuing to care for his portraits even when they were no longer in his possession. For years after completing a portrait he gave advice regarding hanging and re-varnishing. He also acted as a policeman for works in public collections, writing to the Director of the National Portrait Gallery in 1932:

"When visiting the other day ... I found that my portrait sketch of Lord Balfour ... is in a very bad state, and needs to be varnished. May I ask you if I could send someone to varnish the picture – or I might be able to come myself – and if so, at what hour?"[37]

Sitters and press alike celebrated de László's talent for capturing a likeness. He was therefore particularly sought during wartime. As one opens the dusty boxes in the archive time seems to stand still, but few letters are as poignant as those written during the First World War. De László was frequently called upon by families whose husbands and sons were off to the Front. There is a sense of the snapshot about many of these portraits – of men in service dress, a great coat thrown casually over shoulders, a hand resting on a Sam Browne belt, gazing directly at the viewer. A portrait of Captain Maurice Trouton is inscribed by de László "during one sitting"; Lord Londonderry was painted in just three hours; Major Johnson-Ferguson was "done in only two sittings. Every stroke is of value – nothing superfluous."[38] Sir John Lavery encouraged his fellow artists to paint portraits of those going off to fight, the fee of £50 for each portrait to be presented to the Artists' General Benevolent Institution. De László, perhaps mindful of his own five sons too young to fight, did not seem to refuse many commissions. He painted so many, especially during 1915, that Lucy wrote to her husband: "Of course they all want de László's brush for their husbands. You really should wear khaki as being the first portraitist to the Expeditionary Force!"[39]

Inevitably, obituaries of some of de László's sitters began appearing in the newspapers. In the archive cuttings are carefully pinned to the original commissioning letters that echo with the unspoken fear that the men would not return. Lord Rothermere (cat. 117) wrote in November 1916 thanking de László for the "wonderful likeness" of his son.[40] At the bottom of the letter, written in pencil, is a draft of de László's condolence letter sent soon after: "I was so distressed to see in this evening's paper of the news about your son, that he too had joined those who have nobly laid down their lives for their country. I beg you and Lady R to accept my heartfelt sympathy in your great sorrow." Families found the portraits a great comfort: Lord Buxton's son, Denis sat for de László in January 1917 and his father was "extremely glad to have the portrait, especially just now".[41] Lt Buxton died in action in October 1917 at the age of nineteen. Some obituaries, such as the one for Viscount Wendover, who died aged twenty-one of wounds, included a reproduction of de László's portrait alongside the tribute.[42] Crosses appear in de László's sitters' book beside the names of men who did not return from the war.

Several women were painted in their Red Cross uniform, although some, like Lady Stanley, did so reluctantly, at her husband's request:

"Lyulph is (I think rather foolishly) anxious to have a picture of me done in the Red Cross Commandant's dress. It is rather an unpaintable costume I am afraid (Red dress, dead white apron, collar & cap). And I wonder if you [could] make a rather sketchy picture of me for him."[43]

The war meant changes in circumstances for potential patrons. Beryl Stanhope wrote: "I shall have to postpone the great pleasure of being painted by you til later – you will understand how very busy my life is just now. Munitions give me *no* time to myself at all."[44] Others felt the effects of the war financially. Captain Winfield Sifton wrote regarding a portrait of his wife: "... although I am very anxious indeed to have it done, it is still Wartime, and I cannot afford to pay full before the War prices".[45]

De László contributed to the war effort in other ways. He gave portraits to charity sales, including one of Miss Muriel Wilson in her uniform: "The 'Cross Red Nurse' was a huge success & thank you for making me so beautiful – it was sold 10 minutes after the Sale opened to the Duke of Marlborough".[46] He also donated blank canvases to charity auctions, promising to paint the portrait of the highest bidder. A Red Cross sale was held at Christie's in 1915, the contributing artists including Sargent and Orpen: "A stir was caused during the sale of Mr. P. Laszlo's offer of a portrait. With an opening bid of 220 gs. the hammer did not fall until 710 gs. was called."[47] It was an unusual way to gain a sitter, but, not surprisingly, de László soon struck up friendships with many of these sitters, too. He made many charitable donations throughout his career, and in 1934 Mrs Simon Marks, of Marks & Spencer, bought a portrait at an auction. De László wrote to her: "If I was able to do the Cheyne Hospital a good turn, I was amply rewarded in that it brought me such a charming sitter, and gave me the opportunity to make your acquaintance".[48]

Other commissions came from those whose husbands and sons did not return from the Front. Lord and Lady Maxwell of Cardoness in Scotland lost their only son, killed in action at Dardanelles (fig. 46):

"Sir William Maxwell and myself feel indebted to you for your kindness in saying you would under the circumstances be willing to paint a Portrait of our dear son from Photographs ... we will try to give every facility we can to help, as we know the difficulties connected with posthumous portraits .... I am venturing to enclose two Photographs of our son, one in uniform taken just before he went out & one in mufti – that you may see something of what he was like. He was good, & pure & true, brave & fearless with a deep earnestness which shone in his eyes. It might be said of him in Chaucer's lines:-

'He loved Chivalry
Truth and honour, freedom and courtesy
He was a very perfect gentle Knight.'[49]

De László's relationships with his sitters were so intrinsic to the success of his work that he did not find posthumous portraits easy or pleasing, and refused many requests. For favourite patrons, however, or in response to particularly touching letters, he would undertake such commissions. Miss Emma Watts from Richmond, Kentucky wrote:

"My dear Mr. de László,

Some years ago, my mother and I saw one of the exhibitions of your paintings in London. She admired them very much and said, 'That is the only artist who shall paint my portrait'.... Since her death last year, I have thought of it many times .... I know that you are the only artist who could do justice both to her colouring and to the strength and charm that show clearly in the pictures and if you

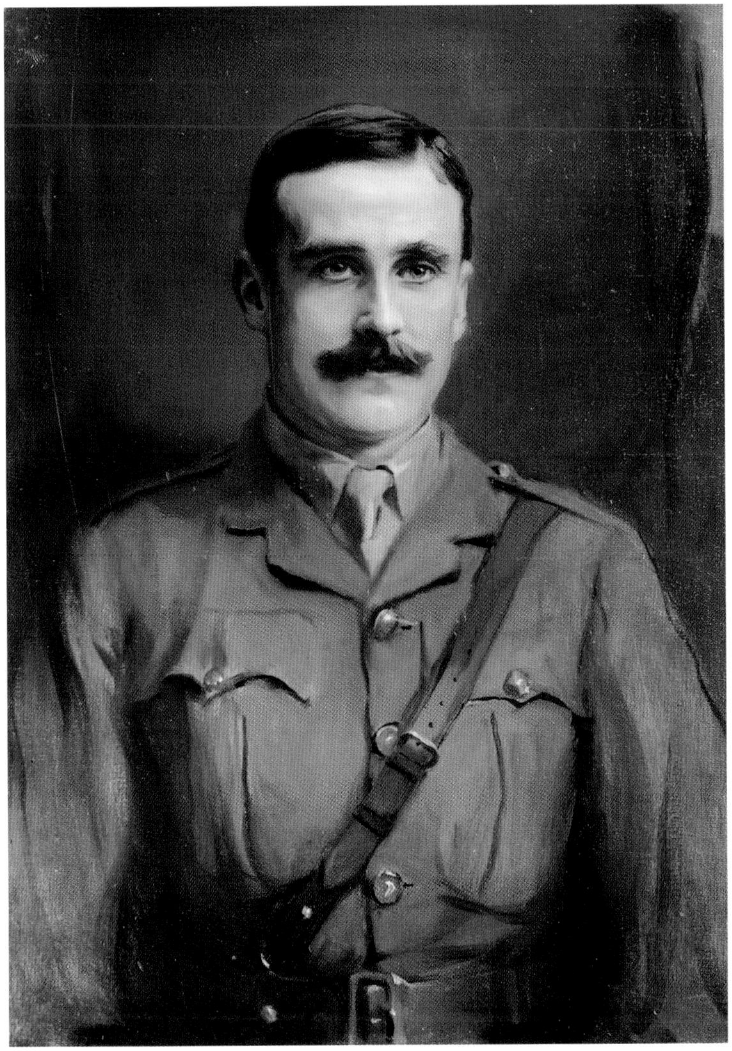

FIG. 46
The Only Son [name not known] *of Lord and Lady Maxwell, ca.* 1916
Oil on canvas
Untraced

would consider a portrait under these circumstances, it would be a joy and a comfort to me always."[50]

De László initially refused many such requests and in this case suggested Miss Watts send photographs and a lock of hair for him to pass on to Sydney Kendrick, his most favoured copyist. The artist then changed his mind and agreed to paint the portrait: "It is quite unusual for me, but I felt from your letters how devoted you were to your Mother, and I know so well what it has meant to me to have my Mother's portrait. It gave me great pleasure to do it for you."[51] Miss Watts was extremely pleased and wrote of the portrait's reception once it had reached Richmond:

"Everyone says, 'How could the artist give such a wonderful expression of her personality when he had never seen your mother?' ... The negro servants simply say, 'It is Miss Mary' .... it is a most striking likeness of one who was always beautiful and beloved and who brought happiness to many."[52]

Some patrons were more demanding than others, and had strong opinions about how the sitting should be tackled. In 1913 the music professor Dr Sophie Weiss commissioned a portrait of one of her most acclaimed students, Sir Donald Tovey, Reid Professor of Music at Edinburgh:

"Will you forgive me if I venture to send you a few lines about my dear Donald's portrait .... Firstly Donald's face is unusually crooked, and the left side ... is much better than the right – indeed the right corner of his mouth is spoilt by some unavoidable dentistry .... I fear he will not be an easy sitter; he is both the most modest and unaffected man personally, and the proudest as an artist, and yet he can be quite self-conscious at times and quite 'unschön' – dreadful though it is to say! ... Don't tell Donald I am having him painted. Make him play you some of your beloved 'ernste musik'."[53]

Dr Weiss wrote several more letters offering her views before signing off: "I shall be only too grateful to leave it all to you. It is afflicting that Donald is looking his most hideous at this moment! and he is terribly old; but that can't be helped."[54]

The archive contains hundreds of tributes from delighted patrons and sitters: "THE PICTURE has arrived! What a splendid gift to us & one we shall especially & always value as the outcome of the kind heart of a friend", wrote Sir Reynolds-Stephens; "Thank you for the lovely picture. It really is charming, we are all delighted with it", wrote the Duchess of Devonshire; "Not only is it a speaking likeness, but it is full of Soul and Poetry", wrote Mrs Pellier-Johnson; and Lady Ellenborough: "It may amuse you to know that even my baby aged 15 months runs towards my picture saying 'Mum Mum' & tries to kiss it!"[55]

There were some patrons, however, who were dissatisfied and requested alterations: Lady Wemyss thought her mouth had "a very severe & bad tempered look", William Younger thought his wife's portrait made "her look older than she looks".[56] Elizabeth, Duchess of York (cat. 98), wrote that her portrait was "marvellous", but worried that her head looked a "trifle large".[57]

If, during its creation, a portrait was not going well, de László had a firm policy: "I never go on trying to put it right, but start an entirely new picture".[58] In some cases he started several new canvases. As a consequence, when a commission was declared complete it meant that de László was satisfied with his work, and complaints were not well received. Some he retouched, albeit reluctantly, but his usual response was that he did not touch portraits after signing them – the spontaneity of his work being part of its value and not something to be reviewed.

One sitter, perhaps afraid of de László's reaction, called in reinforcements in the shape of Joseph Duveen, famed art dealer to Henry Clay Frick, William Randolph Hearst and John D. Rockefeller. Charles McCann, an attorney from New York, wrote:

"It is a source of great sorrow to me, and I know it would be to you, to have the portrait so poorly received by so many of our friends .... In order that I might get an unbiased opinion from one who is an expert and whose opinion is recognized all over the world on portraits, I asked Lord Duveen to come down to Long Island one weekend, and as a favor to me, after luncheon, he examined your portraits of the family .... he said the one of Mrs. McCann was not in keeping with the best work that he had seen you do, and did not consider it a fair presentation of Mrs. McCann .... He said that on his visit to London, he intended making it a point of seeing you and expressing his opinion.

Lord Duveen, as we both know, is entirely a fearless critic, and one who really knows portraits probably better than some of my friends. The question now comes up as to whether you feel that anything further can be done with this portrait of Mrs. McCann, or shall it have to be relegated to obscurity."[59]

De László responded:

"It is most unusual for me to touch my work again once it is finished, but I will gladly make an exception in your case, remembering how happy our association has always been .... Please realise that this is my only reason for making an exception in this case – certainly not because of the outside criticism you mention, even when it is that of a man who knows, and deals in, pictures."[60]

De László's impressive reputation for verisimilitude makes some of the complaints less than credible, and they perhaps say more about the sitter's view of themselves than the quality of the portrait. Lord Curzon (cat. 54) wrote:

"When the agreed Exhibn is over and before my picture goes to be copied will you be willing to make the few alterations on it which everybody suggests.

a. colour little less high on the face

b. jaw and cheeks little less square and full & fat

As everybody without exception agrees about this I think we must all be right!"[61]

Few of de László's patrons required so diverse a range of portraits as Curzon – authoritative, formal portraits of himself; a scandalous portrait of his lover (Elinor Glyn, cat. 55); and a portrait of his second wife in mourning dress for her first husband. Curzon's relationship with the novelist Elinor Glyn has since been well documented, but when she sat to de László the relationship was a covert one. Curzon, however, barely concealed its true nature when writing to de László:

"Dear Mr de Laszlo,

... A lady who is very [good] looking in a picturesque way and has some fame has written to me from Paris and asked whether it would be likely that you would paint her. Her name is Elinor Glyn the novelist. She is not very well off and I am afraid could not manage anything big. If you were willing to paint her what would be the price of a picture the size of that wicked cocotte from Paris in the corner of your room? You could make a splendid thing of her with her white skin, dark eyebrows, green eyes and Venetian red hair. She lives in Paris but comes here sometimes. Yours, Curzon."[62]

Glyn's novel *Three Weeks* (1907) secured her erotic reputation, with critics drawing parallels between the heroine and the author. It tells the tale of Paul Verdayne, who meets an older woman in a Swiss hotel and who, against a backdrop of tiger skins and heavily scented flowers, is given instruction in the art of love. A popular rhyme of the time asked: "Would you like to sin with Elinor Glyn on a tiger skin?/ Or would you prefer to err with her on some other fur?" Glyn did little to discourage her notoriety and asked de László to play along – suggesting he paint her sitting astride a tiger or posed against a tiger skin. She invited him to come for dinner, promising he would find "this red haired lady dressed up in things & charmes of her former life, when she was not just the virtuous & dull mother of this one, but lived in Venice & was a vampire & let her fancy play!!"[63] Agreeing to paint Glyn for an "exceptional fee of 300 guineas", de László made a sketch of her in February 1914 but delayed starting the oil until December, much to the frustration of Glyn, who worried "if you really do want to immortalise my red head & tigerly aspect!!!"[64] De László was pleased with the portrait: "I was very happy in painting Glyn .... The picture will be diabolic – she feels it and I see it."[65] Indeed the painting was a sensation: a full page illustration appeared in *The Sketch* with the headline: "A Very Much Discussed Painting".[66] Glyn gleefully reported to de László comments she had overheard at the Grosvenor Gallery where the portrait was exhibited:

"'Can't you see the powder on the face?' one said, and another: 'Yes, and the shadows, rather blackish, of the hair – plainly dyed!!!' 'Of course he did it on purpose he is so clever.' 'You can almost touch the make-up.' Then they turned round and saw me and nearly had fits."[67]

Curzon, too, was pleased: "I had a letter from Lord C. saying the portrait was 'a masterpiece of modern times' & would rank with the best of all ages 'besides being a superlative likeness' great praise from him!"[68] De László tactfully sent Curzon a reproduction of the portrait.

To Glyn's distress, Curzon married Grace Duggan in 1916, without warning or explanation. De László went on to paint her twice. The marchioness described Curzon's favourite of the two:

"... a sketch portrait of me in my widow's weeds .... George adored this picture, and had a special case made for it, so that he could take it with him wherever he went. He very seldom moved for more than a few days without it, and always had it in his room wherever he could see it."[69]

De László was invited into the very heart of the commissioning family's life in order to record their most personal moments – a portrait of a beloved spouse; a portrait of a daughter before her marriage; a hasty sketch of a son before he left for the Front; a posthumous portrait of a much-missed parent. In addition, and perhaps unexpectedly, the sitter's later enjoyment of the portrait was often enhanced by the happy memories of time spent with de László in his studio and the remembrance of the beginning of a life-long friendship that evolved alongside the picture's creation.

The de Lászlós were highly sought-after guests, and the archive contains countless invitations, many from patrons – invitations to stay with the Duke and Duchess of Northumberland at Alnwick Castle, at Longleat with the Marquis of Bath, at Chatsworth with the Duke and Duchess of Devonshire, at Carisbrooke Castle with Princess Beatrice. Writing to Lucy from 10 Downing Street in 1936, Mrs Baldwin "wonders whether by any chance you and Mr. de Laszlo would care to see the Trooping of the Colour on the morning of June 23rd from the gardens here?"[70]

Several boxes in the archive are labelled "Royal Court" and contain invitations to royal events. Amongst his closest royal friends de László counted Queen Marie of Roumania, Princess Alice of Greece and Princess Marina; Queen Marie and the artist were keen and affectionate correspondents. Footage in the archive taken with a ciné camera shows a playful Princess Alice in the artist's garden. The de Lászlós attended Princess Marina and Prince George's wedding in 1934: "It was a great and unexpected pleasure to us to receive an invitation to be present at the wedding in Westminster Abbey, as I understand only a limited number are being asked".[71]

The de Lászlós were particularly well received during their visits to America, and the artist's movements were documented in newspapers from coast to coast:

"The lion of the moment, has caught several lions himself. He has just finished portraits of the President and Mrs. Coolidge. Now Secretary Mellon, I understand, is sitting for him. As the guest of Mr. and Mrs. Larz Anderson, in whose home he has a temporary studio, where I imagine he is painting one or the other of them, he is constantly sought after for dinners."[72]

The pioneering spirit appealed to de László: "I admire these self-made men of the United States and the pride they take in their successful careers, which enables them to leave fortunes for the good of mankind and which thereby immortalise[s] them".[73] De László gained many supporters and friends during his trips to America. His sitters included Louis Wiley and Adolph Ochs of *The New York Times*, Frank Kellogg, George Eastman of Eastman Kodak, Harvey Firestone of Firestone Tires & Rubber Company, and Presidents Roosevelt, Harding, Coolidge and Hoover. Some papers referred to de László as "the court painter of the Harding administration". The artist held President Harding in great esteem, and the two visited the Corcoran Gallery together to see the portrait of General Pershing (fig. 47).

Some patrons called for de László to paint many members of their families – for example, the Portlands, de Gramonts, de Castellanes, d'Erlangers, Schroders, Harmsworths and Aberconways – and over the years the artist became a valued friend to many of them. De László's greatest patron was William Cavendish-Bentinck, 6th Duke of Portland. They first met in 1912 and the artist painted nearly thirty portraits of the family. The artist and the duke became close friends, and writing to de László in 1933 the Duke looked back on their enduring friendship: "We have been such good friends for so long & I assure you I much value the affection that exists between us".[74] The closeness of their friendship is confirmed by the fact that the duke was godfather to the artist's youngest son, John. Letters to de László from the duke and duchess contain high praise for his work. In 1912 de László painted the duke and duchess and their daughter, Lady Victoria, and the duke was particularly pleased with the portrait of his wife, calling it: "… not only an exact reproduction of her beautiful self but it also has a ray of Heaven illuminating in her face the charming qualities of her soul … words that were used for other famous portraits may justly I think be applied to this one of yours: 'It has an air of nobility about it. A spirit of humanity within it.' Truth held your pencil, genius guided it, and bowing a humble homage to art and genius,

I am, your assured admirer, Portland."[75]

In 1914 the tenants of the Portland estates in England and Scotland wished to present a portrait to the duke's son, the Marquis of Titchfield, as a coming-of-age present. "Of course you must do it. No one else shall or could", the Duke wrote.[76] A year later de László attended Titchfield's marriage to Ivy Gordon-Lennox – a quiet, family affair owing to the war and lack of a 'season' – and produced a sketch while in the congregation in Welbeck's private chapel. In his memoirs the Duke described the artist as a "welcome guest at Welbeck, Langwell and Grosvenor Square" and, as in other cases, de László, and sometimes Lucy, too, stayed with the Portlands while painting their portraits. The duke recalled that de László "paid us a visit at Langwell – where, incidentally, he went deerstalking and was terribly bitten by midges – and there he painted a portrait of my second son, Morven, as a schoolboy, also a head of my wife".[77] Writing to Professor Nuttall de László wrote: "We have just returned from glorious Welbeck Abbey, where we spent a very happy three days with the Portland family. I was so pleased to see all my works there again, there is a special room of my portraits of the whole family"[78] – called 'the László Room'. De László's work was cherished by the family: "Your portrait of the Duchess of Portland came back here yesterday, safe and sound – but alas, not the special case which was made for it (I believe under your direction) for its frequent journeys between Welbeck and Scotland. It is a double case; the outer one is of rough wood, the inner one stained & polished, with brass handles and lined with red baize."[79] The duke was equally enthusiastic about works of himself and described a charcoal sketch, done by de László in 1932 (fig. 48) as "the best portrait of me that has ever been drawn".[80]

During one visit to Welbeck de László painted an exterior view of the house and presented it to the Portlands as a gift. He often gave such pictures to his hosts – a sketch of the Vatican garden was presented to Pius XI; a small painting of Shane's Castle, the seat of Lord O'Neill, has recently been discovered. The artist painted three landscape studies of Floodgates in West Sussex, the home of Sir Merrik Burrell, and gave one to his host (fig. 49). Burrell sat to the artist, as did his wife and daughter, and commissioned the portrait of singer Anny Ahlers (cat. 123). After her untimely death de László, seeing Burrell's grief, gave him the portrait. Writing to her husband, Lucy paid tribute to the men's friendship: "I am glad you have made a friend's contact with him – the Annie A. picture will always be a bond."[81]

Antoine-Armand, 12th duc de Gramont (fig. 50), was de László's keenest patron in Europe. De László painted three generations of de Gramonts – around twenty portraits – between 1902 and 1931. Antoine-Armand was the son of de László's original patron, Antoine-Agenor, 11th duke, and became one of the artist's closest friends, one on whom he often called for advice. The duke was both a scientist and an artist, and permitted de László to share his studio when he was in Paris. Here, at 42bis Avenue Henri Martin, de László painted a number of important portraits, including Maréchal Lyautey and General Pershing. One letter asks the duke to lunch with the artist and General Pershing and to visit the Palais de la Legion d'Honneur to see where the general's portrait would hang. For important commissions in Paris de László took his studio assistant, Harwood, and his secretary, Miss Abernethy, with him. The duke's own assistant tended to the artist's portraits in Harwood's absence:

"And now, dear friend, may I ask you to make arrangements with Jean immediately to buy a bottle of Vibert's 'Vernis à Retoucher', with a broad, flat brush, and go over very slightly the picture of General Pershing. Tell him not to rub with the brush, but to move it quickly. I shall be most grateful if he will do this."[82]

De László used the duke as his eyes and ears in Paris. He sought the duke's opinion as to which portraits he should exhibit and requested, "You must not fail to go to the opening of the Salon and let me know how the pictures are placed".[83] The duke watched de László's success with pleasure: "I just have seen in The Studio the fine

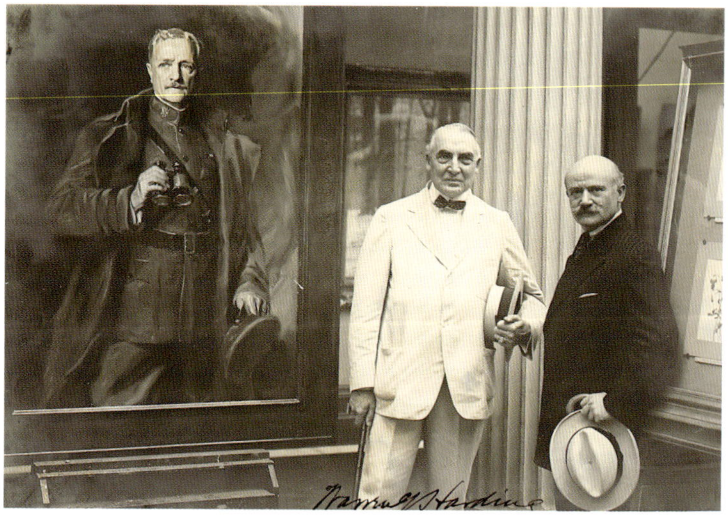

FIG. 47 Philip de László and President Harding beside the artist's portrait of General Pershing, photograph inscribed *On the 13th July The President visited with me the Corcoran Art Gallery in Washington to view the portraits of General Pershing and Elihu Root*, 1921

reproduction of the latest study of Pss. Marina – who is charming and your photo in The Tatler! ... how smart!"[84] A great many letters between the duke and duchess and de László survive in the archive, and de László valued their support and friendship very much:

"I would like to take this opportunity to express to you again my deepfelt gratitude for all the kindness and interest you showed towards me and my work while I was in Paris. I assure you I esteem it very highly, and knowing that you do not do these things often, I appreciate it more than I can say."[85]

One sitter who became like family to the artist and his wife was Jewell Allcroft, whose country seat, Stokesay Court in Shropshire, the de Lászlós often visited. Artist and sitter were equally delighted with her portrait, painted in 1934 (fig. 51). De László declared it "amongst my outstanding portraits" and Allcroft wrote: "I love my picture it is simply beautiful & it was sweet of you to take so much trouble with my ugly face, thank you a thousand times .... I wish you were starting it again as I did enjoy my time with you so much."[86] Their relationship was that of siblings – de László wrote to his "dearest cleanfaced sister", signing off "ever your honorary brother de László". Allcroft was a champion carnation-grower and often sent the artist flowers. When de László became ill towards the end of his life he convalesced in Hove, where Allcroft sent him boxes of flowers which delighted and inspired him: "So lovely that I wished to paint them but the word and will of the doctor silenced this my ardent desire but later on *I must* paint your flowers".[87] He painted a bunch of carnations in 1937, just before his death, and the flowers Allcroft sent to his funeral were laid on his grave. After his death Lucy became

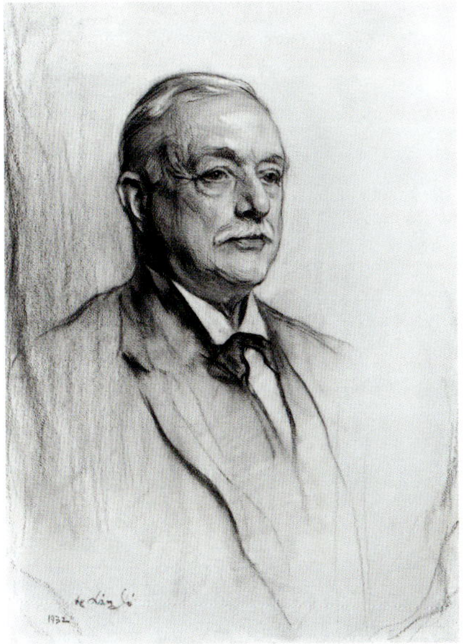

FIG. 48
William Cavendish-Bentinck, 6th Duke of Portland, 1932
Charcoal on paper,
84 × 56 cm
Private collection

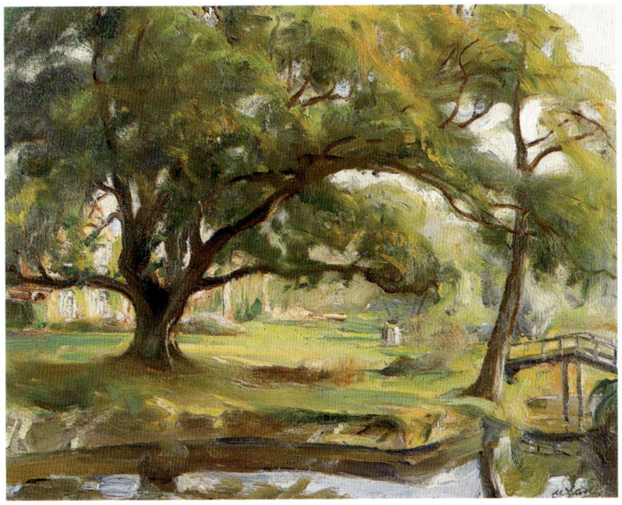

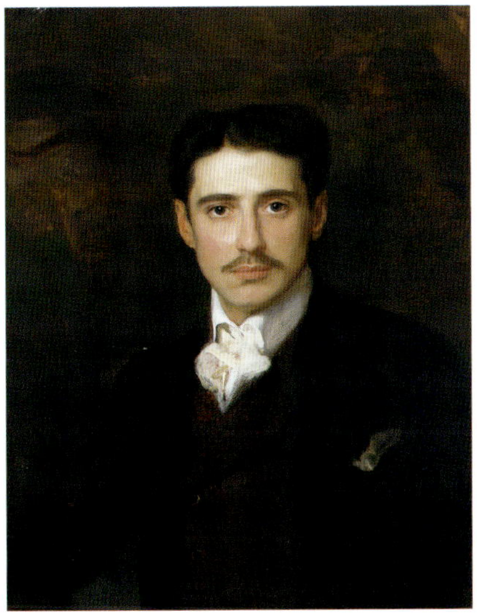

ABOVE FIG 49
The Oak Tree, Floodgates, 1927
Oil on canvas, 40 × 50 cm
Private collection

FIG. 50
Antoine XII-Armand, duc de Guiche (later 12th duc de Gramont), 1902
Oil on canvas, 73 × 56 cm
(cut down from a large group portrait)
Private collection

even closer to Allcroft: "Your friendship Jewell is dear to me knowing his liking for 'clean faced girl' & your warm appreciation of him".[88] A few years later Lucy also sent her a present:

"Dearest Jewell

This is the shawl Philip painted you in, & you must have it. I love to know it in your possession, knowing your love & admiration of him. He got this shawl in Rome I believe. When he was painting Pope Leo XIII & before we married."[89]

De László was interned in the autumn of 1917 – falsely accused of being an enemy alien – and at no other time were his friendships more tested than during this most difficult time of his life. The artist was interned in Brixton Prison and at Holloway internment camp. Suffering from ill health, he was moved to a nursing home in Ladbroke Gardens in Notting Hill, where he was under house arrest, and then to the country home of his solicitor, Sir Charles Russell. De László's friend, art critic, artist and sometimes sitter, Alfred Lys Baldry (cat. 81), was the only non-relative allowed to visit him during his internment. In June 1919, after much lobbying from his family and friends (most of whom were patrons), he was freed, exonerated and his British citizenship confirmed. The press tried to use his good relationships with his patrons against him:

"By virtue of his position as a fashionable painter, he naturally moved in the highest circles, associating with people who are possessed of secrets of the greatest importance. He enjoyed the society of men having intimate and foremost knowledge. He was friend of the Emperor of Austria and the Kaiser."[90]

Only a couple of his patrons and sitters failed him in his desperate times. One, Mrs Max Müller, was cited in the charges against him, claiming that in a conversation with her he had shown himself to be disaffected or disloyal to the king. Another, the press magnate Lord Northcliffe, allowed his newspapers to defame the artist's good name. Friends called upon as witnesses at an enquiry before an Advisory Committee included Mr Lockett Agnew, Sir Luke Fildes, Sir Arthur Lee and William Waldegrave Palmer, 2nd Earl of Selborne (fig. 52). De László painted Selborne several times, and also his wife, and completed a posthumous portrait of their second son, who had been killed in Mesopotamia, in 1916. He was steadfast in his support: "I first met Mr. de Laszlo in the Autumn of 1910, when he painted my portrait. I met him socially a good many times between that and the beginning of the war .... I had many conversations with Mr. de Laszlo of an open and friendly nature. He struck me as being rather inclined to be indiscreet in conversation .... He spoke to me about the Kaiser, whom he had painted, in very hostile terms .... I have had many opportunities of forming an opinion as to Mr. de Laszlo's character and views. In my opinion he is a man of strict honour and integrity, and quite incapable of any disloyal or dishonourable act so far as his country is concerned."[91]

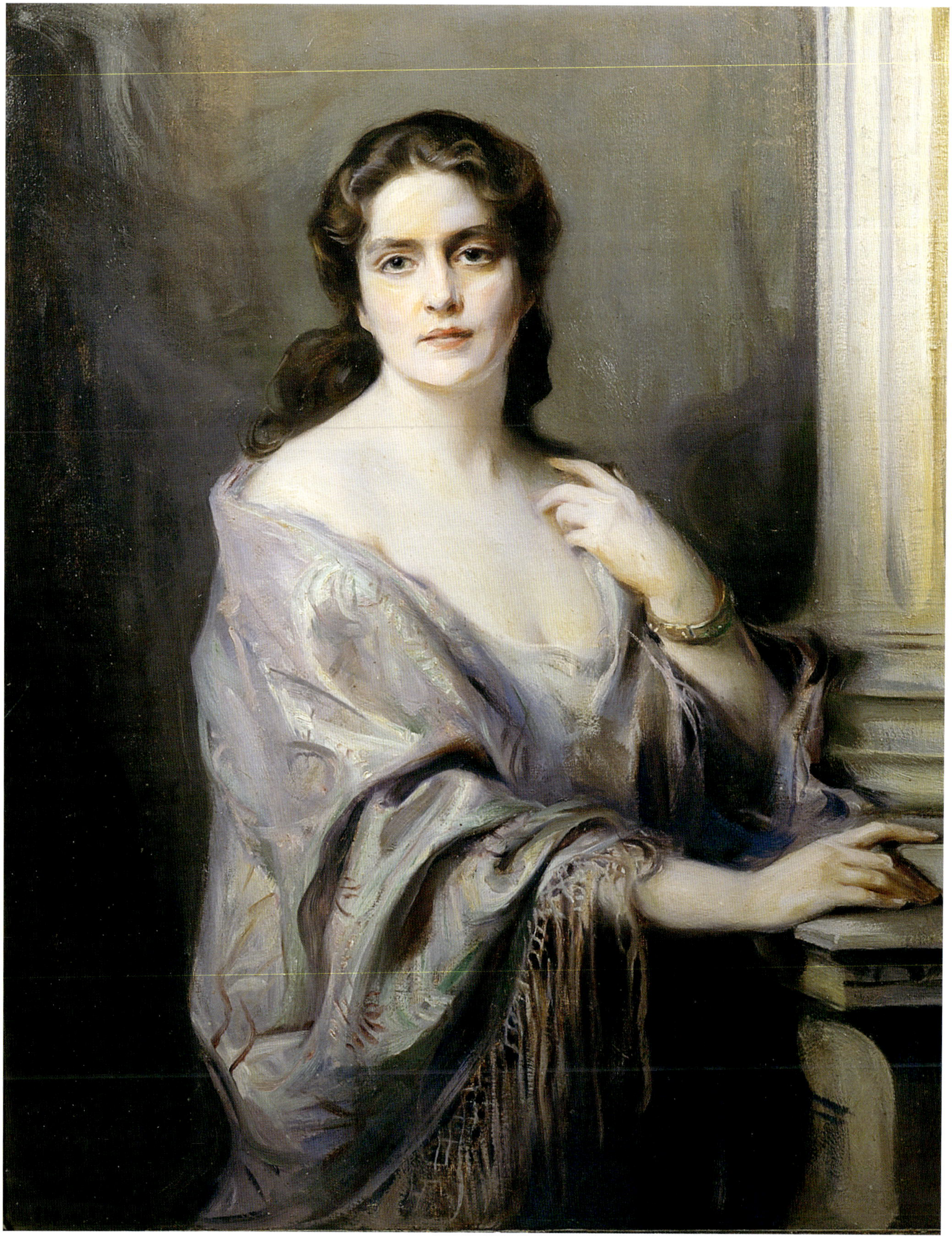

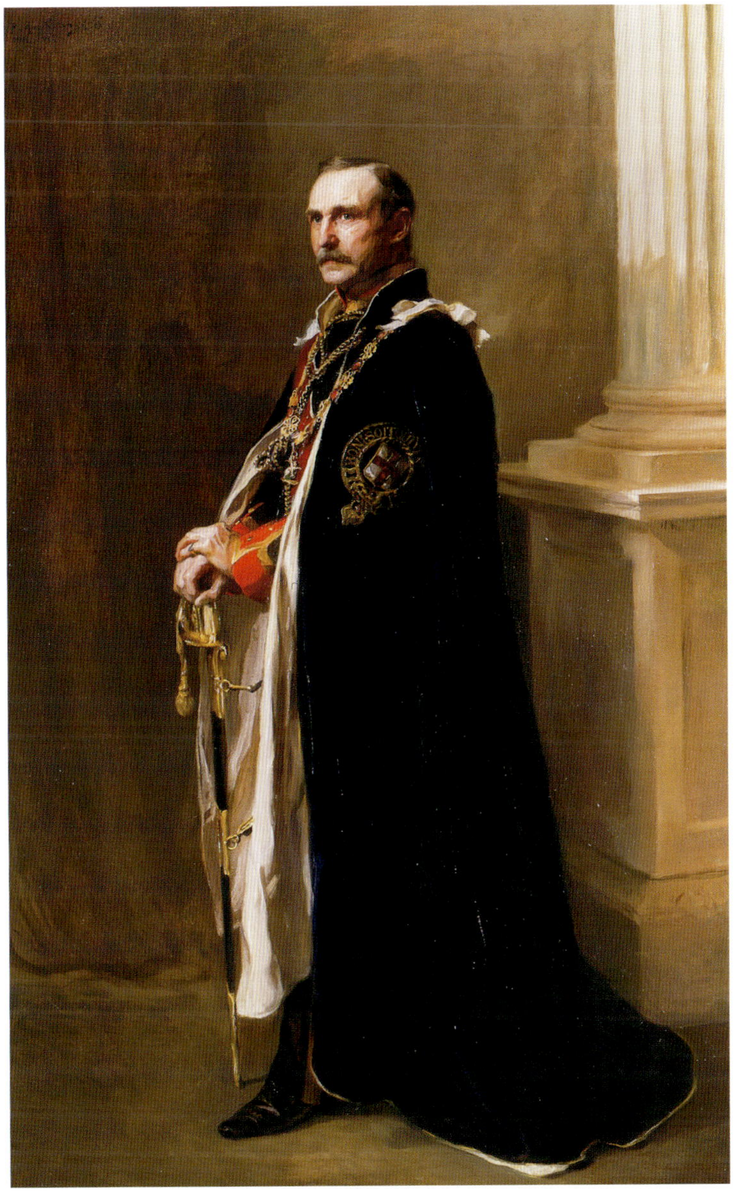

FIG. 51
Miss Jewell Allcroft, 1934
Oil on canvas, 101.6 × 80 cm
Private collection

FIG. 52
William Waldegrave Palmer, 2nd Earl of Selborne, 1911
Oil on canvas, 231.1 × 94 cm
The Worshipful Company of Mercers, Mercers' Hall, London

Lucy rallied support to clear his name, sending a telegram to the Duke of Portland:

"WILL YOU PLEASE VOUCH FOR PHILIP'S CHARACTER AND LOYALTY IN WRITING AND SEND SAME TO OUR SOLICITOR … PHILIP HAS BEEN INTERNED ON GROUNDS OF WHICH I KNOW HE IS INNOCENT THE CASE COMES BEFORE ADVISORY COMMITTEE ON 28TH DO USE YOUR INFLUENCE LETTER FOLLOWS FROM LUCY LASZLO."[92]

De László's solicitor wrote to Portland asking him for a reference: "What opinion did you form as to his personal character and sense of honour?" The Duke answered: "The highest".[93]

Sir Arthur Lee, M.P., and his wife sat several times for the artist (cat. 88), and he and Lucy were frequent guests at the Lees' home, White Lodge in Richmond Park. Lee had been particularly supportive when de László's mother died, and the artist had paid tribute to their friendship then: "The sign of true friendship not only shows in sunny days, but also when one feels the grip of a true friend's hand in sorrow, which I assure you, I appreciate fully".[94] Now Lee proved just as loyal and "offered to go bail for me in any sum that should be named and asked if I might stay with him during the proceedings, but was refused".[95]

The artist's career, far from being tainted by his ordeal, was restored very quickly and flourished again after his exoneration in 1919. De László, however, never forgot those who had supported him: "I am proud to say that all my friends and the leading men of this country stood by me and remained loyal throughout, to my great moral satisfaction".[96]

De László's talent – both as an artist and a friend – were widely acknowledged during his lifetime. Sitters and patrons not only showered the artist with written tributes but also bestowed upon him a great many orders and honours – some given only to those particularly close to the monarchy, such as the Victorian Order (MVO), which de Laszlo received after painting Edward VII. His son Paul wrote in 1934: "My dearest Dads, First let me congratulate you on your latest honours. You now have five stars and when you return we must do a picture of you looking like a Xmas tree. It is a great triumph."[97]

His dedication to his art and his devotion to his patrons were largely responsible for de László's early death. Throughout his career his family and friends urged him, in vain, not to over-exert himself. Letters to friends also reveal that he sometimes longed to escape his relentless schedule and demanding patrons. Some, like the art critic Baldry, felt that portraiture thwarted de László's talents:

"I should greatly like to see you doing just what you want to do to please yourself without having on your mind any idea of pleasing a sitter. I am sure that it would be a joy to you to break away from the portrait convention … and to launch into an expression of yourself.”[98]

Lee wrote: “I am delighted to hear that you contemplate giving up painting society portraits of French men and women. They really are not worth it, and you must give our English landscape a turn.”[99]

There are several references in the archive to de László’s desire to paint a war picture, focusing on the suffering of women in war, but it was not realised. His plans to abandon portraiture came to nothing, which, it seems, can largely be attributed to his loyalty to his patrons and his constant striving for self-improvement. One of his last commissions before his death was another portrait of the Duchess of Northumberland (cat. 138). He explained his reasons for taking on the commission to Princess Helen of Greece:

“I was already very tired from my many activities and I really should not have accepted this last picture, but you will understand how difficult it was to refuse such an inspiring and picturesque subject. Art is not an occupation, it is one’s second nature and the longing to do daily something better keeps one in constant enthusiasm.”[100]

The artist died on 22 November 1937 at the age of sixty-eight. His patrons and sitters wrote hundreds of final tributes. Lucy wrote: “I’ve received hundreds of letters, so warmly appreciative of him – and they still keep coming”.[101]

NOTES

My very special thanks go to Sandra and Damon de Laszlo. It has been an honour to carry out research in the de László Archive and I am particularly grateful to Sandra for the advice and support she has given me in the course of my investigations. She has generously shared her exemplary scholarship for the forthcoming de László catalogue raisonné with me and this has been an invaluable contribution to my endeavours. I would also like to thank Marilyn Inglis for her guidance and encouragement, Lyn Calzia, Deborah Bates Conservation, Susan and Christopher de Laszlo, Vanessa Kastner, Caroline Knight, Victoria Lynnes, Richard Ormond, Robert Satow, Tessa Wild and Christopher Wood. All correspondence quoted is quoted from by the de László Archive (de Laszlo Foundation), unless otherwise stated, and has been reproduced exactly as written by the correspondents.

1. *Daily Express*, 7.6.1929.
2. *Sunday Herald*, 27.11.1927.
3. ‘Every Court But China’, *Time*, XIX, no. 4, 25.1.1932, pp. 26–8.
4. Owen Rutter, *Portrait of a Painter: The Authorised Life of Philip de László*, London: (Hodder & Stoughton) 1939, p. 366.
5. Letter from Chavasse, 21.10.1937.
6. Letter from Tweedie, 21.1.1935.
7. *Free Press*, Burlington, Vermont, 11.5.1928.
8. Rutter 1939, p. 299.
9. ‘Painting a King by Philip de László’, *The Evening News*, date unknown.
10. Anthony Tahi, *The Studio*, October 1901.
11. Letter to Burrell from McKergow, 5.11.1933.
12. Letter from Cromer, 28.12.1926.
13. Letter from Royden, 24.1.1933.
14. Letter to Royden, 28.11.1932.
15. Letter from Graham, 12.7.1925.
16. Letter to Baldry, 17.6.1935.
17. Letter from Nuttall, 20.5.1932.
18. Letter to John Robertson, 30.7.1935.
19. Letter to Reading, 14.1.1927.
20. Letter from Vay, 1904.
21. *Daily Sketch*, 24.8.1927.
22. *The Evening Standard*, 7.9.1929.
23. *The Pioneer*, Allahabad, 2.2.1927.
24. Letter from Graham, 1.3.1920.
25. Letter to Jardine, 20.2.1928.
26. Letter from secretary to Jardine, 22.8.1928. Portrait destroyed in the Blitz.
27. Letter from Temple, Archbishop of York, 9.9.1934.
28. Letter from Davson, 24.4.1931.
29. Letter from Ralli, 20.9.1922.
30. Letter from Castlereagh, 1912.
31. Letter to Bendir, 26.7.1930.
32. Letter to Cottenham from de László’s secretary, 1.11.1935.
33. Letter from Cottenham, 4.7.1936.
34. Letter from Cottenham, 27.7.1936.
35. Letter from Lucy de László, 13.1.1933.
36. Letter from Colefax, 1916.
37. Letter to Hake, 16.6.1932.
38. Letter from Mrs Johnson-Ferguson, 17.6.1917.
39. Rutter 1939, p. 298.
40. Letter from Rothermere, November 1916.
41. Letter from Buxton’s secretary, 10.5.1917.
42. *The Illustrated London News*, 29.5.1915.
43. Letter from Stanley, 16.10.1916.
44. Letter from Stanhope, undated.
45. Letter from Sifton, 13.10.1915.
46. Letter from Wilson, 15.12. [year not known].
47. *Yorkshire Observer*, 17.4.1915.
48. Letter to Marks, 19.7.1934.
49. Letters from Maxwell, not dated, *ca.* 1916. Portrait untraced.
50. Letter from Watts, 8.1.1935.
51. Letter to Watts, 17.6.1935.
52. Letter from Watts, 10.9.1935. Portrait untraced.
53. Letter from Weiss, 13.7.1913.
54. Letter from Weiss, 28.7.1913.
55. Letters from Reynolds-Stephens, July 1935; Devonshire, 6.4.1920; Pellier-Johnson, 1929; Ellenborough, 21.2.33.
56. Letters from Wemyss, 1908; Younger, 10.11.1912.
57. Letter from York, 9.10.1931, de László Archive (de L. C.)
58. Letter to Baldry, 1.12.1933.
59. Letter from McCann, 1.5.1936.
60. Letter to McCann, 21.5.1936.
61. Letter from Curzon, 9.7.1918.
62. Letter from Curzon, 29.7.1913, de László Archive (de L.C.)
63. Letter from Glyn, 31.12.1913, de László Archive (de L.C.)
64. Letter from Glyn, 13.10.1914, de László Archive (de L.C.)
65. Rutter 1939, p. 299.
66. *The Sketch*, 21.4.1915.
67. Rutter 1939, p. 299.
68. Letter from Glyn, undated, the de László Archive (de L.C.)
69. Grace Elvina Curzon, *Reminiscences*, London (Hutchinson) 1955, p.88.
70. Letter from Baldwin, 7.5.1936.
71. Letter to duchesse de Gramont, 6.11.1934.
72. *The Washington Herald*, 7.3.1926.
73. Letter to Dr Munz, 15.5.1926.
74. Letter from Portland, 14.7.1933.
75. Rutter 1939, p.275.
76. Letter from Portland, 28.2.1914.
77. W. Cavendish-Bentinck, 6th Duke of Portland, *Men Women and Things: Memories of The Duke of Portland, K.G., G.C.V.O.*, London (Faber & Faber) 1937, pp.220–2.
78. Letter to Nuttall, 10.8.1934.
79. Letter from Portland’s secretary, 4.7.1931.
80. Cavendish-Bentinck, *op. cit.* (note 77), p.221.
81. Letter from Lucy de László, 2.11.1934.
82. Letter to de Gramont, 5.10.1933.
83. Letter to de Gramont, 12.4.1935.
84. Letter from de Gramont, 25.12.1935.
85. Letter to de Gramont, 18.6.1934.
86. Letter to Allcroft, 14.1.1935; letter from Allcroft, 1.1.1935. All Allcroft correspondence from The Allcroft Archive.
87 Letter to Allcroft, September 1936.
88. Letter from Lucy de László to Allcroft, 25.12.1938.
89. Letter from Lucy de László to Allcroft, 15.10.1940.
90. *Cork Constitution*, 8.10.1917.
91. Statement from Selborne, not dated.
92. Telegram from Lucy de László to Portland, 1917.
93. Letter from Portland to Russell, 12.6.1919.
94. Letter to Lee, 3.3.1915, Lee of Fareham Papers, Courtauld Institute Book Library.
95. Rutter 1939, p. 322.
96. Letter to General Sir Kaiser Shumsher Jung of Nepal, 22.11.1935.
97. Letter from Paul de László, 31.5.1934.
98. Letter from Baldry, 18.7.1935.
99. Letter from Lee, 21.10.1930.
100. Letter to Princess of Greece, 20.8.1937.
101. Letter from Lucy de László to Allcroft, 28.1.1938.

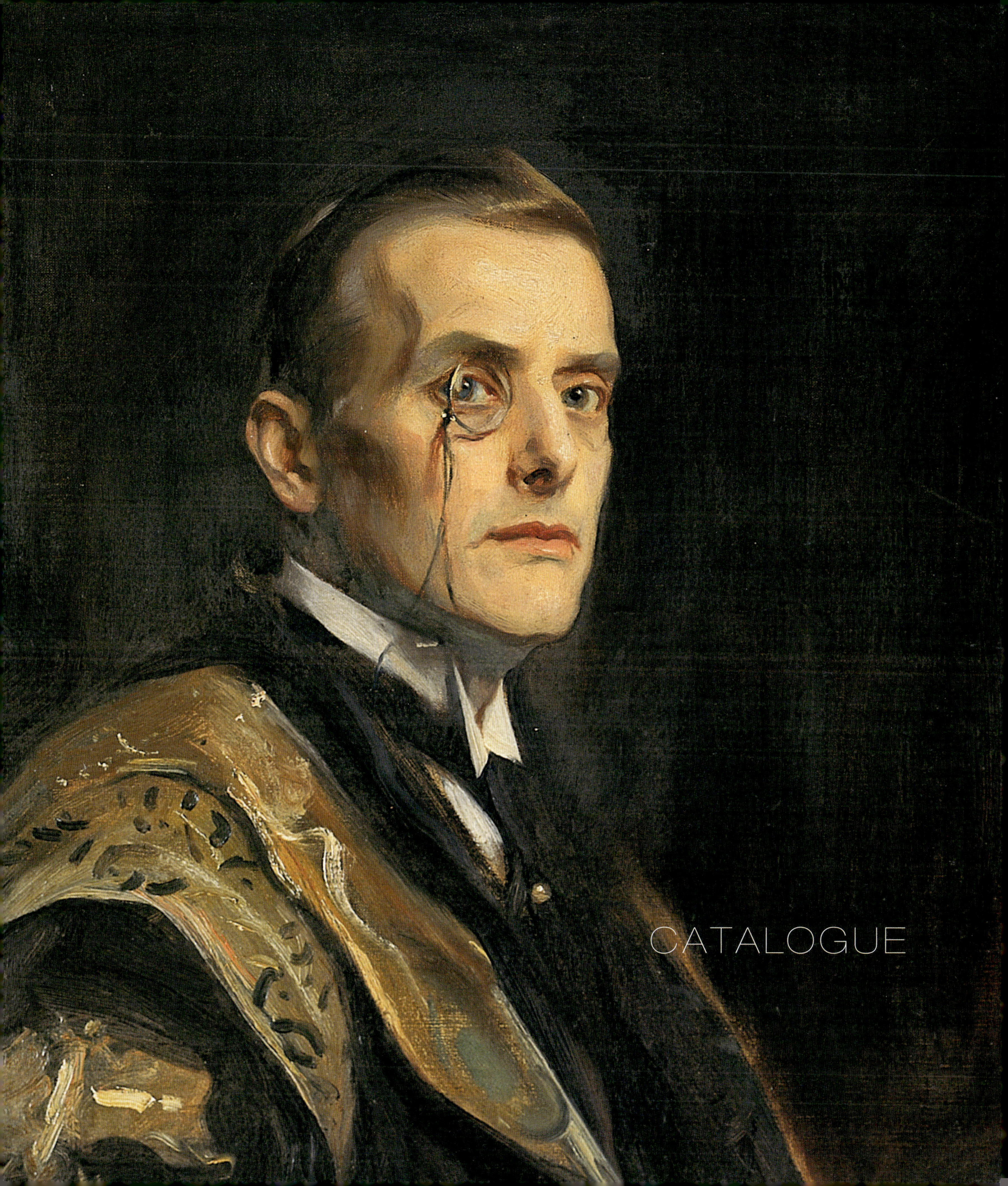

CATALOGUE

Main sources used in this catalogue and their abbreviations

ASB: the Artist's Sitters' Book, in two volumes, used by de László both as a studio visitors' book and as a sitters' book. The first signature, of 1899, is that of the King of Hungary, Emperor Francis Joseph, who signed in the Royal Palace in Budapest, and the last of the Duke of Connaught: *Arthur – Bagshot – 1937*. De László left these books to the British Museum on his death; they are now in the British Library.

N.P.G. Albums: De Lászlo made a unique photographic record of his work (but not complete or perfectly chronological), which was deposited with the National Portrait Gallery, London, after his death. It is a collection of nineteen clothbound albums with the names of the sitters written (mostly by the artist) beneath each photograph. There is no printed word at all in these volumes.

Almost all the photographs in the albums were taken by Paul Laib, a portrait photographer active in London from (certainly) 1900 to 1937. He had a studio in Thistle Grove, South Kensington. Little more is known about him. A large collection of his plate-glass negatives is held in the Witt Library at the Courtauld Institute, London. His portrait by de László also hangs there.

The Studio: *The Studio. An Illustrated Magazine of Fine and Applied Art*, founded by Charles Holme in 1893, was published at the offices of 'The Studio', 5, Henrietta Street, Covent Garden, London. De László's work was frequently discussed and illustrated in this publication from 1899 until 1934. Charles Holme retired in 1919 and was succeeded in his editorship by his son, Charles Geoffrey Holme.

Schleínítz 1913: Otto von Schleínítz, *Künstler Monographien, Nr. 106, Ph. A. von László*, Bielefeld and Leipzig (Velhagen & Klasing) 1913

Williams 1921: *Selections from the Work of P.A. de László*, foreword by comte Robert de Montesquiou, edited by Oakley Williams, London (Hutchinson) 1921

Modern Painting, 1921: *Modern Painting II. The Work of P.A. de László, M.V.O.*, foreword by A.L. Baldry, London (The Studio Limited) 1921

Painting a Portrait, 1934: *Painting a Portrait* by Philip de László, recorded by A.L. Baldry ('How To Do It' Series, No.6), London and New York (Studio Publications) 1934

Rowcliffe 1938: Gregory Rowcliffe & Co., Will Trust, Inventory of Portraits, Pictures, Studies, Sketches, Drawings etc. by Philip Alexius László de Lombos, M.V.O. etc, privately printed, London, 1938

Rutter 1939: Owen Rutter, *Portrait of a Painter, The Authorised Life of Philip de László*, London (Hodder & Stoughton) 1939

Clifford 1969: Derek Clifford, *The Paintings of P.A. de László*, London 1969

All measurements of works of art in the catalogue are sight size.

All catalogue paintings are lent from British private collections unless stated otherwise.

1 A Young Boy 1887

Pencil and charcoal heightened with white on paper, 46 × 36 cm (18⅛ × 14 inches)
Signed, indistinctly inscribed in Hungarian and dated, lower right: *Laszlo F / 87Szept / A modell elmaradása miatt / nem keszült el* [The picture is unfinished as the model did not turn up]
PROVENANCE In the possession of the artist on his death; Patrick de Laszlo, his fourth son
LITERATURE Schleínítz 1913, ill. p.5; Rutter 1939, ill. facing p.32; Clifford 1969, monochrome ill. pl.2

This drawing is one of the earliest signed and dated by de László. It was his first portrait drawing from life, made in September 1887, when he was just eighteen and a relatively new student at the Mintarajziskola (Drawing School, later known as the Academy of Fine Arts) in Budapest. According to his first biographer, Otto von Schleinitz, it was this first drawing that occasioned de László's immediate entry into the painting class of the great Károly Lotz (1833–1904).

Although he had no family antecedents who had been inclined to the visual arts, de László showed a precocious talent from a very early age. At the age of nine he was taken on as a junior scene painter at the People's Theatre in the studio of Moritz Lehmann. After working for an architectural sculptor and a sign-painter, in 1884, aged fifteen, he was apprenticed to the well-known photographer Sándor Strelisky, retouching and colouring photographs. Two evenings a week and on Sunday mornings he was free to study at the Iparrajziskola, the Budapest School of Applied Arts, where he received a sound foundation in drawing from classical casts. Even after entering the Academy in 1886 he continued to work in the evenings for Strelisky to earn money.

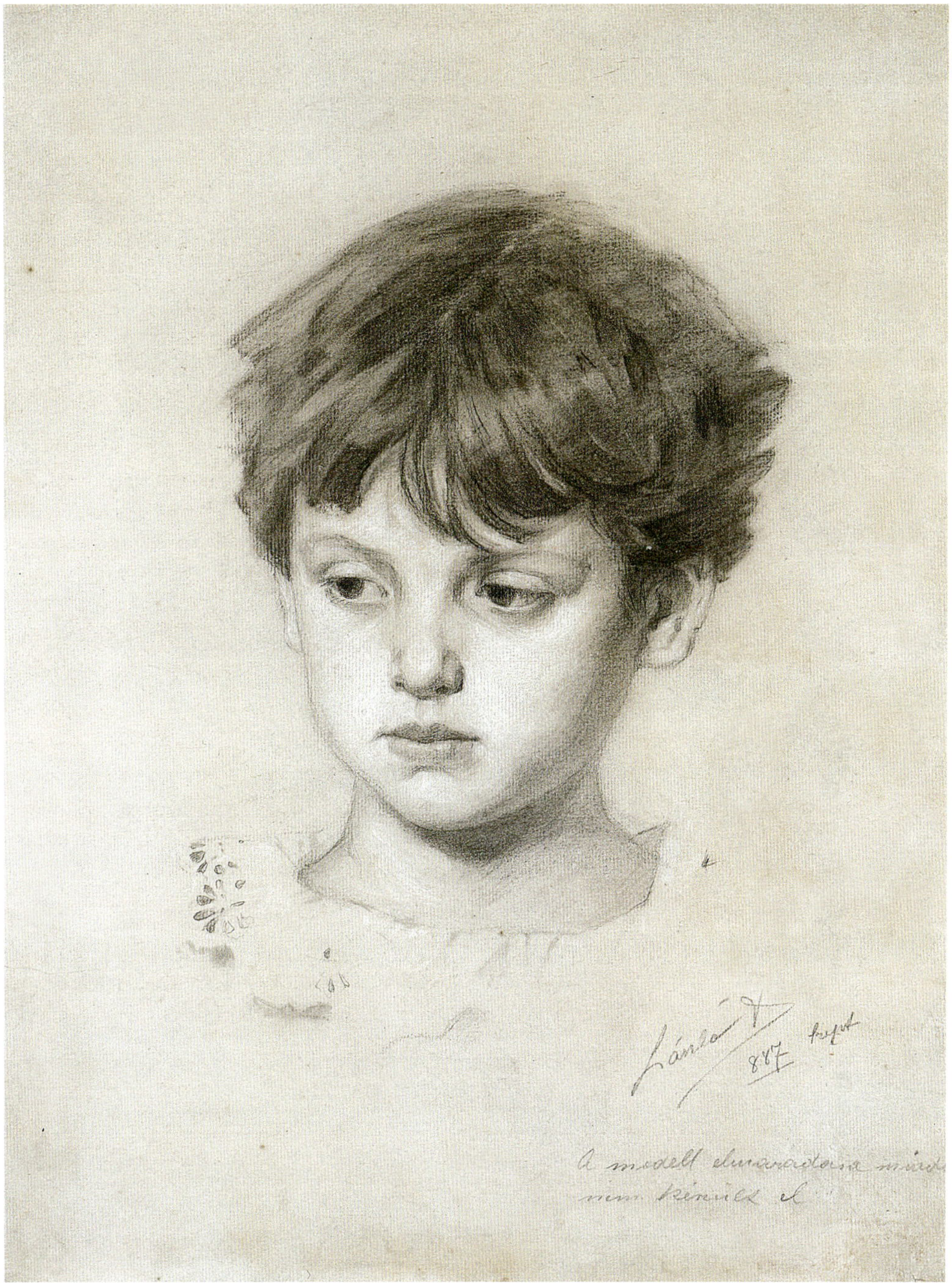

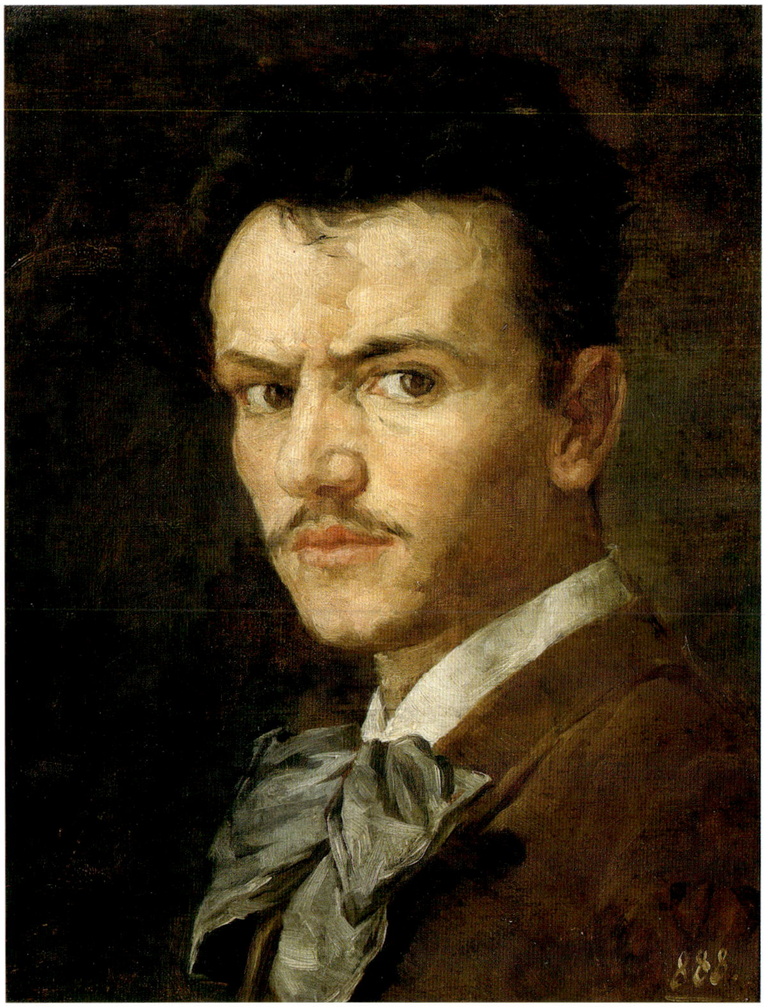

2 Self-portrait 1888

Oil on canvas, 42.5 × 32.7 cm (16¾ × 12⅞ inches)
Dated, lower right: *888*
PROVENANCE In the possession of the artist on his death; John de Laszlo, his youngest son

For the first six months after entering the Academy, de László's work was limited to drawing in pencil and chalks; it was not until later that he could progress to painting in oils, and even then at first in his free time. This is not only the earliest known self-portrait, it is also one of the earliest works in oil by de László to have survived. The pose, with the head turned over his shoulder to fix the viewer with a piercing gaze, was one he continued to favour for self-portraits (cat. 48).

In 1888, an important year for de László, he had a picture (*The Goose Girl*) chosen for public exhibition for the first time. The following year he won a Hungarian State Scholarship and decided to go to Venice, but he contracted typhoid and was forced to return to Budapest.

3 Otto Friedrich 1890

Oil on canvas, 133 × 77 cm (52⅜ × 30¼ inches)
Signed, inscribed and dated, lower left:
meinem Freund/O.Fridrich/1890 László
Private collection, Vienna
LITERATURE Rutter 1939, pp.54, 68–9, 70, 109–10, 114, 116, 128

In 1889 de László began studying at the Royal Bavarian Academy of Art in Munich under the distinguished Austro-Hungarian painter Alexander von Liezen-Mayer, but again fell seriously ill with typhoid and had to return to Budapest. In 1890, after his recovery, he won a Hungarian State Scholarship, and in late autumn that year went to Paris to study at the Académie Julian under Jules Lefèbvre and Benjamin-Constant. While in Munich de László had met the fellow painter Otto Friedrich. Friedrich was "Viennese, very talented and serious …". They became friends, de László holding Friedrich in high regard: "I admired him as a man, saw him often, and also painted him – my first half-length portrait." Friedrich, too, moved to Paris in 1890, where this portrait was most probably painted, and their friendship deepened. The artist wrote in his memoirs: "I loved Friedrich …. He was the one painter with whom I became really intimate in my student days. He was the only man I knew who carried out Leonardo da Vinci's precept that if a painter wishes to preserve and to develop his individuality, he should live and create as much as possible quite alone, since, if he consorts continually with his fellows, he is liable to become unconsciously influenced by them and will end by trying merely to please his friends." Unlike many of de László's early portraits, which show a tendency towards self-consciousness from a desire to please his client, Friedrich's portrait reveals freshness and intensity. The focus of attention on the face, the sketchiness of the clothing and the gestural brushstrokes, particularly in the background, anticipate de László's later style.

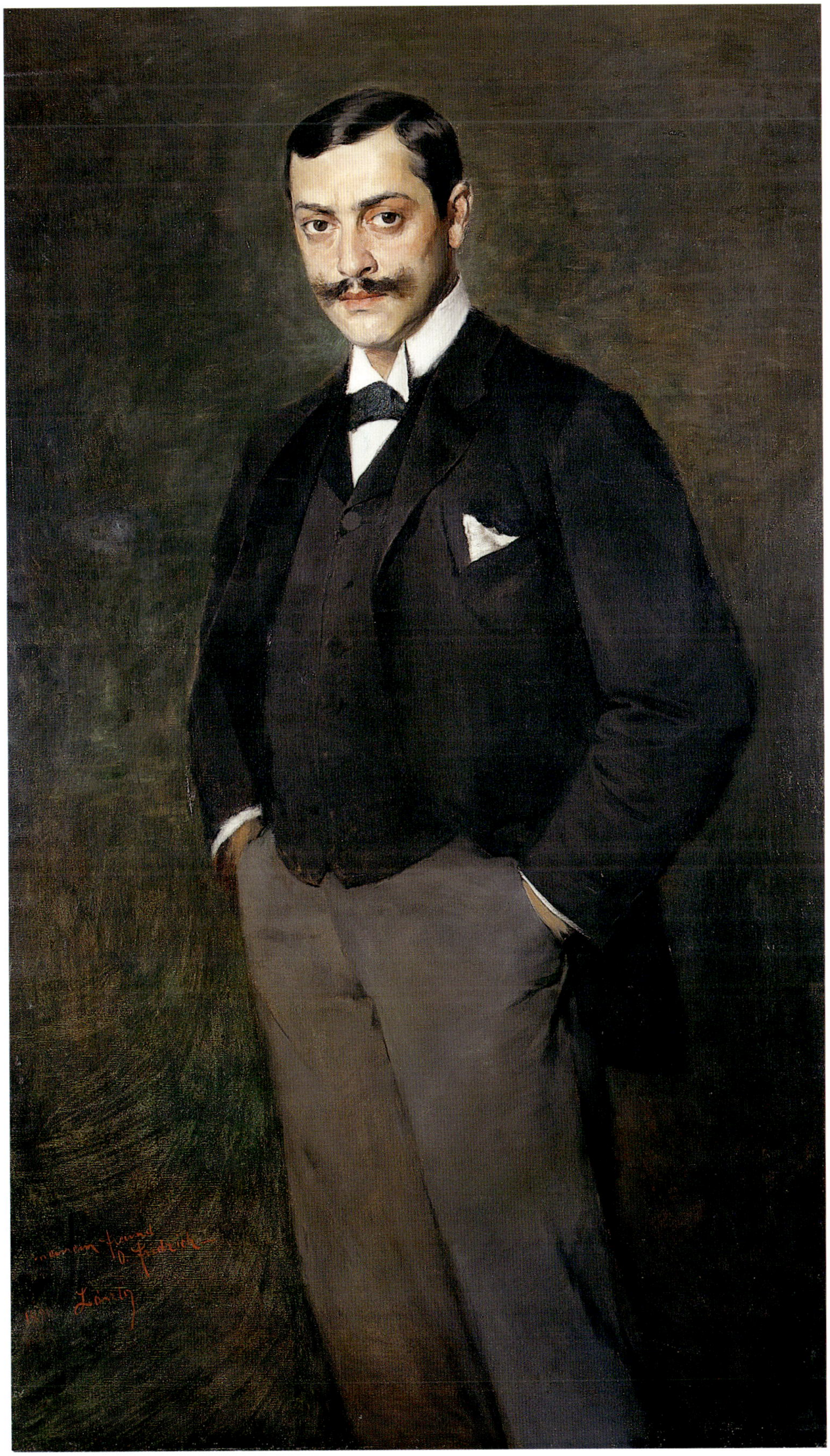

Otto Friedrich was born in Raab (now Györ in Hungary) in 1862. He was brought up in Vienna, where he studied from 1878 at the Academy of Fine Art. From 1885 to 1890 he was at the Academy in Munich under Wilhelm von Lindenschmit and concentrated almost exclusively on history painting. Until 1894 he was working in Paris. He returned to Vienna and in 1897 was a founder member of the Vienna Secessionist movement. He abandoned history painting, becoming an editor of the Secessionist periodical *Ver Sacrum* in 1900. From then on his work showed the distinct decorative characteristics of the *Jugendstil*. He concentrated on genre and landscape painting, exhibiting regularly at the Secession, but also became a distinguished portrait painter. He was known for his illustrations and lithographs, and as a teacher: for thirty years he taught at the Vienna Academy for Women. He was a quiet, solitary man, with an inclination to muse over the problems of his art. In his last years he was forced by ill health to give up painting. He died in Vienna in 1937.

Information on Friedrich from Künstlerarchiv der Österreichischen Galerie Belvedere, Vienna

4 Female Nude 1891

Oil on canvas, 77 × 47.9 (30½ × 18⅞ inches)
Signed, inscribed and dated, lower right:
László / Paris / 1891 V
PROVENANCE In the possession of the artist on his death; by descent in his family
LITERATURE Schleínítz 1913, p.18, ill. p.10; Rowcliffe 1938, p.14 (no. 81); Rutter 1939, pp.63–71

This is a life study from de László's time at the Académie Julian in Paris, in 1890–1. In de László's own words: "The Académie Julian was an old building, in the pre-Revolutionary style: square and sombre, without any artistic or architectural beauty – and a great lack of cleanliness .... In the studio we were given six mornings to make studies of a given size. I think this an excellent idea. The student was obliged to see and to understand the whole body, not only from the point of view of character or colour, but of movement also .... It is vital that the student should understand the following principles: first to know the *construction* of everything in nature; *only* then is it possible for him, if he have a *real vocation* for art, to reduce what he sees to its relative importance, and to create, either in drawing or in painting, the expression of movement and colour values which is the spiritual part of art. All this I began to realise for the first time during my student days in Paris." According to Schleínítz, de László won a prize for this study.

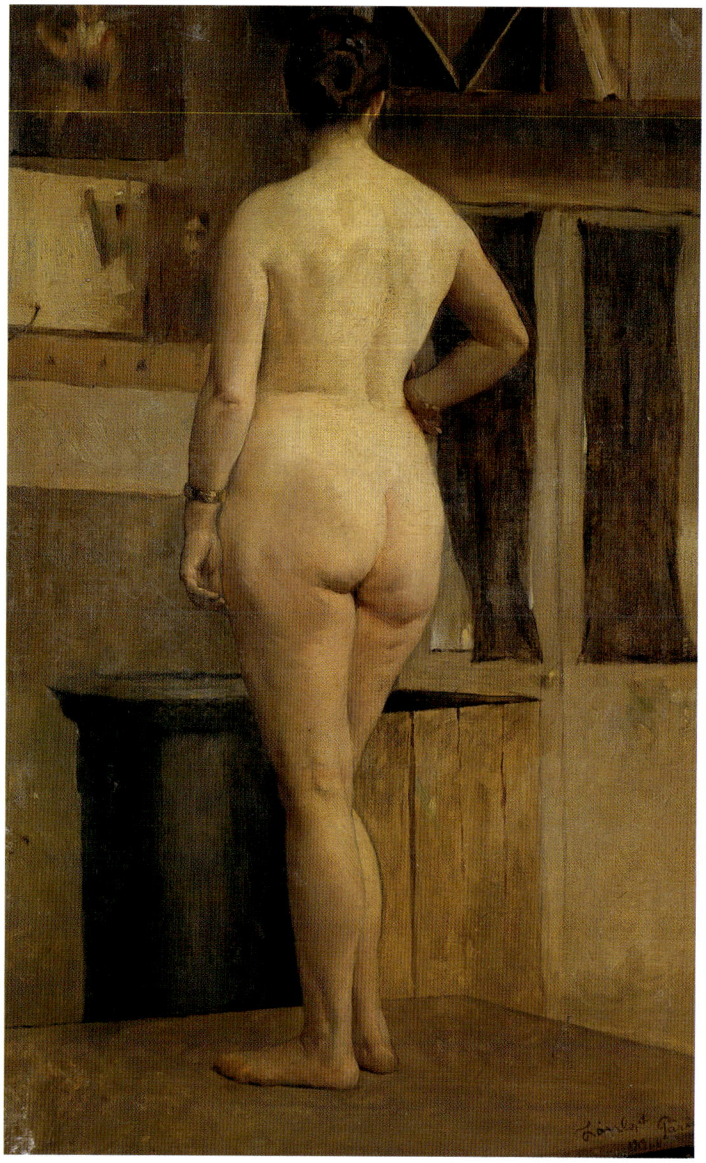

5 An Early Sketchbook *ca.* 1890

Clothbound; 26 numbered pages, mainly genre studies, almost all in pencil and small in scale;
17 × 25 × 2 cm (6⅝ × 9⅞ × ¾ inches)
The Hungarian National Gallery, Budapest
PROVENANCE Acquired by the National Gallery in 1926

Stylistically the book may be dated to the years around 1890. The two pages on view show pencil studies of men and women of varying

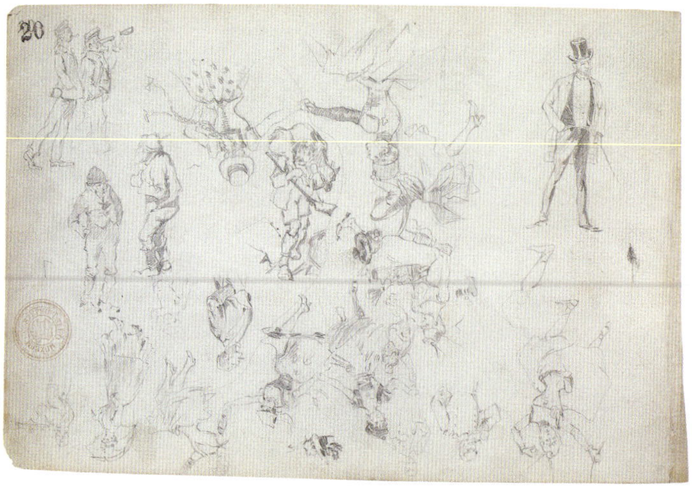

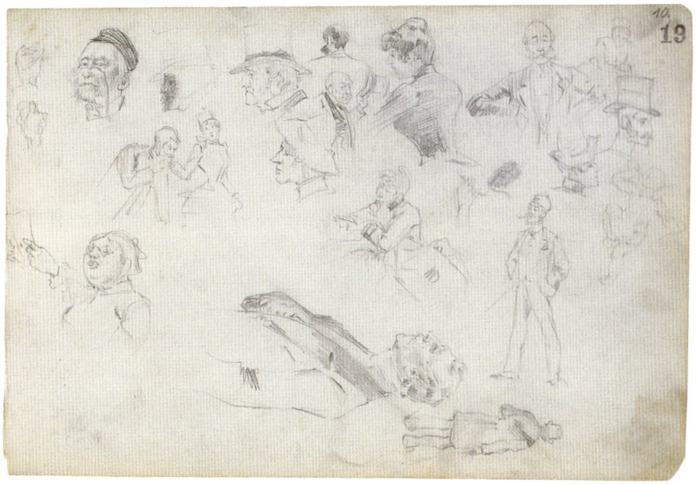

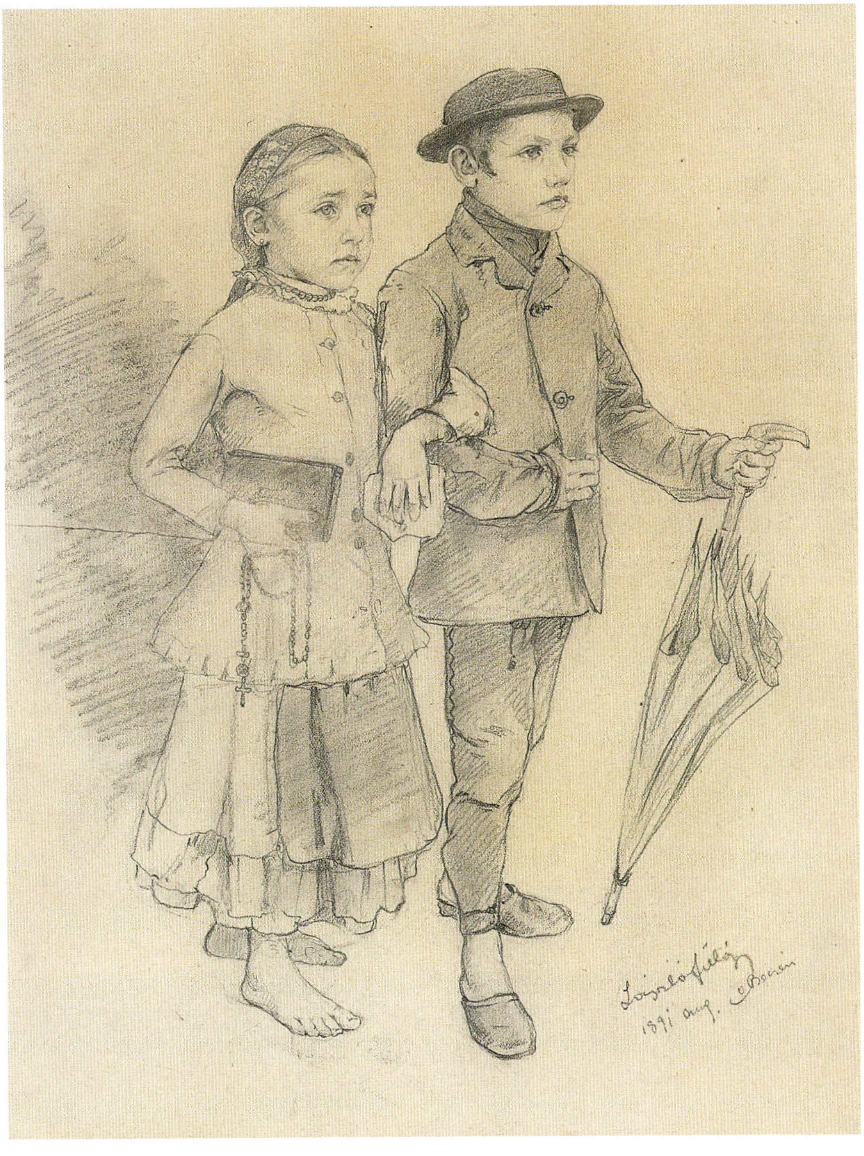

sizes and attire, some theatrical, some rustic, some in evening dress; also studies of hands and a naked child or putto.

6 On the Way to Church 1891

Pencil on paper, 33 × 25.4 (13 × 10 inches)
Signed, inscribed and dated, lower right: *László Fülöp / 1891 aug. O Becsem* [my O-Becse]
Private collection, Paris
PROVENANCE In the possession of the artist on his death; John de Laszlo, his youngest son
EXHIBITED (according to label on back) *Treasures of Famous Children Exhibition*, The Society of Graphic Art (date unknown; after the artist's death), no.1: *Study of Hungarian Peasant Children*
LITERATURE Schleínitz 1913, p.14; Rowcliffe 1938, p.139 (no. 19); Clifford 1969, p.51, monochrome ill. pl.6

During his student years de László spent his summer holidays in the little town of O-Becse in Southern Hungary (now part of Serbia) with the family of Paul Galambos, a local lawyer and landowner. During these visits, which the artist considered to be among the happiest times of his life, he made several paintings and drawings of local worthies (fig. 51), peasants in colourful costumes and scenes from Hungarian country life. In August 1891, when this drawing was made, de László was making his third and last visit to O-Becse, just after finishing two terms at the Académie Julian.

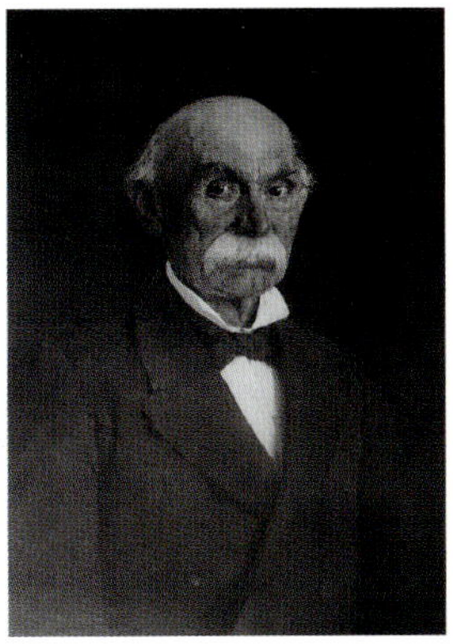

FIG. 53
An Old Man of O-Becse (Herr Grünbaum)
Oil on canvas
Untraced

7 L'Incroyable 1891–2

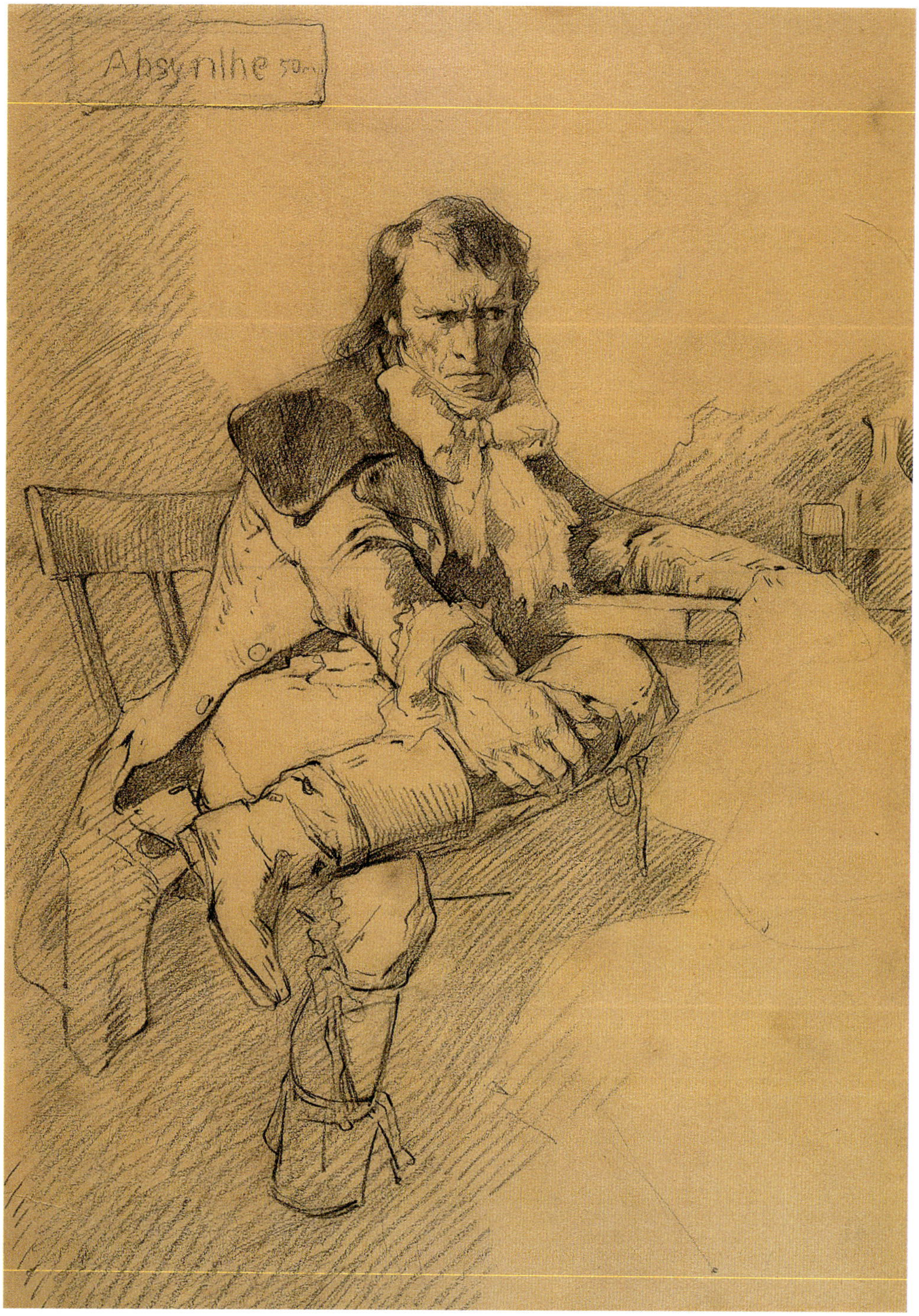

Pencil on paper, 43.2 × 30.5 cm (17 × 12 inches)
PROVENANCE Sir Arthur Guinness, K.C.M.G., nephew of the artist's wife
LITERATURE Rutter 1939, pp.79–81

In 1891, after returning from Paris to resume his studies in Munich, de László was inspired by Carlyle's *French Revolution* to paint a picture of an 'Incroyable', a counter-Revolutionary dandy. Having been provided by the Academy with a period costume, he still lacked a model. His landlady, however, saw a group from the Hoftheater sitting outside on the pavement between rehearsals. Among the actors he spotted the very man he wanted: "He was a member of the chorus (although he gave one the impression of being a much more important person), tall and thin, with a Celtic-looking face and deep-set eyes. He corresponded exactly to my idea of L'Incroyable .... Next morning he came to my studio and proved an excellent model .... We became friends, and I gave him a sketch I made of him, and bought a watch-and-chain for his son. I remember that, among many subjects, we talked of love, about which we had a great dispute .... His excitement in the heat of the discussion gave his face just the expression I wanted for 'L'Incroyable', and I painted it while we argued." According to de László, his tutor Liezen-Mayer "had become too academical to approve of any spontaneity in composition" and did not approve of de László wanting to paint the model "with the face of a passionate French 'Incroyable', with all the culture and intelligence of his race and period. But I could not have painted such a picture in any other way: it would have been simply that of a dressed up model."

The finished picture, for which this is one of several preparatory sketches, remains untraced, but depicted "the Incroyable sitting brooding at a table in a Rembrandtesque light, with a revolutionary paper in his left hand and a bottle of absinthe in front of him." It was apparently exhibited, and sold, at the Budapest Winter Exhibition in 1892.

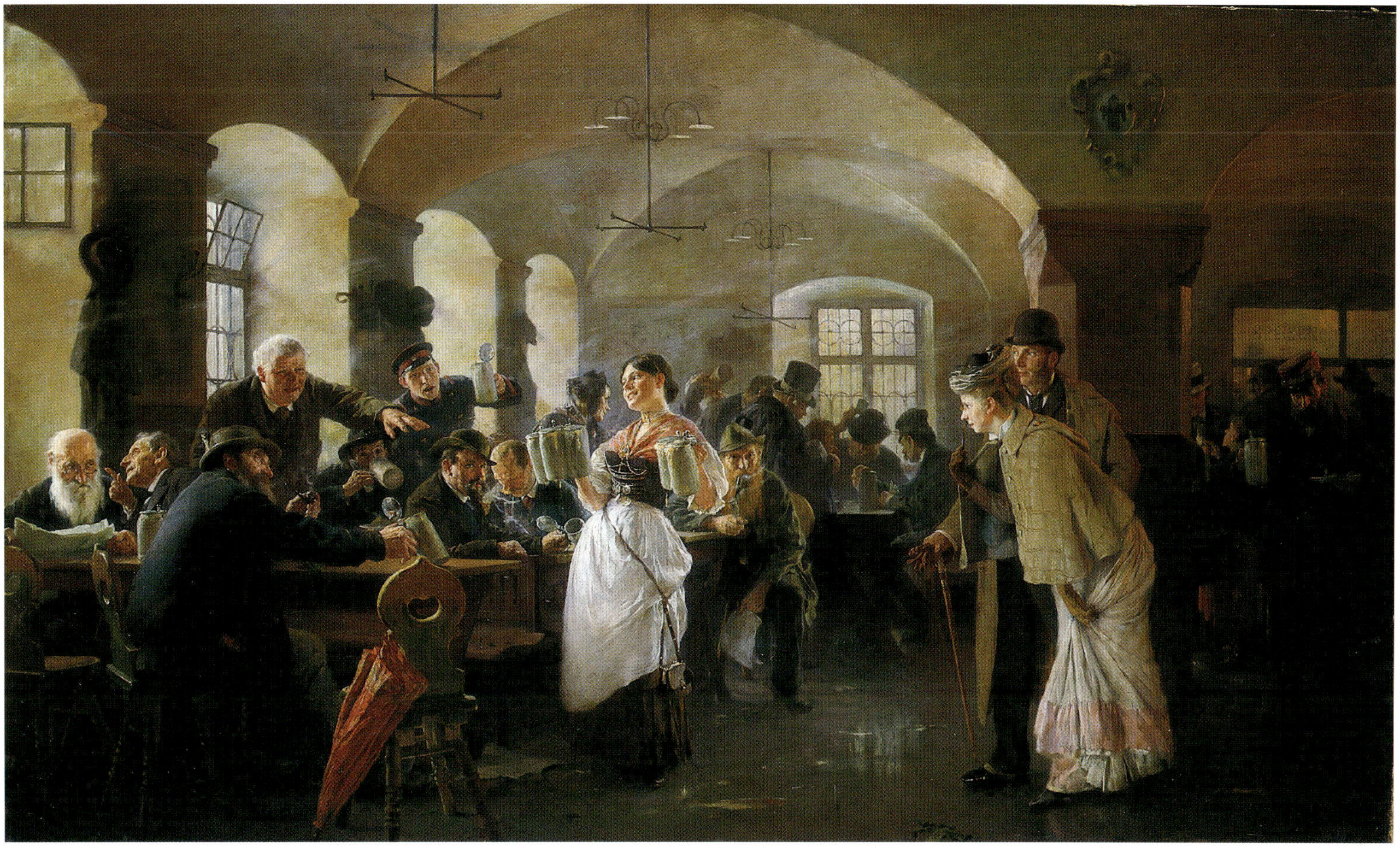

8 The Hofbräuhaus, 1892

Oil on canvas, 78.1 × 127.3 cm (30¾ × 50⅛ inches)
Signed, inscribed and dated, lower right:
László F. 892 München
Hungarian National Gallery, Budapest
PROVENANCE The architect Ignác Ritter von Wechselmann, who bought it from the artist; later presented to the Hungarian National Gallery by a private collector
EXHIBITED The Munich Academy, 1892
LITERATURE Schleínitz 1913, p.13, ill. pl.14; Rutter 1939, pp.81–2, 85, 87, 92, 96, 98–9, 105, 106, 120, 121, 122, 128, 209, ill. facing p.96; Clifford 1969, monochrome ill. pl.9; *Bavaria – Hungary – One Thousand Years*, catalogue of the exhibition at the Oberhausmuseum, Passau, 8 May–28 October 2001 (and at the Nemzeti Múzeum, Budapest in 2002), no.7.3, p.334

Already during his first stay in Munich de László had determined to paint a picture of the Hofbräuhaus, the tavern in which he would eat regularly after work. He was fascinated by the people he saw there: "that wonderful crowd of men drawn from every class … the buxom Bavarian waitresses in their national costumes … a soldier, a cabman, a small official and a business man, a student joking with a waitress …. One day, as I sat watching, I saw a couple of English tourists going round and gazing at the scene. They just fitted into my picture".

On his return to Munich from Paris he made a number of studies from life (cat. 9–12), and in his studio, which he equipped with a table, chairs and even beer mugs similar to those in the Hofbräuhaus (going so far as to reproduce the lighting with the help of a gas-reflector), he built up the complicated composition until it contained a total of twenty-three figures. The impoverished student even bought himself a large camera to help with the poses, salving his guilty conscience with the excuse that the great Munich painter Franz von Lenbach also used photographs for his compositions. In February 1892, after meeting his future wife, Lucy Guinness, at a fancy dress ball in Munich, he asked her to pose for him as one of the English tourists he had included to the right of the composition (see further below, and fig. 53, overleaf). The model for the other head was a Court coachman.

De László exhibited the finished oil painting at the Munich Academy in 1892 together with *L'Incroyable* (cat. 6), and was awarded the Silver Medal.

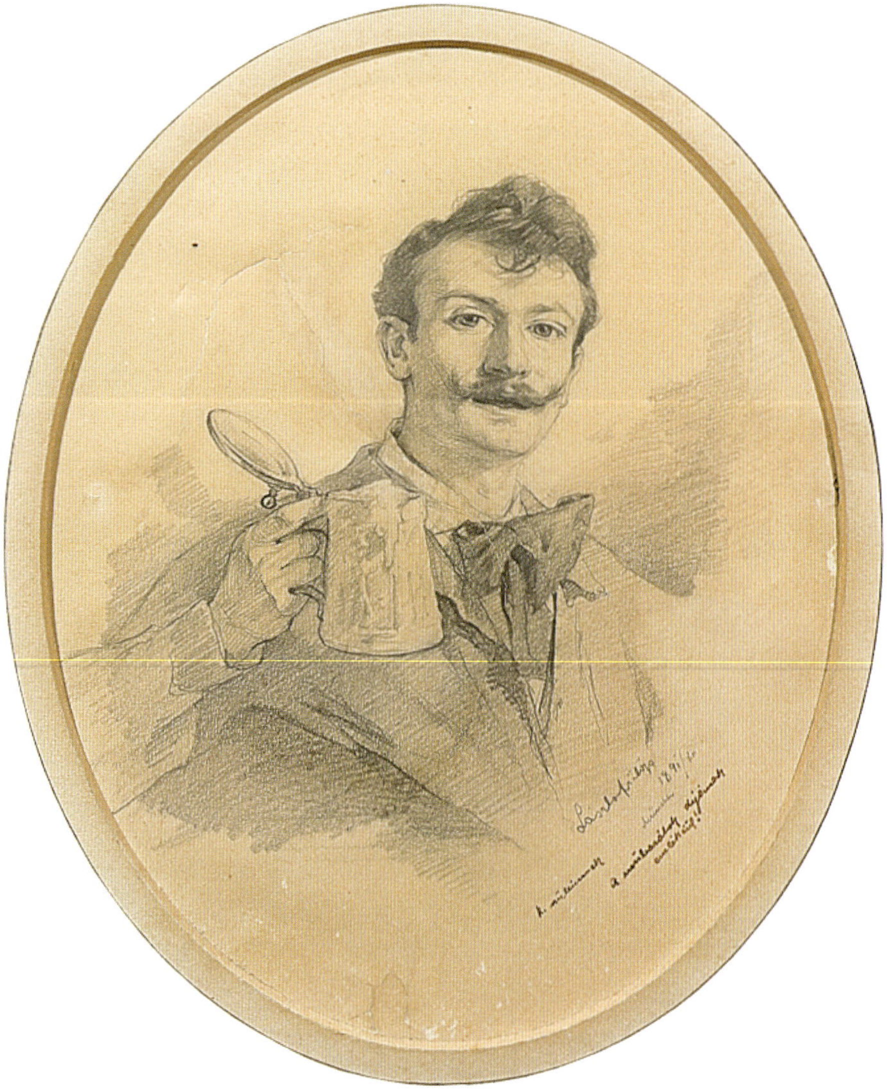

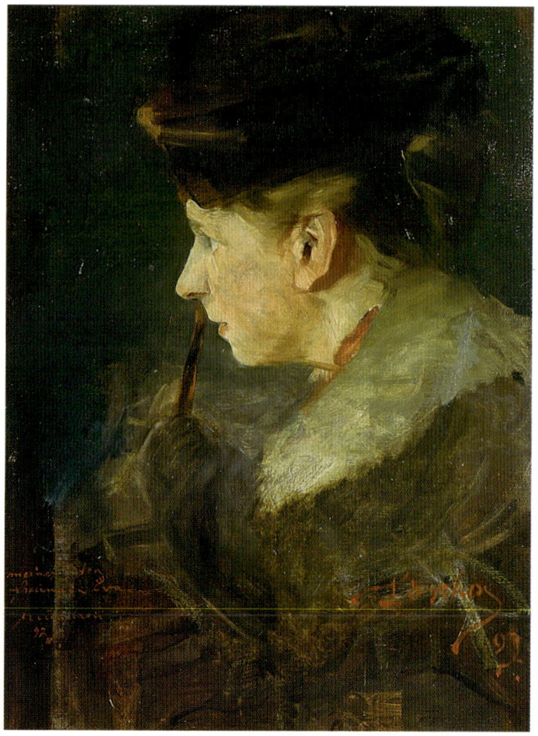

FIG. 54
Miss Lucy Guinness, 1892
Oil on canvas, 59.1 × 61.5 cm (23¼ × 16⅝ in.)
Private collection

9 Self-portrait 1891

Pencil on paper, in an oval mount, 31.1 × 25.4 cm (12¾ × 10 inches) visible
Signed, dated and indistinctly inscribed, lower right: *László Fülöp/1891/xii/München* /[in ink] *k[edves] szüleimnek/a mübarátok dijának/emlékéül!* [To my dear parents/ in memory of the Friends of Art Prize!]
PROVENANCE The artist's parents, Adolf and Johanna, and thence to Marczell László, the artist's brother, and by descent from his second wife

When he made this self-portrait de László, aged only twenty-two but encouraged by Liezen-Mayer, had just re-enlisted at the Munich Academy as a 'composition student', with a studio of his own provided and paid for by the Bavarian State. It is likely that he used the drawing as a preparatory study for *The Hofbräuhaus* (cat. 8), on which he was working at the time.

De László explained to Rutter the circumstances surrounding the inscription on the self-portrait: at Christmas 1891 he heard from his brother Marczi that his painting *The Storyteller* had won the Friends of Art Prize. "I spent days of anxiety waiting for the confirmation and imagining the joy of my family if the news were true. At last the official intimation came. It arrived with a letter from my mother and many notes of congratulations from my friends, followed by cuttings from the newspapers. I felt happiest among the happy. It was an honour of which I had never dreamed." Until this time de László had been receiving state scholarship money. He now wrote to the Ministry of Arts in Budapest thanking them for all their help, but begging them to allow him to surrender the scholarship in favour of some other needy young artist. The prize money, however, which amounted to 1,500 florins, then about £125, he gave to his sister Rózsa as part of her dowry.

De Lászlo used several different models for the figures of *The Hofbräuhaus*, but most significant among them was his future wife, Lucy (fig. 54), whom he had just met at a fancy-dress ball.

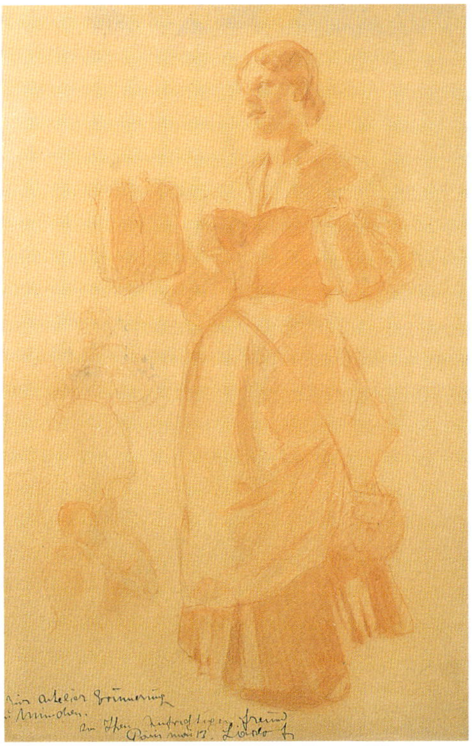

10 A Waitress from The Hofbräuhaus 1892

Sepia chalk on buff paper, 14×28.9 cm ($17\frac{7}{8} \times 11\frac{3}{4}$ inches)
Signed, indistinctly inscribed and dated, lower left: *Zur Atelier Erinnerung / in Munchen /von Ihrem Aufrichtigen Freund / Paris. Mai.13. László F.* [A souvenir of the studio in Munich from your sincere friend, Paris, 13 May László F]
PROVENANCE Given by the artist to his future wife, Miss Lucy Guinness, for whom it was inscribed

Several fine studies for *The Hofbräuhaus* in the possession of the artist on his death are now in the collections of his descendants. Here de László has established the form of the buxom serving girl, but it still lacks the movement, the swing of the hips and the tilt of the head, that define her character in the final version. The artist dedicated it to his future wife with an inscription in hesitant German.

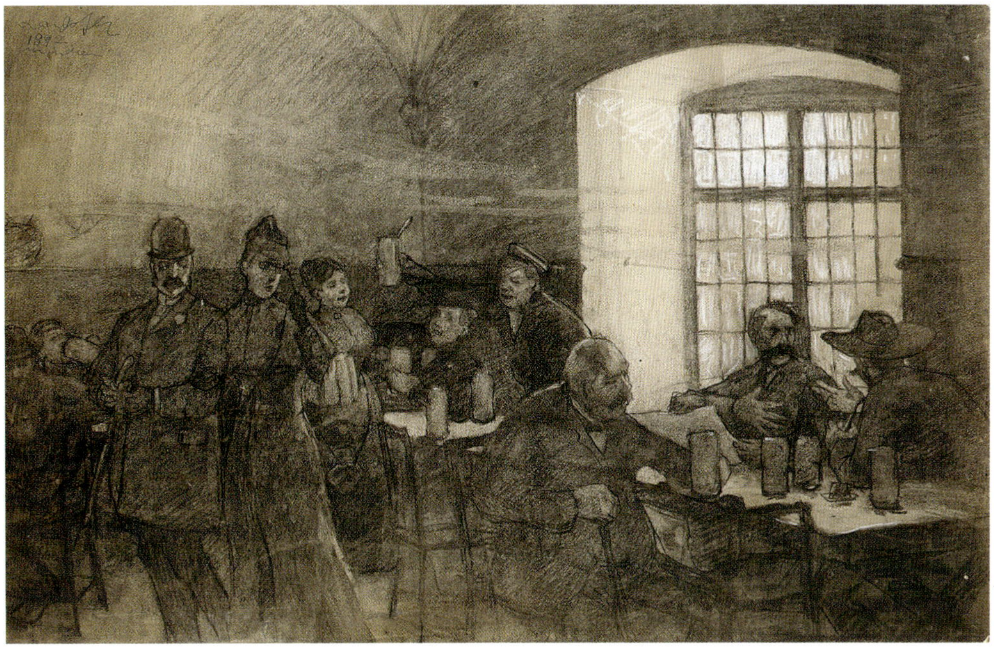

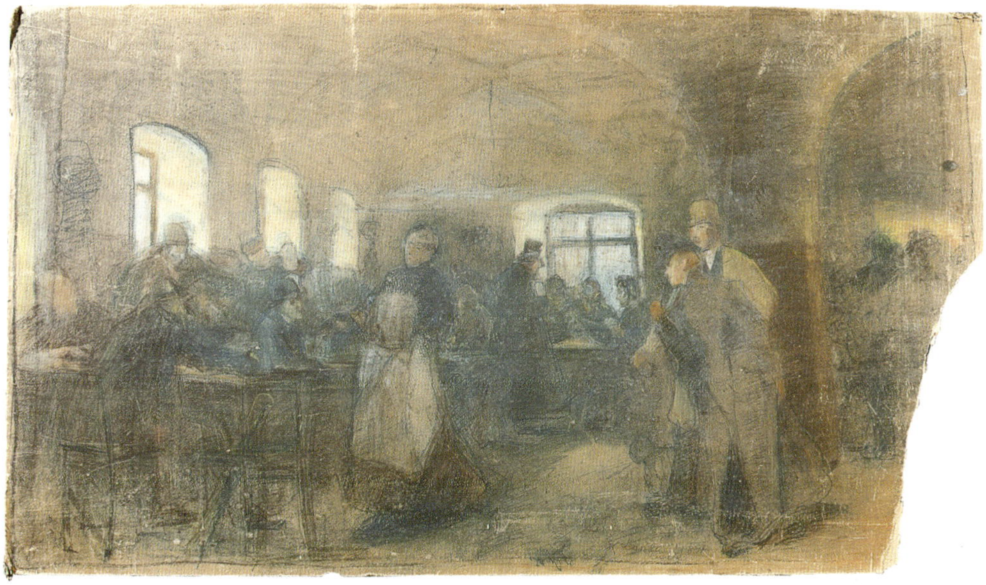

11 The Hofbräuhaus 1891

Coloured chalks and pastels on board, 51.8×89.2 cm ($20\frac{3}{8} \times 35\frac{1}{8}$ inches)
Signed, indistinctly inscribed and dated, lower right: *..László 1891 / Munche*
PROVENANCE In the possession of the artist on his death; Paul de Laszlo, his third son
LITERATURE See cat. 8

12 The Hofbräuhaus 1892

Charcoal and pencil on board, 40.5×61.5 cm ($16 \times 24\frac{1}{2}$ inches)
Signed, inscribed and dated, upper left: *László F.E / 1892 / München*
PROVENANCE In the possession of the artist on his death; Patrick de Laszlo, his fourth son
LITERATURE See cat. 8

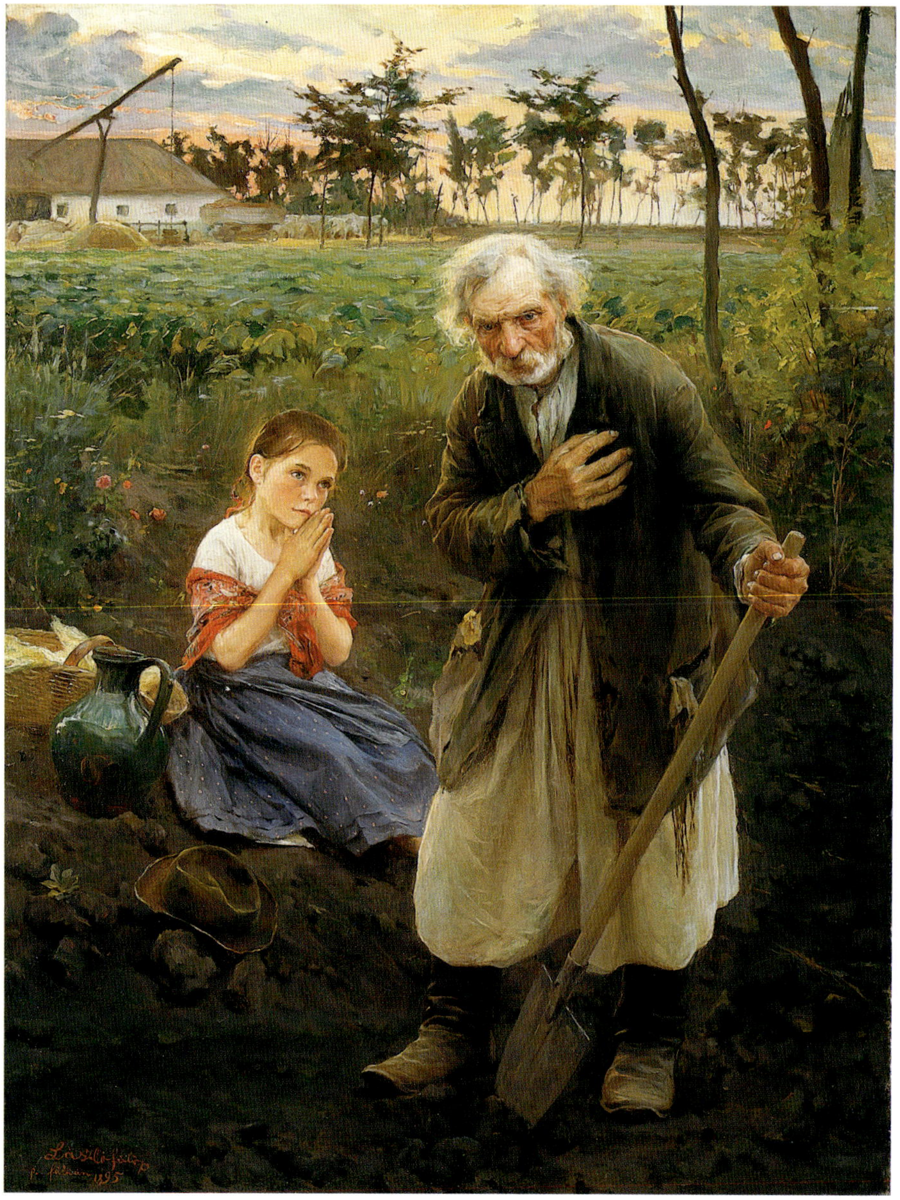

13 At Vesper Bell (Ave Maria) 1895

Oil on canvas, 97.5 × 73 cm (38⅜ × 28¾ inches)
Signed, inscribed and dated, lower left:
László Fülöp p. / fábián. 1895; also inscribed lower centre: *LÁSZLÓ FÜLÖP AVE MARIA*
Hungarian National Gallery, Budapest
PROVENANCE Purchased from the artist in 1896

Early in 1895 de László returned from Sofia to Budapest, having completed the commission which marked the beginning of his career as an international portrait painter – to paint the Bulgarian royal family (see fig. 6, p. 17).

His mentor, Alexius de Lippich, the secretary of the Fine Arts Department of the Ministry of Arts and Education, had a number of portrait commissions arranged for him, but felt that, to build his reputation in his native country, de László should continue to work on historical and genre subjects. *Ave Maria*, painted that year, is actually more typical of his pre-Paris years, although it is not as strong in composition or subject-matter as those with which he had previously won prizes. Nevertheless, the painting was purchased the following year by the Hungarian National Gallery, who may even have commissioned the picture.

14 Falling Leaves 1895

Oil on panel, 80 × 64 cm (31⅛ × 25 inches)
Signed and dated, lower left: *LÁSZLÓ F. 1895*
Private collection, Budapest
PROVENANCE Dr. Pál Majowszky (1871–1935), art collector and Counsellor in the Department of Art of the Ministry of Education 1894–1917; he donated his collection to the Szépmüvészeti Múzeum (Museum of Fine Arts) in 1914
EXHIBITED *Országos Magyar Képzömüvészeti Társulat, Téli kiállítás* (Hungarian Society of Fine Arts, Winter Exhibition), 1895, no.69
LITERATURE Schleínítz 1913, ill. p.17, pl.19; Rutter 1939, pp.151, 153, 163; Clifford 1969, p.23, ill. pl.11

In his memoirs de László writes of this painting: "It depicted an old pensioner of '48 sitting on a bench in a wood, with his thoughts far away in the past and the yellow autumn leaves falling round him. I had many such subjects in mind; they gave me pleasure to paint and … I should have liked to have done more of that type of picture, but the need of money and my ardent desire to help my people compelled me to paint various portraits for 400 or 500 Florins, a sum which meant much to me in those days!"

The old soldier is a veteran of the 1848–49 War of Independence against the Habsburgs. De László's picture was painted in the year Hungary commemorated the thousandth anniversary of the occupation and settlement of the Carpathian Basin by the Magyars in 896. The festivities gave rise to a wave of national sentiment, and the theme of the picture may be seen as a nostalgic and proud reminder of

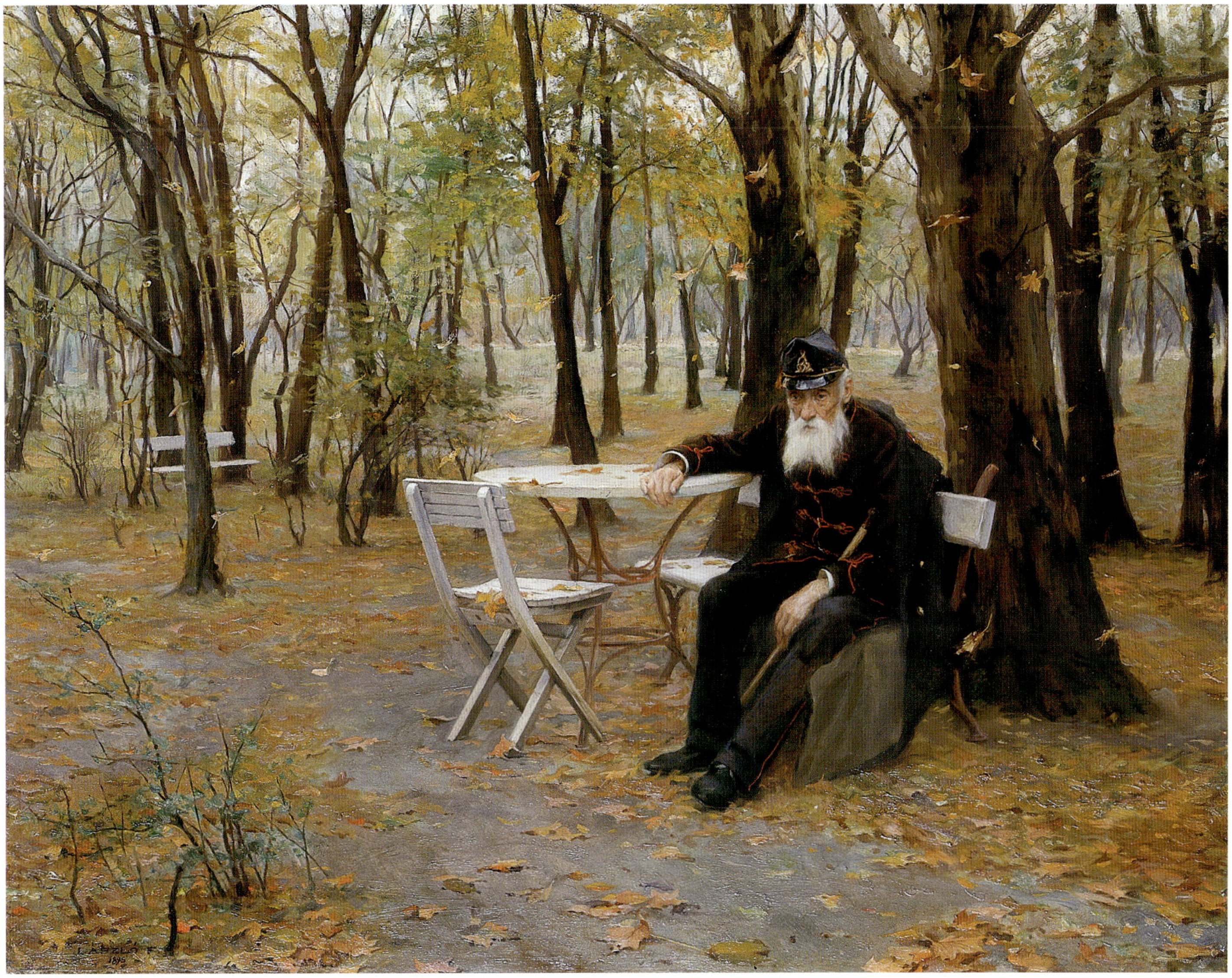

Hungary's struggle for independence.

The inspiration for the painting comes from the first poem, '*Mindvégig*' (To the very end), of an elegiac, melancholy cycle of lyric poems entitled "*Öszikék*" (Autumn crocuses, 1877) by János Arany (1817–1882), the great epic poet and translator of Shakespeare. A literal translation reads: 'Why, this life is beautiful / Until its end, if you are careful / With what's left of it; / But when Autumn comes / And your leaves have fallen / Do not yearn for Summer.'

Schleinitz, who mistakenly attributes the painting to 1892, describes it as "full of gloomy, backward looking and no doubt allegorically meant autumnal mood. The picture was painted in a park in Budapest.... Here on our painting we see an old soldier, a Honvéd (literally 'Defender of the Fatherland') veteran from 1848, over whose home no doubt the well known dedication to invalids might have been written: '*Laeso sed invicto militi*' (To the wounded but unconquered soldier). Contemplating the falling leaves, he feels that his hour too has come to enlist in the Great Army of the Eternal Host. Immersed in the memory of a year (1848) that was so eventful and meaningful for Hungary and brooding over changing times, in this autumnal picture the man conveys to us in the most concise way his story, told without words."

De László was clearly proud of this painting, as he took a reproduction of it with him when he first met his future mother-in-law in London in 1898. He must have created a good impression on Mrs Guinness, whose verdict was, "A most fascinating but dangerous man".

With thanks to Dr. P.T. d'Orbán for information on the historical and literary background

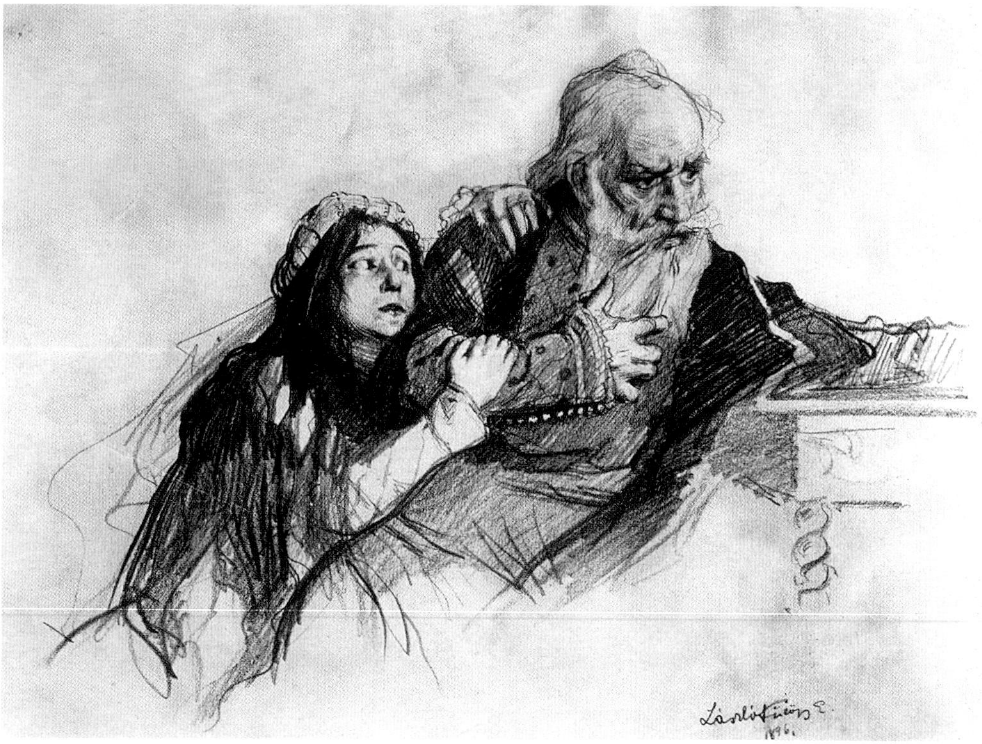

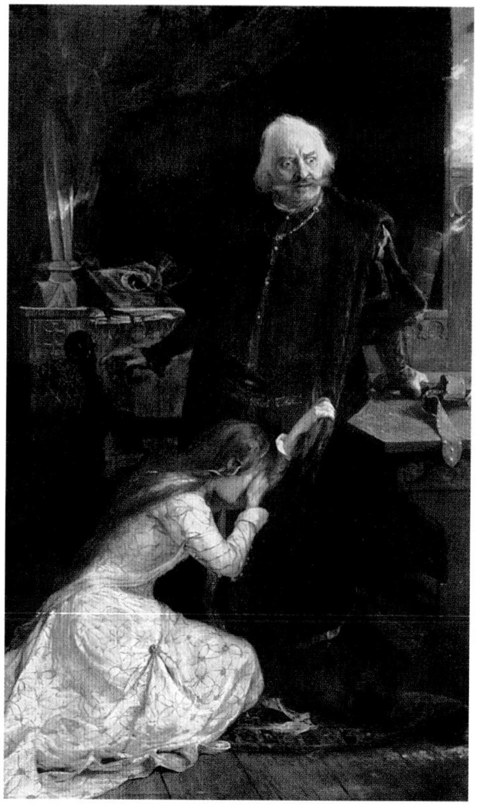

FIG. 55 *Zách Felicián and his daughter Klara*, 1896
Oil on canvas, 217.2 × 156.8 cm, private collection

15 Zách Felicián 1896

Soft pencil on buff paper, 26 × 34 cm
($10\frac{1}{4} \times 13\frac{3}{8}$ inches)
Signed and dated, lower right: *László Fülöp E. / 1896.*
PROVENANCE In the possession of the artist on his death
LITERATURE Schleinitz 1913, ill. p.23, pl.26; *The Studio*, LXXXI, 1920, p.54, ill.; Rutter 1939, p.151; Clifford 1969, pp.20, 23, 59, ill. p.93, pl.13

In 1896 de László also painted a full-size historical painting (fig. 55), for which this is a preparatory study, depicting the story of Zách Felicián. Zách Felicián was a prominent Hungarian nobleman, and his daughter Clara was a lady-in-waiting to Queen Elizabeth, wife of King Robert Charles (died 1348). From the house of Anjou, rulers of Naples, Robert Charles had succeeded in 1308 when the house of Árpád, the original line of Hungarian kings, died out. His queen was a Polish princess. The brother of the queen, Casimir (later King Casimir the Great of Poland), while visiting the Hungarian Court, violated Clara. Attempting to murder the royal family in revenge, Zách Felicián was killed on 17 April 1330 by the king's attendants, and a terrible vengeance was exacted on his own kin.

Zách Felicián's attempt to kill the king and queen was depicted in the *Képes Krónika* (Illustrated Chronicle, 1374–6), but the reason for the attempt is not recorded, and the story of his daughter's rape may be apocryphal. It is also told in a poem by János Arany, and in another by the great Sándor Petöfi, and the accomplished Hungarian painter Madarász Viktor had painted the same scene almost forty years before, in 1858. De László's finished painting is very different from the present drawing, but both depict the scene when Clara tells her father about the rape. With it de László once again exploited the nationalist euphoria of the Millennium celebrations (see cat. 14). The story appealed directly to this sentiment as King Robert Charles and his wife were both foreigners and had introduced pernicious foreign influence at Court.

Just before beginning his painting in Budapest, de László had been sent to Dresden to copy a portrait in the Royal Collection by the eighteenth-century painter Ádám Mányoki of Prince Ferenc Rákóczy II, who had fought against Austria for Hungary's independence. De László also used this visit to study the other paintings in the collection and gain portrait commissions, among them the Crown Princess of Saxony and the Austro-Hungarian Minister to the Court.

With thanks to Dr. P.T. d'Orbán for the historical background in this description

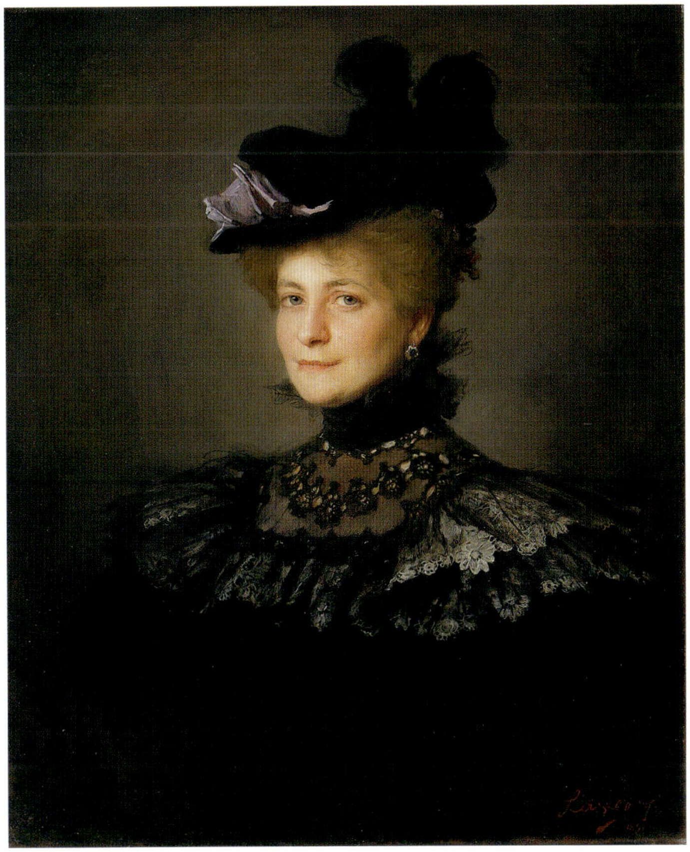

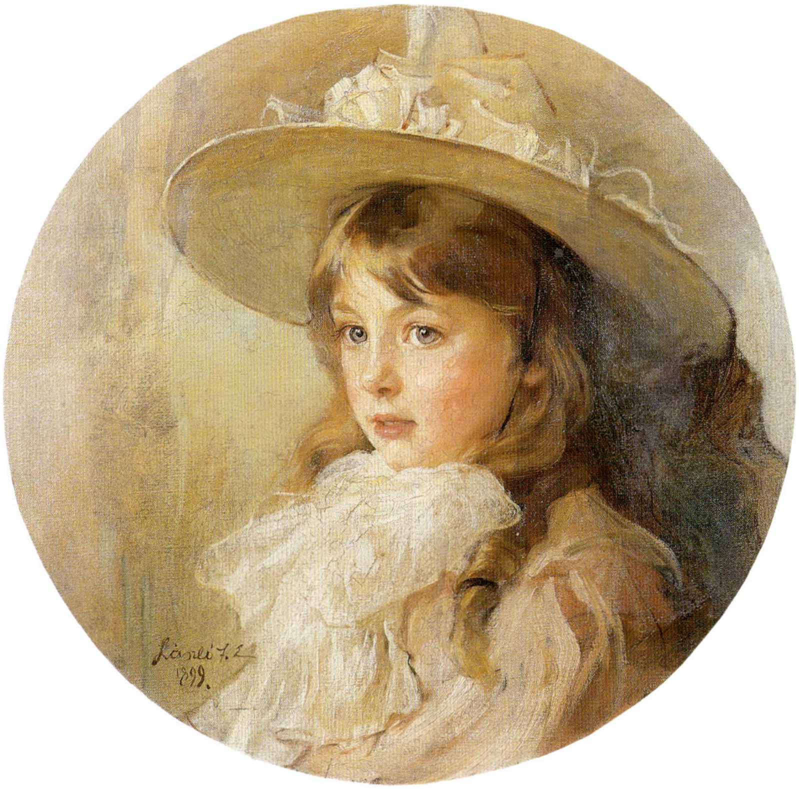

16 A Lady in Black 1897

Oil on canvas, 90.8 × 72.4 cm (35¾ × 28½ inches)
Signed and dated, lower right: *László F. / 1897*
Hungarian National Gallery, Budapest

Also entitled *The Woman in a Black Hat*, this picture was painted in 1897, a year of considerable achievement for de László. Having received the large Millennium Medal from the Hungarian Government the previous year, he became acquainted with Prince Max Ratibor, and was commissioned to paint the prince and several members of his family – portraits which were to bring him great acclaim. The Prince was the German Consul-General in Budapest and introduced de László to the great families of Germany, many of whom became considerable patrons, thus beginning de László's reputation as court painter to all Europe.

17 A Young Girl 1899

Oil on canvas, circular, 49.5 cm (19½ inches) diameter
Signed and dated, lower left: *László FE / 1899*
PROVENANCE In the possession of the artist on his death; Stephen de Laszlo, his second son
LITERATURE Rowcliffe 1938, p.17 (no. 102)

The year 1899, too, was a busy one for the thirty-year-old de László. He painted Francis Joseph, Emperor of Austria and King of Hungary, in Budapest early in the year (fig. 19, p. 32) and went on to Berlin to paint the German chancellor Prince Chlodwig Hohenlohe-Schillingsfürst, later winning the Gold Medal for that portrait at the Paris Salon. He met the German Emperor for the first time in Berlin. He then travelled to Vienna to carry out a number of commissions, returning to Budapest in May to paint the Prime Minister, Count Julius Szapáry, before leaving again for Cologne and Silesia, then to Paris for his first French commission, and finally to Ireland where he became officially engaged to Lucy Guinness seven years after their first meeting. In October he came to England and carried out numerous commissions. From this huge range of possibilities, it has until now been impossible to identify the girl in this portrait or even establish her nationality.

18 His Holiness Pope Leo XIII 1900

Oil on canvas, 111.8 × 93.99 cm (44 × 37 inches)
Signed, inscribed and dated, lower right:
László F.E. / ROMA / 1900 III
Hungarian National Gallery, Budapest
PROVENANCE Presented to the National Gallery by the artist in 1900
EXHIBITED *L'Exposition Universelle*, Paris, 1900, p.437, no.78: *S.S. le pape Léon XIII*; *Jahresausstellung*, Munich, 1903, MALEREI, László, Fülöp, Kat.662: *S.Heil. Papst Leo XIII*; International Society of Art's Exhibition, 1904; *Philip A. László, Portrait Paintings and Drawings*, Fine Art Society, London, May–June 1907, no. 38: *H.H. Pope Leo XIII*; *Exposition P. A. de László*, Hotel Jean Charpentier, Paris, June 1931,
LITERATURE *The Studio*, XXIV, 1901, ill. p.7; 'Fülöp László in the Vatican', *Új Idök* , Yr 7, no. 9, 24 February 1901; *The Studio*, XXXI, 1904, p.69, ill.; Robert de Montesquiou-Fezansac, 'Un portraitiste lyrique, Philipp Laszlo', *L'Art et les artistes*, II, 15 June 1906, p.94; 'Pape Léo XIII', *Je sais tout*, 15 July 1910, ill.p.47; Schleínítz 1913, p.43, pl.47; Williams 1921, pp.33–6, ill. facing p.32 (in colour in the de luxe edition); *The Graphic*, 24 January, 1925, p.122; Rutter 1939, pp.184, 186, 187–92, 193, 195–6, 197, 198–204, 233, ill. facing p.192; Clifford 1969, p. 27, monochrome ill. pl.16

1900 can be considered de László's *annus mirabilis*. Having painted several members of the German imperial family, in early March he travelled to Rome to paint Pope Leo XIII.

Earlier that year Bishop Vilmos Fraknói, the head of the Theological College for Hungarian students in Rome, having befriended de László in Budapest, had suggested to the Pope that an Hungarian artist should paint his portrait for the Hungarian National Gallery to commemorate the nine-hundredth anniversary of the baptism and coronation of St Stephen as first King of Hungary in 1000. As de László wrote in a letter to *Új Idök* (New Times) magazine: "Leo XIII graciously consented, and I was the fortunate person to whom the great task was entrusted ...."

Having made two exceptionally intuitive drawings (Hungarian National Gallery and another untraced, illustrated in *The Studio*), de László had to abandon his first attempt at a likeness in oil after only two sittings as the Pope thought it made him look like Voltaire (fig. 57). The rejected but partly finished head and shoulders portrait (fig. 56) was cut down and kept by the artist during his lifetime. After his death it was sent to the Vatican Museums, where it remains today.

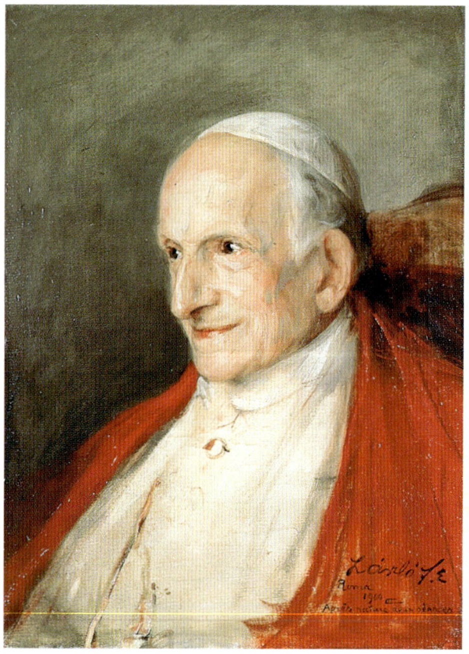

FIG. 56 *Pope Leo XIII*, 1900
Oil on canvas, 58.4 × 43.2 cm (23 × 17 in.),
Monumenti Musei e Gallerie Pontificie, Rome

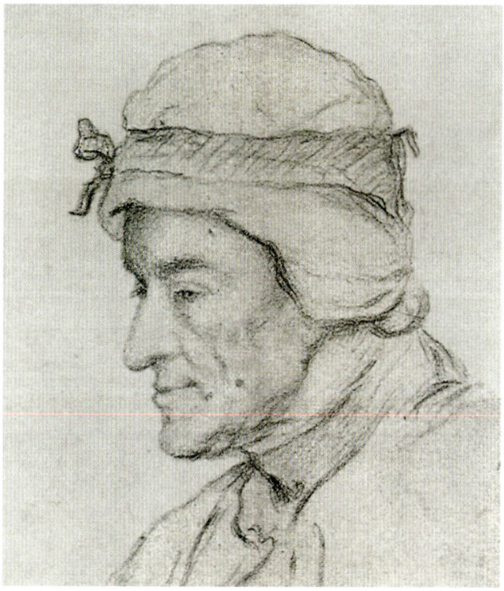

FIG. 57 Thomas Worlidge (1700-1766)
Voltaire (François-Marie Arouet)
Chalk, whereabouts unknown

De László's letter continues: "With gracious benevolence the Holy Father sat for me four times, and I think that with this second attempt I was able to reproduce that impression which I had felt in the first seconds [of our meeting]. During these sessions, in which His Excellency Bishop Fraknói was present throughout, His Holiness showed a lively interest in his portrait. Finally, he conversed with His Excellency Bishop Fraknói about a great variety of subjects; political, religious, social, artistic and scientific questions, and also about Hungary .... I can say that I have never met a man whose innermost feelings were revealed so expressively, and who would be more deserving a model to be studied by an artist." De László completed the portrait with the help of a friend and patron, Baron Rodolphe d'Erlanger, who, according to a descendant, sat for the painting of the robes and the final details of the Pope's hands.

The final portrait obviously pleased the Pope as he gave the artist his papal cap and a handkerchief. The Order of Pope Leo XIII was conferred on him, and he was presented with the Papal Gold Medal of Leo XIII as an additional token of the sitter's admiration. At the Paris International Exhibition in April 1900, de László was awarded the Grand Gold Medal for the portrait.

Count Vincent Joachim Pecci (1810–1903) was ordained priest in 1837, consecrated Archbishop of Perugia in 1846, ordained cardinal in 1853, and in 1878 succeeded Pope Pius IX as Leo XIII. The twenty-five-year-long papacy of this successful international diplomat has been called brilliant. He is known also for his advanced thinking on questions of socialism and modern biblical study.

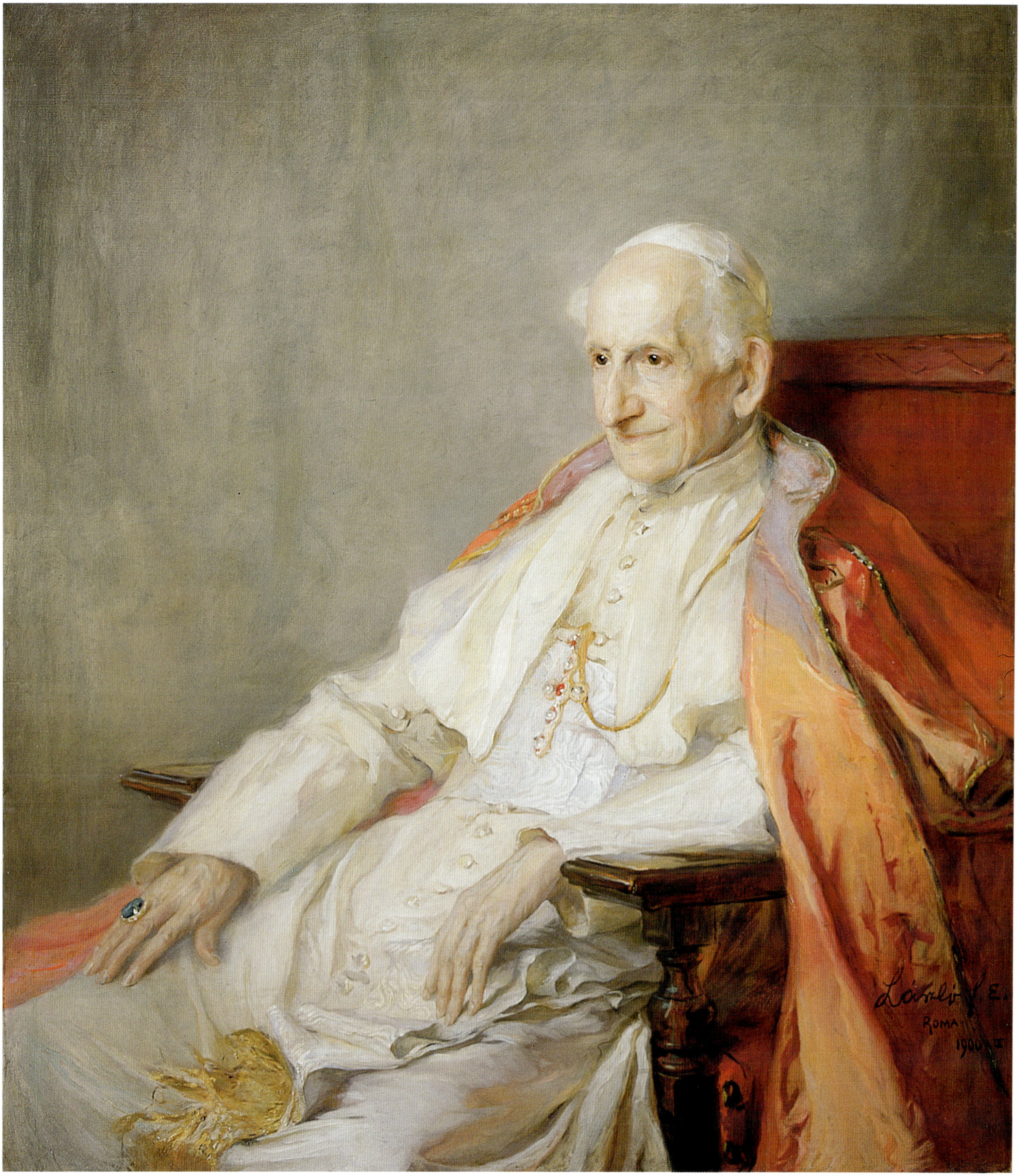
ROMA
1900

19 Cardinal Mariano Rampolla 1900

Oil on canvas, 110.5 × 94.6 cm (43½ × 37¼ inches)
Inscribed and dated, upper left:
MARIANUS CARDINALIS RAMPOLLA / DEL TINDARO.ANNO IUB MCM.
Hungarian National Gallery, Budapest

PROVENANCE Donated by the artist in 1929

EXHIBITED *International Exhibition*, The Paris Salon, 1900; Venice Biennale, April 1901, p.24, no. 15, pl. p.64; Künstlerhaus, Vienna, 1902; International Exhibition, Düsseldorf, 1903; *Jahresausstellung*, Munich, 1903, MALEREI, László, Fülöp, Kat. 663; *International Society's Exhibition*, 1904; *Portrait Paintings and Drawings by Philip A. László*, The Fine Art Society, London, May–June 1907, no. 35: *H.E. Cardinal Rampolla*; The Royal Hibernian Academy of Arts, Dublin, 1909, no.105: *H.E. Cardinal Rampolla*; *Autumn Exhibition*, Liverpool, 1912, no. 207: *His Eminence Cardinal Rampolla, oil. No price*; *Paintings by Philip A. de László*, Corcoran Gallery of Art, Washington, February–March 1921, no.27, *His Eminence Cardinal Rampolla (Late Cardinal Secretary of State to His Holiness Pope Leo XIII)*; *Paintings by Philip A. de László*, M. Knoedler & Co., New York, April 1921, no. 7: *His Eminence Cardinal Rampolla (Late Cardinal Secretary of State to His Holiness Pope Leo XIII)*; *XIX Biennale d'arte di Venezia 1934*, Venice, p.94, no.484: *Il Cardinale Rampolla*

LITERATURE ASB, Vol.I, p.37: *M. Card. Rampolla del Tindaro / (Rom. 1 Avr./ III. 24)*; *Új Idök* , 'Fülöp László in the Vatican', Yr. 7, no. 9, 24 February 1901; Robert de Montesquiou-Fezansac,'Un portraitiste lyrique, Philipp Laszlo', *L'Art et les artistes*, II, 15 June 1906, p.94; Schleínitz 1913, p.42, pl.46; Williams 1921, pp.29–32, ill. facing p.28; *The Graphic*, 24 January 1925, p.122; *Painting a Portrait*, 1934, p.54, ill. (detail of hands only), p.55, pl.XXII; Rutter 1939, pp.185, 186, 190–5, 196, 198, 199, 200–1, 203, 204, 233

Cardinal Rampolla del Tindaro (1843–1913), the Papal Secretary of State, was instrumental in the arrangements for de László's portrait of Pope Leo XIII (cat. 18). At the request of the Hungarian Minister of Arts and Education, Julius Wlassics, de László then painted the Cardinal himself.

Williams wrote of this painting: "The whole picture is conceived in the grand style. Seated erect in his chair of state, the Cardinal, clad in his splendid robes, confronts the spectator squarely and uncompromisingly. As a colour-harmony of rich reds and crimsons, emphasised by the black ribbon of the only decoration the Cardinal, as Grand Master of the Knights of Malta, always worn, it challenges the eye. The brilliant sheen of the watered silk of the cape, against the soft fold of the lace soutane, is an admirable example of László's mastery of technique. But inherent in the dignity of the setting as a whole as these accessories may be, they do not distract the attention from the face .... The interest is from the first focused on the face in the high light, while the figure and setting are put back into the shadow. The impassive face, the firm-set mouth that seems to suppress a smile almost of arrogance, and the steady, watchful glance exercise a curious fascination. The characteristic droop of the right eyelid over the blind eye enhances the enigmatic, sphinx-like expression of the strong face."

De László had a great admiration for Velázquez, and although there is no record of de László having seen Velázquez's masterly, and Machiavellian, portrait of Pope Innocent X (fig. 58) while he was in Rome, it is tempting to assume that he was influenced by it in his rendition of the face and character of the Cardinal. De László believed that it was important to observe character in his sitters' hands, and this detail of the Cardinal's portrait was chosen for discussion by A.L.Baldry in the book *Painting a Portrait*. He writes: "The Cardinal was physically a man of large frame, but mentally he was exceedingly subtle, and he had hands that belonged to his mind rather than his body. De László, recognizing this, dwelt specially on them, and his arrangement of the portrait gave them particular prominence. When he came to the painting of them he asked the sitter to put them in the position in which they appear in the picture and to keep them without moving as long as possible; the Cardinal remained absolutely still for an hour and in that time they were

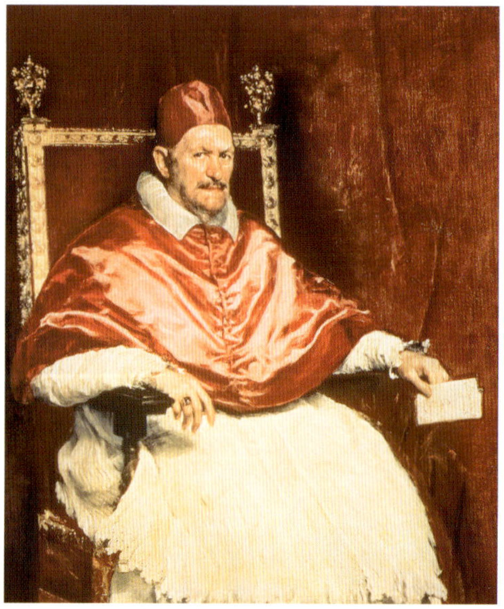

FIG. 58 Diego Velázquez
Pope Innocent X, 1650
Oil on canvas, 141 × 119 cm
Galleria Doria Pamphilj, Rome

finished." De László considered them the best hands he had ever painted.

The portrait of the Cardinal received much praise, winning the Gold Medal awarded by Austrian Government at the Künstlerhaus exhibition in Vienna in 1902 and the special gold medal at Düsseldorf the following year.

Rampolla had been elected Cardinal in March 1887 and became Foreign Secretary to Pope Leo XIII three months later. A controversial and powerful figure in the Vatican, he incurred the displeasure of the Emperor Francis Joseph through his opposition to a Catholic burial for Crown Prince Rudolf, who committed suicide in 1889. Moreover, he was a supporter of the nationalist ambitions of the Slavs in the Austrian Empire, and sanctioned the morganatic marriage of the new heir apparent Francis Ferdinand to a Bohemian countess. On the death of Leo XIII in 1903, Rampolla's hopes of succeeding him were crushed by an Austrian veto.

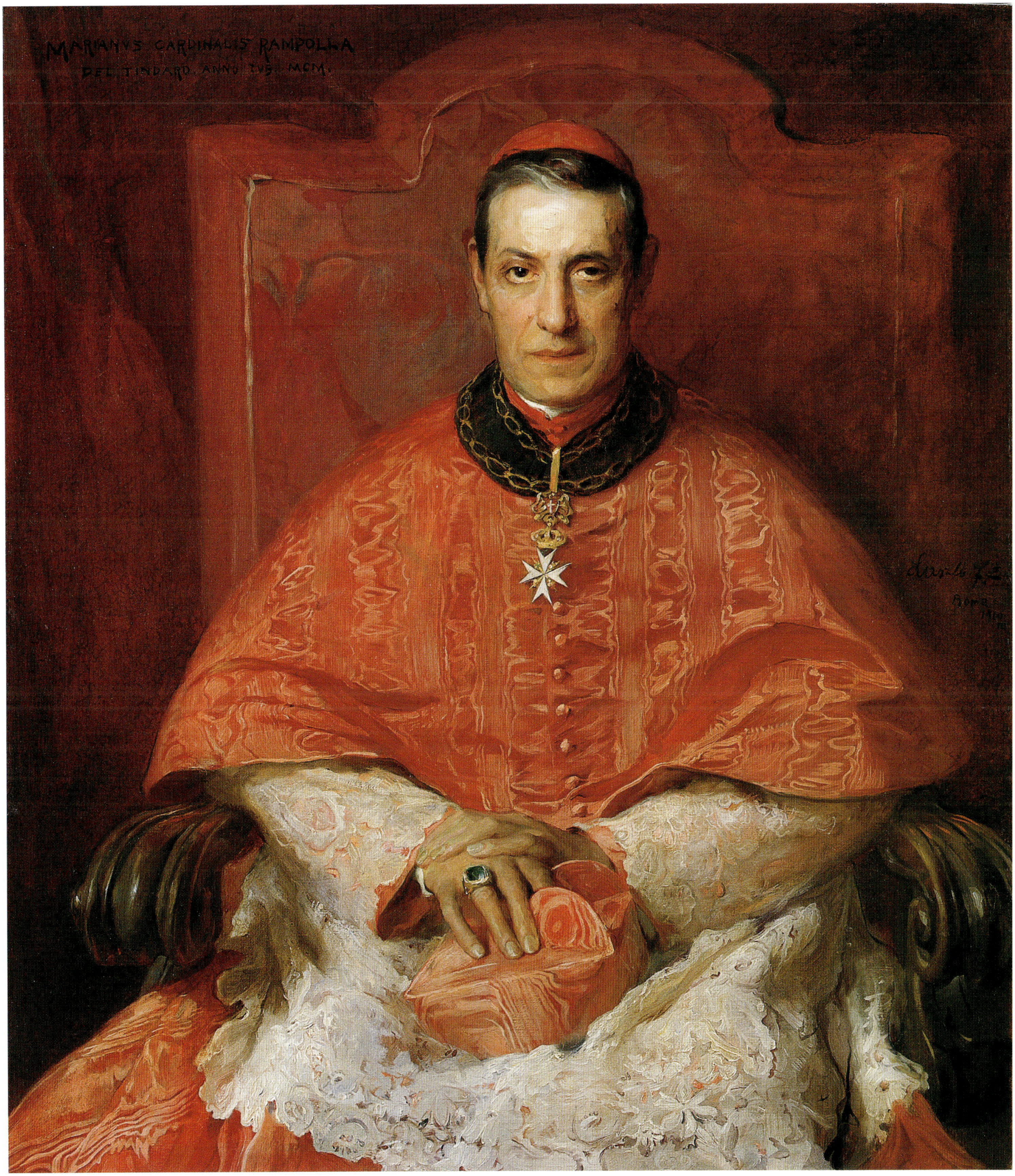
MARIANVS CARDINALIS RAMPOLLA
DEL TINDARO ANNO SVO MCM

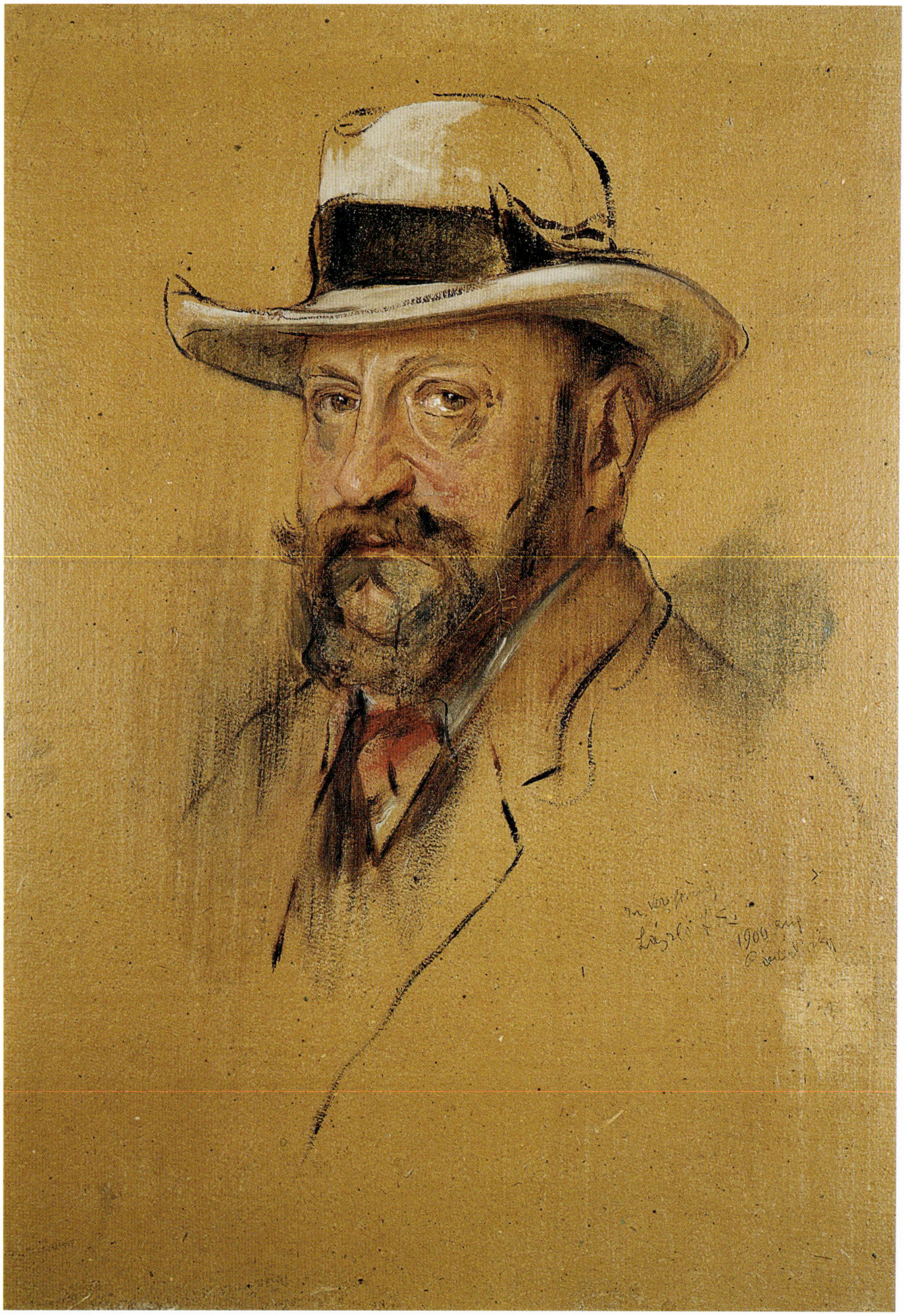

20 Sir Ernest Cassel 1900

Oil on board, 68.6 × 48.3 cm (27 × 19 inches)
Signed and dated, lower right: *László F.E. / 1900*
PROVENANCE Mrs Edward Jenkins, the sitter's niece; Marjorie, Countess of Brecknock, daughter of Mrs Jenkins
EXHIBITED *Portrait Paintings and Drawings by Philip A. László*, The Fine Art Society, London, May–June 1907, no.48: *Sir Ernest Cassel*
LITERATURE ASB, Vol.I, p.34: *E Cassel 2 Mars 1900*; Rutter 1939, pp.202, 209

In June 1900 de László married Lucy Guinness, but their honeymoon in the Lake District was interrupted by a command from Queen Victoria to paint General Sir George White, who had recently returned from the Boer War. Soon after, they received an invitation from Sir Ernest Cassel, whom the artist had met in Rome, to continue their holiday at his home in the Swiss Alps. There de László made this study, which was exhibited at the Fine Art Society exhibition in 1907, and, as a pendant, one of Sir Ernest's sister, Wilhelmina. That same year, during a brief return visit to London, he painted another, very conservative portrait of Sir Ernest. He also made a formal portrait of his daughter, Maud, who married Wilfrid Ashley.

Ernest Joseph Cassel was born in 1852 and died in 1921. The Cassel family were strict Orthodox Jews with a small banking business in Cologne. At the age of sixteen Ernest left for England with only a bundle of clothes and a violin. Just over ten years later, in September 1878, he married Annette, daughter of Robert Thompson Maxwell, becoming a British subject the same day. In 1879 a daughter, Maud, was born. In 1881 his wife died of consumption. His daughter also died of consumption, aged only thirty. Her elder daughter, Edwina Ashley, married Lord Louis Mountbatten in 1922 (cat. 93, 94).

Ernest Cassel had remarkable financial acumen, and was renowned for his absolute honesty and integrity. In England he played the leading role in the construction of the Central

London underground railway, and made a string of acquisitions from which grew Vickers, the foremost armaments manufacturer of the age and the Allies' main arsenal in the Great War. He became financial advisor to King Edward VII, with whom he had established a warm friendship on the racetrack. The king described him as "the cleverest head in England". He was a considerable collector of Old Master paintings, furniture and *objets d'art*, and a talented violinist. It is estimated that in his lifetime he gave away altogether some £2,000,000 for philanthropic causes.

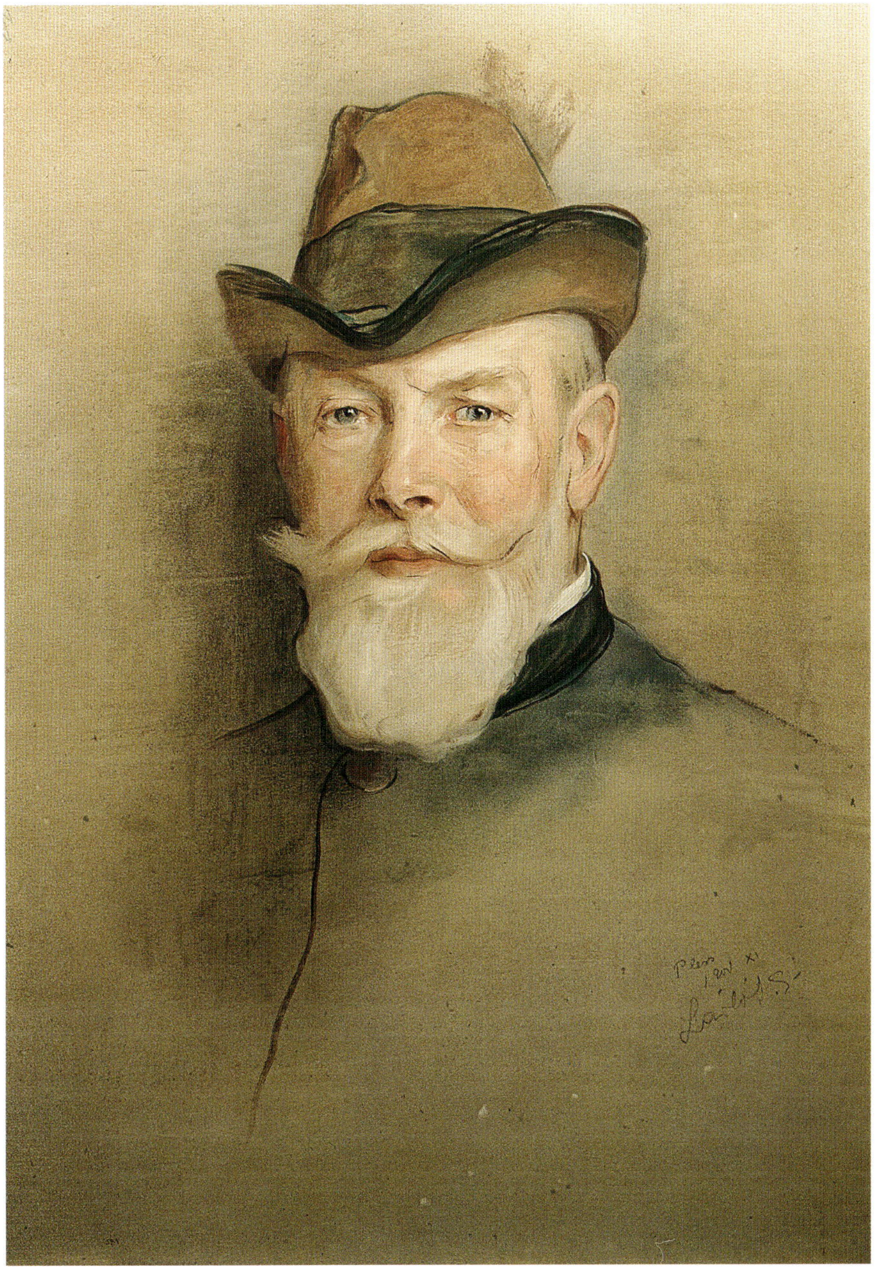

21 Hans Heinrich XI, Prince of Pless 1900

Oil on board, 68.6 × 47.63 cm (27 × 18¾ inches)
Signed, inscribed and dated, lower right:
Pless / 1900 XI / László F.E.
PROVENANCE By descent in the family
LITERATURE ASB, Vol.I, p.49: *Fürst von Ples Pless d.19.xi.1900*

After a short period of settling into the new house he had built for his bride in Budapest (figs. 8, 9, p. 19), in November de László returned to Rome to complete several Vatican commissions resulting from the success of his portrait of Pope Leo XIII (cat. 18). It must be assumed that he fitted in the present portrait, painted in Pless in Silesia, on his way to or from Rome. It ranks among the very finest de László ever painted, both for the sensitive likeness of a very remarkable man and for the quality of the brushwork and palette. De László has portrayed him wearing a Pless hat, which, like the Pless hunting horn, was the sitter's own invention.

Hans Heinrich XI, Fürst und Herzog von Pless, Graf von Hochberg, Freiherr zu Fürstenstein, was born in Berlin in 1833. This distinguished soldier, landlord, courtier, politician, industrialist, educationalist, philanthropist and entrepreneur was the head of an ancient dynasty dating back to the twelfth century whose principality was in the Riesengebirge, Silesia, now part of Poland. His estates were vast and he kept a private army.

His first wife, Marie von Kleist, died in 1883. Their only son, Heinrich, later married Daisy Cornwallis-West, well known for her diaries. In 1886 Hans Heinrich married Mathilde Burggräfin und Gräfin zu Dohna-Schlobitten. They had a son and a daughter.

Hans Heinrich was much beloved, and when Emperor William II made him Duke of Pless in 1905 the act was universally popular. After this he built himself a new palace in Potsdam, but died in Schloss Albrechsberg near Dresden in 1907.

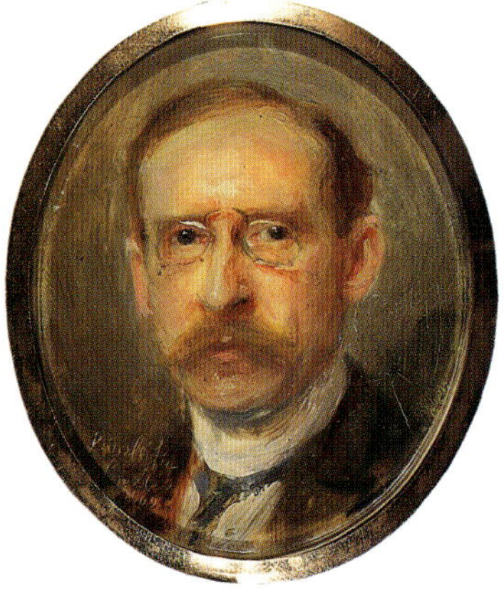

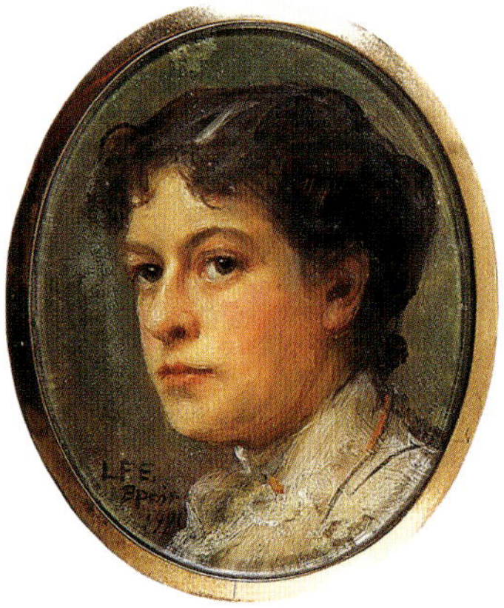

22 Henry Seymour Guinness 1900

Oil on card, 6.4 × 5.1 cm (2½ × 2 inches), oval in a gold frame
Signed and indistinctly inscribed and dated, lower left: *László F.E. / London / 1900*
PROVENANCE By descent in the family

23 Mrs Henry Seymour Guinness, née Mary Bainbridge 1901

Oil on card, 6.4 × 5.1 cm (2½ × 2 inches), oval in a gold frame
Signed, inscribed and dated, lower left: *L.F.E./Bpest/ 1901*
PROVENANCE By descent in the family
LITERATURE ASB, Vol.I, p.4: *M M Bainbridge H.S. Guinness* beneath signature of Field Marshal Sir George White, which is dated 30 June 1900; Rutter 1939, pp.163, 207

Henry Seymour Guinness (1858–1945) was the artist's brother-in-law, his wife Lucy's eldest brother. For sixteen years Henry was in the Government Service in Burma, building the railway to Rangoon. In 1893 his father died and he returned to Ireland, expecting to become the head of the family bank, Messrs Guinness Mahon in Dublin. When his brother Howard, the Senior Director, refused to cede his position, Henry joined the Bank of Ireland, where he worked for many years, becoming Governor twice. During this time he greatly improved and enlarged the estate he had inherited on his father's death together with the family home, Burton Hall. The house was damaged by fire during the Troubles, and by about 1927 both it and the land had been sold. In 1925 he left the Bank after the first Lord Iveagh had invited him to become a director of the Guinness brewery. Before retiring he became a Senator of the Irish Free State Government.

Mary Middleton Bainbridge (1871–1954), was the daughter of K.S. Bainbridge of Co. Durham. Coming from farming stock, farming fascinated her, especially poultry, and, unusually for that date, she took a degree in agriculture at Reading University. She became a Ministry Advisor on animal husbandry, bicycling about the country teaching people how to look after their hens.

Henry and Mary married in November 1900, five months after Philip and Lucy, and took a six-month honeymoon in North Africa and Greece. They had four daughters.

The year 1900 was one of intense activity and constant travelling for de László, and the miniature of Henry must have been painted in June 1900, immediately after de László's own honeymoon, and one of the few times he was in London that year. The miniature of Mary was painted the following May in Budapest as she and Henry were returning from their honeymoon.

24 Mrs Philip de László, née Lucy Guinness 1901

Sepia chalk on paper, 50.2 × 40 cm (19¾ × 15¾ inches)
Signed and dated, lower right: *László F.E. 1901 / IV* and further inscribed, centre right: *LUCY*
PROVENANCE In the possession of the artist on his death; Stephen de Laszlo, his second son
LITERATURE *The Studio*, 1901, XXIV, no.103, pp.16–17, ill.; Schleínitz 1913, p. 62, ill. p.46, pl.52; Rowcliffe 1938, p.136 (no.4)

This drawing was most probably made in preparation for a half-length portrait of Lucy in a very similar pose painted in Vienna in 1902 (fig. 59). It was exhibited to great acclaim at the St Louis International Art Exhibition in

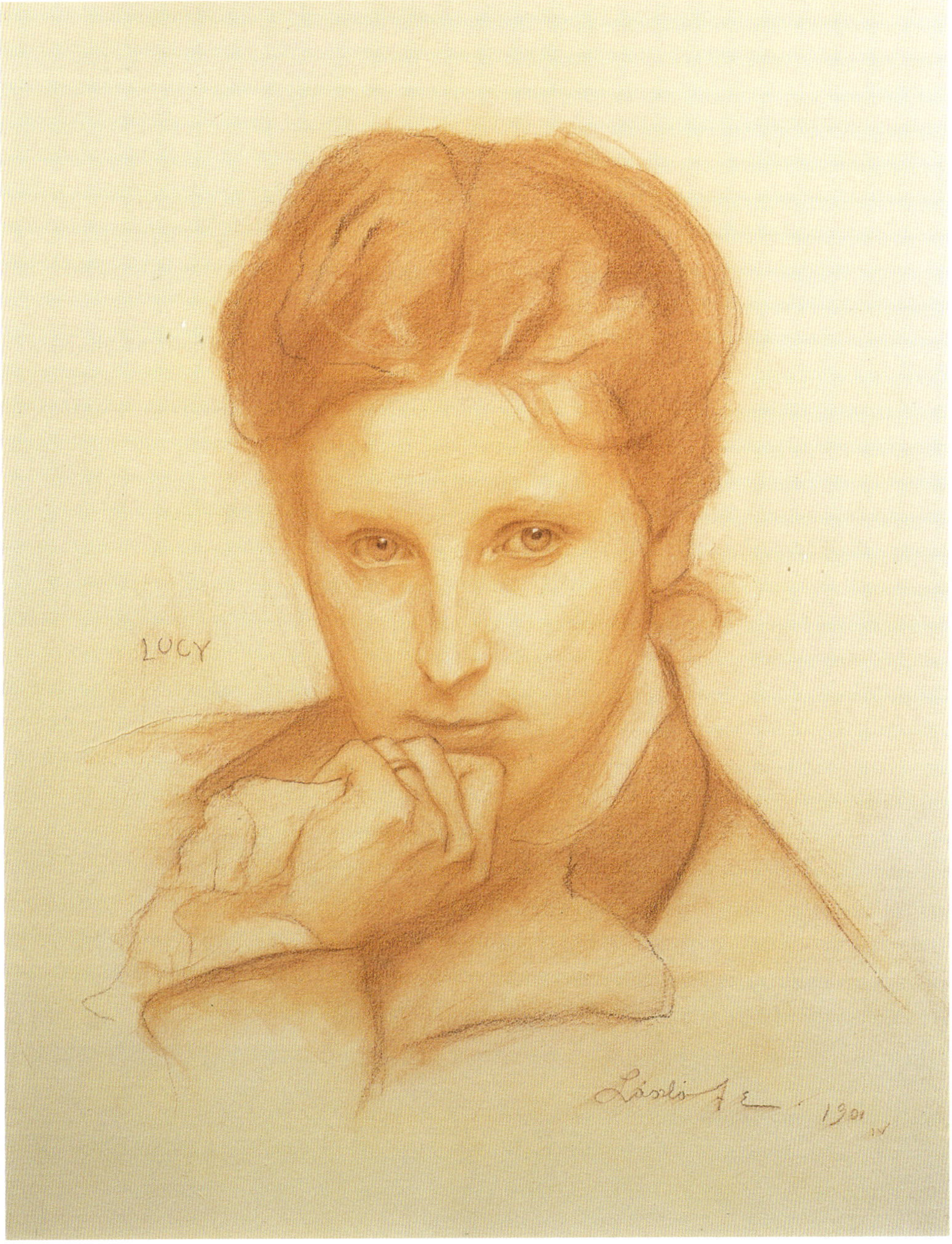

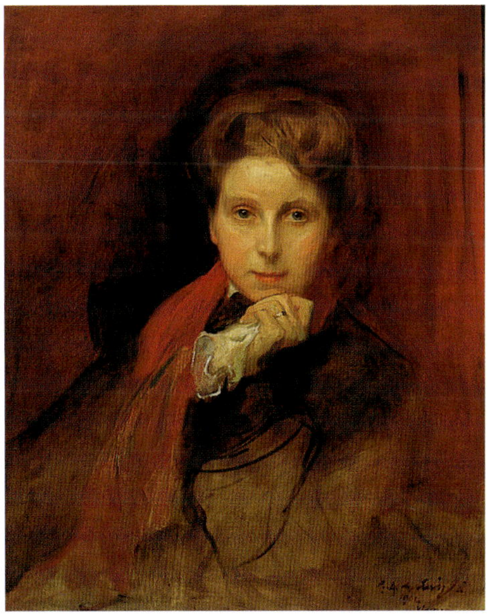

FIG. 59 *Mrs Philip de László*, 1902
Oil on canvas, 73.7 × 58.4 cm (29 × 23 in.)
Private collection, USA

1904, winning a gold medal for de László. A number of lithographs were made from the drawing.

Lucy Madeline Guinness was born on 22 December 1870, the daughter of Henry Guinness of Burton Hall, Stillorgan, Co. Dublin, of the banking firm of Guinness, Mahon and Co. and his wife Emelina (cat. 21). She and her twin brother Noel were the tenth and eleventh of twelve children (see fig. 60, overleaf). In 1892 she met the impoverished young painter in Munich, while travelling on the Continent with her sister Eva. For many years her family opposed their marriage, but on 7 June 1900 she married de László in Stillorgan Church. This drawing was made the following April. Together they had six children, five sons, Henry, Stephen, Paul, Patrick and John, and a daughter, Eva, the second child, who died in infancy. Lucy died in London on 27 December 1950. She is buried with Philip and other family members in Tilford Churchyard, Surrey.

25 Mrs Henry Guinness, née Emelina Brown 1901

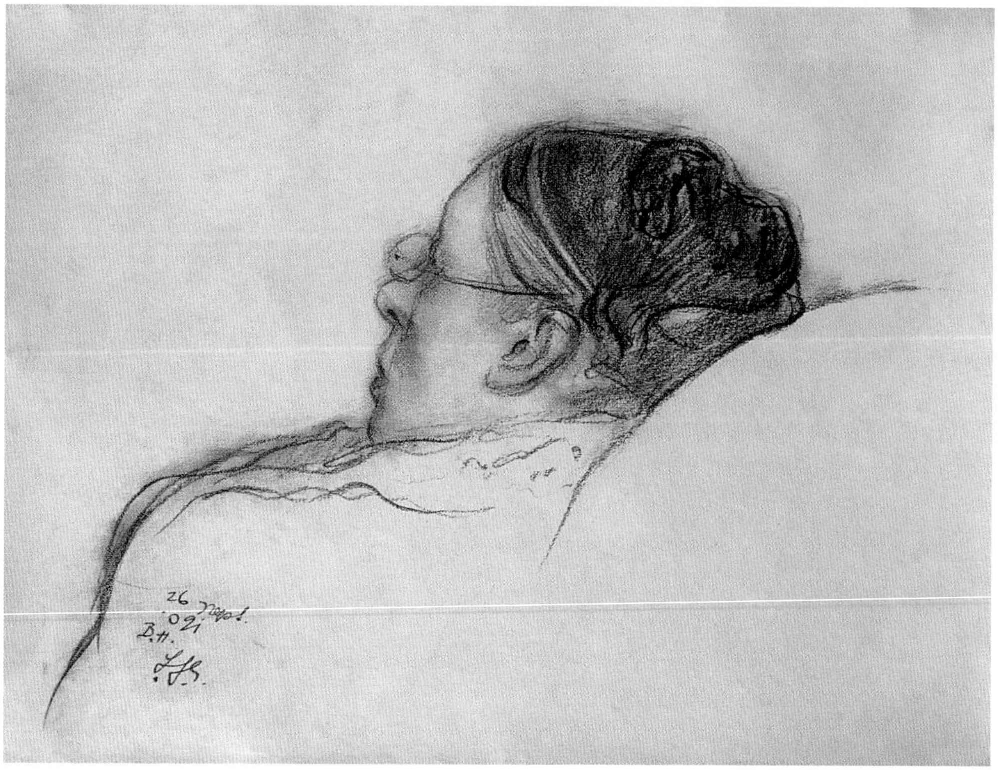

Charcoal on white card, 23.2 × 30.2 cm
($9\frac{1}{8} \times 11\frac{7}{8}$ inches)
Indistinctly dated, inscribed and signed, lower left:
26 Sept / 091 / B.H. / L.F.E.
PROVENANCE Miss Bridget Craig-Brown, niece of the artist's wife and grand-daughter of the sitter

Emelina (Amy) Brown (1829–1906) was the daughter of James Brown of Edinburgh, the supposed illegitimate son of David Ogilvy, 5th Earl of Airlie. She married Henry Guinness in 1858 and together they had twelve children.

Henry Guinness died in December 1893, just under two years after their daughter Lucy had fallen in love with the young de László. His widow described herself as being in "black misery" after her husband's death, and their

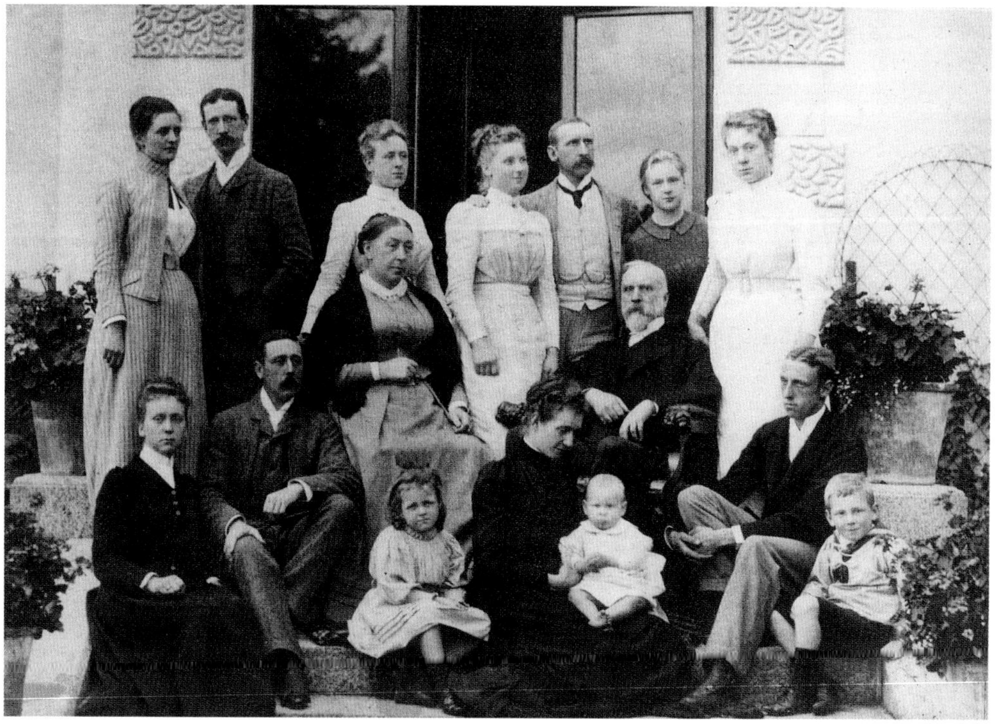

FIG. 60 The Guinness family at Burton Hall, Stillorgan, Co. Dublin, 1890

BACK ROW (left to right): *Mary Alice (May) Guinness (m. Howard Rundell Guinness, 1887), Howard Rundell Guinness, Beatrice Grace Guinness (m. Christopher du Toit, 1911), Lucy Madeline Guinness (m. Philip de László, 1900), Henry Seymour (Harry) Guinness (m. Mary Middleton Bainbridge, 1900), Constance Ellen Guinness (m. Col. Ernest Craig-Brown, 1903), Eva Guinness (never married).*

MIDDLE ROW *Emelina Guinness (née Brown), Henry Guinness of Burton Hall*

FRONT ROW (left to right): *Mary Katherine (Molly) Guinness (m. Capt. John Falls, 1895), Eustace Guinness (m. Isabel Bell, 1898), Evelyn Hill, Ethel Mary Guinness (m. Charles F. Hill, 1885), Constance Emily Hill (on her mother's knee), Richard Noel Guinness (Lucy's twin, m. Mary Stokes, 1894), Cecil Hill*

Of the twelve children of Henry and Emelina, two are missing from the picture: *Amy Henrietta Guinness (m. Edward Wills-Sanford-Wills, 1889); Geoffrey Gwynne Guinness (m. Severine Curutchet, 1886)* declared opposition to the match was continued by Mrs Guinness for some five more years until de László had proved himself worthy of her daughter by his constancy and his artistic successes.

There exists a photogravure of this drawing, which remains in the collection of one of the descendants of the artist. In the inscription *B.H.* refers to Burton Hall, the family home. *L.F.E.* are the artist's initials in the Hungarian manner: *László Fülöp Elek*. As for the date, de László was notoriously imprecise in his writing. Stylistically, the most likely date for this drawing is 1901, the year after Lucy and he were married. Thus it would seem he has used the Hungarian tradition of writing the date without the millennium digit and reversed the numbers 0 and 9.

26 Miss Cassie Falls 1905

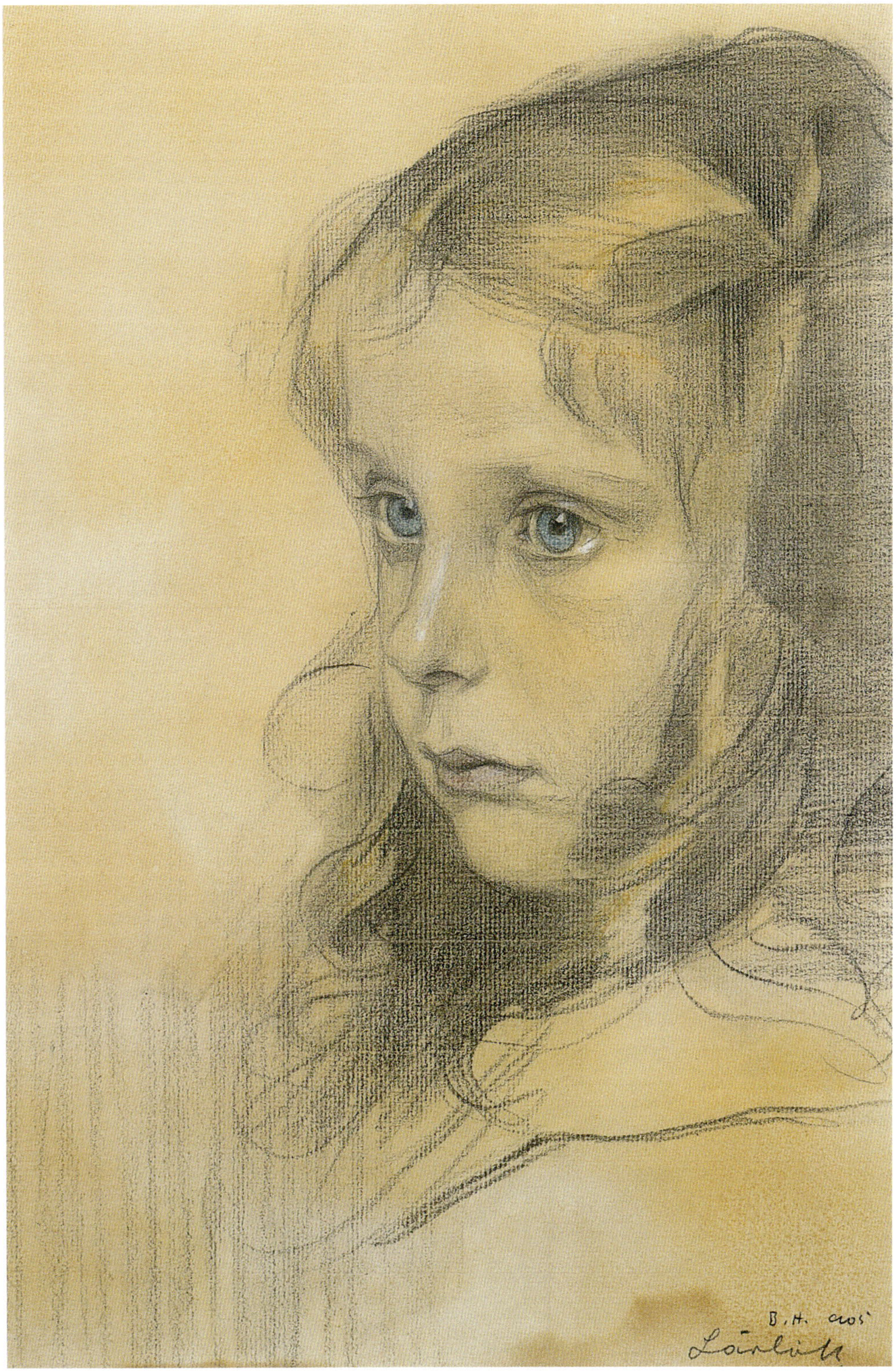

Soft pencil, white and coloured chalks on buff paper, 34.9 × 23.5 cm (13¾ × 9¼ inches)
Signed, inscribed and dated, lower right:
B.H. 905 / László F.E.
Verso: Portrait in terracotta chalk of Henry de Laszlo, eldest son of the artist as a young boy, head only
PROVENANCE In the possession of the artist on his death
LITERATURE Rowcliffe 1938, p.140 (no. 25)

Kathleen 'Cassie' Falls was born in 1899, the daughter of Captain John Falls and Mary Katherine, née Guinness, one of Lucy de László's elder sisters. She died in 1917, aged only eighteen.

De László and his wife were living in Vienna at the time the drawing was made, but during a visit to Burton Hall (*B.H.*) in the late summer of 1905 he made a study of some roses in the garden there, a portrait of his wife (dated September), a family friend, Miss Gerard Little, and the drawing of Cassie.

A number of fine photolithographic or photogravure reproductions were made of the drawing, most of which remained with the descendants of the artist; one was also probably given to Gábor de Térey, a close friend who accompanied the artist to Ireland for his wedding; he bequeathed it to the Hungarian National Gallery.

27 Baroness Emile d'Erlanger, née Catherine de Robert d'Aqueria de Rochegude 1900

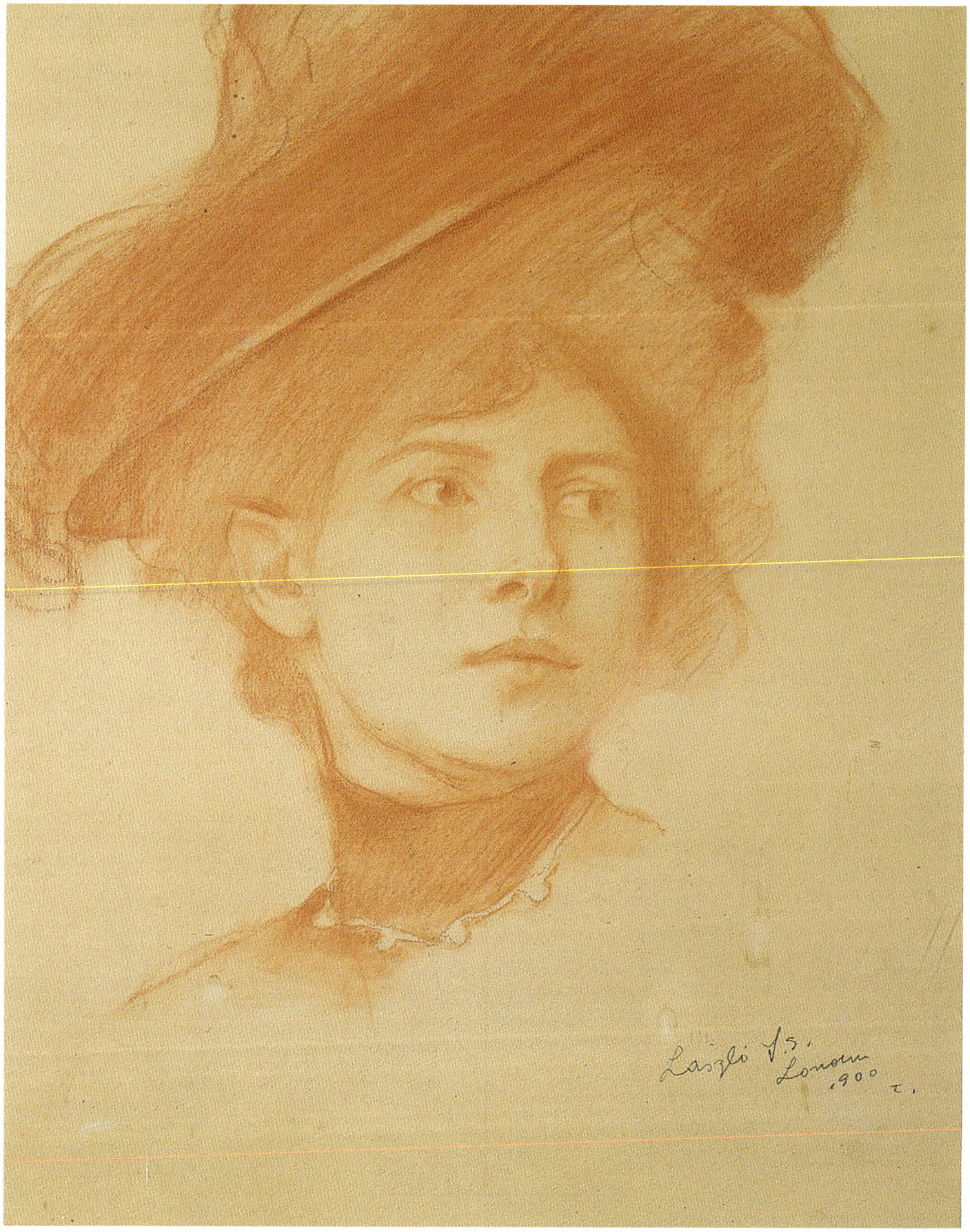

Sepia chalk on paper, 40.6 × 33 cm (16 × 13 inches)
Signed, inscribed and dated, lower right:
László FE / London / 1900

LITERATURE *The Studio*, XXIV, no.103, 1901, pp.14–15, ill.; Rutter 1939, p.181

Catherine ('Mimi') de Robert d'Aqueria de Rochegude, daughter of the Marquis d'Aqueria de Rochegude, was born in Paris in 1874 and brought up in the family château near Orange in Provence. In 1895 she married the financier and railway magnate Baron Emile Beaumont d'Erlanger. They had four children, one of whom died in infancy.

De László had met the d'Erlanger family in Paris in 1899, while carrying out his first commission in France, portraits of Count and Countess Jean de Castellane. There he painted a head study of the Baroness. The present drawing was made in London in 1900, probably during the interruption in his honeymoon (see cat. 20). De László painted two further portraits of the Baroness, in 1905 and 1913. Over the years he also painted several other members of the family, including her husband in 1933.

According to Rutter, the d'Erlangers thought so highly of de László's work that already in 1899 the Baroness had written to Messrs Thomas Agnew & Sons, asking them to exhibit his portrait of the Grand Duke of Saxe-Weimar in their gallery and suggesting that they might be the first to arrange a one-man exhibition for him. This in fact took place in 1907 at the Fine Art Society, but Agnew's held two successful exhibitions of his work in 1911 and 1913.

The couple lived for many years in Lord Byron's former home, 139 Piccadilly, where Baroness Mimi established a famous artistic and musical salon and became indeed one of the great European society hostesses of the first decades of this century. She and her husband were both very supportive of de László during his early career in London, promoting him throughout England. She was also a patron of Diaghilev and the Ballets Russes, and of Cecil Beaton. Perhaps Baroness d'Erlanger's most lasting achievement was her restoration, with her friend Bertie Landsberg, of Palladio's Villa Malcontenta, just outside Venice.

After her husband's death in 1939 she moved to Hollywood, where she lived until her death in 1959.

28 General Arthur de Görgei 1901

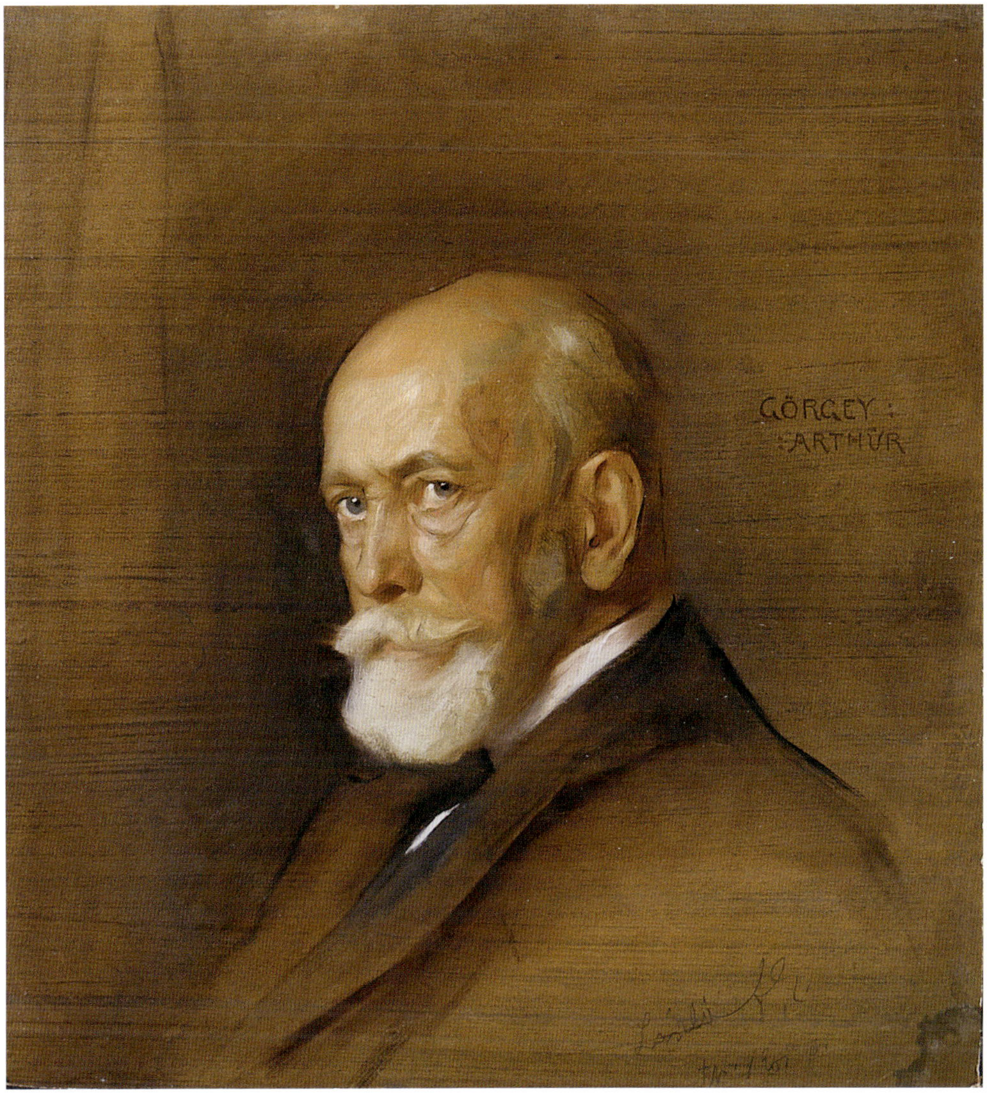

Oil on board, 57.2 × 52.1 cm (22½ × 20½ inches)
Signed, inscribed and dated, lower right: *László F. E. / 1901. III.*, and centre right: *GÖRGEI / ARTHUR*
Private collection, Budapest
LITERATURE ASB, Vol.I, p.50: *Görgei Arthur / Budapest, 1901. február 17. vasárnap* [Sunday 17 February]; Schleinítz 1913, p.23, ill. p.14; Williams 1921, p.37; Rutter 1939, pp.209–10, 233; *Koréh Ferenc beszél New Yorkból* [F. Koréh speaking from New York], published by Viza Kft.,Veszprém, 2001, pp.81–2

This oil study, so similar to the 1901 portrait drawing of the same sitter, is a fine example of de László's startling ability to achieve a consistent likeness and to paint and draw the subject several times over during the same sittings. General de Görgei was depicted five times by de László, and a contemporary copy was made of one of these images. The artist stated in his memoirs that he had painted some 2,700 portraits, which is taken to mean 2,700 sitters. If General de Görgei were a typical example, then his overall output could be calculated at around 13,000 works!

Arthur de Görgei was born in 1818 of a noble Saxon family which had converted to Protestantism and moved to Hungary. After serving in the army he studied chemistry before taking over his father's estates. With the outbreak of the Hungarian Revolution in 1848 he offered his services to Lajos Kossuth's Government. Having inflicted a number of defeats on the Austrians, in March 1849 he was made commander-in-chief of the Army and drove the Austrians out of Hungary. In April Kossuth proclaimed a republic and de Görgei, despite misgivings about the new regime, became Minister of War while retaining command of the Army. The Russian Army now invaded and Kossuth, finding his position impossible, resigned as dictator, to be succeeded by de Görgei, who was still fighting in the field. Two days later, on 13 August, unable to break through the enemy lines, de Görgei surrendered with 24,000 men to the Russians to prevent further bloodshed. He was sent to Klagenfurt in Austria, where he worked as a chemist until he was allowed to return to Hungary in 1867. There, however, the surrender and the fact that he had not even faced a court martial (most of his generals had been executed) had led to accusations of treason and he found no further role in public life. For some years he worked as a railway engineer.

Despite attempts by a large number of his old comrades, rehabilitation and recognition did not come until the turn of the century, when his State pension was restored and de László's three-quarte-length seated portrait of the general was bought by the Hungarian Government for 6,000 florins. It now hangs in the National Museum in Budapest. The present portrait de László gave to his sitter.

De László clearly admired the general. In a letter to his sister de Görgei wrote: "Most of [de László's] time is taken up with my portrait; it is his firm intention that it should become one of his most successful works …". In another letter he describes how he usually sat for de László until around 11 a.m., because the artist preferred the morning light. "Every day

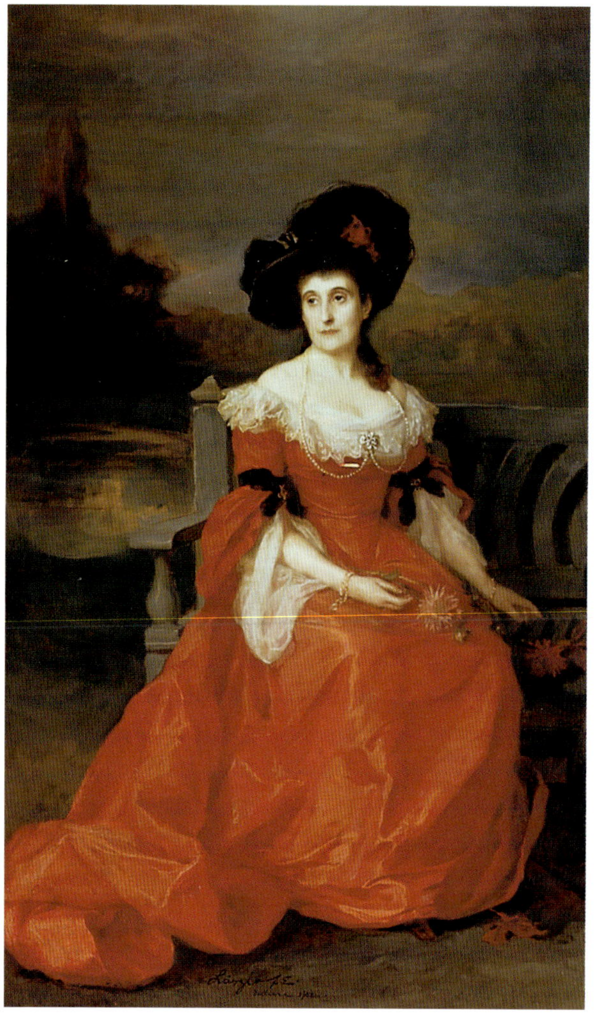

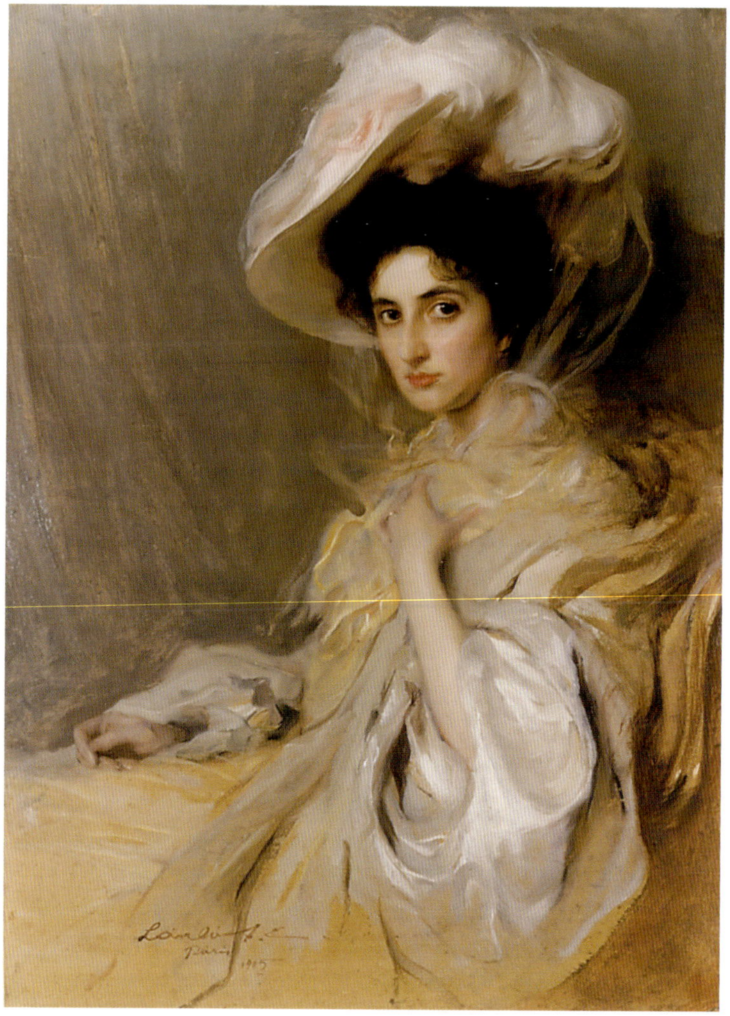

LEFT FIG. 61 *Marguerite Alexandrine, duchesse de Gramont, née de Rothschild*, 1902
Oil on canvas, 215.9 × 127 (85 × 50 in.)
Musée Basque, Bayonne

RIGHT FIG. 62 *Elaine, duchesse de Guiche, née Greffulhe*, 1905
Oil on board, 103.5 × 77.5 cm (40¾ × 30½ in.)
Private collection, Paris

he finds something new in my facial expression. It is amazing to see in this man the strictness of his self-criticism allied to his untiring zeal for work .... The deficiencies are seen only by his eye ...". In Rutter's words, "... de László made no use of the trappings of uniform and orders. He painted the General in the sombre frock-coat of the private citizen, thus directing the attention of the dignity of that wise old face with the keen eyes under their white brows."

General de Görgei died in 1916, aged ninety-eight.

29 Antoine XII-Armand, duc de Guiche 1902

Oil on board, 73.7 × 48.3 cm (29 × 19 inches)
Inscribed, dated and signed, lower left:
Souvenir amicale/de Vallière 1902 / XII / 9 László F.E.

PROVENANCE By descent through the family

LITERATURE ASB, Vol.I, p.60: *Armand de Gramont, duc de Guiche*, together with other signatures dated 1902; Robert de Montesquiou-Fezansac, 'Un Portraitiste Lyrique, Philipp Laszlo', *L'Art et les artistes*, II, no. 15, June 1906, pp.100–1, ill. 100, labelled: *Portrait de M. le Duc de Guiche / D'après l'étude de Philipp LASZLO*; Rutter 1939, pp. 210, 278, 282, 353, 355, 390

The de Gramont family were among de László's most considerable patrons, and he painted some twenty portraits of three generations of the family over the years 1902 to 1931. He painted Armand on at least seven occasions, twice in 1902, in 1909, in 1913, twice in 1922 and in 1931. The present portrait was painted during de László's first visit to château Vallière, the de Gramont family home, where he went at the request of the sitter's father, Antoine XI-Agenor, 11th duc de Gramont, to paint a pair of large family group portraits. De László later divided these two into six individual portraits as his patron wanted to hang a tapestry in their place. The portrait of Marguerite, Armand's mother, née de Rothschild (fig. 61), was one of the six resulting canvases.

Antoine-Armand de Gramont, duc de Guiche (1879–1962), originally intended to become an artist. At the turn of the century he mixed with the artistic community of Paris and counted among his friends Jacques-Emile Blanche, Marcel Proust and the portrait painter Giovanni Boldini. Since studying in Paris in 1890 de László had been part of this circle and in time the two entered into a lifelong friendship. Armand lent de László his studio in the Avenue Henri-Martin, where he painted many distinguished portraits over the years. In 1904 Armand married Elaine Greffulhe (fig. 62), only daughter of Henri, comte Greffulhe and of Elisabeth, princesse de Caraman-Chimay, the ubiquitously talented doyenne of Parisian arts and society at the turn of the century. They had four sons and a daughter. Armand eventually decided to pursue a scientific career, becoming an eminent physician and later founding L'Institut d'Optique in Paris in 1916, as a result of which France became the leading nation in optical research for many years. He succeeded his father as 12th duc de Gramont in 1925. In 1931 he was elected to the Académie des Sciences and became its President in 1956.

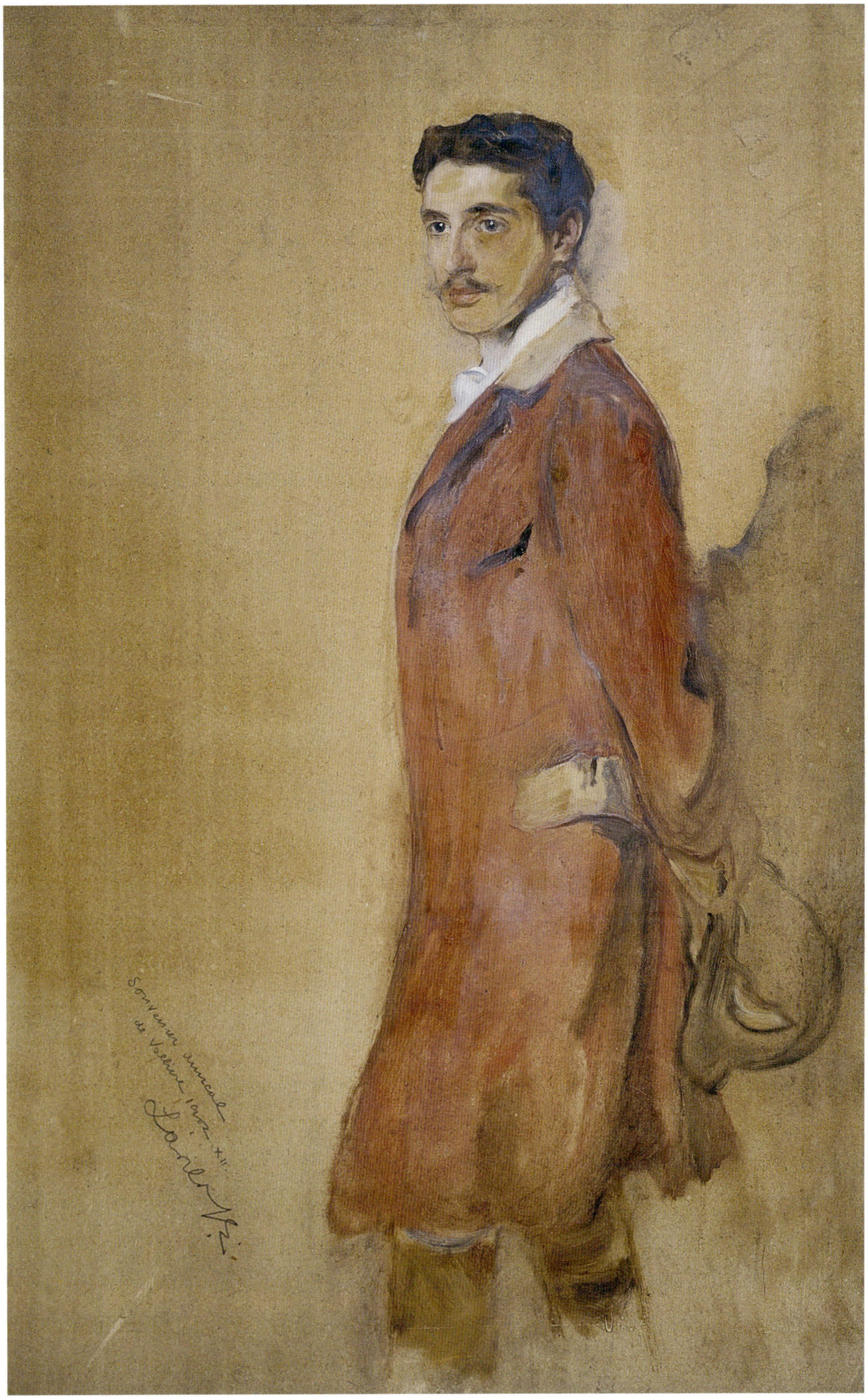

30 Jan Kubelik 1903

Oil on canvas, 71.1 × 57.8 cm (28 × 22¾ inches)
Signed and dated, upper left: *P.A. László / 1903*
PROVENANCE In the possession of the artist on his death; Patrick de Laszlo, his fifth son
EXHIBITED *Portrait Paintings and Drawings by PhilipA. László*, The Fine Art Society, London, May–June 1907, no.40: *Kublik*
LITERATURE Schleínítz 1913, p.80, ill.p.58; Williams 1921, p.45; Rutter 1939, pp.219–20, 225; Clifford, 1969, monochrome ill. pl.17

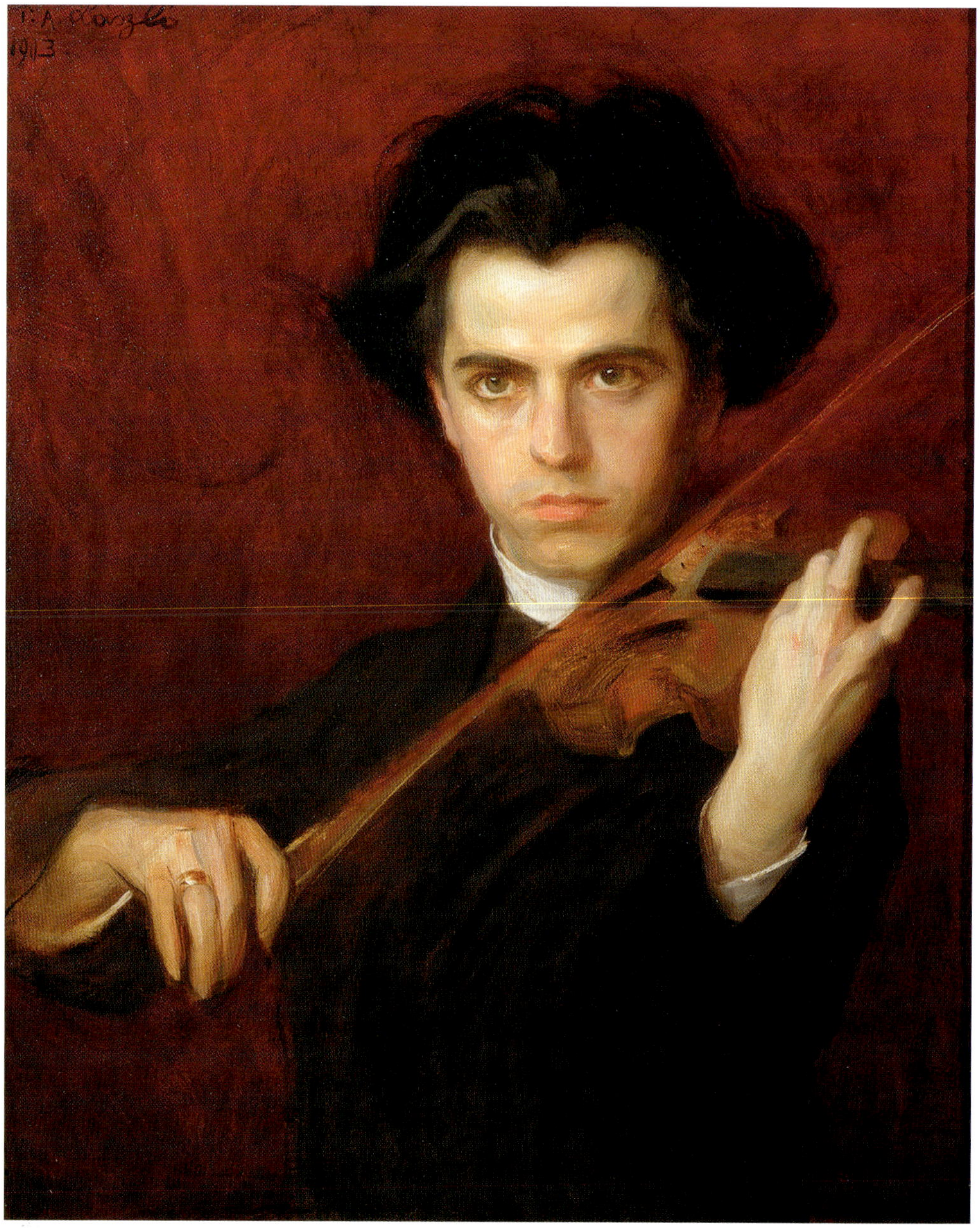

Jan Kubelik (1880–1940) was one of the greatest violinists of his time. De László and his wife, herself a talented violinist, first heard Kubelik play in Vienna in 1903, soon after they had moved there, and they met often afterwards before de László made this portrait of him. They were also friends with the other giant among violinists of the day, Joseph Joachim, whom de László painted twice in 1900. In 1905 he made a portrait of Lucy with her violin of which Williams wrote: "A great violinist has pointed out that the angle at which the violin is held, and the touch of the fingers on the strings, make this, like László's portrait of Kubelik, one of the few pictures of a violinist playing his instrument, not as the painter would have it played, but as the musician knows it can only be played."

Kubelik was born near Prague, the son of a gardener. His father, a talented amateur, started his elder son on the violin at seven but soon found that five-year-old Jan was keener, and after six months a better player, than his father. At the outset of his career in 1898 he was hailed as 'a second Paganini' and in 1900 he made his debut in London. With a good manager and an astute agent masterminding his career from Budapest, there began a decade of triumphs that earned him vast wealth. In 1903 he married Countess Marianne Czáky-Szell and acquired an estate in Silesia, where he spent as much time as he could with his rapidly increasing family (they had five daughters, all violinists, and three sons including the conductor Rafael).

Kubelik's performances dazzled his audiences, his dark looks and slim build enhancing his technical brilliance. In the years before World War I, however, his popularity began to wane, and he became the victim of a number of unlucky business speculations. By 1915 he had retired to concentrate on composition and had six concertos, a symphony and a number of shorter works published. In 1920 he resumed his concert career, touring around the world and once again filling the concert halls in Britain and New York.

31 Professor Johann Nepomuk Oser 1904

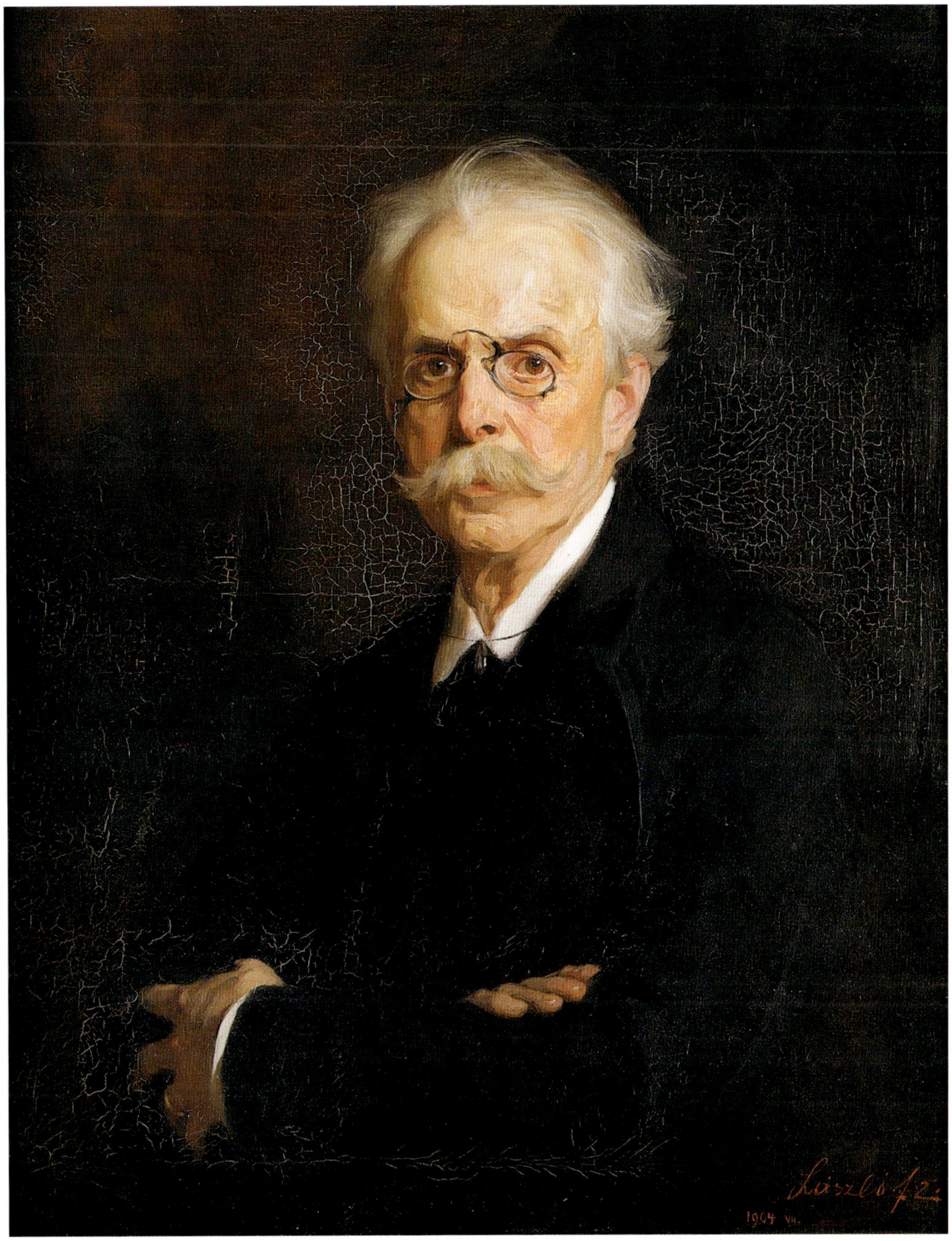

Oil on canvas, 85.1 × 66 cm ($33\frac{1}{2}$ × 26 inches)
Signed and dated, lower right: *László F.E. / 1904 VII*
PROVENANCE Lydia Oser-Wittgenstein, youngest daughter of the sitter
LITERATURE ASB, Vol. I, opp. p. 49: *Dr. Johann Oser* [undated but on a page with other signatures dated 1900]; Rutter 1939, p.221

Johann Nepomuk Oser was born in 1833. His father was a forestry commissioner; his mother was of farming stock and learnt to cook in one of the large monasteries near Grafenegg. Johann was educated at the monastery school of Melk on the Danube and later studied at the Academy of Forestry in Mariabrunn near Graz. He also obtained a doctorate in philosophy at Graz University and then studied chemistry in Paris. He returned to Mariabrunn as Professor of Chemistry, transferring in 1876 to the Polytechnical High School for Inorganic Chemistry in Vienna as Professor, Dean of the Chemistry School, and later as Rector. According to his granddaughter, behind a fierce face hid a very gentle and sociable person who enjoyed hunting and parties afterwards.

In September 1872 Johann married Josephine Wittgenstein, the daughter of Hermann Wittgenstein from Leipzig. The sitter's brother-in-law, Karl Wittgenstein, the father of the philosopher Ludwig and the pianist Paul, had gone into the steel business with the Kupelweiser family (cat. 94). His house in Vienna contained works by Klimt and other leading artists of the day (he was honorary president of the Vienna Sezession), and regular visitors included his cousin Joseph Joachim (whom de László painted in 1903), Brahms, the young Pablo Casals and Bruno Walter. With this circle the newly married de Lászlós first became acquainted in 1900. Already that year de László painted Frau Oser (private collection), a portrait admired by the Emperor when it was exhibited at the Künstlerhaus. He later painted Karl Wittgenstein's wife (destroyed) and, according to Ludwig Wittgenstein's biographer Brian McGuinness, Karl himself, though this portrait remains untraced. The present work was painted in 1904 as a pair to the portrait of Frau Oser. The sitter died in 1912.

32 The Artist's Mother 1904

Soft pencil and black and sepia wax crayon on yellowing white card, 42.5 × 27.9 cm (16¾ × 11 inches)
Indistinctly inscribed, signed and very indistinctly dated in pencil, lower right: *My mother / Bad Königssee / 1904 ...Pest / Laszlo / 12*, and very faintly lower right: *Lucy*, and just visibly half cut off at bottom of card: *My mother* (both in pencil)
Verso, indistinctly inscribed in pencil on dark brown paper: *..Ilonkának* [for Ilonka] / *Fülöp... / London / 1912, Juni 11*

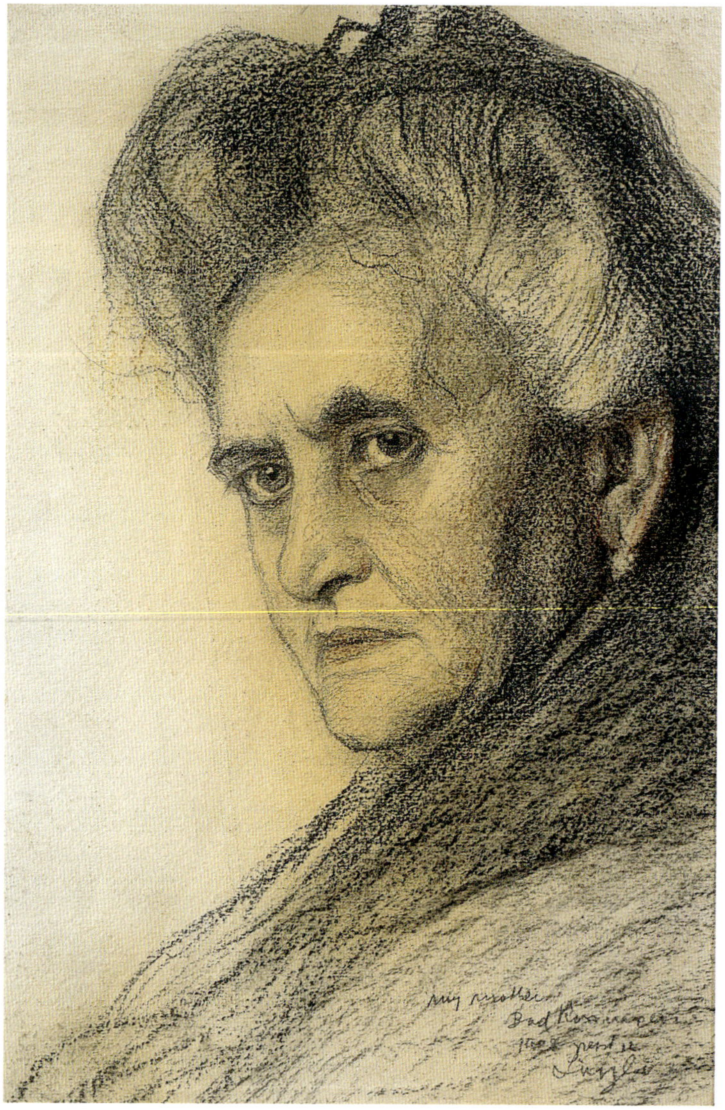

De László was devoted to his mother, Johanna, as she was to all her children, taking a central role in their lives. She was evidently of exceptional character, a strict Catholic, strong and noble in spirit, and very capable. By contrast, her husband Adolf was a somewhat shadowy figure in the young de László's life. In one of the few references he made to him, de László describes him as "the tyrant, the man who never respected his wife or children", and it was his mother's brother Philip Balogh who took a fatherly interest in the boy's welfare and talents. Adolf ran a small business, apparently as a lady's tailor, but not a very successful one; his wife helped him with the work. One of de László's first memories was a fireside scene, while he sat beside his mother during the short winter afternoons as she made garments for the family on her sewing machine.

When he became successful, de László took great trouble to provide for his family and particularly his mother. In the summer he would send her to a resort such as Bad Königssee, in southern Bavaria near Salzburg, where this drawing was made in 1904. De László signed the drawing again in Budapest in 1912 and inscribed it to his favourite niece, Ilonka Krämer, the daughter of his sister Rózsa.

From the end of 1903, until they moved to London in 1907, de László and his family were living in Vienna (cat. 30) and during this 'Vienna period' his mother visited them quite frequently. After the death of her husband, in about 1906, Johanna went to live with her daughter Rózsa in an elegant flat provided for them by the artist in a six-storey apartment building that he had bought. Philip would write frequently from London to his mother and other Hungarian relations, even in wartime, risking his liberty in doing so. Johanna died quite unexpectedly in 1915 in Budapest after a short illness.

33 An Indian Prince 1906

Oil on canvas, 83.8 × 50.8 cm (33 × 20 inches)
Signed, lower right: *P.A. László / Wien / 1906 II*
PROVENANCE The Corcoran Gallery of Art, Washington, D.C., given by the artist in 1921; 'deaccessioned' in 1979
EXHIBITED Annual exhibition, Royal Society of British Artists, 1908, *Study of an Indian*, £300; Renwick Gallery, Washington, D.C., 1971–9

It has not so far been possible to identify the sitter in this portrait, which was painted in Vienna in February 1906. The following year de László and his family moved to London, taking the painting with them. It was exhibited at the Royal Society of British Artists in 1908, the year de László was elected member. Although it remained unsold, from the price of £300 quoted for this painting in the catalogue, it seems that de László was commanding prices more than double those of his contemporaries. At that time he was charging up to £600 for a full-length portrait.

Elinor Glyn (cat. 55) was fascinated by the portrait, referring to it in a letter to de László as "your weird Indian prince" and suggesting that a study of her face and hair coming out of the darkness would make a perfect pendant. The portrait remained with the artist until 1921, when he gave it to the Corcoran Gallery in Washington, probably for the exhibition of his works held there to herald his arrival in Washington to paint President Harding. The link with the Corcoran Gallery continued over a number of years. De László was lent a studio at the Corcoran Museum during his visit to paint President Hoover and his wife in the winter of 1931–2.

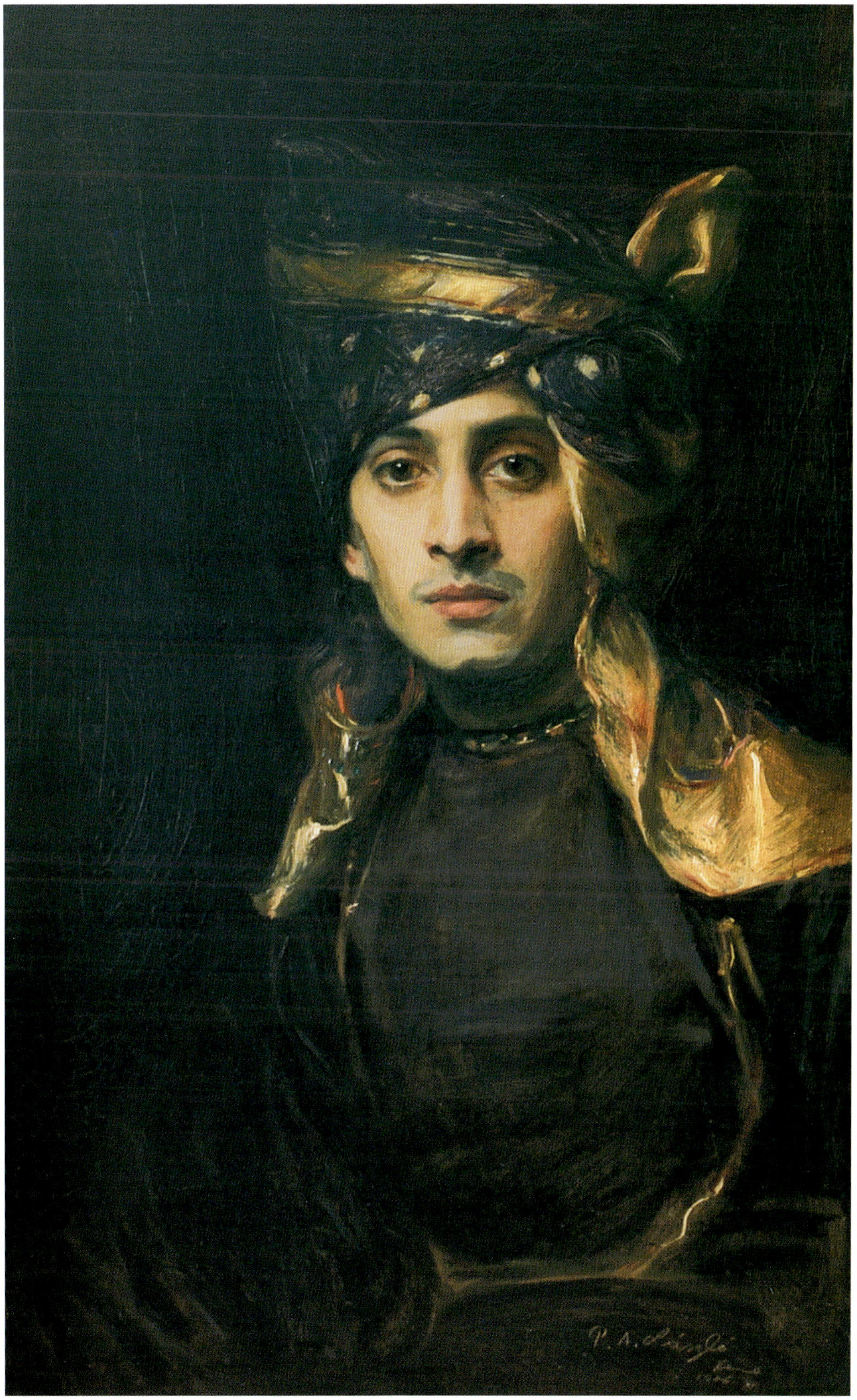

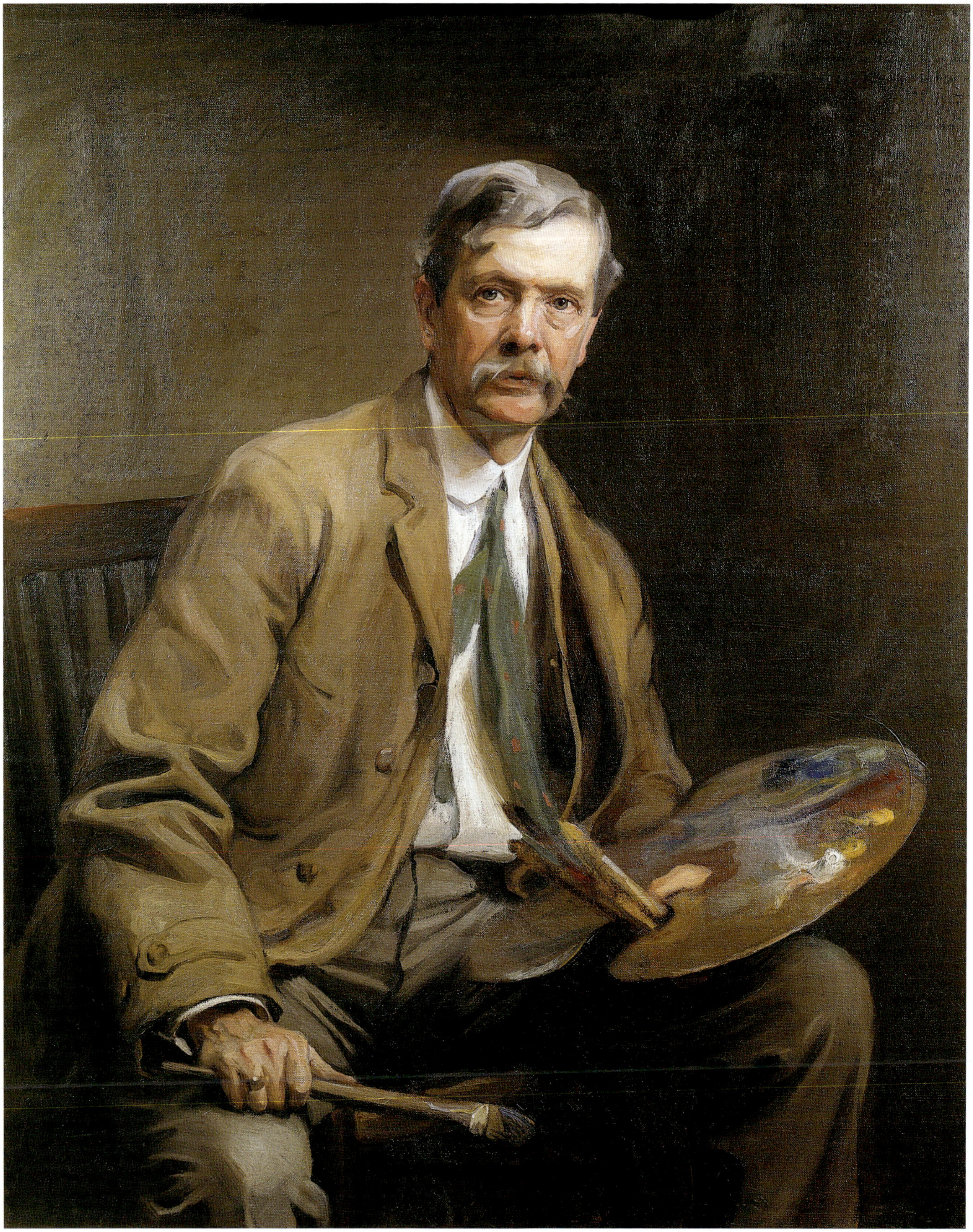

34 Alfred East, A.R.A., P.R.B.A 1907

Oil on canvas, 120.7 × 94.9 cm ($47\frac{1}{2} \times 37\frac{3}{8}$ inches)
Signed, inscribed and dated, upper right: *In great admiration / to Alfred East / P.A. László / 1907 / London*
EXHIBITED *Autumn Exhibition*, Liverpool, 1907, no.1057, ill. p.123: *Alfred East, Esq. A.R.A., P.R.B.A., 48 × 38 / P.A. de László*; Paris Salon, 1908, *hors concours*, no.1023, p.94, ill.p.94: *Portrait d'Alfred East, A.R.A.*; *Winter Exhibition*, Royal Society of British Artists, 1909, no.66: *Alfred East, Esq., P.R.B.A., A.R.A.*; *Spring Exhibition*, Leeds Museum and City Art Gallery, 1910, no.43a: *Alfred East, Esq., P.R.B.A., A.R.A.* (no selling price); Royal Society of British Artists, 1937, no.353: *Sir Alfred East, R.A., P.R.B.A.*
LITERATURE *The Studio*, 1908, XLIV, p.134; Schleínitz 1913, ill. pl.85, pp.72, 102; Rutter 1939, pp.246, 263; Sir Alfred East, *Brush and Pencil Notes in Landscape. Thirty reproductions from water-colour sketches, and twenty-nine from sketches in pencil; with an introduction by Edwin Bale and a portrait frontispiece by P. A. de László*, London (Cassell) 1914, ill. frontispiece

According to Schleínitz, "When László came over to England the most outstanding contemporary portrait painters must have come to his attention. Among these I name above all John S. Sargent, Hubert von Herkomer, J.J. Shannon, John Lavery and the very promising and talented William Orpen. However, László's most intimate friend among the artists is Sir Alfred East, known for his attractive and atmospheric landscapes."

The present portrait was painted in East's studio and given to him by de László as a token of his admiration. In December that year de László and East travelled to St Ives together, where de László made some of his first landscape studies since his student days (cat. 32) and, under East's tuition, his first (and indeed only known) etching (fig. 63). In 1911 he painted the sitter's youngest daughter, Mildred, and later presented the picture to her as a wedding present.

Alfred East was born in 1849. He studied at the government school of art in Glasgow and then at the Ecole des Beaux-Arts and the Académie Julian in Paris. On his return from France, East lived in Glasgow for a while, before moving to London. He travelled regularly and visited Japan in 1889.

A Dewy Morning, painted at Barbizon, was his first work exhibited at the Royal Academy, in 1883. He went on to exhibit regularly at Burlington House, with the Society of Painter-Etchers and with the Royal Society of British Artists. He became President of the RBA in 1906, a post to which de László was elected in 1930, succeeding Walter Sickert. East often exhibited abroad and earned many distinctions, among them the gold medal at the Paris exhibition in 1900. In that same exhibition de László won the gold medal for his portrait of Pope Leo XIII (cat. 18). East excelled at landscape painting and etching. He was elected A.R.A. in 1899, knighted in 1910, and elected R.A. in 1913, a few months before his death. He was also an honorary member of several foreign art societies and academies and was made Cavaliere of the Crown of Italy for his services for the Venice international exhibition of 1903.

In 1874 East married Annie Heath. They had one son and four daughters. He died in London in 1913.

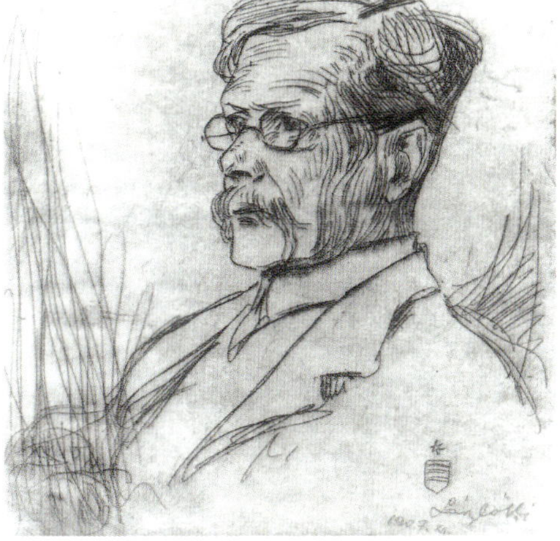

FIG. 63 *Sir Alfred East*, 1907
Etching, 15.2 × 10.2 cm (6 × 4 in.)
Untraced

35 Moored Ships in the Harbour at St Ives 1907

Oil on panel, 32.4 × 40 cm ($12\frac{3}{4} \times 15\frac{3}{4}$ inches)
Signed, inscribed and dated, lower left: *St. Ives 1907 XII / P.A. de László*
PROVENANCE In the possession of the artist on his death; the artist's widow; by descent in his family
LITERATURE Clifford 1969, ill. p.13, pl.II.: *St. Ives. 13 × 16"*

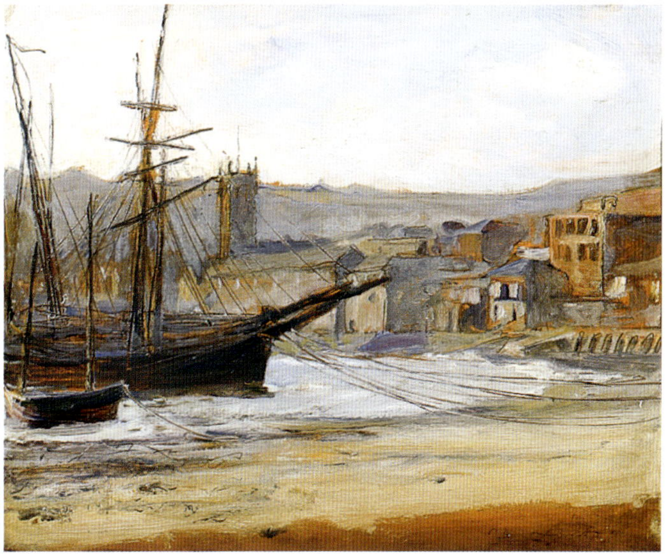

36 H.R.H. Princess Andrew of Greece, née Princess Alice of Battenberg 1907

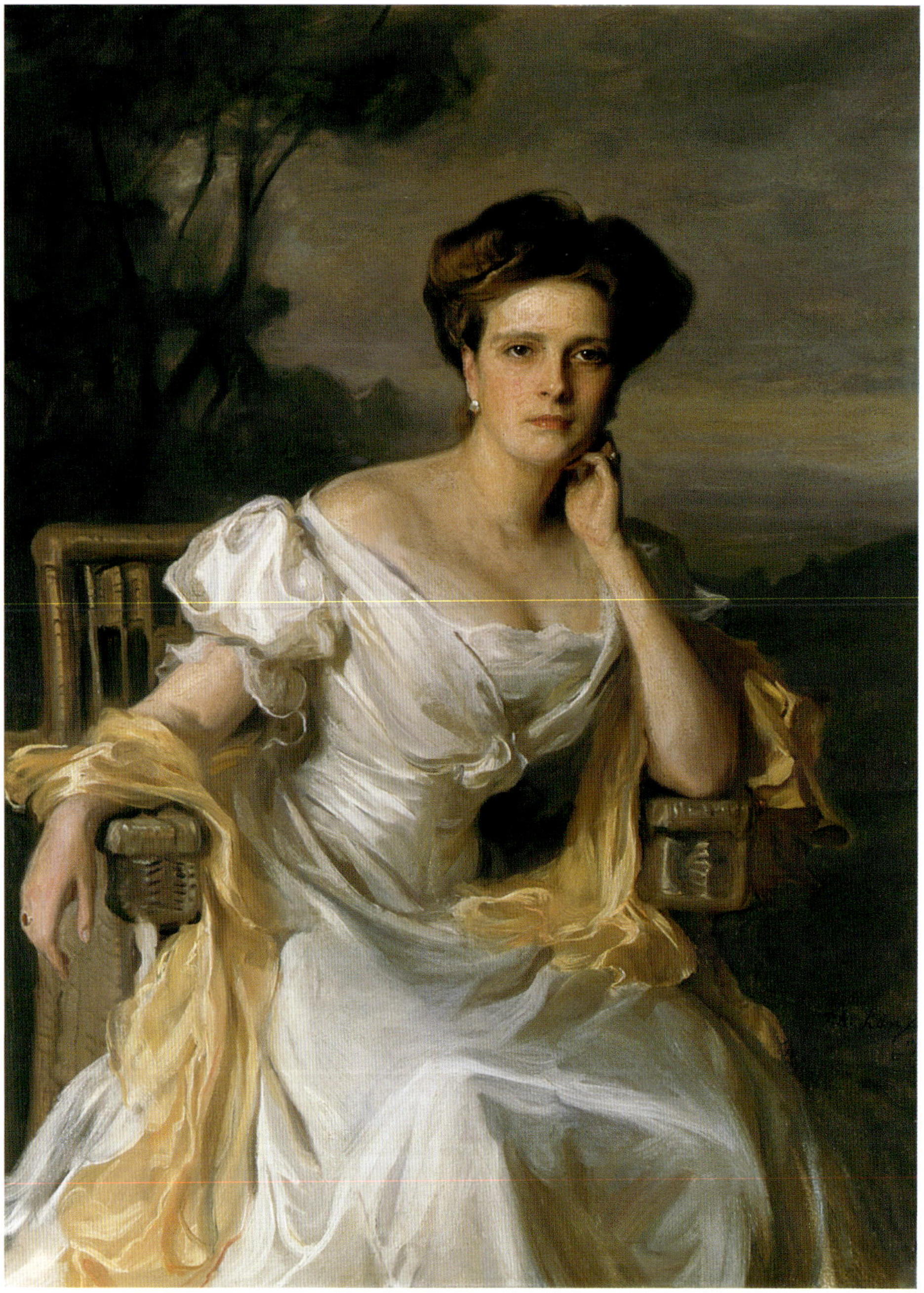

Oil on canvas, 130.5 × 95.3 cm (51⅜ × 37½ inches)
Signed and dated, lower right: *P.A. László 1907. VII*
His Royal Highness The Duke of Edinburgh
EXHIBITED *An Exhibition of Portraits by Philip A. László*, Dowdeswell Galleries, London, June–July 1908, no.23: *HER ROYAL HIGHNESS THE PRINCESS ANDREW OF GREECE*
LITERATURE ASB Vol.I, p.78: *Alice / Prinzessin Andreas von / Griechenland*, directly under that of her husband, dated July 1907; Schleínítz 1913, ill. p.82, pl.98; Williams 1921, p.65; Rutter 1939, p.246; Richard Hough, *Louis and Victoria, the First Mountbattens*, London 1974, ill. the portrait in progress in the artist's studio, pp.202, 203; Hugo Vickers, *Alice, Princess Andrew of Greece*, London 2000, pp.78, 179, 187–8, 197, 198, ill. front cover and spine (detail)

Princess Victoria Alice Elizabeth Julia Marie of Battenberg was born in 1885, the eldest child of Prince Louis of Battenberg (cat. 40) and Princess Victoria of Hesse-Darmstadt, a granddaughter of Queen Victoria. Alice was born at Windsor Castle, with the Queen present at her birth, and brought up in England, Darmstadt and Malta. She was apparently quite deaf from birth, but learned to lip-read remarkably well, and in several languages. In 1903 she married Prince Andrew of Greece (cat. 34). They had four daughters and a son, Philip, the present Duke of Edinburgh.

Soon after painting King Edward VII in 1907, de László was invited to stay at the Heiligenberg, the family home of Princess Alice's grandfather, Prince Alexander of Hesse, set in the hills above Darmstadt, to paint her portrait. De László began sketching on 15 July and finished the portrait five days later. Through modesty Alice made her younger sister Louise sit in her place when the artist was doing her knees, though in the portrait these are covered by the dress. It is told that, during his visit, de László entertained the household singing Hungarian songs with the famous singer Conny Pauer.

Princess Alice's life was marked by wars, revolutions and long periods of exile. She was deeply affected by the murder of her beloved Aunt Ella (Grand Duchess Elizabeth) during the Russian Revolution and by the turmoil of Greek politics throughout the first quarter of the century. Eventually she and her husband separated and she became a religious. She emerged for her daughter-in-law's coronation in 1953, "a contrast", in Cecil Beaton's words, "to the grandeur, in the ash-grey draperies of a nun". She died at Windsor in 1969.

37 H.R.H. Prince Andrew of Greece 1913

Oil on canvas, 103.8 × 78.4 cm (47⅞ × 30⅞ inches)
Signed, inscribed and dated, lower left: *P A de László / London . 1913. XI*
His Royal Highness The Duke of Edinburgh
EXHIBITED *Royal Portraits by Philip A. de László* M.V.O., M. Knoedler & Company Inc., London, 27 November–8 December 1934, no.5: *His Royal Highness Prince Andrew of Greece, brother of H.R.H. Prince Nicholas*
LITERATURE ASB Vol.I, p.94: *Andrew / Prince of Greece Nov. 7th 1913 London;* NPG 1913–15 Album, p.14; *The Illustrated London News*, 1 December 1934, p.868, ill.: *Uncle to the Bride: H.R.H. Prince Andrew of Greece. Younger brother of Prince Nicholas of Greece;* Rutter 1939, pp. 283, 286, 289; David Duff, *Hessian Tapestry*, London 1967, ill. facing p.320; Hugo Vickers, *Alice, Princess Andrew of Greece*, London 2000

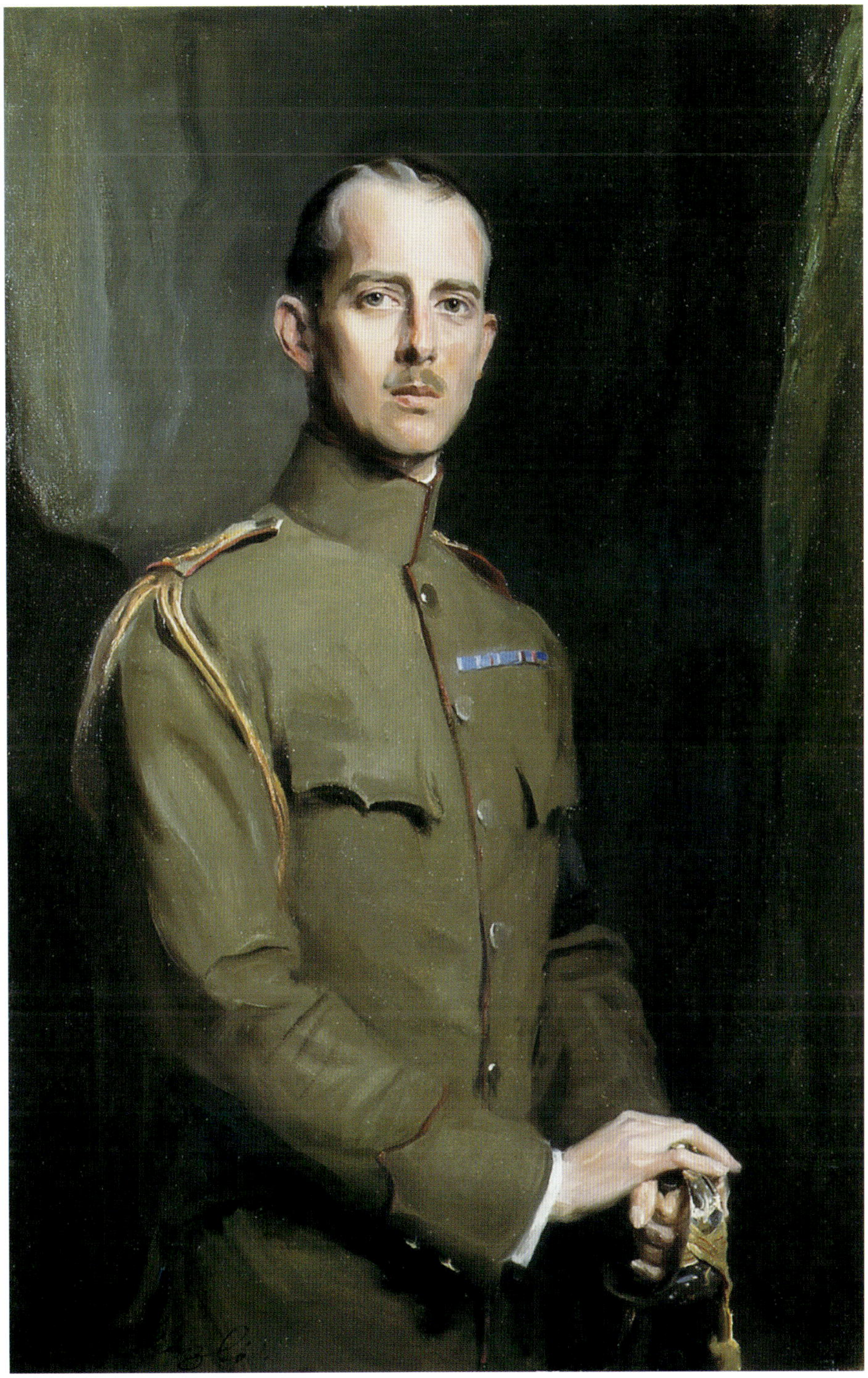

Five years after painting the sitter's wife (cat. 33), de László painted the portrait of Prince Andrew in the uniform of a Colonel of the Greek Cavalry.

H.R.H. Prince Andrew of Greece, G.V.C.O. (1882–1944), was the fourth son of King George I of the Hellenes, the brother of Queen Alexandra, and his wife Olga (cat. 54), grand-daughter of Tsar Nicholas I. He was a tall, impressive looking man: Princess Alice told her grandson the Prince of Wales that on her first sight of him in London in 1902 she found "He was exactly like a Greek god". Of all his brothers and sisters he was the one who most identified with Greece, even speaking Greek to his parents. From an early age he was prepared for a military career and he saw front-line action in the First Balkan War in 1912. The present portrait was painted in London in November 1913, while Prince Andrew was there with his wife, who was to be decorated by King George V with the Royal Red Cross "in recognition of her services in nursing the sick and wounded among the Greek soldiers during the recent war".

Following the overthrow of King Constantine (cat. 56) in 1917, Prince Andrew was dismissed from the Greek Army. In 1922, after the defeat of Greece in the war against Turkey and the military coup that led to the exile of the king for the second time, Prince Andrew was arrested and risked execution. He was released on the intervention of King George V and Lord Curzon. He drifted apart from his wife, dying in Monte Carlo in 1944.

38 The Rt Hon James Lowther M.P. 1907

Oil on board, 78.7 × 52 cm (31 × 20½ inches)
Signed, dated and inscribed, lower left:
To Mrs Lowther / 1907 XII / P.A.László / Hutton John
The Treasurer and Masters of the Bench of the Inner Temple
PROVENANCE Speaker's Hall in Westminster
LITERATURE ASB, Vol.I, p.79: *James W. Lowther / Hutton John Penrith, Dec 18 / 07*; Schleínitz 1913, p.106; Rutter 1939, p.247; Hugh Owen, *The Lowther Family*, Sussex 1990, ill. p.398, pl.99

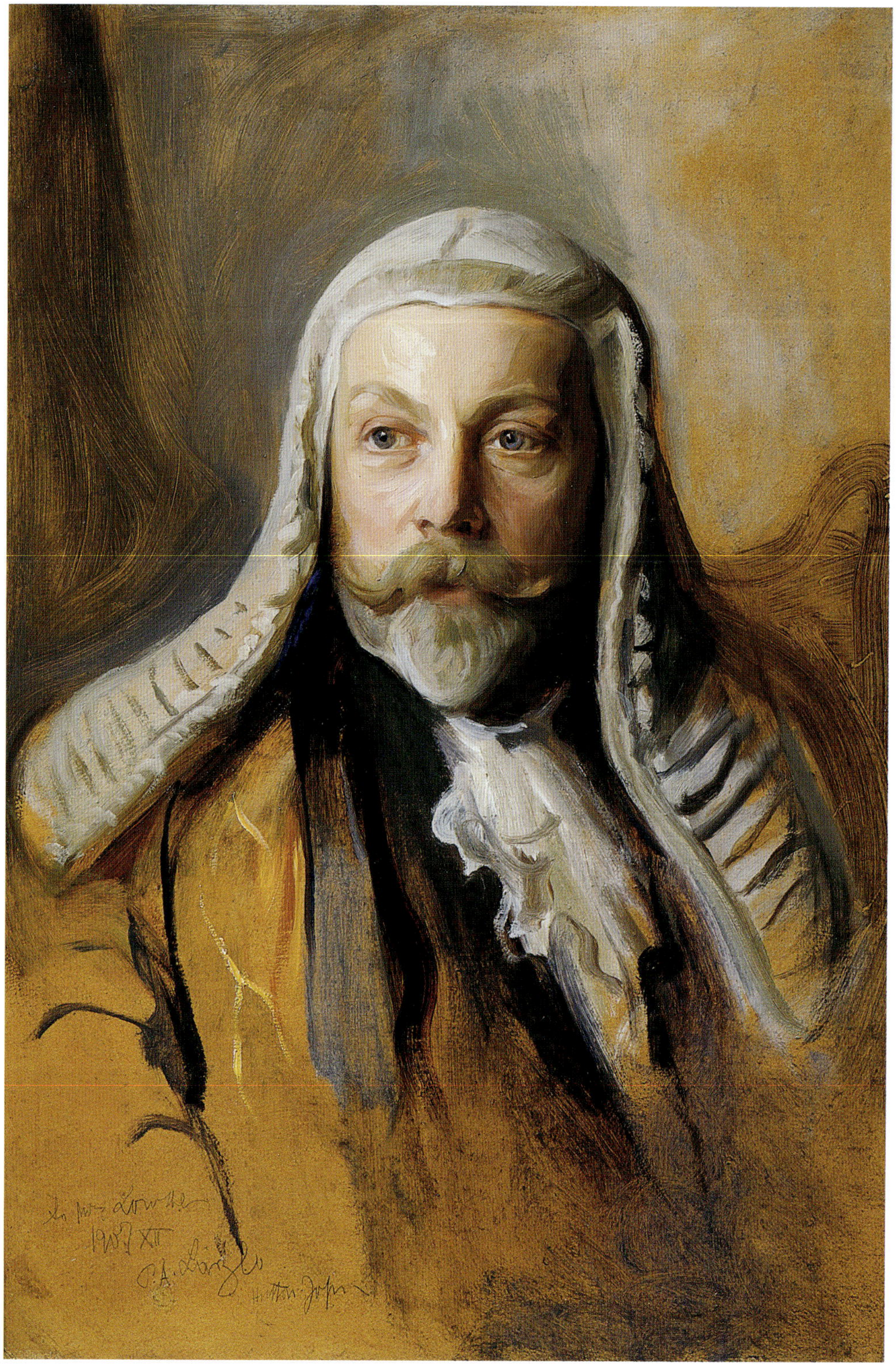

De László's arrival in London from Vienna in May 1907 was marked by an exhibition at the Fine Art Society attended by King Edward VII and Queen Alexandra. This resulted in the King commissioning de László to paint him, the Queen (figs. 26, 27, p. 36) and Princess Victoria (National Portrait Gallery), and a flood of commissions followed. Among these was one to paint James Lowther, the Speaker of the House of Commons. Although it was painted at their home, Hutton John near Penrith, and dedicated to Mrs Lowther, the portrait was destined for the Speaker's Hall in Westminster and now hangs in the Inner Temple, of which Lowther was a Bencher.

De László was introduced to Lowther through Arthur Lee (later Viscount Lee of Fareham), whom de László himself had only met and painted recently, but who was to become one of de László's closest friends and a great promoter of his art (cat. 88).

James William Lowther (1855–1949) was Conservative M.P. for Penrith from 1886 to 1921 and Speaker of the House of Commons from 1905. He was created Viscount Ullswater in 1921. De László carried out two paintings of Speaker Lowther, the present portrait and in 1908 a three-quarter-length portrait for the Grand Jury Room of the Courts in Carlisle. An unsigned and undated preparatory oil sketch on board for the latter was in the artist's collection at his death.

39 The Baronesses Dorothee and Marga Schröder 1908

Oil on board, 101.6 × 76.2 cm (40 × 30 inches)
Signed, inscribed and dated, upper left: *DOROTHE / MARGA*; lower right: *P.A. László / 1908*
PROVENANCE Baron Bruno Schröder; Baroness Marga Schröder; Mr and Mrs John Schroder
EXHIBITED *An Exhibition of Portraits by Philip. A. László*, Dowdeswell Galleries, London, June–July 1908, no.7: *BARONESS D. AND M. DE SCHROEDER.*
LITERATURE Schleinitz 1913, p.112, ill. p.87, pl.103

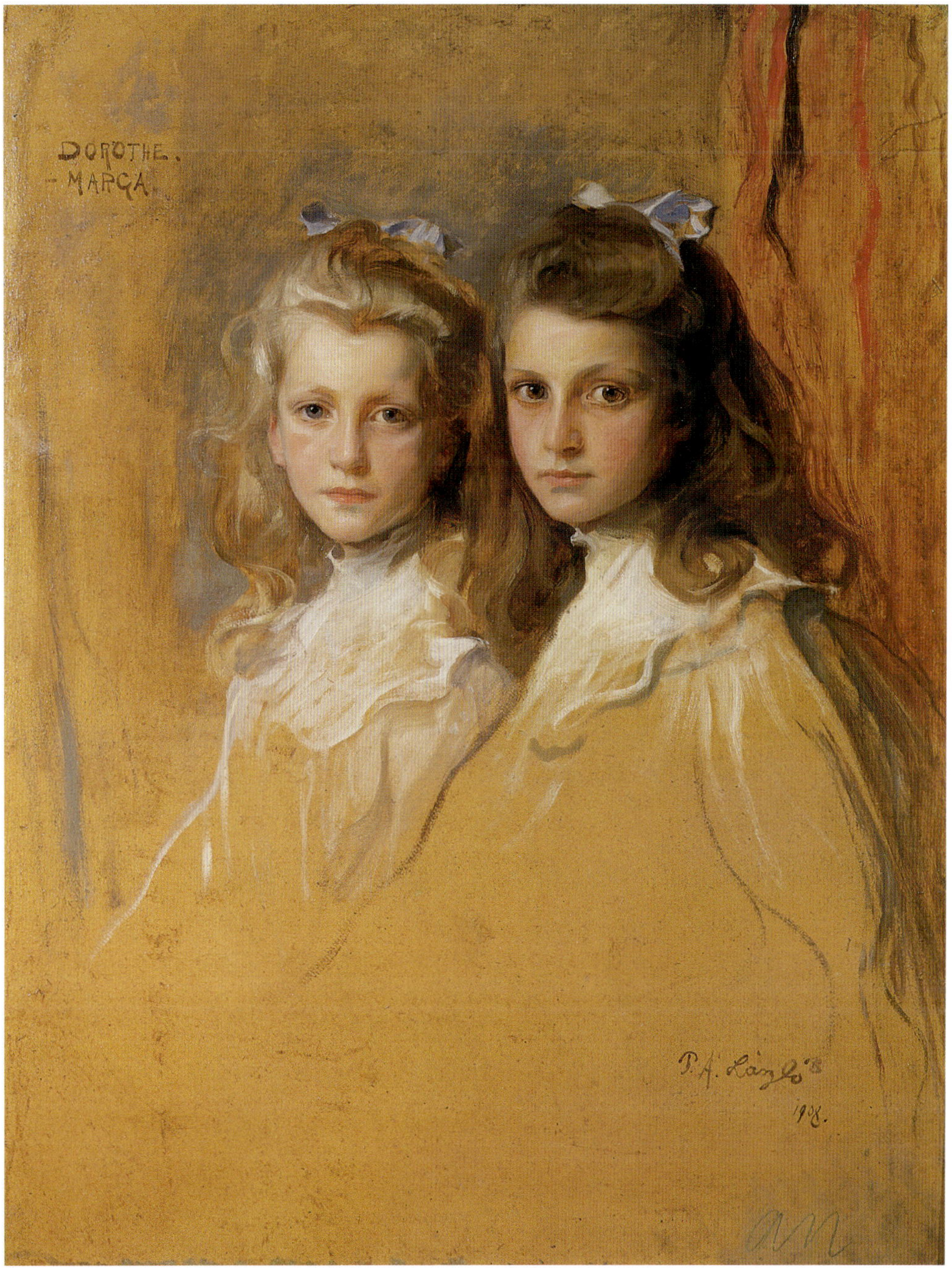

Dorothee (1897–1985) and Marga (1898–1977) were the daughters of Baron Bruno von Schröder (cat. 64) and his wife Emma. The present painting was the first of more than twelve portraits that de László painted of the Schröder family over the years from 1908 to 1935. The Scröders became close friends, de László often visiting them at their home, Dell Park, in Surrey. On his first visit he was invited to discuss painting a portrait of the girls' mother. She later wrote, "Mr. László said he had not much time to paint my portrait, but that he would LOVE to do our two girls .... He was to have an exhibition in Berlin in a few months' time and wanted to show their portrait there. I have ever since chaffed him about this – how he tried to avoid painting my portrait, choosing my two nice girls instead!"

The double portrait was a great success. Apparently when the German Empress saw the portrait in Berlin she said to de László: "Yes, I can see that they are the children of Baron and Baroness Schröder, as the one has the eyes of her father and the other has the hair and blue eyes of the Baroness".

De László painted Dorothee again in 1915, and also in 1923 on the occasion of her marriage to her cousin, Baron Heinrich Schröder. Marga remained unmarried and continued to live at Dell Park for the rest of her life. She ran a small dairy herd, and always believed she was preserving the property for the next generation. The sisters are credited with saving the family bank by loyally holding on to their shares in difficult times.

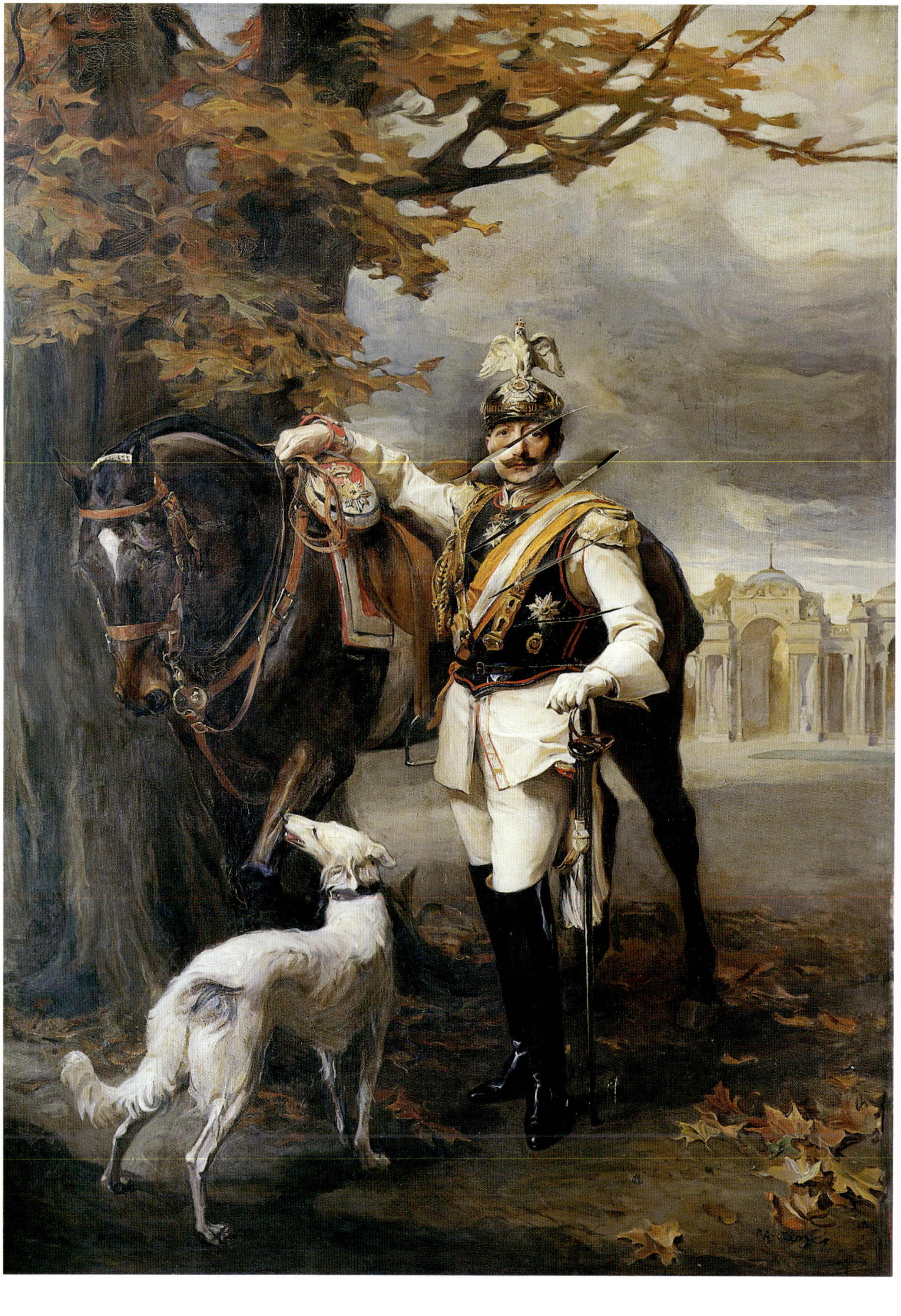

40 H.I.M. Emperor William II of Germany 1910

Oil on canvas, 326 × 232 cm (128⅓ × 91⅓ inches), the canvas damaged by four diagonal slashes to the figure of the Emperor

Signed, dated and inscribed, lower right: *P.A. László / 1910 III / Neues Palais*

Stiftung Preußische Schlösser und Gärten Berlin-Brandenburg

EXHIBITED *On Behalf of the Artists' General Benevolent Institution. Exhibition of Portraits by Philip A. László, M.V.O.*, Thos. Agnew & Sons, London, May–June 1911, no.1, *His Imperial Majesty the German Emperor*; also probably Royal Hibernian Academy of Arts, Dublin, 1913, no.184: *H.I.M. the German Emperor*

LITERATURE ASB. Vol.I, p.82: *Wilhelm / I.R. II / XII 1908*; on the opposite page: a photograph of the artist offering schnapps to the Emperor, inscribed by the artist on the verso: *1909 / Aug: / Wilhelmshöhe / während eines / Ausfluges mit / dem Kaiser* [during an excursion with the Kaiser]; Schleínitz 1913, pp.107–9, *111, 114, 128*, ill. pl.118, p.103 and p.114; Count Robert Zedlitz-Trützschler, *Twelve Years at the German Court*, London, 1924, p.232; Daisy, Princess of Pless, *From My Private Diary*, London 1931, p.285; Rutter 1939, pp.268–9; Joachim von Kurenberg, *The Kaiser: a Life of Wilhelm II*, translated by Russell and Hargen, London 1954, p.179; Clifford 1969, pp.35, 36; Katharine MacDonogh, *Reigning Cats and Dogs, A History of Pets at Court since the Renaissance*, London 1999, p.275; Ludwig Freiherr von Flotow, *Erinnerungen*, ed. Erwin Matsch, Vienna 1982, p.272

Between 1899 and 1913 de László painted some twenty portraits of members of the German imperial family. In November 1908 he went to Potsdam to paint a formal three-quarter-length portrait of the Empress Victoria Augusta (Huis Doorn, Holland), her daughter Princess Victoria Louise (presently untraced), and Crown Princess Cecilie (Schloss Cecilienhof, Potsdam).

In autumn 1908, the forty-nine-year-old William had been on the throne for twenty years. It had been a dreadful year for him, with one personal or political crisis following another. Already in October he was considering abdication, and at the end of November he suffered a nervous breakdown. Two weeks later de László made his first head study of the Emperor (fig. 64), on which he later based the head of the present portrait. When Princess Victoria first saw this study, of which a popular reproduction was made, she exclaimed delighted, "*Endlich der Papa und nicht der Kaiser!*" [At last Papa and not the Kaiser!]. In August 1909, de László was summoned to the Summer Residence at Wilhelmshöhe to paint an official portrait of the Emperor.

Schleínitz wrote in 1913: "In this masterpiece, dominated by the excellently modelled head, we see an idealized image of the monarch and yet at the same time an entirely life-like, true Emperor and Supreme Commander revealing his quintessential character. Here no less than in nearly all his paintings László excels in the ability to refine and ennoble stark realism with a certain poetry of execution. Vigour is expressed in most of his male portraits. The Emperor's posture seems unforced, natural and vivacious; the look in his eyes is serious but not severe, and hints at concerns that even he cannot turn away from. Ultimately, the artist has invested his features with such an uncommonly sympathetic expression that its attractive, arresting nature dominates over everything else."

Daisy, Princess of Pless, was not so complimentary: "The state portrait painted by Laszló [*sic*] to hang with those of his ancestors in the gallery adjoining the throne room in the Royal Palace in Berlin is not a success. The Emperor wears the white Cuirassier Guards' uniform with silver breast-plate and silver eagle-crowned helmet of which he was so fond, and which was certainly very 'paintable'. He stands beside what is, I think, supposed to be a horse: the colour scheme is pink and white and chocolate boxy, and the whole thing is deplorable. The Emperor quite liked it, because he had no more knowledge of pictures (in spite of his delusions to the contrary) than the average Royalty has. In how few Palaces are there any good modern pictures!" Lockett Agnew (cat. 44), however, thought it "an admirable portrait – rather more sad than his usual expression. It looks to me as if it was painted when all his friends were being prosecuted in the police court!"

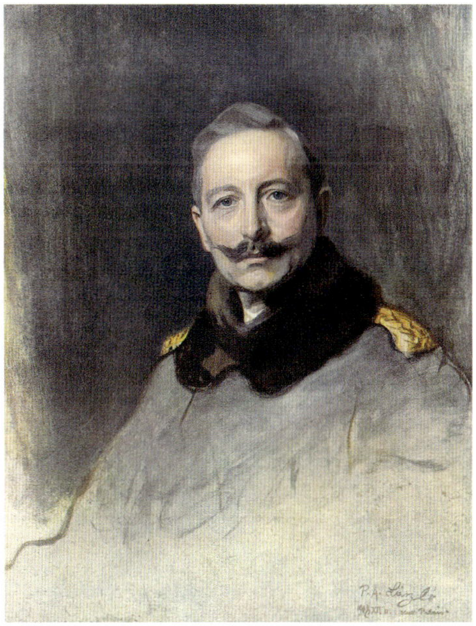

FIG. 62 *H.I.M. Emperor William II of Germany*, 1908
Coloured lithographic reproduction on grey paper, 37.1 × 27.6 cm (14⅝ × 10⅞ in.), private collection

Rutter describes how "Princess Victoria took a keen interest in the success of the portrait, and seeing that the groom was having difficulty in making the horse stand still – for the sun was hot and the flies were troublesome – she insisted that she could do more with it than anyone else. For several hours Her Imperial Highness stood under the blazing August sun in the great shadeless courtyard of the palace, holding the horse's head, while de László worked at his canvas and the groom kept the flies off them both."

Despite the prominence of the handsome borzoi in the finished portrait, the Emperor's personal preference was for dachshunds, and a dozen "biting, snarling little brutes" would accompany him everywhere, attacking anyone in sight. By contrast the borzoi was synonymous with elegance and imperial prestige and therefore more fitting for an Emperor's official portrait. According to Rutter, the Emperor "had specially ordered a

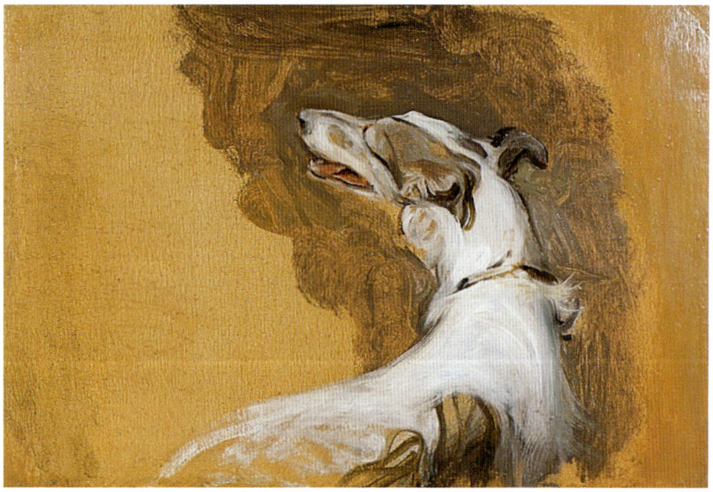

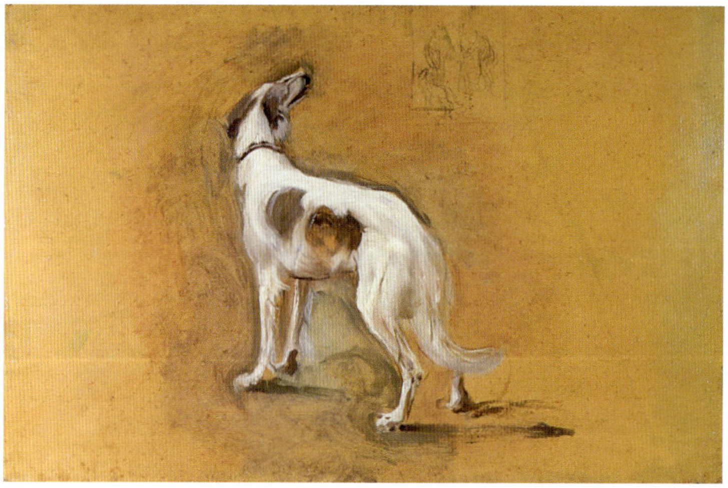

couple of Borzoi dogs from Chemnitz as additional decoration". "Such were the exigencies of this commission that, very unusually, de László made use of photography to record the composition in the courtyard, and before beginning the picture de László had several photographs taken in order to obtain the best pose for his restless models [fig. 65]." A letter dated 13 December 1909 from the artist to Lady Muriel Herbert refers to a projected appointment to go to Wilton House to paint the "fine dog for my picture of the German Emperor". Two studies of borzois remain in the collection of the artist's family (cat. 38, 39).

De László was allowed to take the Emperor's uniform back to England to complete the details and he finished the background from studies made in Kensington Gardens. Three preparatory oil sketches on board, one of which remains untraced and the rest with the artist's family, all show a different interpretation of the architecture in the background. The final version shows the triumphal arch behind the Neues Palais (New Palace) in the park at Potsdam. The Emperor did not see the completed work until 1911, when he opened the artist's exhibition at Agnew's in Bond Street while on a short visit to London for the unveiling of the Victoria Memorial. He was delighted with the portrait but jokingly remarked on the background,

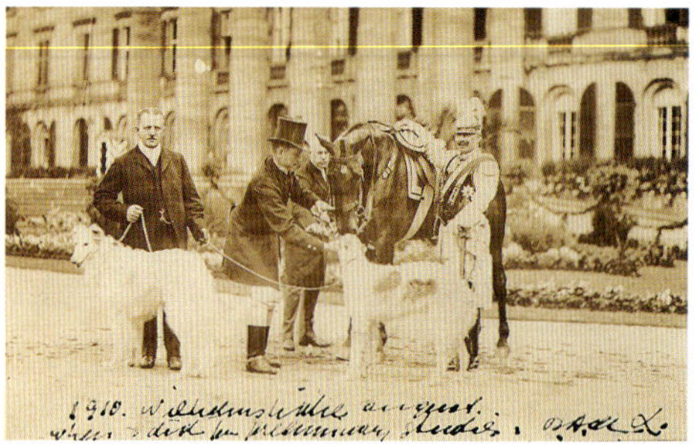

FIG. 62 In the courtyard at Wilhelmshöhe, 1909

"Why Autumn? Am I a falling leaf?"

For the portrait de László received 20,000 marks. At the Emperor's wish a copy was made for the Crown Prince to take to India with him on his tour to the East, as a present to the Viceroy Lord Hardinge (untraced).

For many years the portrait is believed to have been in store in the royal childrens' gymnasium at the Neues Palais. The painting, having been attacked allegedly with bayonets, most probably by occupying Russian troops at the end of the Second World War, has recently been cleaned and conserved for exhibition.

With thanks to Giles MacDonogh for biographical advice for this entry

41 A Borzoi

Oil and pencil on board, 49.5 × 60.3 cm ($19\frac{1}{2} \times 23\frac{3}{4}$ inches)
Verso, inscribed: *The Borzois Dog*
PROVENANCE In the possession of the artist on his death; Patrick de Laszlo, his fourth son
LITERATURE Rowcliffe 1938, p.31 (no. 164); Rutter 1939, pp. 268–9; Clifford 1969, monochrome ill.pl. 21; Katharine MacDonogh, *Reigning Cats and Dogs, A History of Pets at Court since the Renaissance*, London 1999, ill. between pages 256 and 257

42 A Borzoi

Oil on board, 51.4 × 74.9 cm ($20\frac{1}{4} \times 29\frac{1}{2}$ inches), cut down
Verso: Another study of the same subject
PROVENANCE In the possession of the artist on his death; Patrick de Laszlo, his fourth son
LITERATURE Rowcliffe 1938, p.31 (nos. 165 and 165Rev.); Rutter 1939, pp.268–9; Katharine MacDonogh, *Reigning Cats and Dogs, A History of Pets at Court since the Renaissance*, London 1999, ill. p.275

43 H.S.H. Prince Louis of Battenberg, 1910

Oil on board, 93.3 × 70.5 cm ($36\frac{3}{4} \times 27\frac{3}{4}$ inches)
Signed, inscribed and dated, lower left:
Study / 1910 P.A. de László
His Royal Highness The Duke of Edinburgh
LITERATURE ASB, Vol.I, p.86: *Louis Battenberg / Vice Admiral* (undated but with six other Battenberg signatures, the page inscribed by the artist *909 April 2/in my studio/ London*; Rutter 1936, pp.267–8, 272–3

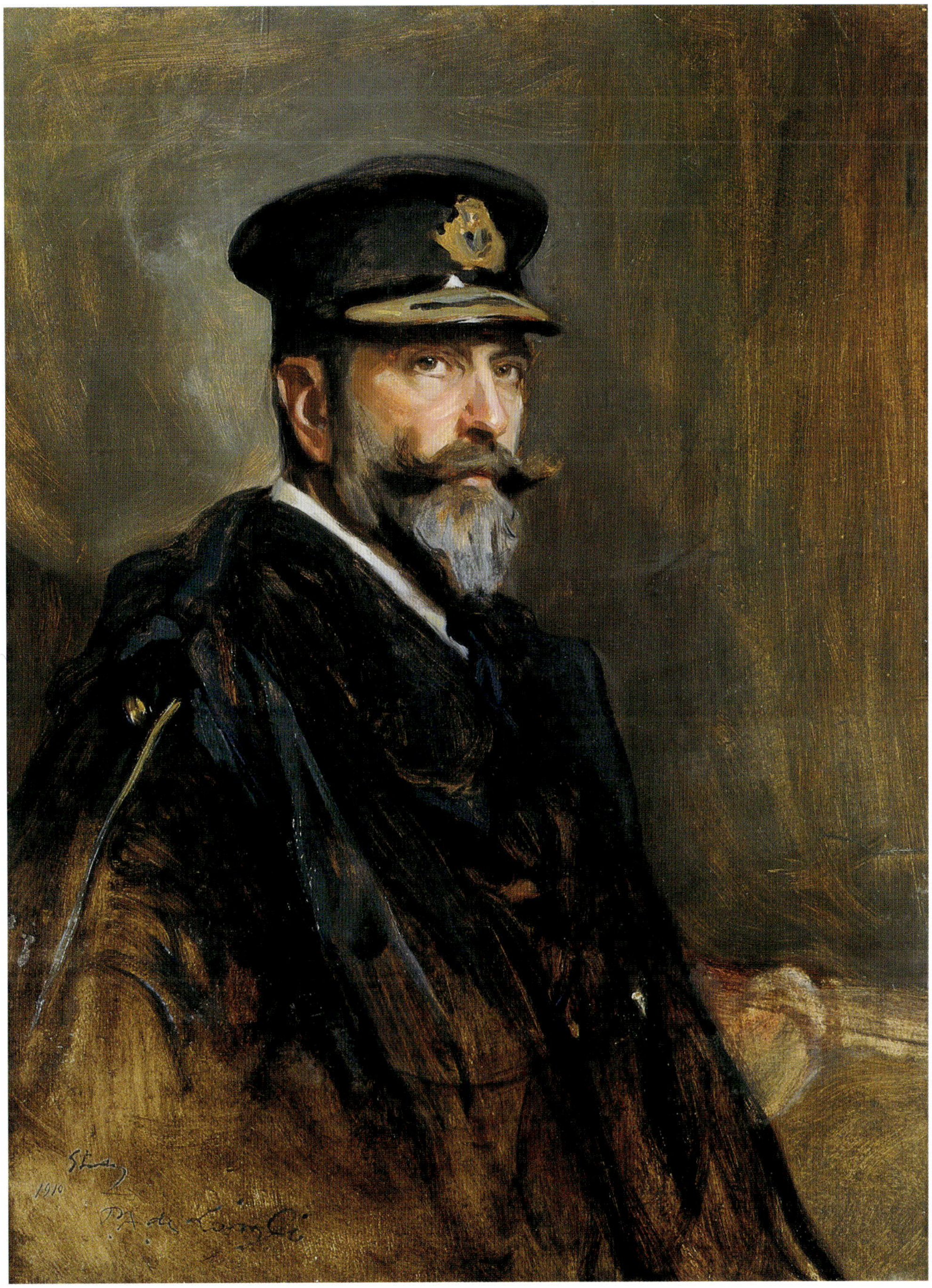

This study shows Prince Louis in the uniform of a Vice Admiral. De László painted the sitter on three other occasions, in a three-quarter-length portrait, a head-and-shoulders portrait drawing dated 1909, and a half-length portrait dated 1914.

Prince Louis Alexander of Battenberg was born in 1854 at Graz in Austria. He was the eldest son of Prince Alexander of Hesse and his morganatic wife Countess Julia von Haucke. In 1868 he joined the Royal Navy as a cadet and became a naturalized British subject. Prince Louis, with his commanding presence and great charm, looked the "beau ideal of the British Naval Officer". Queen Victoria followed his promising career with interest.

Appointments followed: Battenberg was made Director of Naval Intelligence (1902–5), Rear Admiral (1904), Commander-in-Chief of the Atlantic Fleet (1908–10), Vice-Admiral (1910) and finally First Sea Lord (1912). However, with the outbreak of World War I, despite his staunchly British sympathies, he felt his German origins were incompatible with his position and he resigned as First Sea Lord in October 1914. In July 1917, at the request of the king to his relations to change their German titles to English ones, Prince Louis anglicized the family name to Mountbatten and was created Marquess of Milford Haven. He was promoted to Admiral of the Fleet in 1919.

Prince Louis took a keen interest in British naval history. He was the first president of the Society of Nautical Research and was particularly interested in the Navy Records Society. With Admiral Percy Scott he was involved in the invention of the cone signalling apparatus.

On 30 April 1884 he married his cousin Princess Victoria of Hesse-Darmstadt, the eldest daughter of Louis IV, Grand Duke of Hesse-Darmstadt, and Princess Alice, a daughter of Queen Victoria. They had two daughters and two sons, all of whom were painted by de László; Alice (cat. 36), Louise (1889–1965), later Queen of Sweden, George, later 2nd Marquess (1892–1938), and Louis (cat. 90). Lord Milford Haven died in 1921 in London.

44 Vita Sackville-West 1910

Oil on canvas, 116.5 × 80 cm ($45\frac{7}{8} \times 31\frac{1}{2}$ inches)
Indistinctly signed and dated, upper right:
P.A. László. 1910. II
Sissinghurst Castle, Kent
EXHIBITED *On Behalf of the Artists' General Benevolent Institution. Exhibition of Portraits by Philip A. László,* M.V.O., Thos. Agnew & Sons, London, May–June, 1911, no.14: *Hon. Victoria Sackville-West*
LITERATURE ASB, Vol.I, p.84: *Vita Sackville West Feb. 25th 1909*; Rutter 1939, p. 273; Nigel Nicolson, *Portrait of a Marriage,* London 1973,p.82, ill. between pp.30 and 31; Victoria Glendenning, *Vita, The Life of V. Sackville-West,* London 1983, p.36, ill. p.110

According to the sitter's family, her mother Lady Sackville had heard that de László thought her daughter one of the loveliest young women he had ever seen. "Then do you not think you owe it to your art and her beauty to paint her portrait without a fee?" she asked him. It seems he was forced to agree. Lady Sackville then decided exactly what her daughter should wear for the sittings. This again was unusual, as de László had strong views about his lady sitters retaining a "timeless beauty". On occasions he designed the sitter's dress himself and on canvas endlessly re-invented his lady sitters' chosen finery. Here, the amber beads certainly belonged to the sitter; she wore them all her life. Lady Sackville herself had been painted by John Singer Sargent, but thought the portrait not flattering enough and immediately commissioned a charcoal drawing from Sargent to replace the oil.

Vita was not quite eighteen at the time the portrait was painted. After inheriting it she hid it in the attic, thinking it "too smart" for Sissinghurst. De László painted another three-quarter-length portrait of her, which remained unfinished, unsigned and in the artist's possession until his death. That portrait was later destroyed, in 1947, by the executors of de László's estate in accordance with his wishes that work not worthy of him should not survive him. In 1915 de László painted Vita's father-in-law, Sir Arthur Nicolson, later 1st Lord Carnock (private collection).

The Hon. Victoria Mary (Vita) Sackville-West was born at Knole near Sevenoaks in March 1892, the only child of Lionel, 3rd Lord Sackville and his wife Victoria, illegitimate daughter of 'Pepita' and his uncle Lionel Sackville-West, 2nd Lord Sackville. In 1913 she married the diplomat and writer the Hon. Harold Nicolson (who was knighted in 1953). She was a vital, gifted and complex woman, who made her mark as a poet, novelist and journalist. In 1927 she won the Hawthornden Prize for her extended poem *The Land*, in which she expressed her close sympathy with the life of the soil of Kent. Her novels include *The Edwardians* (1930), *All Passion Spent* (1931) and *The Easter Party* (1953). *Knole and the Sackvilles* (1923) and *Pepita* (1937) are studies of her family and origins. She was also the most influential English gardener of the twentieth century, creating with her husband the gardens at Sissinghurst Castle, Kent. They had two sons, Lionel Benedict, born in 1914, and Nigel, born in 1917; but she was known, too, for her passionate affair with Violet Trefusis and her intense relationship with Hilda Matheson and Virginia Woolf. Vita Sackville-West died in 1962.

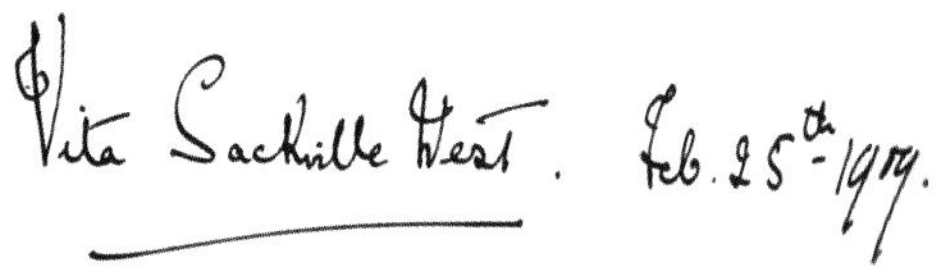

FIG. 66 Vita Sackville-West's signature in the artist's sitters' book

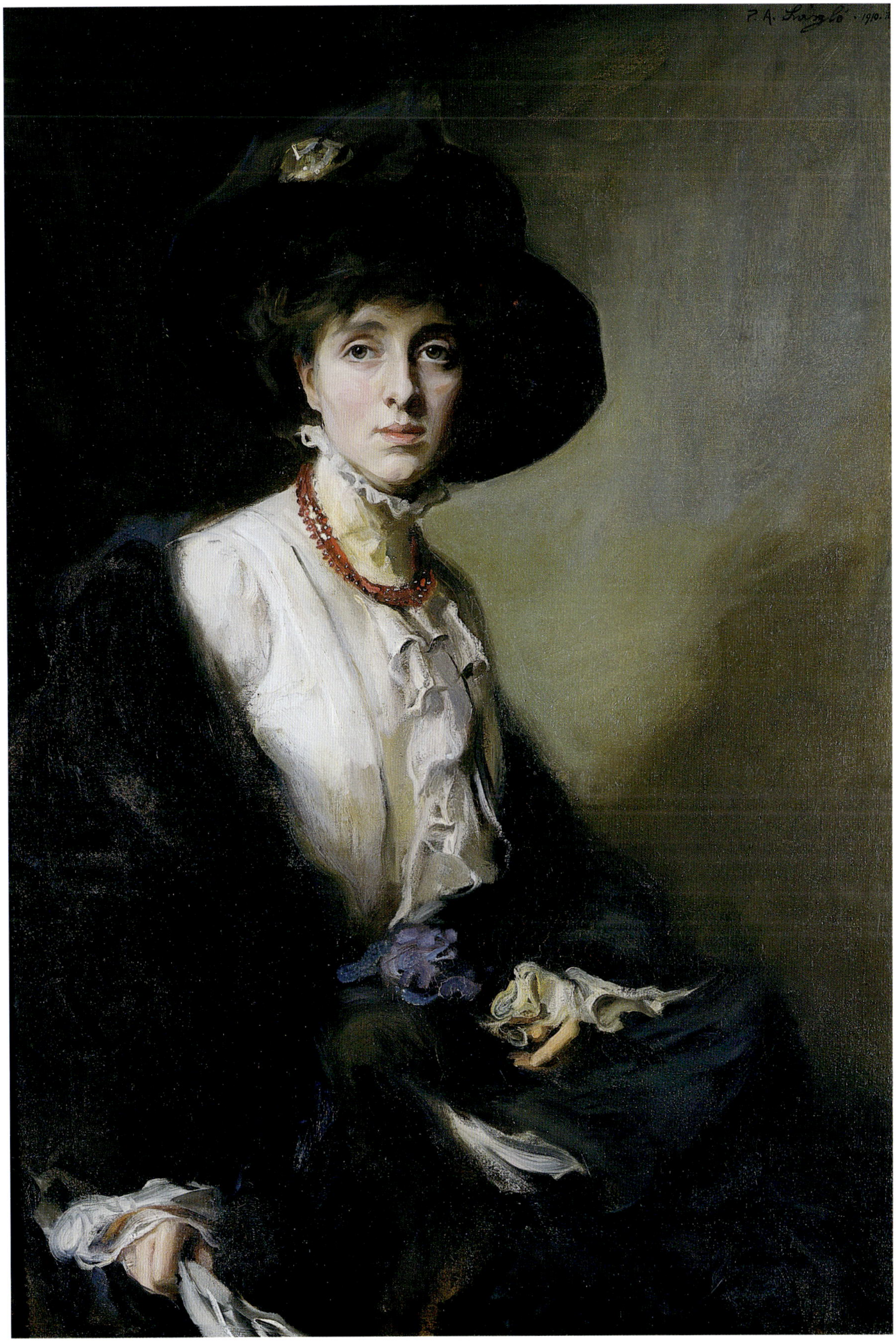

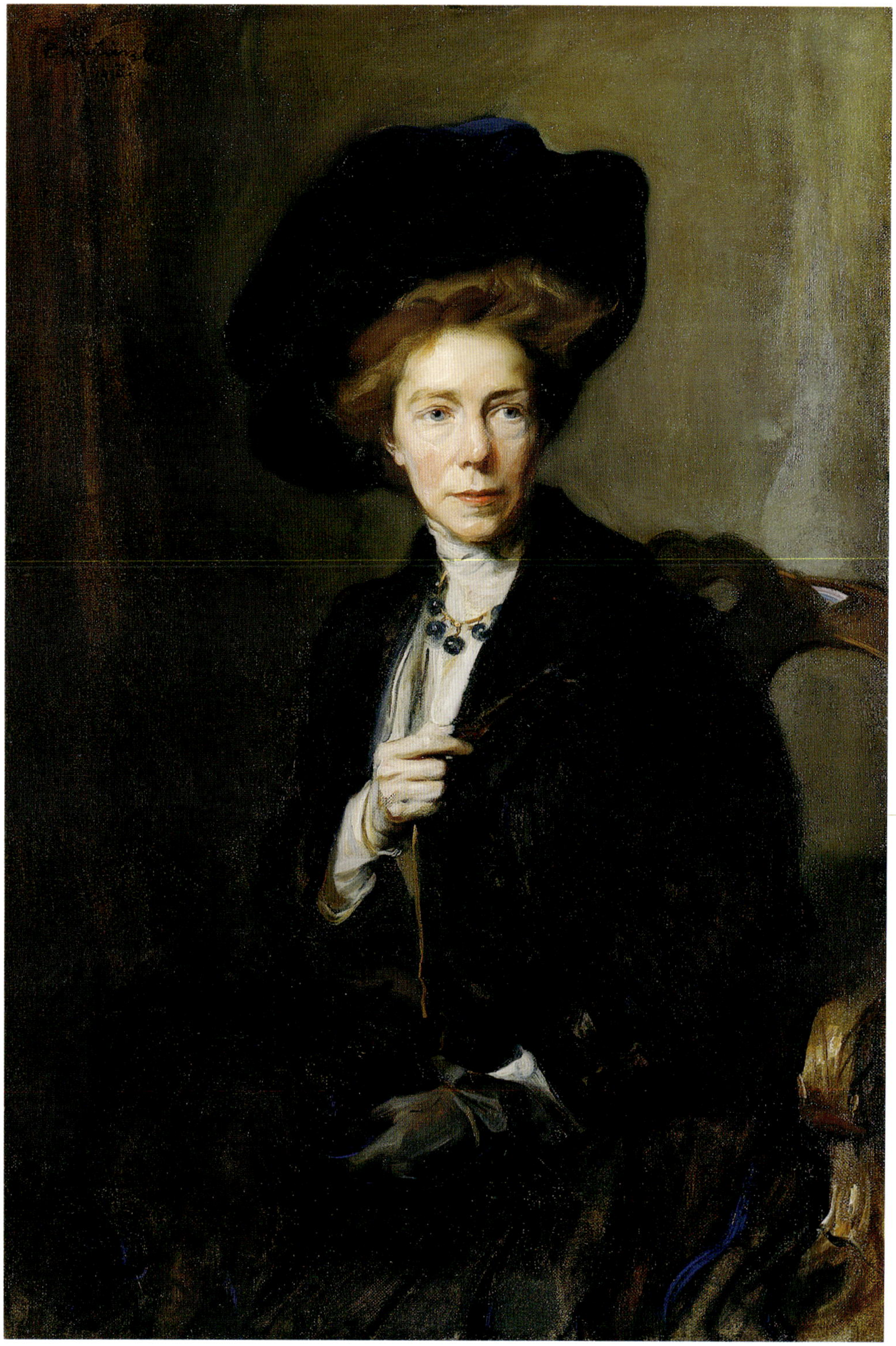

45 Miss Elizabeth Guinness 1910

Oil on canvas, 112.4 × 76.2 cm (44¼ × 30 inches)
Signed and dated, upper left: *P.A. László / 1910*
Royal Holloway, University of London
PROVENANCE Presented to The Royal Holloway College by its past and present members, 1911
EXHIBITED *Spring Exhibition*, Royal Society of British Artists, 1911, no.99, *Miss E.M. Guinness*
LITERATURE ASB, Vol.I, p.55: *Elizabeth M. Guinness / April 18. 1909*

Elizabeth Maude Guinness (1869–1960) was a second cousin to the artist's wife. She was among the earliest students of Royal Holloway College and immediately after gaining Honours in English in 1892 she joined the academic staff there, becoming Librarian, Tutor and Lecturer in English. From 1899 until 1908 she was Vice-Principal of the College under Miss (later Dame) Emily Penrose, whom

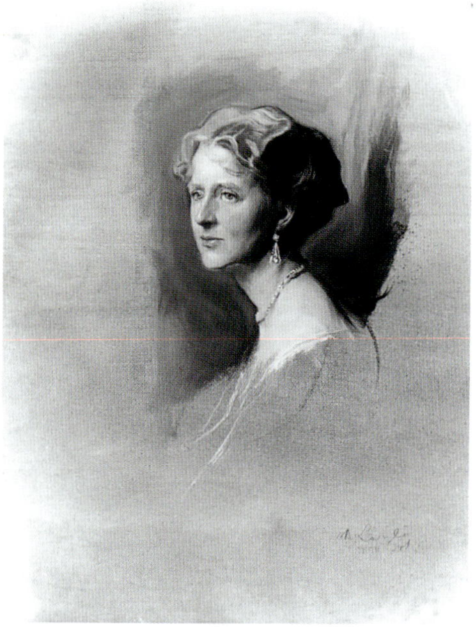

FIG. 67 *Lady Susan Townley, née Lady Susan Keppel*, 1911
Oil on board, 61 × 45.7 cm (24 × 18 in.)
Private collection

de László painted in 1907 (Royal Holloway College). With Miss Penrose's departure for Oxford, Miss Guinness left to be Vice-Principal of Cheltenham Ladies' College.

De László has painted her as a smart and stylish dresser, reflecting the charm of manner and fineness of mind that were long remembered at Royal Holloway. "When she met students", wrote one, "she became the leader of a salon, a touchstone for taste".

46 Lady Wantage, née the Hon. Harriet Jones Loyd 1911

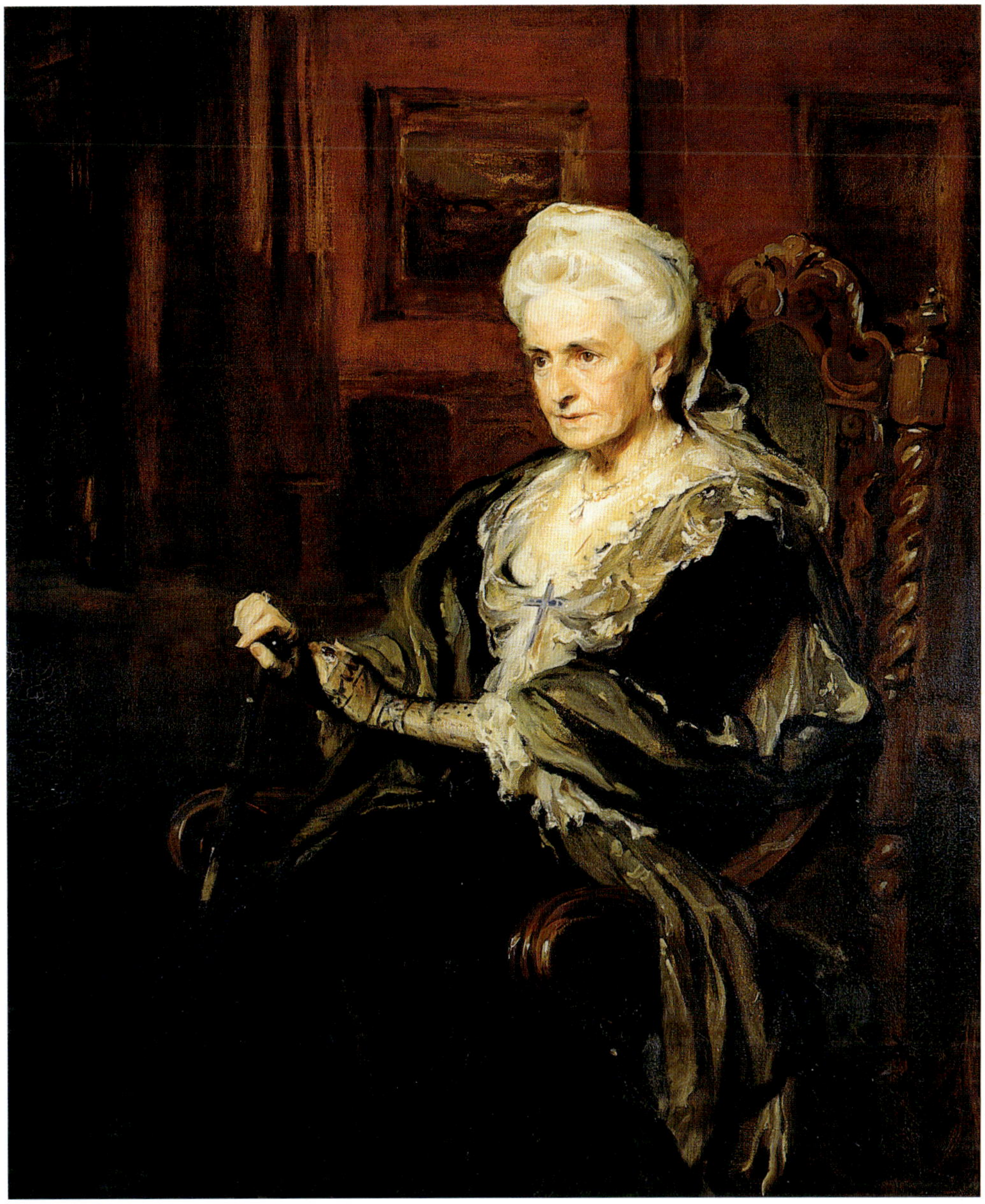

Oil on canvas, 138.4 × 113 cm (54½ × 44½ inches)
Signature not visible, probably lower left in darkened paint area
From the Loyd Collection
EXHIBITED The Royal Academy, 1911, no. 338; *International Art Exhibition*, Amsterdam, 1912 (winner of the *diplome d'honneur*, the highest award); Paris Salon, 1914, p.19, no.677; Birmingham Museum and Art Gallery, 1945–52, no.22
LITERATURE ASB, Vol.I, p.84: *Harriet S. Wantage Dec. 13th / 1909*; Williams 1921, pp.149–52, ill. facing p.148; Rutter 1939, p.267, ill. facing p.272; M. Chamot, D. Farr and M. Butlin, *Tate Gallery Catalogues, The Modern British paintings, drawings and sculpture*, I, 1964, p.373, no.2957; Clifford 1969, monochrome ill. pl.26; *The Loyd Collection Catalogue*, no. 39

Tate Britain, London, has a preliminary study for this portrait dated July 1911, painted one Sunday morning, showing Lady Wantage in a large black hat and veil and holding a prayer book, having just returned from church. The present work was de László's first to be accepted for show in the Royal Academy, in 1911, although to his mind it was very poorly hung. In 1912 it won the *diplome d'honneur*, the highest award at the International Exhibition in Amsterdam. A copy of the portrait hangs in the dining room of Wantage Hall at Reading University.

While staying with Lady Wantage, de László, following his custom of making spontaneous study portraits of other house guests during commissions, also painted, with great rapidity, Lady Susan Townley (fig. 67) and her late husband's cousin Lady Jane Lindsay, and, on his departure, sketched Lady Wantage's Pekinese in the visitors' book.

Harriet Sarah Jones Loyd was born in 1837, the only child of the banker Samuel Jones Loyd, 1st Baron Overstone, and his wife Ichabod Wright. In 1858 she married Robert James Lindsay, who assumed the name of Loyd-Lindsay and bought the estate of Lockinge, near Wantage. Sir Robert Loyd-Lindsay, V.C., K.C.B., created 1st Baron Wantage in 1885, died in 1901. They had no children. Lady Wantage published a memoir of her late husband. She died in 1920. Lockinge House was demolished in 1947.

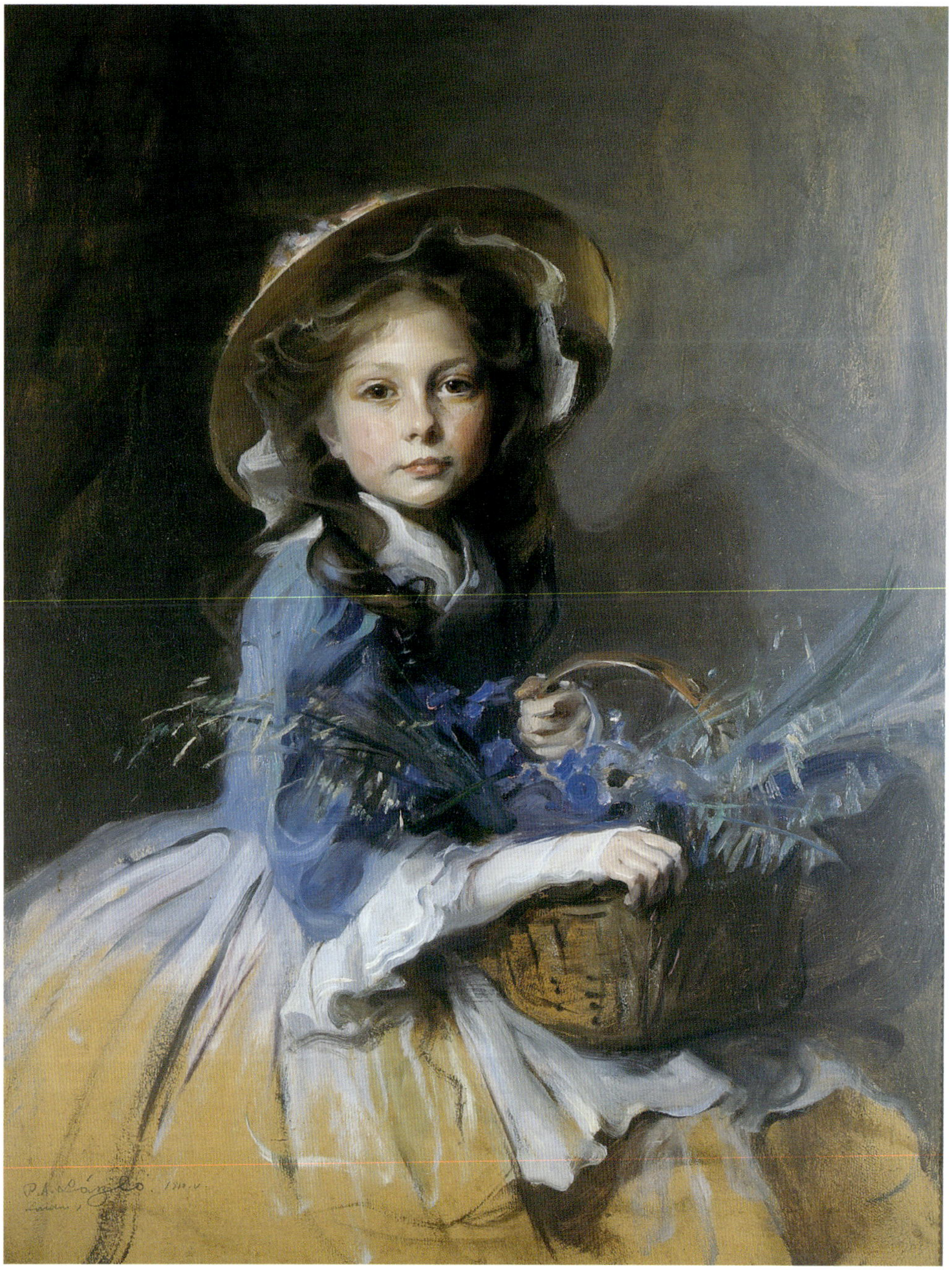

47 Miss Olive Trouton 1910

Oil on board, 90.5 × 70.2 cm ($35\frac{5}{8} \times 27\frac{5}{8}$ inches)
Signed, inscribed and dated, lower left:
P.A. László 1910. V. / London
EXHIBITED *Exhibition of Portraits by Philip A. Laszlo,* Thomas Agnew & Sons, London, May–June 1911, no.2: *Miss Olive Troughton*; *Exhibition of Paintings by Philip A. de László, M.V.O., In Aid of the London Hospital and The Artists' General Benevolent Institution,* Wildenstein & Co., Ltd., London, November–December 1937, no.34: *Olive, Daughter of the Late Professor Trouton and Mrs. Trouton*
LITERATURE National Portrait Gallery, 1903–14 Album, p.54, and 1907–13 Album, p.7; *The Studio,* LIII, 1911, p.262, ill.; Schleinitz 1913, ill. p.118, pl.132

Anne Mabel Olivia (Olive) was the daughter of Frederick and Annie Trouton. She was born in Dublin in 1900, the eldest of the three daughters. Of her four elder brothers, two were killed during the First World War (cat. 66) and a third during the Blitz in London in 1944. She trained as an architect, and in 1929 married a fellow architect, Adrian van Montagu. Before the Second World War they worked together with Barbara Acworth, concentrating on pubs and on domestic architecture imbued with her own particular colour schemes. They had one son, John Patrick, born in 1930. Olive continued to work informally as an architect, designing for friends and family, and on a few occasions for Henry de Laszlo, the artist's eldest son. She died in 1986 in Buckinghamshire.

48 Self-portrait 1911

Oil on canvas, 55.9 × 46 cm (22 × $18\frac{1}{8}$ inches)
Signed, inscribed and dated, lower right: *Nemzeti Szálón-nak / London 1911 / László F.E.*
The Hungarian National Gallery, Budapest
PROVENANCE The National Salon, Budapest; acquired by the Hungarian National Gallery
LITERATURE Schleínítz 1913, ill. no.1, facing p.1

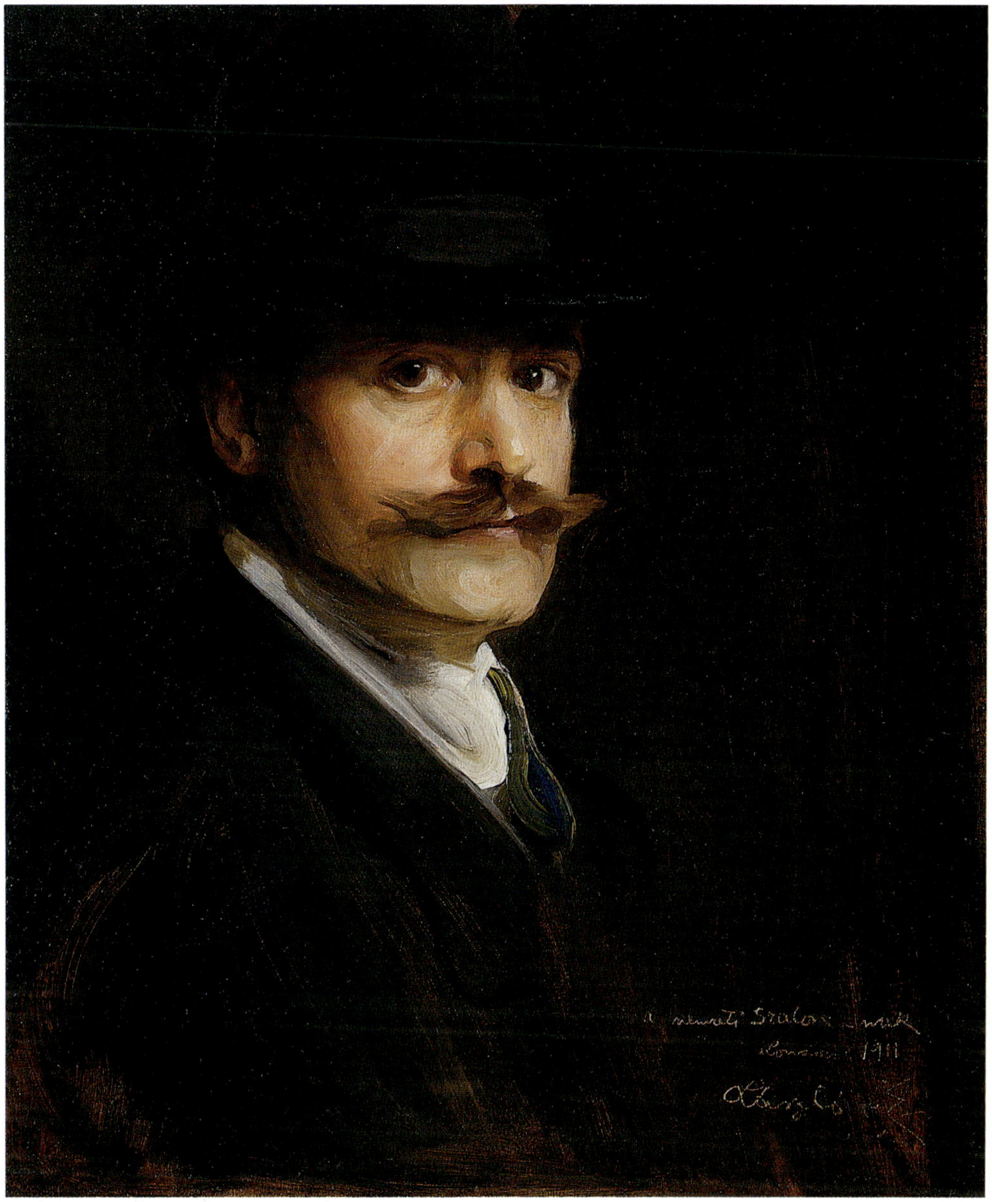

The year 1911 saw de László at the peak of his international career, and accepting considerably more commissions throughout Europe than in previous years. Following the success of his exhibition at Agnew's in spring 1911, the critic A.L. Baldry (cat. 81) pointed out: "now that [de László] has all his faculties under discipline and that he has acquired a true understanding of the way in which they can best be used, there is no fear he will lapse into convention or stray into extravagance. He is a sane, sincere, and well-balanced artist who knows not only what he intends to do but also how his intentions can best be realized; and he is too wholesomely ambitious to be content even with the large measure of success that he has already secured." This confidence is displayed in the present self-portrait, painted in London for the foundation of a national institute of Hungarian portraiture in Budapest. In the same year the Uffizi Gallery in Florence commissioned de László to contribute to its celebrated collection of self-portraits by prominent artists (fig. 68). In both portraits de László has shown himself looking intently over his shoulder, as in his self-portrait of 1888 (cat. 2), but here his gaze is accentuated by the unusual close-cropped composition and by the brim of the hat pulled down over his brow. This format he used again later in his portrait of Lord Albemarle (cat. 67).

The painting was later acquired by the Hungarian National Gallery from the 'national salon' in lieu of a debt.

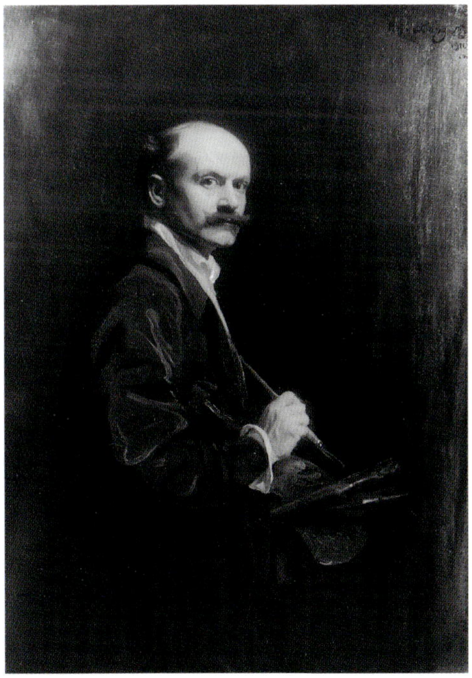

FIG. 68 *Self-portrait*, 1911
Oil on canvas, 122 × 86 cm (48 × 34 in.)
Gallerie degli Uffizi, Florence

49 The Duchess of Portland, née Winifred Dallas-Yorke 1911

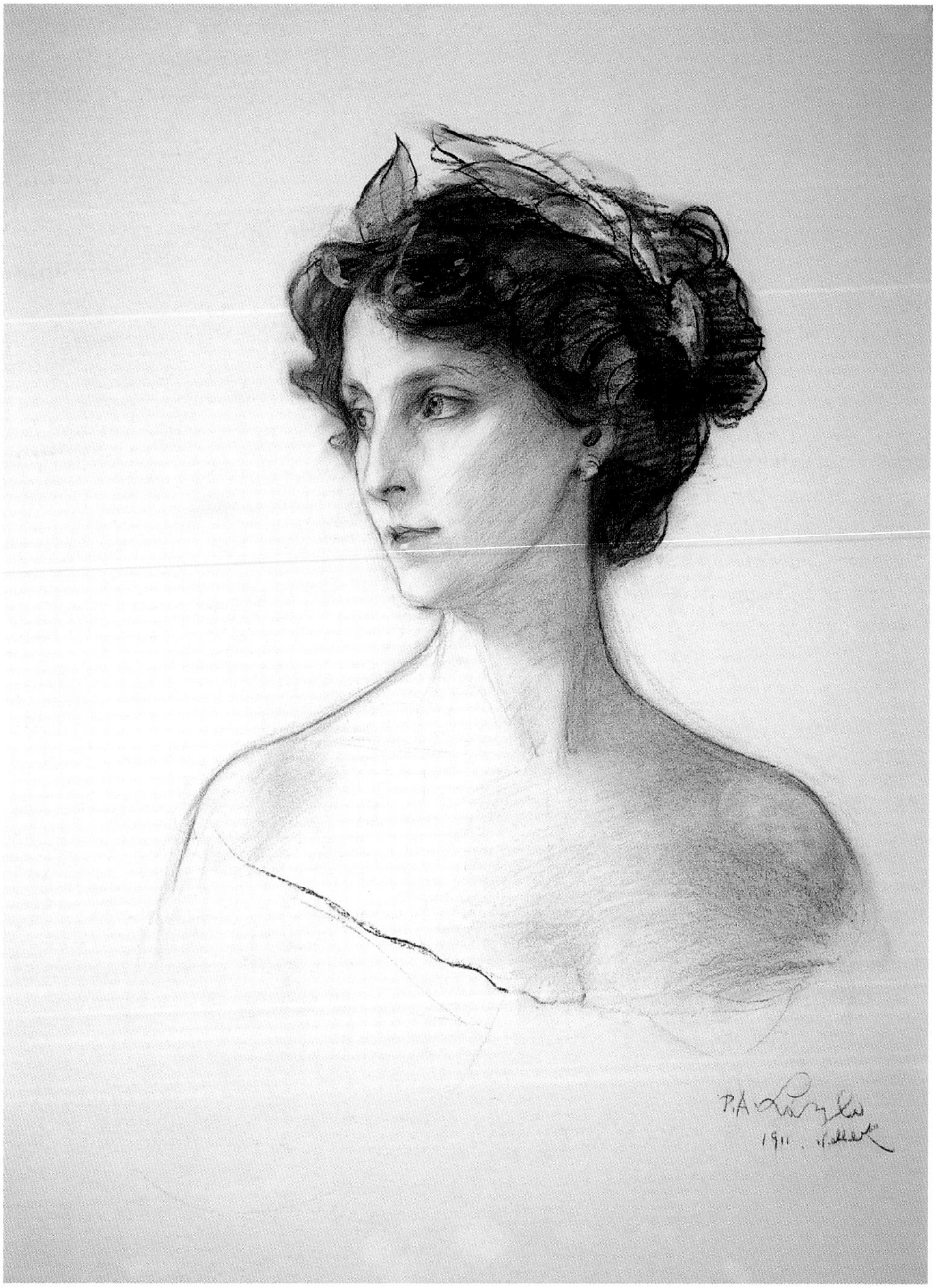

Charcoal on paper, 72.1 × 52.4 cm
($28\frac{3}{8} \times 20\frac{5}{8}$ inches)
Signed, dated and inscribed, lower right:
P.A. László / 1911. Welbeck.

LITERATURE *The Sketch*, 29 May, 1912, ill.; Schleínitz 1913, ill. p.124, pl.140; *The Graphic*, 15 November 1913, ill.; *The Studio*, LIX, 1913, ill. between pp.300 and 305; Richard W. Goulding, *The Catalogue of Pictures. The Duke of Portland*, Cambridge 1936, no.925; *The Graphic*, 24 January 1925, p.122, ill.; William Cavendish-Bentinck, 6th Duke of Portland, *Men, Women and Things, Memories of the Duke of Portland, K.G., G.C.V.O.*, London 1937, p.221; Rutter 1939, pp.275, 359, 364

The Duke of Portland was probably de László's greatest patron and friend in England. The artist painted nearly thirty portraits of the family over the years 1911 to 1937, the present portrait being one of the first. He was often a guest at their home, Welbeck Abbey, Worksop, where the Duke hung his portraits together in the 'László Room'. In 1912 he painted two oil portraits of the Duchess in the same laurel crown, which is thought to have been owned by the artist, as other distinguished sitters were painted in it over the years. There exists a contemporary lithograph of this drawing, much smaller than the original, one copy of which remains in a private family collection in Scotland. The Duchess's beauty was captured by de László in no less than six portraits, the most famous of which, the 'Queen Mary's pearls' portrait (fig. 32, p. 41), has only just been rediscovered.

Winifred Anna, the only daughter of Thomas Dallas-Yorke of Walmsgate in Lincolnshire, was born at Murthly Castle in Perthshire in 1863. In 1889 she married William Cavendish-Bentinck, 6th Duke of Portland. They had two sons, William ('Chopper' or 'Sonny'), later 7th Duke, and Francis Morven, and a daughter, Victoria. She was Mistress of the Robes to Queen Alexandra from 1913 to 1925, and a J.P. in Nottinghamshire, D.B.E. and D.J.St.J. A considerable philanthropist, she spent much time working with hospitals and founded Portland College, originally for those disabled by injuries sustained in mining accidents. She was also the founder of the Royal Society for the Protection of Birds. She died at Welbeck in 1954.

50 Robin Vane-Tempest-Stewart, Lord Stewart, later 8th Marquess of Londonderry 1911

Black crayon on paper, 66 × 57.2 cm
(26 × 22½ inches)
Signed and indistinctly dated, lower right: *P.A. László / 1911. / July*, and inscribed, centre left: *Robin*

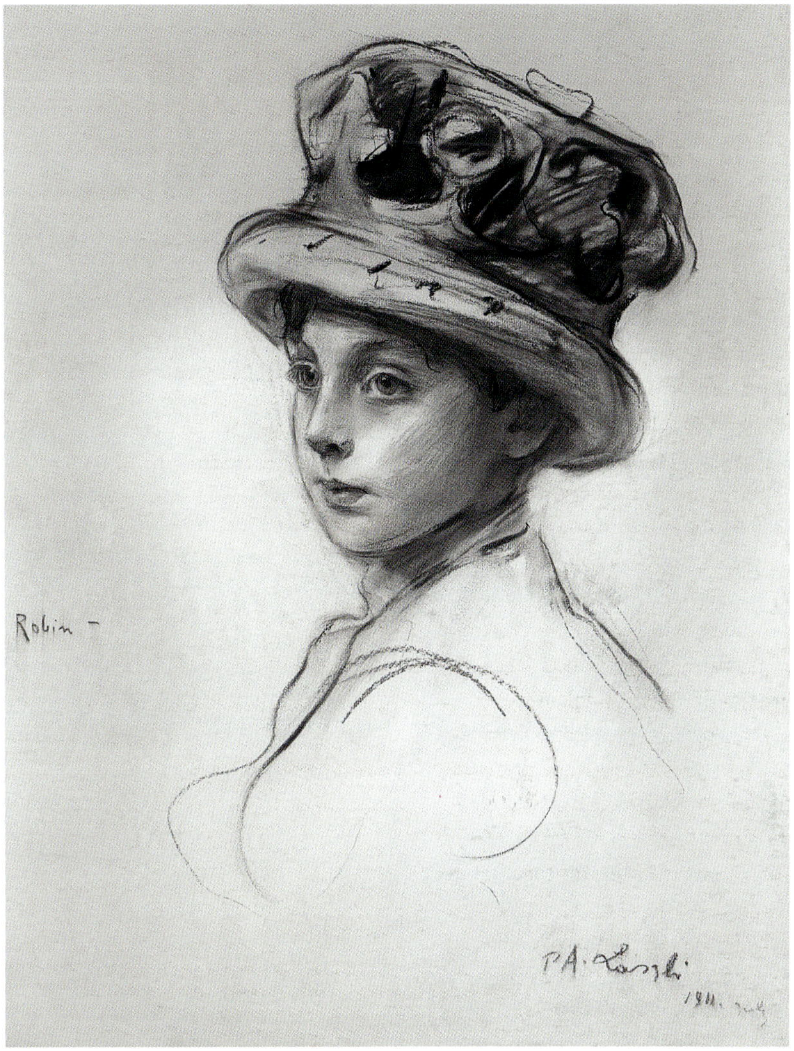

The present drawing is one of the first of a number of portraits de László made of three generations of the Londonderry family. He was commissioned to paint Lord Stewart (1902–1955), the only son of Viscount and Viscountess Castlereagh (cat. 56, 57), in his uniform in order to commemorate his acting as page to his grandfather, the 6th Marquess of Londonderry, at the Coronation of King George V (fig. 69). During a break in the sittings, the boy placed his grandfather's coronet upon his own head and de László spontaneously made this drawing. De László had hoped to be allowed to paint the coronation (on 22 June 1911) but to his disappointment the king appointed John Henry Bacon as official artist.

The oil painting of Lord Stewart (dated 1912) is one of only two known portraits the artist signed 'László de Lombos'. De László was ennobled by Francis Joseph, Emperor of Austria and King of Hungary, in 1912. His full title thereafter was Philip Alexius László de Lombos, but soon decided to style himself simply 'de László', and thenceforward signed his pictures thus.

Edward Charles Stewart Robert Vane-Tempest-Stewart, Lord Stewart, the only son of the 7th Marquess of Londonderry and the Hon. Edith Chaplin, was born on 18 November 1902. He was brought up mainly in Ireland. He sat as M.P. for County Down between 1931 and 1945. He was a Tory who had friends from all parties and frequently entertained at home, supported by his much loved wife Romaine, née Boyce-Combe. He became Viscount Castlereagh in 1915 and 8th Marquess of Londonderry in 1949. He died in 1955.

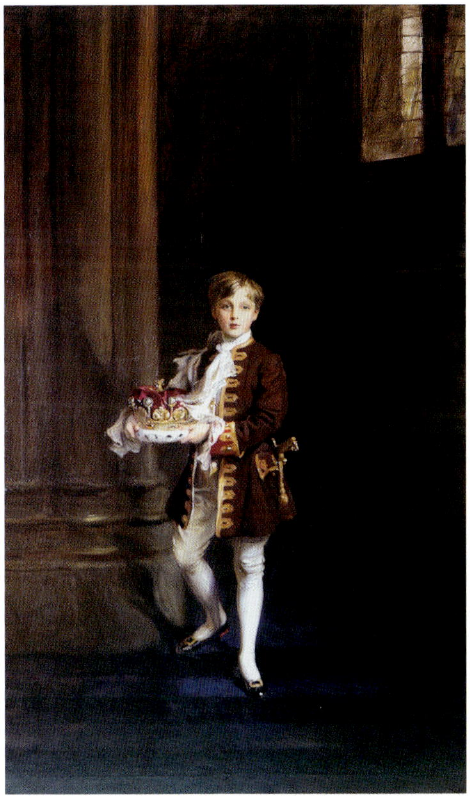

FIG. 69 *Lord Stewart, later Viscount Castlereagh*, 1912
Oil on canvas, 287 × 195.6 cm (113 × 77 in.)
Private collection

51 The Marchioness of Londonderry, née Lady Theresa Chetwynd-Talbot 1912

Oil on board, 85.7 × 67.3 cm (33¾× 26½ inches)
Signed and dated, lower right: *P.A. de László / 1912 – ×*
PROVENANCE Most probably the daughter of the sitter, Lady Helen Mary Theresa, 6th Countess of Ilchester

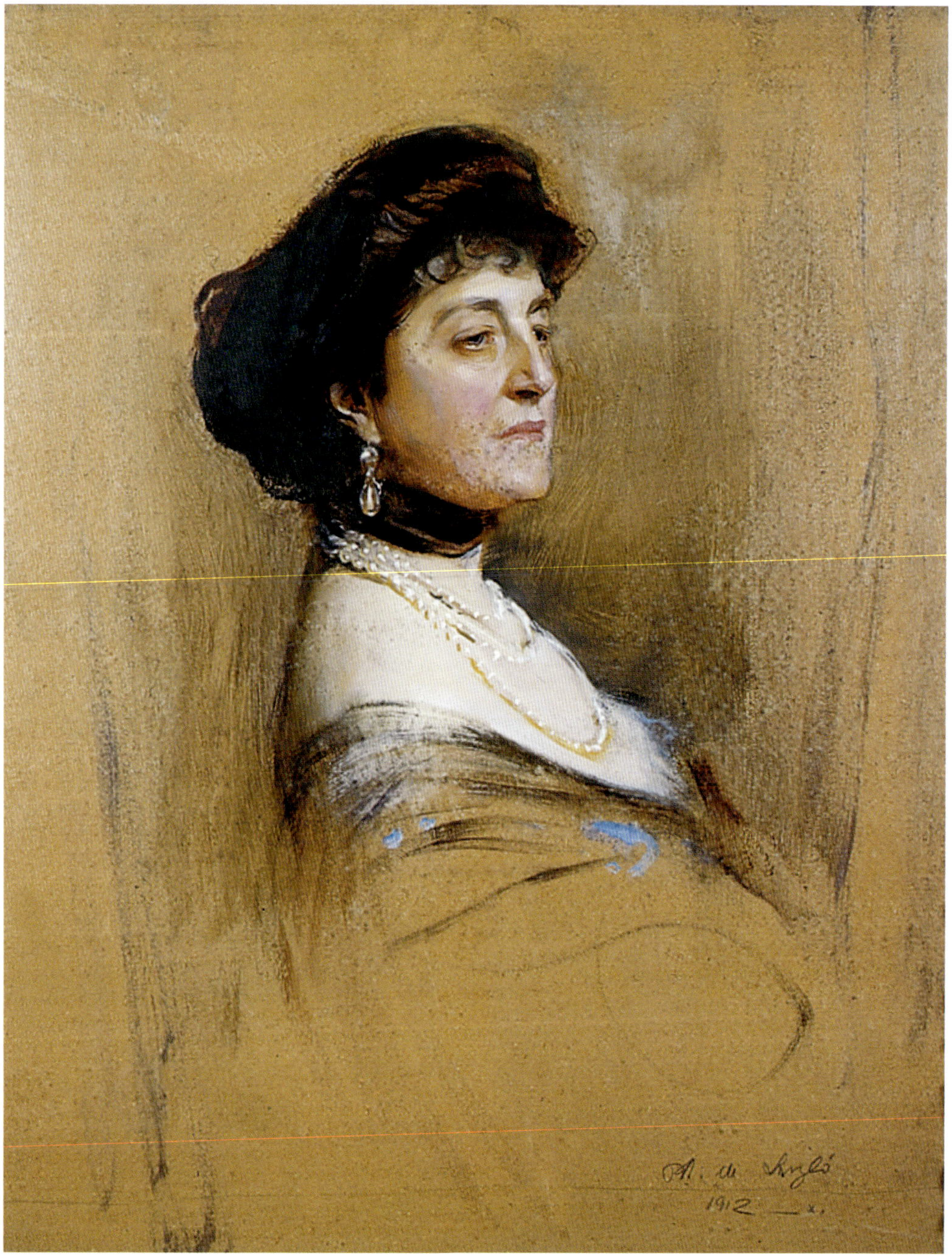

Lady Theresa Susey Helen Chetwynd-Talbot, known as 'Nellie', the eldest daughter of the 19th Earl of Shrewsbury, was born at the family home, Inglestone. In 1875 she married Charles Stewart, Viscount Castlereagh, later 6th Marquess of Londonderry, and thereafter lived mainly at Wynyard Park, Stockton-on-Tees. In 1909 she was painted by Sargent.

Nellie was, apparently, a strong-willed woman. She was well-known in racing circles, George Lambton writing in *Men and Horses I Have Known* that she "knew as much and more about a horse than most men". De László's friend the Duke of Portland, describing Lord and Lady Londonderry in his *Memoirs of Racing and Hunting*, wrote: "Lady Londonderry became quite an expert in her knowledge of pedigrees and in the practical management of a stud farm and racing stable. I am afraid, however, that [the Londonderrys'] luck on the turf never quite equalled their zest and keenness." Nonetheless, she had quite a reputation as a tipster and under a *nom de plume* wrote articles mainly about the family's racehorses. Latterly, Lord Londonderry became Lord Privy Seal and held a number of other Cabinet appointments while Lady Londonderry became a political hostess, presiding over Londonderry House in Park Lane (demolished in the 1960s).

She had two children, Charles Stewart Henry, born in 1878, who succeeded as 7th Marquess, and a daughter, Helen Mary Theresa. A younger son died in 1899. Lady Londonderry died in 1919 in London, a victim of the Spanish influenza epidemic.

52 Francis Korbay 1912

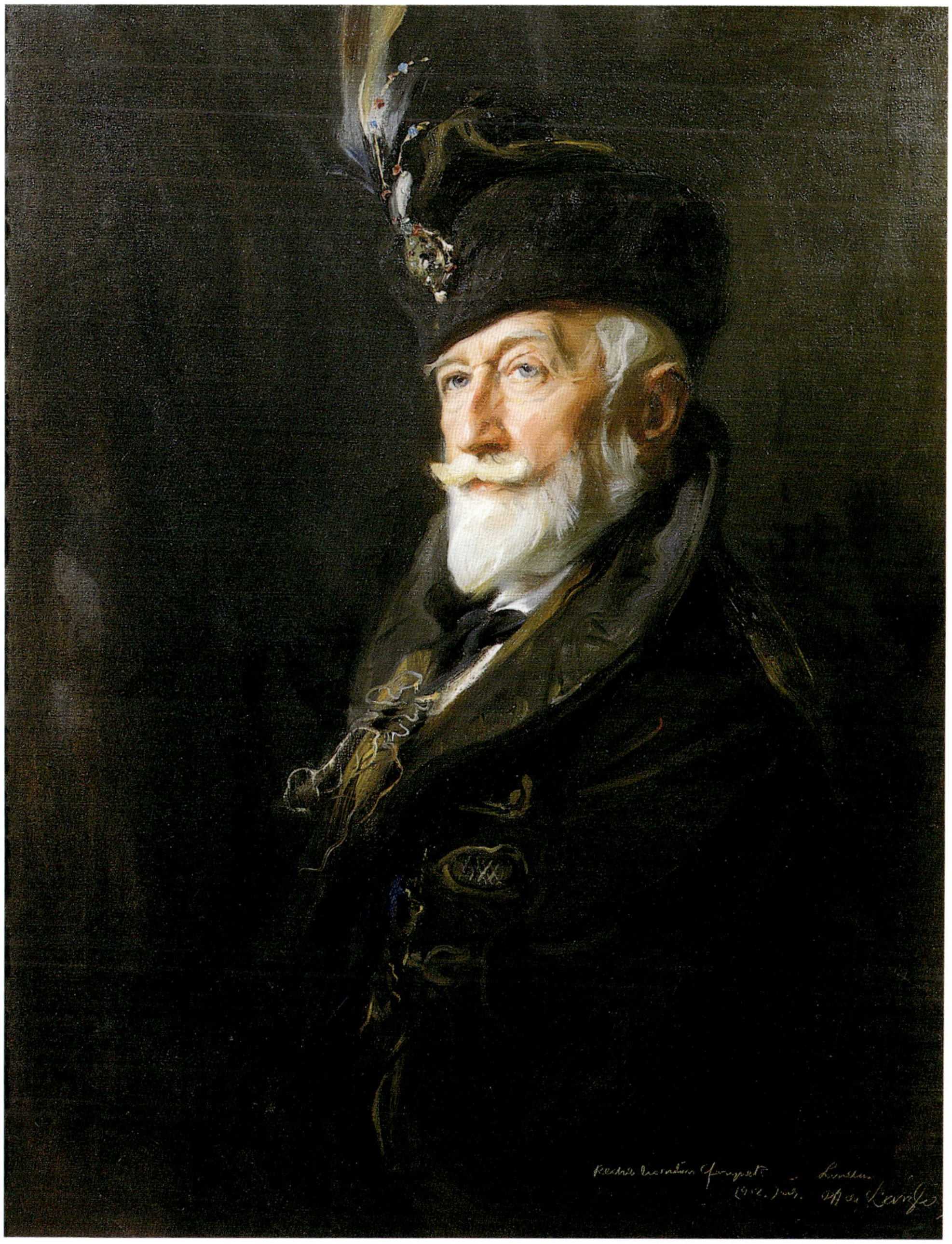

Oil on canvas, 90.2 × 69.9 cm (35½ × 27½ inches)
Signed, indistinctly inscribed in Hungarian, and dated, lower right: *Kedves barátom Ferencznek* [To my dear friend Francis]- *London / 1912. July. P A de László*
LITERATURE ASB, Vol.I, p.64: *Francis Korbay July 29th 1912;* N.P.G. Album 1903–14, p.70, and 1907–13, p.48, where annotated by de László: *Korbay Francz / my souvenir / 1912;* Williams 1921, pp.113–4, ill. facing p.112

"Monsieur Korbay was one of László's closest friends in England. His death in 1913 – a loss to musical society in London, and a lasting grief to the many friends he had in this country – moved László deeply. Born a son of one of the families of the lesser Magyar nobility, whose fortunes had been overshadowed by the troubles of the '48 [cat. 14], he devoted himself to music almost before he was out of his teens. A favourite pupil of Abbé Liszt, he became, in the judgement of many qualified critics, the finest exponent of his master's works …. László's portrait of him, done quite shortly before his death, preserves the distinguished and attractive personality of the man, his charm of manner and innate distinction. A thorough citizen of the world in every sense of the word, there was a note of old-world chivalry and courtly gallantry, more especially towards women, that made him the type of old-world aristocrat to his fingertips, of the aristocracy of wit and intellect as well as birth. So attractive a personality could not, apart from personal friendship, fail to appeal to the artist in László, just as it did to Sargent, another close friend of his. [Sargent had drawn and painted him around 1880.] Like most Hungarians, intensely jealous of their common nationality, László decided to depict his friend in the picturesque garb of a Magyar gentleman, of which both were equally proud." In March 1912 the artist himself had been raised to the hereditary Hungarian nobility by the Emperor Francis Joseph.

Francis Alexander Korbay was born in Budapest in 1846, the son of amateur musicians. He studied the piano with various masters and composition under Mosonyi and Robert Volkmann. He sang opera at the National Theatre of Budapest from 1865 to 1868. The continued exertion was too much for his voice, and he took to the piano on the advice of his godfather, Liszt. After touring in Europe as a pianist, he went to the U.S.A. in 1871 for two years. By this time his voice had recovered sufficiently to enable him to give song recitals, accompanying himself, and to teach singing. It was his arrangements of Hungarian national songs into English that made his reputation in England. Korbay lived in London from 1894 and was a professor of singing at the Royal Academy of Music from that year until his death.

53 William Lockett Agnew
1912

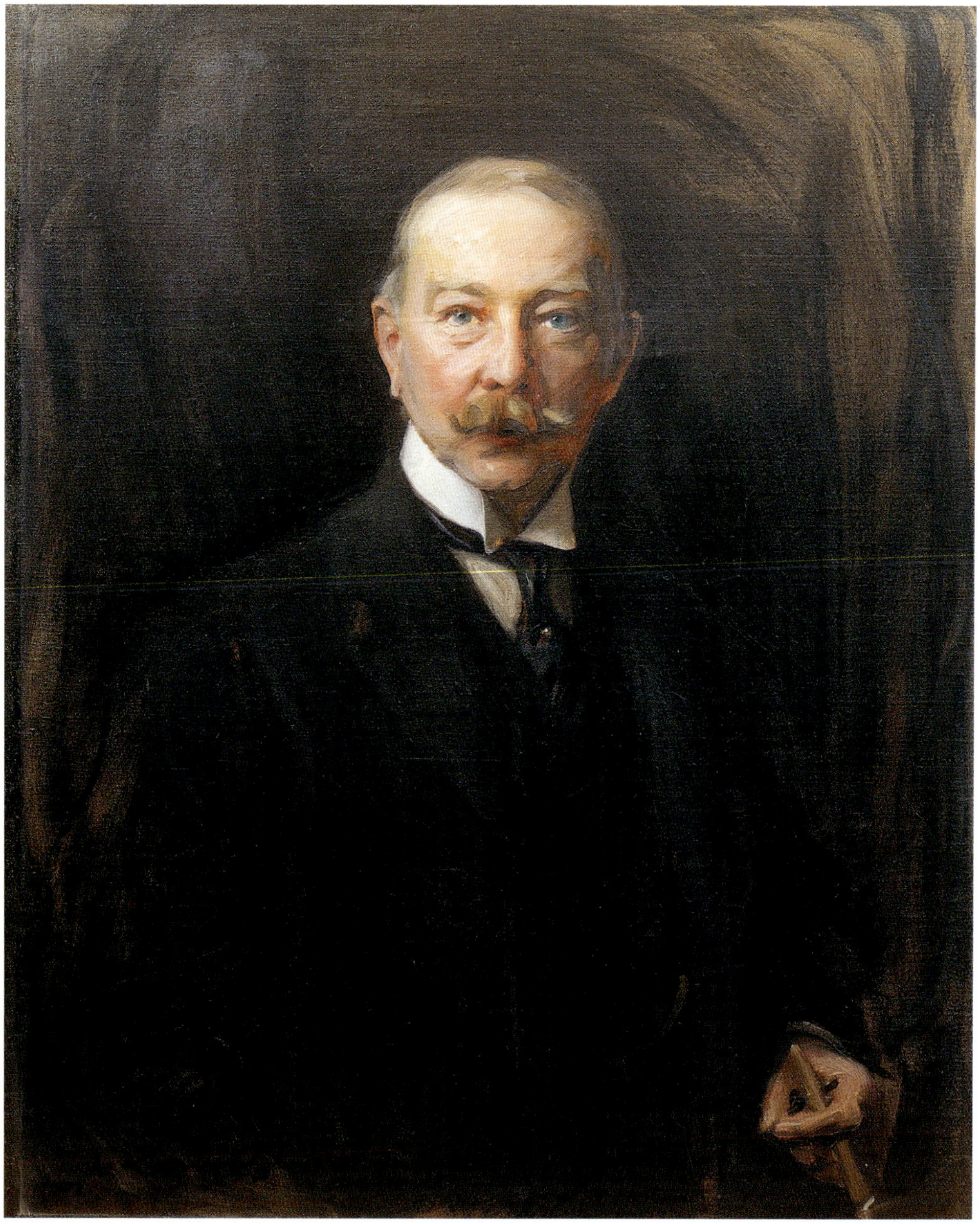

Oil on canvas, 90.2 × 69.9 cm (35½ × 27½ inches)
Signed and dated, lower left: *P.A. László / 1912.II.*
PROVENANCE Mrs Lockett Agnew, Whitehall Gardens
EXHIBITED *On Behalf of the Artists' General Benevolent Institution. Exhibition of Portraits by Philip A. László, M.V.O.*, Thos. Agnew & Sons, London, June–July 1913, no.28: *W. Lockett Agnew, Esq.*
LITERATURE N.P.G. Album 1913–15, p.30; Williams 1921, p.221; Rutter 1939, pp.266–7, 279, 322, 329, 288

Williams noted that this portrait was distinguished for its directness and unaffectedness. The strongly modelled face is lit up by a shrewd yet cheery smile, with a twinkle of humour lurking in the corner of his eyes. The impression is that of an English businessman with the open-air tastes of a country squire. He adds, "How decoratively the subfusc expanse of the Londoner's customary garb of civilization can be broken by the delicate blue spiral from a good cigar, in which the sitter was on every available opportunity wont to seek solace from the cares of business".

The following year de László painted the sitter's wife Josephine, née Shiel. Both portraits were exhibited at the artist's exhibition at Agnew's in 1913. William Lockett was a loyal friend of de László's, and a great support to him during his internment in 1917. He was born in 1858 in Salford, Manchester. His grandfather Thomas had been apprenticed to the antiquarian Vittore Zanetti, eventually becoming a partner in his thriving firm of framemakers, gilders and dealers in coins and prints. At that time the business was largely in Manchester, and it was the joint enterprise of the Agnews (father and son) which was instrumental in bringing the company south in 1860. In 1881, Lockett joined what by then had become the family firm of art dealers and publishers, and became senior partner in 1913, a post he held until his death. He invited de László to exhibit three times in his galleries, twice in 1911 (on the first occasion specially to show de László's recently completed portrait of Emperor William II, cat. 40) and in 1913.

Generous and charming, William Lockett was also a competent sportsman, and very knowledgeable about racing. He had no children, but was devoted to his beautiful wife, sisters and two nephews, to whom he was known as 'Uncle Spoof'. He died in London in 1918.

54 George Nathaniel, Earl Curzon of Kedleston 1913

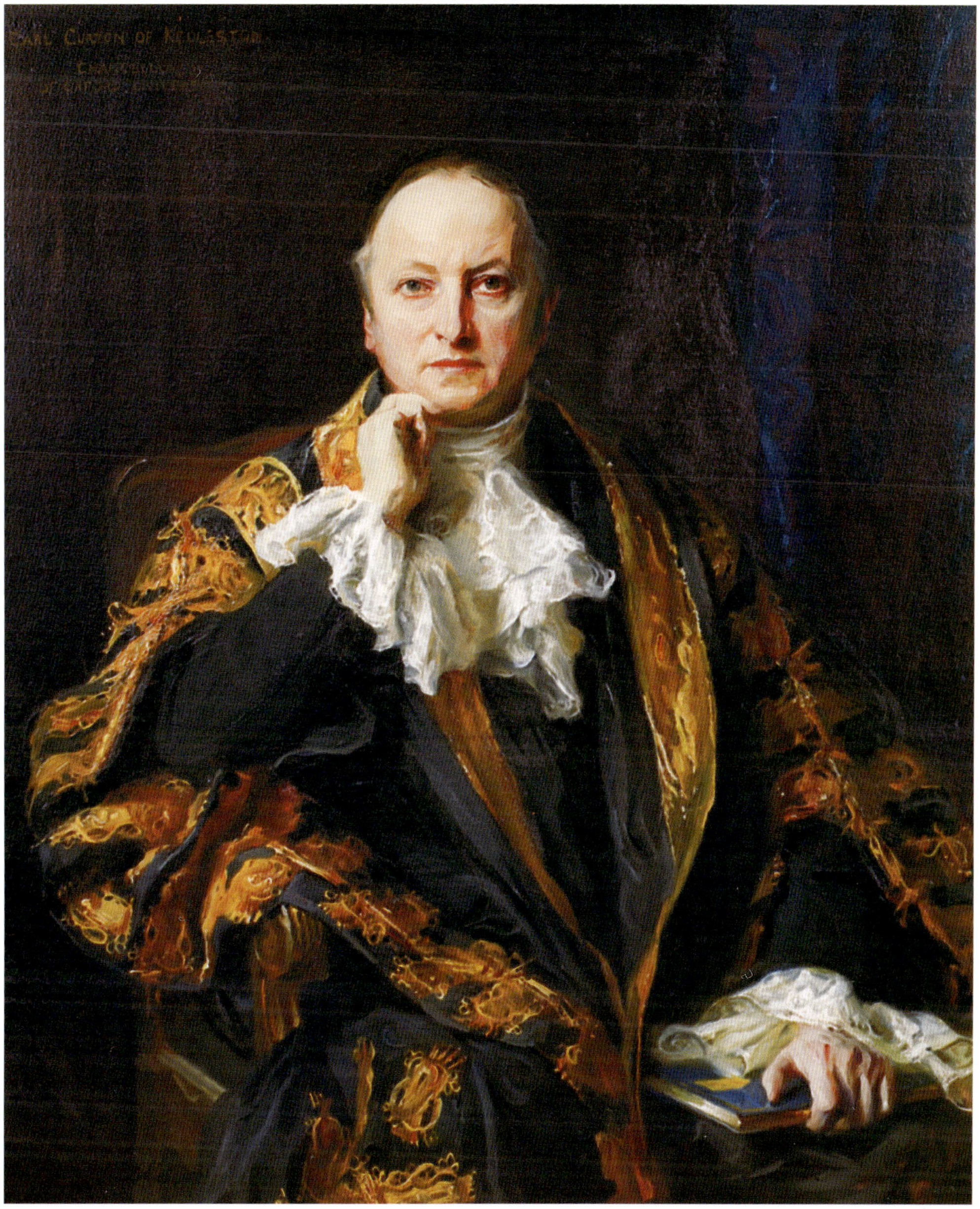

Oil on canvas, 118.1 × 96.5 cm (46½ × 38 inches)
Signed and dated, lower left: *P. A. de László. / 1913 / MAR*; upper left: *EARL CURZON OF KEDLESTON / CHANCELLOR / OF OXFORD UNIVERSITY*
The Warden and Fellows of All Souls College, Oxford
PROVENANCE Presented to All Souls College by the sitter
EXHIBITED *On Behalf of the Artists' General Benevolent Institution. Exhibition of Portraits by Philip A. László, M.V.O.*, Thos. Agnew & Sons, London, June–July 1913, no.2: *The Earl Curzon of Kedleston, P.C., G.C.S.I.*
LITERATURE ASB, Vol.I, p.92: *Curzon of Kedleston / March 15th. 1913*; Williams 1921, pp.197–200, ill. facing p.196; Mrs Reginald Lane Poole, *Catalogue of Portraits in the Possession of The University, Colleges, City and County of Oxford*, Oxford 1912–25, Part II, III, pp.203–4; Rutter 1939, pp.278, 293, 298–9; Jane Abdy, *The Souls*, London 1984, p.29; David Gilmour, *Curzon*, London 1994, head study ill. on cover and spine

There exist two authorized copies of the present portrait, by Frederick Cullen (Balliol College, Oxford), and Sydney Percy Kendrick (School Hall, Eton College), and at the time he painted the present portrait, in March 1913, de László also made a head and shoulders study which he gave to the sitter as a 'souvenir' (private collection). The following year Lord Curzon was painted by Sargent (fig. 35, p. 46).

George Nathaniel Curzon, Marquess Curzon of Kedleston, K.G., P.C., G.C.S.I., G.C.I.E. (1859–1925), was the eldest son of Baron Scarsdale. He gained a fellowship at All Souls in 1884. A man of great self-confidence, Lord Curzon had unshakeable faith in his own infallibility, which earned him an unfortunate reputation for unapproachability and pomposity, but his energy and ability and his courage in the face of bitter disappointments stamp him as one of the outstanding figures of the century. He became Under Secretary of State for India in 1891, and from 1895 to 1898 Under Secretary of State for Foreign Affairs. In 1898, at the age of thirty-nine, he was made Viceroy of India. Disagreements brought on by his dynamic regime forced his resignation and return to England in 1905. In 1907 he was elected Chancellor of Oxford University and Honorary Fellow of Balliol College. It was during this period that de László painted this portrait of Lord Curzon in his Chancellor's robes, holding a bound copy of the University Statutes.

In 1911 he was made Earl Curzon of Kedleston. In 1915 he returned to politics as Lord Privy Seal and was Lord President of the Council and member of the War Cabinet from 1916–19. He fulfilled his ambition of becoming Foreign Secretary (1919–24), but was thwarted in his hopes for the premiership by the selection of Stanley Baldwin in 1923. From 1916 to 1924 he was Leader of the House of Lords. He was created Marquess in 1921.

For some years Curzon's name was linked with that of Elinor Glyn (cat. 55).

55 Elinor Glyn 1914

Oil on canvas, 111.8 × 81.3 cm (44 × 32 inches)
Signed and dated, lower right:
P.A. de László / XII. 1914. LONDON
PROVENANCE Sir Rhys Rhys Williams Bt., D.S.O., K.C., and by descent in the family
EXHIBITED Grosvenor Gallery, London, 1914; *Paintings by Philip A. de László*, The Corcoran Gallery of Art, Washington, February–March 1921, no.18: *Mrs. Elinor Glyn*; *Paintings by Philip A. de László*, M. Knoedler & Co., New York, April 1921, no.14: *Mrs. Elinor Glyn*; *Elinor Glyn*, Ferrers Gallery, London, October–November 1974, no.1
LITERATURE ASB Vol.I, p.95: *Elinor Glyn Oct. 14th 1914*, and p.100: *Elinor Glyn November 5th / 1914*; *The Studio*, LXVIII, 1916, pp.145–56, ill.; *The Sunday Chronicle*, 13 October 1935, p.2, article by Beverley Nichols: N.P.G. 1915–16 Album, p.12; Rutter 1939, pp. 298–9; Jane Abdy, *The Souls*, London 1984, p.29; Meredith Etherington-Smith and Jeremy Pilcher, *The IT Girls*, London 1986, pp.167, 211

"Dear Mr de László, A lady who is very [good] looking in a picturesque way and has some fame has written to me from Paris and asked whether it would be likely that you would paint her. Her name is Elinor Glyn the novelist. She is not well off and I am afraid could not manage anything big." So wrote Lord Curzon in July 1913, a few months after de László had painted his own portrait (cat. 54). "You could make a splendid thing of her," he continued, "with her white skin, dark eyebrows, green eyes and Venetian red hair." Glyn had her own ideas about her portrait. She wanted to be painted in black transparent drapery sitting on a long-haired Manchurian tiger-skin whose orange coat would match her hair. She explained to de Laszlo: "If you knew the strange effect tiger skins have on me! the touch of the tiger awakens some far-off savagery – some former life when I was unhampered, and could kill – or love – when I desired, without having to consider civilisation. Now I am in a cage and live off bread and milk, and wear sapphires." The price of 300 guineas was agreed but pressure of work meant that it was not until February 1914 that de László could travel to Paris to make a preparatory study (Prado, Madrid). Then the war broke out and de László was overwhelmed with commissions to paint men leaving for the front. In desperation Glyn wrote to him in October: "I do believe it is because you don't want to paint my portrait at all that you keep putting me off?! You perhaps dislike weird red hair and white faces, & prefer the sweet cows' milk English ladies that one sees staring in their strength from the walls of the Academy!"

Unable to resist her charms, de László changed some appointments and the final version of the portrait was completed in London in December. The tiger skin was left out but, according to Rutter, Glyn was nevertheless delighted with the portrait, despite reservations that the hair was "a trifle too orange red". Lord Curzon was also pleased: as Glyn wrote to de László, "I had again a letter from Lord C. saying the portrait was 'a masterpiece of modern times' & would rank with the best of all ages besides being a 'superlative likeness' – great praise from him!" It also created a stir at the Grosvenor Gallery when it was exhibited there soon after it was painted. De László wrote to his wife: "I was very happy painting Glyn. The picture will be diabolic – she feels it, and I see it."

The novelist Beverley Nichols went to the exhibition with Glyn, particularly to see her portrait. "I stared at the portrait, I stared at the original," he wrote. "Finally I turned to her and said: 'Which is which?' She smiled, and shrugged her shoulders. Only a great artist could have painted that picture. Elinor Glyn is an enigma, and so is the picture."

De László painted Glyn's mother the following year, and between 1923 and 1925 painted two versions each of her daughters, Margot and Juliet.

Elinor Glyn was born in Jersey in 1864, the second daughter of Douglas Sutherland (1830–1865), a civil engineer from Toronto, and his wife Elinor, of Ontario. Her father died only the year after she was born. In 1871 her mother married David Kennedy (1810–1888), apparently to fulfil her first husband's wish that their two daughters should be brought up in Europe. The family settled in St Helier, where the characterful girls were taught by a succession of governesses. In April 1892 she married Clayton Glyn J.P., a personable Essex landowner. They lived in lavish style, entertaining and being entertained in large country houses, and Glyn gained a reputation for her exotic looks and behaviour.

Her husband was a financial failure, however, and soon she was writing her romantic novels and short stories out of necessity. In 1915 Clayton Glyn died. For some years her name was linked with that of Lord Curzon, after he had fallen for her when he saw her playing in a dramatization of her novel *Three Weeks* in London in July 1908. Curzon was for Elinor the great romantic figure, "the sun, moon and stars to the end of time". The announcement of his engagement to Grace Duggan in 1916, without a word to her before or afterwards, was a bitter blow.

She had a first brief acquaintance with film around this time. Her novel *The Reason Why* was filmed as a silent two-reeler in 1915, and, according to Etherington-Smith and Pilcher, she herself had been filmed by George Eastman while de László was painting her. In 1922 Elinor Glyn went to Hollywood for five years and later to New York, where she wrote articles for the daily press and stories for magazines. She wrote *It* and the screenplay for the film which made Clara Bow the 'It' girl. In 1927 de László painted a third portrait of her. Afterwards she wrote in his sitters' book: "a life's gratitude for three hours of divine inspiration / great artist! – homage! June 25 1927."

After losing a certain amount in films, the later years of her life she spent in London, and continued writing articles for both the British press and the Hearst newspapers in America. In 1940 her family, fearing for her safety in the Blitz, sent her to their family home in Wales. However, dissatisfied there, she returned to London, where she died in a nursing home in 1943, aged seventy-eight. Ironically, the 1927 portrait was destroyed in a bombing raid while in storage in Cardiff.

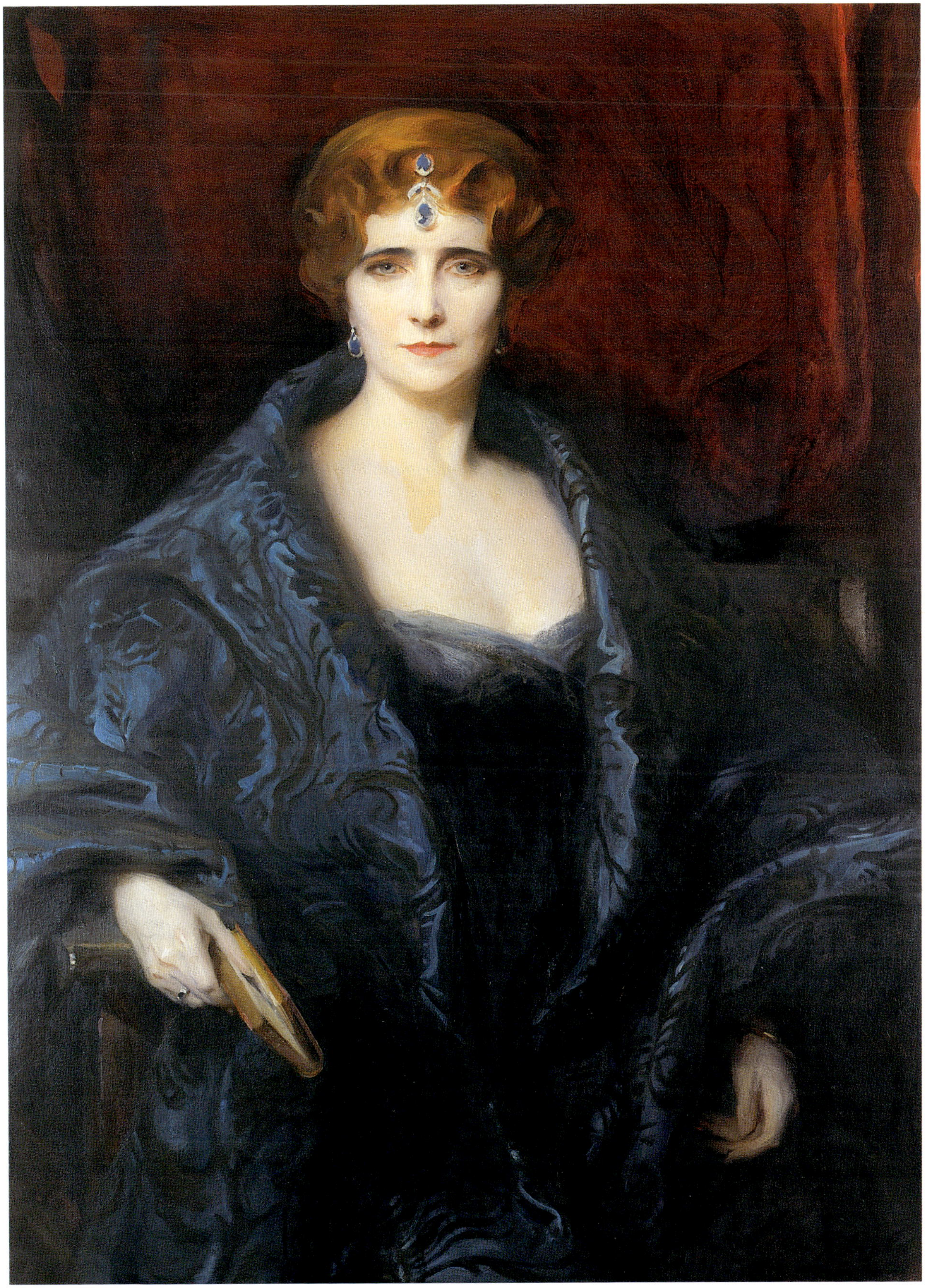

56 The Marchioness of Londonderry, née the Hon. Edith Chaplin 1920

Oil on canvas, 87 × 55.9 cm (34¼ × 22 inches)
Indistinctly signed and dated, lower right:
de László / 1920
The Imperial War Museum, London
PROVENANCE Presented by the artist to the Imperial War Museum in 1920
EXHIBITED *A Series of Portraits and Studies By Philip A. de László, M.V.O.*,The French Gallery, London, June 1923: *The Marchioness of Londonderry / Kindly lent by the Imperial War Museum. A gift to the Nation by the Artist*; *Society Portraits, 1850–1939*, Colnaghi and The Clarendon Gallery, 30 October–14 December 1985, no.74, pp.164–5, ill.
LITERATURE N.P.G. 1917–21 Album, p.117; 'Rally Cry to Northern Women', *North Mail & Newcastle Chronicle*, 26 October 1931, ill.; *The British Legion Journal*, March 1933, p.307, ill.; *The British Legion Journal*, May 1933, p. 388 (correction); Rutter 1939, pp.277, 345

The painting was made in two full days in May 1920. De László painted the sitter without her hat at the request of the Trustees of the Imperial War Museum, and he made no charge for the commission. The sitter is seen wearing the uniform of the Women's Army Auxiliary Corps, later called the Women's Legion, which she was instrumental in raising during the First World War. For this she was honoured with the first military D.B.E. in 1917.

De László had painted the sitter in 1913 when she was Viscountess Castlereagh (cat. 57), and was to paint her again in 1927.

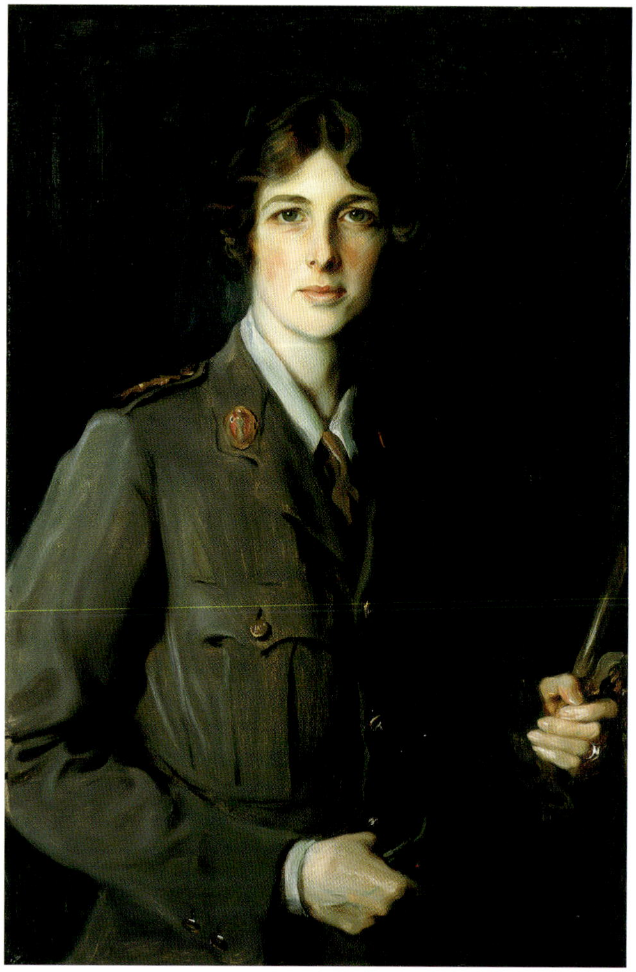

57 Viscountess Castlereagh, née the Hon. Edith Chaplin 1913

Oil on canvas, 182.9 × 116.8 cm (72 × 46 inches)
Signed and dated, lower right:
P. A. de László / 1913 Aug
Mount Stewart, Londonderry Collection by permission of the Honourable Lady Mairi Bury, J.P.
EXHIBITED *Exhibition of Portraits by Philip A. de Laszlo, M.V.O.*, Thos. Agnew & Sons, London, June–July 1913, no. 4: *The Viscountess Castlereagh*
LITERATURE *Die Woche*, issue 35, Berlin 1913, ill. p.1486; Williams 1921, pp. 205–8, ill. facing p.204; Hugh Montgomery Hyde, *Londonderry House and its Pictures*, London 1937, ill. pl. XXXVII: *EDITH, MARCHIONESS OF LONDONDERRY / Philip de Laszlo*, and in index with other de László portraits, p.57; Rutter 1939, p.277; Anne de Courcey, *Circe, The Life of Edith Marchioness of Londonderry*, London 1992, ill. on dust cover (detail)

Lady Castlereagh and de László co-operated in the design of this portrait, which was to be hung in the great portrait gallery in Londonderry House among the paintings by Gainsborough, Reynolds and Lawrence, and so strove to achieve a timeless quality in the dress, colouring and composition. The portrait did not completely satisfy Lord Castlereagh, however, who requested certain alterations, but de László stood his ground. In 1920 the Marchioness of Londonderry, as she had become, was painted again by de László in

W.A.A.C. uniform (cat. 56). Sargent also made a charcoal sketch of her during the war.

In 1924 de László painted a portrait of her husband, seated, most probably in Londonderry House, beneath a portrait of the 2nd Marquess by Lawrence. It would seem that a pendant portrait of Lady Londonderry was to be painted, but only a sketch for this is thus far recorded.

The Hon. Edith Helen Chaplin, born in 1878 in Blankney, Lincolnshire, was the eldest daughter of 1st Viscount Chaplin. She married Charles Stewart Henry Vane-Tempest-Stewart, Viscount Castlereagh, later 7th Marquess of Londonderry, in 1899. They had one son (cat. 50) and four daughters. Following the example of her mother-in-law (cat. 51) she became the most distinguished political hostess of her day, hosting Eve of Parliament receptions for the Conservative Party between the wars and receiving up to two thousand guests in an evening at Londonderry House. Her remarkable spectrum of friendships was reflected in the membership of The Ark, the dining club she founded in 1915, whose members, including Winston Churchill, Ramsay Macdonald and the Prince of Wales, were given the names of birds, beasts or mythical animals. She also founded the Women's Legion and was an early and influential supporter of women's suffrage.

A brilliant gardener, plantswoman and botanist, she created the Mount Stewart gardens and arboretum in County Down (now National Trust) while her husband was Minister of Education in the Northern Ireland government from 1921 to 1926. According one of her daughters, she had a good sense of humour and a tremendous enthusiasm for life. She remained very energetic, even when suffering from bone cancer for the last two years of her life. A nephew who had been wounded in the First World War gave her his electric wheelchair, which, 'zuped up', enabled her to speed about her garden right to the end of her life. She was always surrounded by dogs of various breeds and she bred dachshunds. De László has painted her with her favourite lurcher. She died in 1959 at Mount Stewart.

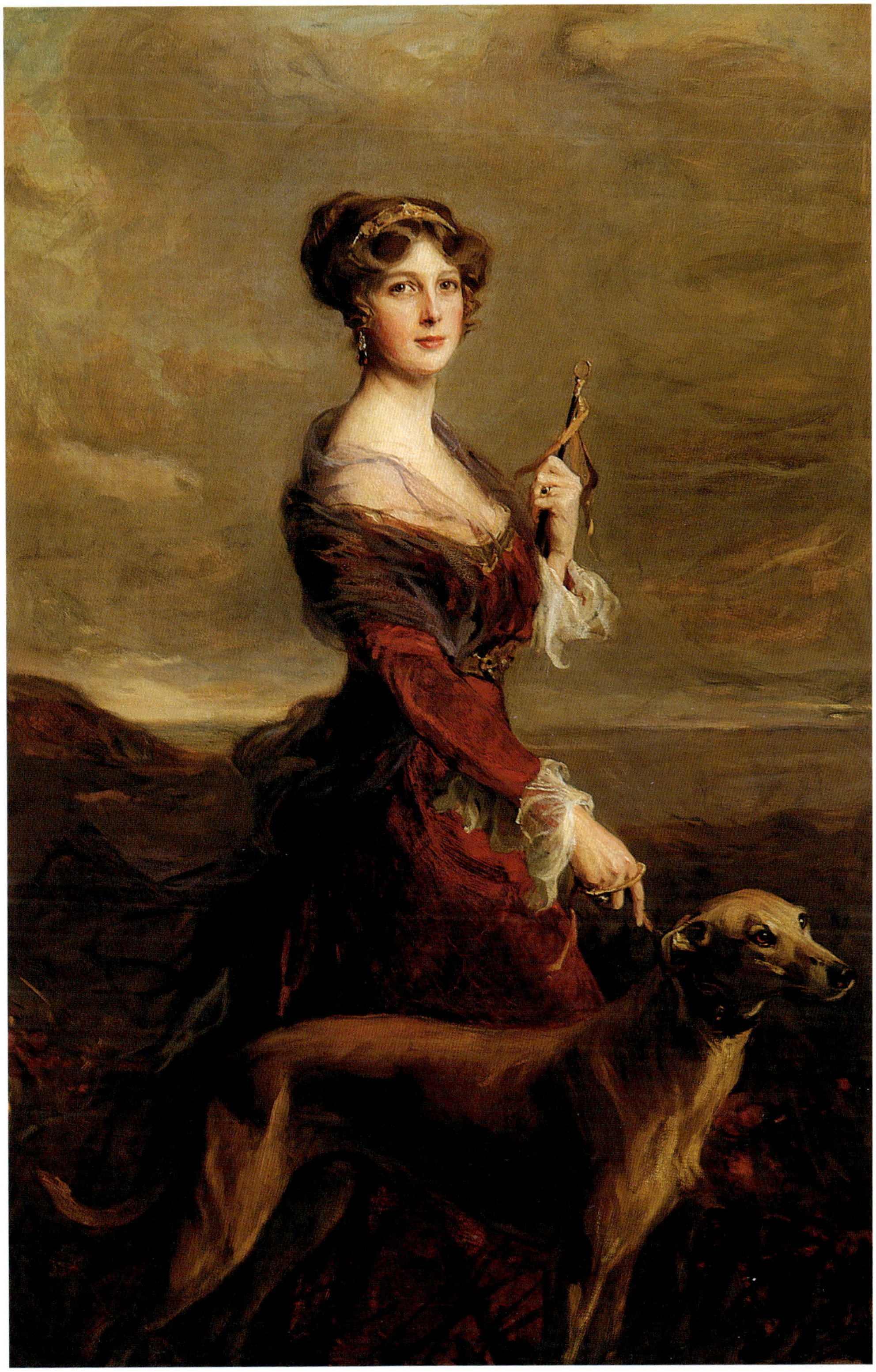

58 H.M. Queen Olga, Queen Mother of the Hellenes, née Grand Duchess Olga of Russia 1914

Oil on canvas, 147.3 × 101.3 cm (58 × 40½ inches)
Signed, inscribed and dated, upper left: *P. A. de László / ATHEN. / 1914. iv.*; upper right, the Greek Royal and Russian Imperial Arms

PROVENANCE H.R.H. Princess Helen of Roumania

EXHIBITED *Royal Portraits by Philip A. de László, M.V.O.*, M. Knoedler & Company, Inc., London, 27 November–8 December 1934, no.13: *Her Majesty the Late Queen Olga of Greece, wife of H.M. the late King George of Greece and sister-in-law of H.M. Queen Alexandra. Kindly lent by H.R.H. Princess Helen of Roumania*

LITERATURE ASB, Vol.I, p.96: *Die Kunst ist meine feurige Liebe / die zur Heimat führet / Athen März 1914. Olga / Königin Mutter der Hellenen, Prinzessin von Dänemark, Grossfürstin von Russland* [Art is my burning love that leads [me] home. Athens March 1914. Olga / Queen Mother of the Hellenes, Princess of Denmark, Grand Duchess of Russia]; and p.98: *Olga*, on a page with the signatures of Queen Alexandra, Maria Feodorovna, the Dowager Empress of Russia, King Manuel and Queen Auguste Victoria of Portugal, several of which are dated 1914; Rutter 1939, pp. 285–92

In February 1914 de László and his wife were spending a holiday near Toulon in France, when an unexpected telegram arrived from Prince Andrew of Greece, whom de László had painted in London the previous year (cat. 37), on behalf of his brother, King Constantine (cat. 60), inviting him to come to Greece to paint portraits of the royal family. After an arduous journey by train via Paris and Milan and then by steamer from Brindisi to Athens, de László finally arrived on the evening of 27 March.

Early the next morning they were received by the Queen Mother, Queen Olga, dressed in deep mourning, her husband of forty-six years having been assassinated the previous year. She personally showed them around the old Royal Palace, finding a large room with a north light for de László's use as a studio. Sittings began immediately for Queen Olga's portrait, for which she wore the blue sash and badge of the Grand Cross of the Royal Order of the Saviour of Greece, and an extraordinary rapport developed between sitter and artist. As de László himself described her, "Her Majesty was a dignified and handsome lady, with a lovely smile, and very Slavonic in type .... Her gracious manner put me at my ease immediately .... Her nobility of mind and her goodness of heart were coupled with great modesty .... Unfortunately she could not see without glasses, and at first I had some difficulty in getting the expression of her eyes." Nevertheless she noticed the artist's arm shaking with tiredness as he held his increasingly heavy palette and numerous brushes in his left hand, and arranged to have a smaller one made with the thumb-hole padded with chamois leather, writing a personal inscription on the reverse. "It would be difficult to give a better example of her tenderness of heart. She radiated love." Such was the affection she commanded within the royal family that while her portrait was being painted the studio became its members' daily meeting place.

During his stay de László painted some seven portraits of immediate members of the Greek royal family. At the end, Queen Olga specially requested that de László accompany her to England. He brought the paintings with him to complete, and in June three Queens visited his studio in Fitzjohn's Avenue to see them – Queen Alexandra, The Empress Marie of Russia and Queen Olga herself.

Queen Olga was born in 1851, daughter of Grand Duke Constantine, niece of Tsar Alexander II and grand-daughter of Tsar Nicholas I. In 1867 she married King George I of the Hellenes (1845–1913), born Prince William of Denmark, who had been elected King of Greece in 1863. Together they had eight children, their eldest son succeeding to the Greek throne as King Constantine I.

"How charming Olga of Greece is!" Queen Victoria had written to her daughter Empress Frederick, "so handsome & so dear and charming. She has *none* of the *bourgeoisie* of the rest of the Russian family even including our dear excellent Marie [Duchess of Edinburgh]." She was also much loved by her sister-in-law Queen Alexandra and by King Edward VII, and particularly by the young Prince George (later King George V). She spent the First World War and Revolution in Russia with her other sister-in-law, the Dowager Empress Marie, where she established and ran a hospital in Pavlovsk, near St Petersburg. Rescued from Russia in 1918 under Danish diplomatic protection, she went to Switzerland to join her son, Constantine, then in exile. She returned to Greece on the death of her grandson, King Alexander I, in 1920, and became Regent until Constantine's restoration in December of that year. After the declaration of a Republic in 1924, she lived in exile at first in London and then in Rome, where she died in June 1926. She was buried in the crypt of the Orthodox Church in Florence alongside the coffin of her son Constantine, but her remains were re-interred in Greece on the restoration of the Monarchy in 1935. She was renowned for the philanthropic works she instituted in Greece and it was on her initiative that the Bible was translated into modern Greek.

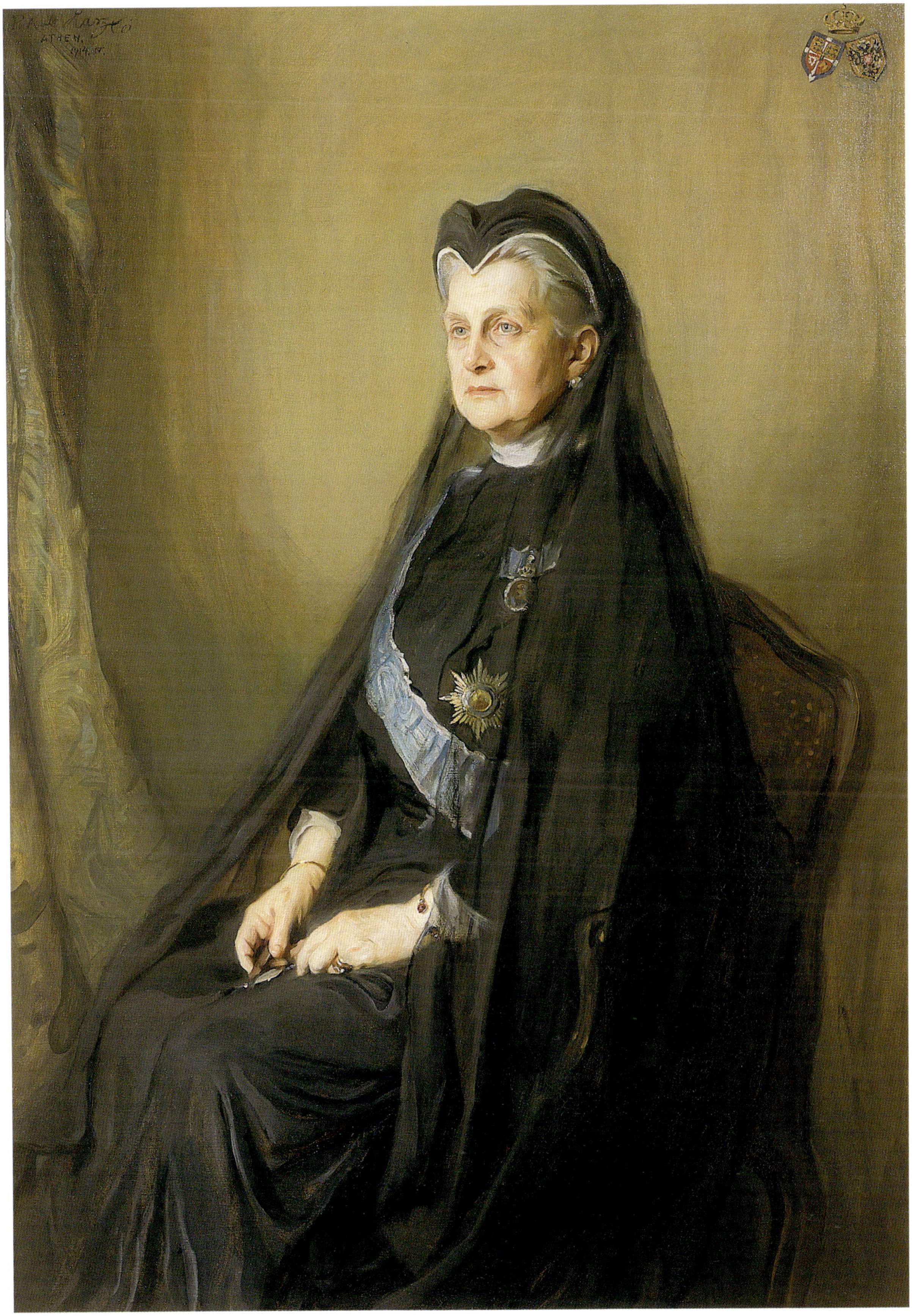

59 H.R.I.H. Princess Nicholas of Greece, née Grand Duchess Elena Vladimirovna of Russia 1914

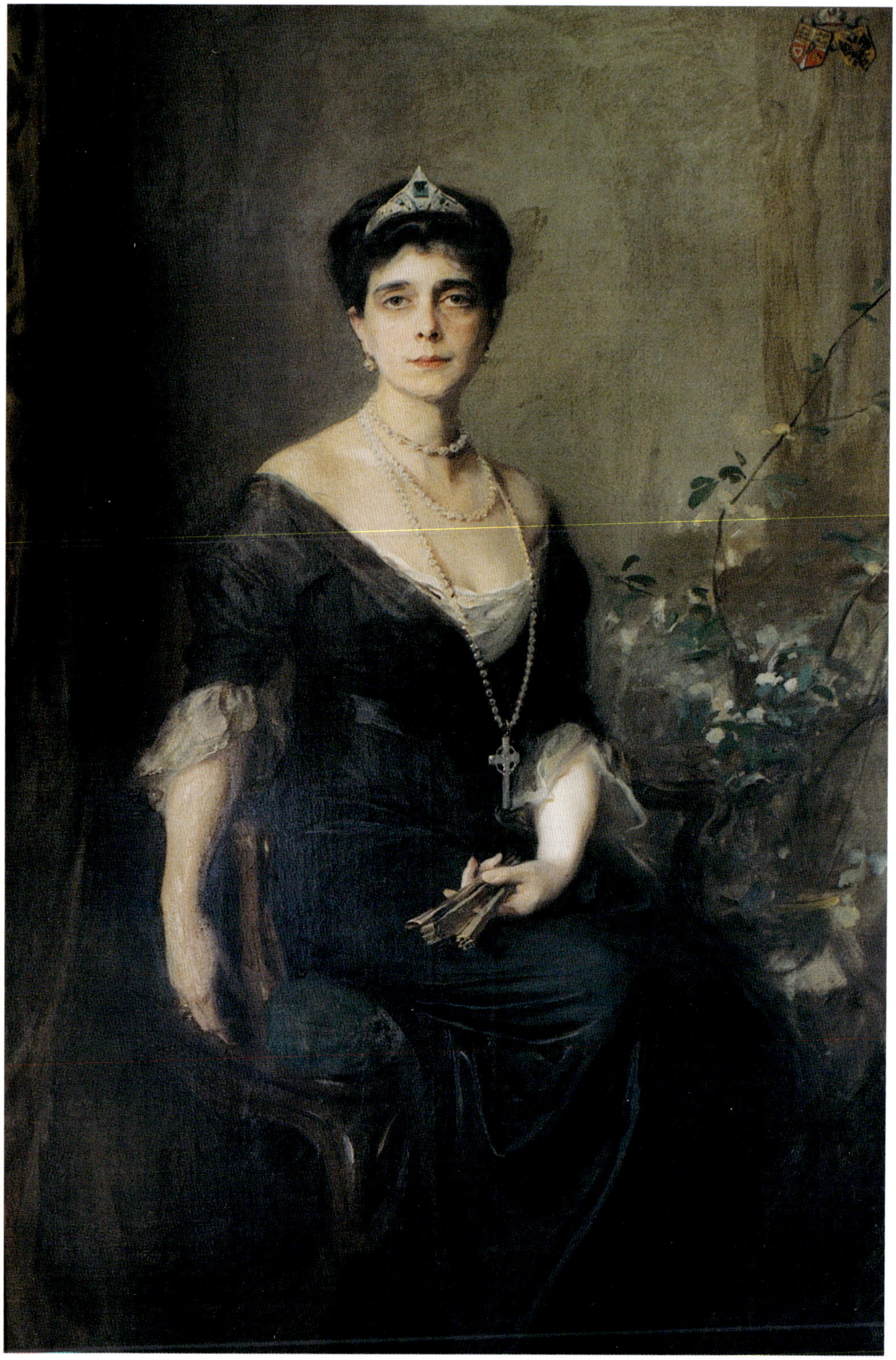

Oil on canvas, 158.8 × 103.2 cm (63½ × 40⅝ inches)
Signed and dated, lower left: *P.A. de László . Athens 1914 . IV.*; upper right, the Royal and Imperial Arms of Denmark and Russia

PROVENANCE The late Princess Marina, Duchess of Kent, daughter of the sitter

EXHIBITED *Royal Portraits by Philip A. de László, M.V.O., Loan Exhibition In aid of The Wedding Gift Fund for St. George's Hospital (at the special request of H.R.H. The Duke of Kent)*, M. Knoedler & Company, Inc., London, November–December 1934, no: 11: *Her Royal and Imperial Highness Princess Nicholas of Greece, mother of H.R.H. Princess Marina; Exposition P. A. de László*, Hotel Jean Charpentier, Paris, June 1931

LITERATURE ASB, Vol.I, p.96: *Helene / Prinzessin von Griechenland / Grossfürstin von Russland Athen, April 1914* [Helen / Princess of Greece / Grand Duchess of Russia Athens, April 1914]; Wedding Present List of H.R.H. the Duke of Kent and Princess Marina, 29 November 1934, no.1047: *T.R.H. Prince and Princess Christopher of Greece. Framed portrait of H.R.H. Princess Nicholas of Greece by P. de László; The Illustrated London News*, 1 December 1934, p.867, ill.: *The Bride's Mother: Her Royal and Imperial Highness Princess Nicholas of Greece.*; Prince Michael of Greece and Alan Palmer, *The Royal House of Greece*, London 1990, p.70, ill.; Geoffrey C. Munn, *Tiaras. A History of Splendour*, Woodbridge 2001, p.184, ill. pl.164; Hugo Vickers, *Alice, Princess Andrew of Greece*, London 2000

De László painted more than fifty portraits of the British and Greek Royal Families over the years 1907 to 1935, two years before he died. This portrait was given to the Duke of Kent and Princess Marina, the daughter of the sitter, on the occasion of their marriage in 1934 by Prince and Princess Christopher of Greece.

De László also painted a study portrait of the sitter in Athens in 1914, which is inscribed by the artist: *In grateful remembrance of my happy Easter in Athens.* Furthermore, there are two preparatory drawings in the collection of a descendant of the artist, one of which is indistinctly inscribed by the artist: *1914, July / … a few days before the war.*

Princess Nicholas of Greece, Grand Duchess Elena of Russia (known as Ellen) was born in 1882. An austere and commanding woman, she was the daughter of Grand Duke Vladimir, a son of Tsar Alexander II, and his wife, the formidable Maria Pavlovna, née Princess of Mecklenburg-Schwerin. The infamous Prince Felix Yussopov, the murderer of Rasputin, claimed in his memoirs that he had been in love with Ellen for years. "Her beauty fascinated me," he wrote, "she had the loveliest eyes imaginable and everyone fell under their charm." In 1902 she married Prince Nicholas (born 1872), the third son of George I, King of the Hellenes, and Queen Olga (cat. 60), who was not only a professional soldier but a talented painter and playwright. They had three daughters, Olga, Elizabeth and Marina (cat. 127). According to Hugo Vickers, "her priorities were 'God first, then the Russian Grand Dukes, then the rest'." Crown Princess Marie, née Bonaparte, thought her "superb" but was scared by "her beauty and her pride".

In 1917 Prince Nicholas and his wife followed his brother, King Constantine (cat. 60), into exile in Switzerland. They returned to Greece in 1920, but after 1923 settled in Paris. In 1935 the family returned to Greece, where Prince Nicholas died in 1938. Throughout the German occupation Princess Nicholas refused to leave, preferring to remain near her husband's tomb. She died in Athens in 1957.

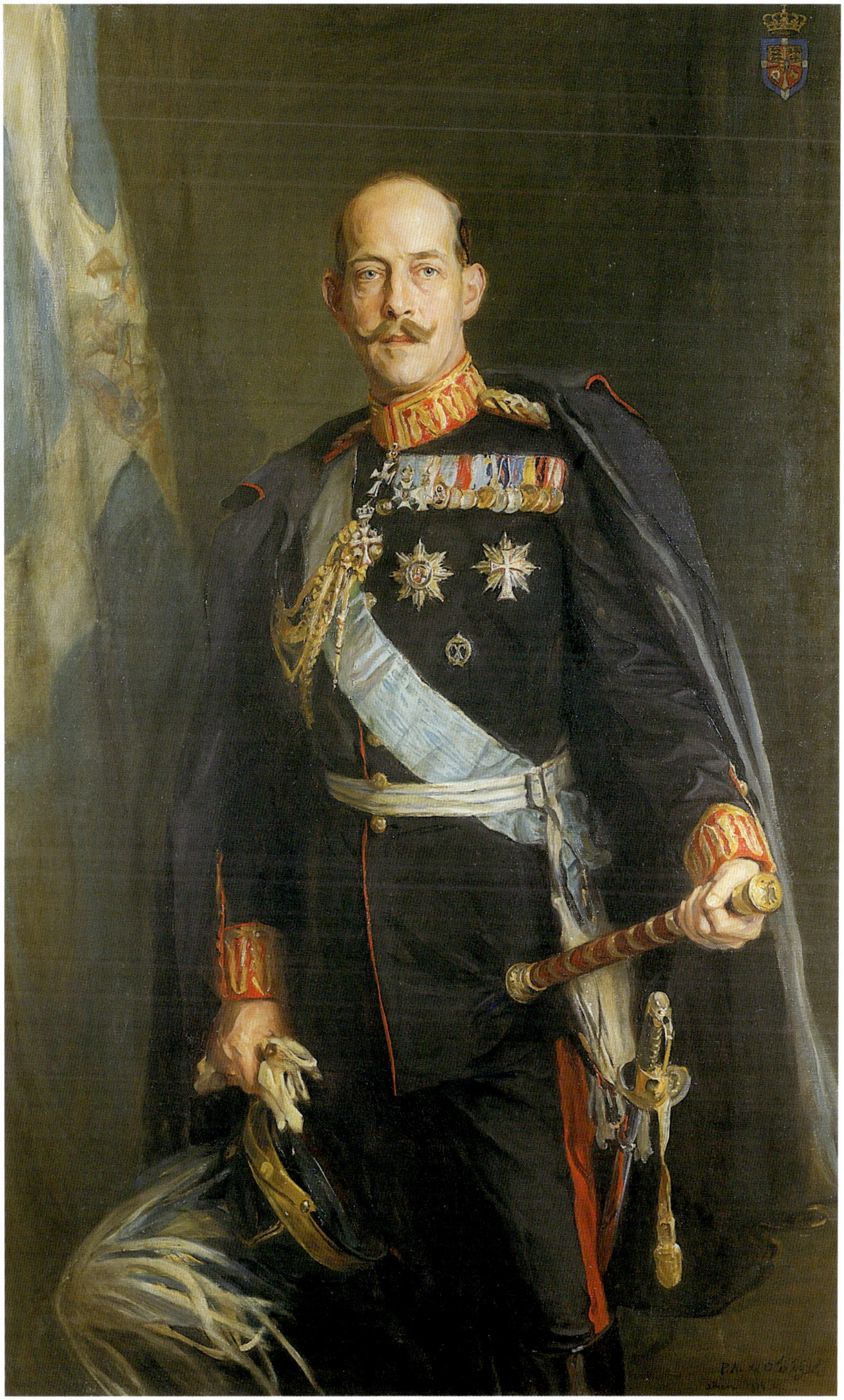

60 H.M. King Constantine I of the Hellenes 1914

Oil on canvas, 179 × 109.9 cm ($70\frac{1}{2} \times 43\frac{1}{4}$ inches)
Signed, inscribed and dated, lower right: *P.A. de László / Athen 1914.iv.*; upper right: the Royal Arms of Greece

PROVENANCE Her Royal Highness Princess Helen of Roumania

EXHIBITED *Royal Portraits by Philip A. de László,*

M.V.O., M. Knoedler & Company, Inc., London, 27 November–8 December 1934, no.3: *H.M. The Late King Constantine of Greece, brother of H.R.H. Prince Nicholas of Greece. Kindly lent by H.R.H. Princess Helen of Roumania*

LITERATURE ASB, Vol.I, p.97: *Constantine R. / Athen 1/14 April 1914*; Rutter 1939, pp. 285–92

On 14 April 1914 de László began his portrait of the King Constantine, the king standing for five hours so that he was able to finish the underpainting. De László depicted him in the full dress uniform of a General of the Infantry of the Greek Army with the blue sash and badge of the Grand Cross of the Royal Order of the Saviour of Greece, the Cross of the Danish Order of the Danebrog, and the Greek Military Cross at his neck. The Field Marshal's baton in the king's hand had just been presented to him by the Army in recognition of the manner in which he had led them in the recent war with Turkey. The sittings were very informal, usually followed by tea, and surrounded by the king's children, who took to calling the artist 'uncle'. The king sat to him every day until the portrait was finished on 20 April (fig. 70), when he invested de László with the Cross of Commander of the Royal Order of the Saviour of Greece, and left to visit his brother-in-law, Emperor William II, at Corfu.

As well as the present formal portrait of the king, de László made two fine studies of him, one head-and-shoulders and one half-length, dated April and May respectively. Such was the bond forged during that visit in 1914 that in ensuing years de László was to paint some twenty more portraits of members of the Greek Royal Family, in both his London and Paris studios.

Constantine of Greece and Denmark was born in 1868, the son of King George I of the Hellenes and Grand Duchess Olga of Russia. He was proclaimed *Diadoch* (successor) in 1884, aged sixteen. In 1889 he married Princess Sophie of Prussia. Together they had six children, three sons and three daughters. He became Inspector General of the Army in 1911, and two years later the popular prince, a

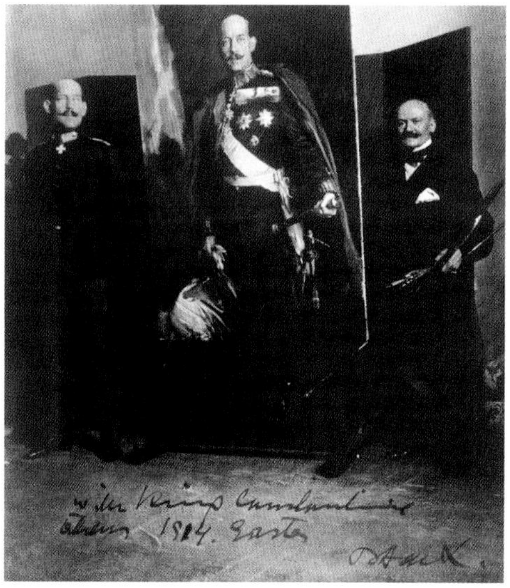

FIG. 70 King Constantine and the artist and his portrait, Athens, 1914

forceful, impressive personality, succeeded to the throne, following the assassination of his father. On the outbreak of the First World War, he remained reluctant to support either side, while the nationalistic Prime Minister Venizelos orchestrated a campaign against him, claiming his reluctance to join the war was caused by his wife's relationship to the Kaiser. With the support of Britain and France, in 1917 Venizelos forced King Constantine to abdicate in favour of his second son, Alexander (his eldest son George was also suspected of German sympathies). Constantine went into exile in Switzerland. He returned to Greece in 1920, and was restored to the throne by a plebiscite in December that year. Soon Greece was at war with Turkey again and in 1922 was crushingly defeated by the Turks at Smyrna. Fearing civil war, Constantine abdicated once more and was now succeeded by his eldest son, as King George II. He went into exile to Italy, where he died in Palermo in January 1923, and was buried in the crypt of the Orthodox Church in Florence. Both the king and his wife were re-interred in Greece in 1935.

61 Hudson Ewbanke Kearley, 1st Viscount Devonport 1914

Oil on canvas, 238 × 129.5 cm (94 × 51 inches)
Signed and dated, lower left: *P. A. de László / 1914 XII;* upper right, family crest
On loan from the present Viscount Devonport to Cranleigh School, Surrey

LITERATURE N.P.G. 1913–15 Album, p.83; Rutter 1939, pp.293, 328, 333–4, 345, 359; letters, 296–7, 303, 323

This portrait shows Lord Devonport wearing the robes and court dress of a Privy Councillor. The following year de László painted Lady Devonport and made two further portraits of Lord Devonport, in 1921 and in 1925, for the Port of London Authority Building. Lord Devonport also commissioned portraits from de László of his friends David Lloyd George, Field Marshal Lord Roberts (fig. 34, p. 45) and of the M.P. Timothy Healey .

In August 1914 de László became a naturalized British subject, Lord Devonport being one of his four sponsors. The present portrait was rejected by the Royal Academy in the summer of 1915, on grounds of the artist's country of birth being an enemy of Britain. Lord Devonport was extremely indignant about this. "Yes, indeed," he wrote, "you were right in your conception of the meanness to which jealous rivals will descend. I confess that I had a broader view of my countrymen. But they have belied me. To describe such a mean and petty excuse for the exclusion of your work as scandalous is to put it in mild terms. They know as well as I do that you are a British subject, and that as such you are entitled to equal terms and equal treatment with the best of them. We all know that success breeds 'envy, hatred and malice' among those who grudge it because they cannot command or gain it for themselves. It is their only refuge! But you have your triumph in standing at the top of the tree in the 'empty frame' competition at Christie's last week. Easily first! And Sargent a respectable second! What more can you desire?" Sir Luke Fildes was one of the Royal Academicians who would not associate himself with the Society's attitude, and he wrote de László a kind letter. Lord Devonport applauded it, and, referring again to "the specious devices" of de László's envious friends, said, "They should be compelled to answer the conundrum of their own making – When is an Englishman not an Englishman? Their answer (from their conscience) would probably be, 'When he paints *too well*.'" Throughout de László's later internment as a suspected enemy alien, Lord Devonport remained a loyal friend and a great support to him. He played an instrumental part in securing the artist's release and in clearing his name and reputation.

Hudson Ewbanke Kearley (1856–1934) left Cranleigh School in Surrey at the age of fifteen and, after eight months unpaid work in a City coffee sale-room, joined the tea merchants Tetley & Sons. In 1876 he founded the firm of Heseltine & Kearley (later International Stores and Kearley and Tonge) and became a successful pioneer of the modern chain-store.

In 1892 he turned to politics, and was elected as Liberal Member for Devonport. In 1909 he gave up his political career to become the first Chairman of the newly constituted Port of London Authority, a position he held until 1925, and a Privy Councillor. In 1910 he was raised to the peerage as Baron Devonport, of Wittington in Buckinghamshire. In November 1916 Lloyd George appointed him first Food Controller and he developed a voluntary scheme of rationing. He resigned from office on the grounds of ill health in May 1917 and was advanced to a Viscountcy.

The far-sighted development programmes which he inaugurated at the Port of London represented Devonport's most notable public service. In 1888 he had married Selina, youngest daughter of Edward Chester, of Blisworth, Northamptonshire. They had two sons and a daughter.

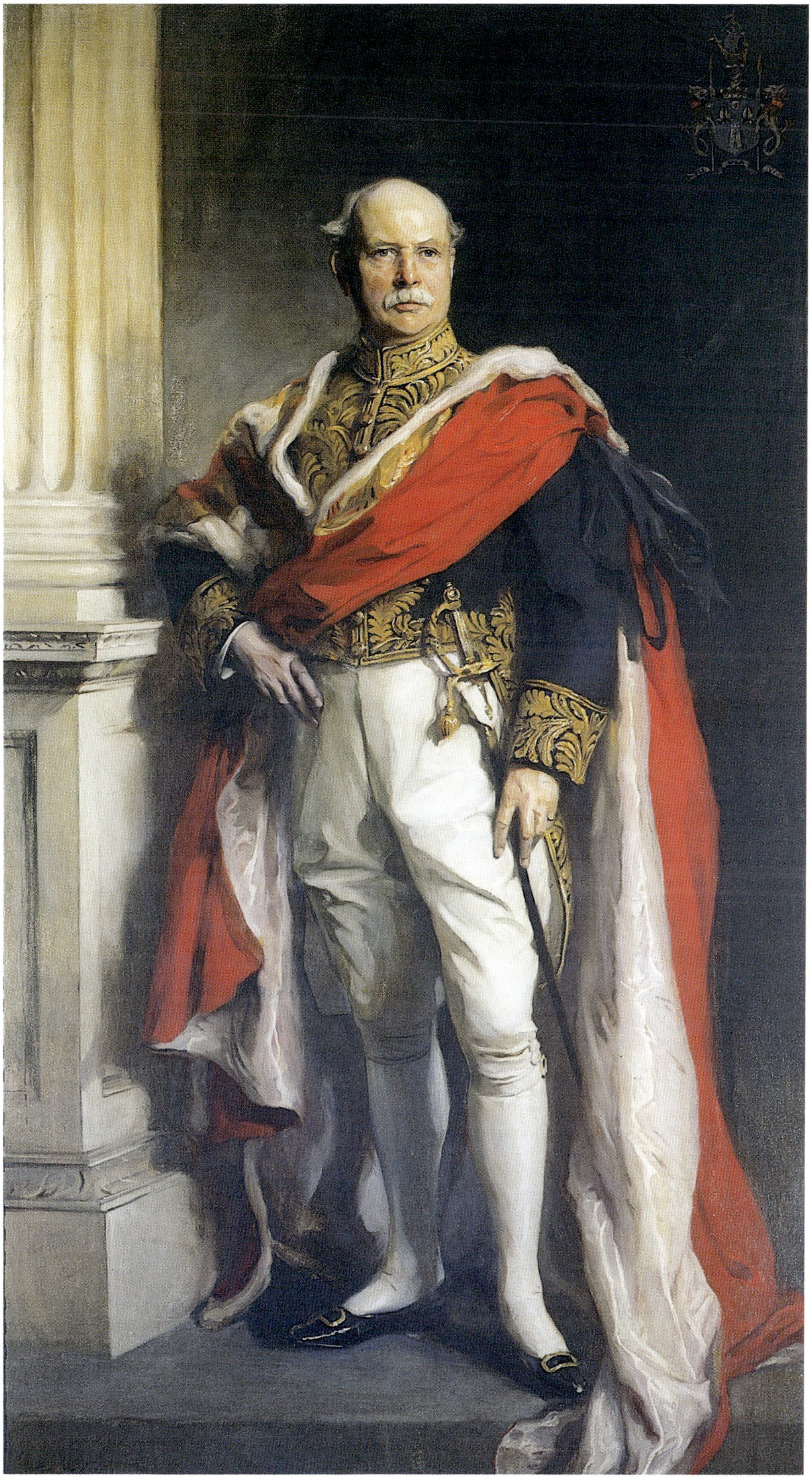

62 The Artist's Mother 1914

Oil on canvas, 90.2 × 70.2 cm ($35\frac{1}{2} \times 27\frac{5}{8}$ inches)
Signed, inscribed and dated, lower left: *Portrait of my dear mother /1914 .II.London / P.A.de László*
PROVENANCE In the possession of the artist on his death; Patrick de Laszlo, his fourth son and grandson of the sitter
EXHIBITED *A Series of Portraits and Studies By Philip A. de László,* M.V.O., The French Gallery, London, May–June 1929, no.9: *Mr. deLászló's mother; The Autumn Exhibition of Autumn Paintings,* Ferens Art Gallery, Hull, October 1929, no.131: *My Mother*
LITERATURE N.P.G. 1913–15 Album, p.89; Clifford 1969, monochrome ill. pl.31: *My Dear Mother;* Rutter 1939, pp.282, 299–310, ill. facing p. 288

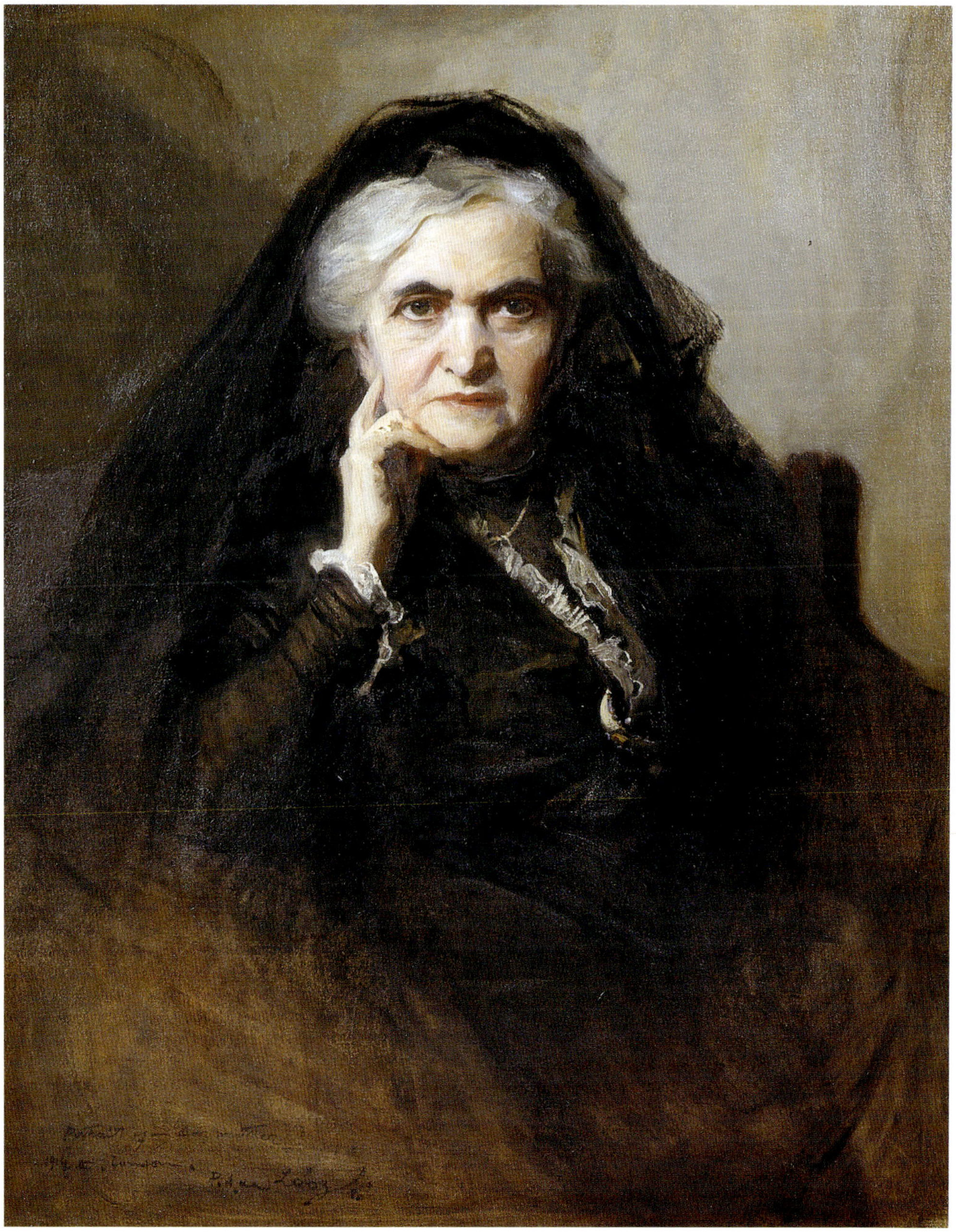

In early 1914 de László's seventy-five-year-old mother (also cat. 32) came to London with his niece Ilonka, and in February he made this final portrait of the beloved matriarch. On 15 February the family travelled together to Calais, where they parted company, Johanna and Ilonka returning to Budapest, Philip and Lucy to take a holiday in the South of France. It was the last time he was to see her.

With the outbreak of war, the Austrians confiscated de László's bank account in Vienna, from which he had been providing for his mother and family in Budapest. Fearing for his mother's welfare, at the risk of compromising his own position as a recently naturalized British subject, he arranged for letters and sums of money to be sent on to Hungary through friends in neutral Holland.

In early February 1915, Johanna died unexpectedly in Budapest after a short illness. In a letter in reply to one of condolence from one of his sitters, de László wrote: "Many thanks for your sympathy in my great sorrow, which comforted me very much. It is the separation at such an hour, when I could have lightened my dear mother's last hours, that will always remain a life long sorrow with me. I am so grateful now to have painted her just last year – which will remain as a sign & example to my children's children of one of the most noble mothers, which ever lived." In another letter he wrote: "In my studio there stands on my easel the last portrait of her, which I was so happy to paint last year. It is the very best I have ever painted. And so I am not alone."

63 Baroness Conrad de Meyendorff, née Nadine Vladimirnova Louguinine 1914

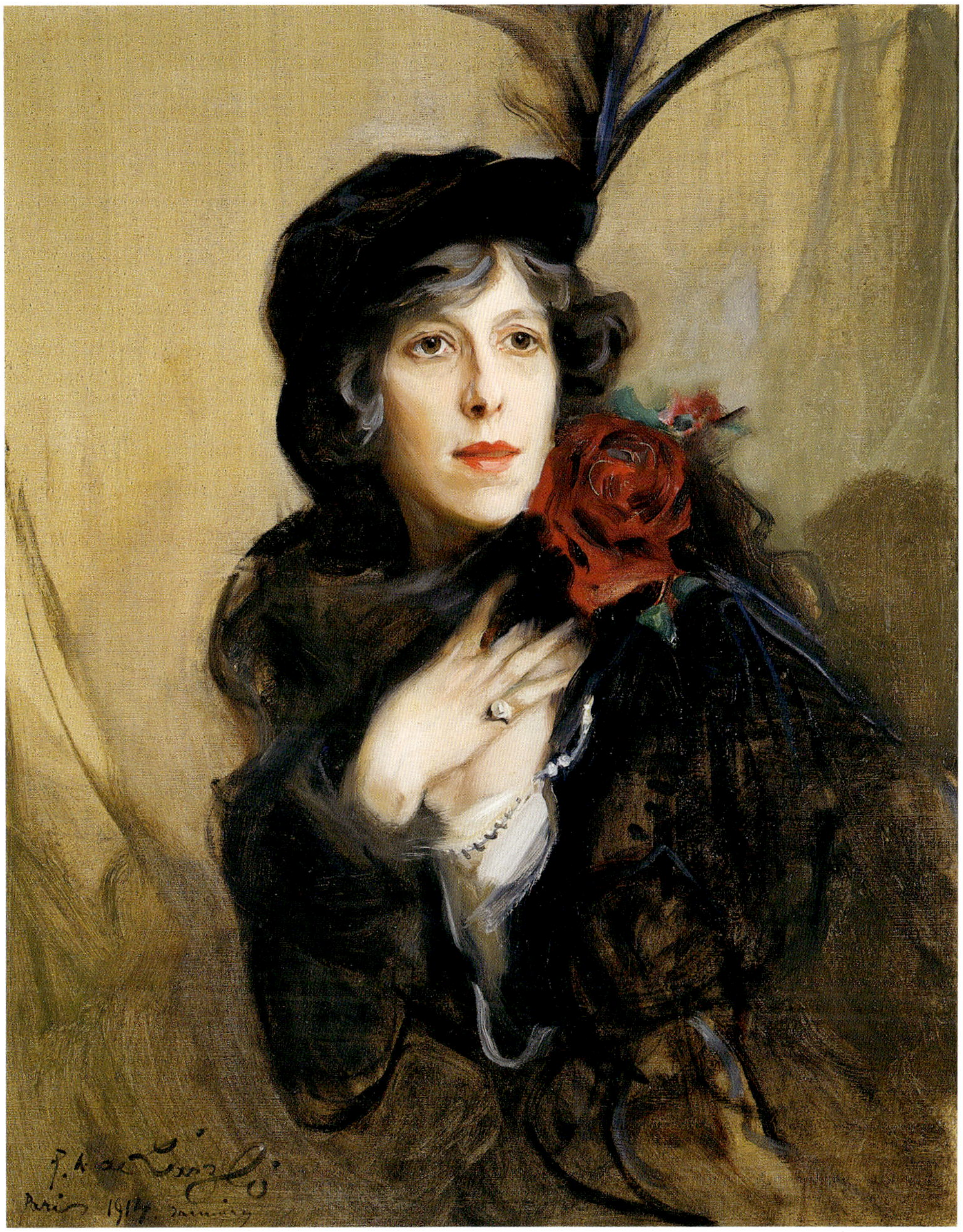

Oil on canvas, 80 × 63.5 cm (31½ × 25 inches)
Signed, dated and indistinctly inscribed, lower left:
P.A. de László / Paris 1914
LITERATURE ASB, Vol. I, p.95: *Nadine de Meyendorff / January 1914*; Rutter 1939, pp.282, 301, 307

According to Rutter, "Early in 1914 [de László] went back to Paris, where he stayed with his friend the Duc de Guiche [cat. 29] and was fêted everywhere. He painted the Vice-President Jean Dupuy, M. et Mme. de Bruyn, Baron Meyendorff, and his wife, the Countess de Pourtalès and the Countess de Fontenay."

Nadine de Meyendorff was the daughter of Wladimir Feodorovitch Louguinine (1834–1911) and his wife Maria Petrovna Minier. Her father was a remarkable scientist in the field of thermodynamics, working in Paris and St Petersburg. Early in 1903 she married Baron Conrad de Meyendorff, an officer in the Russian Navy and later first Secretary at the Russian Embassy in Madrid. The de Meyendorff family, originally from the Baltic Peninsular (a branch of the Üxküll family), came to Russia in 1856.

Baron Conrad and his wife were both intrepid explorers. They spent their two-month honeymoon on the Inca trails in Peru and Bolivia, where Nadine took some two hundred photographs and wrote a diary which was published as *L'Amazonie d'une baronne Russe, Des Andes à l'Atlantique en 1903*. In 1909 she and her husband jointly wrote and published the book *L'Empire du Soleil: Pérou et Bolivie*.

Nadine was also a courageous and expert mountain climber. Her father had a property at Chiètre, near Bex, in Switzerland, and by the time she was eighteen she had already climbed all the Alpes Vaudoises and the Dents du Midi. Later she became the first woman to reach the peak of Cerro Tolosa (5730 m) in the Aconcagua Mountains in Argentina. The Baron and Baroness had two sons, George and Waldemar, both of whom died in an accident in 1924.

De László painted another portrait of Baron Conrad in London in 1916 (which remained in the collection of the artist and was subsequently destroyed in a warehouse fire) while the baron was on a visit from the Russian Embassy in Madrid. He was sympathetic to the artist's difficulties in communicating with his family in Hungary during the War and tried to give him practical assistance to get much needed money to de László's relatives in Budapest, but without success.

64 Mrs George Sandys, née Dulcie Redford 1915

Oil on canvas, 241.30 × 125.73 cm (95 × 49½ inches)
Signed and dated very indistinctly, upper left: *P.A. László / 1915*
LITERATURE ASB, Vol.I, p.61: *D.E.A. Sandys / 26-1-16*; N.P.G. 1915–16 Album, p.83, where dated by the artist 1916; *The Studio*, LXVIII, 1916, p.154, ill.

The portrait was painted soon after the birth of the sitter's first child, in June 1915. In one of his most dramatic and Van Dyckian compositions, de László has here draped a swathe of material about the sitter and positioned her dogs, a Pekinese and a Japanese spaniel, so as to create a graceful pyramidal shape. In the same sittings he made a fine portrait drawing of Mrs Sandys, which he presented to her as a gift.

Dulcie Edythe Angela Redford was born in 1893 in Ayr, the daughter of Sir Edward Redford, C.B., and his wife Florence, the 'beautiful Lady Redford'. She grew up in Edinburgh and became known as one of the 'Three Belles' of Edinburgh. In 1914 she married George Owen Sandys (1884–1971), son of Edwin Del Sandys, at St Mary's Cathedral, Edinburgh. On the outbreak of the First World War her husband joined the Westmoreland & Cumberland Yeomanry, and in 1915 they moved into Greythwaite Hall, Lancashire. Their son Myles was born that year and in 1920 they had a daughter, Evangela.

Mrs Sandys was a very beautiful woman, inheriting her good bone structure from her mother. Although she preferred the London life with its theatre and bridge parties, she enjoyed tennis, loved Ascot, learned to shoot and was a fine skater. She was also a chain smoker. Mrs Sandys died in London aged seventy-nine, in March 1972, just six weeks after her husband.

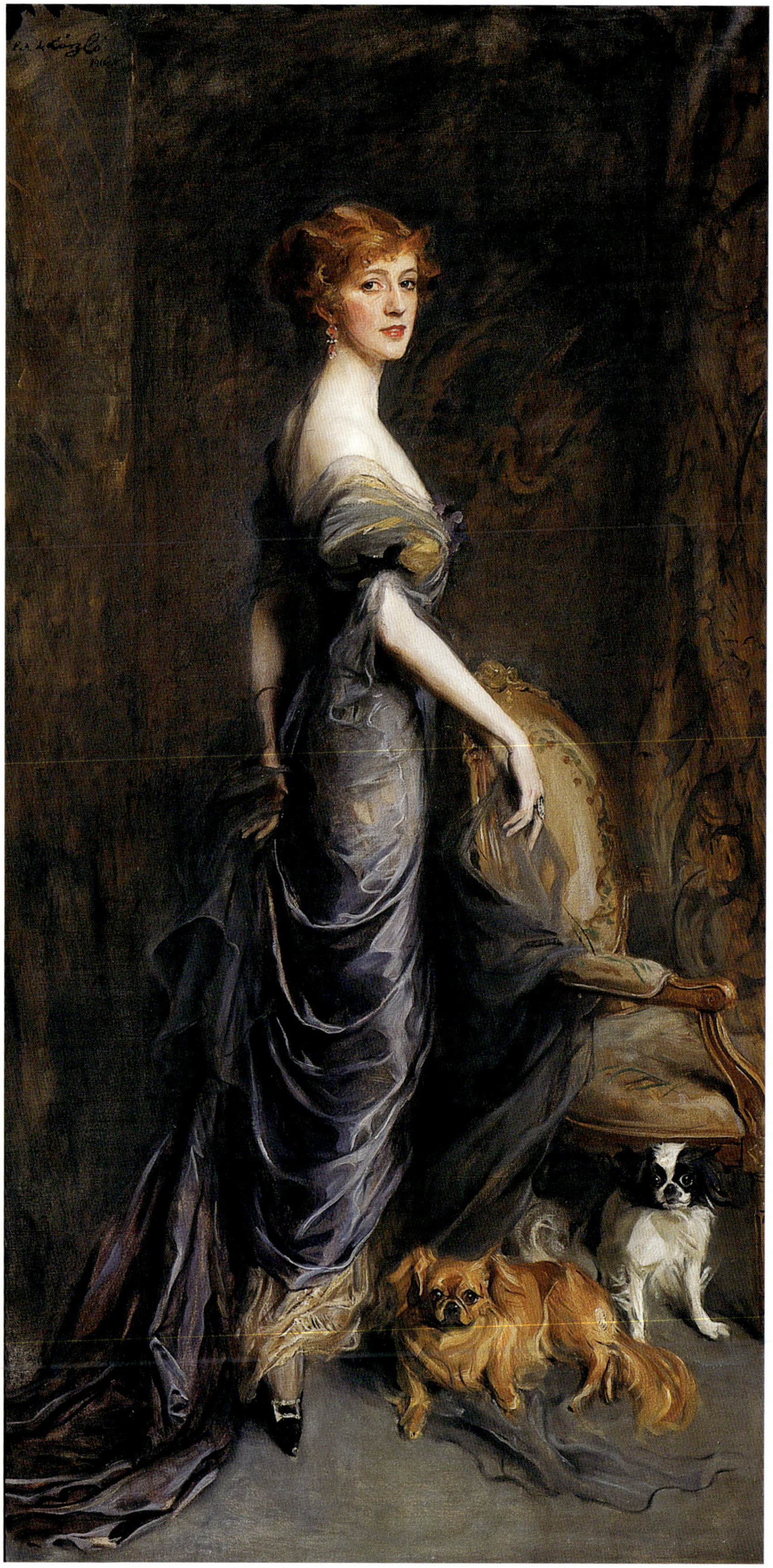

65 H.R.H. The Princess Louise, Duchess of Argyll 1915

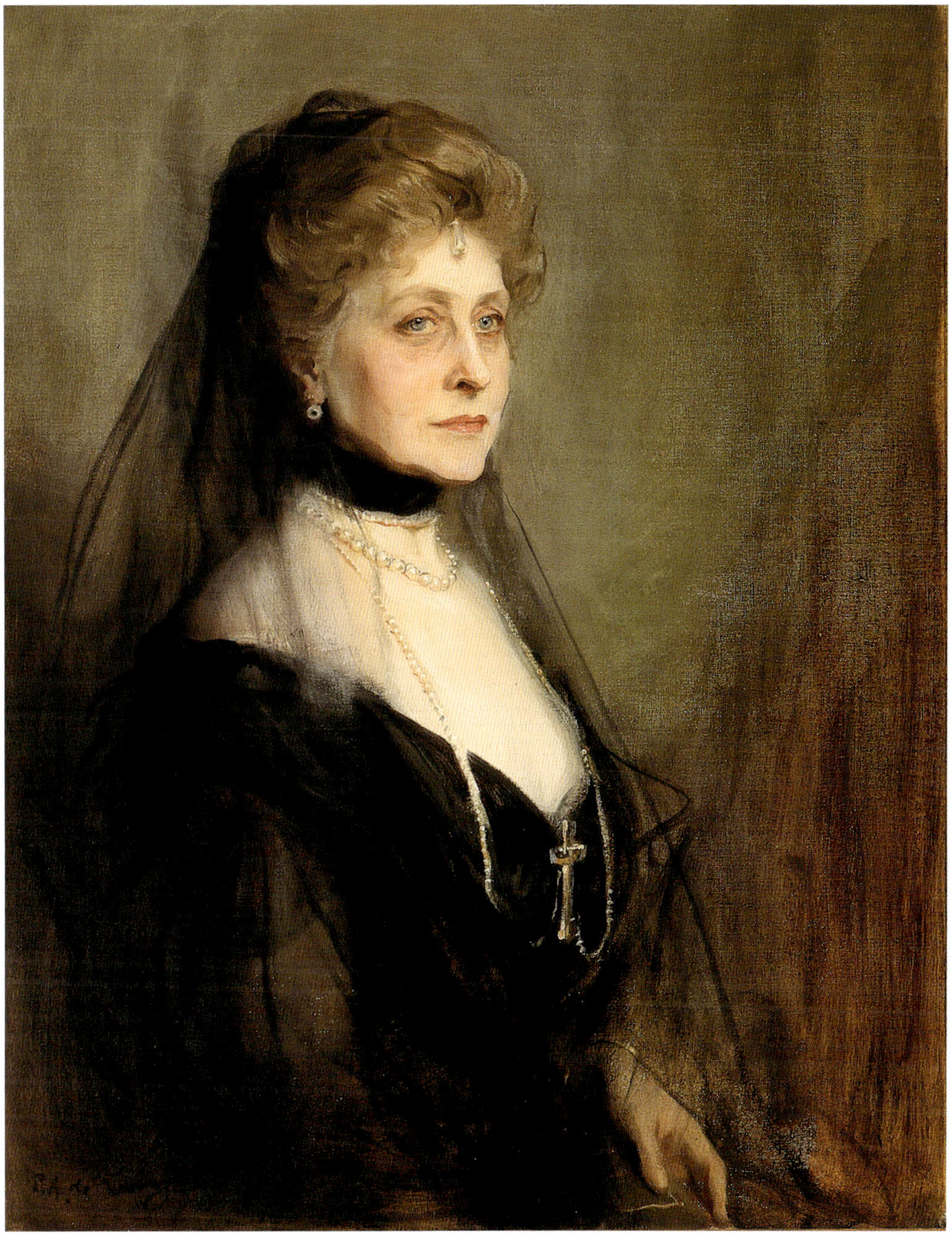

Oil on canvas, 90.2 × 69.9 cm (35½ × 27½ inches)
Signed and indistinctly dated, lower left: *P.A. de László / 1915. III.*

EXHIBITED *A Series of Portraits and Studies By Philip A. de László, M.V.O.*, The French Gallery, London, , June 1923, no. 6: *H.R.H. The Princess Louise, Duchess of Argyll*

LITERATURE ASB, Vol.I, p.86: *Louise*, on a page dated by the artist 1909; *The Studio*, LXXXVI, September 1923, ill. p.130; Jehanne Wake, *Princess Louise, Queen Victoria's Unconventional Daughter*, London 1988, p.81, and ill.

Princess Louise Caroline Alberta was born at Buckingham Palace in 1848, the sixth child and fourth daughter of Queen Victoria and Prince Albert. In 1871 she married John Douglas Sutherland, Marquess of Lorne (1845–1914), who succeeded his father in 1900 as 9th Duke of Argyll. They had no children. From 1878 to 1883 Lord Lorne was Governor-General of Canada, and in honour of Princess Louise's stay there Lake Louise in the Rocky Mountains was named after her.

Princess Louise, who was renowned for her wit and beauty, led with her husband a quiet and retiring life. They both enjoyed the same literary and artistic tastes and at their home in Kensington Palace they regularly entertained sculptor and artist friends such as Sir J.E. Boehm, Sir Alfred Gilbert, J. Seymour Lucas and Sir Lawrence Alma-Tadema. The Princess was herself a talented artist and sculptress. One of her best-known works is the marble statue of Queen Victoria at Kensington Palace overlooking the Round Pond. She also made the monument to Prince Henry of Battenberg in Whippingham Church, near Cowes, Isle of Wight, and designed the memorial in St Paul's Cathedral to the Canadian soldiers who fell in the South African War. She wrote for magazines under the nom de plume of 'Myra Fontenoy'.

Princess Louise was a patron of the Ladies' Work Society, which enabled poor women to gain a living from needlework, and with her strong encouragement the National Union for the Higher Education of Women was founded in 1872. She was its first president and is remembered for her influential work in the advancement of secondary education for girls. After the Duke's death in 1914 the Duchess lived a still more secluded life between London and Roseneath House in Dumbartonshire. In 1919 she was given the Colonelcy-in-Chief of the Argyll and Sutherland Highlanders. The Duchess died in 1939 at Kensington Palace in her ninety-second year.

66 Lieutenant Desmond Trouton 1915

Oil on board, 80 × 54.9 cm ($31\frac{1}{2} \times 21\frac{5}{8}$ inches)
Signed and dated, lower right:
P.A. de László / 1915. May 16
PROVENANCE Maurice Trouton, brother of the sitter
LITERATURE ASB Vol.I p.103: *Desmond Gardiner Trouton / May 16th 1915*

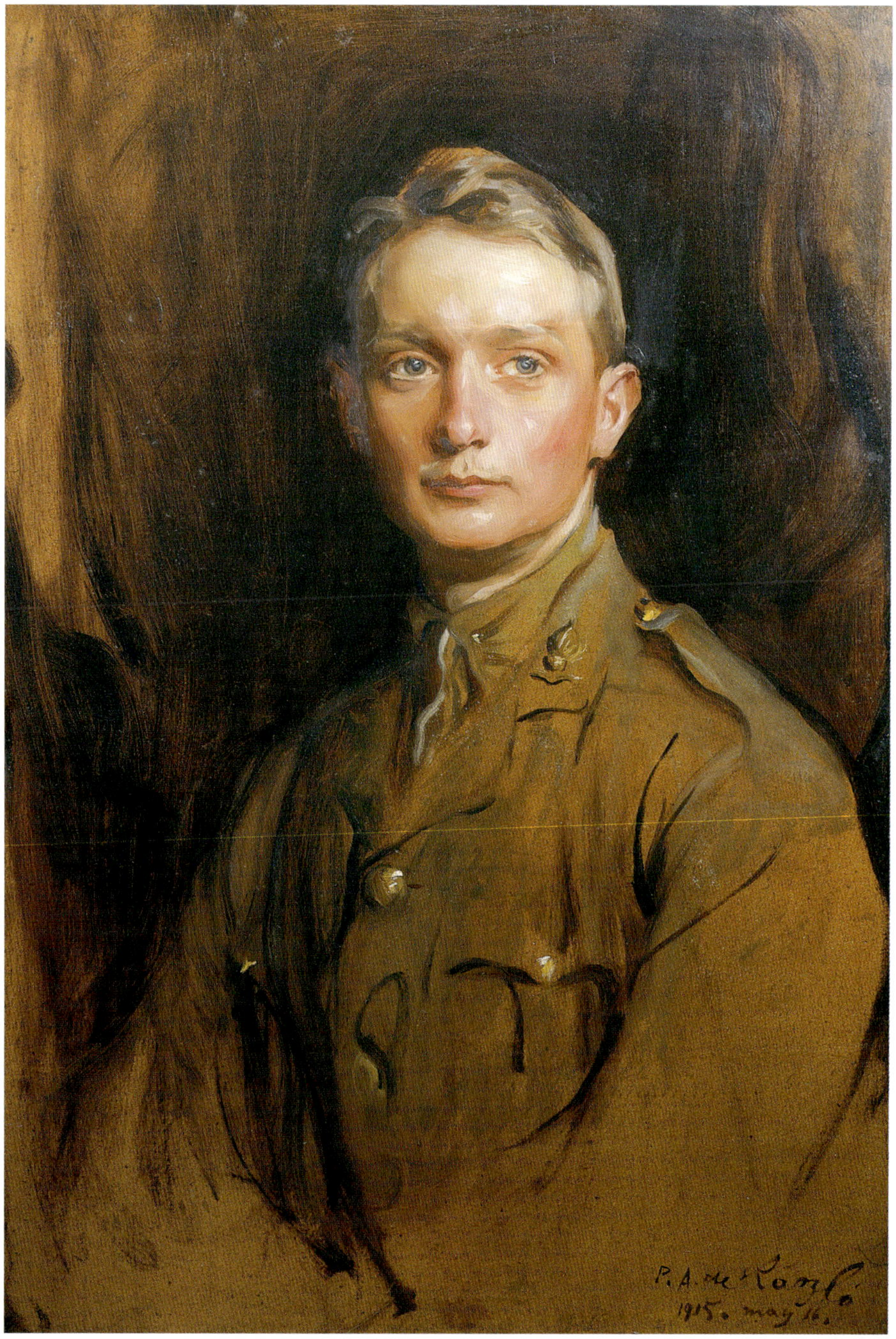

De László painted or drew almost every member of the Trouton family (cat. 47), with whom he and his wife were good friends. Lucy de László was a cousin of Desmond's father and both families spent summers in Tilford, in Surrey, where the Troutons owned a house, as did Lucy's sister Eva. Both the artist and his wife are buried in Tilford churchyard.

The portrait of Desmond Trouton is typical of those that de László was commissioned to paint during the First World War, particularly in 1915, of officers going to the front. According to a daughter one of de László's wartime sitters, the artist offered to paint portraits of these young soldiers, perhaps home on a short leave, for a very modest fee, about £100. None of these men wanted to spend much time in an artist's studio and, as de László was extremely quick at achieving an excellent likeness, he was much sought after. De László actually inscribed his portrait of the sitter's younger brother, Maurice, "during one sitting", and it can be assumed that the present portrait was also painted in a matter of hours. In April de László had made a portrait drawing of their eldest brother Eric (fig. 71). He was killed just five months later at Loos. In his sitters' book de László put a cross beside the signatures of soldiers who never returned.

Desmond Gardiner Trouton was born in Dublin in 1893, the second of four sons of the distinguished physicist Professor Frederick Trouton and his wife Annie, née Fowler. They also had three daughters. Desmond served in The Royal Artillery, reaching the rank of Major. He died in the Battle of Passchendaele on 13th October 1917.

His portrait was inherited by his brother Maurice. During the Blitz in 1944 his London flat was bombed, and Maurice, his wife and Maurice's portrait by de László all perished. Desmond's portrait survived.

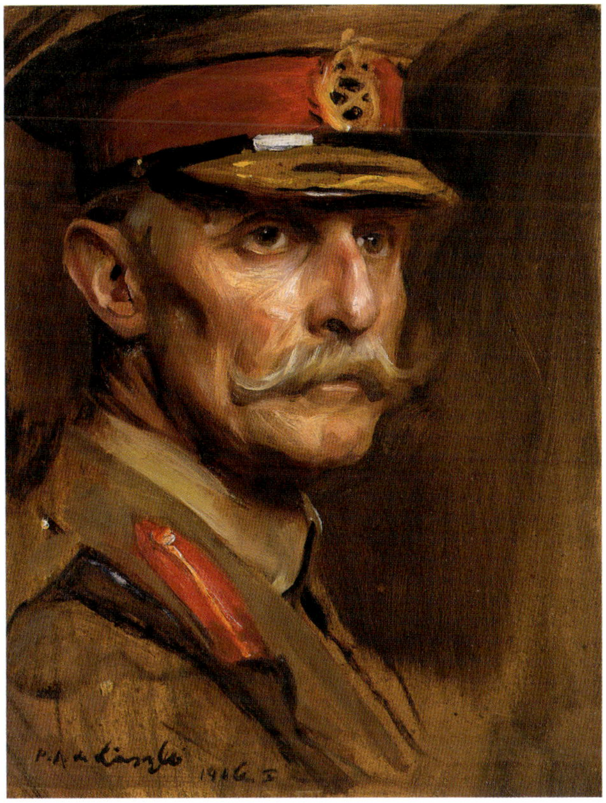

67 Brigadier-General the Earl of Albemarle 1916

Oil on board, 43.2 × 31.8 cm (17 × 12½ inches)
Signed and dated, lower left: *P.A. de László / 1916. I*
LITERATURE ASB, Vol.I, p.104: *Albemarle / Jan. 10. 1916*; N.P.G. 1915–16 Album, p.1a

De László also painted a portrait of the sitter's wife in 1909 and their son, Viscount Bury, in 1915. He painted the sitter's daughter-in-law, Lady Judith Wynn-Carrington, in 1911, and his grandson's first wife, Lady Mairi Vane-Tempest-Stewart, as a child in 1923.

Arnold Allan Cecil Keppel, 8th Earl of Albemarle, was born in 1858. In 1881 he married Gertrude Lucia, the only child of the 1st and last Earl Egerton of Tatton. They had four sons and a daughter. From 1892 to 1894 he was M.P. for Birkenhead. In South Africa in 1900 he served as a Lieutenant-Colonel, and became Brigadier-General in 1906. After the First World War he was A.D.C. to King Edward VII and to King George V, and Lord in Waiting between 1922 and 1924.

In his private life, he was a sculptor of considerable talent. He studied in professional sculptors' studios in London, and had a number of his most successful pieces cast in bronze. His *Drummer Boys* (the subject taken from Kipling's short story) now stands outside the Borough Council offices in Woodbridge, Suffolk, having been presented to the town by his daughter-in-law on her husband's death in 1979. He was skilled with his hands in every way: when his children were young he built his own yacht, in which he would take his family on sailing expeditions. He was a fine shot, and occasionally had King Edward VII to shoot at the family home, Quidenham Park in Norfolk. He died in 1942 and was succeeded by his eldest son.

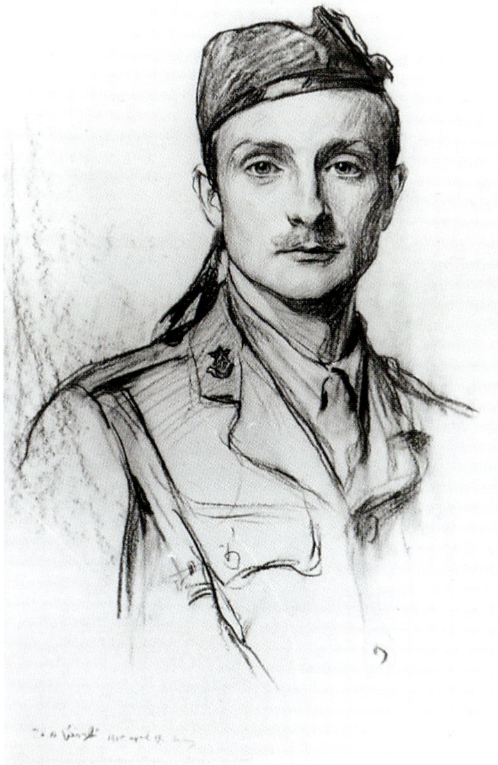

FIG. 71 *Lieutenant Eric Trouton*, 1915
Charcoal, 73.7 × 53.3 cm (29 × 21 in.)
Private collection

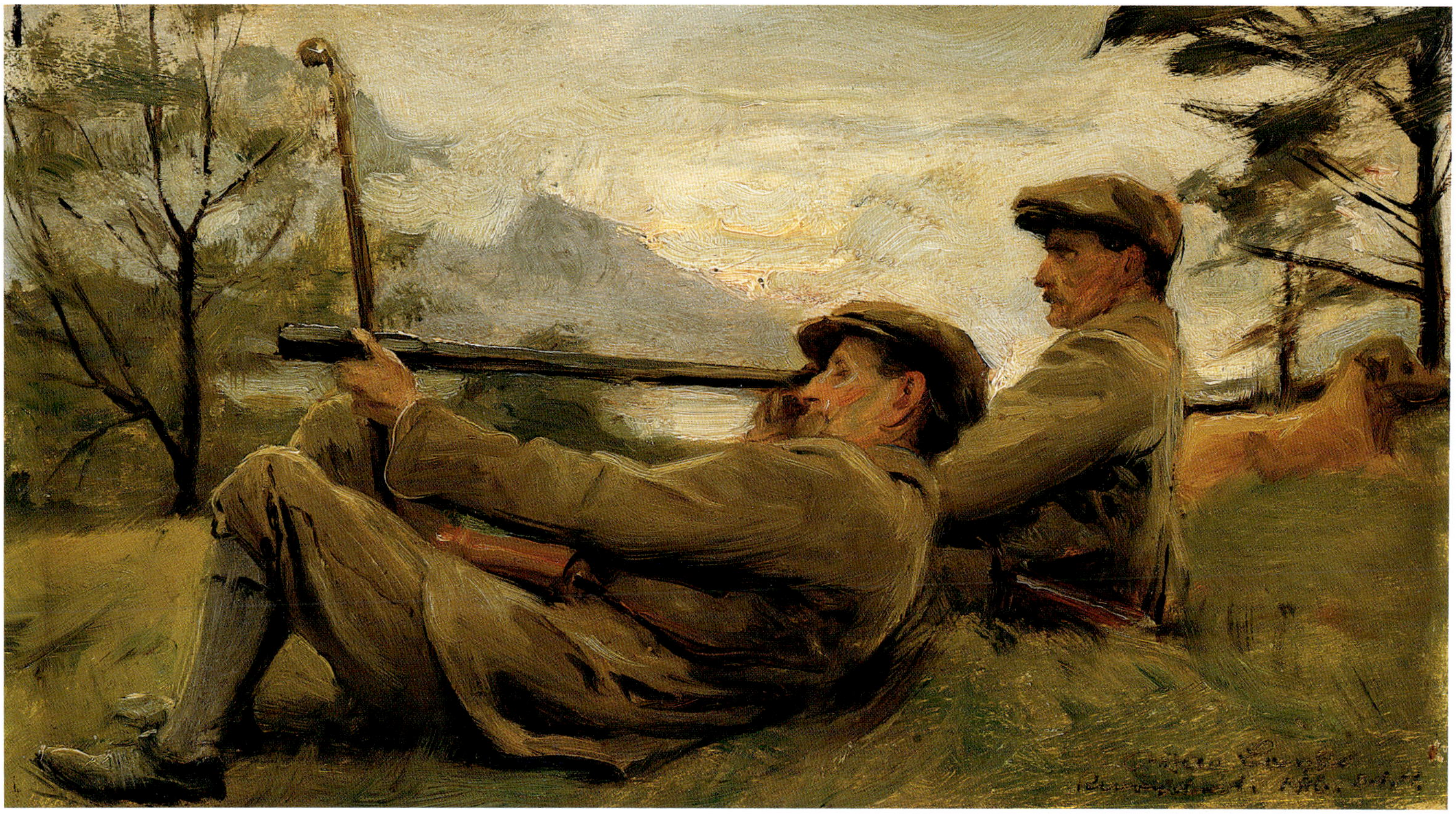

68 The Stalkers 1916

Oil on panel, 15.2 × 25.4 cm (6 × 10 inches)
PROVENANCE In the possession of the artist on his death
LITERATURE N.P.G. 1912–16 Album, p.47, where labelled by the artist: *My Gillies during my last / stalking at Knoydart – / 1916*; Clifford 1969, monochrome ill. pl.33: *The Deer Stalkers*

When he carried out commissions at their residences de László was often welcomed by his patrons as a friend, enthusiastically taking part in the activities of the house party. In 1912, he had been a guest at the Portlands' Scottish estate. The Duke later mentioned in his memoirs, "... de László subsequently paid us a visit at Langwell – where, incidentally, he went deerstalking and was terribly bitten by midges." Here we find him on the hill with his brushes in Invernessshire. Knoydart was a large sporting estate owned from 1890 to 1930 by the Bowlby family, whose portraits de László painted in 1914 and 1915. In 1915 he also made two landscape studies at Knoydart, and it may be that the artist signed this study later, putting on the wrong date. In 1930, the estate was bought by the Brocket family, of whom de László painted portraits from 1935 to 1937. The hill (Sgurr Coire na Coinnich) in the present picture can also be seen behind Lady Brocket in his portrait of her (fig. 72). According to one of her descendants, de László did not visit Knoydart again, but used photographs from the family albums (or even the present painting) to paint the background of her portrait in his studio in London.

69 Charles Clare 1916

Pencil on paper, 50.2 × 35.6 cm (19¼ × 14 inches)
Signed, inscribed and dated, lower left: *To my master Clare / Melbreck / 1916 May 6. P.A.de László.*
PROVENANCE The sitter and by descent in the family, thence to the present owner
Hankley Common Golf Club, Surrey

Melbreck, where this drawing was made, was near Tilford, Surrey, the home of the Trouton family and a summer resort of the de László family (cat. 47 and 66). Hankley Common was the site of the local golf course and until 1918 the professional there, de László's "master", was Charles Clare. De László remained an enthusiastic golfer all his life, listing the game as his recreation in *Who's Who*. In 1925 he wrote in a letter: "I got so keen over golf that I played about four hours every day, with the result that on my return home I had an attack of overstrained heart, which meant that I had to rest and entirely give up all work for about two weeks." Lucy, however, saw no health hazard in a round of golf, writing in November 1934: "Laczi darling, have a good time in America, & please if you love me as you say, do not press, and work quietly & play golf." Nonetheless in 1935 he wrote: "I got too ambitious, and the golf-links were too lovely, and after playing continuously for nine days I got nose-bleedings [*sic*] which lasted for five days, and the doctor stopped my playing. I will take it up again soon, but will not play continuously, only weekly. I am inclined to forget I am not twenty-five years old."

Charles Edmund Clare was born in Southport in 1882. He joined Hankley Common Golf Club in 1904.

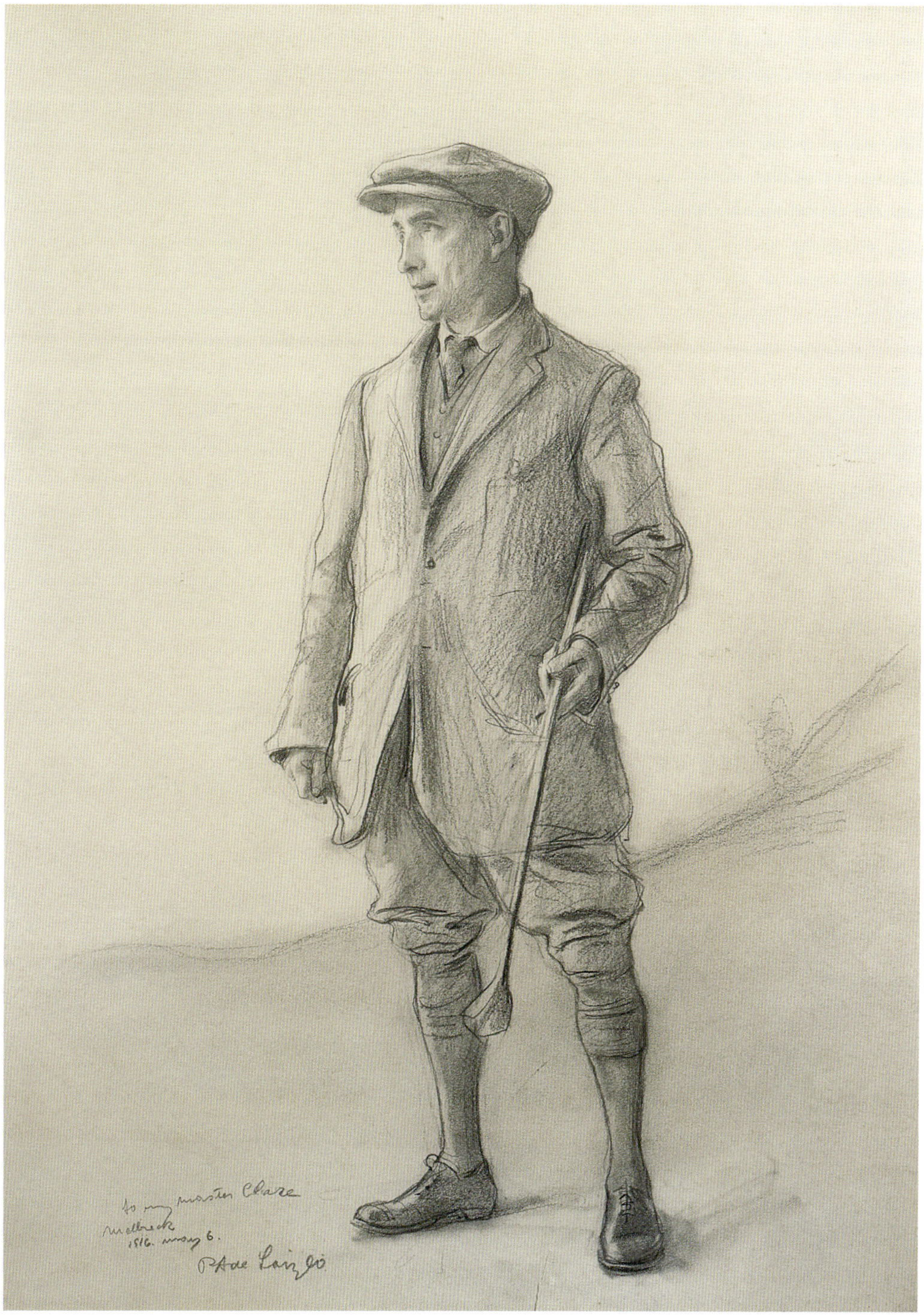

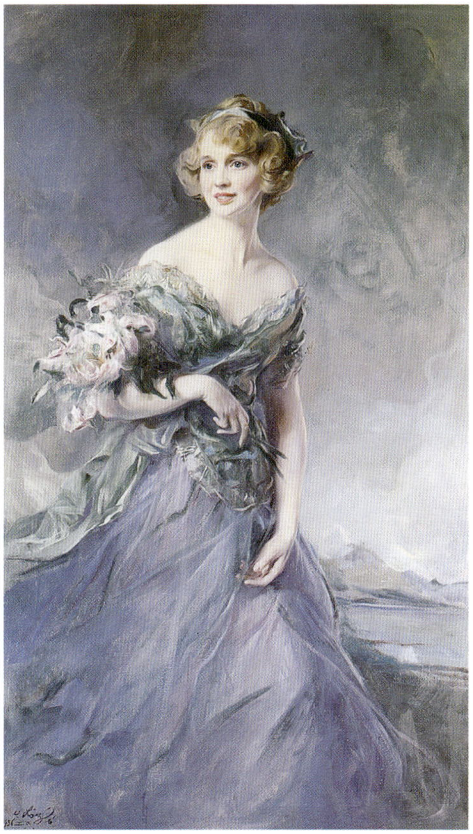

FIG. 72 *Lady Brocket*, 1936
Oil on canvas, 175.3 × 101.6 cm (69 × 40 in.)
Private collection

70 Lt-Col. Rasaldar Jagat Singh and Lt-Col. Rasaidar Man Singh 1916

Oil on board, 90.2 × 69.9 cm (35½ × 27½ inches)
Signed, inscribed and dated, lower right: *P.A. de László / 1916. May 1*
PROVENANCE In the possession of the artist on his death
EXHIBITED 88th Annual Exhibition, Royal West of England Academy, November 1933–February 1934, no. 172: *Sikh Officers, no price*
LITERATURE ASB, Vol.II, p.5: *Rasaldar Jagat Singh. 12th Cavalry / Rasaidar Man Singh 21st Cavalry*, among other signatures dated between May and June 1916; *The Studio*, LXVIII, 1916, p.156, ill.; Rutter 1939, p.306; Clifford 1969, monochrome ill. pl.34

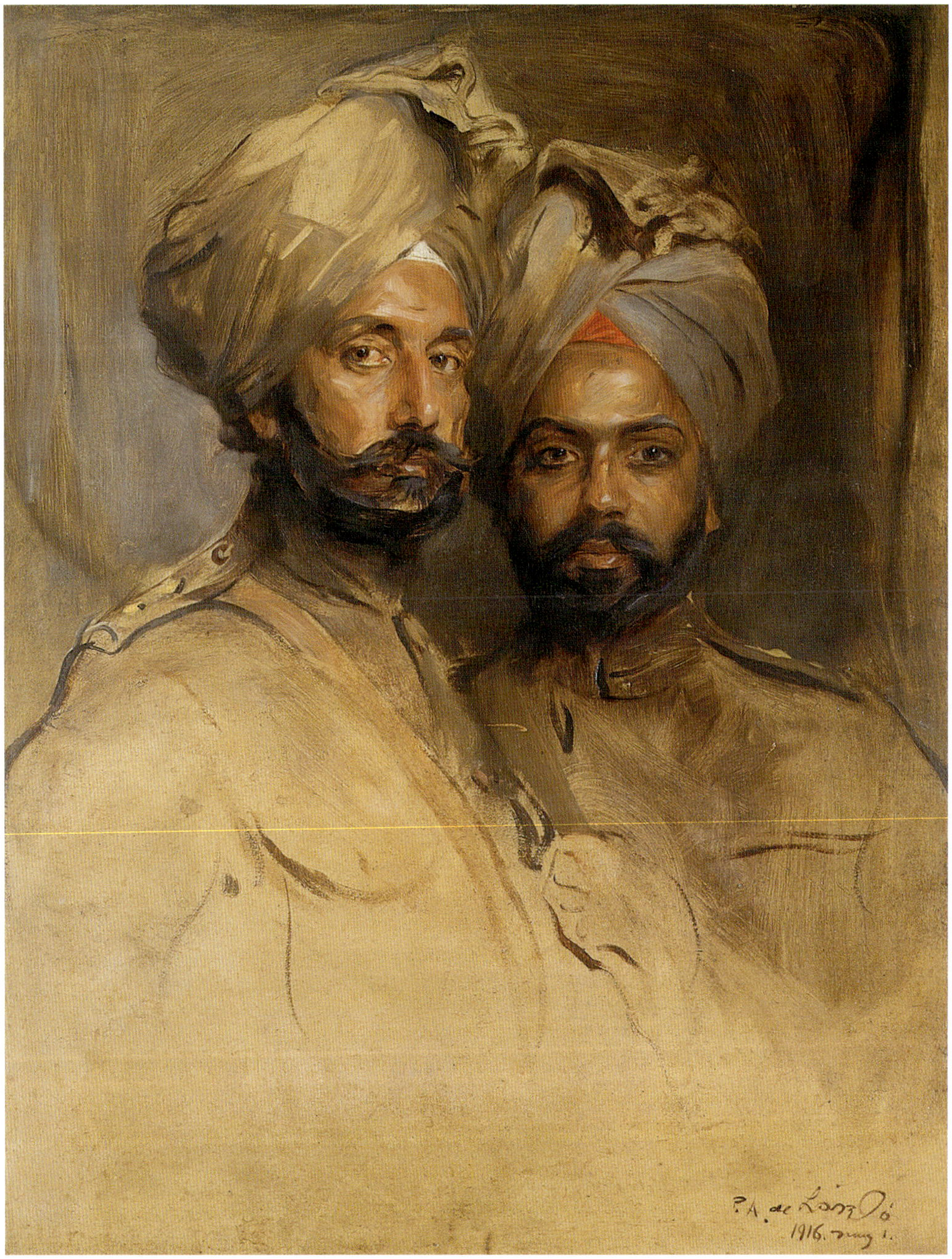

The sitters are likely to be brothers, given their similar names – Rasaldar Jagat Singh on the left and Rasaidar Man Singh on the right. Derek Clifford, who prepared his book of 1969 with the help of the de László family, calls them "the Sikh A.D.C.s". A number of Indian Cavalry officers visited de László's studio in London in May 1916, possibly to see his portrait of the Indian prince (cat. 33), carefully entering their names and regiments in his sitters' book in English and Punjabi, leaving their addresses in India. De László never visited the sub-continent, but nevertheless, according to Rutter, painted this double portrait for himself. It was greatly admired by Austen Chamberlain, the Secretary of State for India, who asked de László to produce a small version for a Red Cross sale in Bombay which was being organized by Lady Willingdon, the wife of the Viceroy. Instead, de László painted a one-sitting sketch of another Indian officer for the nominal fee of 50 guineas, which was raffled in Bombay for £650. That portrait now remains in a private collection.

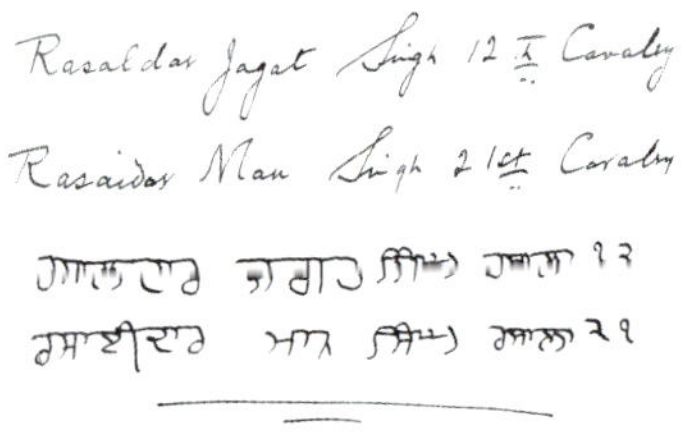

FIG. 73 Detail of a page from the artist's sitters' book with the names of the Singh brothers

71 Mrs Archie Graham, née Dorothy Shuttleworth 1917

Oil on canvas, 170.8 × 102.2 cm (67¼ × 40¼ inches)
Signed and dated, upper left: *P A de László / 1917*
LITERATURE ASB Vol.II, p.8: *Dorothy Graham. Oct: 19th. 1916.*; N.P.G. 1917–21 Album, p.5

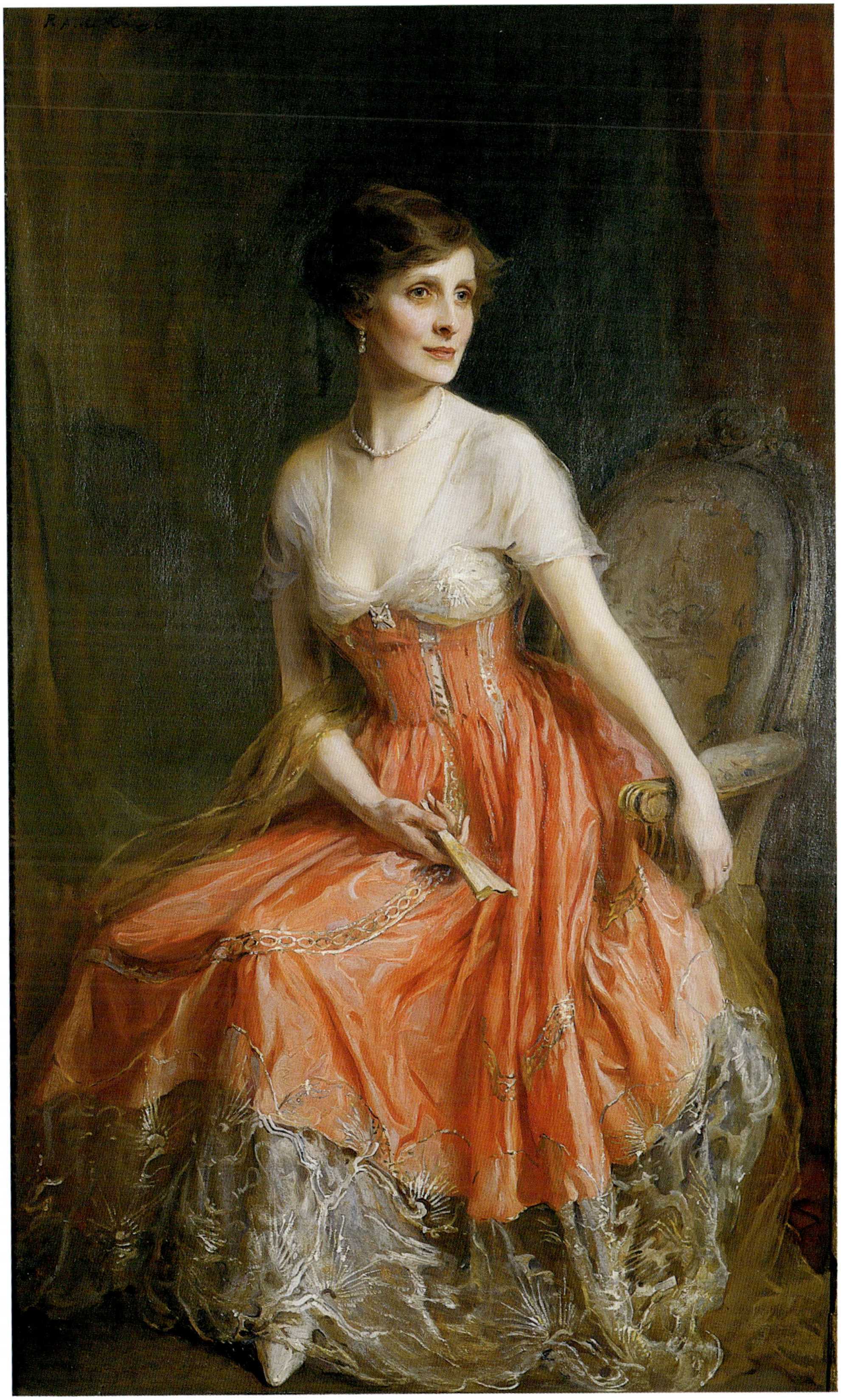

Mrs Graham's sister Emmeline had been painted by Sir John Lavery, but it was to de László that her husband went to commission this portrait. It was painted, together with a half-length portrait in the same dress, in the artist's studio in West House, Campden Hill.

For such an important commission the artist would make several preparatory drawings and oil sketches in different poses, in order to establish which was likely to be the most successful. One such survives of Mrs Graham (fig. 74), which became the verso of a painting of one of the artist's sons.

De László himself chose the colour of the silk and designed the dress for Mrs. Graham, though she herself was a talented dressmaker.

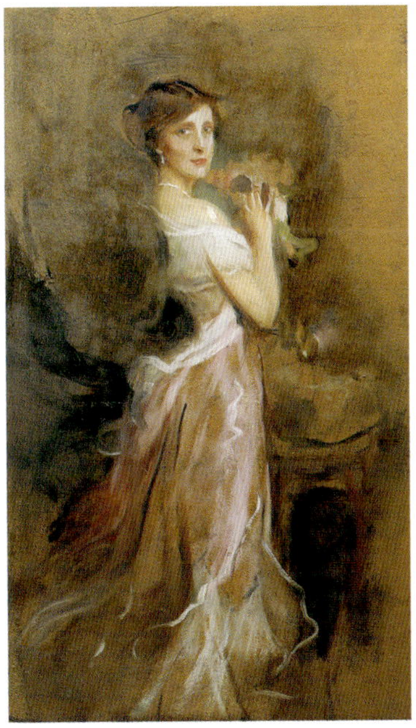

FIG. 74 *Mrs Archie Graham, 1917*
Oil on canvas, 63.5 × 38.1 cm (25 × 15 in.)
Private collection

It is known to have cost £50, which deeply shocked her mother-in-law, who received the bill at the family home, Airthrey Castle, near Stirling, while coping with the absence of her eight sons and considerable war-deprivations at the time.

Dorothy Phoebe, the seventh of the thirteen children of Allen Thornton Shuttleworth of the Indian Forestry Commission and his wife Laura Beetham, was born in 1884. In 1910 she married Archie K. Graham (1882–1968), a Director of John Graham & Co., dealers in jute and other raw materials from the Indian sub-continent, and William Graham's Trading Co. in London. They lived both in India and in London. They had four daughters, Hermione, Noel, Christina and Bridget.

Mrs Graham was a renowned beauty, known as 'the Belle of Bombay'. Despite delicate health, she was an accomplished and courageous horsewoman, and a beautiful dancer. She was a gentle and much beloved lady, with a wonderful sense of humour. She died in London in 1953.

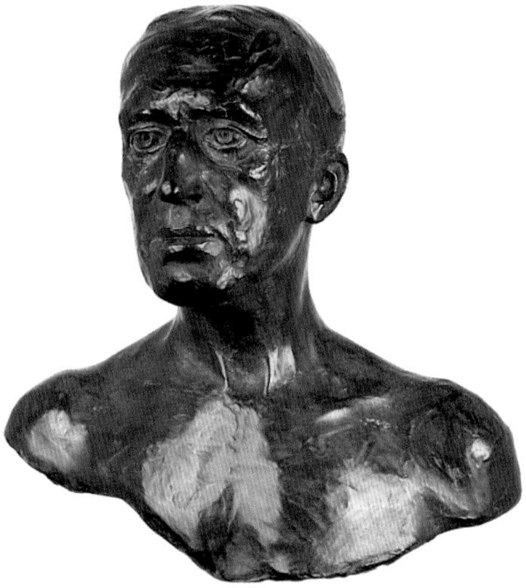

72 Baron Bruno von Schröder 1917

Bronze on marble plinth, 45.7 cm (18 inches) high
Signed, behind: *de László*
LITERATURE ASB Vol.II, p.10: *Bruno Schröder – April 1917*

73 Baron Bruno von Schröder 1917

Oil on canvas, 175.3 × 101.6 cm (69 × 40 inches)
Signed, dated and inscribed, lower left: *de László / 1917 June 12. Heath Lodge.*
LITERATURE ASB Vol.II, p.10: *Bruno Schröder – April 1917.*; N.P.G. 1917–21 Album, p.23; Richard Roberts, *Schroders Merchants & Bankers*, London 1992

Bruno von Schröder (1867–1940) was born in Hamburg but came to London in around 1905, as the chosen heir of his uncle Baron Sir John Schröder, to run the family banking house of J. Henry Schröder & Co. In 1894 he had married Emma von Deichmann of Cologne, with whom he had four children, Rudolf, who died in 1915, a second son, Helmut, and two daughters, Dorothee and Marga (cat. 39).

De László had already painted Baron Bruno in 1911, and was to paint him again in 1926 for the bank. The present portrait was considered to be a very fine likeness by the sitter's wife, who called it a "wonderful tour de force". She wrote, "Mr. de László always makes his sitters stand very straight; even in those days my husband, owing to his great height, stooped a little, but I think this is on the whole an excellent portrait .... It is quite marvellous how the hands are painted – they give you the real feeling of pulsing blood." To soften the lines of the evening dress de László lent the Baron his opera cape, lengthening it in the portrait to give it the right line for his height. The inclusion of the column was also intended to show off his stature. An oil sketch for the portrait exists in the same collection, with the figure standing to the left and without the addition of the cape.

This portrait would have been one of the last de László painted before his internment in September 1917 (cat. 77). Later asked by an official why he had painted the German baron, he replied quietly, "He is my friend". It was most probably while painting this portrait that de László also made the bust of Baron Schröder (cat. 71), one of only three he is known to have executed – the other two are of his wife Lucy (1930) and of Alfred Lys Baldry (cat. 82). The original plaster model for the bronze also remains in the collection of a descendant of the sitter.

Bruno von Schröder was the eighth of nine children born to Johann Rudoph I and Clare Louise Schröder. Johann Rudolph was the younger brother of the head of the Hamburg firm Schröder Gebrüder and a nephew of John Henry Schröder of J. Henry Schröder & Co., London. He would have joined the family firm in Hamburg, if John Henry Schröder had not invited him to succeed him in the London company, an "exceptional chance of a lifetime" that he accepted. However, he remained close to his family in Hamburg and kept a house there, which he visited most summers. He was a generous benefactor of Hamburg charities, a magnanimity recognised in 1904 when he was created a Freiherr by Emperor William II.

The declaration of war by Britain on Germany at midnight on 4 August 1914 created a crisis for Schröder and his company. Avoiding sequestration, on Friday 7 August 1914 Baron Bruno was issued with a naturalization certificate from the Home Secretary and a license to reside and trade signed by King George V.

Baron Bruno inherited from his uncle a keen interest in horticulture and particularly orchids. He had a country residence at Heath Lodge (subsequently enlarged and renamed Dell Park), where this portrait was painted, and one of the finest collections of orchids in the country, for which he won many 1st-class certificates. He won his first Royal Horticultural Society Medal in 1912.

He died in December 1940. Helmut Schroder became senior partner of Schroder's on his father's death.

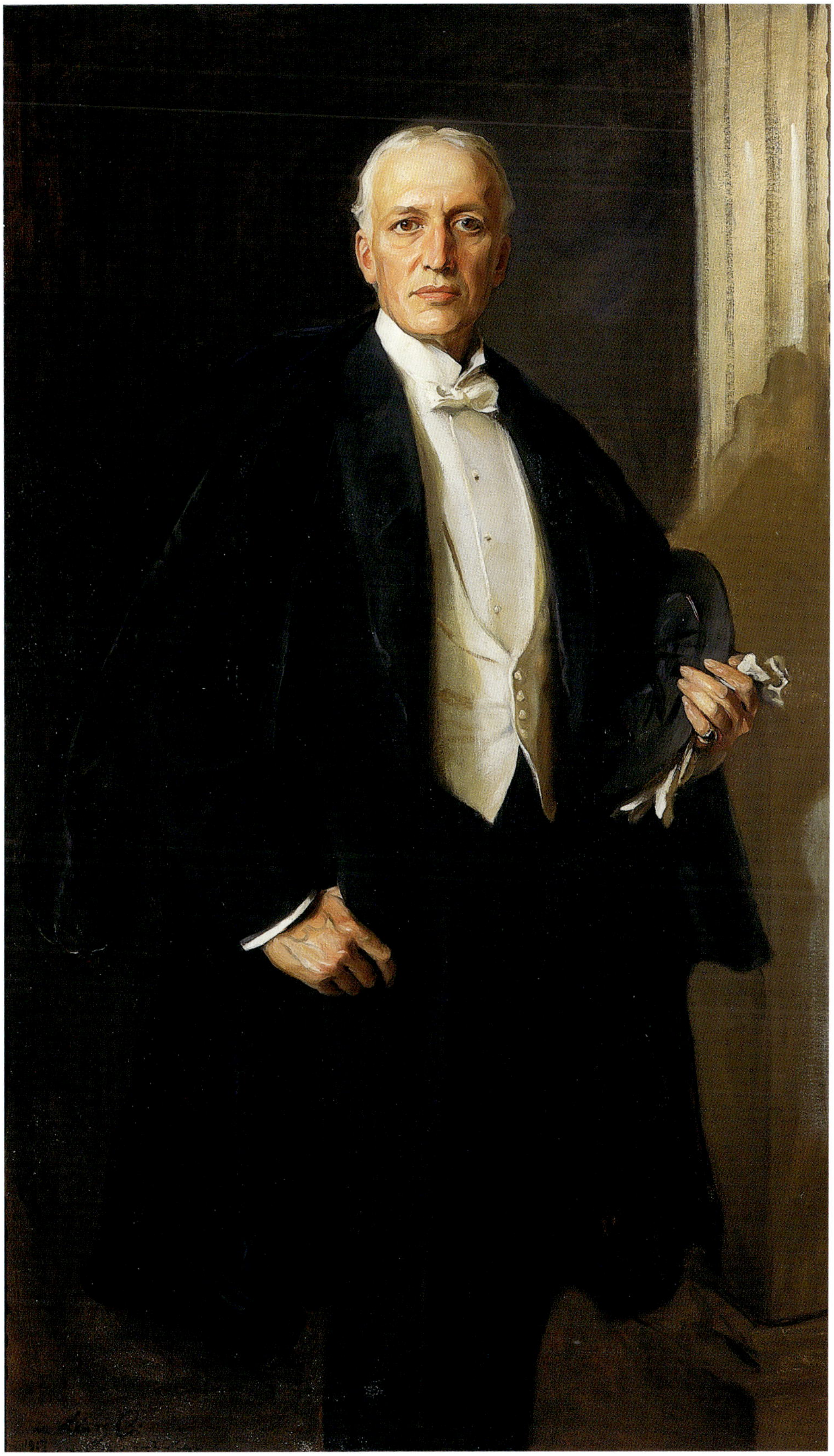

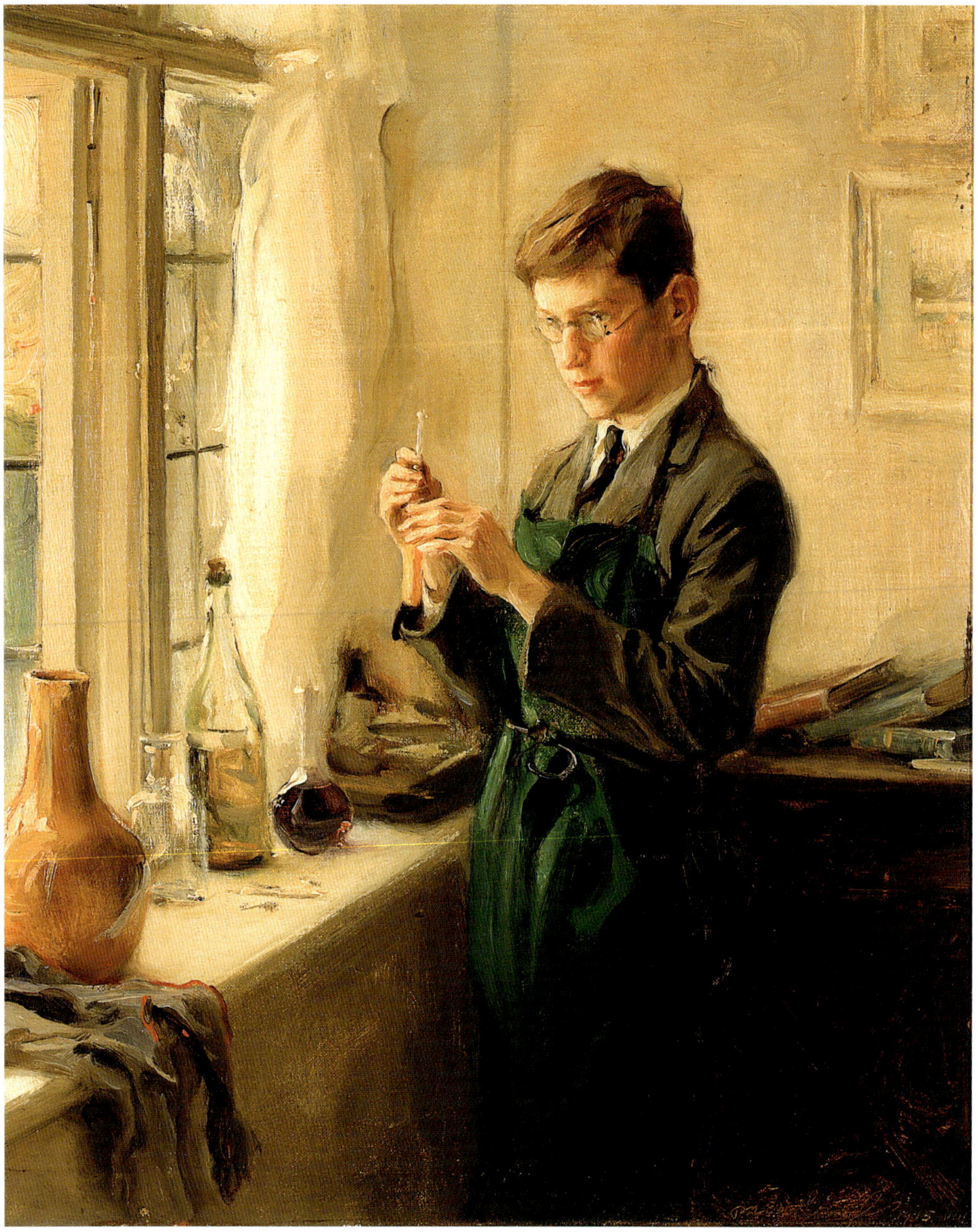

74 Henry, the Artist's Eldest Son 1915

Oil on board, 50.8 × 40.6 cm (20 × 16 inches)
Signed and dated, lower right: *P A de László / 1915 VIII*
PROVENANCE In the possession of the artist on his death
LITERATURE N.P.G. 1915–16 Album, p.16a, where labelled by the artist: *Our Henry / 1914 at Hammondswood*; Rutter 1939, p.298

Henry was born in Budapest on 11 June 1901. According to a member of the family, "At the time the picture was painted Henry was attending Rugby School, where he excelled in Sciences, particularly chemistry. Philip and Henry decided that Henry should be painted doing what he loved most (at least at school) so Henry borrowed a considerable amount of chemistry equipment and set some up on a large table – beakers, glasses, Bunsen burner, etc, with the idea that he would be painted in the middle or towards the end of a complex and successful experiment. Philip, when he saw the set-up, had Henry dismantle the experiment, empty the beakers, remove most of the pieces and substitute coloured water." Henry was not amused.

De László was a man of consummate energy and, even when taking time away from London, he was constantly on the go. When not painting commissions, he was writing letters, composing and painting family portraits, or interiors, or recording a landscape view for his own satisfaction. Hammondswood was a cottage in the village of Frensham in Surrey.

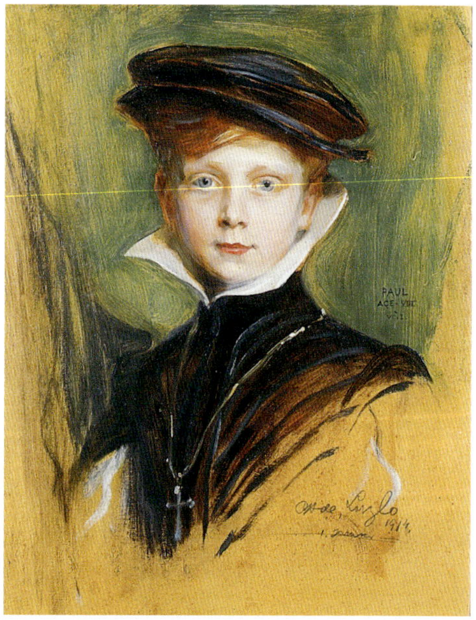

75 Paul, the Artist's Third Son 1914

Oil on board, 61 × 47.6 cm (24 × 18¾ inches)
Signed and indistinctly dated, lower right: *P A de László / 1914 / 1 Januar*, and inscribed, centre right: *PAUL / AGE VIII / VI.I*
PROVENANCE In possession of the artist on his death; Paul de Laszlo, his third son and the sitter
LITERATURE N.P.G. 1913–15 Album, p.27b

De László much admired seventeenth-century Spanish painting and Velázquez in particular. He kept a wardrobe of Spanish ruffs, black velvet doublets and hose and other such in his studio and would invite his sons, and friends with Spanish connections, to sit for him in these costumes. The black velvet doublet in the present portrait appears frequently in his domestic oeuvre (cat. 81, 86, 111) and remains in the family's possession.

6 January was the sitter's birthday. Paul Leonardo had been born in Vienna in 1906. He was called Leonardo after Leonardo da Vinci. He was educated at Rugby and Balliol College, Oxford. In 1929 he was called to the Bar. In 1933 he married Miss Josephine McConnell, and they had three children, Christopher, Ann and Jane.

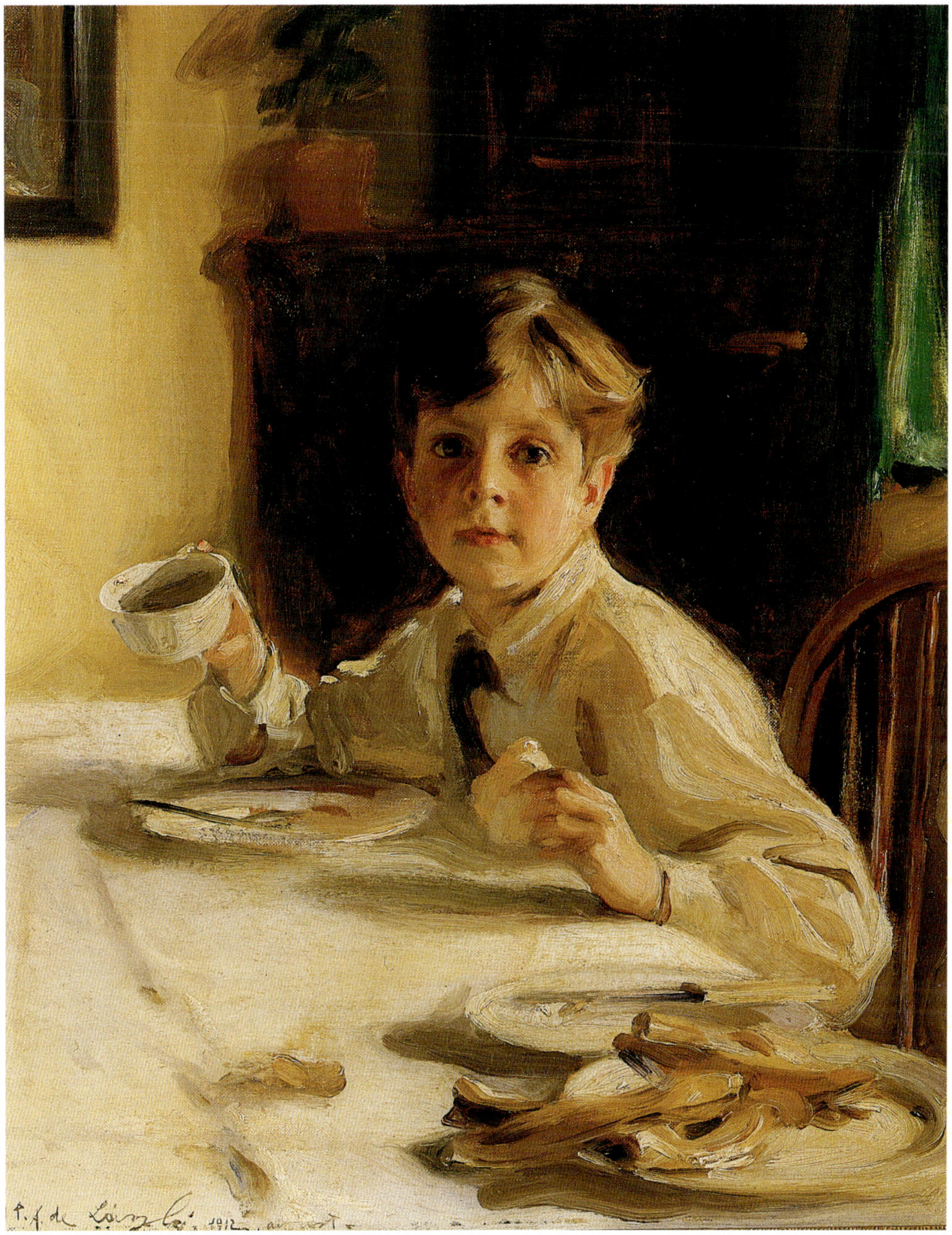

76 'Top o' the Morning': Stephen, the Artist's Second Son 1912

Oil on canvasboard, 53.3 × 43.2 cm (21 × 17 inches)
Signed and dated, lower left: *P A de László 1912 August*
PROVENANCE In the possession of the artist on his death; Henry G. de Laszlo, his eldest son
EXHIBITED *Portraits by Philip A. de László, M.V.O., Loan Exhibition held in aid of The Artists' General Benevolent Institution*, M. Knoedler & Company, Inc., London, June–July 1933
LITERATURE N.P.G. 1903–14 Album, p.36, and 1912–16 Album, p.7; Williams 1921, pp.177–8, ill. facing p.177; Clifford 1969, monochrome ill. pl.28

"On the following morning the summer sun was shining, and as he entered the breakfast-room of his cottage among the Surrey pine-woods his young son Stephi waved his coffee cup towards him in joyous welcome of his father's unexpected arrival. The sunlight and the buoyancy of the welcome stirred all the artist in Laszlo."

Stephen was born in Vienna on 6 July 1904. The artist and his family often went to Surrey to stay with the Troutons (cat. 47, 66 and 69) or to visit Lucy's sister Eva, who lived at The Willows, Tilford. On occasions de László took a house nearby for the summer called Hammondswood, in Frensham (cat. 74), but when their parents were away the children would stay with their aunt. They later recalled much enjoying there their freedom from the formality of their London existence. The present picture might have been painted at either of those cottages.

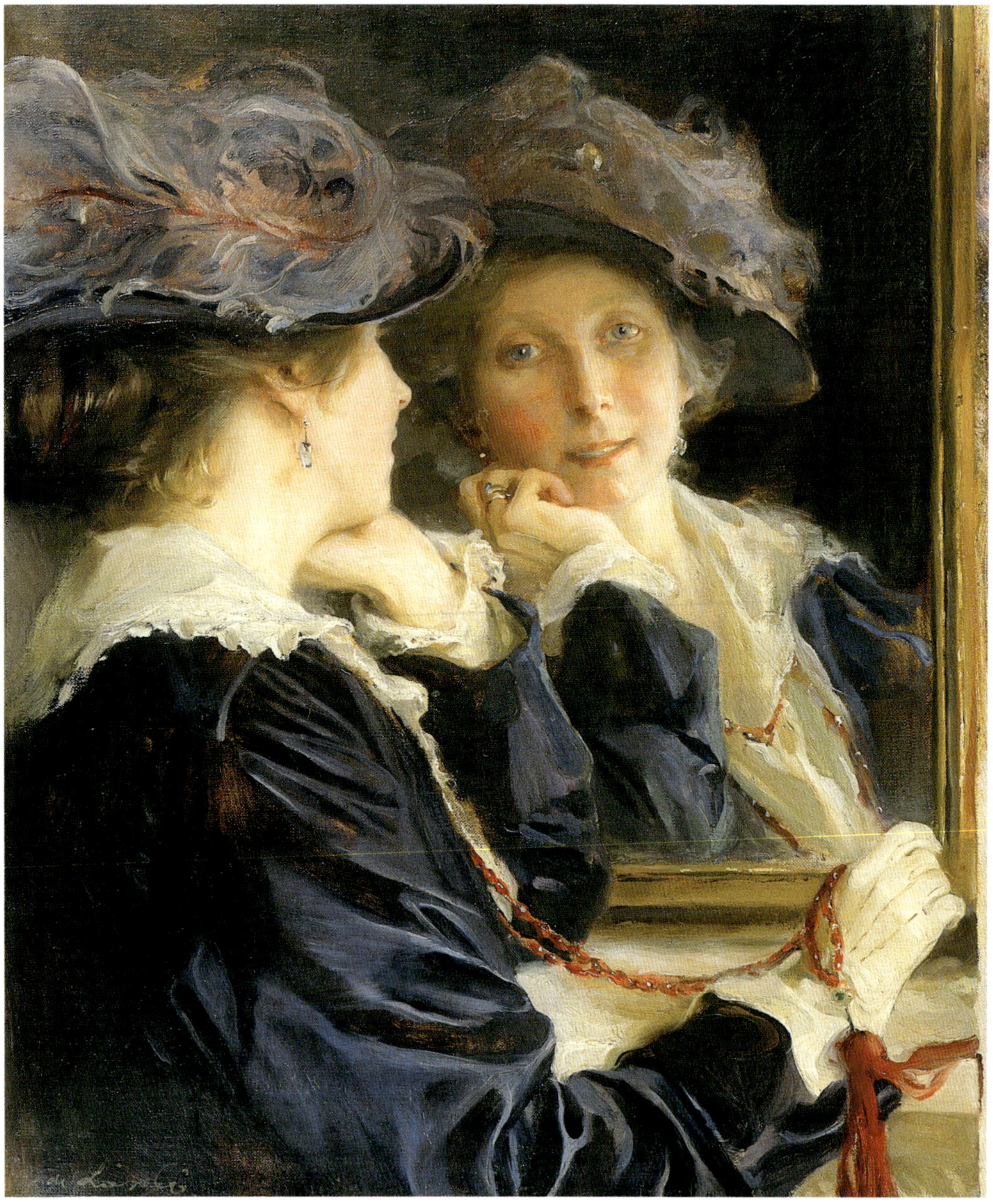

77 Lucy de László, the Artist's Wife 1918

Oil on canvas, 71.1 × 57.8 cm (28 × 22¾ inches)
Signed and dated, lower left: *de László / 1918 August*
PROVENANCE In the possession of the artist on his death; Paul de Laszlo, his third son
EXHIBITED Paris Salon, 1927, *hors concours*, p.57, ill.p.42, no.1112: *portrait Mme de Laszlo*
LITERATURE N.P.G. 1917–21 Album, p.50; Clifford 1969, monochrome ill. pl.35

De László was arrested and interned in September 1917 under Section 14B of the Defence of the Realm Regulations, and spent seven weeks in Brixton Prison in humiliating circumstances. After this, he was moved to Holloway Internment Camp, where he stayed until his health broke down so completely that finally, in May 1918, the authorities were persuaded to move him to a nursing home in Ladbroke Gardens in London. He remained, however, under strict house arrest and was only allowed to see his wife and children. Just once a month his good friend the art critic A.L.Baldry (cat. 81, 82) was permitted to visit him. This study of Lucy was made in August 1918 while at Ladbroke Gardens.

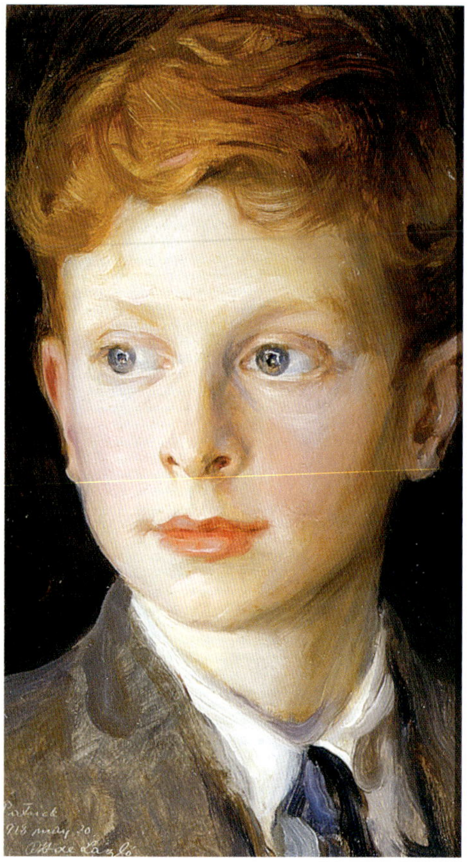

78 Patrick, the Artist's Fourth Son 1918

Oil on board, 25.4 × 14 cm (10 × 5½ inches)
Signed, inscribed and dated lower left: Patrick / 1918 May 20 / P A de László
PROVENANCE In the possession of the artist on his death; John de Laszlo, fifth son of the artist; Patrick de Laszlo, the sitter and fourth son of the artist
LITERATURE Rowcliffe 1938, p.81 (no. 436); Rutter 1939, p.330

This picture was the first portrait de László painted in the nursing home at 20 Ladbroke Gardens, after being released from internment in Holloway Prison. In his diaries he wrote, "After I had been there three days, enjoying the lovely grounds, the quiet garden and listening to the birds, I had, for the first time in nine months, the pleasure of holding the dear palette in my hand again and with great delight I started a sketch of my son Patrick before he left home to enter Twyford School. It was wonderful to be surrounded by my old friends the colour tubes and brushes after so long. It was a lovely day, with just the light I wanted, and I painted from three o'clock until seven, with a short interval for tea. I forgot myself in my work and finished the portrait. I am happy about it and shall treasure it as my first painting after my arrest. So long as I had my dear palette and my brushes in my hands I felt young, as I always do, but after I had finished my strength gave way and I collapsed."

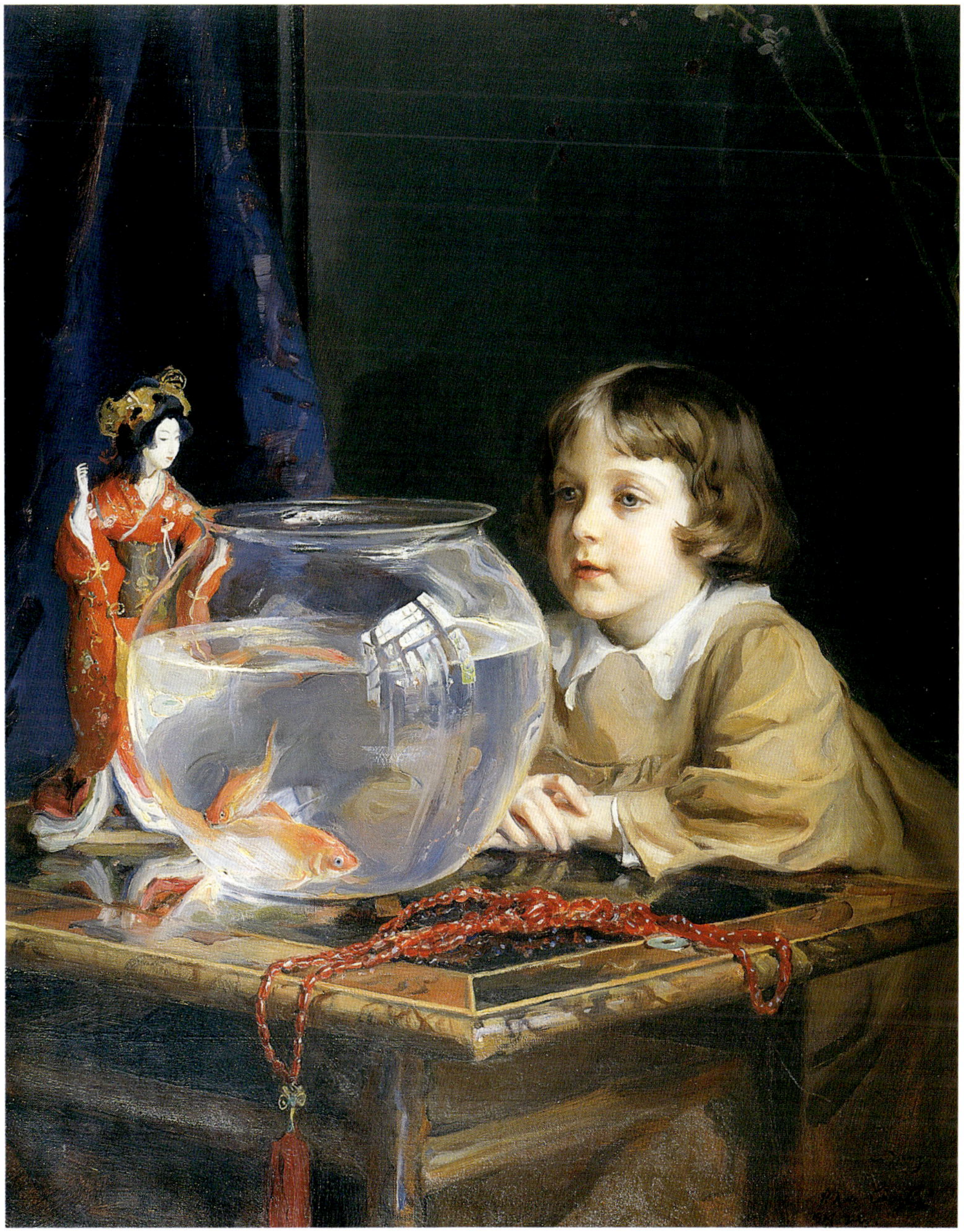

79 John, the Artist's Fifth Son 1918

Oil on canvas, 90.8 × 70.5 cm (35¾ × 27¾ inches)
Signed, inscribed and dated, lower right:
Our Johny. / P A de László / 1918 July
Verso: *In devotion dedicated to my Lucy / this picture of our Johny / has been painted / during my greatest sorrows / but justice must prevail / when truth will be known. / 1918 VII. P. A. de L.* (in oil paint on the canvas) and *The Chinese figure / was presented with others / by the last Empress of China to Mrs G Roosevelt at White House- / this one was given to Lucy as a souvenir of the time when I painted / President Roosevelt's portrait in 1908 Spring – Washington* (in ink on the stretcher)
PROVENANCE In the possession of the artist on his death; Paul de Laszlo, his third son
EXHIBITED Autumn Exhibition, The Royal Glasgow Institute of Fine Arts, 1934, no.70: *John with Goldfish*
LITERATURE Rutter 1939, pp.331–2; N.P.G. 1921–3 Album, p.31

John Adolphus de László was born in London on 20 October 1912. This study was made a month after de László arrived at the nursing home in Ladbroke Gardens, having suffered a nervous breakdown in Holloway Prison. In his diary he wrote: "27th June. I have been painting a picture of John with a bowl of goldfish, and made good progress with it this morning. How interesting it is to watch the movement of the fish in the water …. Life is full of interest if only we gave more time to the observation of it: but we pass life by and miss so much." "5th July. To-day I finished the picture. It has many good qualities in colour and composition, and I think it has caught the character of the boy. I know it might have been much better, but I am too conscious of my present humiliating circumstances."

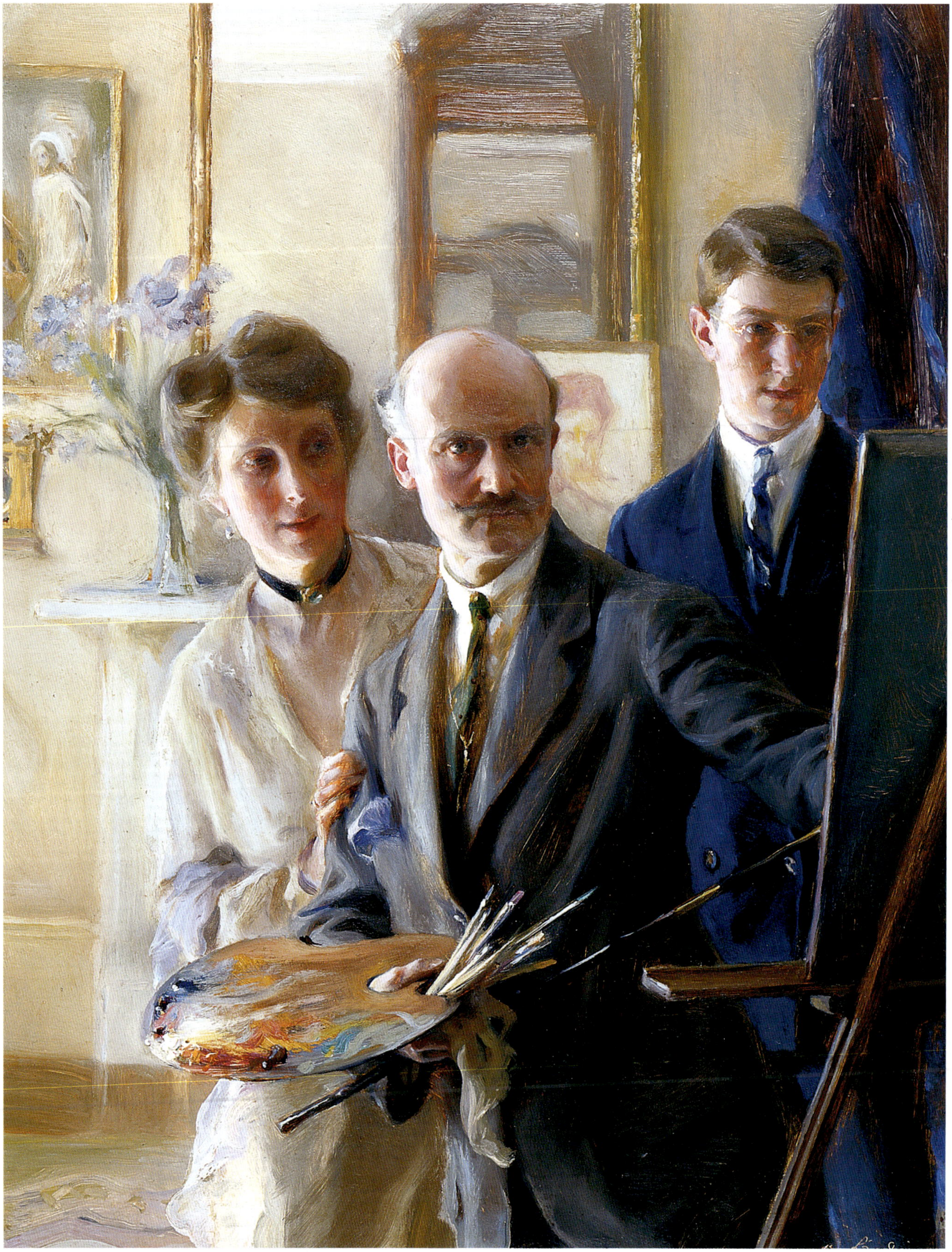

80 The Artist, his Wife Lucy and their Son Henry 1918

Oil on board, 45.1 × 33.3 cm (17¾ × 13⅛ inches)
Signed, inscribed and dated, lower right: *de László / 1918 Sept. London*, and on verso in pencil: *Finished this trio portrait of us on the 27th of Sept. 1918 in the days of distress and hope for happier times to come*
PROVENANCE In the possession of the artist on his death; Paul Leonardo de Laszlo, his third son
LITERATURE N.P.G. 1917–21 Album, p.49; *The Studio*, LXXXI, February 1921, no.335, p.53, ill; Clifford 1969, monochrome ill. pl.36

This painting of the artist supported by his wife and eldest son was painted in September 1918 at Ladbroke Gardens, when, though his health was somewhat restored, he still had no idea as to when he might be released. The painting of Christ on the wall behind, a rare watercolour by the artist (fig. 74), painted in Holloway, testifies to his re-found faith. De László identified himself with Christ, with His innocence and the cruelty He suffered.

During his time in the nursing home he considered painting a picture of the Crucifixion, writing, "In the restless past I scarcely ever had the opportunity to pass so much time in meditation as I do now. It is a great help to me. Only now do I realize how much the Almighty has granted me. In my adversity and solitude I have learnt to understand much. It is a warning for the future to live more wisely, and to appreciate what I possess in love and gifts."

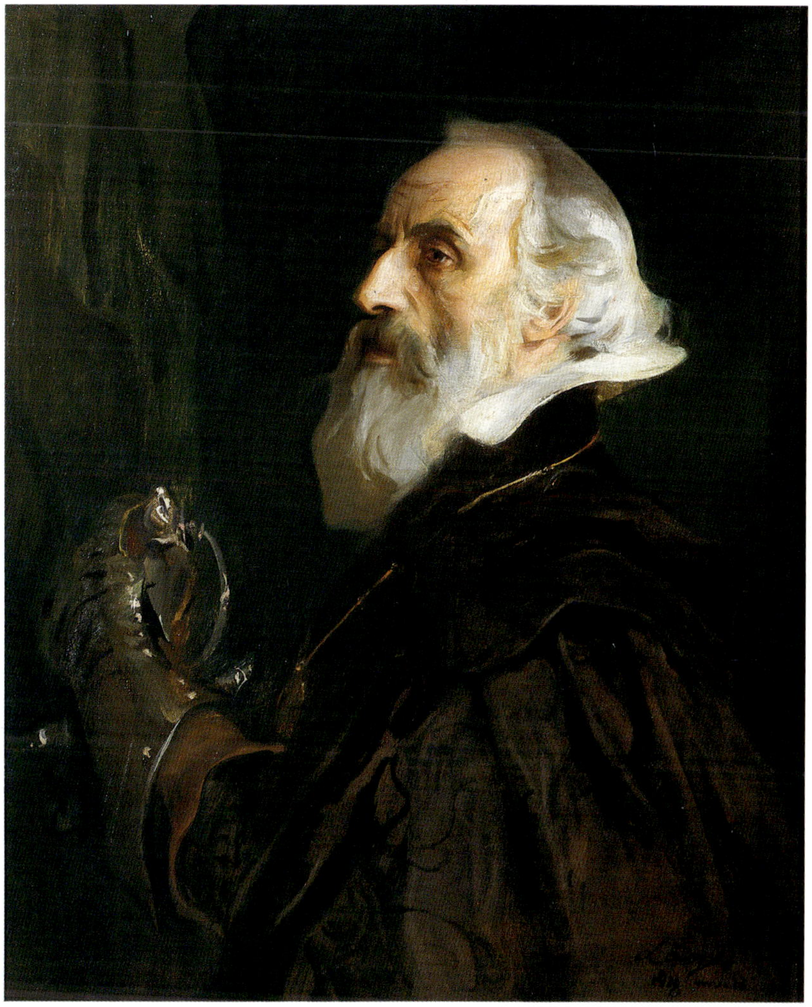

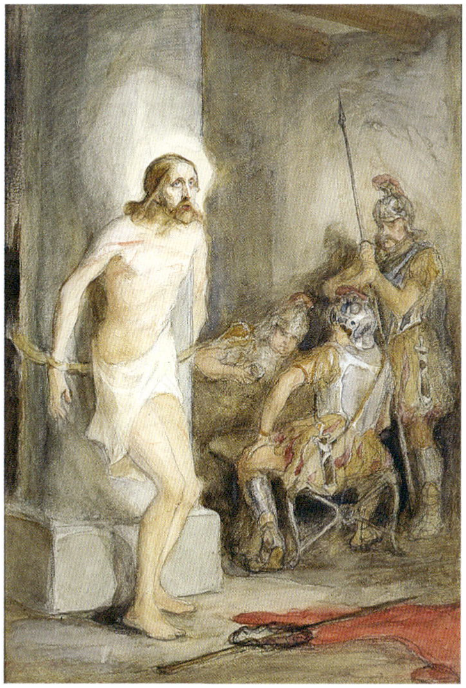

FIG. 74 *Christ and the Roman Soldiers*, 1918
Pencil and watercolour, 53.3 × 35.6 cm (21 × 14 in.)
Private collection

81 Alfred Lys Baldry 1918

Oil on canvas, 80 × 64.1 cm (31½ × 25¼ inches)
Signed and dated, lower right: *László / 1918 Nov. 16*
PROVENANCE In the possession of the artist on his death; Patrick de Laszlo, his fourth son
LITERATURE ASB Vol.II, p.12: *A.L. Baldry. / Dec. 14th 1918.*; N.P.G. 1927–9 Album, p.23b; Rutter 1939, pp.333, 344–5, 381, 384, 389, 273

With his aquiline profile, long white hair and beard, Baldry made the perfect subject for this fine illustration of de László's appreciation for Spanish portraiture.

Alfred Lys Baldry was an artist and art critic who wrote his first article on Philip de László in 1911, after the artist's successful exhibition at

Agnew's that year. He soon became de László's firm friend and was the only visitor outside his family allowed at the Ladbroke Gardens nursing home during the dark days of internment.

Baldry, himself of Spanish descent, was born in Torquay in 1858, the son of Alfred Baldry. In 1877 he won a scholarship to The South Kensington School of Art in 1877 and later became a pupil of Albert Moore. He began exhibiting in the early 1880s. In 1887 he married Annie Lilian Brocklehurst. They lived at Wolmer Wood in Buckinghamshire and had one son.

As well as writing frequently for *The Studio*, Baldry was art critic of *The Globe* from 1893 to 1908 and London art critic of *The Birmingham Post* for about thirty years. He also made contributions to the *Encyclopaedia Britannica* and enjoyed theatre and opera. He published some eight art books, including monographs on Albert Moore (1894), Sir John Everett Millais (1899), Hubert von Herkomer (1901) and G.H. Boughton, R.A. (1904). He died in 1939. De László painted a number of portraits of Baldry over the years, some very informal (fig. 75), and in 1920 painted his wife and son.

In 1933, de László made one of his very few portrait busts of his friend. It is interesting to note how de László, who had only a little early training in sculpture, treated the material exactly as though he were painting, with the same regard to the surface and the architectural formation, character and expression. Indeed the pose seems to have been taken from that in the present portrait (or *vice versa*).

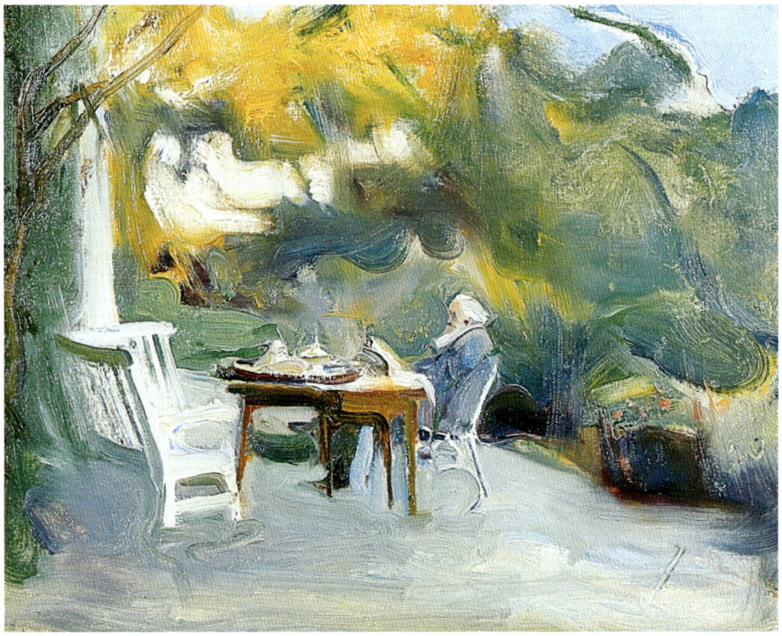

FIG. 75 *Alfred Lys Baldry seated at a Table in the Gardens at The Kennels*, 1917
Oil on canvas, 30.5 × 35.6 cm (12 × 14 in.)
Private collection

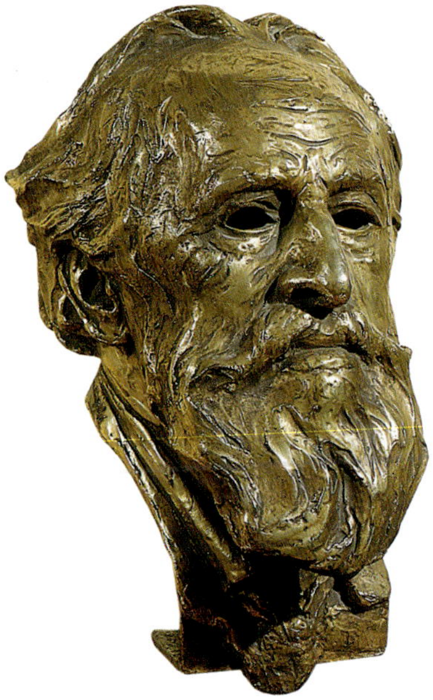

82 Alfred Lys Baldry 1933

Bronze, 34.9 cm ($13\frac{3}{4}$ inches) high, excluding stand
Signed, on collar, right: *de László*, and indistinctly dated *1933*
PROVENANCE In the possession of the artist on his death; Patrick de Laszlo, his fourth son
EXHIBITED *Exhibition of Paintings by Philip A. de László, M.V.O., In Aid of the London Hospital and The Artists' General Benevolent Institution*, Wildenstein & Co., Ltd, London, November–December 1937, ex-catalogue
LITERATURE *Painting a Portrait*, 1934, ill. p.9 (clay model)

83 Henry and John, the Artist's Eldest and Youngest Sons 1919

Pencil and coloured pastels heightened with white on grey paper, 52 × 34.9 cm ($20\frac{1}{2} \times 13\frac{3}{4}$ inches)
Signed, inscribed and dated, lower left: *Henry reading / to / Johny / 1919. Easter / P A de L.*
PROVENANCE In the possession of the artist on his death; Lucy de Laszlo, the artist's wife; John de Laszlo, his youngest son
LITERATURE Rowcliffe 1938, p.140 (no.26)

This drawing was made in Easter 1919 at Littleworth Corner, the house lent to de László by his solicitor, Sir Charles Russell (cat. 85), to which he was able to move from Ladbroke Gardens. It is interesting to compare this charming informal study of the family at home – typical of the work de László produced at Littleworth – with another, made the previous year (cat. 84): the latter drawing is by contrast tightly composed and cropped, creating an almost photographic and abstracted image of childhood, and was quite justly chosen for illustration in *The Studio*.

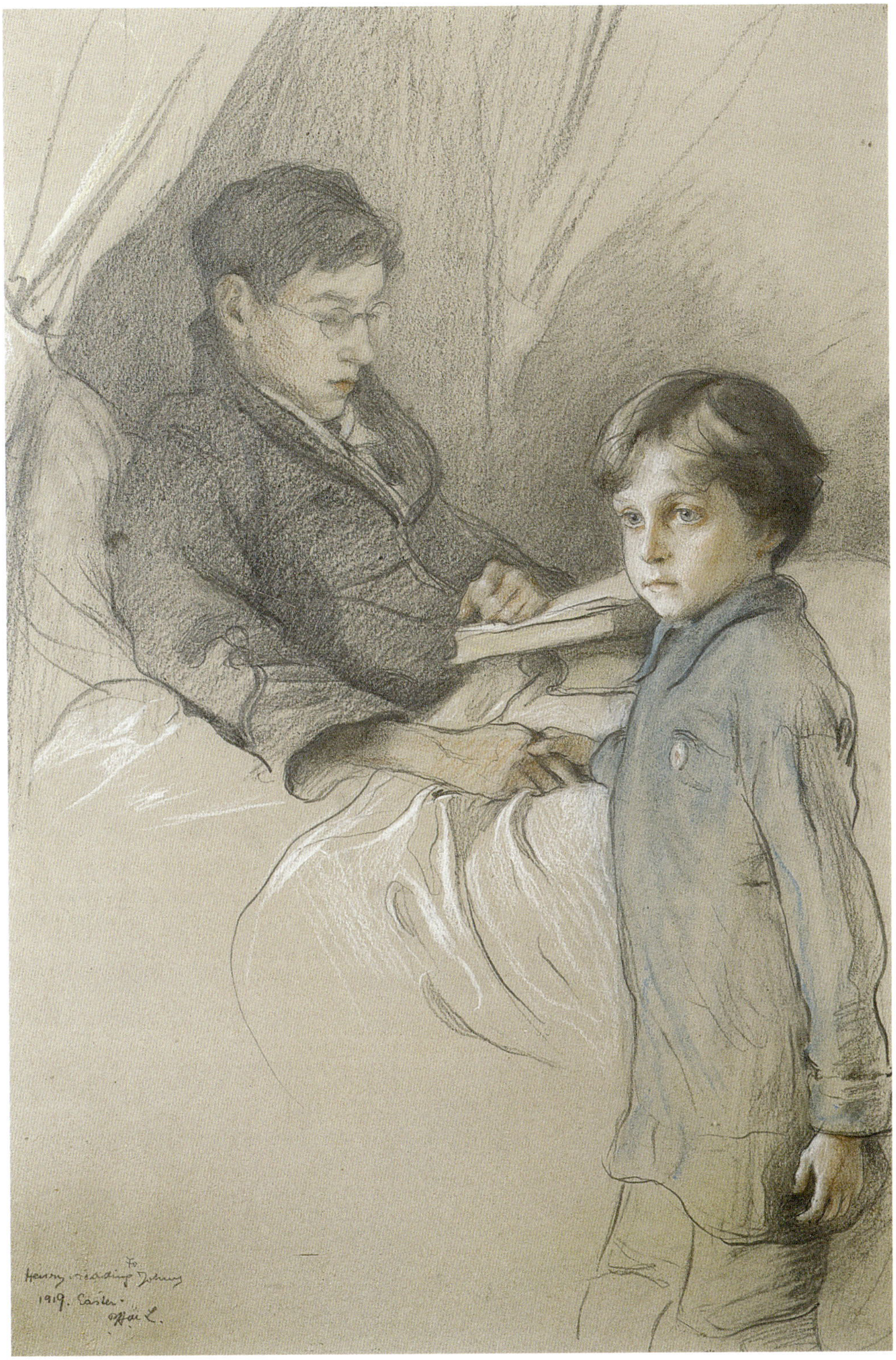

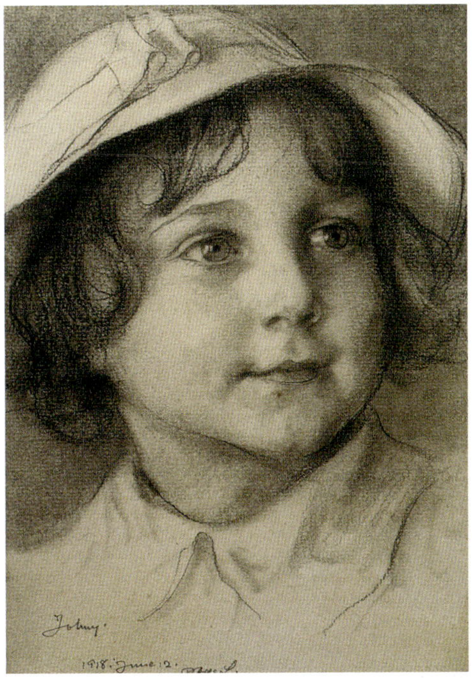

84 John, the Artist's Youngest Son 1918

Charcoal and soft pencil on buff card, 26.4 × 18.1 cm ($10\frac{3}{8} \times 7\frac{1}{8}$ inches)
Signed, inscribed and dated, lower left: *Johny. / 1918: June 12. / P.A. de L.*
PROVENANCE In the possession of the artist on his death; John de Laszlo, the sitter
LITERATURE *The Studio*, LXXXI, 1921, ill. p.50

On the backboard is a well preserved label from the framers that de László frequently used – E. Remy of 153, King's Road, Chelsea.

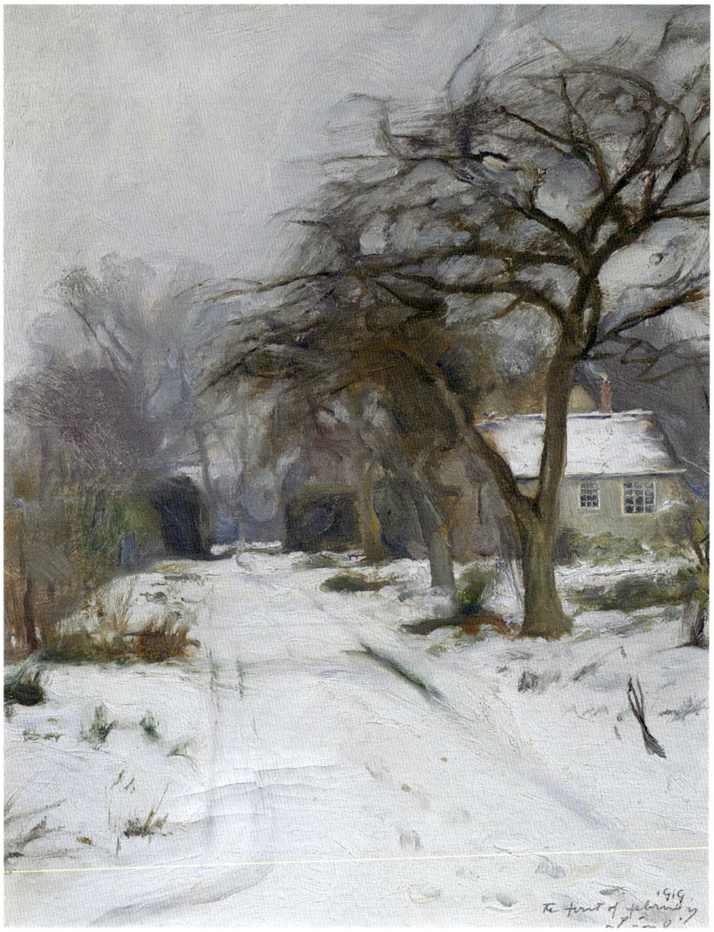

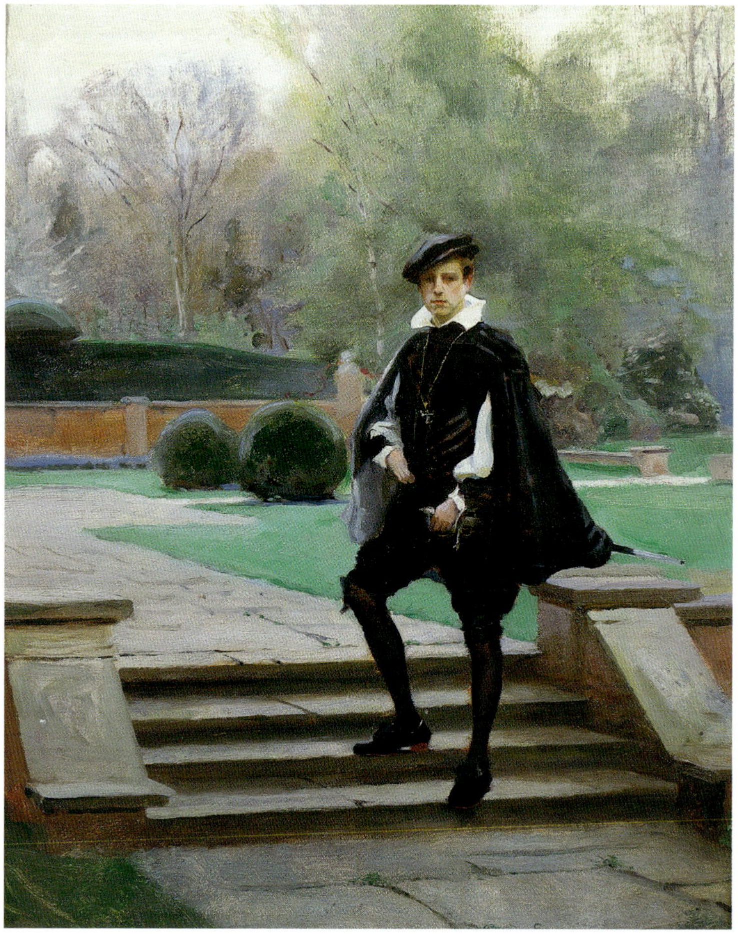

85 'The First of February' The Driveway at Littleworth Corner in the Snow 1919

Oil on canvasboard, 49.5 × 39 cm ($19\frac{1}{2} \times 15\frac{3}{8}$ inches)
Signed, inscribed and dated, lower right: *1919 / The first of February / László*
PROVENANCE In the possession of the artist on his death
LITERATURE Clifford 1969, frontispiece

In December 1918, de László's solicitor Sir Charles Russell offered his country house, Littleworth Corner, at Burnham Beeches in Buckinghamshire, to the artist and his family, and, thanks to the intervention of Lord Devonport (cat. 61), the Home Secretary gave his permission for de László to move there on medical grounds. He remained on strict parole, however. A detective from Scotland Yard paid periodical visits, and he was not permitted to go more than three miles from the end of this drive. De László's bleak mood and frustration can be imagined from this study, his only snow scene.

Sir Charles insisted on waiting for the hostility of public opinion against British citizens of foreign origin to die down, and it was not until June 1919 that de László's case came up before the Revocation Committee. At the hearing the Committee found no evidence of any disloyalty or disaffection to his adopted country, clearing de László's name and exonerating his reputation. He was immediately given the freedom to resume his life and work, and his British citizenship was duly confirmed.

86 Stephen, the Artist's Second Son 1919

Oil on canvasboard, 50.8 × 39.4 cm (20 × $15\frac{1}{2}$ inches)
PROVENANCE In the possession of the artist on his death; John de Laszlo, his youngest son
EXHIBITED *Exhibition of Paintings by Philip A. de László, M.V.O., In Aid of the London Hospital and The Artists' General Benevolent Institution,* Wildenstein & Co., Ltd, London, November–December 1937, no.28: *Stephen, Littleworth Corner*

De László painted some of his finest informal paintings during the time that he and his family were living at Littleworth Corner, including, besides this work, his fine drawing of his eldest and youngest sons together (cat. 83), his study of his wife in an interior (cat. 87), other interior scenes, still lives, landscapes, portraits of Sir Charles and his family – amounting to about forty pictures. This is a fine essay in placing a full-length figure against a landscape, the garden at Littleworth. De László also painted a more traditional portrait of Stephen in costume, visible in the background of his portrait of Lucy in an interior.

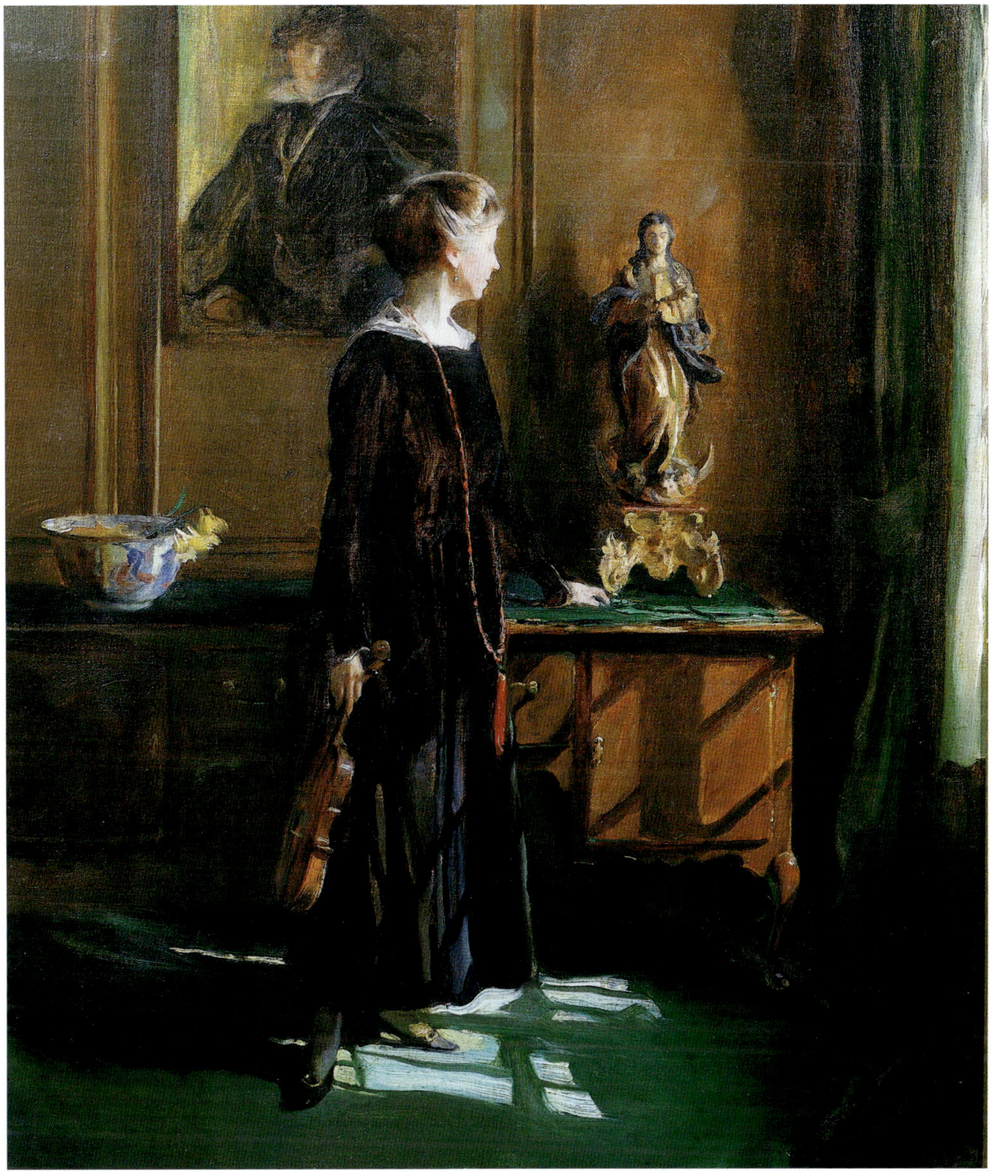

87 Lucy de László, the Artist's Wife 1919

Oil on canvas, 67.9 × 50.2 cm (26¾ × 19¾ inches)
Signed, inscribed and dated, lower right: *de László. Easter 1919* (partly obscured by the frame), and on the verso indistinctly: *My Lucy. she loved the madonna. /she inspired me to do this / summery inspiration. / Easter 1919 / P. A. de L.*
PROVENANCE In the possession of the artist on his death; Paul de Laszlo, his third son
LITERATURE *The Studio*, LXXX, 1920, p.101, ill.; N.P.G. 1931 Album, p.16b; *Painting a Portrait*, 1934, ill. p.49, pl.XIX

De László called this painting "an interesting problem of light and colour". After he had been deprived of the opportunity to paint in oils whilst interned, the period at Littleworth Corner between December 1918 and June 1919 was one of intense activity for de László. This picture of his wife holding her violin, with the recently painted portrait of his son Stephen in Spanish dress on the wall behind, a statue of the Madonna, the daffodils in the Chinese bowl, and the scene bathed in sunlight, is a highly evocative depiction of all that de László held dear during his incarceration. The first Easter of peace-time had still not brought de László any indication of how long his ordeal would last.

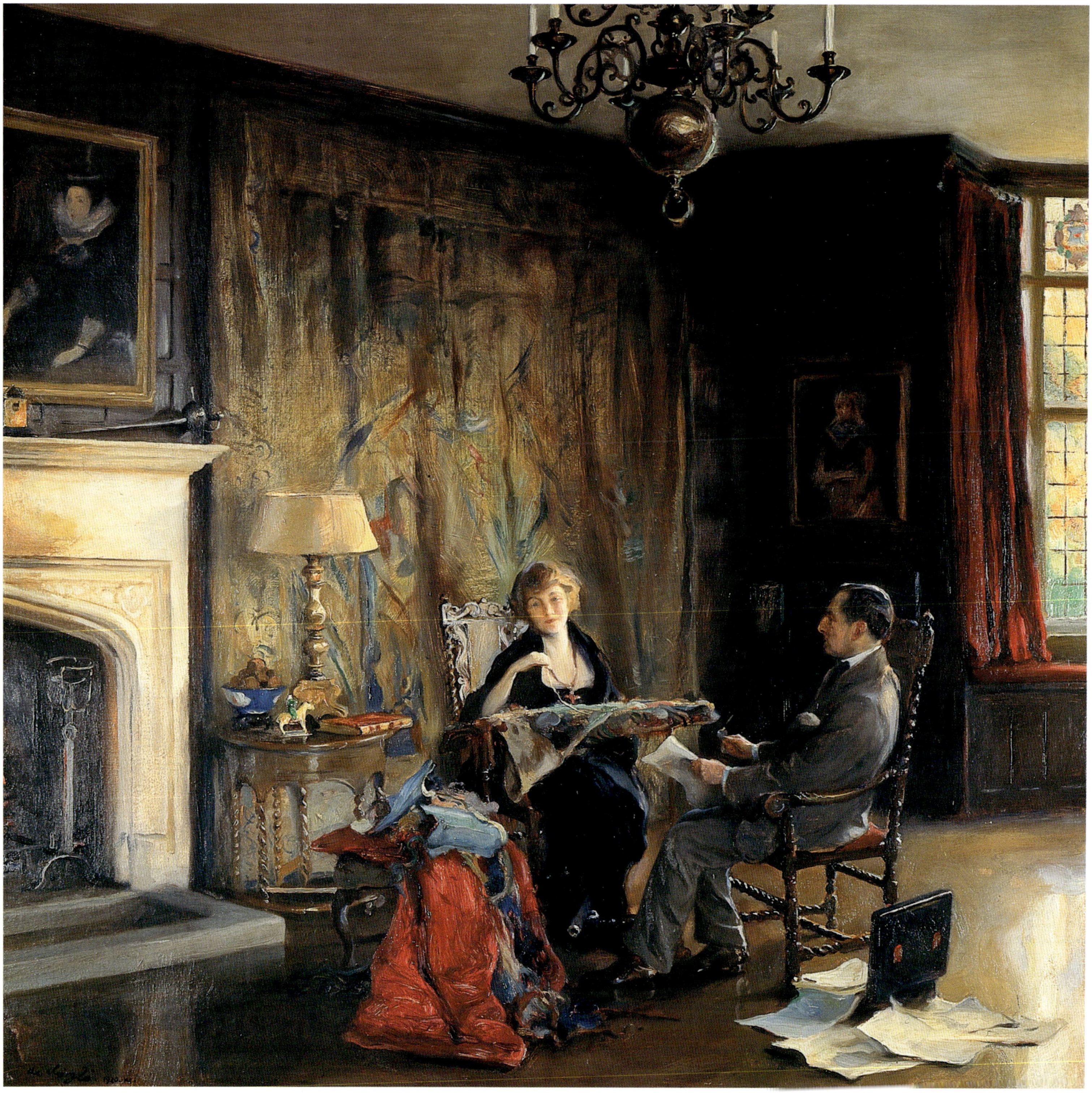

88 'The Last Days at Chequers' Lord and Lady Lee of Fareham in the Hawtrey Room 1920

Oil on canvas, 90.8 × 90.8 cm (35¾ × 35¾ inches)
Signed and dated, lower left: *de László 1920. XI*
The Collection of the Chequers Trust
LITERATURE ASB, Vol.II, p.18: *Ruth Lee of Fareham 7 November 15th Chequers / Bucks 1920*; *Modern Painting*, 1921, ill.; Rutter 1939, pp.246–7, 249, 263,278, 293, 322, 326, 328, 359; Peter Lasko, 'L'institut Courtauld et l'histoire de l'art en Grande-Bretagne', *Revue de l'art*, no.30, 1975, ill. p.88, pl.1; Norma Major, *Chequers, The Prime Minister's Country House and Its History*, London 1996, pp.88, 89, ill. p. 126

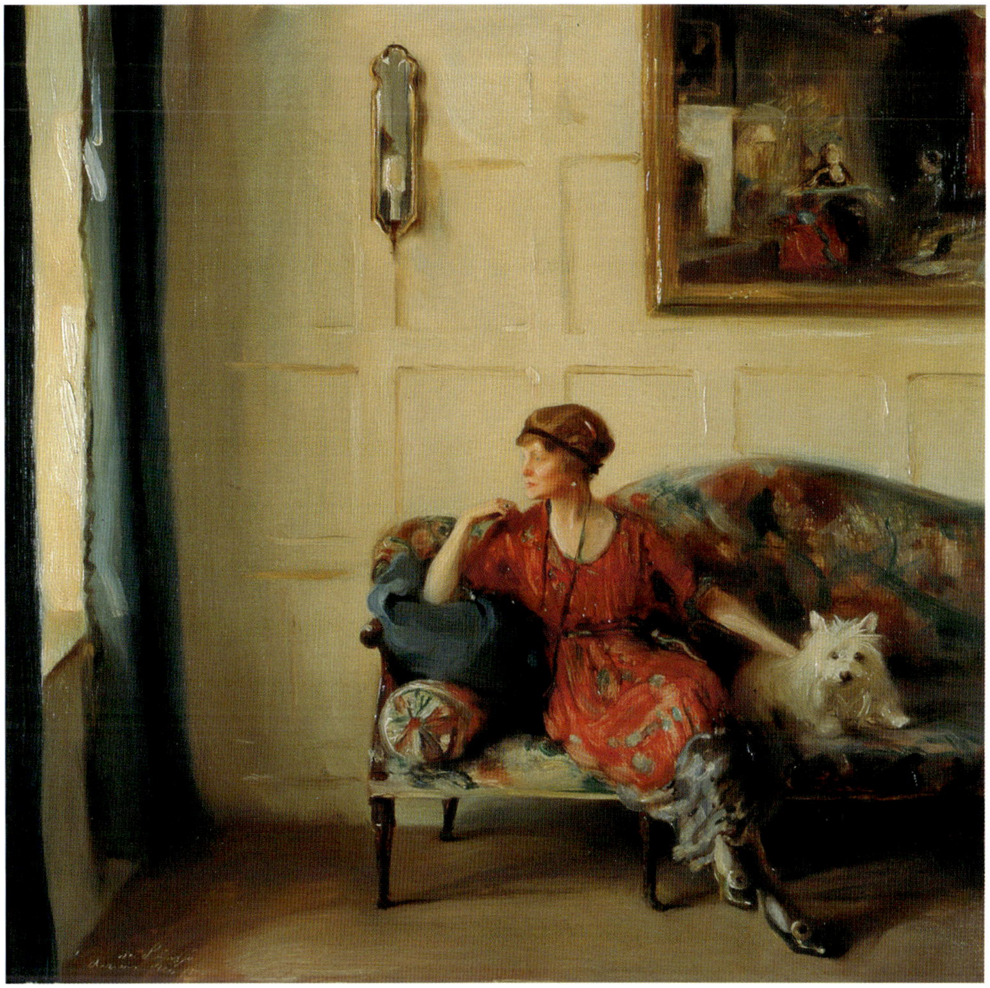

FIG. 76 *Miss Faith Moore at Chequers*, 1920
Oil on canvas, 53.3 × 53.3 cm (21 × 21 in.)
By kind permission of the Trustees of the Chequers Estate

De László first met Arthur Lee (1869–1947) and his wife at a garden party at Windsor in the summer of 1907. A deep and long-lasting friendship developed between de László and the Lees, who brought him a number of commissions, including the portraits of James Lowther, the Speaker of the House of Commons (cat. 38), and, in 1908, President Theodore Roosevelt (fig. 11, p. 23). In 1914 Lee, together with Arthur Balfour, Lord Devonport and Howard Guinness, acted as de László's sponsor in his application for British citizenship. The present portrait would seem to be one of the last of some ten paintings and drawings, both official and intimate, that de László made of the Lee family over the years between 1907 and 1925. De László also painted Mrs Lee's aunt, Ella L. Moore, in 1908 and her sister, Faith Moore, on four occasions – on one (fig. 76), showing *The Last Days* hanging on the wall behind her.

The half-American son of a clergyman, Arthur Hamilton Lee was born in Bridport in Dorset. He was educated at Cheltenham College and, after Sandhurst, was commissioned into the Royal Artillery. While military attaché to the United States Army in Cuba he became a very close friend of Teddy Roosevelt, and was later military attaché at the British Embassy in Washington. He retired in 1900 and was elected Conservative M.P. for Fareham. On the outbreak of the Great War, he rejoined the Army as a colonel. He was created K.C.B. in 1916, and, in 1918, G.B.E. and 1st Baron Lee of Fareham. In August 1919 he was appointed President of the Board of Agriculture, soon becoming Minister of Agriculture and Fisheries. He held this position until 1921, when he became First Lord of the Admiralty. In 1922 he was created 1st Viscount Lee of Fareham.

An enthusiastic collector, Lee had a great knowledge of the fine arts, especially painting, and became a trustee of the Wallace Collection and of the National Gallery, and a member of the Royal Fine Art Commission from 1926.

In 1899, while in Washington, Lee married Ruth Moore, the eldest daughter of John Godfrey Moore, an American financier. In 1909 they took over the lease of Chequers, and in 1917 Lady Lee and her sister Faith purchased the freehold. They handed it immediately to Arthur Lee, who, since they had no children, arranged to bequeath the house to the nation, with an endowment of £100,000 for its upkeep, for the use of future Prime Ministers.

De László's painting was executed in November 1920 to mark their planned departure from the house on Armistice Day. They finally left in January 1921.

89 The Rt Hon. Austen Chamberlain, P.C., M.P. 1920

Oil on canvas, 90.2 × 59.7 cm (35½ × 23½ inches)
Signed, inscribed and dated, lower right:
de László / 1920. XII
LITERATURE ASB, Vol.II, p.19: *Austen Chamberlain. / Dec. 18. 19. 1920*; *Modern Painting*, 1921, ill.; Rutter 1939, pp.282, 306, 308, 323, 328, 329, 337, 344–5; letter 304

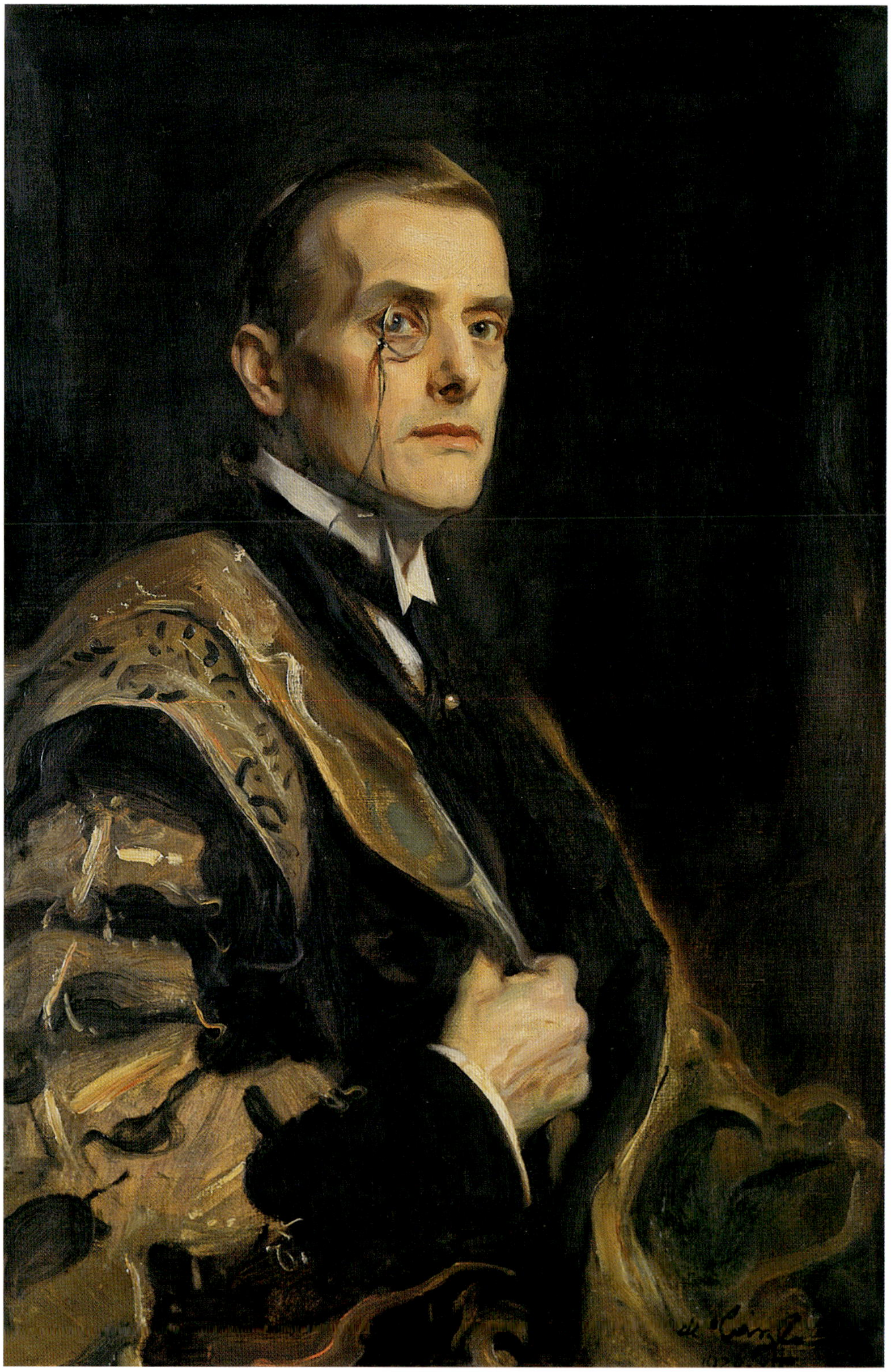

It can be assumed that de László first met Austen Chamberlain when he commissioned his first portrait in 1913 and, not unusually for de László, the two became friends. The artist painted some nine portraits of the family over the years. The friendship between the two families extended to the next generation and has been renewed in the third as a result of the compiling of de László's catalogue raisonné.

After de László's arrest, Chamberlain was among the first to go before a Parliamentary Advisory Committee to testify that de László was of good character, and loyal to his adopted king and country. The Committee was unable to decide on de László's case, and he remained in detention. In the early spring of 1918, a year and a half later, Chamberlain, together with Lord Devonport (cat. 61), Sir Arthur Lee (cat. 88) and Lord Selborne (fig. 52, p. 63), formed a deputation to the Home Secretary, but to no avail. It was not until 1919 that the Revocation Committee heard his case and, on the positive evidence of a number of important figures, including Chamberlain, the artist's name was finally cleared, and his reputation restored.

(Joseph) Austen Chamberlain (1863–1937) was the eldest son of the statesman Joseph Chamberlain and half-brother to Neville Chamberlain. He was Chancellor of the Exchequer from 1903 to 1906 and from 1919 to 1921, Secretary for India 1915–17, a member of Lloyd George's War Cabinet, Lord Privy Seal, Leader of the House and Unionist leader from 1921–2. As Foreign Secretary from 1924 to 1929 he was made a Knight of the Garter and received a Nobel Peace Prize for negotiating the Locarno Pact in 1925.

The present painting was, according to the sitter's daughter, painted towards the end of his second term as Chancellor of the Exchequer, as a farewell present from his Treasury colleagues. De László made another study of Chamberlain for his own pleasure, in 1929.

90 Miss Diane Chamberlain 1920

Pencil on cream paper, 48.3 × 34.3 cm
(19 × 13½ inches)
Signed, dated and inscribed, lower right: *as a souvenir of the 18th / anniversary of our dear / friends Austen and Mrs Chamberlain's /wedding day* – (1924 in another hand) *de László / 1920 / XII /Xmas*
LITERATURE ASB, Vol.II, p.19: *Diane Chamberlain*, not dated but between entries for 10 and 11 December 1920; *The Studio*, LXXXI, 1921, no.335, ill. by p.47; Rutter 1939, p.345

De László made this drawing at the same time as he painted the portrait of the sitter's father (cat. 89), in preparation for an oil painting, completed in the same year. He had painted her mother in 1915, and made a double portrait of the sitter with her brother Joseph in 1917. He painted Diane again, twice, as a young woman in 1933 and 1935. At that time she was working for her father as his Personal Private Secretary.

Both drawing and painting were presented to the family as gifts, both to mark the eighteenth wedding anniversary of the sitter's parents and in gratitude for their friendship and support during the artist's internment. It would have been at this time that Diane wrote to the artist in which she made a sketch of him (included in the collection of memorabilia at the exhibition this book accompanies).

Beatrice Diane Chamberlain, born in London in 1912, was the second child and only daughter of Austen Chamberlain and his wife Ivy Dundas. In 1935 she married Arthur Terence Maxwell (1905–1991), only son of Brigadier-General Sir Arthur Maxwell. They had a daughter, Valerie, and two sons, Patrick and David.

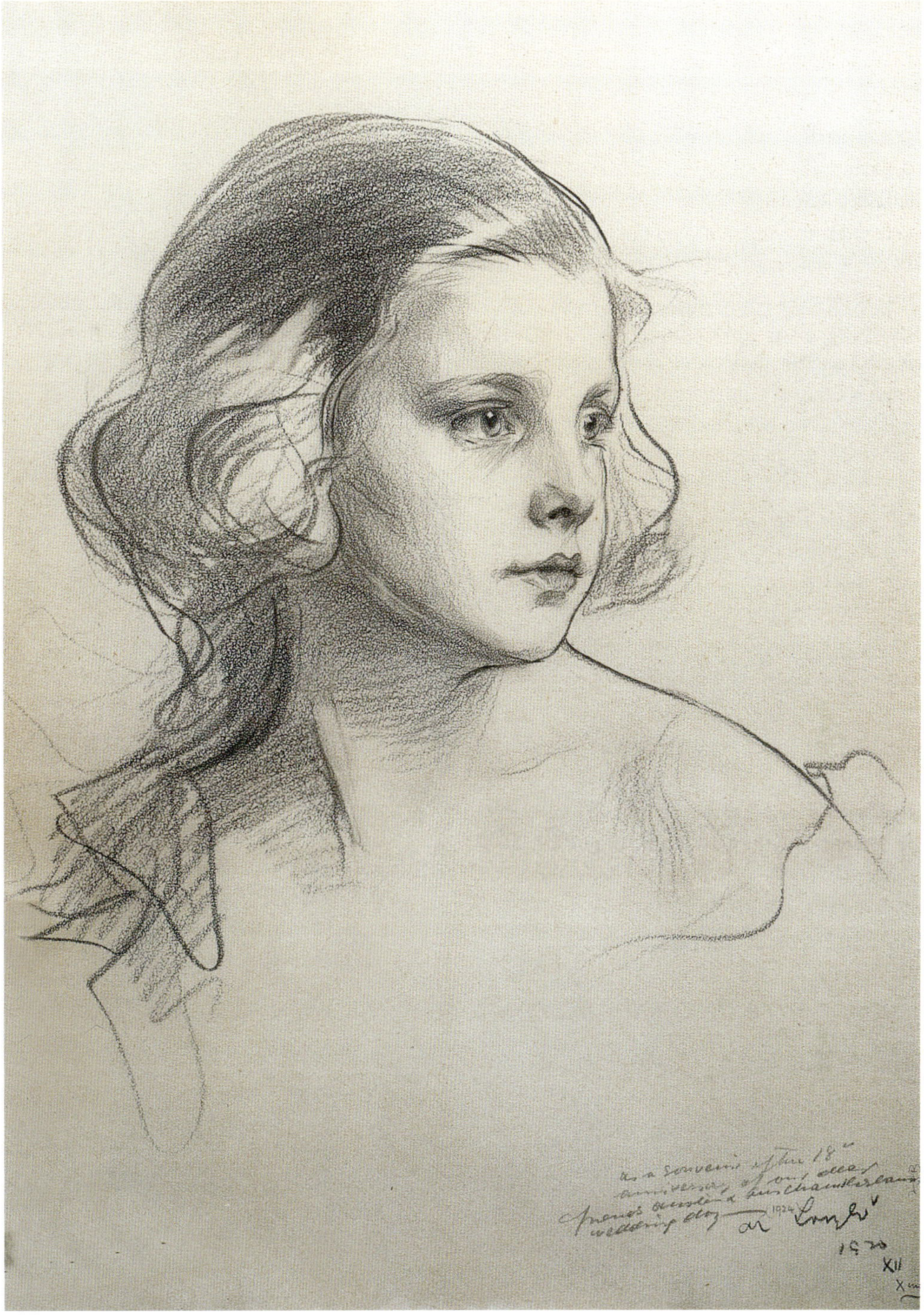

91 Master Godfrey and Miss Diana Ralli 1922

Oil on canvas, oval, 101.6 × 81.3 cm (40 × 32 inches)
Signed and dated, lower right: *de László / 1922.Oct.*
LITERATURE ASB, Vol.II, p.31: *Godfrey.* and *Diana.* with the date *Oct 18th 1922.* in another hand; N.P.G. 1921–23 Album, p.14

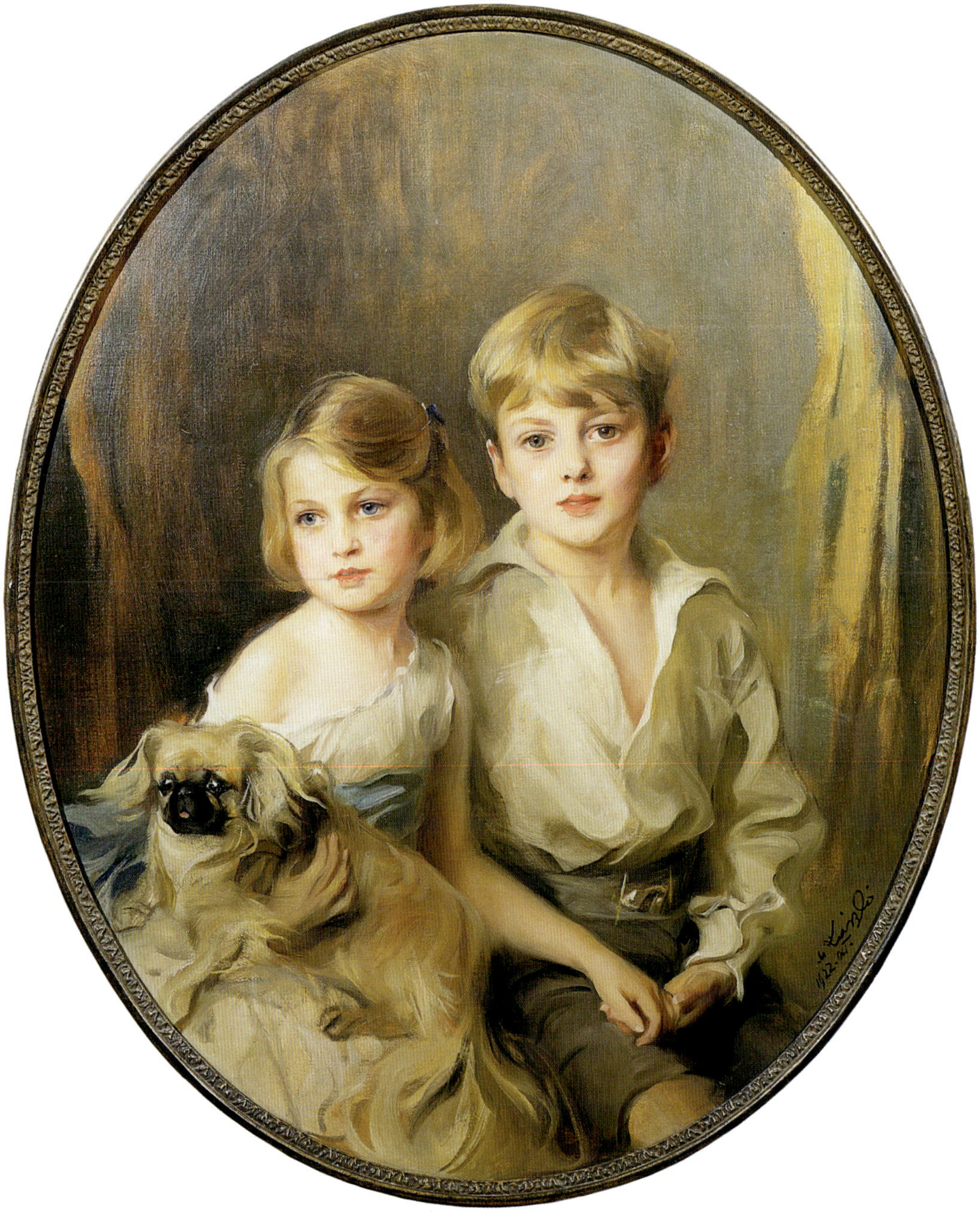

Two preparatory drawings for this portrait remain in the collection of a descendant of the artist. De László also painted a portrait of the children's mother, Mrs Eustratio Ralli, in 1923. In a letter written in 1992, Diana (Didie) described the painting of "the two rather 'Goody Goody' looking Ralli children painted at the age of four and six years old". The artist ended up tying Didie to one of the columns in his studio with the wide blue sash of her dress. According to her nephew, "Whilst the great artist was starting the painting, he decided that Didie might like a doll to hold. As, even at that early age, Didie really thought of herself as a boy ... she certainly did not appreciate the doll. To compound the problem, Philip de László said, 'What beautiful hair you have. It is quite outstanding.'... After that sitting ... Didie hacked away at her hair under her bonnet .... To his great credit, the artist was able to remember what her hair looked like .... It was because she kept fidgeting and getting up that he did indeed tie her to a pillar to keep her still! ... It was of course a masterpiece to let her hold the family Pekinese dog, 'Teeny', as she infinitely preferred dogs to dolls."

In 1999, Godfrey Ralli recalled: "de László let me watch while he painted the dog's face. It was an experience I shall never forget. With very few strokes he had the outline of his head. In perhaps a quarter of an hour he had the expression exactly, and I knew that dog very well. It was uncanny to watch. As a child, little did I realize that I was watching a master at work. It was so quick and quite brilliant."

Godfrey Victor Ralli, born in 1915, was the eldest son of Eustratio Lucas Ralli (1876–1964) and his wife Louise Warrington Williams (1890–1982). After he leaving the army he followed a successful career in the City. Diana (Didie) Myrtle Ralli, born in 1918, shot her first stag by the age of twelve, with a rifle her father had used during the Boer War. She married Lt-Col. John Herbert Walford, D.S.O, an officer in the Seaforth Highlanders. She died on 8 June 2001.

92 Mrs John Walter, née Phyllis Foster 1924

Oil on board, 85.2 × 68.6 cm ($35\frac{1}{2}$ × 27 inches)
Signed and dated, lower left: *de László / 1924 / VI*
PROVENANCE Mrs Pamela Landegger, daughter of the sitter
LITERATURE ASB, Vol.II, p.40: *Phyllis Walter. May 16th 1924*, beneath the signature of her husband

During a fancy dress ball in London in 1924 de László asked for an introduction to Mrs Walter, whose full Spanish costume of a black flounced dress and lace mantilla had caught his eye, and on that first meeting persuaded her to sit for a portrait. The same year, he was commissioned to paint her husband. He made two portraits of her in this costume, one of which was taken by a member of her family to Budapest, and was lost, presumed destroyed, in the Second World War. The present portrait was also taken east, to Prague, in 1936, and also disappeared during the war. It was returned anonymously, by post, in 1955, in perfect condition.

(Phyllis) Charlotte Hilda Foster was born in 1876, the youngest daughter of Col. and Mrs Charles E. Foster of Long Buckley Hall, Northamptonshire. In 1903 she married John Walter V, the last of that dynasty to own *The Times*. On the outbreak of the First World War the family went to live in Madrid, where John Walter was Press Attaché at the Embassy. They

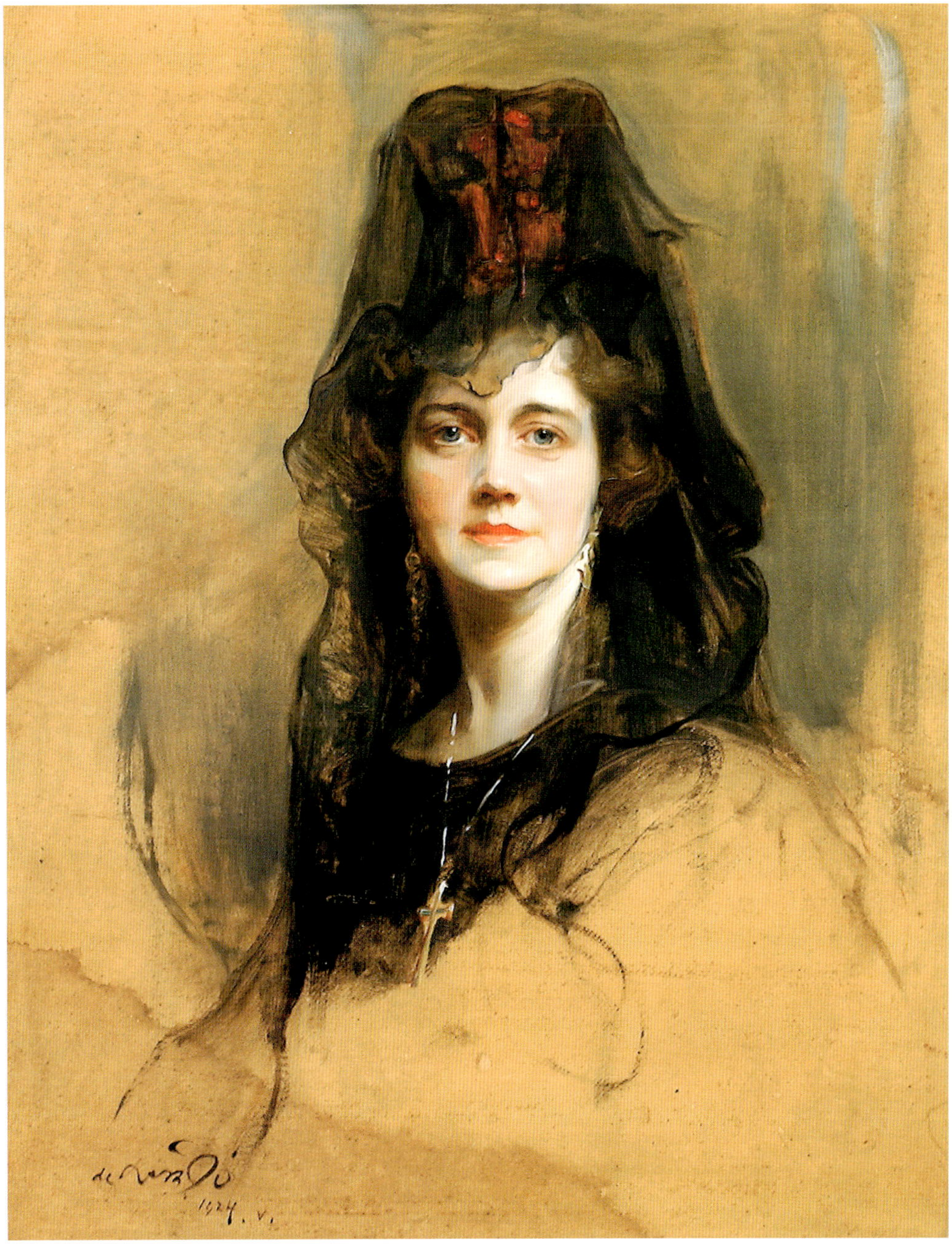

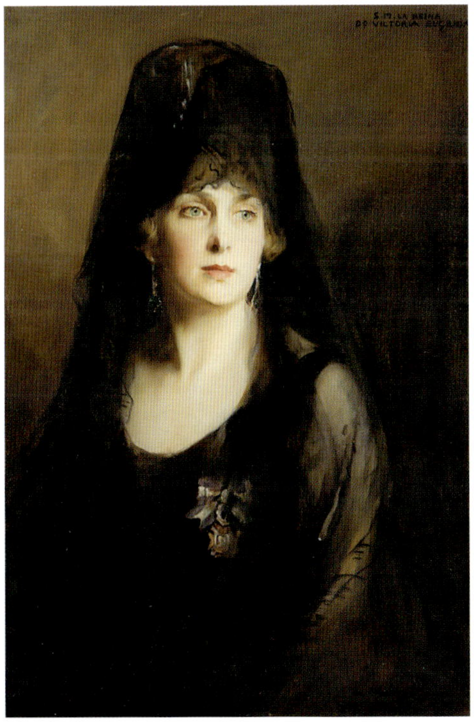

FIG. 77 *H.M Queen Victoria-Eugenia of Spain*, 1927
Oil on canvas, 88.9 × 61 cm (35 × 24 in.)
Museo del Prado, Madrid

had four children. Pamela, the eldest, recalled how her mother, Spain's English Queen 'Ena' (Victoria-Eugenia) and a few other English women would meet for sewing and tea, and talk longingly about England and the danger of the war: "The Queen and my mother were both simple souls who saw things in black and white, and knew very little about politics or economics, or other more subtle reasons for the Great War." For his portrait of the Queen of Spain, in 1927, de László used the costume and composition of Mrs Walter's portrait, with the additional subtlety of the turn of her head to the right (fig. 77).

Mrs Walter remained enchanted all her life by Spain and most things Spanish, as was reflected in the furnishings of her houses in Spain and, later, England. She died in 1937.

93 Lady Louis Mountbatten, née the Hon. Edwina Ashley 1923

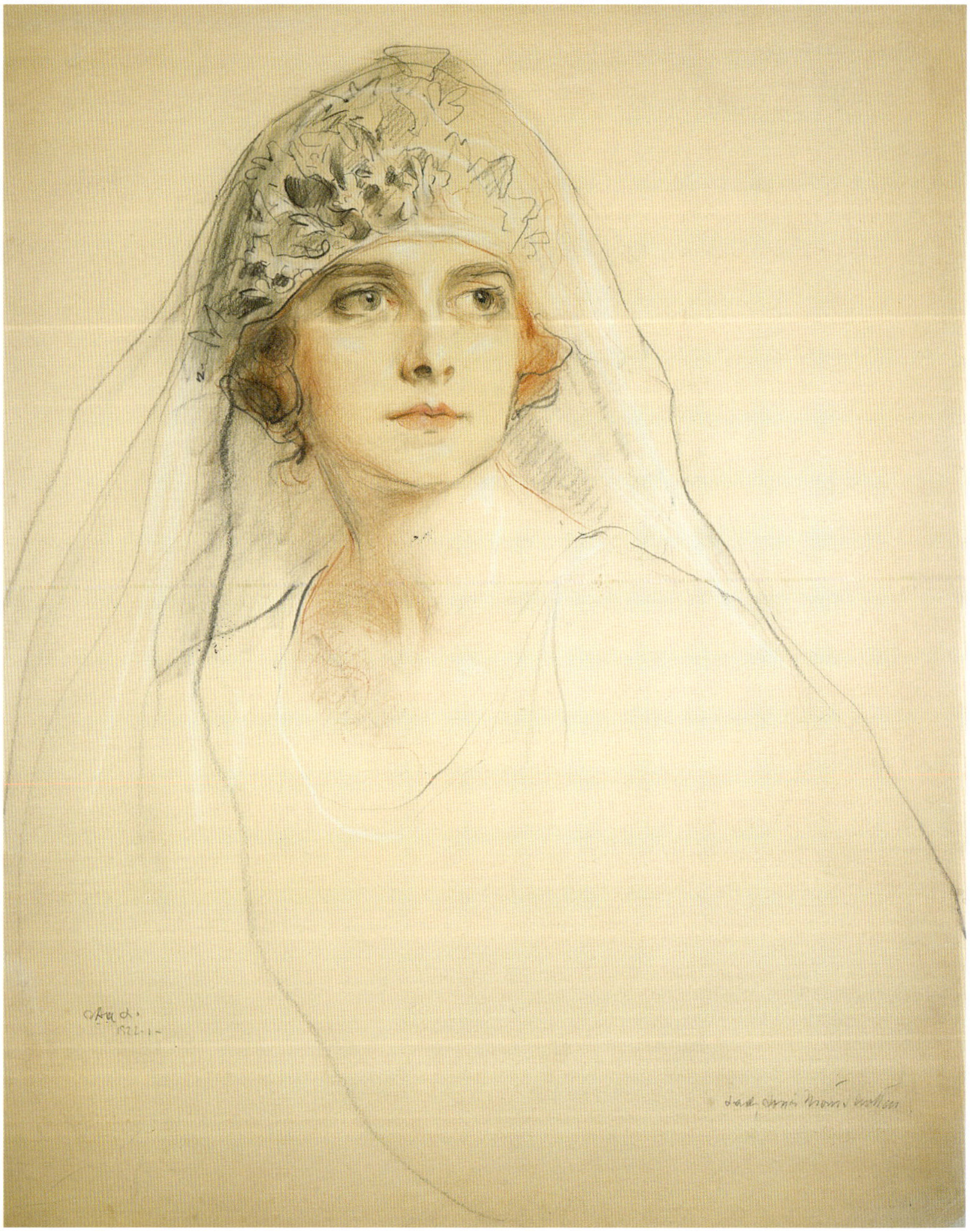

Pencil and red chalk on white paper, 60.1 × 48.9 cm (24 × 19¼ inches)
Signed, inscribed and dated, lower left: *P.A. de L. / 1923 -I-*, and lower right: *Lady Louis Mountbatten*
PROVENANCE In the possession of the artist on his death
LITERATURE ASB, Vol.II, p.35: *Edwina Mountbatten January 17 23*; Rowcliffe 1938, p.145 (no. 21)

The Hon. Edwina Ashley married Lord Louis Mountbatten (cat. 94) on 18 July 1922. The present drawing would certainly seem to be a preparatory study for the wedding portrait that de László painted of Lady Louis, which he inscribed *In memory of 18th July 1922*, although he actually painted it in 1923, during the same sittings as the present drawing. He painted a further study portrait of her in 1924. Sargent had made a portrait drawing of the younger Edwina in 1912.

Edwina was born in London in 1901, the daughter of Colonel Wifrid W. Ashley, later Baron Mount Temple, and Amalia Mary Maud, only daughter of Sir Ernest Cassel (cat. 20). Her godfather was King Edward VII. On her grandfather's death in 1921 she inherited some £2.3 million and a fine collection of paintings. Her marriage the following year at St Margaret's, Westminster, was a high point of the London season. On her father's death in 1939, she inherited Broadlands, which came indirectly from the Palmerston family. The outbreak of World War II marked the beginning of a distinguished career of service with the Order of St John.

After Lord Louis was appointed Supreme Allied Commander, South East Asia, in 1943, she proved tireless in her inspections of hospitals and schools in the Far East, and in organizing welfare services for returned allied prisoners of war and internees. Lady Mountbatten accompanied her husband to India when he was appointed last Viceroy in 1947. Her many acts of social as well as political conciliation were vital in strengthening ties between the British and Indian peoples.

On her return from India she took on even more responsibilities, and severely taxed her health. While on an exhausting tour for the St John Ambulance Brigade she died unexpectedly in her sleep in Borneo on 21 February 1960. Lady Mountbatten was buried at sea off Plymouth with naval honours.

She had two daughters, Patricia, born in 1924, who married the 7th Baron Brabourne in 1946, and Pamela, born in 1929, who married the designer David Hicks in January 1960.

94 Lord Louis Mountbatten 1925

Oil on board, 96.5 × 71.1 cm (38 × 28 inches)
Signed and dated, lower right: *de László / 1925. I.*
Verso: Preparatory oil sketch of the Kupelweiser family, a compositional essay for a group portrait

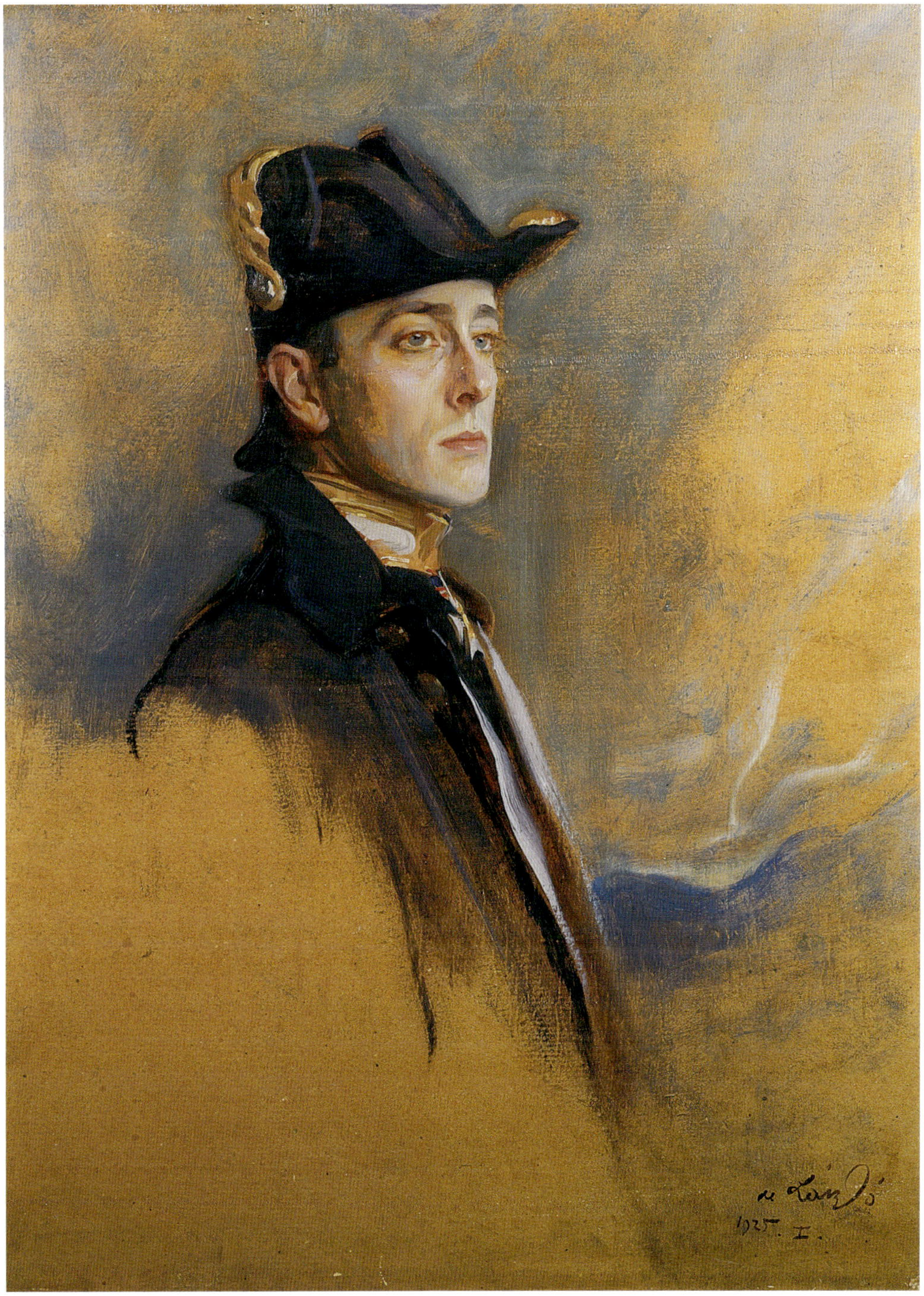

The present study portrait of Lord Louis from January 1925 is a pair to a study portrait in oils of his wife painted in 1924. De László also painted a formal wedding portrait in oils of each of them, hers dated 1922 and his 1924. He painted many other members of their extended families, some several times.

Prince Louis of Battenberg was born at Frogmore House, Windsor, in 1900, the younger son of Prince Louis of Battenberg, later Louis Mountbatten, 1st Marquess of Milford Haven (cat. 43), and Princess Victoria of Hesse. His great-grandmother Queen Victoria and Tsar Nicholas II were his sponsors. In 1922 he married Edwina Ashley (cat. 93). After a distinguished career in the Navy, in 1942 he was appointed Chief of Combined Operations and in 1943 Supreme Allied Commander, South East Asia. He was created 1st Viscount Mountbatten of Burma in 1946, in recognition of his work in Asia, and then appointed the last Viceroy of India in February 1947, presiding over the delicate transition to independence. In recognition he was created 1st Earl Mountbatten of Burma.

In 1955 he became First Sea Lord (as his father had been) and later Chief of Defence Staff for six years, before retiring in 1965. He was killed in his boat off the coast of County Sligo, Ireland, by an I.R.A. terrorist attack on 27 August 1979. His elder daughter Patricia succeeded to the title as 2nd Countess Mountbatten of Burma.

The verso, a compositional sketch for a portrait of the Kupelweiser family, whom de László knew in Vienna between 1902 and 1907, illustrates the artist's habit of recycling his painting boards, but this one is unusual in being re-used many years later. The Kupelweisers were a prominent family of Austrian industrialists for whom de László painted an enormous family group, eventually completed in 1907, and certainly the largest and most complex commission he had carried out until then. It remains with a descendant of the sitters.

95 Chief Medicine Eagle
1923

Oil on board, 69.9 × 49.5 cm (27½ × 19½ inches)
Signed and dated, lower left: *P A de László / 1923.*, and inscribed, centre left: *Medicine Eagle*
Verso: Preparatory oil sketch of Count Leopold Berchtold, the Austro-Hungarian Ambassador to Russia, whose formal portrait was exhibited at de László's first London exhibition, at the Fine Art Society, in 1907
PROVENANCE In the possession of the artist on his death; Patrick de Laszlo, his fourth son
EXHIBITED *A Series of Portraits and Studies By Philip A. de László, M.V.O.*, The French Gallery, London, June 1924, no.48: *Study of a North-American Indian*

When the impressario 'Buffalo Bill' Cody first brought his 'Wild West Show' to Europe in the 1880s, it started a fascination for 'cowboys and Indians', which, from the earliest days of cinema, filmmakers were quick to exploit. One of the first classic Westerns was *The Covered Wagon*, released by Paramount in 1923.

That year, Chief Medicine Eagle came to England, possibly to lecture on the Native American Indian way of life. He appeared at an exhibition in London where he was seen by de László and his fourteen-year-old son, Patrick, who suggested his father should paint him. According to family legend, de László approached the Canadian High Commissioner to persuade Medicine Eagle to sit for his portrait. He was at first reluctant to be painted in his full headdress, but was eventually persuaded, and apparently he sat unblinking and immobile for two hours, in which time this portrait was painted.

At the same time de László made two drawings of Chief Medicine Eagle: one he gave to the Chief (untraced), the other (fig. 78) was subsequently reproduced as a postcard to promote *The Covered Wagon*.

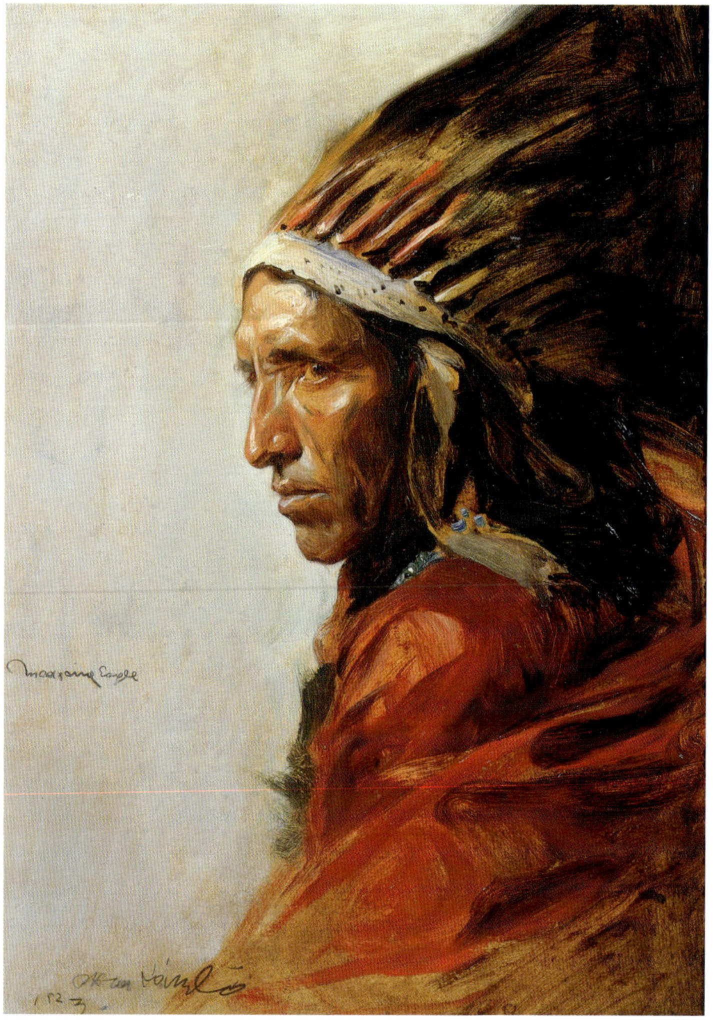

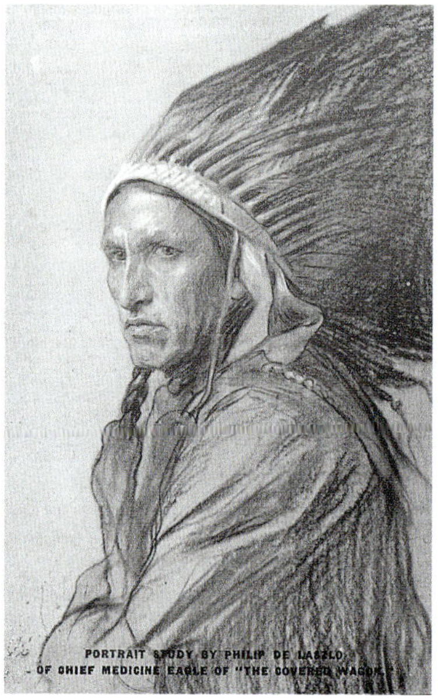

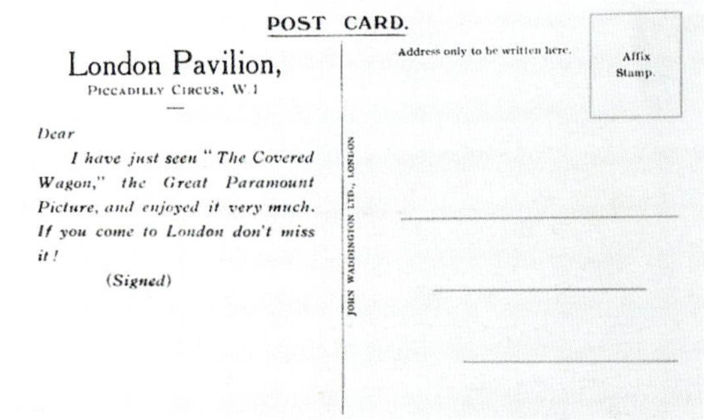
POST CARD.

London Pavilion,
PICCADILLY CIRCUS, W 1

Dear
I have just seen "The Covered Wagon," the Great Paramount Picture, and enjoyed it very much. If you come to London don't miss it!
(Signed)

Address only to be written here.

Affix Stamp.

JOHN WADDINGTON LTD., LONDON

FIG. 78 Postcard of *Chief Medicine Eagle* advertising *The Covered Wagon*, based on a drawing in charcoal and graphite, 1923
Donated by Jonathan King

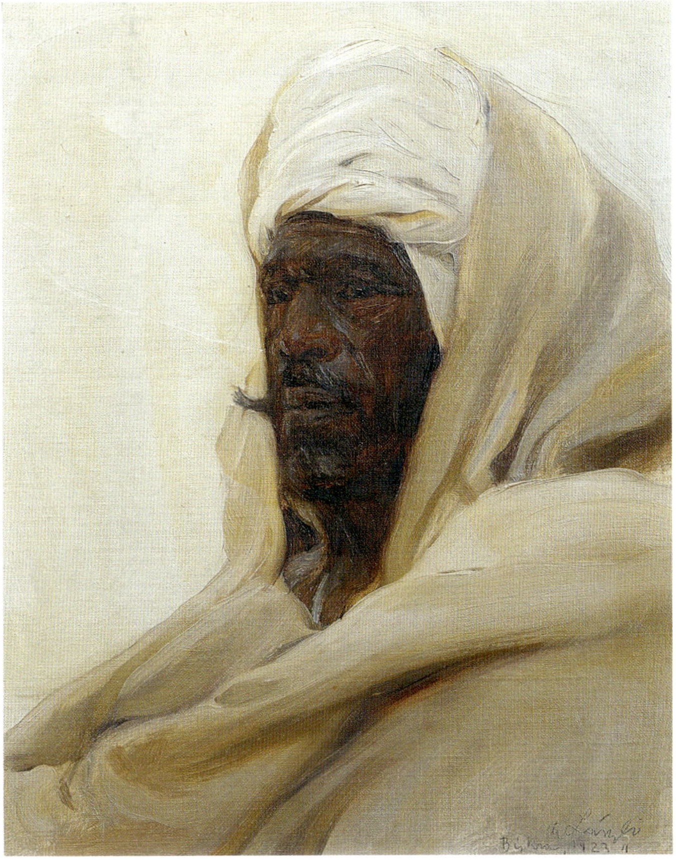

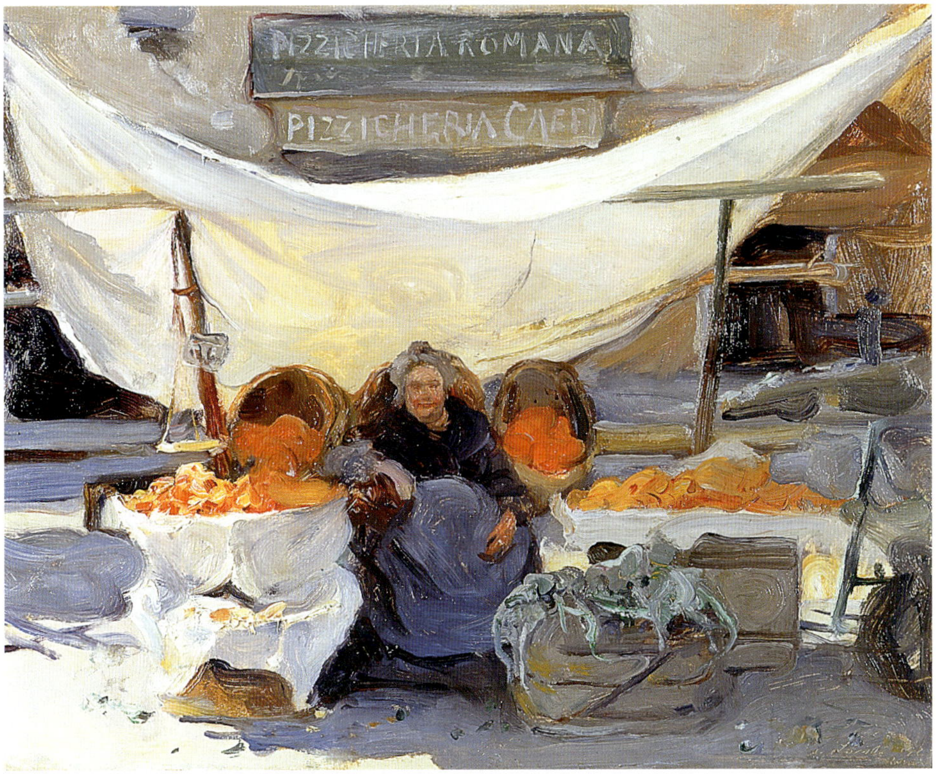

96 An Arab at Biskra 1923

Oil on canvasboard, 39.4 × 31.1 cm
(15½ × 12¼ inches)
Signed in pencil and indistinctly inscribed and dated, lower right: *de László /Biskra, 1923 II.*
PROVENANCE In the possession of the artist on his death
LITERATURE *The Studio,* LXXXVI, 1923, ill. p. 134; Rutter 1939, p.348

In 1923 de László took his wife on their first real holiday since the war. According to Rutter, "They spent some time in Algeria. He was excited and delighted by all he saw, and enjoyed painting Arab types …."

97 The Orange Seller 1923

Oil on panel, 31.8 × 39.4 cm (12½ × 15½ inches)
Signed, inscribed and dated, lower right: *de László 1923 / Rome*
PROVENANCE In the possession of the artist on his death; Patrick de Laszlo, his fourth son
EXHIBITED *Exhibition of Paintings by Philip A. de László, M.V.O., In Aid of the London Hospital and The Artists' General Benevolent Institution,* Wildenstein & Co., Ltd., London, November–December 1937, no.55: *A Roman Orange Seller*
LITERATURE Clifford 1969, ill. front dust cover and p.25, pl.V.

At Easter 1923, on his return from Algeria, de László stopped off in Rome to paint Mussolini (untraced). While there he painted one of the most successful of all his sketches, a study of a market woman. In Clifford's words, "This with its relaxed economy of means, uninhibited colour sense, is fresh, crisp, immediate and complete, and he rarely equalled it."

The exhibition at Wildenstein's, New Bond Street, which opened two days after de László's death in November 1937 included a larger number of studies and landscapes than had ever been included in his shows before. He showed some 26 still-life and landscape paintings to 37 portraits and portrait drawings.

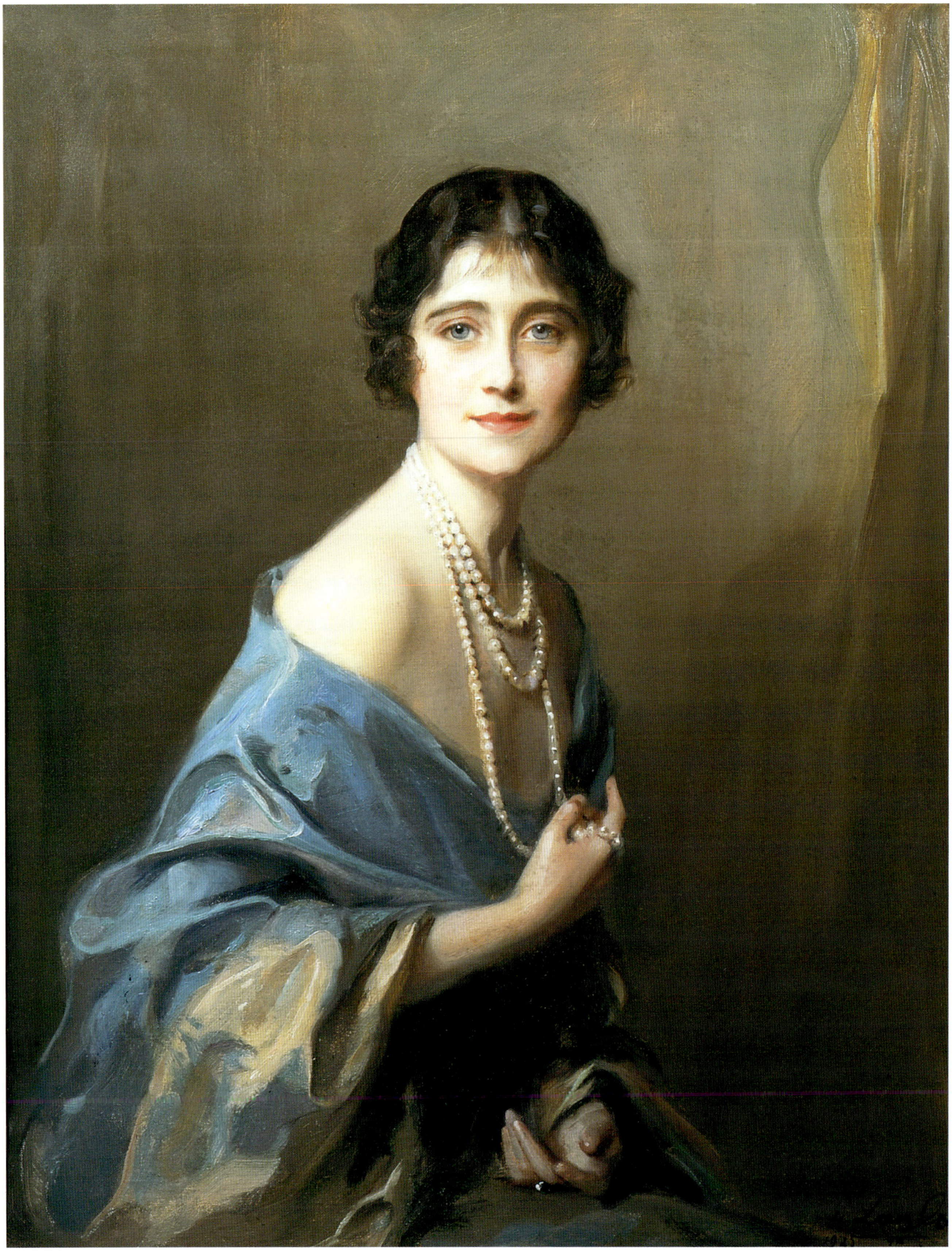

98 Her Late Majesty Queen Elizabeth the Queen Mother, when Duchess of York 1923

Oil on canvas, 90.2 × 68.6 cm (35½ × 27 inches)
Signed and dated, lower right: *de László / 1925. VIII*
Lent by Her Majesty the Queen
PROVENANCE The Hon. Sir David Bowes Lyon, K.C.V.O., brother of the sitter
EXHIBITED *Paintings & Drawings*, The National Portrait Gallery, 27 June–28 September 1980, no.E: *August 1925 Philip de Laszlo. Lent by Her Majesty the Queen and the Hon. Lady Bowes Lyon*; *Exposition P. A. de László*, Hotel Jean Charpentier, Paris, June 1931
LITERATURE ASB, Vol.II, p.45: *Elizabeth / August 2nd 1925*, with her parents' signatures either side, signed in 1931; N.P.G. 1919–25 Album, p.4; Lady Cynthia Asquith, *The Duchess of York*, London 1927, ill. frontispiece and dust cover; Rutter 1939, pp. 358, 374; John W. Wheeler-Bennett, *King George VI: His Life and Reign*, London 1958, p.152, ill. facing p.154; *The Queen Mother: A Celebration*, National Portrait Gallery, 27 June–28 September, 1980, ill.; 'The Queen Mother: A Celebration', *The Connoisseur*, vol.205, August 1980, ill. front cover, article p.300; Christopher Warwick, *King George VI & Queen Elizabeth, A Portrait*, London 1985, ill. dust cover; 'The Queen Mother and her Painters: A 90-Year Love Affair', *The Sunday Times Magazine*, 29 July 1990, ill. p.29

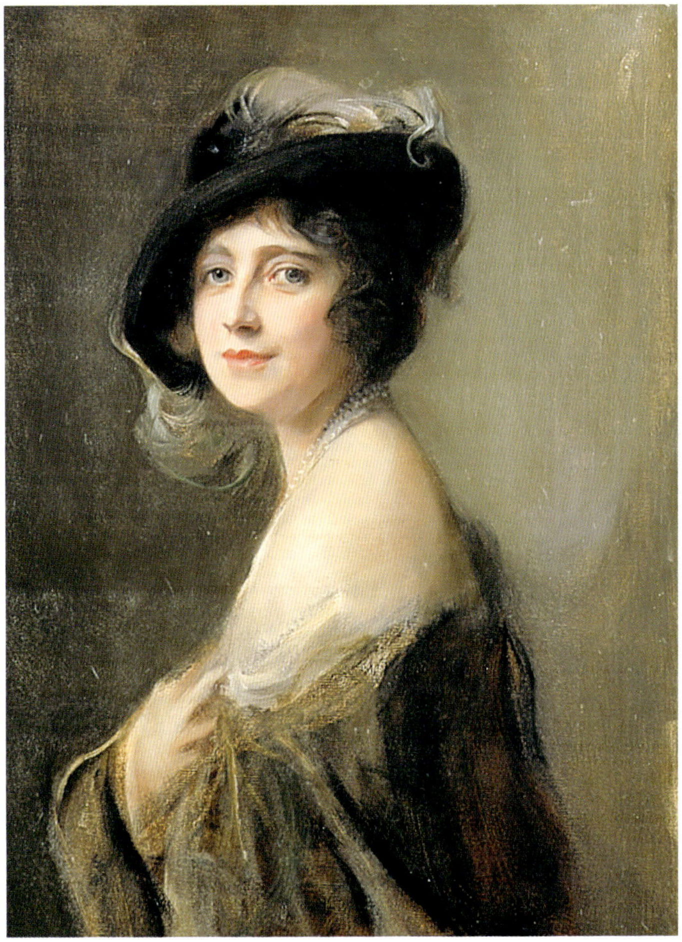

FIG. 79
H.M. Queen Elizabeth the Queen Mother when Duchess of York, 1931
Oil on canvas, 88.9 × 68.6 cm (35 × 27 in.)
John Hardy, London

According to de László family legend, the artist was staying at Glamis, the sitter's family home, when the Duke and Duchess of York became engaged. De László had painted the Duchess's sister Lady Rose in 1917, and in July 1925 their mother, the Countess of Strathmore, asked de László to make the present portrait, which she had envisaged as a sketch: "She felt that her daughter was so young that a head alone would not typify her and wanted her figure, even if described by only a few strokes. She also told him that she was very anxious that the portrait should be under life-size, to emphasize her small but graceful figure. De László carried out these wishes, but instead of a sketch he painted a finished portrait of Her Royal Highness." Lady Strathmore was so delighted with the portrait that she arranged to have it copied in 1926, without the artist's permission and much to his displeasure. That copy remains at Glamis to this day. The name of the copyist remains unknown.

Years later Queen Elizabeth clearly recalled the artist draping her with a swathe of blue material from his studio. She enjoyed sitting to him, especially as he painted so very quickly. She recalled his painting the "marble shoulder", and that he talked to entertain his sitter, but not too much. In 1929 he painted her sister Lady Mary, after her marriage to Lord Elphinstone (cat. 101), and in 1931 de László painted the Duchess again, with a paired portrait of the Duke of York.

He made a further undated study of the Duchess (fig. 79), wearing a large feathered hat, most probably also in 1931, although the sitter had no idea that another portrait had been painted of her during those sittings. In that same year, de László also painted her parents (cat. 120, 121) and her brother, the Hon. David Bowes Lyon.

There also exist a number of modern replicas of this portrait: a photographic replica on canvas remains in the Lansdowne Club in London, and another two replicas in private family collections have thus far been recorded.

Lady Elizabeth Angela Marguerite Bowes Lyon was born on 4 August 1900, the youngest of the four daughters and ninth of the ten children of Claude, 14th Earl of Strathmore and Kinghorne and his wife Celia Cavendish-Bentinck. On 26 April 1923 she married H.R.H. The Duke of York (1895–1952), later H.M. King George VI. Her Majesty Queen Elizabeth the Queen Mother died at Windsor, in her one-hundred-and-second year, on 30 March 2002.

99 Sir Ernest Rutherford 1924

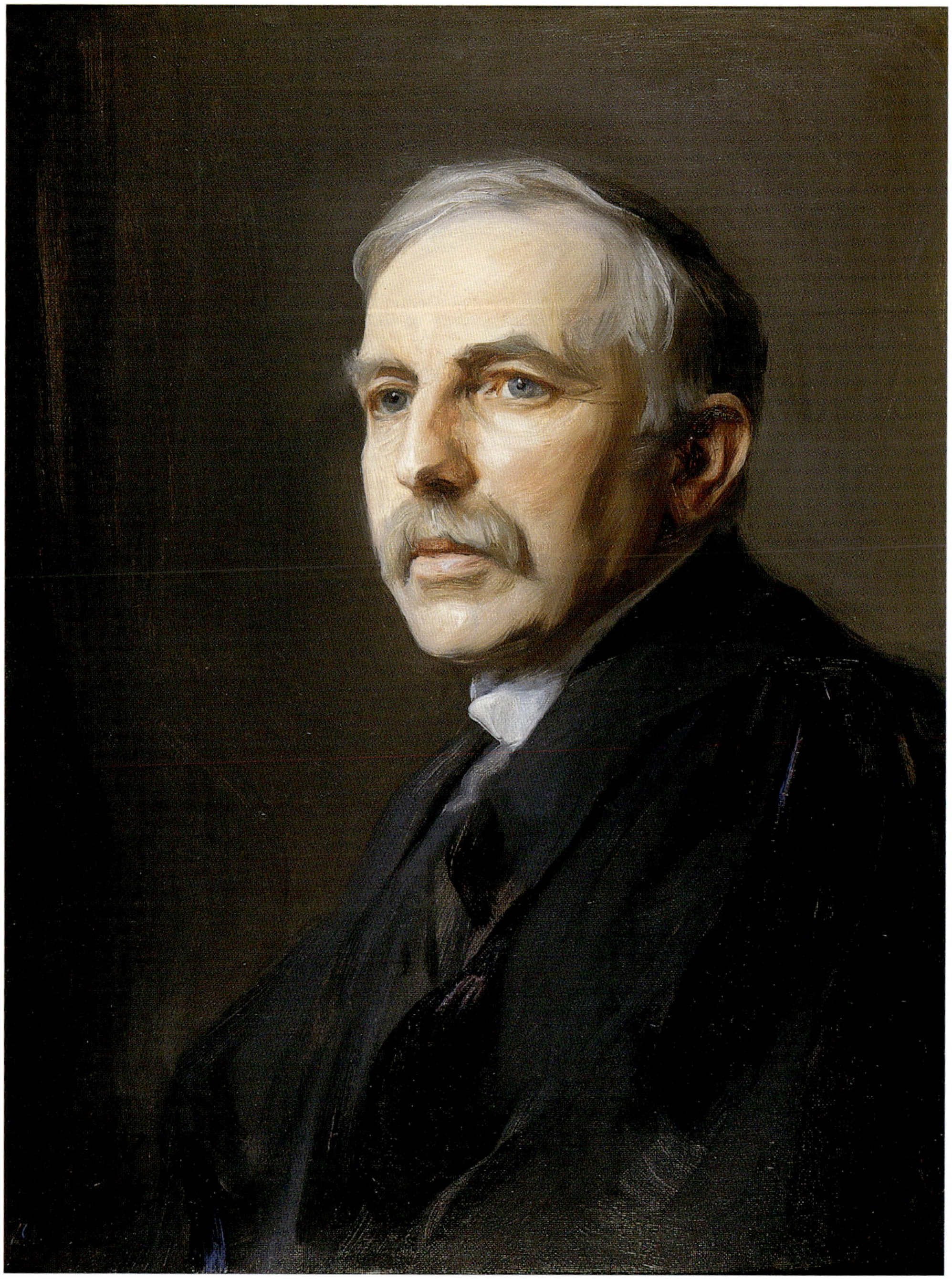

Oil on canvas, 73.3 × 56.8 cm (28⅞ × 22⅜ inches)
Indistinctly signed and dated, lower left:
de László / 1924
Trinity College, Cambridge
PROVENANCE Presented by Lady Rutherford to Trinity College, Cambridge
EXHIBITED *A Series of Portraits & Studies by Philip A. de László, M.V.O.*, June 1924, The French Gallery, London, no.24: *Sir Ernest Rutherford, Professor of Physics, Cambridge*; *Exhibition of Paintings by Philip A. de László, M.V.O., In Aid of the London Hospital and The Artists' General Benevolent Institution*, Wildenstein & Co., Ltd., London, November–December, 1937, no.6: *The Late Ernest Rutherford, O.M., F.R.S., 1st Baron Rutherford*
LITERATURE ASB, Vol.II, p.41: *E. Rutherford June 20 1924*

Ernest Rutherford was born in Nelson, New Zealand, in 1871, the son of James and Martha Rutherford. He was educated at Nelson, Canterbury College, Christchurch, then New Zealand University. He went to Cambridge University in 1894. He married, in 1900, Mary G. Newton, and they had one daughter. He was professor at Montreal from 1898, at Manchester from 1907, and in 1919 he became a fellow of Trinity College, Cambridge. He was also Director of the Cavendish Laboratory and remained at Cambridge until his death.

In 1908, he was awarded the Nobel Prize for Chemistry, and was knighted in 1914. In 1925 he received the O.M. and became President of the Royal Society, of which he had been a Fellow since 1903. In 1931 he was created Baron Rutherford of Nelson. A pioneer of modern atomic science, his main researches were in the field of radioactivity, and he was the first to recognize the nuclear nature of the atom. He died in Cambridge in 1937. His portrait was draped with black cloth (fig. 80) at the Wildenstein exhibition in the winter of 1937; a bust of de László himself was similarly draped.

As related in Suzanne Bailey's essay (p. 52), the artist had planned also to paint Albert Einstein, who had agreed, but de László was forced by his programme of work to cancel.

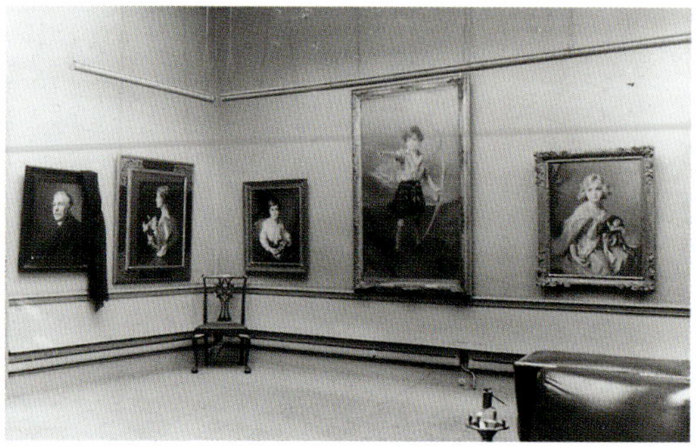

FIG. 80 The show rooms at Wildenstein's, London, during de László's 1937 exhibition, in which Rutherford's portrait is displayed with a black drape. In this year the artist also died, and his bust was also presented in the rooms with a black drape.

100 Dr Alfred Cort Haddon 1925

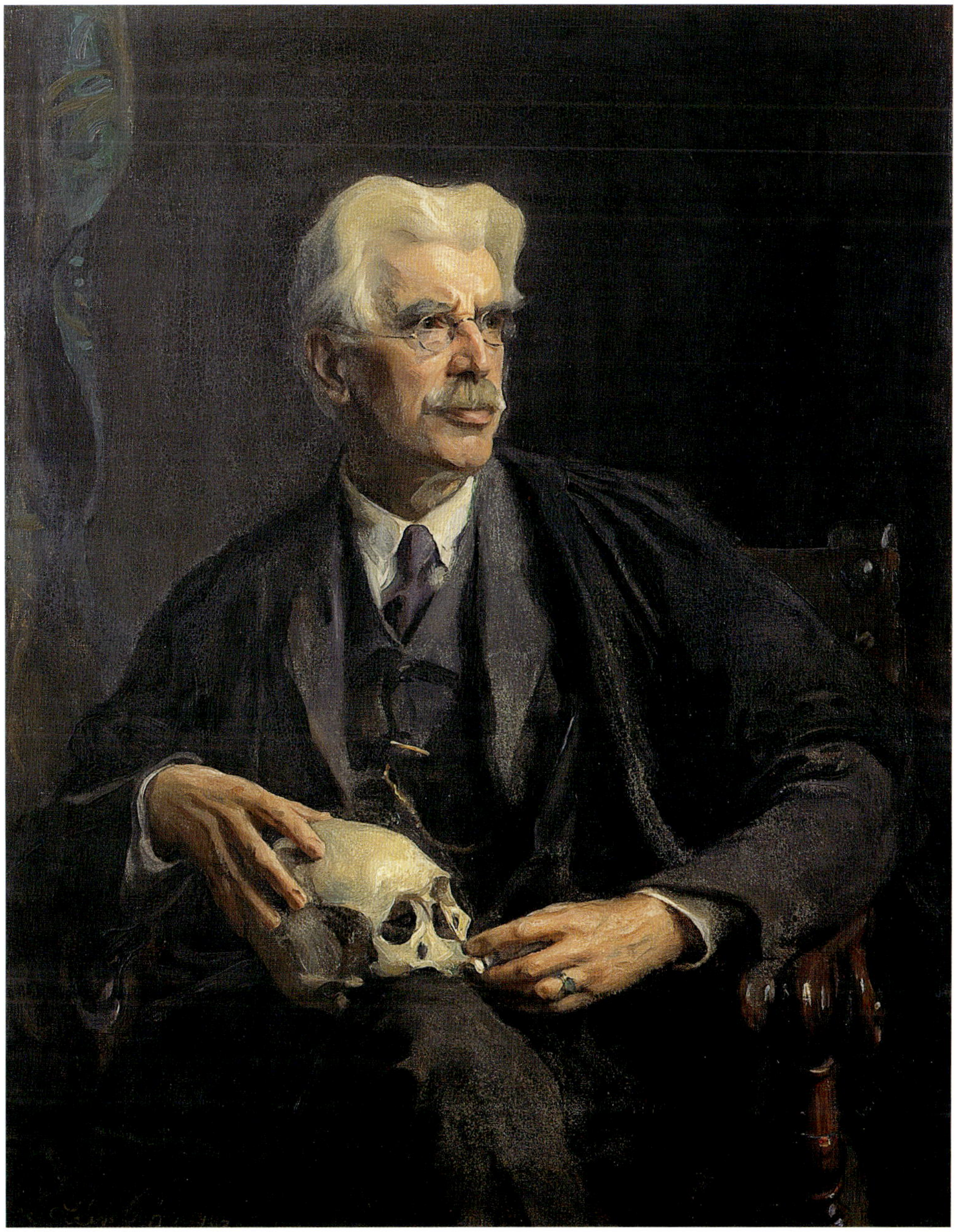

Oil on canvas, 110.5 × 85.7 cm (43½ × 33½ inches)
Signed and dated, lower left: *de László. 1925.*
Haddon Library, Museum of Archaeology and Anthropology, Cambridge

EXHIBITED *Exhibition of Portraits by Philip A. de Laszlo, M.V.O.*, M. Knoedler & Co., New York, October 1925, no.9: *Alfred Cort Haddon, Esq., M.A., Sc.D., F.R.S.*; *Special Exhibition of Portraits by Philip A.de László, M.V.O.*, The Baltimore Museum of Art, December 1925–January 1926, no. 14: *Alfred Cort Haddon, Esq., M.A., Sc.D., F.R.S.*; Autumn Exhibition, Liverpool, 1927, no.940: *Alfred C Haddon, ScD, FRS, oil. No price*

LITERATURE ASB, Vol.II, p.43: *Alfred C. Haddon 20 February 1925*; N.P.G. 1919–25 Album, p.28, where labelled: *Prof. Haddon*; *Christ's College Magazine*, XXXIV, no.108, Lent Term 1926, p.185; Rutter 1939, pp.359, 367; A.Hingston Quiggin, *Haddon the Head-Hunter*, Cambridge 1942, pp.144, 146; *Christ's College Magazine*, no.221, 1996, p.28

This portrait was commissioned by Dr Haddon's friends and pupils for the Museum of Archaeology and Anthropology at Cambridge on the occasion of his seventieth birthday in May 1925. De László painted two more half-length portraits of Dr Haddon in 1925: one remains in the collection of Christ's College, Cambridge, and the other was given to the sitter for his family. A study portrait on board of the sitter remained in the artist's studio on his death, but is as yet untraced.

The eminent anthropologist Alfred Cort Haddon was born in London in 1855, the son of John and Caroline Haddon, devout Baptists. He entered Christ's College, Cambridge, in 1875. After a time as curator of the Zoological Museum at Cambridge, in 1880 he was appointed Professor of Zoology at the Royal College of Science and Assistant Naturalist to the Science and Art Museum in Dublin. While doing pioneer work there in the scientific classification of sea anemones, he developed an ethnographical interest in western Irish life.

Between 1888 and 1889 he made zoological and ethnographical investigations in the Torres Straits. Consequently, in 1898–9, he organized and conducted a Cambridge Anthropological Expedition to the Torres Straits, New Guinea and Sarawak.

From 1900 he was University Lecturer and later Reader in Ethnology at Cambridge until 1926. He was President of the Royal Anthropological Institute in 1902–3, and of the Antiquarian Society and the Folk-Lore Society.

In 1881 Haddon married Fanny E. Rose. They had a son and two daughters. They lived in a large house in Cranmer Road, Cambridge, filled with trophies from his many travels. He loved his garden, sharing his enthusiasm with visitors. His son has described his father as having an acute and inquiring mind with a keen sense of humour, and as bringing a breath of fresh air into a static and staid society. He died in Cambridge in 1940.

101 The Hon. Andrew Elphinstone 1925

Oil on canvas, 124.5 × 86.4 cm (49 × 34 inches)
Signed and dated, lower right: *de László / July 1925*
EXHIBITED *Exhibition of recent Portraits and Studies by Philip A. de László, M.V.O.*, Victoria Art Galleries, Dundee, September 1932, no.13: *The Hon. Andrew Elphinstone Lent by Rt. Hon Lrd Elphinstone*; *Exhibition of Paintings by Philip A. de László, M.V.O., In Aid of the London Hospital and The Artists' General Benevolent Institution*, Wildenstein & Co., Ltd., London, November–December 1937, no.13: *The Honble. Andrew Elphinstone, son of Lord and Lady Elphinstone*
LITERATURE ASB, Vol.II, p.45: *Andrew Elphinstone* and *2 July 1925* in the artist's hand

De László painted the sitter's parents in 1929. His mother, Lady Mary Bowes Lyon, was an elder sister of Her Late Majesty, Queen Elizabeth, the Queen Mother (cat. 98). The formal portrait of the sitter's father hangs in the Head Office of the Bank of Scotland, on The Mound, in Edinburgh.

The Hon. Andrew Elphinstone was born in 1918, the younger son of Sidney Herbert, 16th Baron Elphinstone. He served with The Cameron Highlanders in the Second World War, and was Aide de Camp to the Viceroy of India, Lord Linlithgow, from 1941 to 1943. In 1946 he married Jean Hambro, daughter of Angus Hambro, M.P. of Milton Abbey in Dorset. They had two children. In 1950 he was ordained into the Church of England, working in Wimborne Minster and later as Rector in Worplesdon, Surrey.

A proud Scot, Andrew Elphinstone was happiest when in Scotland. He loved shooting and the countryside, and was a keen gardener. He was an accomplished pianist and organist, and a good linguist: he learnt Gaelic and, when in India, Urdu. A much loved parish priest, he retired in 1964 owing to ill health. He died in 1975 at Worplesdon. His book, *Freedom, Suffering and Love*, was published posthumously.

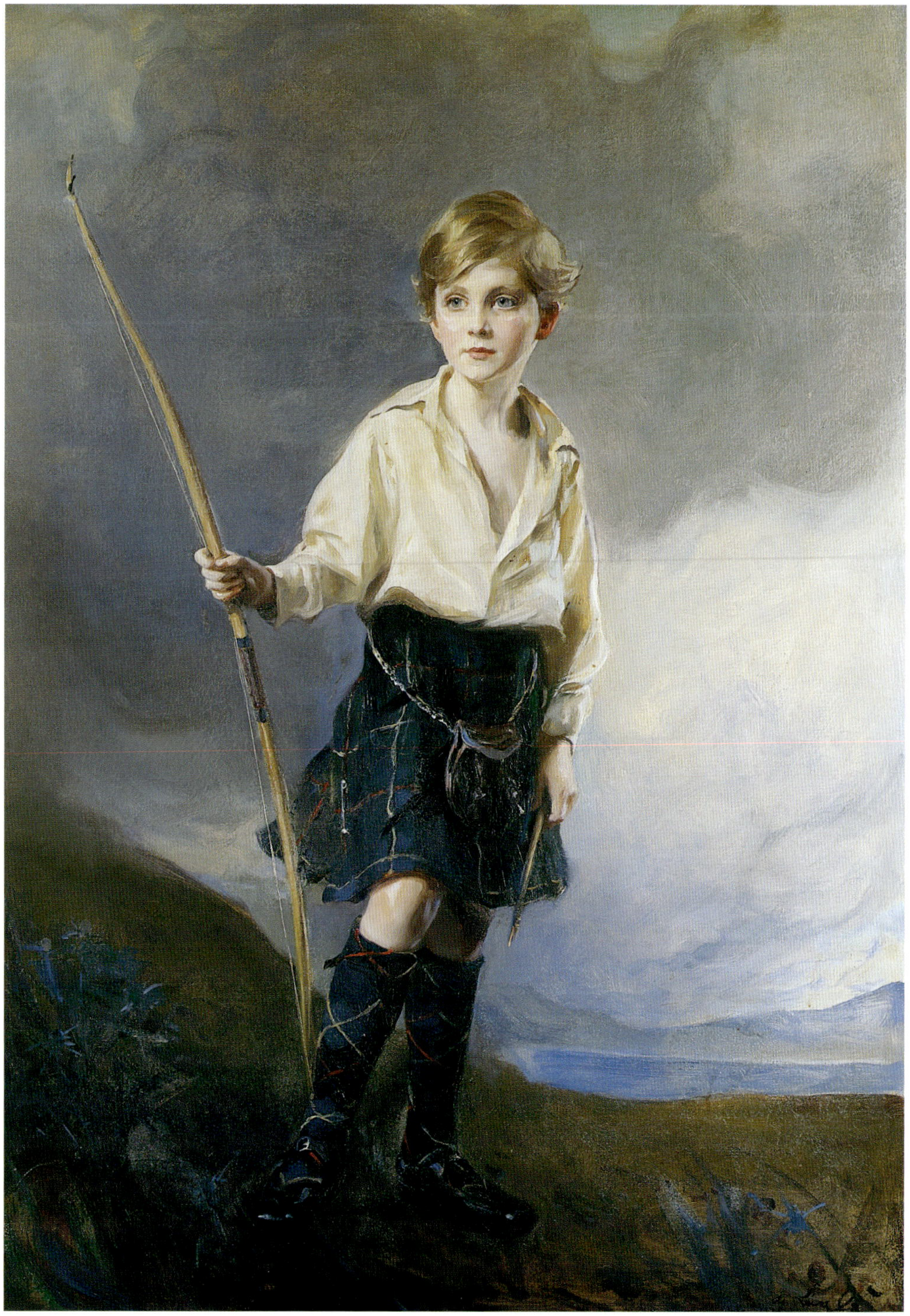

102 Miss Christian Hilda Guthrie of Guthrie 1935

Oil on canvas, 84.5 × 66 cm ($33\frac{1}{4}$ × 26 inches)
Signed and dated, lower right: *de László / 1935 I*
EXHIBITED *Exhibition of Paintings by Philip A. de László, M.V.O., In Aid of the London Hospital and The Artists' General Benevolent Institution*, Wildenstein & Co., Ltd., London, November–December 1937, no.14: *Christian Hilda, daughter of Colonel and Mrs. Guthrie*
LITERATURE ASB Vol.II, p. 80/81: *Christian Guthrie January 9th 1935*; N.P.G. 1935 Album, p.8

There exists a pencil and pastel preparatory sketch for this portrait. The portrait was commissioned by the sitter's mother, who had a fine collection of paintings. She also kept an aviary, which might account for the falcon in the picture. So far as is known, de László included a bird in very few other portraits.

Christian Hilda was the second of the two daughters of Lieutenant Colonel Ivan Douglas Guthrie, 20th of Guthrie Castle, Angus, and Kathleen Mona, younger daughter of Colonel the Hon. George Gough. Her mother was a prominent Irish Revivalist during the early years of the century and much involved in the artistic circles of Ireland at that time. Christian Hilda was born on 12 October 1924. In 1947 she married James Rattray, of Craighall-Rattray, Perthshire. Together they had five children. She died aged only thirty-nine in 1963.

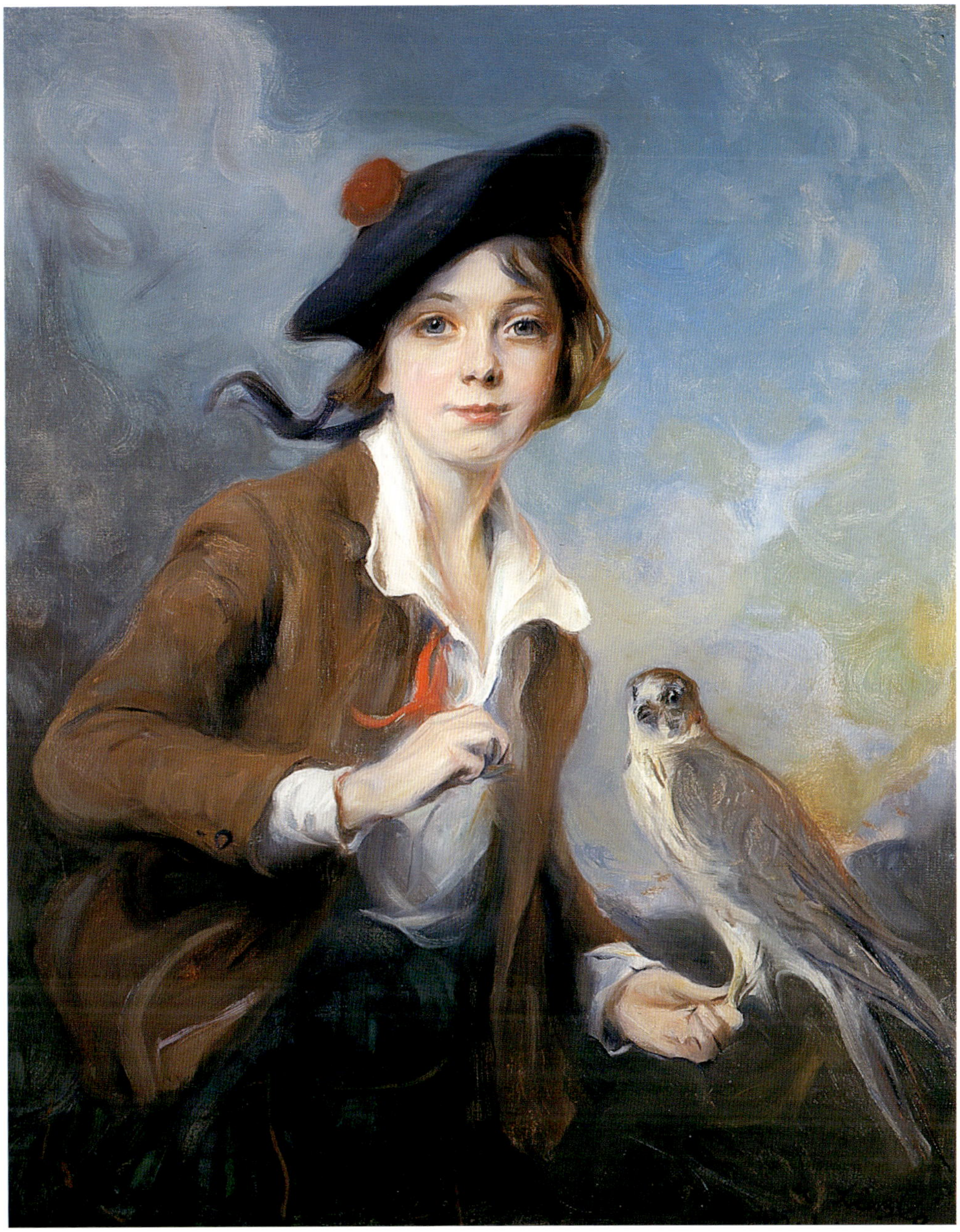

103 Lady Alastair Graham, née Lady Meriel Bathurst 1925

Oil on canvas, 90.8 × 70.2 cm (35¾ × 27⅝ inches)
Indistinctly signed and dated, lower left: *de László / 1925. VII*

EXHIBITED *A Series of Portraits and Studies By Philip A. de László, M.V.O.*, The French Gallery, London, June 1923, no.13: *Lady Meriel Graham*; *Exhibition of Paintings by Philip A. de László, M.V.O., In Aid of the London Hospital and The Artists' General Benevolent Institution*, Wildenstein & Co., Ltd., London, November–December 1937, no.7: *The Late Lady Alastair Graham*

LITERATURE ASB, Vol.II, p.45: *Meriel Graham July 8th 1925*; N.P.G. 1919–25 Album, p.13

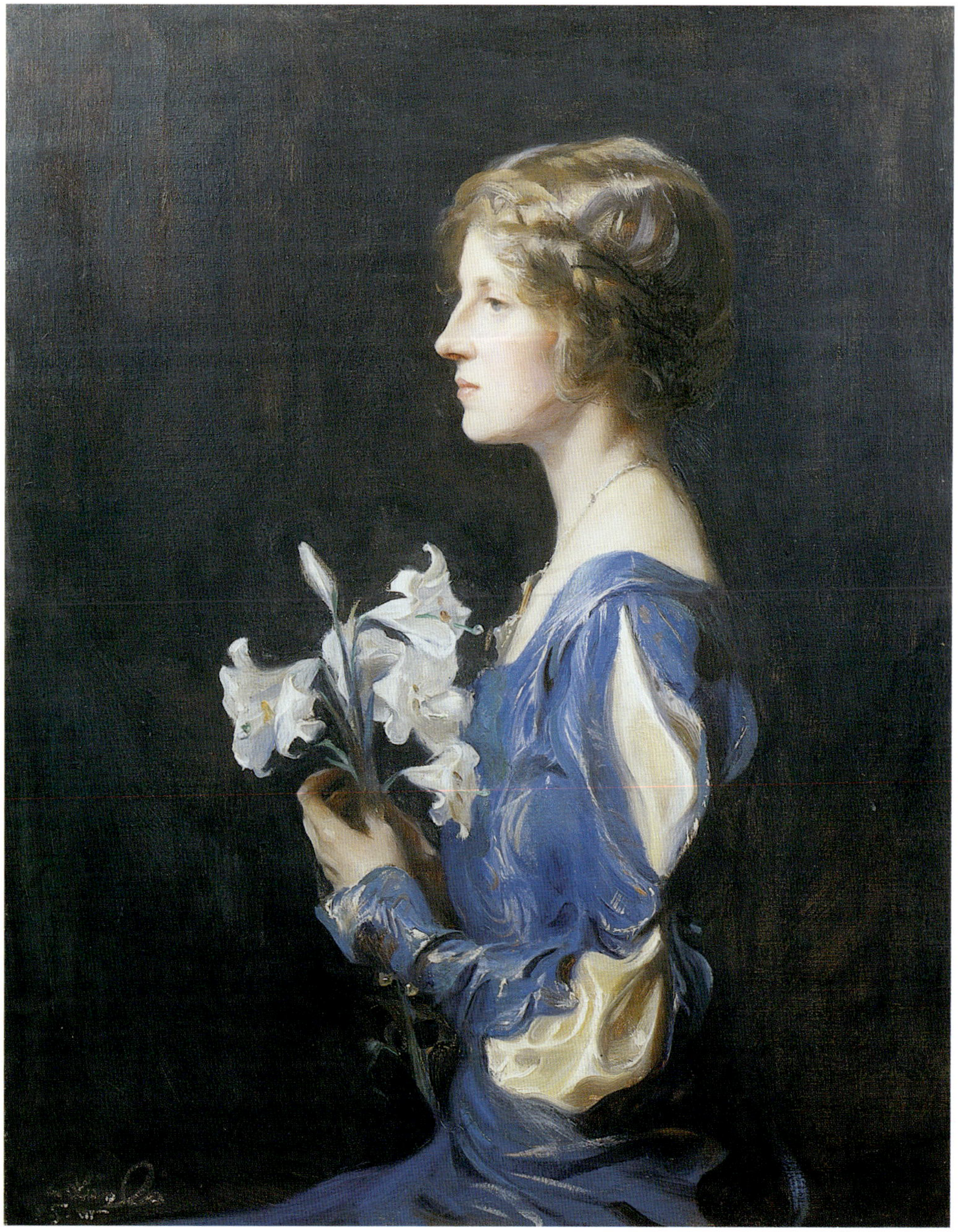

De László painted a number of portraits of the Bathurst family over the years 1919 to 1936. In 1920 he painted a study and another formal portrait of Lady Alastair. In 1925, the year in which he painted the present portrait, and again in 1926, he painted her sister-in-law, Lady Apsley (cat. 104).

Lady Meriel Olivia Bathurst was born in 1894, the only daughter of Seymour Henry, 7th Earl Bathurst, and the Hon. Lilias Margaret Frances Borthwick. In 1916 she married Commander Lord Alastair Graham R.N., the younger son of the 5th Duke of Montrose. Two daughters, Lilias and Margaret, were born in 1917 and 1919, and two sons, Ian, born in 1923, and Robin, born in 1926. Having left the Navy at the end of the War, Lord Alastair worked for Beardmore's Engineering Co. Despite a desire to farm in Scotland, in the end he followed his elder brother James to Suffolk, taking on part of the Rendlesham estate, near Ipswich. A devoted wife and mother, Lady Alastair raised her family in relatively modest circumstances on the farm. She was a devout Christian with a compassionate nature. She was a passionate gardener and her particular love of lilies is reflected in this portrait. She died aged only forty-one in January 1936. Lord Alastair died in 1976.

104 Lady Apsley, née Miss Viola Meeking 1926

Oil on canvas, 128.3 × 86.4 cm (50½ × 34 inches)
Signed and dated, lower left: *de László / 1926*
LITERATURE ASB, Vol.II, p.44: *Viola Apsley May 25th 1925*; N.P.G. 1925–7 Album, p.16

This is the second portrait by de László of Lady Apsley, completed a year after the first. He also painted several other members of her family, including her husband, their two children, and her younger sister Finola, the wife of Arthur, 6th Baron Somers.

Violet Emily Mildred Meeking was born in 1895, the daughter of Capt Bertram Meeking. In 1924 she married Allan Algernon Bathurst, Lord Apsley, D.S.O., M.C., M.P., the eldest son of the 7th Earl Bathurst. Lord Apsley was M.P. for Southampton until 1929, and from 1931 for Bristol Central. He was killed on active service with the R.A.F. in Malta in 1942. The eldest of their two sons, Henry, succeeded his grandfather as 8th Earl in 1943.

Lady Apsley became, in the year of her marriage, President of the Southampton Women's Conservative Association, a post she held until 1929, and from 1943 to 1945 held her late husband's seat as Conservative M.P. for Bristol Central. In 1930 she received her pilot's licence. She was also an author, her books including, in 1932, *To Whom the Goddess* (with Lady Diana Shedden) and *Bridleways through History* (1936).

From 1938 to 1939 Lady Apsley was County Commandant A.T.S. for Gloucestershire, and became Chief Commandant of the A.T.S. in 1940. She was a Member of the Films Council (Board of Trade) from 1943–46, and from 1945 a governor of the Royal Agricultural College, Cirencester. Between 1942 and 1948 she was National Chairman of the Women's Section of the British Legion. She was awarded a C.B.E. in 1952. She died in 1966.

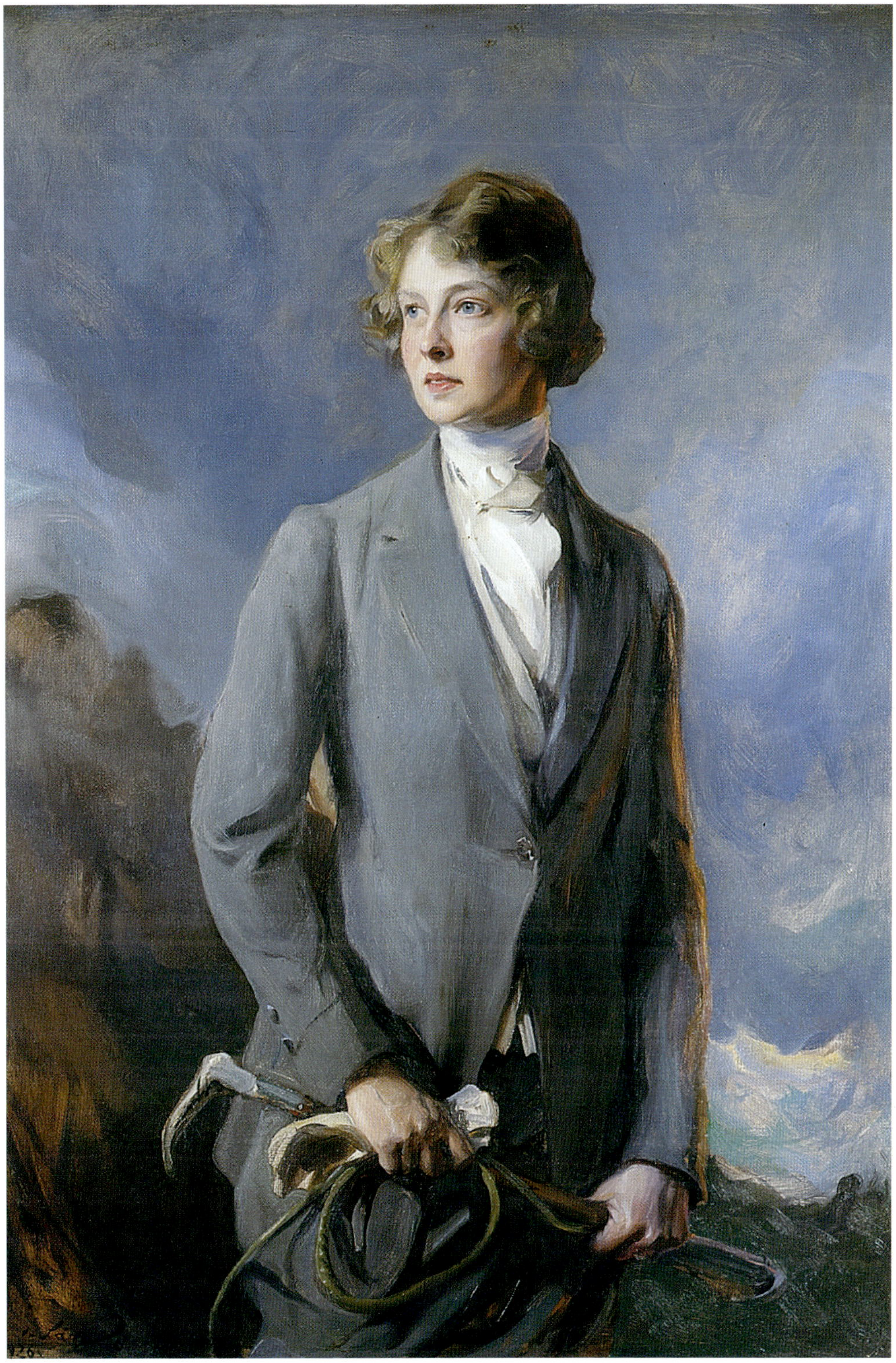

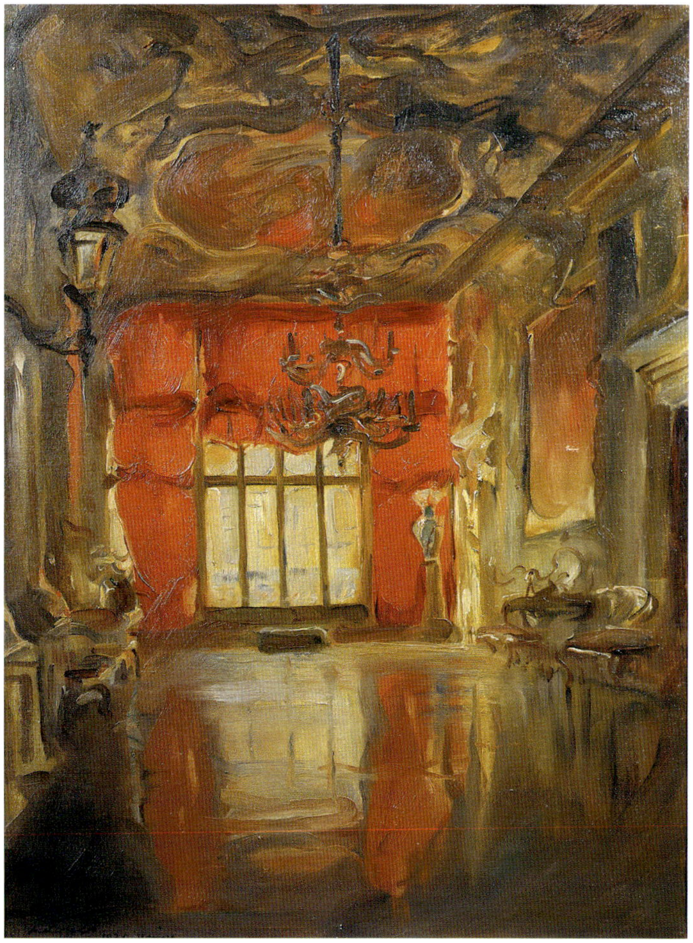

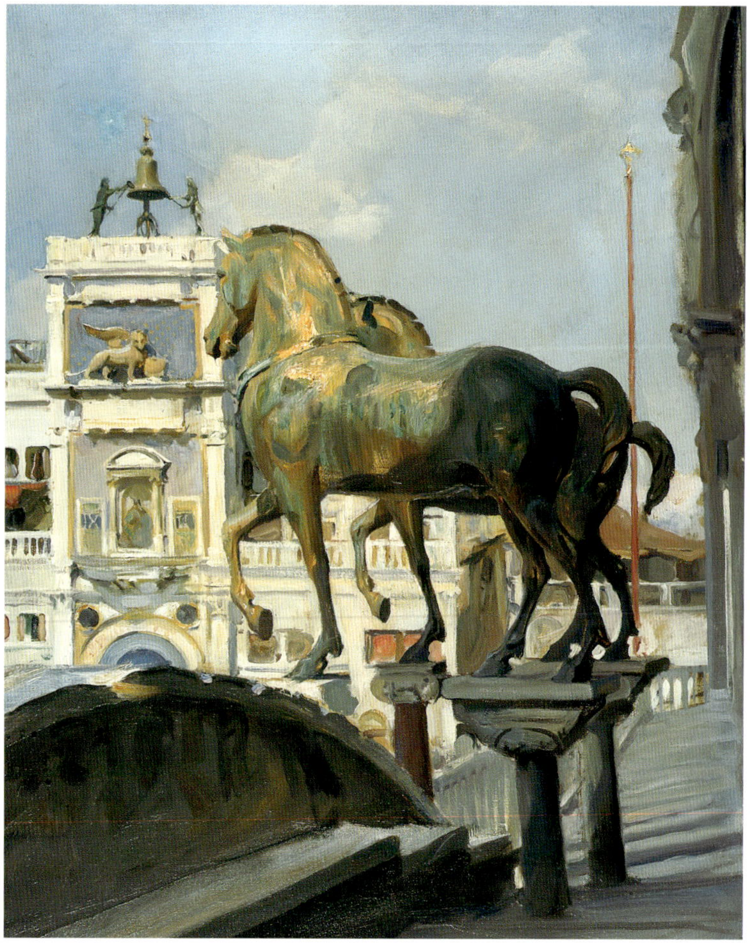

105 An Interior in the Palazzo Albrizzi, Venice 1923

Oil on canvas, 80 × 58.7 cm ($31\frac{1}{2} \times 23\frac{1}{8}$ inches)
Signed and dated, lower left: *de László 1923 Venice*
PROVENANCE In the possession of the artist on his death; Patrick de Laszlo, his fourth son
EXHIBITED *Autumn Exhibition*, Royal Society of British Artists, 1930, no.175: *Study of Palazzo Albrizzi, Venice*
LITERATURE Rowcliffe 1938, p.102 (no. 605)

In 1923, after holidaying in Algeria (cat. 96) and returning via Rome (cat. 97), de László continued north to Venice. For the artist, the great revelation of the 1923 trip was the rediscovery of the colours of nature, and he revelled in his love for the effects of the sun by painting sunsets in the Algerian desert. His fascination for the evening light is also clearly apparent in this Venetian interior. Palazzo Albrizzi preserves one of the few complete interiors in Venice unaltered since the eighteenth century, and still in the possession of the descendants of those for whom it was built.

106 The Bronze Horses of St. Mark's, Venice 1926

Oil on canvas, 68.6 × 53.3 cm (27 × 21 inches)
Signed and dated, lower left: *de László 1926*
Dundee Art Galleries and Museums
PROVENANCE Presented by the artist to McManus Galleries, Dundee, in 1929
EXHIBITED Galeries Charpentier, Paris; Autumn Exhibition, Liverpool, 1927, no.850: *The Horses of St Mark, oil. £300.00*; Victoria Art Galleries, Dundee, *Exhibition of recent portraits and studies by Philip A. de Laszlo, M.V.O.*, September 1932, no.46: *Bronze Horses of St. Mark's, Venice. Lent by Dundee Corporation*; British Academy, Dundee, 1947, no.97

The painting of this picture was captured on film with a 16 mm camera that was given to the artist by George Eastman after de László painted him in 1926. Extracts from the considerable footage taken between 1926 and the artist's death in 1937 will have been shown during the exhibition this book accompanies.

107 A Village in the Italian Tyrol 1926

Oil on board, 19.7 × 24.8 cm ($7\frac{3}{4} \times 9\frac{3}{4}$ inches)
Signed, lower left: *de László*
Indistinctly inscribed verso: *1926 / agst / Sarentino Tyrol / PA de László*
PROVENANCE Marczell László, the artist's brother, and by descent from his second wife

In August 1926 de László spent some time in the Italian Tyrol, until 1918 part of Austria. In Sarentino, a village in the Sarenthaler Alps between Merano and the new capital of Bolzano, he painted this view of the castle and a picture of a carpenter. One other Tyrolean scene has been recorded. All these paintings were painted for the artist's pleasure, and remained in family collections after the artist's death.

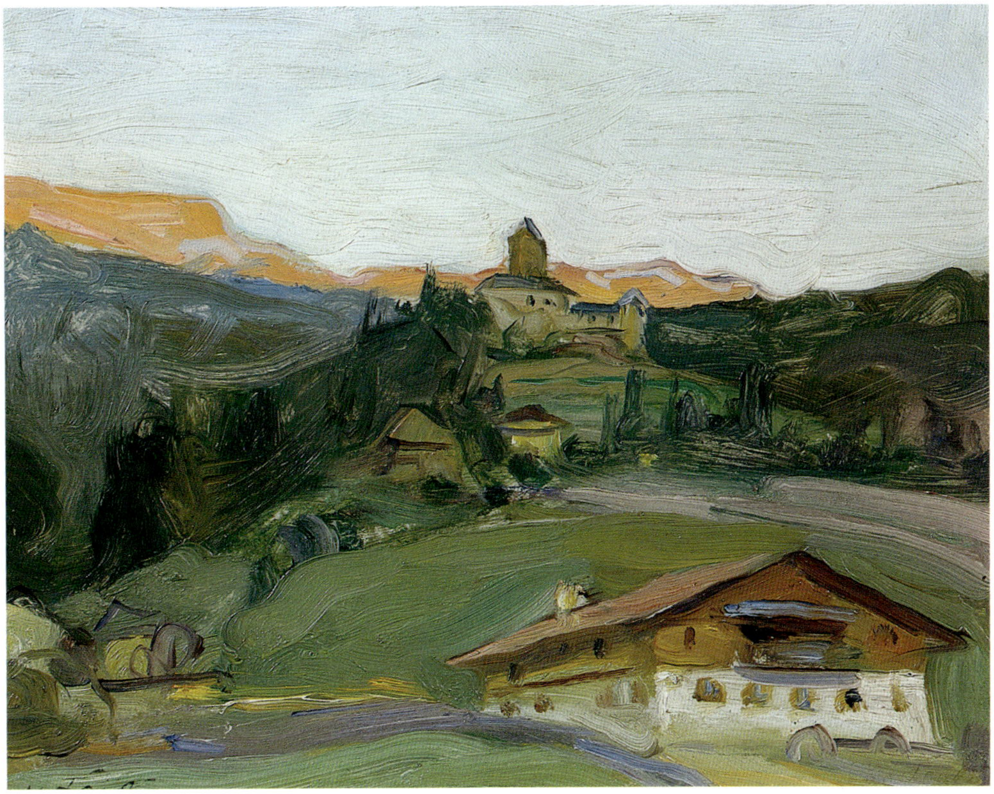

106 St Mark's Basilica, Venice 1926

Oil on board, 20.6 × 24.8 cm ($8\frac{1}{8} \times 9\frac{3}{4}$ inches)
PROVENANCE In the possession of the artist on his death

From the Tyrol de László travelled to Venice. After his thwarted attempt to study there in 1889, de László apparently made three visits to Venice. In 1907 he had been awarded the large Gold Medal at the Academy there for a portrait of his wife. He had last been there in 1923 (cat. 105). Of the five paintings recorded from these visits, two are undated; one of these is this small sketch of the Basilica, drenched in evening sunlight behind the billowing flags. His large study of two of the four bronze horses of St Mark's (cat. 106) is dated 1926, as is an interior view of the Basilica, which notes the precise day – 1 September. The free handling of the paint would suggest the later date for the view from the Piazza, too.

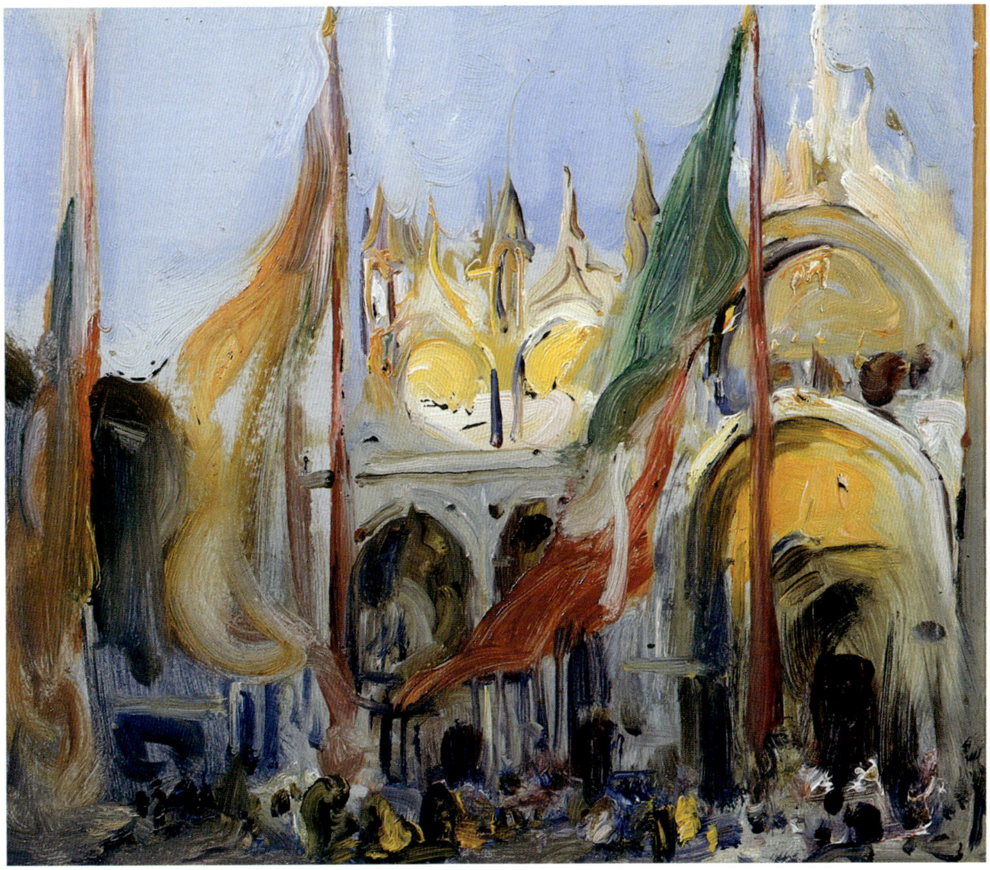

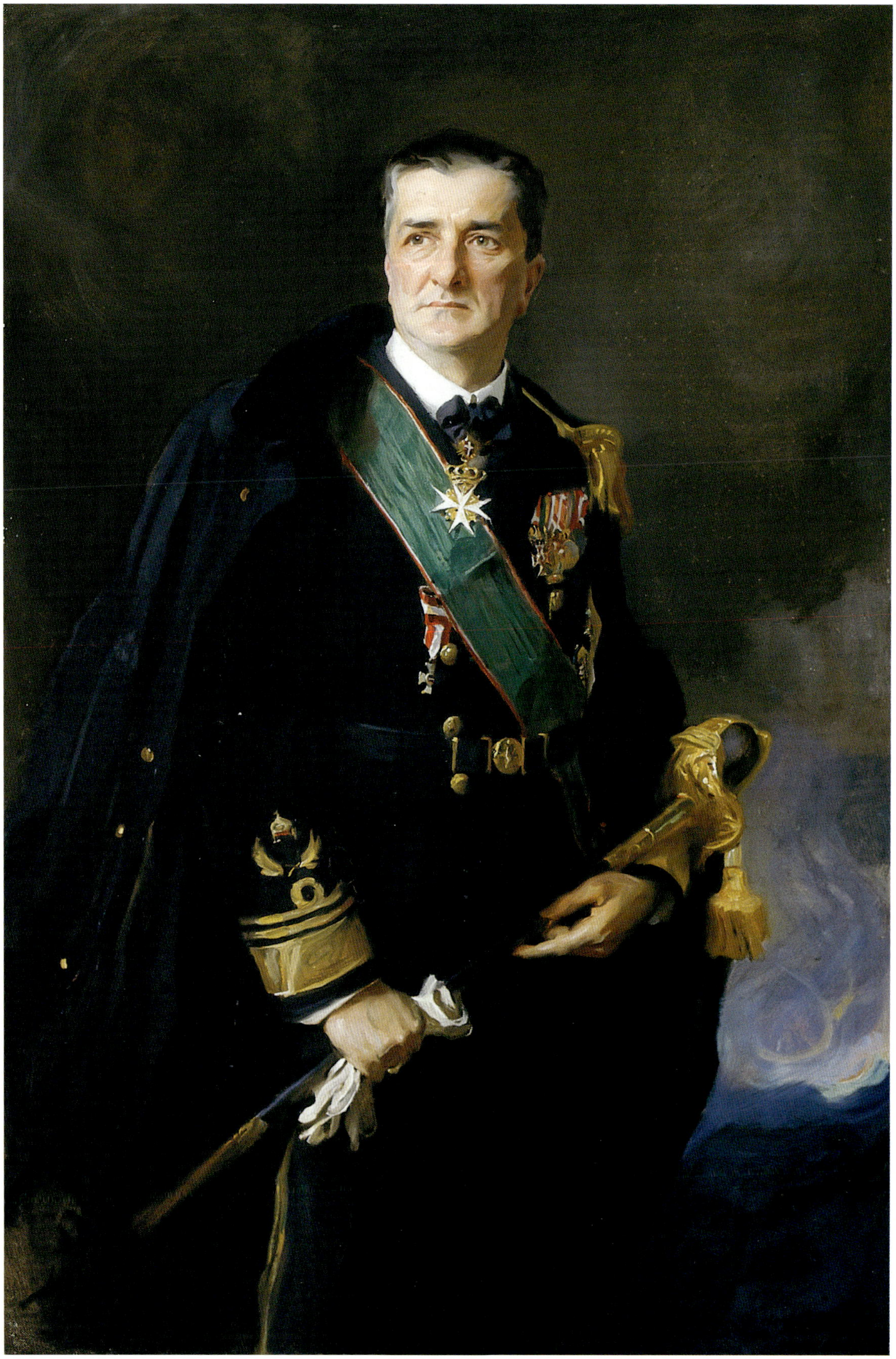

109 Admiral Nicholas Horthy, H.S.H. the Regent of Hungary 1927

Oil on canvas, 160 × 105.1 cm (63 × 41⅜ inches)
Signed, inscribed and dated, lower right: *de László Gödöllö 1927*
Hungarian National Gallery, Budapest
PROVENANCE Donated to the National Gallery of Fine Art, Budapest, in 1929
EXHIBITED *A Series of Portraits and Studies By Philip A. de László*, M.V.O., The French Gallery, London, May–June 1929, no.2: *His Highness the Regent of Hungary*
LITERATURE ASB, Vol.II, p.56: *Horthy / Gödöll 27 / IX 927.*; *Pesti Napló* [Pest Diary], 23 October 1927, ill. pp.78–9 (here fig. 81); Rutter 1939, pp.369, 375–6, 379

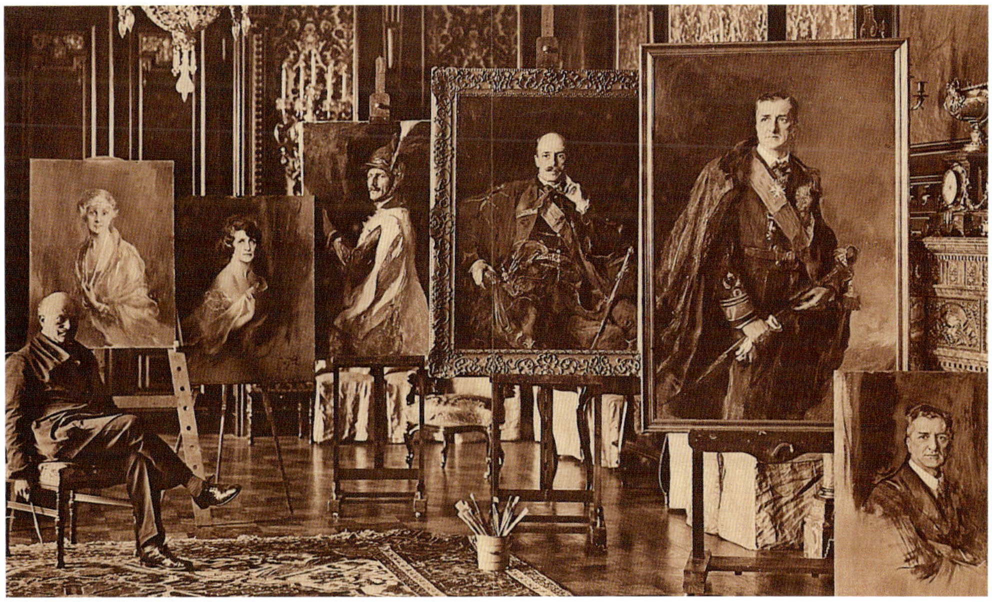

FIG. 81 "Philip de László with his Budapest pictures in the dining room of the Royal Castle. It was here that a studio was put at his disposal …. The portrait of the Regent ... the artist painted for the Museum of Fine Arts …."
(*Pesti Napló* [Pest Diary], 23 October 1927, pp.78–9)

Miklós (Nicholas) Horthy de Nagybánya was born in 1868, the fourth son of István (Stephen) de Horthy and Paulette de Halassy. In 1901 he married Magdalene Purgly de Jószás. They had two sons and two daughters. A naval officer in the Austro-Hungarian Navy from 1886, he was aide-de-camp to the Emperor Francis Joseph from 1909 to 1914. At the battle of Otranto against the Italians in 1917 he was severely wounded, and for his gallantry later awarded the highest Austro-Hungarian order, the Maria Theresia Order. In 1918, he was appointed Commander in Chief of the Austro-Hungarian Navy. In 1919 he became Minister of War in the anti-Communist Hungarian Government, and Commander of the National Army. Despite the abolition of the monarchy in Austria, Hungary remained a kingdom, and in 1920 Horthy was elected Regent, although he resisted two attempts by King Charles IV (Emperor Charles of Austria) to return to the throne in 1921.

Despite his long years in England, de László longed for an invitation to paint the Regent. This finally came in the autumn of 1927, and de László travelled to Gödöllö, the castle outside Budapest which the Emperor Francis Joseph had bought for the Empress Elisabeth, and which the Regent used as his country residence. There he painted Admiral Horthy, his wife and the Hungarian Prime Minister, Count Stephen Bethlen. Rutter states that "when [de László] left for England he was able to feel that his reputation was completely re-established in the country he had never ceased to love". In the same sittings the artist painted a half-length study portrait of the sitter in the same pose as the present portrait, which remains as yet untraced.

The artist painted Horthy once more, in 1935, at the request of the Hungarian Government. On that visit to Budapest de László was greatly fêted by a country which finally "accepted him as one of her most distinguished sons". As he told the *Pesti Napló*, "Most artists stress the Regent's interesting and salient features, but beyond that there is something that attracts me far more – the definite and characteristic individuality that emanates from the Regent. It is something one cannot express in words, and something I have rarely experienced in others. It could not have developed anywhere but on Hungarian soil." The later portrait also remains untraced. A few days before his death, the artist learnt that Horthy had awarded him the Badge of the Corvinus Order of Honour, the highest Hungarian award for artistic or literary merit.

During the Second World War Hungary was allied to Germany and Italy. In 1943, Horthy unsuccessfully attempted to reach a separate peace with the Western powers, and in March 1944 the country came under German occupation. In October, Horthy proclaimed an armistice but was arrested by the Germans, forced to resign and taken to Germany as a prisoner. He was freed by the American forces in 1945, and spent his last years in exile in Estoril, Portugal, where he died in 1957.

110 Baron Sir Rudolf von Slatin Pasha 1927

Oil on board, 57.2 × 50.2 cm (22½ × 19¾ inches)
Signed, inscribed and dated, lower right: *For my friend / from de László / 1927*
Verso: Oil sketch of the Hon. Lady Johnstone, née Antoinette Eno Pichot
LITERATURE ASB, Vol.II, p.55: *R Slatin 5th Septbr 927*; Rutter 1939, p.176

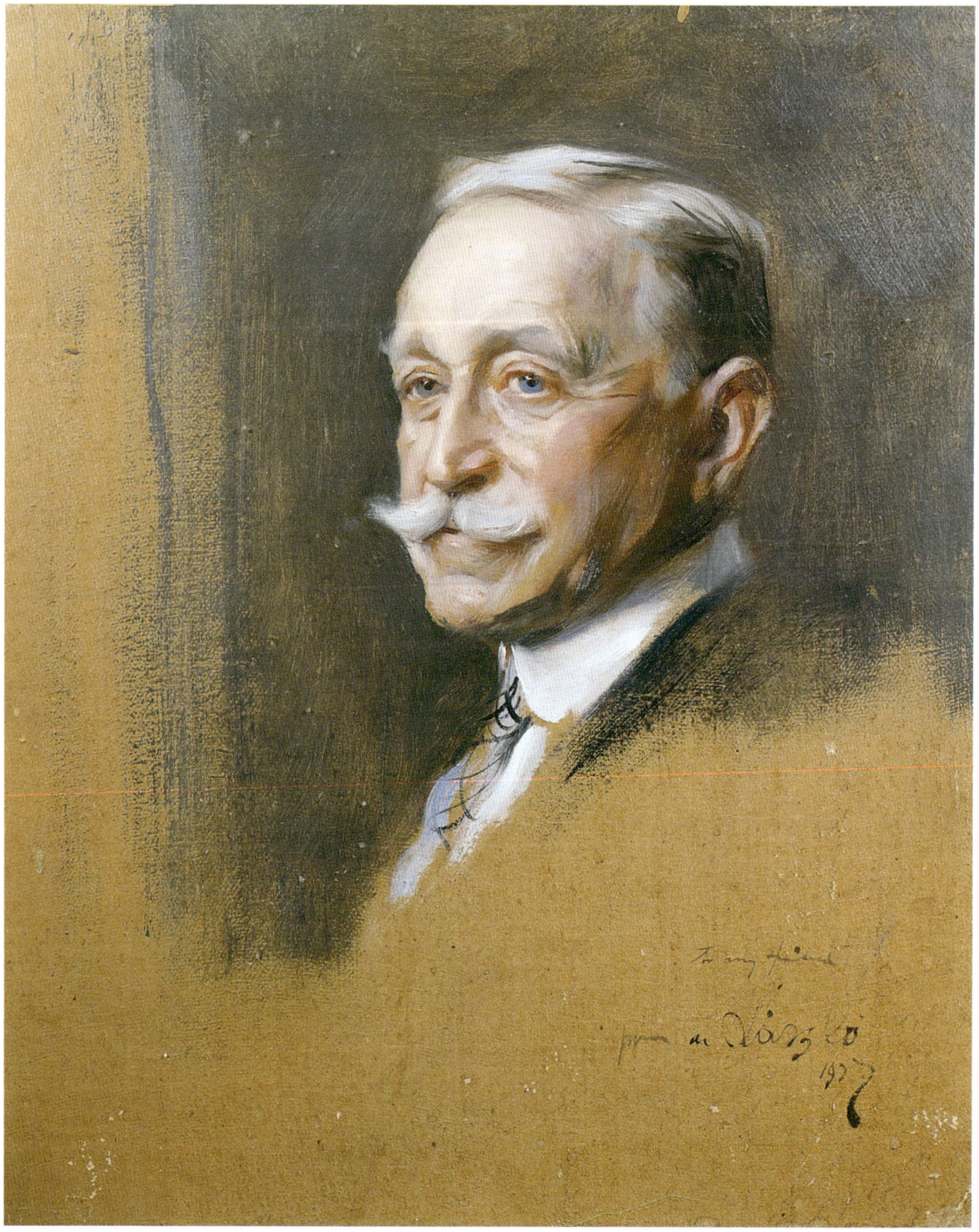

The present portrait was described by the sitter's daughter as being "a brilliant likeness – I have never seen anything more like my father – even a photograph". She remembered clearly that the portrait was achieved in two and a half hours. The artist met Slatin Pasha while he was in Vienna in 1899, and they remained friends until the baron's death in October 1932.

The portrait verso is typical of de László's studio practice. He usually used oil on board for such preliminary studies, and for portraits of his family and personal friends. If a portrait was not going well, he would almost invariably start again, rather than re-work the existing portrait. Thus, Lady Johnstone's portrait was rejected for some reason and, being economical by nature, de László kept it in his studio, and took it up again later to use the other side for this portrait of his friend Slatin Pasha. De László made two other portraits of Lady Johnstone, one of which was exhibited at the Fine Art Society exhibition in 1907.

Rudolf Carl Slatin was born near Vienna in 1857. He first visited the Sudan at the age of seventeen. After fighting with the Austro-Hungarian army in Bosnia, in 1879 he arrived in Khartoum to serve under General Gordon, and was made governor of the province of Darfur two years later. During the Mahdist revolts in 1882, Slatin nominally adopted Islam, his troops having attributed his lack of success during these revolts to his Christianity. Nevertheless, in 1883 he was defeated and surrendered to the Mahdists. Two years later Khartoum fell and Gordon's severed head was brought to him by his captors. After eleven years in captivity he managed to escape, reaching Egypt in 1895, in which year he was also raised to the rank of Pasha by the Khedive, made a C.B., and wrote his book *Fire and Sword in the Sudan*. For his services in the 1897–8 campaigns in Egypt he was created K.C.M.G. in 1898. The following year he was ennobled by the Emperor of Austria. From 1900 to 1914 he was Inspector General of the Sudan, and made a Lt-General in the Egyptian Army.

In 1906 he was raised to Baron of the Austrian Empire, and the next year was made an honorary Major-General in the British army. In 1914 he married Alice, eldest daughter of Baron Victor von Ramberg, whose father had been the Austrian A.D.C. to the Duke of Wellington at Waterloo. They had one daughter, Anne-Marie, in 1916.

His wife died of cancer in 1920, whereupon Baron Slatin moved to the former Austrian spa town of Meran, now in the Italian Tyrol. His daughter recalled that Meran was "full of elderly Austrian Colonels", with whom her father was able to indulge in his passion for stamp collecting. His other great interest was his garden, where annually his attempts to achieve an English lawn were frustrated by the heavy winter weather. He was a very sociable man, and much liked by a large circle of friends, with many English among them.

The Hon. Lady Johnstone (1859–1934) was born Antoinette Eno, only daughter of J.W. Pinchot of New York. In 1892 she married the diplomat the Hon. Sir Alan Vanden-Bempde-Johnstone, K.C.V.O., G.C.V.O., the fourth son of the 1st Baron Derwent. They had one son, Harcourt (1895–1945), who became an M.P. and a Minister in the wartime coalition government.

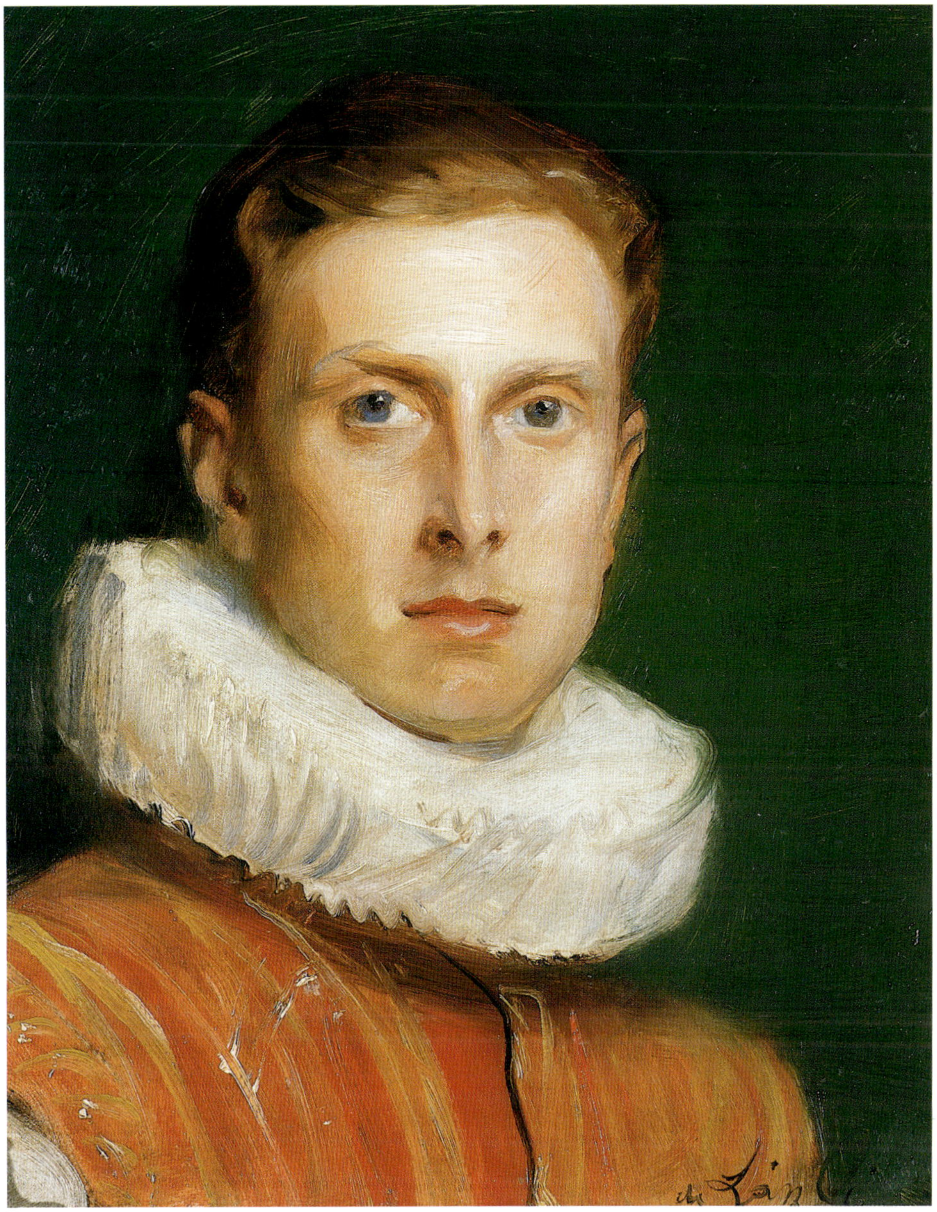

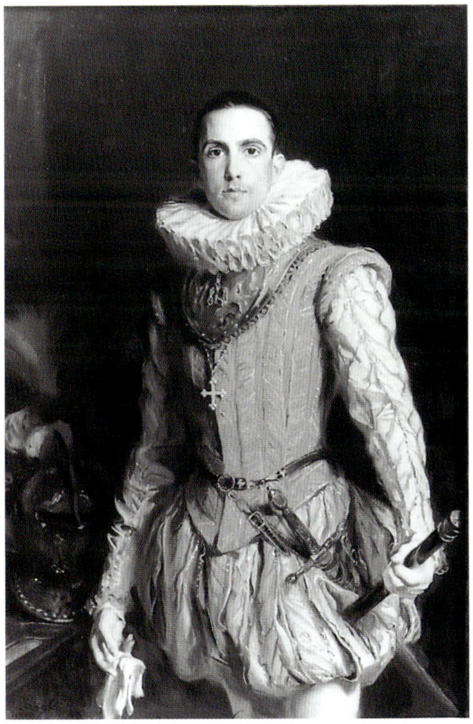

FIG. 82 *Prince Humbert of Savoy, Prince of Piedmont*, 1928
Oil on canvas
Private collection

111 Patrick, the Artist's Fourth Son 1928

Oil on panel, 39.4 × 31.1 cm ($15\frac{1}{2} \times 12\frac{1}{4}$ inches)
Signed and indistinctly dated, lower right:
de László / 1928
PROVENANCE In the possession of the artist on his death; Lucy de László, the artist's wife; Patrick de Laszlo, the sitter and fourth son of the artist
LITERATURE N.P.G. 1927–8 Album, p.31(b)

Patrick David was born in London on 26 March 1909. His father chose his second name in admiration for the French Neoclassical artist Jacques-Louis David. In June 1928 de László went to Turin to paint the Prince of Piedmont (later King Umberto II of Italy) in the costume of his ancestor Emanuele Filiberto (1553–1580), which he was to wear at a court pageant commemorating the first prince of Savoy (fig. 82). Later that year he painted this portrait of Patrick dressed in the Prince's costume.

112 Three Egyptians in a Boat on the Nile 1929

Oil on board, 50.2 × 40 cm (19¾ × 15¾ inches)
Signed and dated, lower right: *de László / 1929*
PROVENANCE In the possession of the artist on his death; Paul de Laszlo, his third son
EXHIBITED Ferens Art Gallery, City of Hull, *The Autumn Exhibition of Autumn Paintings*, 1929, no.137: *My Boat on the Nile Price 200*
LITERATURE Rowcliffe 1938, p.105 (no. 619); Rutter 1939, p.371; Clifford 1969, ill. p.53, pl.XII

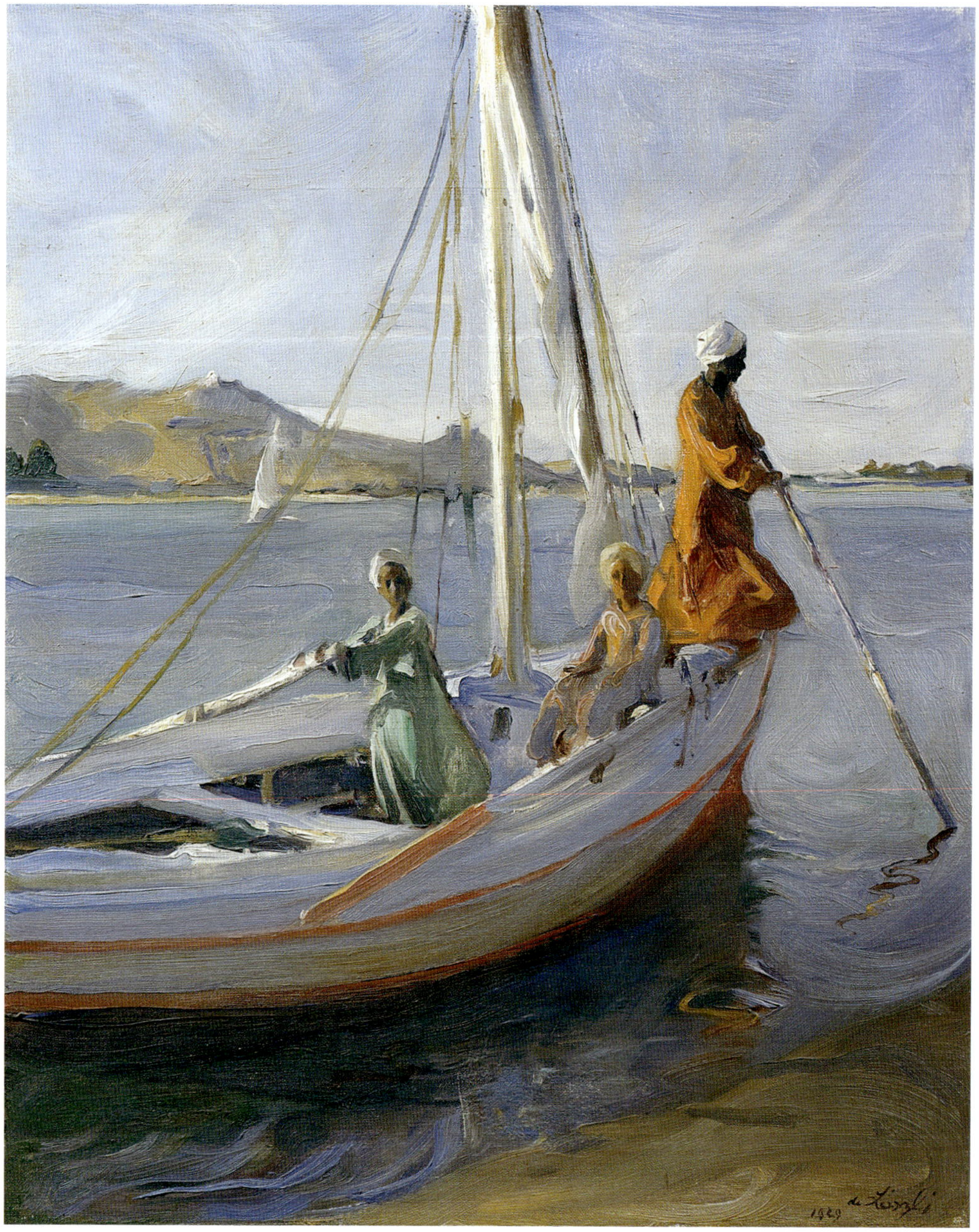

This striking composition was painted on the Nile on 27 February 1929. When the sketch was exhibited in Hull later that year, it was described as 'My Boat on the Nile', on the face of it a very modest mode of transport for someone who had just painted the King of Egypt.

De László arrived in Cairo in January 1929 to paint King Fouad I of Egypt (fig. 83) and his son, Prince Farouk. Once this commission was completed, the artist was joined by his wife and their thirteen-year-old son, Paul. Together they journeyed up the Nile, visiting Karnak, Luxor and Aswan. Indefatigable as ever, de László made a number of oil studies during this trip, including several landscapes and portraits. He also experimented with watercolour, but found it unsatisfactory: "… it needs too much practice," he said.

At the beginning of March they visited Luxor, where de László painted a view of the Court of Rameses II in the Temple of Ammon (cat. 113). Derek Clifford has written: "In the wide range of de László's landscape subjects … it was the natural drama of brilliant sunlight to which he reacted most vigorously. Without the sun his studies often, although not always,

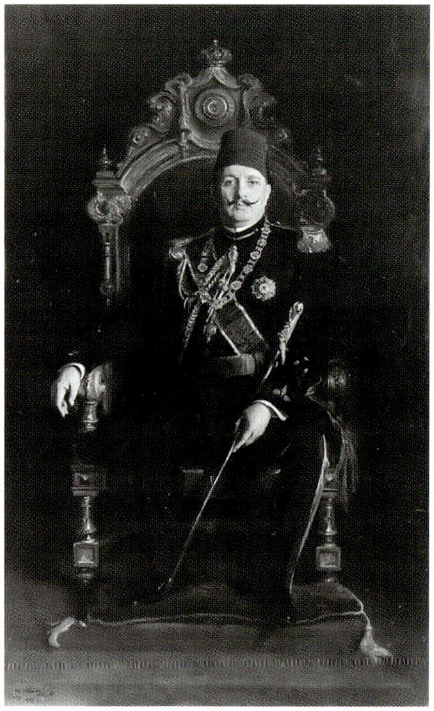

FIG. 83 *King Fouad of Egypt*, 1929
Oil on canvas
Untraced

failed to extract any quality from the scene other than a prosaic statement of fact, but when sunlight drenched stone his work became instantly alive."

113 The Temple at Luxor 1929

Oil on canvas, 79.4 × 58.4 cm (31¼ × 23 inches)
Signed, inscribed and dated, lower left: *de László / LUXOR 1929*; on the verso: *de László Luxor Tempel / 1929 / March / P.A. de László*

PROVENANCE In the possession of the artist on his death; Henry de Laszlo, his eldest son; Patrick de Laszlo, his fourth son

EXHIBITED *84th Annual Exhibition*, Royal West of England Academy, November 1929–February 1930, no.26: *Study of the Luxor Temple no price*; *Exhibition*, Royal Society of British Artists, London, 1930, no.168: *Luxor Temple*; *Exhibition of recent Portraits and Studiesby Philip A. de László*, M.V.O., Victoria Art Galleries, Dundee, September 1932, no.65: *Temple at Luxor*; *Exhibition of Paintings by Philip A. de László, M.V.O., In Aid of the London Hospital and The Artists' General Benevolent Institution*, Wildenstein & Co., Ltd., London, November–December 1937, no.41: *Temple at Luxor*

LITERATURE Rowcliffe 1938, p.102 (no. 604); Rutter 1939, p.371; Clifford 1969, ill. p.57, pl.XIII

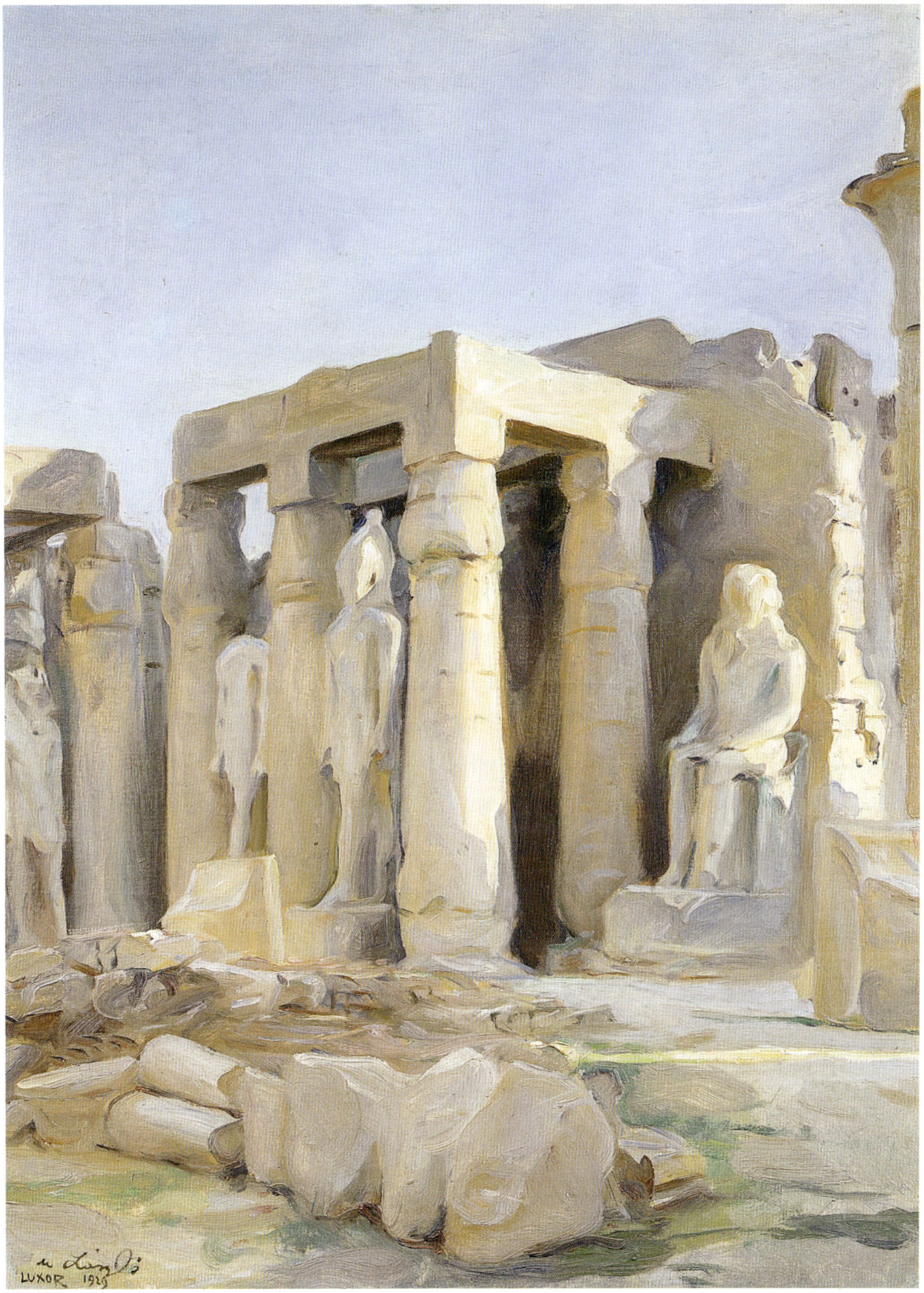

114 A Nubian Serving Boy 1929

Oil on canvasboard, 50.8 × 40.6 cm (20 × 16 inches) Signed, indistinctly inscribed and dated, lower right: *de László / Aswan 1929*; on the verso signed by the artist with initials and inscribed, upper right: *my coffee boy*

PROVENANCE In the possession of the artist on his death; Patrick de Laszlo, fourth son of the artist

EXHIBITED *The Autumn Exhibition of Autumn Paintings*, Ferens Art Gallery, Hull, 1929, no.130: *My Nubian Servant Price 200*; *Exhibition of recent Portraits and Studies by Philip A. de László, M.V.O.*, Victoria Art Galleries, Dundee, September 1932, no.67: *A Nubian Servant*

LITERATURE Rowcliffe 1938, p.53 (no. 271); Rutter 1939, p.371

This quick sketch of his "coffee boy" is thought to have been painted at Aswan, during de László's trip up the Nile in March 1929.

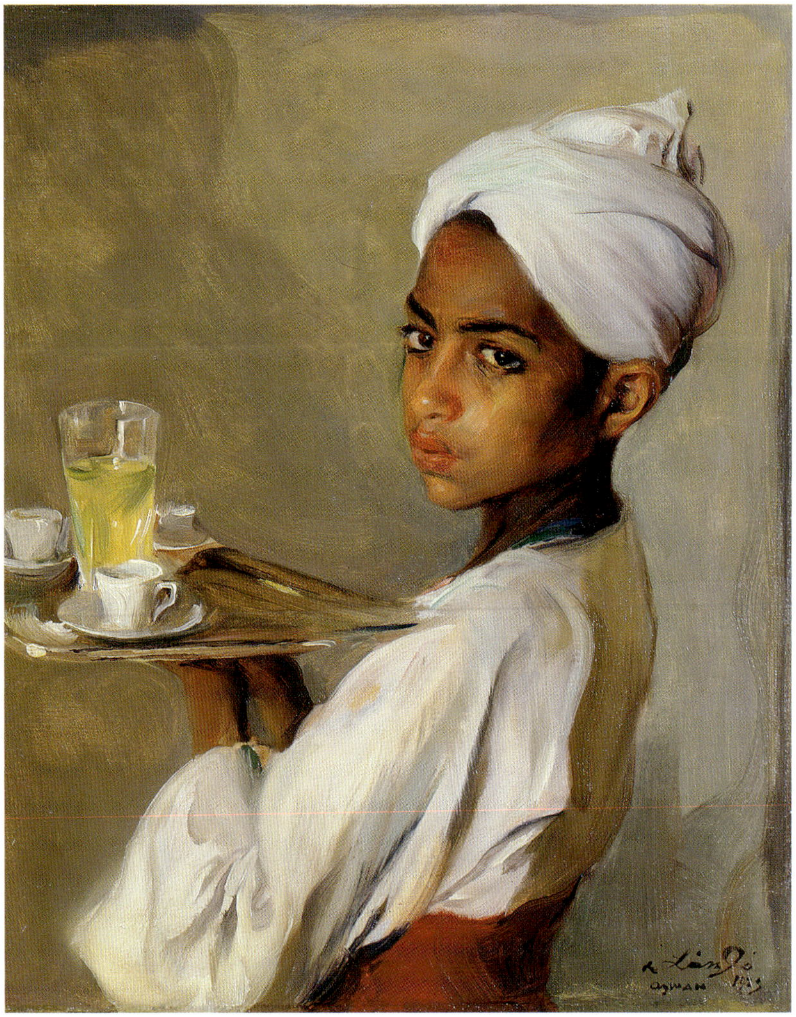

115 A Sailing Boat on the Nile 1929

Oil on board, 20.3 × 25.4 cm (8 × 10 inches)

PROVENANCE In the possession of the artist on his death; Stephen de Laszlo, his second son

LITERATURE Rowcliffe 1938, p.127 (no.749); Rutter 1939, p.371

De László's 'snapshot in oil' was also made at Aswan in March 1929 during his trip up the Nile.

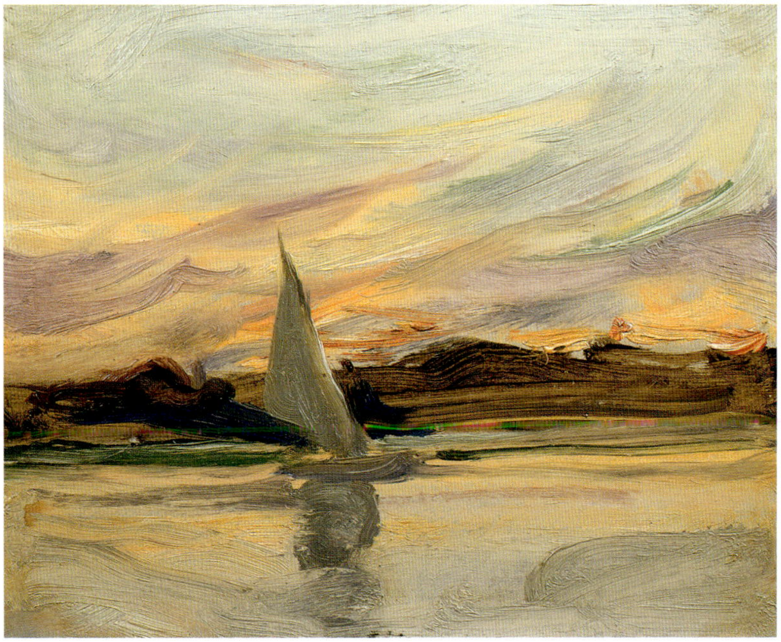

116 James Joicey, 1st Baron Joicey 1929

Oil on canvas, 114.3 × 91.4 cm (45 × 36 inches)
Signed and dated, lower right: *de László / 1929*
EXHIBITED *Exhibition of recent Portraits and Studies by Philip A. de László, M.V.O.*, Victoria Art Galleries, Dundee, September 1932, no.24: *The Rt. Hon. Lord Joicey, J.P., D.L., D.C.L.*
LITERATURE ASB Vol.II, p.62: *Joicey July 23rd 1929*; N.P.G. 1927–29 Album, p.36

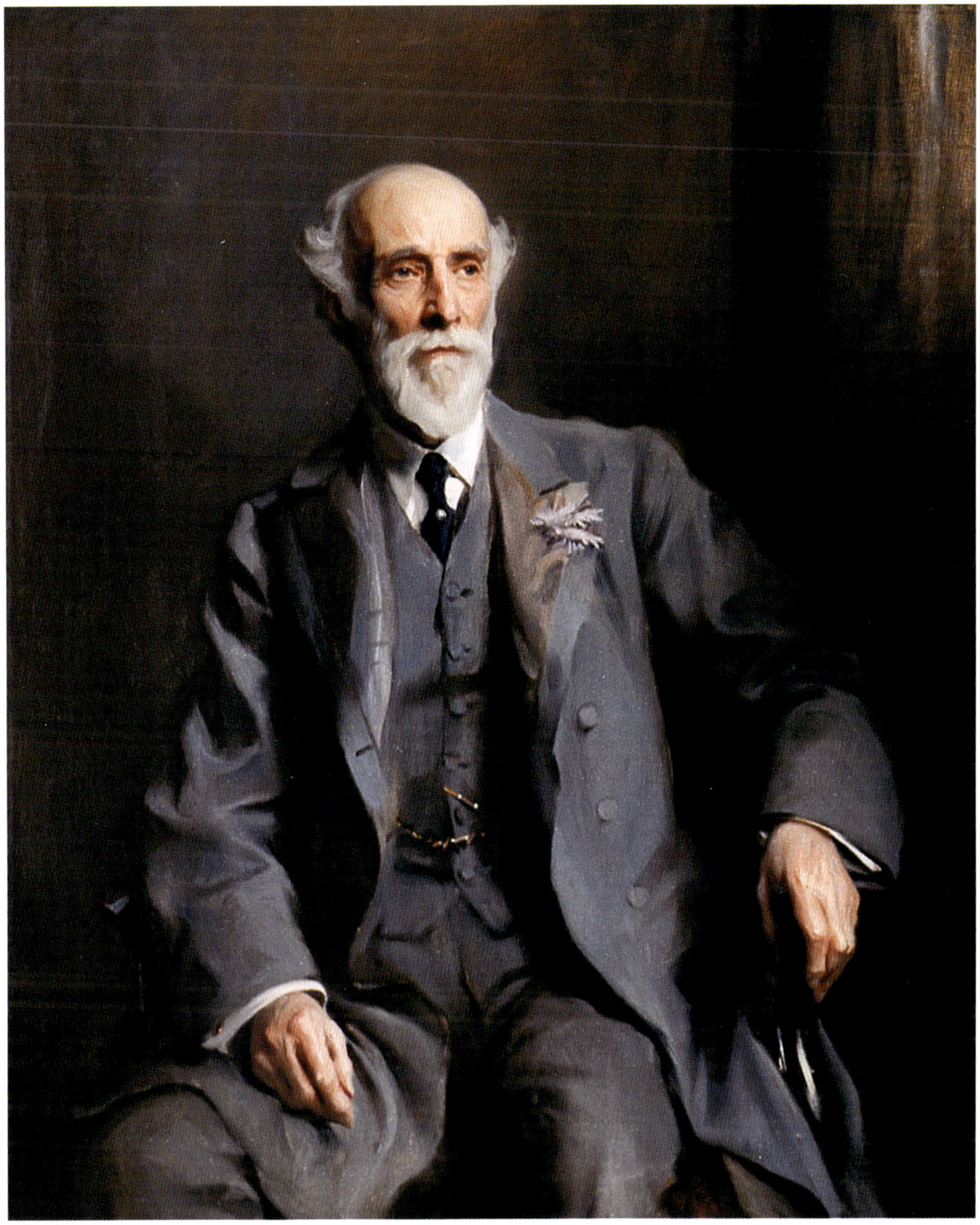

De László made a charcoal drawing of Lord Joicey in 1916 and had already painted his daughter Marguerite, his second son, Hugh, later 3rd Baron, and two of his daughters-in-law before making this portrait in 1929.

James Joicey was born in 1846, and was educated at Gainford School, Co. Durham. He owned several coalmines, was sometime proprietor of the *Newcastle Daily Leader* and M.P. for Durham County. He was also J.P. and Deputy Lieutenant for County Durham. He was created Baronet in 1893 and Baron in 1906. A great philanthropist, he did much to lead the movement to improve the conditions of the men working in the mines in the region. He was beloved by friends and employees alike.

In 1879 he married Elizabeth Robinson and they had two sons. She died in 1881, and three years later he married Marguerite, daughter of Colonel Thomas Drever and granddaughter of General de Fontaine of Fontainebleau. They had two sons and a daughter, Marguerite. Lady Joicey died in 1911.

In 1905 Lord Joicey purchased the Ford Castle estate, to which he retired, and in 1912 bought the Etal estate, near Berwick-upon-Tweed, for one of his sons. He was more than happy living in the country and took up many rural pursuits. After he had lost both his wives, his two younger sons died during the First World War, and his daughter in 1924. Lord Joicey died at the age of ninety in 1936.

117 Harold Harmsworth, 1st Viscount Rothermere 1930

Oil on canvas, 112.4 × 81.9 cm (44¼ × 32¼ inches)
Signed, inscribed and dated, lower left: *László / London / 1930*
Hungarian National Gallery, Budapest
PROVENANCE Given by the artist to the Hungarian National Gallery in 1930
LITERATURE ASB, Vol.II, p.63: *Rothermere 8th July 1929*; p.66: *Rothermere July 21st / 1930*; N.P.G. 1929–31 Album, p.19; Rutter 1939, p.371; Richard Bourne, *The Lords of Fleet Street, The Harmsworth Dynasty*, London 1990, pp.83–4, 116–19

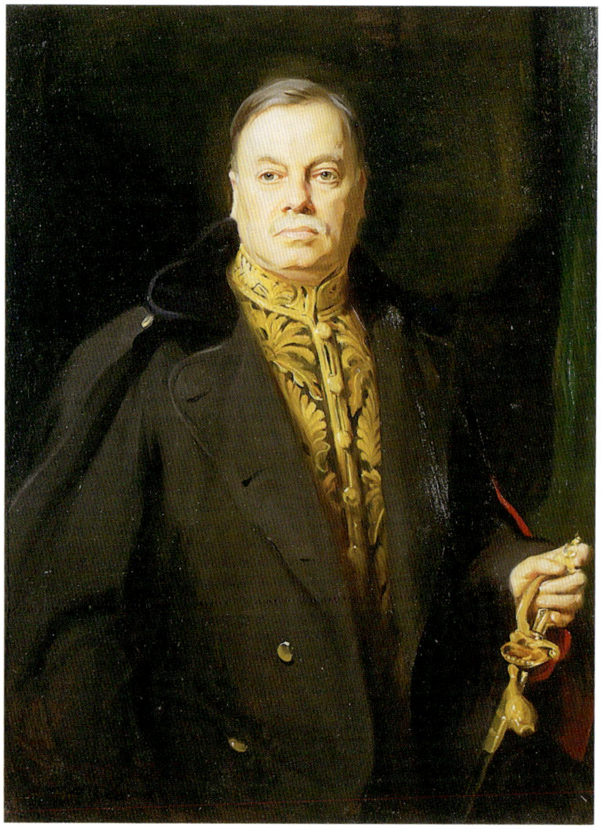

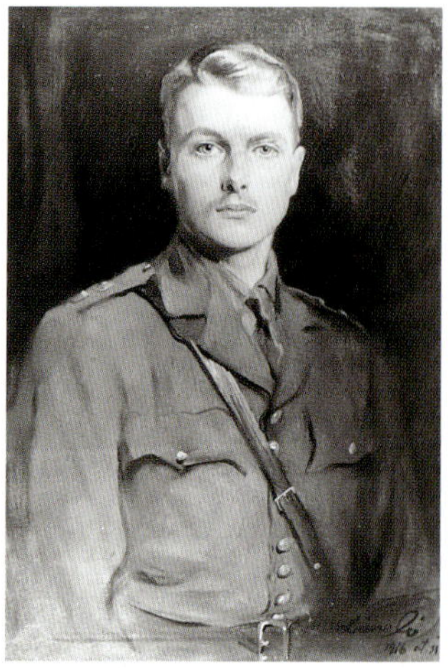

FIG. 84 *The Hon. Vyvyan Harmsworth* (1895–1916), 1916
Oil on canvas, 80.6 × 55.2 cm
(31¾ × 21¾ in.)
Private collection

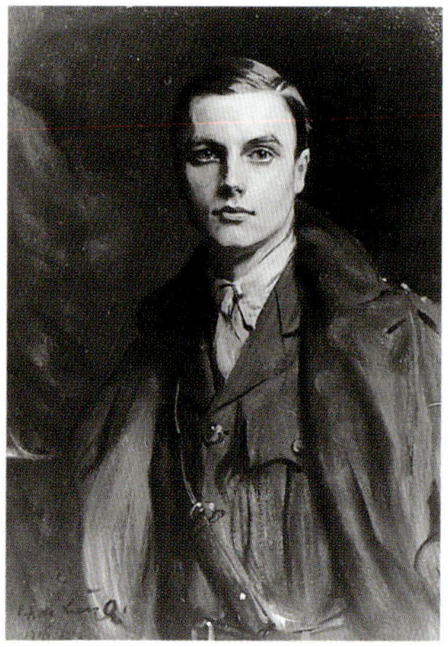

FIG. 85 *The Hon. Vere Harmsworth* (1895–1916), 1916
Oil on canvas, 80.6 × 55.9 cm
(31¾ × 22 inches)
Private collection

De László painted portraits of many members of the Harmsworth family, including the sitter's brother, Lord Northcliffe, in 1910, his mother, Mrs Alfred Harmsworth, and his three sons, Vyvyan (fig. 84), Vere (fig. 85) and Esmond. The two eldest sons were killed in action in the First World War. According to Richard Bourne, towards the end of his life Lord Rothermere hung the two de László portraits of his eldest sons with the portrait of his mother on the wall facing the end of his bed at his home, Stody House in Melton Constabl. A copy of the present portrait by the Hungarian artist Jóseph Mányai remains in the collection of the Inner Temple, London.

Harold Sydney Harmsworth, the second son of Alfred Harmsworth, was born in 1868. In July 1893 he married Mary Lilian Share. He and his brother, Alfred, later 1st Viscount Northcliffe, built up a successful business in periodicals, but in 1894 they branched into daily journalism, buying *The Evening News*. Nine years later they founded *The Daily Mirror*. In 1910 Harold Harmsworth established the King Edward VII Chair of English Literature at Cambridge, and received a baronetcy. He became Baron Rothermere four years later. For the last year of the war he was Air Minister, and in 1919 was elevated to Viscount.

In 1914 he had disassociated himself from his brother to concentrate on *The Daily Mirror*, which by 1922 had a circulation of three million. After his brother's death in 1922, he acquired control of *The Daily Mail* and *The Sunday Dispatch*. He was founder of *The Glasgow Daily Herald* and *The Sunday Pictorial*, Chairman of Associated Newspapers Ltd and Director of Amalgamated Press Ltd. In 1928 he became honorary Bencher of the Middle Temple.

The Treaty of Trianon of 1920, in which Hungary lost more than two thirds of her pre-war territory, provoked Rothermere to write an article on this perceived injustice, which he published in his newspapers. The response to this article was huge, and from 1927 to 1938 he led a campaign to draw attention to the plight of the eleven million Hungarians living outside Hungary's borders and to restore the lost territory. In Hungary Lord Rothermere became a national hero; mementos were made with his name and likeness, statues were raised and plaques unveiled. So great was his popularity, some even advocated that he should be invited to fill the throne of Hungary, empty since the death of Charles IV in 1922. De

László was a great supporter of the campaign and offered to paint Lord Rothermere in 1928. From the Hungarian League for Revision he received the reply: "We are happy to think that by your thoughtful act we are offered an opportunity to show our gratitude to an unselfish and noble champion of Hungary's just cause, and that at the same time a work of art by our greatest portrait painter will be added to the Hungarian National Gallery …we appeal to you, Sir, to paint this portrait and we feel greatly indebted to you for giving us a masterpiece which we value beyond the ordinary standard of works of art."

Lord Rothermere died in November 1940 and was succeeded by his surviving son Esmond. To this day he is remembered with gratitude and respect by many Hungarians. A ciné film of Rothermere and his son was made during one of their visits to Hungary, and will have been showing at the exhibition this book accompanies.

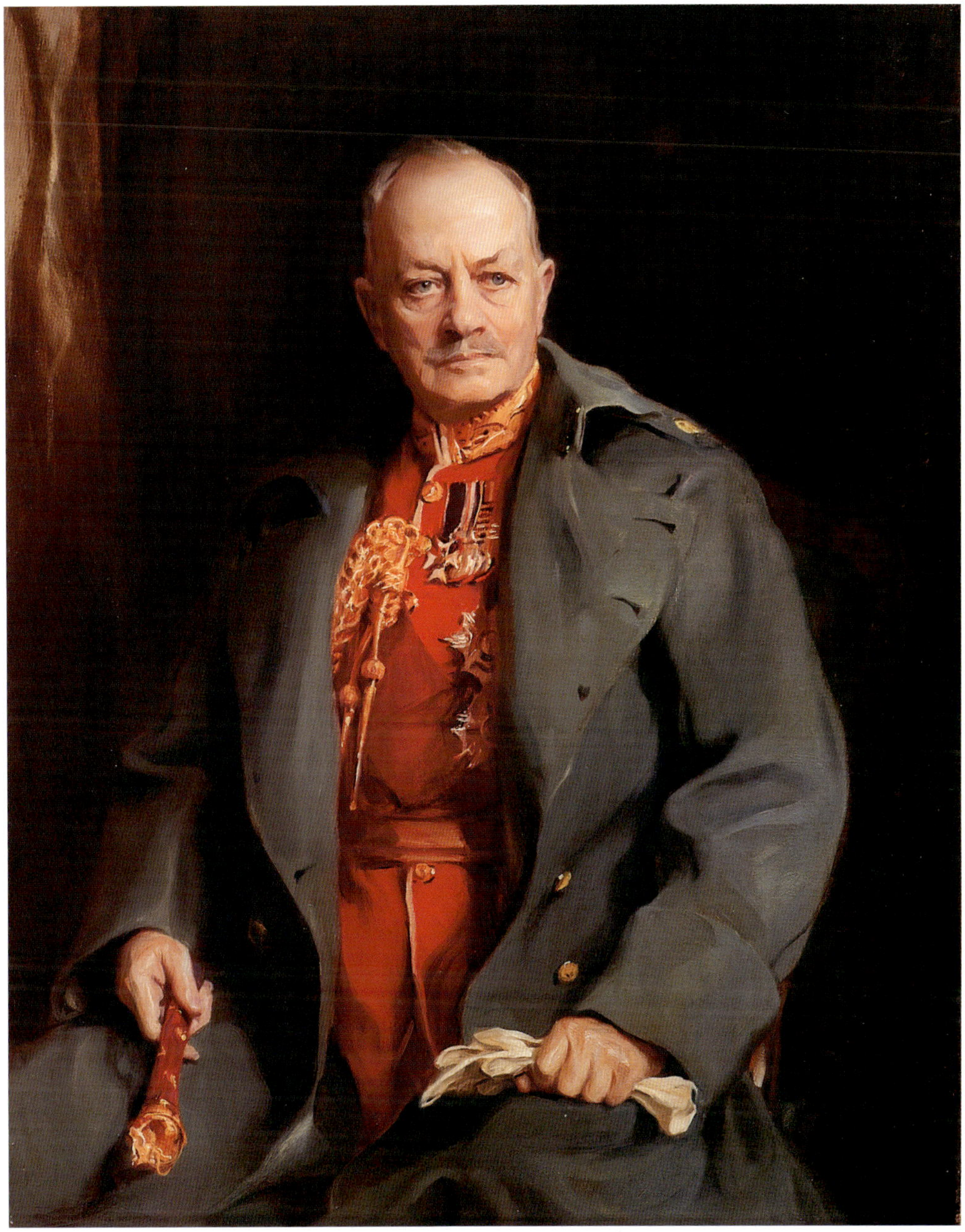

118 Field Marshal the Viscount Byng of Vimy 1933

Oil on canvas, 120.7 × 92.7 cm (47½ × 36½ inches)
Signed and dated, lower right: *de László / 1933 / IV*
The National Portrait Gallery, London, on loan to The King's Royal Hussars Museum, Winchester
PROVENANCE Byng family collection; bequeathed by the widow of the sitter in 1951 to the National Portrait Gallery, London
EXHIBITED *Portraits by Philip A. de László, M.V.O., Loan Exhibition held in aid of The Artists' General Benevolent Institution*, M. Knoedler & Company, Inc., London, June–July 1933, no.22: *Field-Marshal The Viscount Byng of Vimy, G.C.B., G.C.M.G.*
LITERATURE ASB, Vol.II, p.74: *Byng of Vimy Dec. 21st 1932.*; N.P.G. 1932 Album, p. 26; Rutter 1939, p.261; Jeffery Williams, *Byng of Vimy, General and Governor General*, London 1983, ill. pl.36

De László painted Byng and made a fine pencil (head only) study of him as a Brigadier General in 1908 (fig. 86). He also painted Lady Byng in 1917 (untraced).

Julian Hedworth George Byng was born in 1862, the youngest son of George, 2nd Earl of Strafford, and his second wife Harriet, daughter of the 1st Lord Chesham. He was educated at Eton. While gazetted to the 10th Hussars, he saw active service in the Sudan, most notably taking part in the historic charge at El Teb in 1884. During the South African War he commanded the South African Light Horse. On his return he married Marie Evelyn Moreton, only child of the Hon. Sir Richard Charles Moreton. From 1902–4 he commanded the 10th Hussars.

In 1914 he became Major General Commanding in Egypt, before taking over the 3rd Division in France. In May 1915 he was given command of the Cavalry Corps with promotion to Lt-General. In August that year he was sent out to the Dardanelles to command the IX Corps at Suvla. His almost immediate decision to withdraw was indeed so successful that Byng became known as the 'Hero of Gallipoli'. In May 1916 he took over command of the Canadian Corps in France. The Corps' greatest feat, which will forever be inseparably connected with Byng's name, was the capture of Vimy Ridge in April 1917. He was Commander of the Third Army until 1918, and in 1919 he was created Baron Byng of Vimy. In 1921 he was appointed Governor General of Canada, a post he held until 1926. He was raised to Viscount in 1928. Lord Byng was always a passionate sportsman, and both he and his wife particularly loved ice hockey. He died in 1935, leaving no issue, and his peerage therefore became extinct.

When this portrait was painted Byng was Colonel of the 10th Hussars. A contemporary copy of the portrait by Sydney Percy Kendrick, de László's most favoured copyist, hangs in the Cavalry and Guards Club, London.

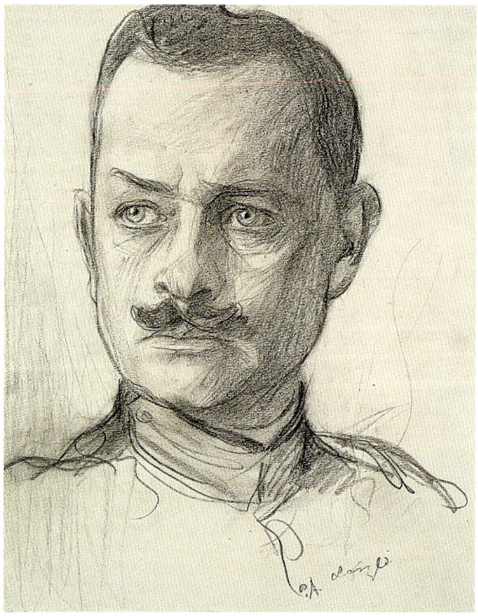

FIG. 86 *Brigadier-General the Hon. H.G. Julian Byng*, 1908
Charcoal, 37.5 × 29.5 cm ($14\frac{3}{4} \times 11\frac{5}{8}$ inches)
National Archives of Canada, Ottawa

119 Mrs Edmund Buchanan, née Doreen Bury 1929

Oil on canvas, 132.1 × 91.4 cm (52 × 36 inches)
Signed and dated, lower right: *de László / 1929*
PROVENANCE Charles A. Buchanan Esq.; Col. Edmund P. Buchanan; Patrick Buchanan Esq., until his death in 1998
EXHIBITED *Exhibition of recent Portraits and Studies by Philip A. de Laszlo, M.V.O.*, Victoria Art Galleries, Dundee, September 1932, no.33: *Mrs. Edmund Buchanan, Lent by C.A.Buchanan, Esq.*
LITERATURE ASB, Vol.II, p.64: *Doreen M. Buchanan / Sept. 6th '29*; N.P.G. 1929–31 Album, p.4

This portrait was chosen to illustrate the cover of *A Brush with Grandeur* as a striking statement to de László's skills. The composition combines the daring vivacity of the 1920s with the graceful strength of the best of European portraiture in previous centuries. Fluidity of brushwork is underpinned by stability of structure to make this one of the most brilliant portraits of de László's career.

De László painted a double portrait of Mrs Buchanan's sisters-in-law, Misses Marjory and Elizabeth Buchanan, in 1923. This portrait was painted six years later. According to Mrs Buchanan's son, his mother was inclined to tell people that she and de László had painted the picture together. Unusually, he would not allow anyone to see the painting before it was finished, keeping it covered with a sheet between sittings. "One day," he recalled, "when it was nearly finished he was called out of the room to the telephone, and [my mother] was alone for the first time with the picture and jumped up and ran over to look at it. She was aghast at how revealing the dress was and that one nipple was almost visible through the material. She knew my grandmother (who went as far as placing a large lampshade in front of the bare breasted woman in an 18th Century tapestry for the sake of modesty) would be horrified. So she took her thumb and rubbed it on the still wet paint and blurred that bit. She said that Mr. de László never noticed, and her contribution remained!"

Doreen Marguerite Bury was born in 1900 in British Columbia, where her father was temporarily practising as a barrister. Her younger years were spent at Downings, the family home in Northern Ireland, where she became an excellent horsewoman and developed a love of hunting. Soon after the death of her parents, she and her sister Esmée (who later married Sir Francis Lascelles) were forced to leave Ireland by the Republicans, who burnt their house to the ground. They went to live with cousins in Somerset, where the hunting was something of a consolation.

In 1926 she married Edmund Pullar Buchanan, a Captain in the Argyll and Sutherland Highlanders, with whom she had three sons, Neil, Patrick and Nigel. From 1926 to 1928 she and her husband were with the regiment in Egypt. The present portrait was painted on their return. In 1935–6 they were in India, but on the death of his father Edmund Buchanan retired from the army as a Major, and returned to run the family estate, Touch, in Stirlingshire.

In 1940 Touch was taken over as a hospital, and in June that year Edmund Buchanan was taken prisoner in northern France with the remnants of the Highland Division. Having moved to a smaller house nearby, whence she ran the estate, Mrs Buchanan started up a 'Comforts Depot', raising money and provisions for 7th Argyll prisoners of war. Her husband was released in 1945 and demobilized as a full Colonel.

In 1958, a brain tumour confined her to a wheelchair for the rest of her life. Despite this she still managed to enjoy life with her family and friends. Mrs Buchanan died in 1986.

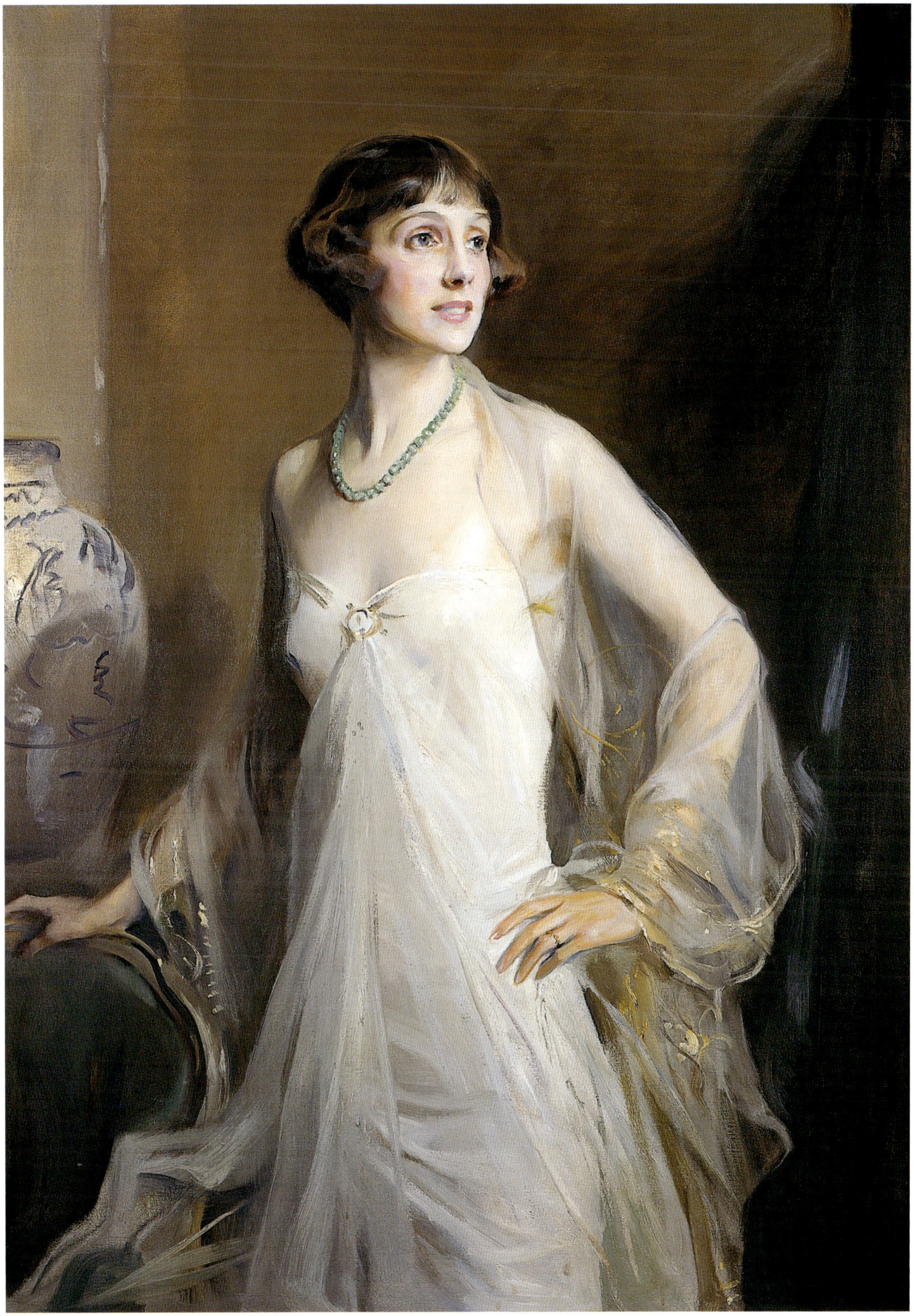

120 Claude Bowes Lyon, 14th Earl of Strathmore and Kinghorne 1931

Oil on canvas, 96.5 × 73.7 cm (38 × 29 inches)
Signed and dated, lower left: *de László / VII 1931*
EXHIBITED *Exhibition of recent Portraits and Studies by Philip A. de László, M.V.O.*, Victoria Art Galleries, Dundee, September 1932, no.5: *The Rt. Hon the Earl of Strathmore, K.T., G.C.V.O.*; *Portraits by Philip A. de László, M.V.O., Loan Exhibition Held In Aid of The Artists' General Benevolent Institution*, M. Knoedler & Company, Inc., London, June–July 1933, no.16: *The Earl of Strathmore and Kinghorne, K.T., G.C.V.O.*
LITERATURE ASB, Vol.II, p.45: *Strathmore / 1931 July 9th*; N.P.G. 1931 Album, p.20; *The Studio*, CVI, 1933, p.149, ill.; Special Coronation Number, *Illustrated London News*, 1936

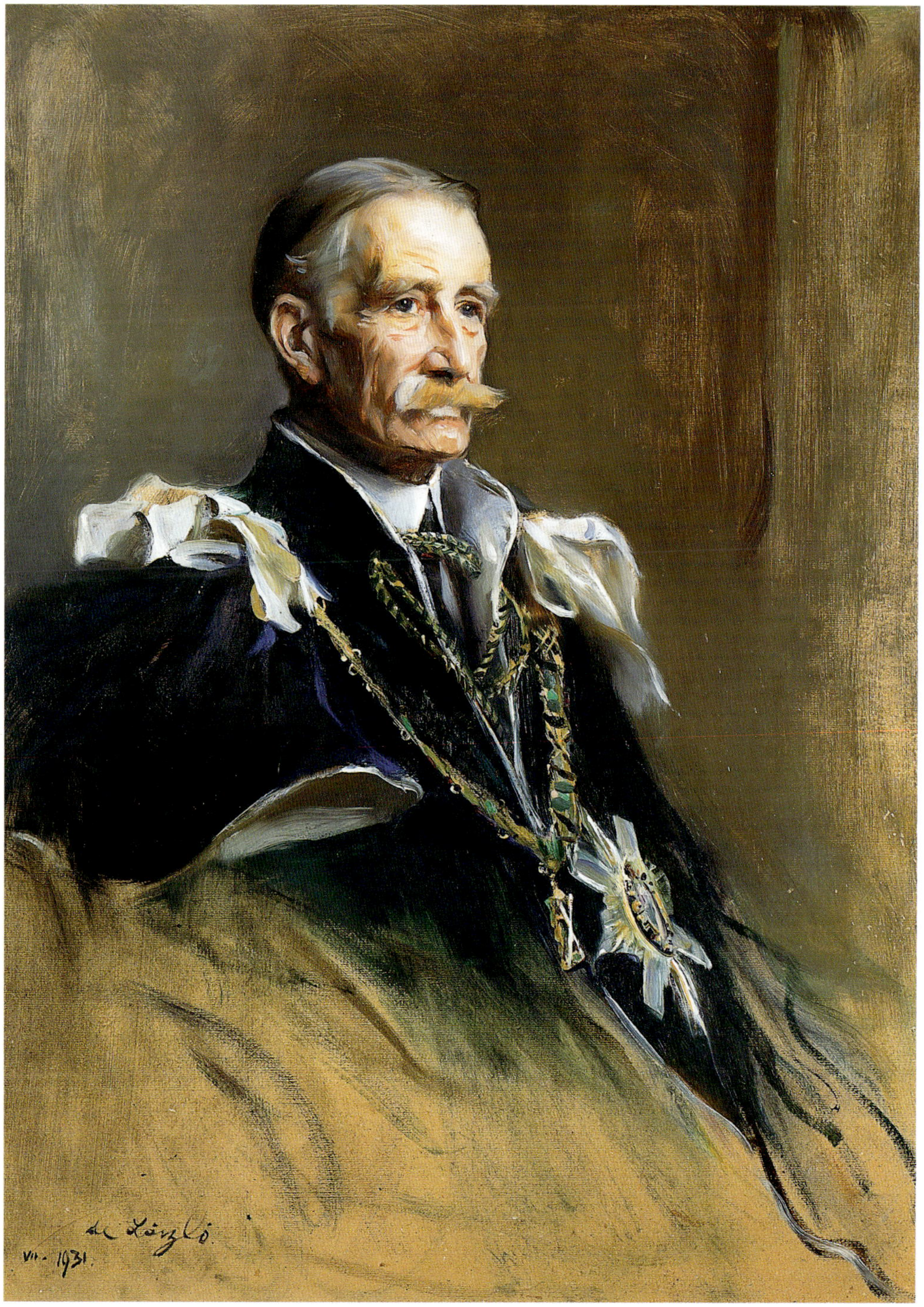

This portrait, showing the sitter in the robes of a Knight of the Thistle, was painted, as a pendant to cat. 121, on the occasion of the Strathmores' golden wedding anniversary in 1931, and presented to the Earl by his tenants and estate workers. In that year de László painted a second portrait of his daughter and her husband, the future King George VI.

Claude George Bowes Lyon was born at Glamis in 1855, the eldest son of Claude Bowes Lyon and his wife Frances Dora Smith. He was educated at Eton and served in the 2nd Life Guards. In 1881 he married Celia Cavendish-Bentinck. He succeeded his father as 14th Earl of Strathmore and Kinghorne in 1904.

According to Grania Forbes, Lord Strathmore loved the outdoor life and took a full part in undertaking even menial tasks on the estate. He was known to be somewhat vague and eccentric: he busied himself with looking after the rhododendrons and chopping and bringing in the firewood, even sometimes at night. His interest in forestry led him to take an active part in the development of the plantations on his estates, and he was one of the first to grow larch from seed, brought over by him from Norway. His father had nearly bankrupted the estate by building Episcopalian churches all over Scotland; so his was not a wealthy family, but Lord Strathmore was renowned as a considerate and generous laird and as a devout Christian. Reading the Bible every day was as important to him as doing the *Telegraph* crossword. Although of a somewhat retiring disposition, he was a welcoming and hospitable host to his children's friends, having a good sense of fun and loving a joke. The Strathmores were one of the last families in Scotland to employ a jester for family entertainments. He himself would quote from *Ingoldsby Legends* and *Alice through the Looking Glass* to his children. He was a fanatical cricketer, and the hugely enjoyable matches at Glamis were taken very seriously. Lord Strathmore died at Glamis in 1944 and was succeeded by his eldest son.

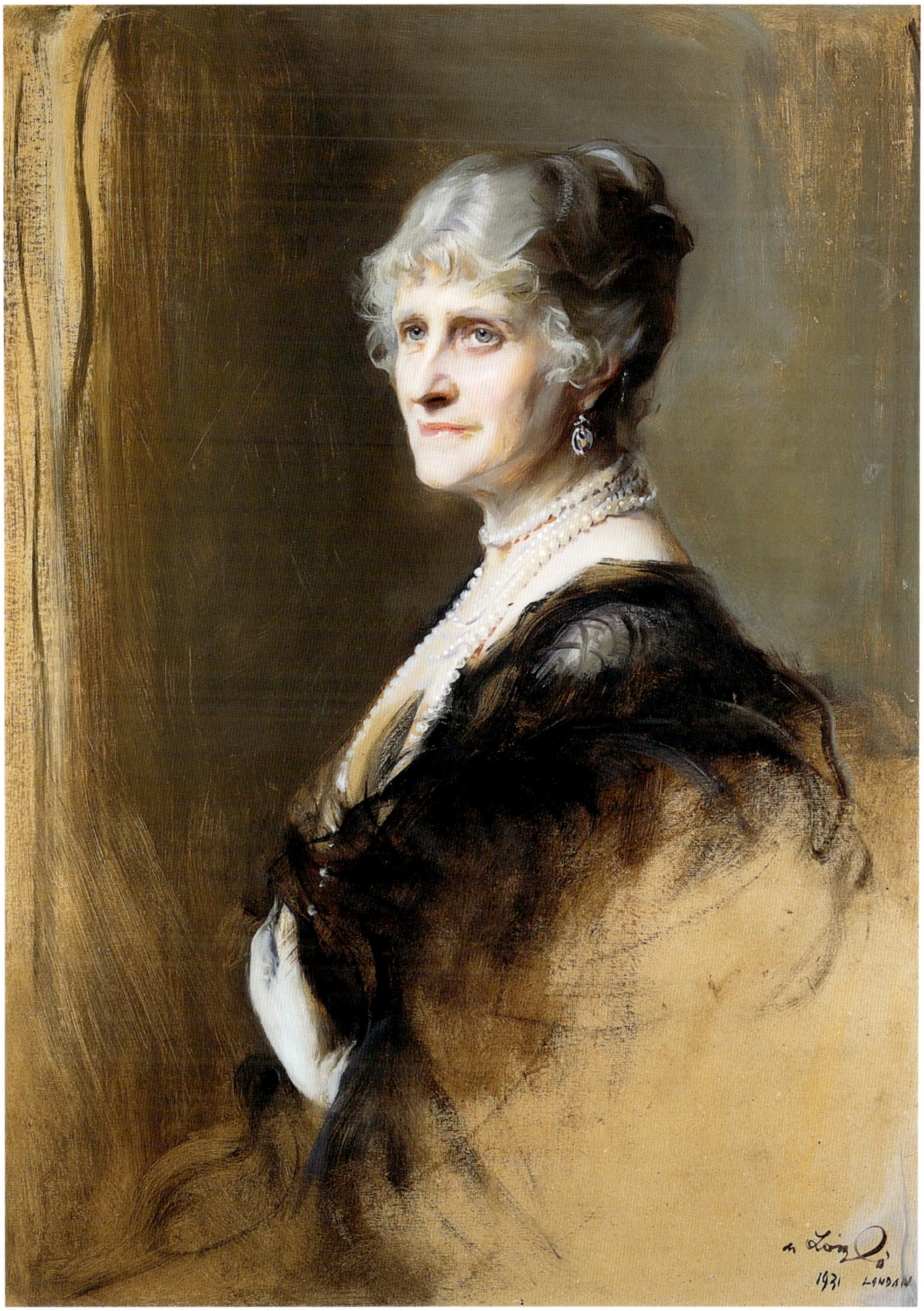

121 The Countess of Strathmore and Kinghorne, née Celia Cavendish-Bentinck 1931

Oil on canvas, 96.5 × 73.7 cm (38 × 29 inches)
Signed, dated and inscribed, lower right: *de László / 1931 LONDON*
EXHIBITED *Exhibition of recent Portraits and Studies by Philip A. de László, M.V.O.*, Victoria Art Galleries, Dundee, September 1932, no.6: *The Rt. Hon the Countess of Strathmore*; *Portraits by Philip A. de László, M.V.O., Loan Exhibition Held In Aid of The Artists' General Benevolent Institution*, M. Knoedler & Company, Inc., London, June–July 1933, no.20: *The Countess of Strathmore and Kinghorne*
LITERATURE ASB, Vol.II, p.45: *Cecilia Strathmore / July 1st 1931* ; N.P.G. 1931 Album, p. 19; *The Studio*, CVI, 1933, p.149, ill.; Rutter 1939, p.358; Special Coronation Number, *Illustrated London News*, 1936

De László had already painted a number of the Bowes Lyon children when he made this portrait of Lady Strathmore and its pair of her husband (cat. 120). Lady Strathmore's was a present from her daughter, the Duchess of York, on behalf of the whole family.

Nina Cecilia (Celia), born in 1862, was the

daughter of the Revd Charles William Frederick Cavendish-Bentinck, a grandson of the 3rd Duke of Portland. On 16 July 1881 she married Claude George Bowes Lyon, later 14th Earl of Strathmore and Kinghorne. They had six sons and four daughters. Their eldest daughter, Violet, died of diptheria, their third son, Alexander, died of a brain tumour in 1911, and then, in 1915, another son, Fergus, was killed in battle at Loos.

Lady Strathmore had a "genius for motherhood" and, unfashionably for the time, breast-fed all her babies. She had a tremendous zest for living and under her influence all her children developed a confident and uninhibited approach to life. She was adored by her family, from whom she expected the highest standards, her motto being "work is the rent you pay for life". Lady Strathmore herself taught her younger children to read and write, starting with Bible stories, and considered music important. A talented musician herself, she often invited distinguished musicians to stay and her dinner parties would be followed by a private concert, performed by family and guests. She and her husband were extremely hospitable to their children's many friends, giving elegant balls and hosting house parties for them, some lasting weeks at a time. She was a skilled needlewoman and gardener, spending nearly a decade creating the Italian garden at Glamis. She was a kind and exacting mistress of the several family homes, running them efficiently and practically, and keeping meticulous account books. During the First World War, she ran Glamis as a hospital. An elegant and stately woman, she wore black over many a year. Lady Strathmore died in 1938.

122 Cosmo Gordon Lang, Archbishop of Canterbury 1932

Oil on canvas, 165.7 × 108.6 cm (65¼ × 42¾ inches)
Signed, inscribed and dated, lower right: *de László / Lambeth Palace 1932*; upper left: coat of arms and inscription: *COSMO / ARCHIEPS / CANTUAR*
Church House, Westminster, London
EXHIBITED *Portraits by Philip A. de László, M.V.O., Loan Exhibition Held In Aid of The Artists' General Benevolent Institution*, M. Knoedler & Company, Inc., London, June–July 1933,no.24, ill.: *The most Honble. and Most Reverend Cosmo Gordon, Lord Archbishop of Canterbury. (By courtesy of the Corporation of the Church House, Westminster)*
LITERATURE ASB, Vol.II, p.73: *Cosmo Cantuar June 29. 1932*; *The Studio*, CVI, 1933, p.148; Rutter 1939, pp.373, 378

De László had painted Archbishop Lang's predecessor Randall Davidson in 1926 (also Church House; fig. 32, p. 44), producing one of the most flamboyant British ecclesiastical portraits of all time. The present portrait of Archbishop Lang is far stronger, if more modest in scale, with a composition surprisingly reminiscent of his celebrated portrait of Cardinal Rampolla (cat. 19), although the two clerics could hardly have been more different in character. The artist painted the archbishop again the following year, for Balliol College, Oxford, where the portrait remains. De László's last portrait of the Archbishop was painted in 1937 in his robes for the coronation of George VI. A very free preparatory oil sketch for that is owned by one of the artist's descendants. The present portrait was commissioned by Church House, where it has remained since.

Cosmo Gordon Lang was born in Aberdeen in 1864, the son of the Very Revd John Marshall Lang, and educated at Glasgow University and Balliol College, Oxford. He was ordained in 1890 and became Dean of Divinity at Magdalen College, Oxford, Bishop of Stepney and Canon of St Paul's in 1901, Archbishop of York in 1908 and Archbishop of Canterbury in 1928. During his primacy, his brother became Moderator of the Church of Scotland– a 'double' which is very unlikely ever to be repeated. On retiring from Canterbury in 1942, he was created Baron Lang of Lambeth. A man of wide interests, he was accepted by all parties in the Church of England. He was friend and counsellor to the Royal Family and played an important role in the Abdication crisis of 1936. As Archbishop of Canterbury, Dr Lang gave the blessing at de László's memorial service held at St Margaret's, Westminster, on 26 November 1937. He died on 5 December 1945. He never married.

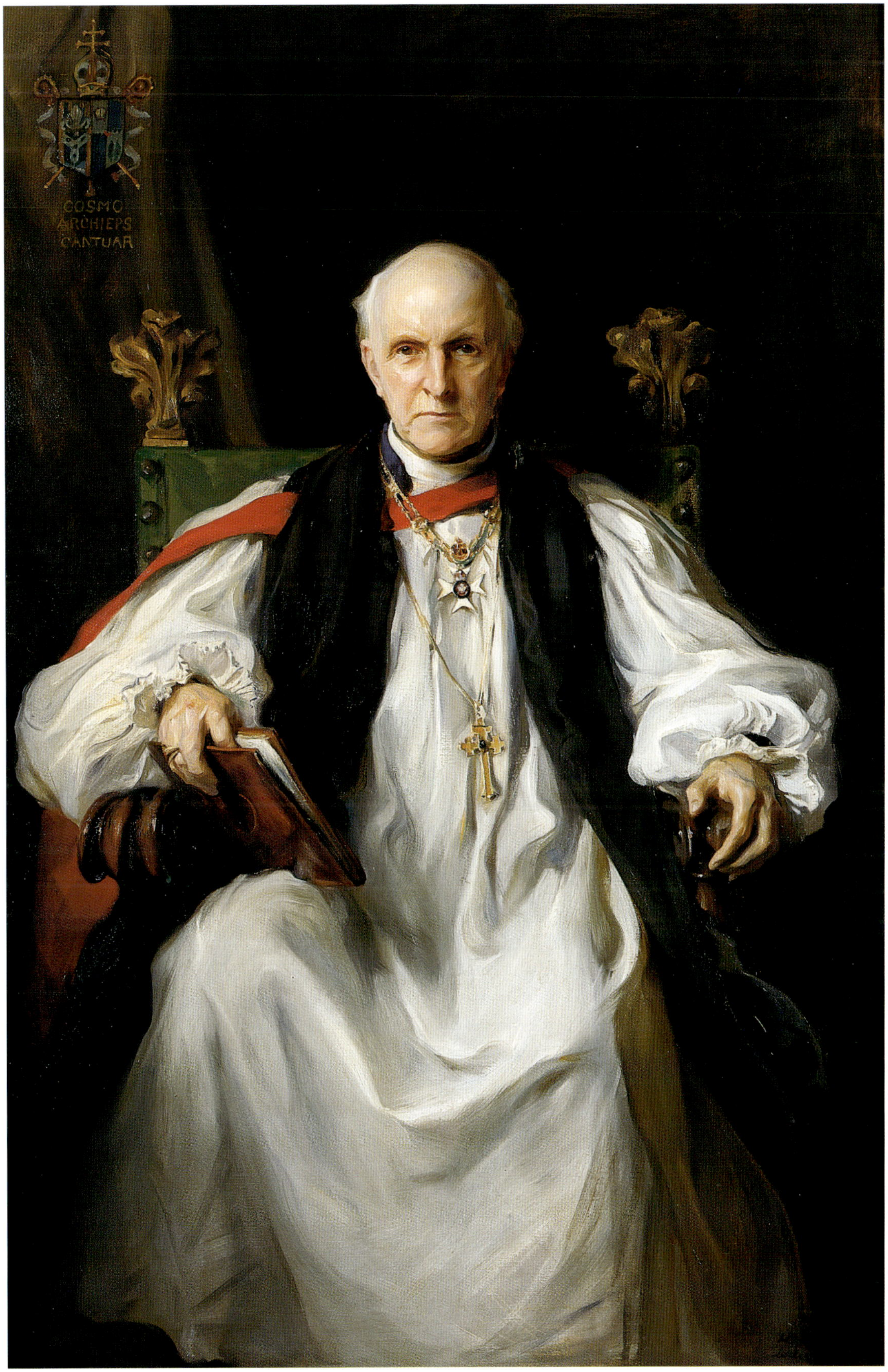
COSMO
ARCHIEPS
CANTUAR

123 Miss Anny Ahlers 1933

Oil on canvas, 172.7 × 116.8 cm (68 × 46 inches)
Signed and dated, lower left: *de László / 1933*
PROVENANCE Sir Merrik Burrell, Bart.
EXHIBITED *Portraits by Philip A. de László, M.V.O., Loan Exhibition Held In Aid of The Artists' General Benevolent Institution*, M. Knoedler & Company, Inc., London, June–July 1933, no.6: *The Late Miss Anny Ahlers*
LITERATURE ASB, Vol.II, p.74: *Anny Ahlers 26 XI 32*; N.P.G. 1933 Album, p.10; Rutter 1939, p.373, ill. facing p.384; Clifford 1969, monochrome ill. pl.46

In 1932, Sir Merrik Burrell, Bt, was taken by his daughter Dreda to see the beautiful and talented German actress and singer Anny Ahlers performing. Recently divorced from his second wife, he was smitten by Anny immediately and commissioned from de László a half-length portrait of her. He had in mind the sort that leading ladies, especially on the Continent, would display in the foyers of theatres. De László, faced with a sitter of such striking appearance, found the commission too subdued, and embarked upon the present full-length portrait. Anny, however, who suffered from bouts of depression, often failed to appear for sittings, which upset de László greatly.

On 14 March 1933, aged only twenty-six, Anny fell from the balcony of her flat and died instantly from a broken neck. The portrait was unfinished. Dreda Burrell was persuaded to sit for the completion of the painting, wearing Anny's dress. She recalled de László painting the actress's hands, shoulder and slippers as she posed for him (fig. 87). The portrait was exhibited to great acclaim at Knoedler's that June, and coloured reproductions of it were sold in aid of the Artists' Benevolent Fund. The *Daily Mail* wrote, "... by the liveliness of Mr de László's rendering [it is] a melancholy reminder of the fragility of life." The *Star* pointed out, "... ever since the exhibition opened the portrait of poor Anny Ahlers has been the centre of an admiring group, and a bowl of Du Barry roses stands in front of it."

Contemporary photographs exist of the portrait in both its unfinished and finished states. The emerald ring on Anny's left hand was a present from Sir Merrik and remains in the possession of the family. After her death, Sir Merrik had a lock of her hair set under glass in the lid of an antique French box and wrote an inscription in her memory, which was placed in the box (on display in the exhibition this book accompanies). Sir Merrik found the portrait somewhat too large for his home, Floodgates, near the family seat, Knepp Castle, in Sussex, but he treasured it nonetheless. De László painted three landscape studies in the grounds at Floodgates (fig. 49, p. 61).

Anny Ahlers was born in Hamburg in 1906. She made her first stage appearance at the age of seven. After the First World War she appeared as a *première enfant-danseuse* at the Vienna Opera House, and then at the Berlin State Opera House. In 1924 she returned to Hamburg to study operatic singing, and that year made her adult debut at the Volks-opernhaus there. Her success continued in Berlin, where she co-starred with Richard Tauber in *The Song of Love*, and in Vienna.

In 1932 she was brought over to London by an impresario, Mr Scott, with whom she was much in love, to appear as Jeanne in *The Dubarry* at His Majesty's Theatre. Once in England, however, apart from presenting her with cheques she hardly knew how to cash, Scott largely ignored her, and she found herself alone with little English and no friends or relations.

After her death, her mother and sister came over from Germany for her funeral and cremation, but only took half her ashes back with them. Some time later the funeral directors contacted the Burrell family: Scott had requested the retention of the rest of the ashes, but had made no further arrangements, practical or financial. Consequently, Sir Merrik had those ashes buried at Shipley, the church close to Knepp Castle. Such was Anny's popularity that the whole cast and orchestra from *The Dubarry* came down from London for the service of committal. The great Heddle Nash sang in the church and there was a tremendous gathering at Floodgates afterwards. There are memorials to both Sir Merrik and Miss Ahlers in Shipley Church.

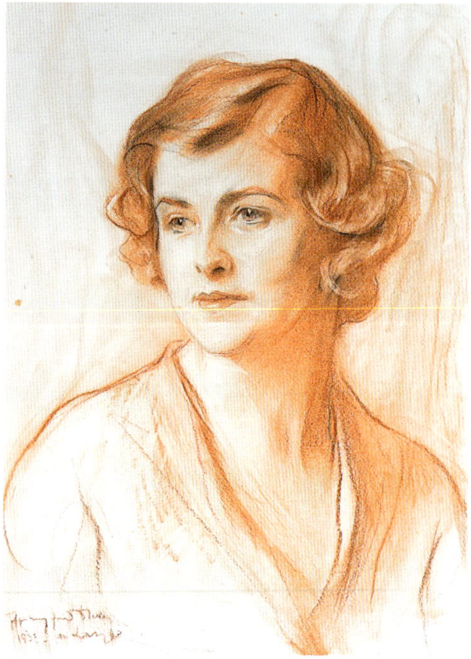

FIG. 87 *Miss Ethdreda (Dreda) Burrell*, 1933
Chalk and pencil, 50.8 × 35.6 cm (20 × 14 in.)
Private collection

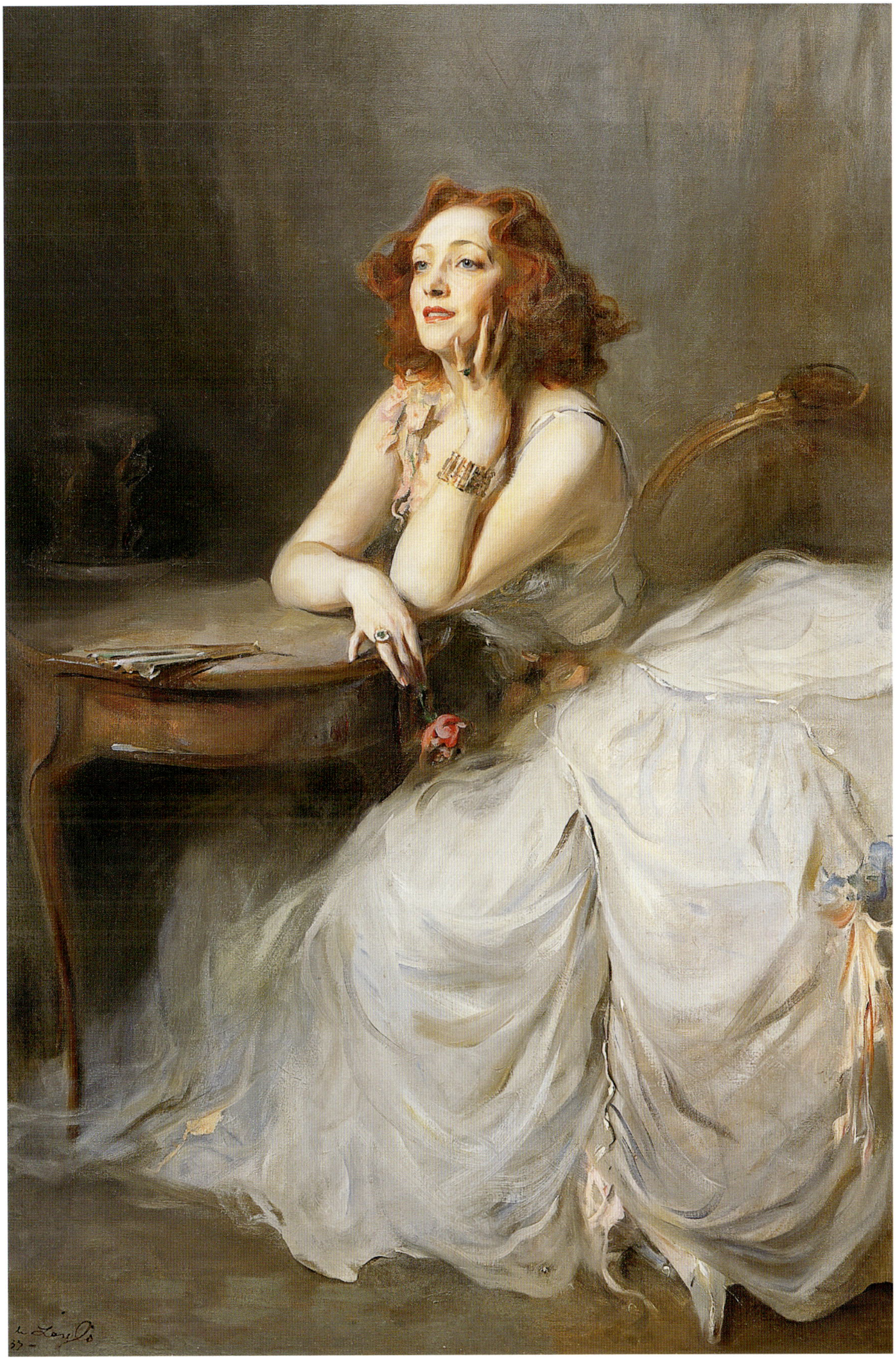

124 Her Majesty the Queen when Princess Elizabeth of York 1933

Oil on canvas, 90.2 × 69.2 cm (35½ × 27¼ inches)
Signed and dated, lower left: *de László* in black ink, / *1933 VI* in blue paint
Lent by Her Majesty the Queen
EXHIBITED *Portraits by Philip A. de László, M.V.O., Loan Exhibition Held In Aid of The Artists' General Benevolent Institution*, M. Knoedler & Company, Inc., London, June–July 1933, no: 18: *Her Royal Highness The Princess Elizabeth of York*; *Autumn Exhibition*, The Royal Glasgow Institute of Fine Arts, 1933, no.238: *HRH The Princess Elizabeth of York*; *Elizabeth II: Portraits of Sixty Years*, National Portrait Gallery, November 1986–March 1987; *Childhood, A Loan Exhibition of Works of Art*, Sotheby's, London, January 1988, no.450; *Golden Jubilee Exhibition, The Royal Society of Portrait Painters*, The Mall Galleries, London, S.W.1. (not in catalogue)
LITERATURE ASB, Vol.II, p.76: *Elizabeth May 25th 1933*; N.P.G. 1933 Album, p.24; Rutter 1939, p.374; John Cornforth, *Queen Elizabeth The Queen Mother, at Clarence House*, London 1996, ill. on front dust cover and facing title page; Jonathan Marsden, *Clarence House Official Souvenir Guide*, Royal Collection Publications 2003, p. 51, ill.

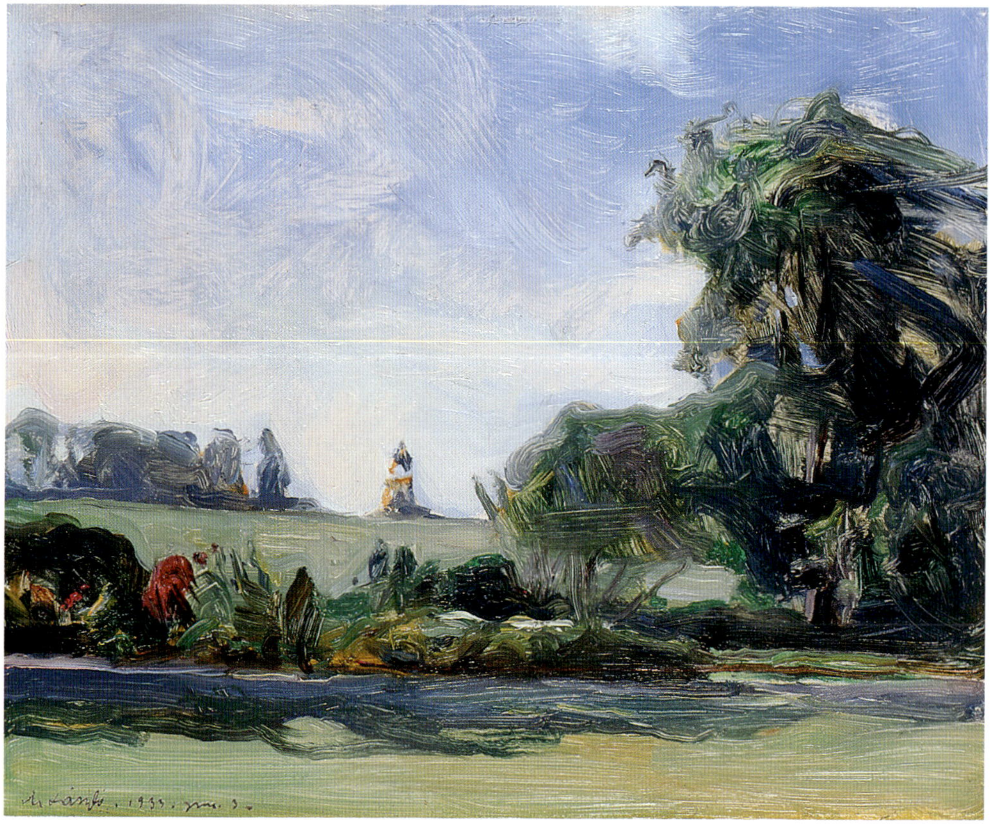

FIG. 88 *The Copper Horse, Windsor Park*, 1933
Oil on canvas, 20.3 × 25.4 cm (8 × 10 in.)
The Royal Collection © 2004 Her Majesty Queen Elizabeth II

According to Rutter, de László described his seven-year old sitter as "intelligent and full of character", but "very sleepy and restless" at her second sitting after having attended Queen Mary's birthday luncheon party.

After Knoedler's exhibition *The New York Daily Times* wrote: "Who are the greatest feminine personalities of the day? Royalty, politicians, and hostesses hurried away from their breakfast tables yesterday, despite the prospect of a long day of receptions, dinner parties, and dances, lasting well into this morning, to discover the judgement of a painter – the famous Mr. Philip de László. The answer was typical of this little wizard of color, whose studio is frequented by so many well-known people – Princess Elizabeth of York and the late Anny Ahlers [cat. 123]. Their portraits were two of the outstanding impressions of this exhibition in Old Bond-street .... Princess Elizabeth sat enthroned among them all, in white frills and a blue sash, but her gilt chair was under a typical English sky, and the glimpse of English countryside was a reminder that she was Elizabeth of England .... The portrait is for the Duchess of York, and the Duke specially requested that the Princess should be given her correct name in the catalog. It is 'Her Royal Highness Princess Elizabeth of York'."

The view of the Copper Horse in Windsor Park, dated 3 June 1933 (fig. 88), was probably made during a break from painting the present portrait. It was very typical of de László, an indefatigable man, always to take the opportunity to paint a view or scene that caught his eye. Many remained in his studio on his death. Some, as in this instance, were presented by the artist to the subject of the commissioned portrait that had occasioned the painting of the landscape study. Christopher Lloyd has recently pointed out that the silhouette of the Copper Horse is just visible in the lower right-hand quarter of the portrait, and it may well have been for this reason that de László made the separate oil sketch of the view from the castle.

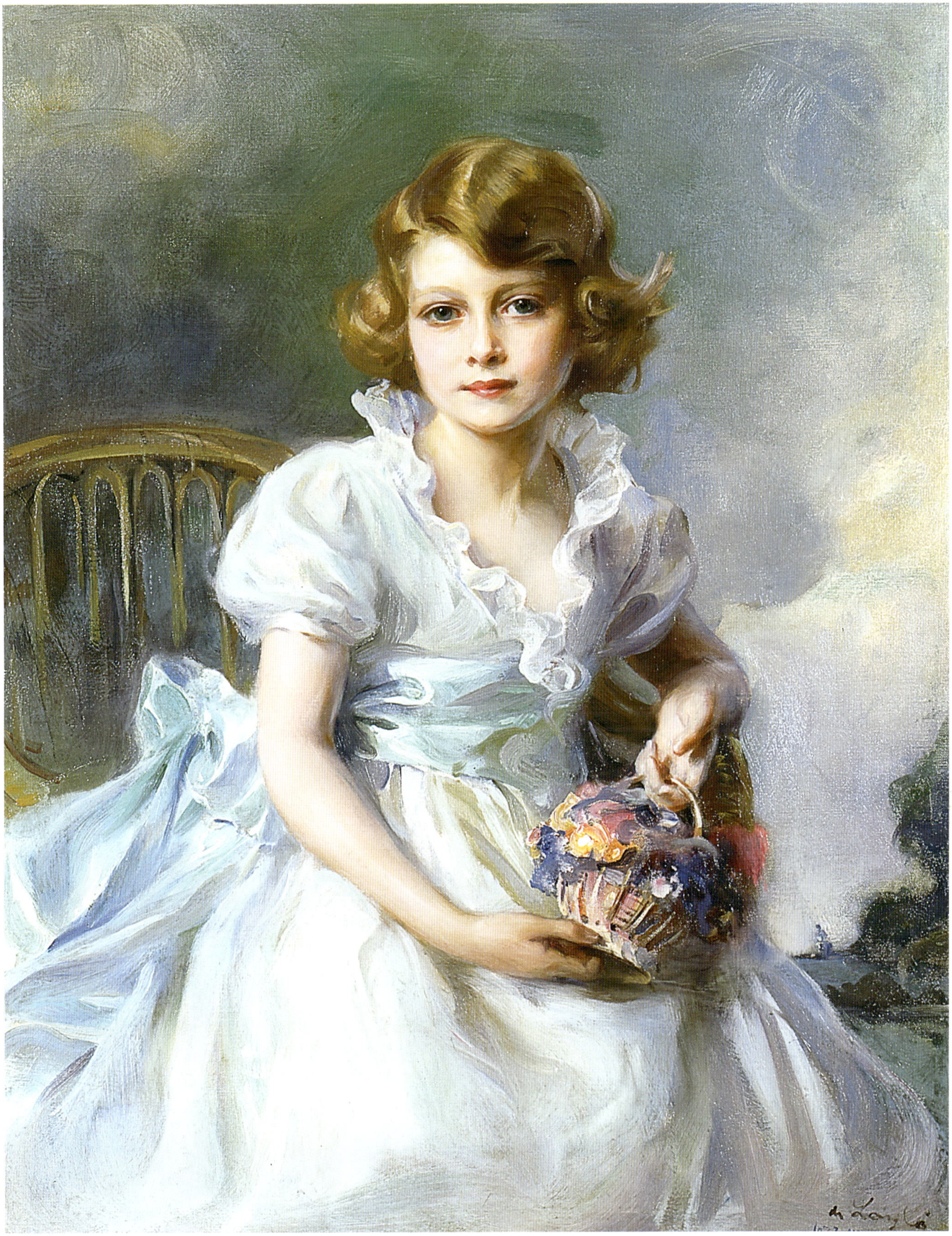

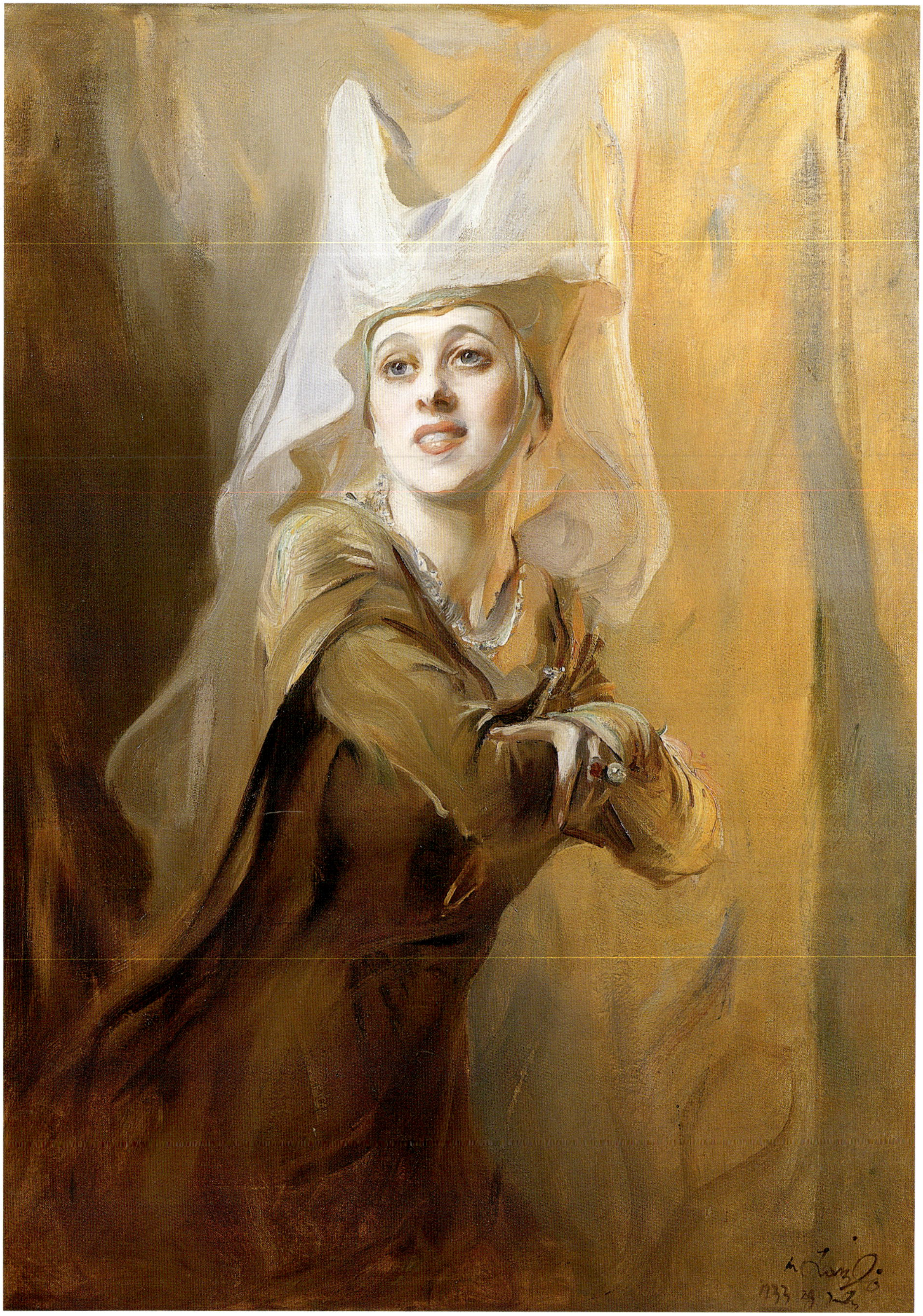

125 Miss Gwen Ffrangcon-Davies 1933

Oil on canvas, 109.2 × 77.5 cm (43 × 30½ inches)
Signed and dated, lower right: *de László / 1933 29 July*
PROVENANCE In the possession of the artist on his death; John de Laszlo, fifth and youngest son of the artist
EXHIBITED *88th Annual Exhibition*, Royal West of England Academy, November 1933–February 1934, no.117: *Miss Ffrangcon-Davis, in Richard of Bordeaux, no price*; Doncaster Museum and Art Gallery, 1935
LITERATURE Rowcliffe 1938, p.3 (no.17); Rutter 1939, p.384; *Painting a Portrait*, 1934, colour ill. frontispiece, black and white ill. pp.19, 21, 23, 25, 27, 29, 31, 33, 35, 37, 39, 41, 43, 45, 47

In 1933 the editor of *The Studio*, C.G.Holme, asked de László to paint a portrait to demonstrate the art of portraiture for his series of 'How To Do It' books. De László agreed, but did not want to appear to be a teacher of portrait painting, so it was decided that, while he painted, his old friend the critic A.L.Baldry (cat. 81) would question him about his technique and Holme would photograph the progress. As a model the versatile actress Gwen Ffrangcon-Davies was chosen. Photographs (fig. 89) demonstrated de László's technique: the 'sight size' method, with the sitter and the canvas placed close together; the artist steps away to compare the two, and back to the canvas to paint what he has observed. This practice is also well illustrated in a contemporary ciné film (shown during the exhibition this book accompanies).

For the sittings Miss Ffrangcon-Davies wore a costume for Gordon Daviot's *Richard of Bordeaux*, in which she was playing Anne of Bohemia opposite John Gielgud. In 1934 de László painted her again, in her costume for the title role in Daviot's *Queen of Scots*, and gave her the portrait as a gift. He also painted another, smaller, portrait of her in that same costume which, like the present portrait, he kept in his studio, and is now in the possession of one of his descendants.

Gwen Ffrangcon-Davies, the daughter of David Ffrangcon-Davies, a well-known baritone of the day, was born in London in 1891. She was educated at South Hampstead School and then studied abroad. As a teenager she went backstage to see Ellen Terry, for whom she recited from *Romeo and Juliet*, and Terry gave her the encouragement she needed. She made her debut in a walk-on part in *A Midsummer Night's Dream* in 1911. In those early days, however, she found work mainly as a singer: she toured in musical comedy shows and sang at concerts. By 1921 she was taking lead roles with the Birmingham Repertory Company, under the great actor-manager Sir Barry Jackson, including, in 1922, Etain in a legendary 216 consecutive performances in London of Rutland Boughton's opera *The Immortal Hour*. She acted in many leading roles alongside the great actors and actresses of the day. Her long association with the Shakespeare's heroines began with Cordelia in *King Lear* and Juliet to John Gielgud's Romeo in 1924, which became her most famous role.

She last appeared on stage in Chekhov's *Uncle Vanya* in 1970, but she continued to act on television and in radio, making her last television appearance at the age of one hundred. Gwen Ffrangcon-Davies had a rare ability to identify herself with the part she was playing to such an extent that while on stage she herself, as she said, "ceased to exist". Fiercely independent, to the end of her life she lived alone with her cat in a seventeenth-century cottage, virtually untouched by modernity, where she enjoyed gardening. She was created D.B.E. in 1991. Dame Gwen died in 1992, just after her one hundred-and-first birthday.

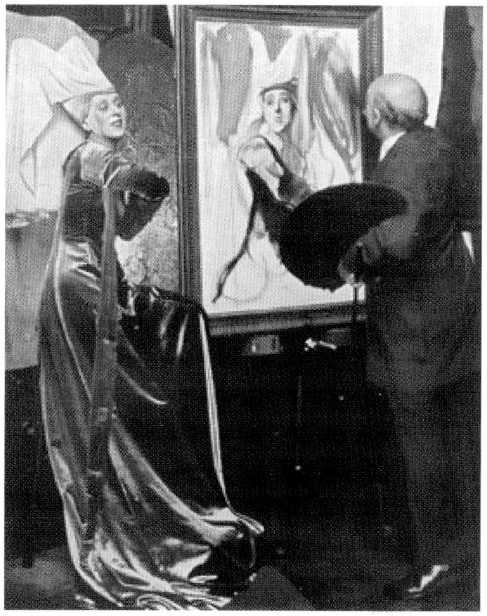

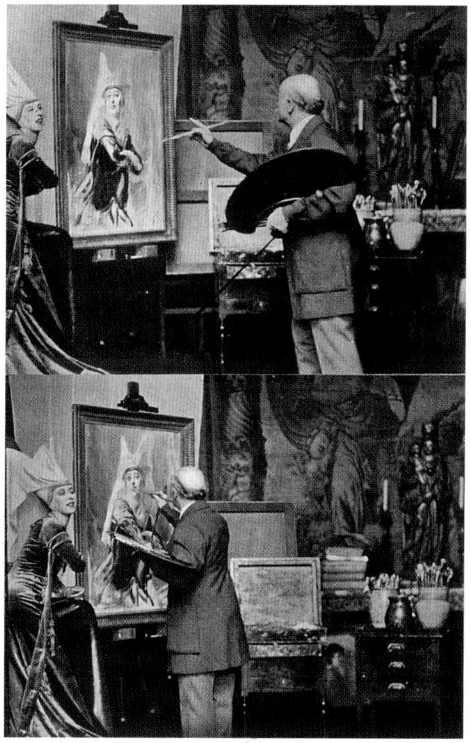

FIG. 89 Photographs from *Painting a Portrait*, 1934, by P.A. de László: "When I stand back I am recording mentally what I am going to put on my canvas when I walk up to it"

126 H.R.H. Princess Marina of Greece, later Duchess of Kent 1934

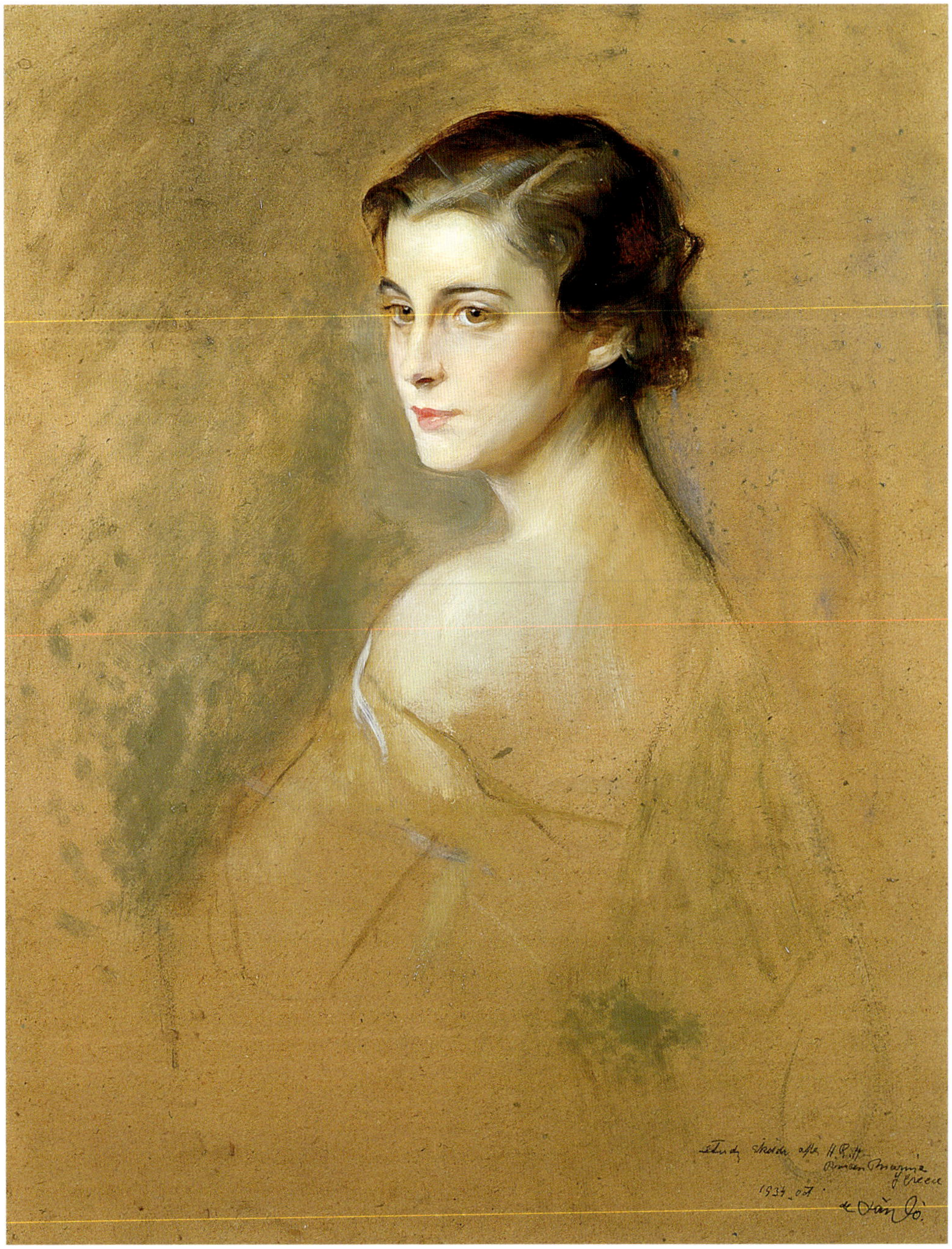

Oil on board, 80 × 62.2 cm (31½ × 24½ inches)
Signed, inscribed and dated, in pencil lower right: *Study Sketch after H.R.H.-/ Princess Marina / of Greece/ 1934. Oct . / de László*
PROVENANCE In the possession of the artist on his death; Patrick de Laszlo, fourth son of the artist
EXHIBITED *Royal Portraits by Philip A. de László, M.V.O., Loan Exhibition In aid of The Wedding Gift Fund for St. George's Hospital (at the special request of H.R.H. The Duke of Kent)*, M. Knoedler & Company, Inc., London, November–December 1934, no.17: *Her Royal Highness Princess Marina (profile study)*
LITERATURE ASB Vol.II, p.79: *Marina / Princess of Greece / and Denmark Sept. 26–1934*; N.P.G. 1934 Album, p.35b; Rowcliffe 1938, p.28 (no.154); *Apollo*, XX, no.120, December 1934, p.354, ill. p.292; Rutter 1939, pp.288, 374, ill. facing p.376

The present portrait was painted in two hours in Paris, probably in the duc de Gramont's studio in Avenue Henri Martin (cat. 29). The artist's wife noted it was never completed as the Princess was unable to give a further sitting. Another study portrait remains in a private family collection. At the same time de László painted a pair of formal portraits of the Duke and Duchess of Kent, commissioned as wedding presents.

Princess Marina of Greece was born in Athens in 1906, the youngest of three daughters of Prince and Princess Nicholas of Greece (cat. 37, 38). She spent her childhood in Athens and the Tatoï Palace at the foot of Mount Parnes. After periods of exile, the family settled in Paris.

In November 1934 she married Prince George, Duke of Kent (1902–1942), son of King George V and Queen Mary. They had three children: Prince Edward, the present Duke, was born in 1935; Princess Alexandra in 1936; and Prince Michael in 1942. In August 1942 the Duke was killed when his aircraft crashed in Scotland. Taking over her husband's role as patron and president of many institutions, the Duchess continued to carry out a full programme of engagements, and devoted herself to causes such as the Royal National Lifeboat Institution, the newly established University of Kent, and the All-England Lawn Tennis Club. She was also Colonel-in-Chief of the Royal West Kent Regiment.

As a young woman, aided by her mother, Princess Marina developed her fine taste in clothes, many of which she made herself. One of the best dressed women of her time, she greatly influenced the style and appearance not only of other members of the Royal Family, but also of the British public. She was herself an artist of accomplishment. Princess Marina died at Kensington Palace in 1968 after a short illness, and was buried next to her husband at Frogmore.

127 Mabell, Dowager Countess of Airlie, née Lady Mabell Gore 1933

Oil on canvas, 104.2 × 72.4 cm (41 × 28½ inches)
Signed and dated, lower left: *de László 1933*
Dundee Art Galleries and Museums, on loan to a private collection, Scotland
PROVENANCE Presented to the town of Dundee by the artist
EXHIBITED *Portraits by Philip A. de László, M.V.O., Loan Exhibition held in aid of The Artists' General Benevolent Institution,* M. Knoedler & Company, London, June–July 1933, no.30: *MABELL, DOWAGER COUNTESS OF AIRLIE, G.B.E*; *Old Dundee: People and Places,* Dundee 1991
LITERATURE ASB, Vol.II, p.75: *Mabell Airlie 7th Feb,* among other signatures dated 1933; N.P.G. 1933 Album, p.11

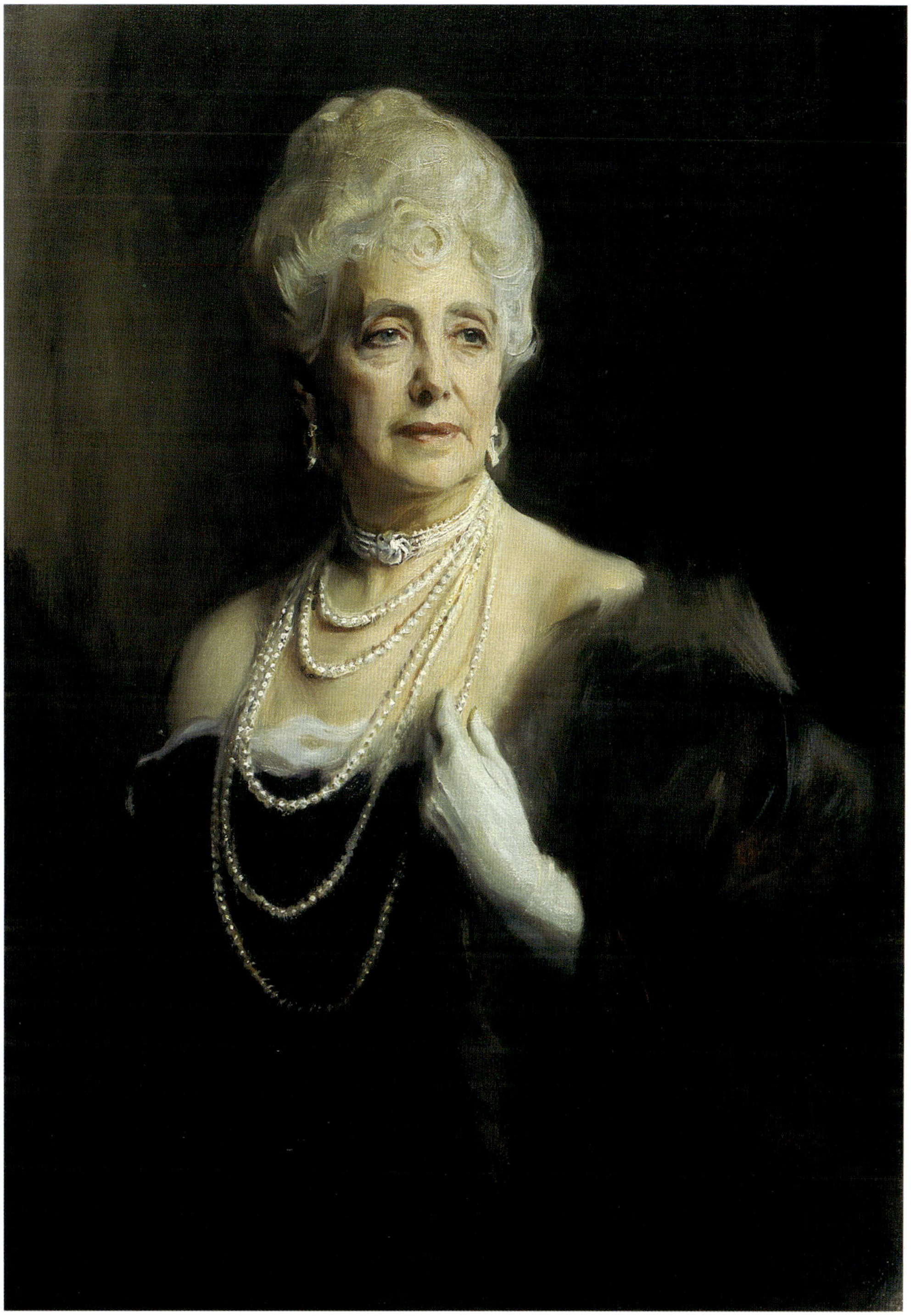

This portrait was presented to the City of Dundee by de László in 1933, after the Town Council had requested a portrait of Lady Airlie in recognition of her charitable work. When the portrait was exhibited at Knoedler's in June that year the *Oban Times* wrote: "Of the portraits shown, which are all of prominent people, that of Mabell, Countess of Airlie ...will be noticed as [a] striking example of elegant and forceful portraiture". Lady Airlie had been drawn by Sargent in 1923, and in 1935 de László also painted her daughter-in-law, the 12th Countess, née Lady Bridget Coke, the mother of the Hon. Sir Angus Ogilvy (private collection).

Lady Mabell Frances Elizabeth Gore was born in 1866, the eldest daughter of the 5th Earl of Arran. In 1886 she married David William Stanley Ogilvy, 11th Earl of Airlie, who was killed in action in South Africa in 1900, leaving her, aged only thirty-seven, to bring up their three sons and three daughters.

She worked indefatigably for charitable causes in and around the city of Dundee, as well as becoming a distinguished author, publishing: *In Whig Society 1775–1818* (1921), *Lady Palmerston and her Times* (1922) and *With the Guards We Shall Go* (1933). She became G.B.E., Hon L.L.D. of St Andrews University, J.P. and Lady of the Bedchamber to H.M. Queen Mary. She died in 1956.

128 H.M. Queen Marie, the Queen Mother of Roumania, née Princess Marie of Edinburgh 1936

Oil on canvas, 150.5 × 92.7 cm (59¼ × 36½ inches)
PROVENANCE In the possession of the artist on his death; Patrick de Laszlo, his fourth son
LITERATURE ASB, Vol.II, p.85: *Marie / Cotroceni / Feb. 1936*; Queen Marie of Rumania, *Diaries*, Vol III 195 rola 489, pp.77, 80–81, National Archives, Bucharest; Rowcliffe 1938, p.86 (no.468); Rutter 1939, pp.175, 352–3, 376; Terence Elsberry, *Marie of Romania, The Intimate Life of a Twentieth Century Queen*, London 1973, pp.263, 265; ed. Diana Fotescu, *Americans and Queen Marie of Romania, A Selection of Documents*, The Center for Romanian Studies, Oxford, 1998, p.119

Despite many requests, de László adamantly refused to visit what he considered "Hungary's enemy": in 1919 the Roumanians had invaded Hungary, occupying and looting Budapest, and, in 1920, had taken large areas of Hungarian territory. De László had first met the then Crown Princess Marie in Vienna in 1899. It was not, however, until she visited London in 1924 that he painted her, at that time writing in his diary: "[The Queen] is uncommonly intelligent, and she knows what she wants; she also knows how to make use of her great charm and lilac eyes. At first I felt rather uncomfortable in her presence, as I despise her cowardly Rumanian people, who owe their present position to the Treaty of Trianon [1920], which dealt most unjustly with Hungary. But I will not go into politics. The Queen knows her duty – and I am an artist of the world, and paint history, not only individuals… [She] is very ambitious and would like to be a kind of Byzantine queen, but I fear the Rumanian kingdom has been built upon marshy ground." This portrait (fig. 21, p. 33) remains in the collection the National Museum of Peles Castle in Sinaia, Roumania, and was on loan to the Cotroceni Museum (formerly Palace) in Bucharest from 1989 to 2000.

Only in January 1936 could de László finally persuade himself "to put his political prejudice aside" when King Carol II commissioned portraits of himself and his mother for the National Bank of Roumania, and of his mistress, Elena Lupescu. Queen Marie sat to him first, which resulted in a formal portrait showing her seated full length in a dark gown; this picture has now been traced to the vaults of the National Museum of Art in Bucharest, together with a posthumous portrait of her husband King Ferdinand I, who died in 1927.

The early part of February 1936 was devoted to the present portrait. The Queen wrote in her diary that de László had arrived at Cotroceni eager to paint "a really royal picture". She continued: "Sitting for him is very entertaining … but yesterday's sitting was exhausting as he insists upon gorgeous and official attire, a thing I have quite given up – so that I had to dig up the old gorgeousness of my royal days and this attire is exceedingly heavy and exhausting to wear …".

In her diary entry for 1 February the Queen wrote: "Day entirely given up to László. It is a joy to see him paint. It is pure magic; the sweetness of his hand, eye, brush is astounding. He arranges a looking glass in such a way that one can see the picture he is making and thus one remains interested all the time. In the morning he made a rough sketch of my head with incredible rapidity and sureness – a marvellous touch and such perfect colouring and feeling for line, knowledge of bone construction bringing out the best in a face. The colour scheme we have

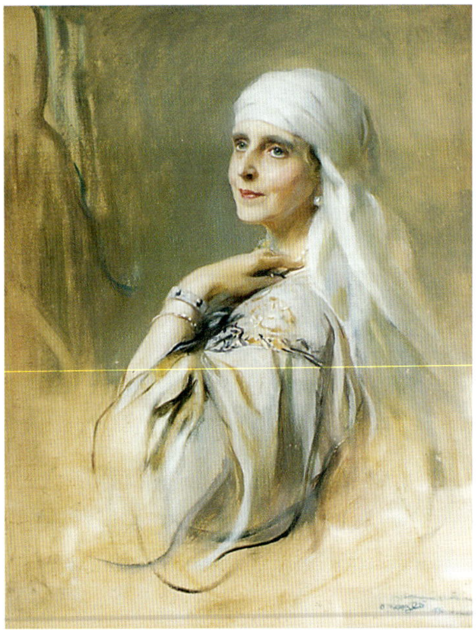

FIG. 90 *Queen Marie of Rumania, née Princess Marie of Edinburgh*, 1936
Oil on canvas, 88.9 × 68.6 cm (35 × 27 in.)
Private collection, Switzerland

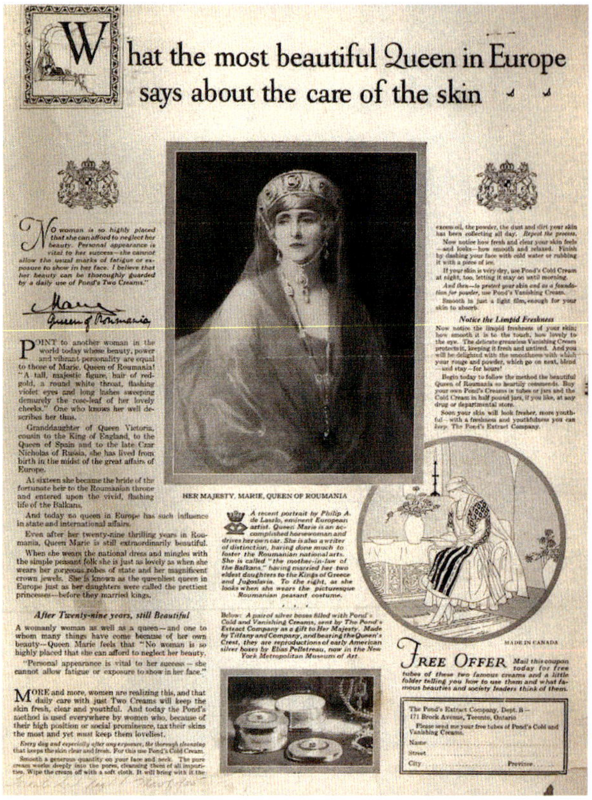

What the most beautiful Queen in Europe says about the care of the skin

"No woman is so highly placed that she can afford to neglect her beauty. Personal appearance is vital to her success—she cannot allow the usual marks of fatigue or exposure to show in her face. I believe that her beauty can be thoroughly guarded by a daily use of Pond's Two Creams."

Marie
Queen of Roumania

POINT to another woman in the world today whose beauty, power and vibrant personality are equal to those of Marie, Queen of Roumania! "A tall, majestic figure, hair of red-gold, a round white throat, flashing violet eyes and long lashes sweeping demurely the rose-leaf of her lovely cheeks." One who knows her well describes her thus.

Granddaughter of Queen Victoria, cousin to the King of England, to the Queen of Spain and to the late Czar Nicholas of Russia, she has lived from birth in the midst of the great affairs of Europe.

At sixteen she became the bride of the fortunate heir to the Roumanian throne and entered upon the vivid, flashing life of the Balkans.

And today no queen in Europe has such influence in state and international affairs.

Even after her twenty-nine thrilling years in Roumania, Queen Marie is still extraordinarily beautiful.

When she wears the national dress and mingles with the simple peasant folk she is just as lovely as when she wears her gorgeous robes of state and her magnificent crown jewels. She is known as the queenliest queen in Europe just as her daughters were called the prettiest princesses—before they married kings.

After Twenty-nine years, still Beautiful

A womanly woman as well as a queen—and one to whom many things have come because of her own beauty—Queen Marie feels that "No woman is so highly placed that she can afford to neglect her beauty.

"Personal appearance is vital to her success—she cannot allow fatigue or exposure to show in her face."

MORE and more, women are realizing this, and that daily care with just Two Creams will keep the skin fresh, clear and youthful. And today the Pond's method is used everywhere by women who, because of their high position or social prominence, tax their skins the most and yet *must* keep them loveliest.

Every day and especially after any exposure, the thorough cleansing that keeps the skin clear and fresh. For this use Pond's Cold Cream.

Smooth a generous quantity on your face and neck. The pure cream works deeply into the pores, cleansing them of all impurities. Wipe the cream off with a soft cloth. It will bring with it the excess oil, the powder, the dust and dirt your skin has been collecting all day. *Repeat the process.*

Now notice how fresh and clear your skin feels—and looks—how smooth and relaxed. Finish by dashing your face with cold water or rubbing it with a piece of ice.

If your skin is very dry, use Pond's Cold Cream at *night*, too, letting it stay on until morning.

And then—to protect your skin and as a foundation for powder, use Pond's Vanishing Cream.

Smooth in just a light film, enough for your skin to absorb.

Notice the Limpid Freshness

Now notice the limpid freshness of your skin; how smooth it is to the touch, how lovely to the eye. The delicate greaseless Vanishing Cream protects it, keeping it fresh and untired. And you will be delighted with the smoothness with which your rouge and powder, which go on next, blend—and stay—*for hours!*

Begin today to follow the method the beautiful Queen of Roumania so heartily commends. Buy your own Pond's Creams in tubes or jars and the Cold Cream in half pound jars, if you like, at any drug or departmental store.

Soon your skin will look *fresher*, more youthful—with a freshness and youthfulness you can *keep*. The Pond's Extract Company.

HER MAJESTY, MARIE, QUEEN OF ROUMANIA

A recent portrait by Philip A. de Laszlo, eminent European artist. Queen Marie is an accomplished horsewoman and drives her own car. She is also a writer of distinction, having done much to foster the Roumanian national arts. She is called "the mother-in-law of the Balkans," having married her two eldest daughters to the Kings of Greece and Jugoslavia. To the right, as she looks when she wears the picturesque Roumanian peasant costume.

Below: *A pair of silver boxes filled with Pond's Cold and Vanishing Creams, sent by The Pond's Extract Company as a gift to Her Majesty. Made by Tiffany and Company, and bearing the Queen's Crest, they are reproductions of early American silver boxes by Elias Pelletreau, now in the New York Metropolitan Museum of Art.*

MADE IN CANADA

FREE OFFER *Mail this coupon today for free tubes of these two famous creams and a little folder telling you how to use them and what famous beauties and society leaders think of them.*

The Pond's Extract Company, Dept. B—
171 Brock Avenue, Toronto, Ontario
Please send me your free tubes of Pond's Cold and Vanishing Creams.
Name
Street
City Province

FIG. 91 'What the most beautiful Queen in Europe says about the care of her skin', *Pond's Extract Company Magazine*, February 1925; the portrait by de László reproduced is here fig. 21, p. 33

decided upon is perfect all in being uncommon.

"László is delighted; he says he never painted a portrait with these colours. I again had lunch brought into the studio … short cozy [*sic*] little meal and we began the big portrait which appeared like magic on the big canvas. It is exceedingly tiring for me as I stand with all these heavy drappings [*sic*] as well as my diadem. But at last it's worthwhile. At 6 I was however dead-tired and delighted to shed my queenly attire."

This portrait, however, remained unfinished, and, with its two related oil sketches, was in the possession of the artist on his death. While in Bucharest he also painted two half-length portraits of the sitter, one in traditional Hungarian costume (fig. 90), which remains in a private family collection, and the other in mourning attire (her cousin King George V had just died), which remains untraced.

Princess Marie Alexandra Victoria was born in Kent in 1875, the daughter of Queen Victoria's second son, Alfred, Duke of Edinburgh (later Duke of Saxe-Coburg-Gotha) and the Grand Duchess Marie, daughter of Tsar Alexander II. In 1893 she married Prince Ferdinand of Hohenzollern-Sigmaringen, Crown Prince of Roumania, who inherited the throne from his uncle Carol I in 1914. They had six children, Carol, Elisabetha, who married George II of Greece, Mignon (Marie), who married Alexander II of Yugoslavia, Nicolas, Ileana, later Archduchess Anton of Austria, and Mircea, who died young. Queen Marie died at the summer residence in Sinaia in 1938.

Queen Marie was a legendary beauty. Her 1924 portrait by de László was put to an unusual (but no doubt very effective) use in the February 1925 issue of *Pond's Extract Company Magazine* (fig. 91).

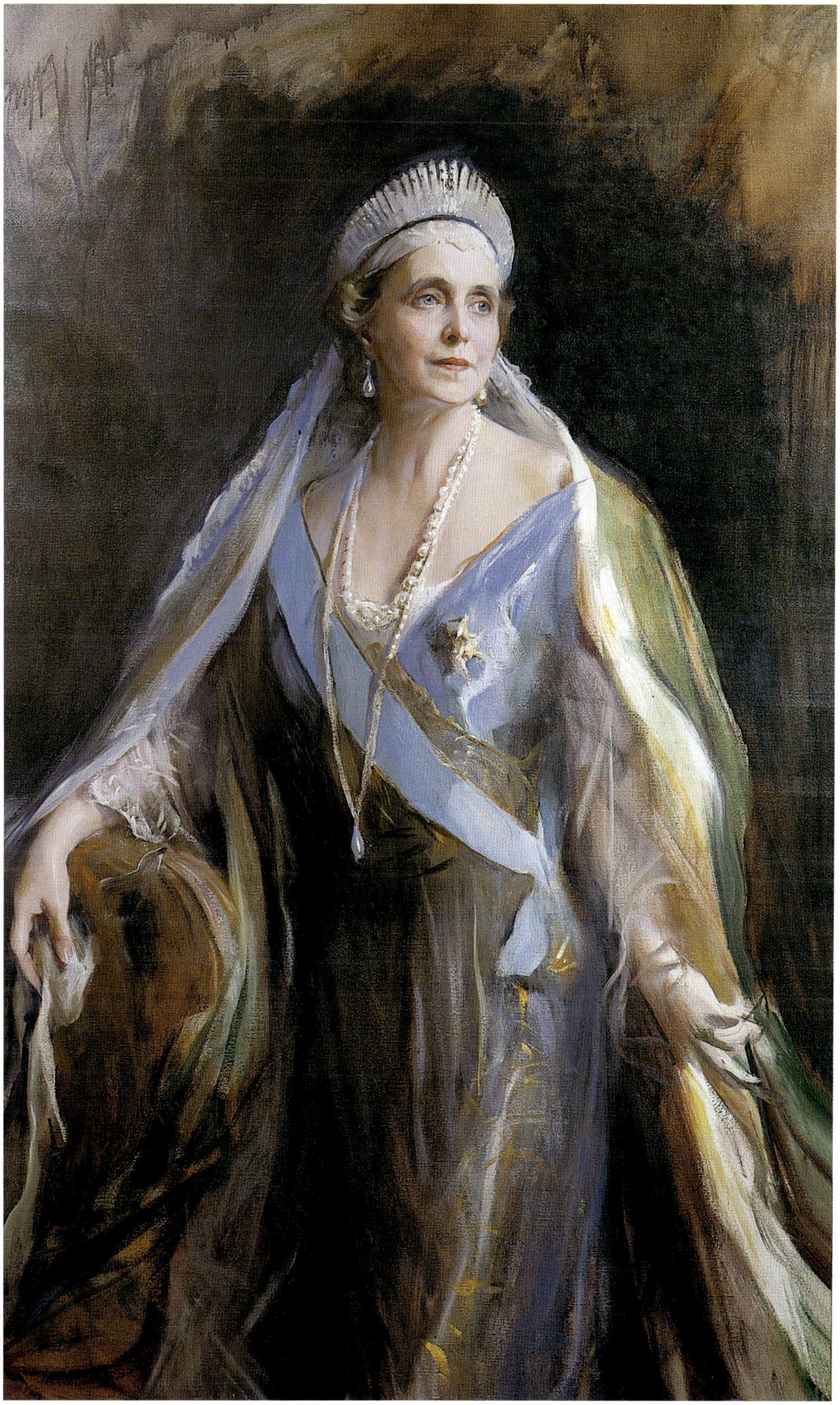

129 A Marrakesh Girl 1934

Oil on canvasboard, 48.9 × 38.7 cm
(19¼ × 15¼ inches)
Signed and dated, lower right: *de László / 1934. III*; on the verso inscribed dated and signed: *Marrakesh / 1934. March / PAde L* in ink
PROVENANCE In the possession of the artist on his death; Patrick de Laszlo, his fourth son
LITERATURE *Painting a Portrait*, 1934; Rowcliffe 1938, p.55 (no.281)

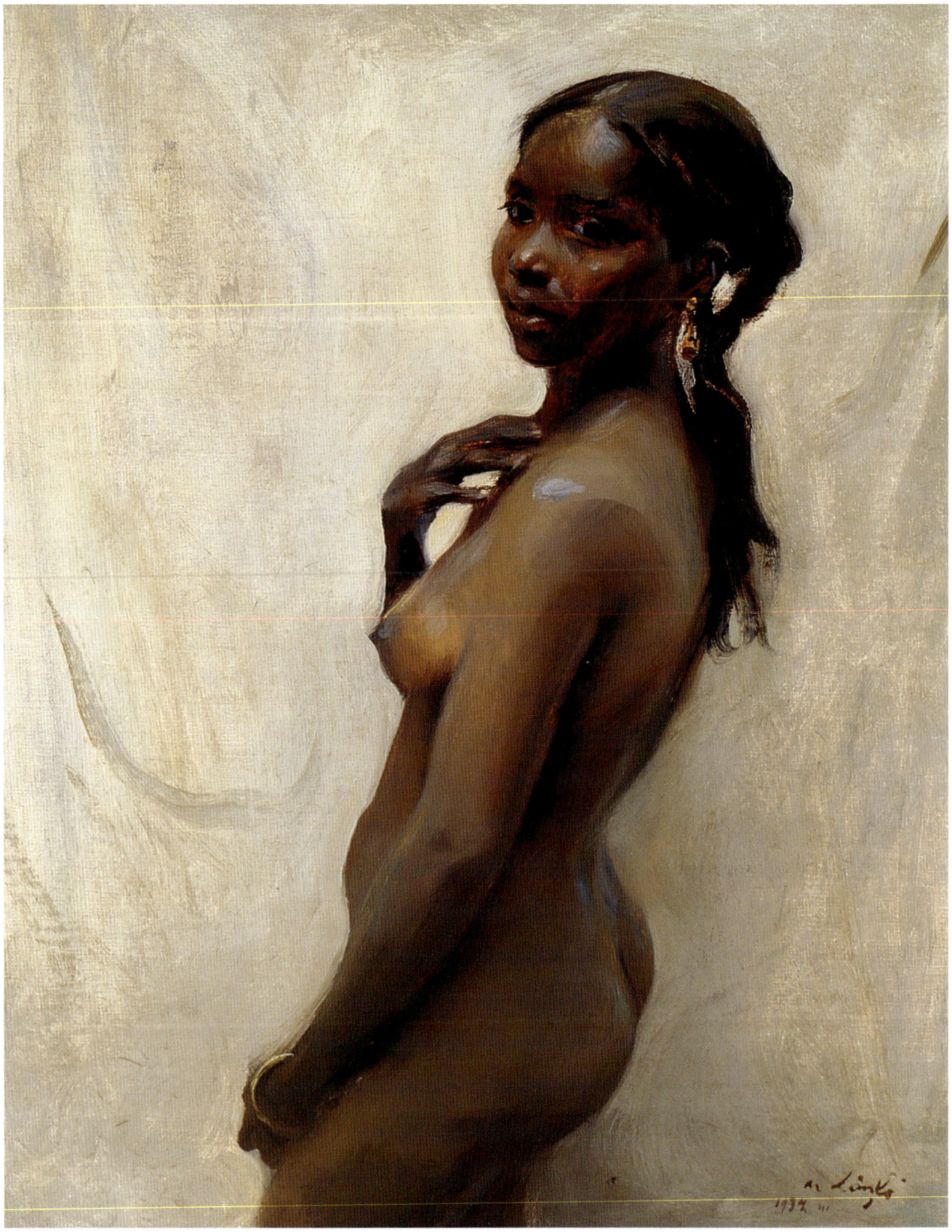

In March 1934 de László travelled to Marrakesh in Morocco for a holiday. He went on to Tangiers at Easter and then returned home. There are five recorded studies of nudes and figures that he produced during this time. Many of them remain in the possession of descendants of the artist. Here, close examination of the painted model reveals an extraordinary range of colours. In the chapter 'The Artist's Palette' in *Painting a Portrait*, the colours on which de László mainly depended were listed, and illustrated (fig. 92): "Here they are, in the order in which I put them on my palette – ultramarine, madder, rose madder, zinc white, light cadmium, dark cadmium, yellow ochre, burnt sienna". He began his pictures primarily by painting the outline on the canvas with a few brush lines: "I draw with my brush and all my painting is drawing", and rarely mixed more than two colours at once on his palette. In preference to linseed oil, he used as his medium poppy oil, which is slower drying: "I like my painting to keep wet as long as possible so that I can finish straight away the part of the picture I am working on before the paint dries; the slow drying is helpful, it enables me to finish more deliberately and it makes the consistency of the paint more pleasant to handle. Work finished while the paint is still wet always looks fresher and more direct."

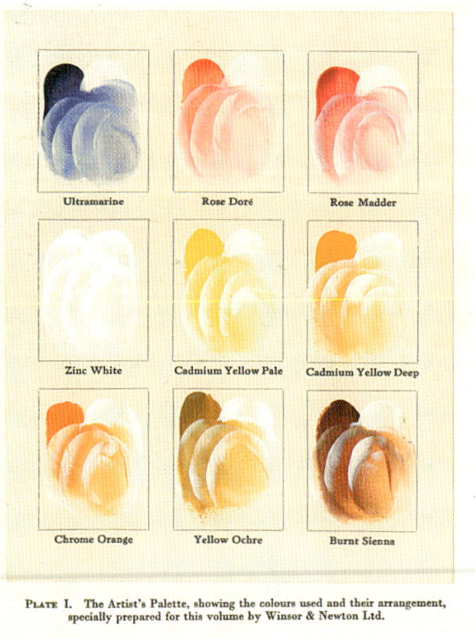

FIG. 91 De László's palette (*Painting a Portrait*, 1934, p.13, pl.1)

130 H.H. Lieutenant-General Sir Sawai Man Singh II, Maharaja of Jaipur 1935

Oil on canvas, 99 × 74.3 cm (39 × 29¼ inches)
Signed, inscribed and dated, lower left:
de László 1935 / LONDON
LITERATURE ASB Vol.II, p.84: *S. Man Singh of Jaipur / 12th July 1935*; N.P.G. 1935 Album, p.21b

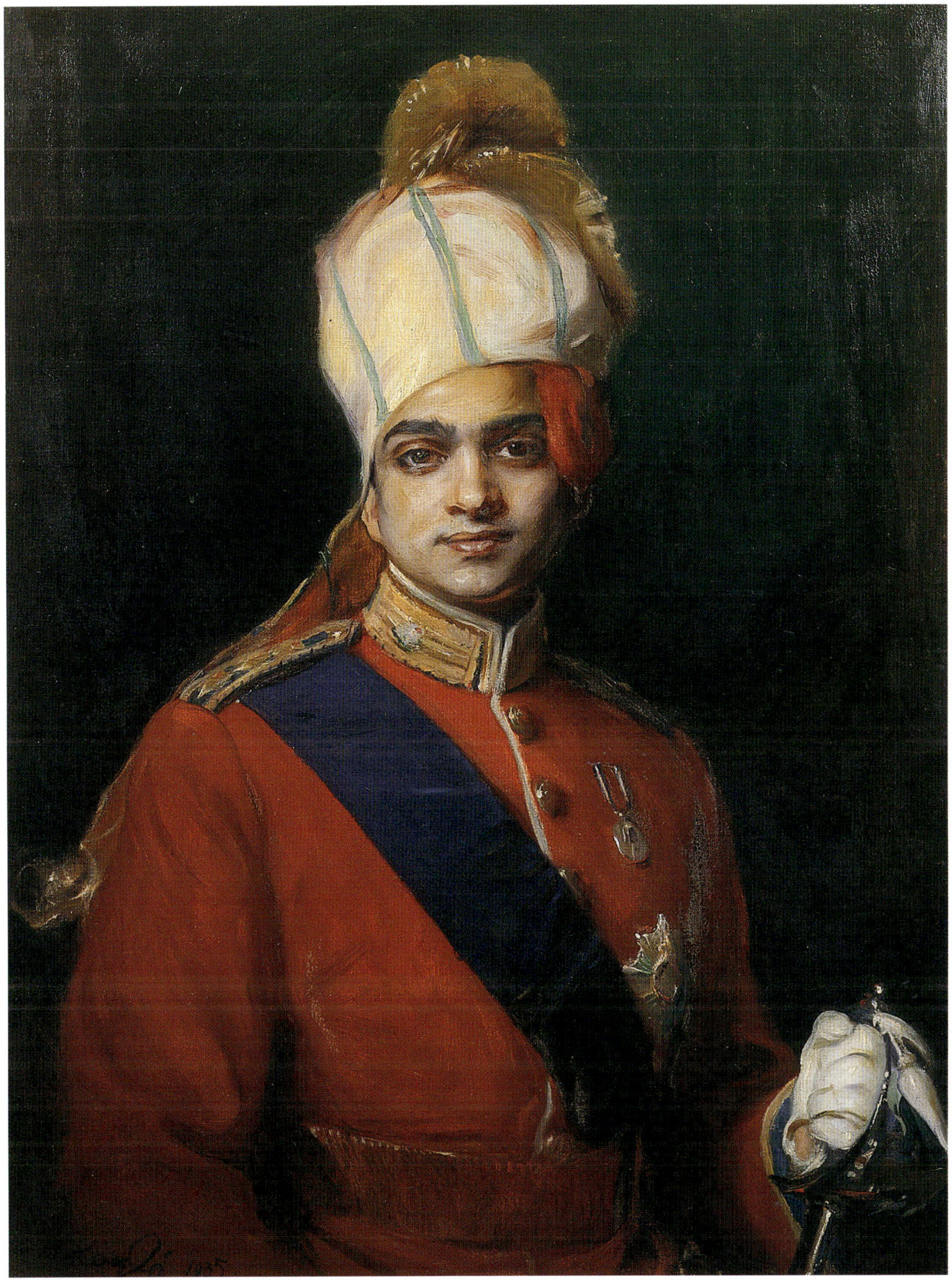

An oil sketch for this painting is in a private collection in America. In the same year, de László painted a less formal study portrait of the Maharaja in a brilliant saffron-coloured turban, which remained in the artist's possession until his death. He also painted the sitter's future mother-in-law, the Maharani of Cooch Behar, on two occasions.

Kumar Mormuket Singh of Isarda was born in 1911 and was adopted by the childless Lt-General Maharaja Sir Sawai Madho Singh Bahadur, whom he succeeded in 1922. At the age of twelve he was married for the first time, to the sister of the Maharaja of Jodhpur, with whom he later had a son and a daughter. In 1932 he married his second wife, the niece of his first, with whom he had two sons. In 1940 he married his third wife, Ayesha, daughter of the Maharaja of Cooch Behar; they had one son.

During the Second World War, he saw active service with the Life Guards in the Middle East, and the Royal Scots Greys in Gaza. His appointment as Liaison Officer for the Indian States brought him back to India for the remainder of the war.

As ruler of Jaipur, he was deeply concerned with the welfare of his people and the improvement of the state, but, by 1944, the reforms in India had reduced his role from autocratic ruler to constitutional monarch. In 1948 he was named Rajpramukh, Head of the new Rajasthan Union of States, with duties more ceremonial than actual. In 1956 this office was abolished. Henceforth he divided his time between India and England, playing an active role as President of the Indian Polo Association. In 1962 the Rajasthan State Assembly elected him to the Upper House. From 1964 to 1968 he was ambassador to Spain. Thereafter he devoted his time to representing the interests of the former rulers of India whose few remaining privileges were in danger of being abolished. He died in 1970, whilst playing polo at Cirencester.

131 Chinky 1934

Oil on canvas board, 32.4 × 40 cm
($12\frac{3}{4} \times 15\frac{3}{4}$ inches)
Signed, inscribed and dated, lower right: *CHINKY / de László / 1934 / P A de L*
PROVENANCE In the possession of the artist on his death; Stephen de Laszlo, his second son

Chinky belonged to Stephen and Diana de Laszlo, second son and daughter-in-law of the artist, and was also killed in the car crash in which they died on New Year's Eve 1938-9. The artist and his wife also had a Pekinese, called Yang (fig. 93), who features in the family ciné films.

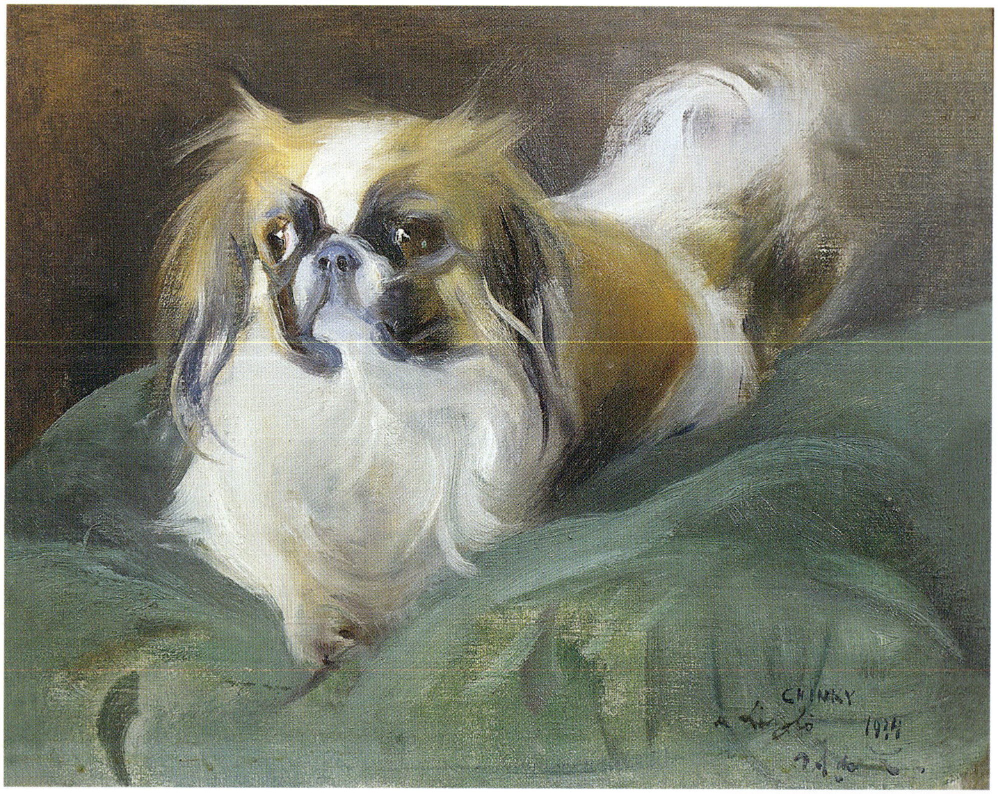

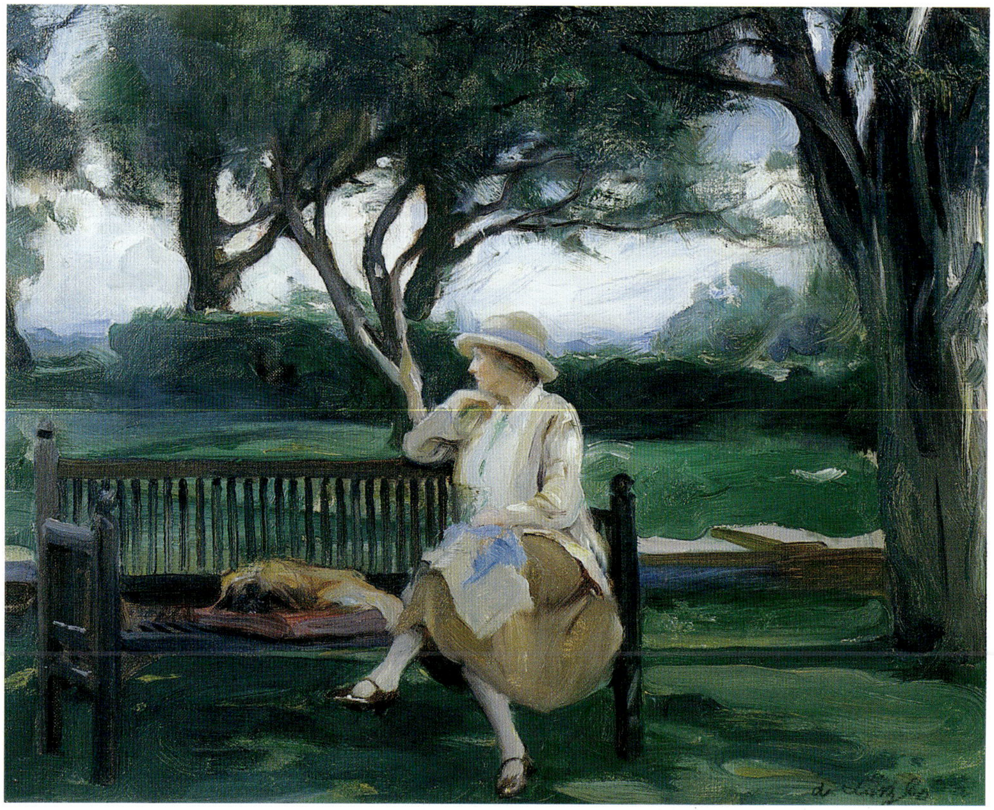

FIG. 93 *Mrs Philip de László with Yang*, 1928
Oil on canvas, 33 × 40.1 cm (13 × 16 in.)
Private collection

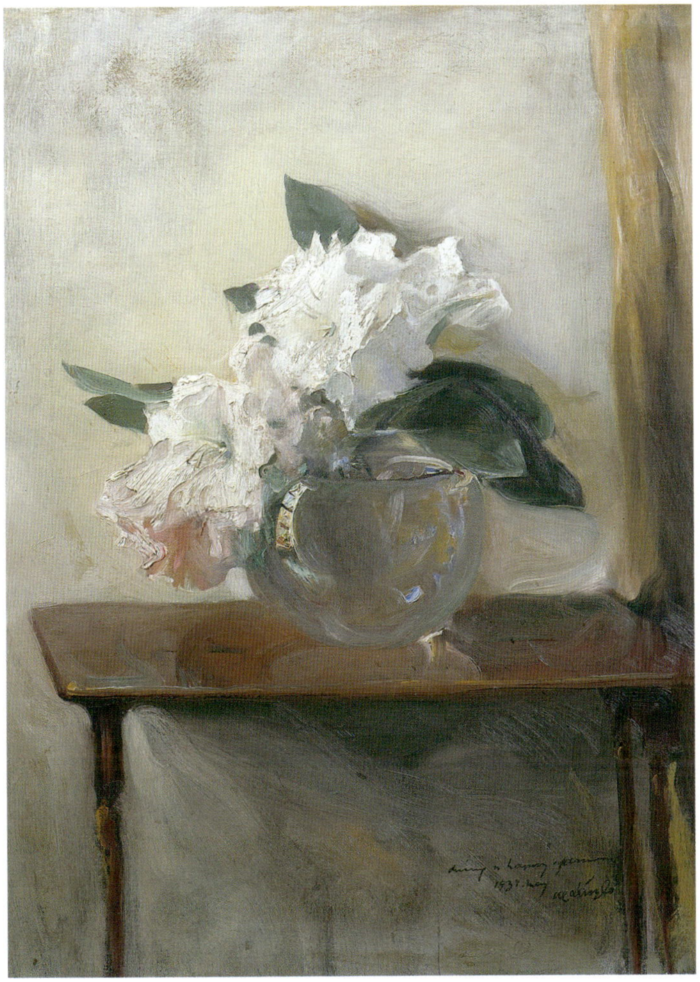

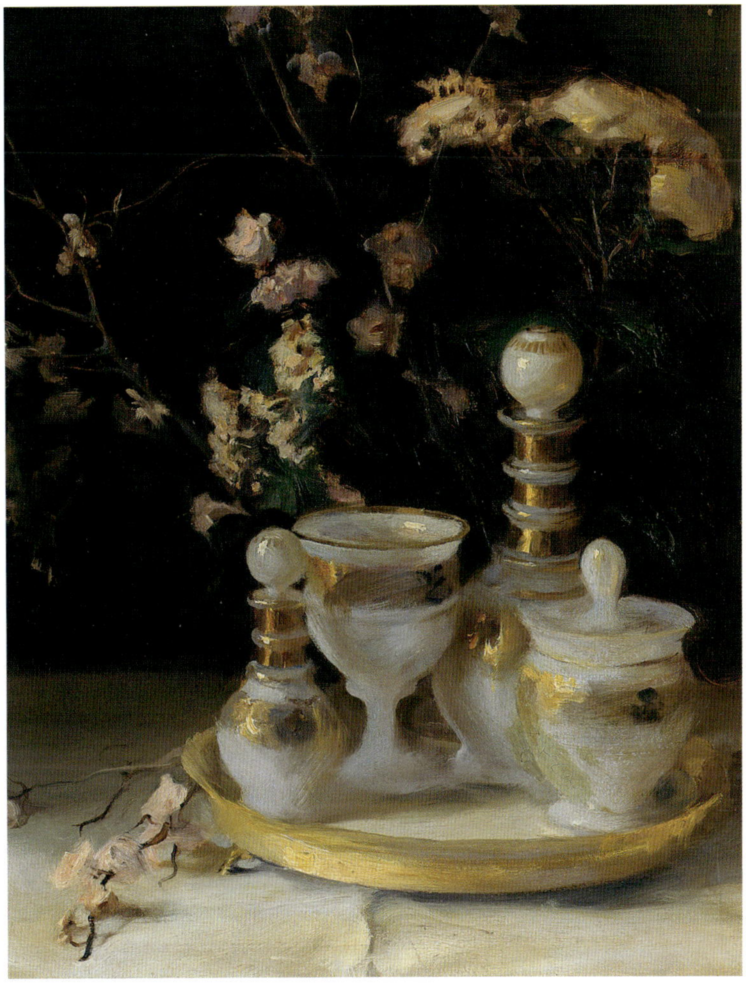

132 Rhododendrons 1934

Oil on canvas, 79 × 55.9 cm (31⅞ × 22 inches)
Signed, inscribed and dated, lower right: *During a happy afternoon / 1934 May / de László*
PROVENANCE In the possession of the artist on his death; John de Laszlo, his fifth and youngest son
EXHIBITED *Exhibition of Paintings by Philip A. de László, M.V.O., In Aid of the London Hospital and The Artists' General Benevolent Institution*, Wildenstein & Co., Ltd., London, November–December 1937, no.54: *Rhododendrons*
LITERATURE Rowcliffe 1938, p.102 (no.603)

This still life, painted in an afternoon at his house in Fitzjohn's Avenue in London on his return from Morocco, shows how de László applied his principles "to make his picture harmonious in design and satisfying in its colour scheme" (*Painting a Portrait*, 1934) to all subjects. The palette is subdued but translucent, the brushwork fresh and spontaneous, and reveals de László at his best, working 'white in white', or rather 'wet in white'.

133 Still Life with Porcelain and Carnations 1937

Oil on canvasboard, 50.8 × 40.6 cm (20 × 16 inches)
Inscribed and dated on the verso: *1937 Villa les Brises*
PROVENANCE In the possession of the artist on his death; Henry G. de Laszlo, his eldest son
LITERATURE Rowcliffe 1938, p.109 (no. 645); Rutter 1939, p.377

De László had suffered a severe attack of angina in August 1936, and had been ordered to rest by his doctor, Lord Dawson of Penn. He had still not completely recovered by the winter, and the doctor advised him not to return to London. Accordingly, he spent the winter at Cap Ferrat in the south of France, in the Villa Les Brises, which had been lent to him by Lord Beaverbrook. He remained there, under strict orders not to exhaust himself by painting more than four days a week, until Easter 1937.

The decanter in the still life is also depicted in another study in the possession of a descendant of the artist. The carnations, which she had herself grown, were brought to him by his dear friend Jewell Allcroft (fig. 51, p.63), who came specially to visit him at Cap Ferrat.

134 View of the Marienkirche, Grossgmain 1935

Oil on canvasboard, 30.8 × 38.4 cm (12⅛ × 15⅛ inches)
Inscription indistinctly written on the verso: *Austria / GrossGmein / 1935.aug / PadeL.*, in black crayon; *Hier, lieber Marczi, waren wir zusammen, mit Fülöp, wie er dieses Bild malte. / Lucy M. de László. / Dec.2.1937.*, in Lucy's hand in black ink [Here, dear Marczi, we were together with Fülöp when he painted this picture]. (The artist had died in November that year.)
PROVENANCE In the artist's possession on his death, given by his widow Lucy to the artist's brother, Marczell László; by descent through his wife

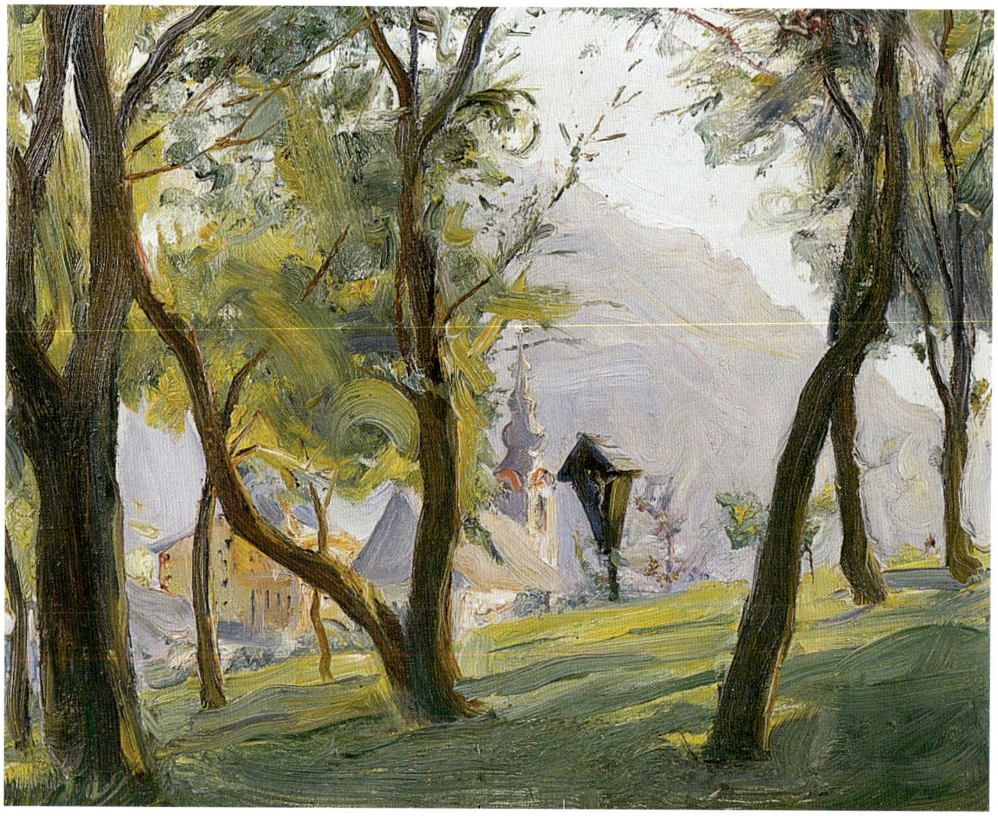

In March 1935 de László went back to Budapest to paint a second portrait of Admiral Horthy (cat. 109). After a hectic schedule he resolved to rest a little in the summer and spent June to September in the Austrian and German Alps.

While staying in Bad Gastein in August he painted this view of the pilgrimage church of St Mary at Grossgmain, some ten miles from Salzburg. His wife accompanied him, and it would seem from the inscription that his brother Marczi joined them for a while. That summer de László made quite a number of landscape studies, which were, as ever, made for his own pleasure. There exists a very similar study of the same scene, probably painted on the same day.

135 View from the Villa Les Brises, Cap Ferrat 1937

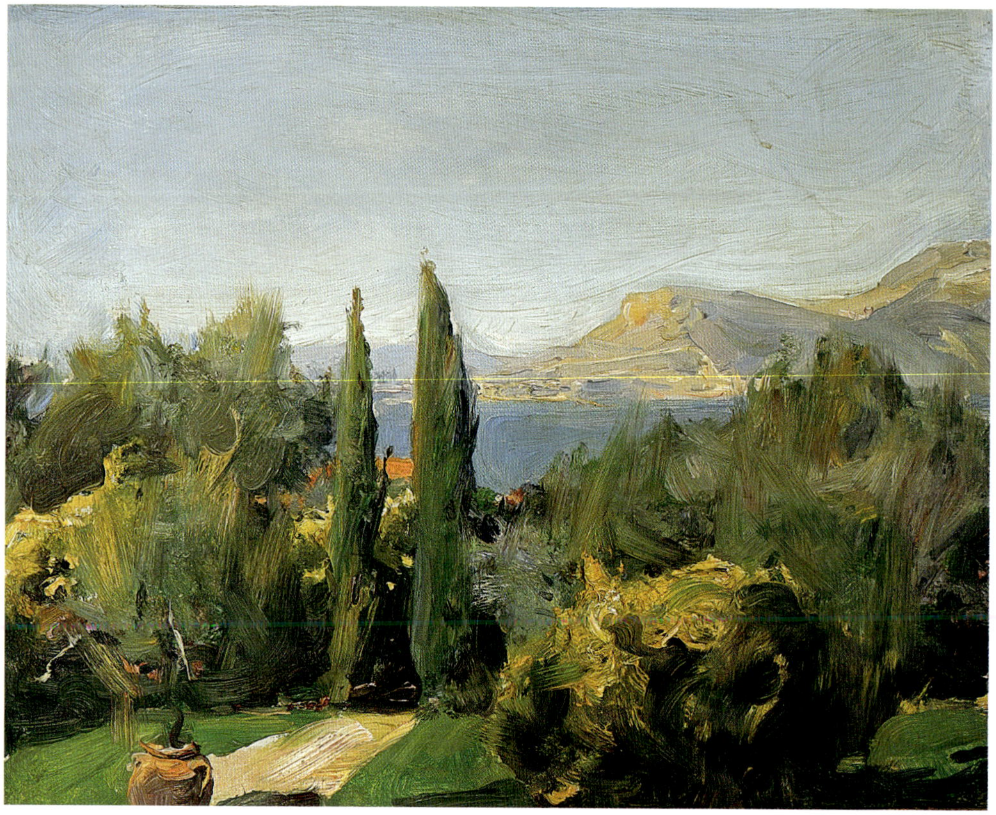

Oil on canvasboard, 40.6 × 33 cm (16 × 13 inches)
Signed, lower right: *de László / 1937 I*; on the verso signed, inscribed and dated: *Villa Les Brisas / Cap Ferrat / 1937 30 – January / painted from / the drawing room windows / during one impression P.A. de László* in ink
PROVENANCE Lucy de László, wife of the artist; Paul de Laszlo, their third son; Christopher de Laszlo, their grandson
EXHIBITED (Probably) *Exhibition of Paintings by Philip A. de László, M.V.O., In Aid of the London Hospital and*

The Artists' General Benevolent Institution, Wildenstein & Co., Ltd., London, November–December 1937, no.40: *At Cap Ferrat*
LITERATURE Rowcliffe 1938, p.119 (no.705); Rutter 1939, p.377

This view from the villa was painted in January 1937, nine months before de László's death. An inscription on the verso states that it was painted "during one impression". In 1923 de László had written: "I feel regretful that I have not painted more landscapes in the past. It seems to me there is only one right method of landscape painting – to paint a résumé of Nature, and to try to do it in one sitting, and a larger picture in not more than three."

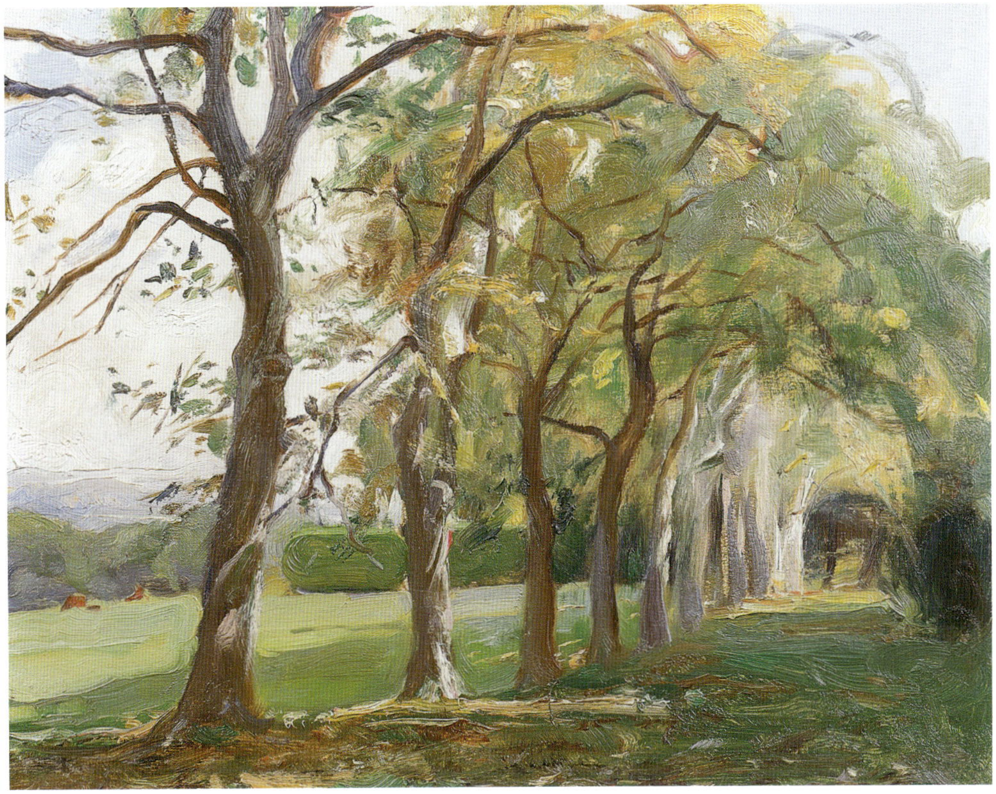

136 An Avenue of Trees, Bedales 1937

Oil on panel, 31.8 × 39.4 cm (12½ × 15½ inches)
PROVENANCE In the possession of the artist on his death; by descent in his family
LITERATURE Rowcliffe 1938, p.120 (no.710)

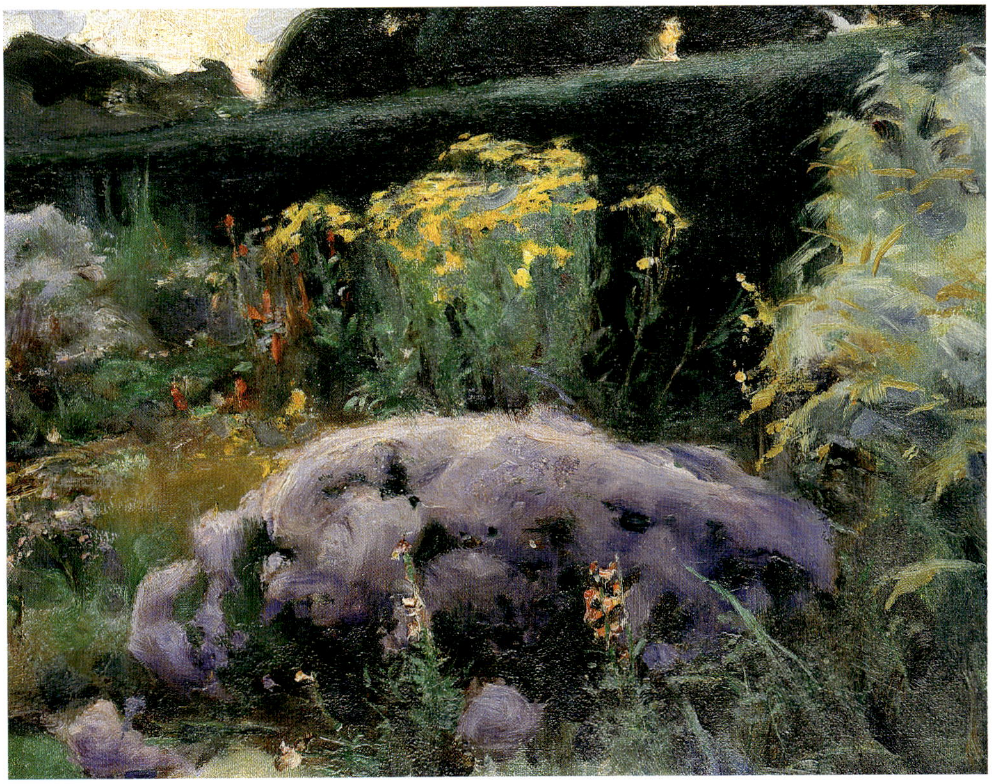

137 Flowers in the Garden at Bedales 1937

Oil on canvasboard, 40.6 × 50.8 cm (16 × 20 inches)
Signed, inscribed and dated on the verso: *At the Bendales* [sic] */- Sussex / 1937 Sept. / P A de László*
PROVENANCE In the possession of the artist on his death; Henry G. de Laszlo, his eldest son
LITERATURE Rowcliffe 1938, p.107 (no.635)

In the summer of 1937 de László rented Bedales, a house in Lindfield, West Sussex, where, regardless of his doctor's advice, he continued to make sketches around the garden. He even felt well enough to undertake a few commissions, especially since, in Coronation year, many of his former patrons wanted to be painted in their ceremonial robes (cat. 138). The study of the garden was signed only eight weeks before the artist's death.

138 The Duchess of Northumberland, née Lady Helen Gordon-Lennox 1937

Oil on canvas, 139.7 × 83.9 cm (55 × 33 inches)
Signed, inscribed and dated, lower right: *de László / Syon / 1937*
Duke of Northumberland, Alnwick Castle
EXHIBITED *Exhibition of Paintings by Philip A. de László, M.V.O., In Aid of the London Hospital and The Artists' General Benevolent Institution,* Wildenstein & Co., Ltd., London, November–December 1937, no.24: *Her Grace the Duchess of Northumberland*
LITERATURE ASB Vol.II, p.87: *Helen Northumberland Aug. 2nd 1937; Catalogue of Paintings,* compiled by the Eighth Duke and Duchess of Northumberland, 1930, no.831; N.P.G. 1936–37 Album, p.20; Rutter 1939, p.378; Diana Scarisbrick, *Ancestral Jewels,* London 1989, p.155, colour ill. p.154, pl.217

De László has portrayed the Duchess in a gown of cloth of gold and a robe of crimson velvet and ermine, with a design incorporating the Percy Lion and Fetterlock, the Gordon Ivy Leaf and the Richmond Rose, all worked in gold thread. She is wearing the family jewels – a *collet rivière* with a diamond cross as a pendant, two emerald and diamond brooches on her bodice, and a strawberry leaf tiara set with diamonds from the ceremonial sword given to the 3rd Duke of Northumberland by King George IV. The tiara was stolen in 1963.

Despite his terminal heart condition, de László came up to London from Bedales to paint Prince and Princess Chichibu of Japan (both portraits later destroyed in a fire), and went to Syon to paint the Duchess of Northumberland in her court dress as Mistress of the Robes. The artist confessed to his friend A.L. Baldry on 18 August 1937: "We came here [Bedales] on the 23rd July, but I have since had to interrupt my rest. It was a temptation which was difficult to refuse. I went to stay for ten days with the Duchess of Northumberland, one of the most beautiful women in this country, and I did a full length portrait of her in reduced size, such as Zoffany used to paint, in her Coronation Robes as Mistress of the Robes to the Queen. This is a historic picture, painted in her own magnificent surroundings at Syon House, and I think I have succeeded in it." De László had been eager to paint the portrait *in situ* at either Alnwick or Syon to help him "do something unusual – not in the studio", and, according to the Northumberland picture catalogue, the portrait was painted in the Ballroom (now known as the Great Dining Room) at Syon. The price agreed was £500. The portrait was finished by September and sent to Alnwick, only to be borrowed for de László's last exhibition in London in November that year. He died of a heart attack two days before the opening, on 22 November 1937.

De László had painted the Duchess three times previously, in 1915 (untraced) and 1916 (fig. 94), and in 1928, with her youngest son, Lord Geoffrey Percy. He painted her husband in 1927 as well as a number of other portraits of members of the family over the years.

Lady Helen Magdalen Gordon-Lennox was born in 1886, the daughter of the 7th Duke of Richmond and Gordon. In 1911 she married Lord Alan Percy, who succeeded as 8th Duke of Northumberland in 1918. They had four sons and two daughters. She was Mistress of the Robes to H.M. Queen Elizabeth from 1937. In 1939 she was appointed Captain of the Women's Transport Services (F.A.N.Y.), a position she held until 1943, then becoming Commander from 1943–46. She was A.D.C. to Princess Alice, Countess of Athlone. She died in 1965.

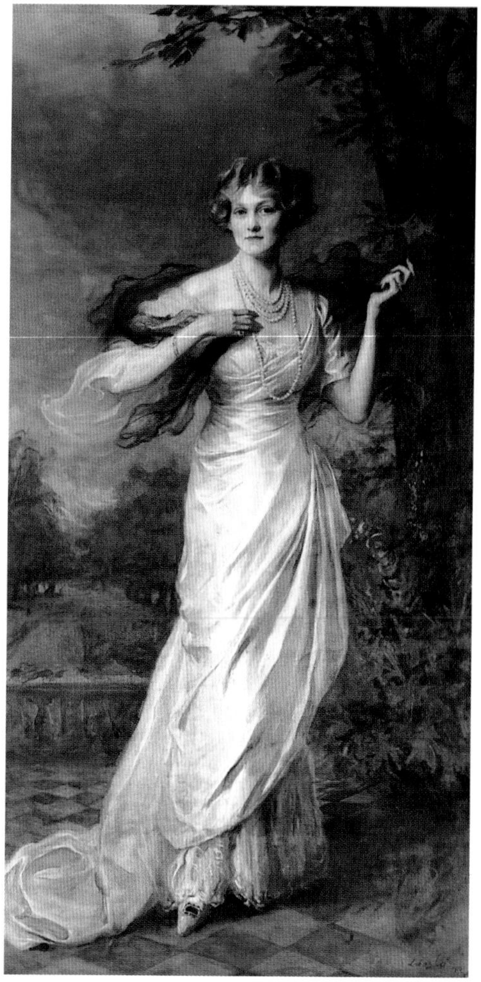

FIG. 94 *The Duchess of Northumberland,* 1916
Oil on canvas, 73.7 × 53.3 cm (29 × 21 in.)
Duke of Northumberland, Alnwick Castle

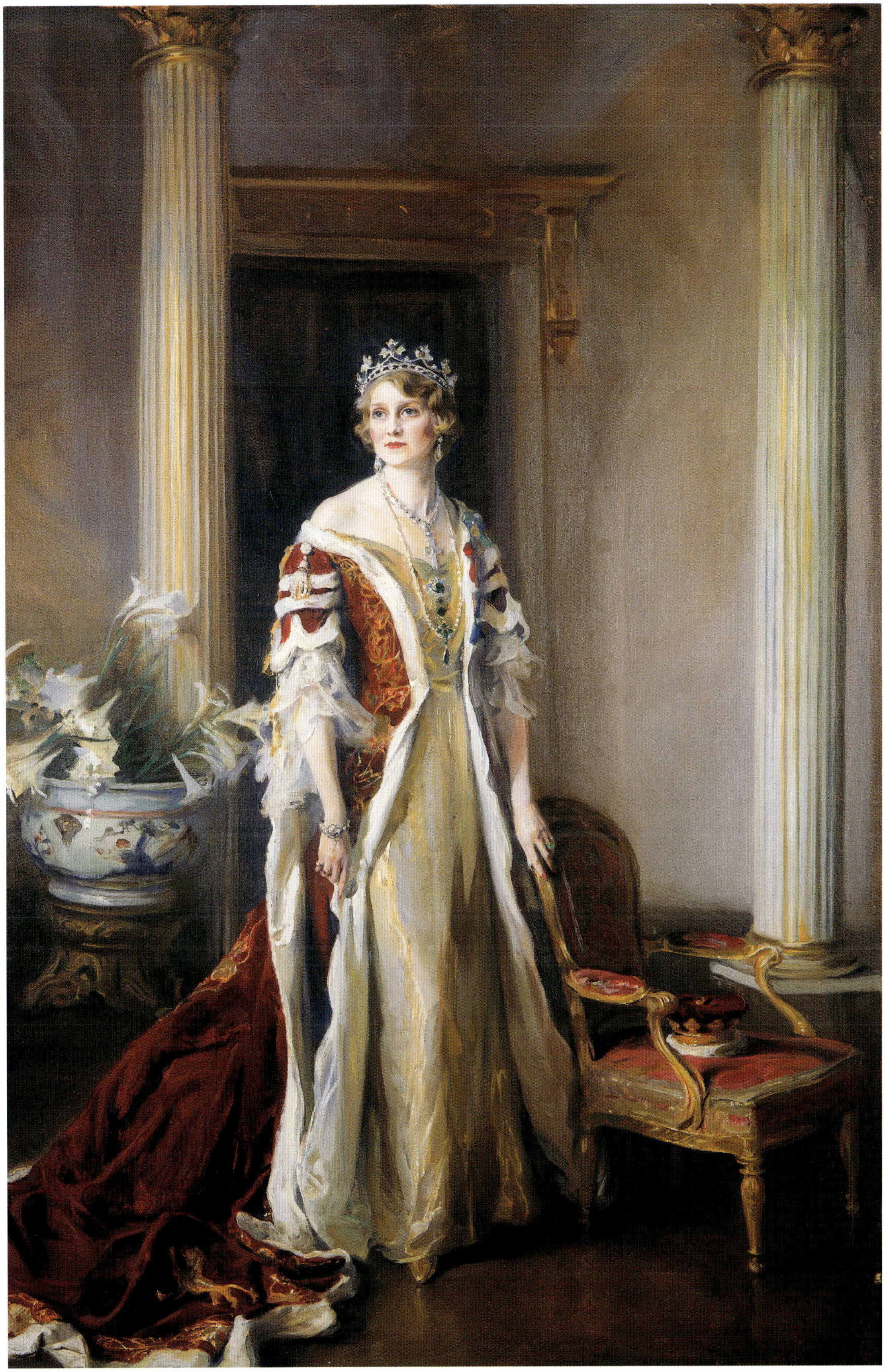

Index

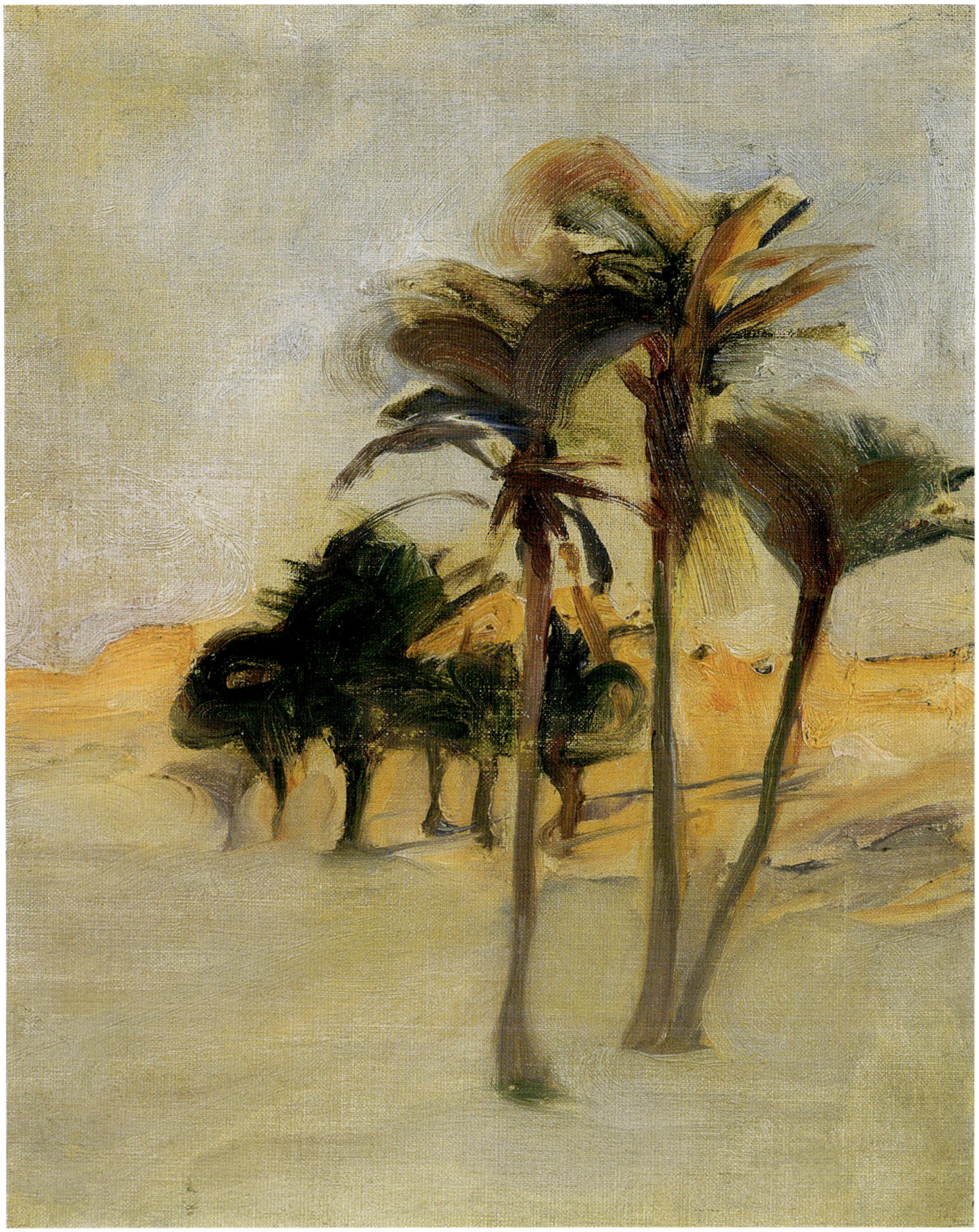

Palm-trees at Touggourt, Algeria, 1923
Oil on canvasboard, 39.4 × 31.4 cm (15½ × 12⅜ in.)
Private collection

Credits

Photography commissioned by the de Laszlo Foundation (© 2004, The de Laszlo Foundation) was ably carried out by Roy Fox.
All works by de László are © 2004 The de Laszlo Foundation. Other copyrights and procurements are acknowledged as follows:
The Bridgeman Art Library, figs. 18, 20, 58; cat. 88;
By Kind Permission of the Trustees of the Chequers Estate, cat. 88;
© Christie's, fig. 31;
© Houghton Hall Collection, fig. 12;
©Londonderry, fig. 69
The Metropolitan Museum of Art, Bequest of Benjamin Altman, 1913. (14.40.619) / Photograph © 1984 The Metropolitan Museum of Art, fig. 22;
© 2001, National Gallery, London, fig. 24;
© National Museum of Peles Castle, Sinaia, Roumania, fig. 21
© the Duke of Northumberland, cat. 138
© The National Portrait Gallery, London, cat. 118;
The Royal Collection © 2003, Her Majesty Queen Elizabeth II, figs. 25, 28, 30, 88, cat. 98, 124;
The Royal Collection © 2003, the Duke of Edinburgh, cat. 36, 37, 43
© Trinity College, Cambridge, fig. 23, cat. 99;
© Photo Vatican Museums, fig. 56
©Witt Library, Courtauld Institute, London, fig. 57

Apart from those already mentioned in the Message and Acknowledgements on pp. 6 and 7, the practical support of the following in the preparation for the exhibition and the catalogue is most appreciatively acknowledged:
Cadogan Tate, shippers;
Emma Cunningham, public relations;
Hamish Dewar (Mason's Yard), restorer;
Green & Stone Ltd, framers;
Larry Jamieson and Tamra Ferguson, video work;
Charles Marsden-Smedley, exhibition designer;
Joanna Payne, conservator of works of art on paper;
Stuart and Jenny Sanderson, restorers;
Sue Wakefield, postcards;
Arnold Wiggins & Sons, framers;

the curators of the Royal Collection, the Portland collection, the Schroder collection and the Winchester Army Museum; the personal assistants of the Cluff, Harmsworth and Schroder collections

all those involved at Christie's;

all those involved at the Hungarian Cultural Centre;

Silvia Benato and all those involved at Graphic Studio, Verona, repro and printing

THE DE LÁSZLÓ CATALOGUE RAISONNÉ

Sandra de Laszlo and Christopher Wentworth-Stanley would be very pleased to hear from any owners of works by de László with whom Sandra has not already been in touch.